THE MYSTERY OF JESUS CHRIST

The Mystery of Jesus Christ is a theology manual for the study of Christology and Soteriology. It provides a useful overview of the many issues in its field – and it does so with clarity, treating complex questions not only in fair and sophisticated ways, but also in ways that the ordinary student will find most helpful.

Monsignor Fernando Ocáriz, professor of fundamental and dogmatic theology at the Pontifical University of the Holy Cross, Rome, is a member of the Roman Pontifical Academy of Theology and a consultor of the Congregation for the Doctorine of Faith.

Lucas F. Mateo-Seco is professor of theology at the University of Navarre and editor of *Scripta Theologia* and *Scripta de Maria*.

José Antonio Riestra is professor of dogmatic theology and deputy dean of the Pontifical University of the Holy Cross, Rome.

June 2013

THEOLOGY TEXTBOOKS

A series devised by members of the faculty of theology
of the University of Navarre

The Mystery of Jesus Christ

A CHRISTOLOGY AND SOTERIOLOGY TEXTBOOK

F. Ocáriz, L.F. Mateo Seco
and J.A. Riestra

FOUR COURTS PRESS

Set in 11 on 13pt Ehrhardt for
FOUR COURTS PRESS LTD
7 Malpas Street, Dublin 8, Ireland
e-mail: info@four-courts-press.ie
www.four-courts-press.ie
and in North America
FOUR COURTS PRESS
c/o ISBS, 920 N.E. 58th Street, Suite 300, Portland, OR 97213.

This translation is by Michael Adams and James Gavigan.
Original title: *El Misterio de Jesucristo*

© F. Ocáriz, L.F. Mateo Seco and J.A. Riestra 1991
Ediciones Universidad de Navarra, S.A.,
Plaza de los Sauces, 1 y 2, Barañain (Navarra), España.

© English edition 1994: Four Courts Press.
Reprinted 2004 with correction.

ISBN 1-85182-127-9

A catalogue record for this book is
available from the British Library.

Printed in England by
Antony Rowe Ltd, Chippenham, Wilts.

Contents

CHAPTER ONE
The Expected Messiah

CHAPTER FOUR

Christ: Way, Truth and Life

CHAPTER FIVE

The Redemption (I)

CHAPTER SIX

The Redemption (II)

Preface

This manual of Christology developed in the normal way for a book of its type: as teachers we felt the need for it, and our teaching helped us to produce it. The fact that this book has three authors derives from a desire to avoid too narrow a focus; it draws on a varied range of teaching experience and yet, we trust, has the necessary consistency and coherence.

This textbook is designed for seminarians and theology students who are meeting this subject for the first time. Dealing with what are traditionally called *De Verbo Incarnato* and *Soteriology*, it tries to cover all the main themes in a systematic way, and avoid less important ones (it is not always easy to choose what to include and what to omit), and it has not tried to strike a purely quantitative balance in the amount of space devoted to each theme.

However, although this is a textbook, our purpose is not merely academic; we particularly want the book to help the reader attain what St Paul says in his Letter to the Christians of Ephesus—"the breadth and length and height and depth, and to know the love of Christ which surpasses knowledge, that you may be filled with all the fullness of God" (Eph 3:18-19). This calls for a *contemplative* approach to teaching and study—contemplation of the mystery of Christ—because "the truth of the Lord is studied with the head bowed; it is taught and preached in expansion of the soul who believes it, who loves it and who lives by it."[1]

It is not enough, then, (even in theology) to *study* Christ; in the words of Blessed Josemaría Escrivá, "we must seek Christ in the word and in the bread, in the Eucharist and in prayer. And we must treat him as a friend, as the real, living person he is—for he is risen. Christ, we read in the Epistle to the Hebrews, 'holds his priesthood permanently, because he continues forever. Consequently he is able for all time to save those who draw near to God, since he always lives to make intercession for them' (Heb 7:24-25). Christ, the risen Christ, is our companion and friend. He is a companion whom we can see only in the shadows—but the fact that he is really there fills our whole life and makes us yearn to be with him forever. 'The Spirit and the Bride say, "Come." And let him who hears say, "Come." And let him who is thirsty come, let him who desires take the water of life without price. . . . He who testifies to these

---

1. John Paul II, Homily, 21 October 1980: *Insegnamenti*, III, 2 (1980) 944.

things says, 'Surely I am coming soon. Amen. Come, Lord Jesus' (Rev 22:17–20)."[2]

2. Blessed J. Escrivá de Balaguer, *Christ is passing by* (Dublin 1982), no. 116.

Abbreviations and Sources

1. BOOKS OF THE BIBLE

Acts	Acts of the Apostles	2 Kings	2 Kings
Amos	Amos	Lam	Lamentations
Bar	Baruch	Lev	Leviticus
1 Chron	1 Chronicles	Lk	Luke
2 Chron	2 Chronicles	1 Mac	1 Maccabees
Col	Colossians	2 Mac	2 Maccabees
1 Cor	1 Corinthians	Mal	Malachi
2 Cor	2 Corinthians	Mic	Micah
Dan	Daniel	Mk	Mark
Deut	Deuteronomy	Mt	Matthew
Eccles	Ecclesiastes (Qohelet)	Nah	Nahum
Esther	Esther	Neh	Nehemiah
Eph	Ephesians	Num	Numbers
Ex	Exodus	Obad	Obadiah
Ezek	Ezekiel	1 Pet	1 Peter
Ezra	Ezra	2 Pet	2 Peter
Gal	Galatians	Phil	Philippians
Gen	Genesis	Philem	Philemon
Hab	Habakkuk	Ps	Psalms
Hag	Haggai	Prov	Proverbs
Heb	Hebrews	Rev	Revelation (Apocalypse)
Hos	Hosea	Rom	Romans
Is	Isaiah	Ruth	Ruth
Jas	James	1 Sam	1 Samuel
Jer	Jeremiah	2 Sam	2 Samuel
Jn	John	Sir	Sirach (Ecclesiasticus)
1 Jn	1 John	Song	Song of Solomon
2 Jn	2 John	1 Thess	1 Thessalonians
3 Jn	3 John	2 Thess	2 Thessalonians
Job	Job	1 Tim	1 Timothy
Joel	Joel	2 Tim	2 Timothy
Jon	Jonah	Tit	Titus
Josh	Joshua	Tob	Tobit
Jud	Judith	Wis	Wisdom
Jude	Jude	Zech	Zechariah
Judg	Judges	Zeph	Zephaniah
1 Kings	1 Kings		

2. JOURNALS, DICTIONARIES ETC.

AAS	Acta Apostolicae Sedis
AC	Ami du Clergé
Ang	Angelicum
AnTh	Annales Theologici
Aquin	Aquinas
BL	Biblica
BLE	Bulletin de Littérature Ecclésiastique
Burg	Burgense
CCC	Catechism of the Catholic Church
CCL	Corpus christianorum, series latina
Conc	Concilium
CT	La Ciencia Tomista
DAFC	Dictionnaire Apologétique de la Foi Catholique
DB	Dictionnaire de la Bible
DBS	Dictionnaire Biblique. Supplément
DC	Doctor Communis
DGHE	Dictionnaire d'Histoire et Géographie Ecclésiastique
DT	Divus Thomas (Piacenza)
Div	Divinitas
DS	Denzinger-Schönmetzer, *Enchiridion Symbolorum*
DSp	Dictionnaire de Spiritualité
DTB	Various authors, *Diccionario de Teología Bíblica* (ed. J.B. Bauer), Barcelona 1967
DTC	Dictionnaire de Théologie Catholique
EB	Estudios Bíblicos
ED	Euntes Docete
EE	Estudios Ecclesiásticos
EL	Estudios Lulianos
EM	Estudios Marianos
EscV	Escritos del Vedat
ETL	Ephemerides Theologicae Lovanienses
FS	Franziskanischen Studien
GCS	Die Griechischen Christlichen Scriftsteller
GER	Gran Enciclopedia Rialp, Madrid
Greg	Gregorianum
ITC	International Theological Commission
Lat	Lateranum
LV	Lumière et Vie
MSR	Mélanges de Science Religieuse
MS	Various authors, *Mysterium Salutis. Manual de teología como historia de la salvación*, Madrid 1971
NovT	Novum Testamentum
NRT	Nouvelle Revue Théologique
PG	J.-P. Migne, *Patrologia Graeca*

PL	J.-P. Migne, *Patrologia Latina*
QLP	Questions Liturgiques et Paroissiales
RB	Revue Biblique
RBI	Rivista Biblica Italiana
RCatT	Revista Catalana de Teología
RET	Revista Española de Teología
RHE	Revue d'Histoire Ecclésiastique
RSPT	Revue des Sciences Philosophiques et Théologiques
RSR	Recherches de Science Religieuse
RT	Revue Thomiste
RTL	Revue Théologique de Louvain
ScEccl	Sciences Ecclésiastiques
Scr	Scripture
ScrTh	Scripta Theologica
SC	La Scuola Cattolica
SCDF	Sacred Congregation for the Doctrine of the Faith
SCh	Sources Chrétiennes
SM	Scripta de Maria
STh	*Summa Theologiae*
ThWNT	Theologisches Wörterbuch zum Neuen Testament
TQ	Theologische Quartalschrift
VD	Verbum Domini
VS	La Vie Spirituelle
WA	M. Luther, *Werke. Kritische Gesmantausgabe* (Weimar edition, 1883)
ZKT	Zeitschrift für katholische Theologie
ZNW	Zeitschrift für die Neutestamentliche Wissenschaft und die Kunde der älteren Kirche

Introduction

In recent years, Jesus Christ, his Person and his mission (the salvation of mankind), has attracted ever more attention, both at the level of personal piety and joyful acceptance of faith and in the field of theological study. All one has to do is to look at the bibliography to see the wealth of material on Christology, the richness and complexity of the subject and the diversity (and divergence) of approaches.[1] Therefore, before entering into our study of Christology proper, it will be helpful to look at some preliminary questions, especially those to do with method.

1. CHRIST, THE OBJECT OF CHRISTOLOGY

Jesus Christ is the central object of the Church's faith. He is also the object of Christology, which, as the word implies, is a discourse or treatise on Christ.[2] It is one of the key areas of theology[3] and constitutes the study, in the light of faith, of what that faith teaches regarding the mystery of Christ and his work of redemption.[4]

1. For a good summary of the main questions and a general assessment, see J. Ratzinger, "Introduzione" in SCDF, *Mysterium Filii Dei: Dichiarazione e commenti* (Rome, 1989), 9-24.
2. "Christology", word made up of "Christ" and "logos" (treatise), means "treatise on Christ" It used to be included as part of the medieval summas but since then has been treated as a separate subject under various titles, e.g., *De verbo incarnato*.
3. Although theology covers a wide range of subjects (and therefore can be divided into separate treatises), these are so closely inter-related that Aquinas described theology as *una in specie atoma*: the formal object, the viewpoint, is one and the same throughout (cf. *STh* I, q. 1, aa. 3 and 4)). *The mystery of Christ* is the thread running right through theology and giving it overall unity. As the Second Vatican Council says. "In the revision of ecclesiastical studies the main object to be kept in mind is a more effective coordination of philosophy and theology so that they supplement one another in revealing to the minds of students with ever increasing clarity the Mystery of Christ, which affects the whole course of human history, exercises an unceasing influence on the Church, and operates mainly through the ministry of the priest" (Decr. *Optatam totius*, 14).
4. Theology is usually defined as that branch of knowledge which deals with God viewed in the light of divine revelation. As St Anselm put it, it is *fides quaerens intellectum*, faith seeking understanding (*Proslogium*, I). Cf. John Paul II: "Faith is the vital and permanent root of theology which emerges, precisely, from the questioning and searching which are intrinsic to faith itself. That is, it comes from its impulse to comprehend itself, both in its radically free option of personal adherence to Christ and in its assent to the content of Christian revelation. Carrying on theology is then a task which belongs exclusively to the believer as believer, a task inspired and sustained by faith at every single moment and by that unlimited questioning and searching" (*Address to teachers of theology*, Salamanca, 1 November 1982).

In a certain way, the profession of faith—*Jesus is the Christ*—is a resume of the Christian faith; and Christology is nothing other than the theological development of the content of that profession.[5] It involves, obviously, not just speculation on something in which the student is not involved, not committed to;[6] rather, it means exercising *reason enlightened by faith*[7] in order to *discover* Christ and repeat the very words the first disciples used when they told each other of their joy at having found him: "Come and see" (Jn 1:39); "We have found the Messiah" (Jn 1:41).

Christianity is the good news of Christ; in fact, we can say that Christianity is Christ. As the *Catechism of the Catholic Church* puts it, "the transmission of the Christian faith consists primarily in proclaiming Jesus Christ in order to lead others to faith in him."[7a] What identifies the Christian is nothing other than identification with Christ. From this it follows that the Church's mission is simply that of preaching the truth about Christ and *changing* people into Christ. What the Encylical *Redemptor hominis* says about the relationship between the Church and the mystery of Christ can in a sense be applied to the theologian: "The Church lives his mystery, draws unwearyingly from it and continually seeks ways of bringing this mystery of her Master and Lord to humanity—to the peoples, the nations, the succeeding generations, and every individual human being—as if she were ever repeating, as the Apostle did: 'For I decided to know nothing among you except Jesus Christ and him crucified' (1 Cor 2:2)".[8]

In this respect, it is useful to emphasise the radical newness of the Christian religion in the context of the history of religions. Christianity is, first and foremost, following a man (Jesus), whom one *confesses* to be the Messiah (*the Christ*) expected by the Jewish people—a man whom one worships, loves and listens to with the same commitment that one has to God the Creator, because one firmly believes that that man, a son of Adam, is also the Only-begotten of the Father, God from God, and Redeemer and Saviour of mankind.

From this perspective, it must be said "that Christology lies at the heart of all Catholic dogma. Catholic dogma is centred on Christ. The mystery of

---

5. Cf. W. Kasper, *Jesus the Christ* (London, 1976), 15.
6. Christology is not an "indirect discourse" (merely asserting, e.g., that the first Christians believed that God raised Jesus of Nazareth from the dead), nor is it an *historicist* study in which the theologian does not commit himself personally. Christology, rather, accepts the testimony of those "chosen by God as witnesses" (Acts 10:41); basing itself on this testimony it unambiguously makes this assertion which continues to "shock": *Jesus is the Son of God, who died and rose from the dead to save mankind*. It explores the implications of that assertion.
7. Theology is grounded on faith and guided by faith; but it is also the product of reasoning. Theological study leads to a deeper understanding of the mysteries of faith and how they interconnect (cf. First Vatican Council, Const. *Dei Filius*, ch. 4, DS 3015-20).
7a. CCC, no. 425. And a little further on it says: "In order to be a Christian it is necessary to believe that Jesus Christ is the Son of God (cf. Acts 8:37; 1 Jn 2:23)" (ibid., no. 454).
8. John Paul II, Enc. *Redemptor hominis* (4 March 1979), 7.

God become man is the 'Holy of Holies' of the Church."[9] It follows automatically that, over and above any other consideration, *Who is Jesus Christ?* is the key question in all Christian belief and conduct. His Person is the basis of the authority with which he addresses his appeal to us and of the commitment his teaching elicits: everything is grounded on *who* this Person is who proclaims it. A good example of this is the Sermon on the Mount: "You have heard that it was said to the men of old. . . . But I say to you" (cf. Mt 5:21). The question, then, of *who* and *what* Jesus Christ is is the key question which neither theologian nor believer can avoid. Therefore, the answer to this question must be clear and unambiguous.

The Church provides such an answer in the *Symbols*, in its Creeds. The Creed of Nicea-Constantinople is a very good example of the clarity of this profession of faith, and it echoes faithfully what we find in the New Testament: "You are the Christ, the Son of the living God", Peter solemnly and significantly confesses at Caesarea Philippi (Mt 16:16).

It is *Christ himself* that man should search for, and not some "image" of him, more or less beautiful, more or less touching. As at Caesarea Philippi, Jesus' question continues to be put to every man, every woman, and put also to that branch of knowledge which wishes to be called "Christology": "But who do you say that I am?" (Mt 16:15). The salvation-bearing reply (the *salutaris confessio*) to this question comes to us from "on high" (cf. Mt 16:17), for it is a response of faith, which is beyond man's natural powers; faith is a *gift* while being at the same time in conformity with reason, a *reasonable service*.[10] Thus, "it is that we receive the belief in Jesus from the Church, and not from philosophical and textual criticism."[11] Consequently, " whoever seeks Christ without the Church, putting his trust in his own insight and what goes by the name of criticism, deprives himself of all possibility of finding the living Christ. Only the living comprehends and affirms the living."[12] In fact, "without the living Church, the Gospels and, indeed, the entire New Testament would be simply a more or less stirring literary composition, raised, it is true, high above all other religious literature, even the Old Testament, but all the same just a body of writing robbed of the breath of life, the fresh inspiration of flesh-and-blood reality."[13]

9. K. Adam, *The Christ of Faith* (London, 1957), 4.
10. Cf. First Vatican Council, Const. *Dei Filius*, chaps. 3 and 4 (DS 3008-20). On the different approaches to the mystery of Christ, cf., e.g., P. Rodriguez, "Actitudes humanas ante Cristo" in ScrTH 21 (1989), 847-66.
11. K. Adam, op. cit., 5.
12. Ibid.
13. Ibid.

2. HISTORICAL STUDY OF JESUS OF NAZARETH

At the same time it must be said that the profession of faith, which governs all theological work, refers to the life of Jesus Christ. "Jesus Christ", we read in an important document from the International Theological Commission, "the object referent of the Church's faith, is neither a myth nor any sort of abstract notion. He is a man who lived in a concrete milieu and who died after having lived his own life within the unfolding of a historical process. It follows that historical research concerning Jesus Christ is demanded by the Christian faith itself."[14] And, more recently, the Pontifical Biblical Commission reminds us that "this research is never detached, is never neutral (*nunquam est neutra*). In fact, the person of Jesus affects (*tangit*) every human being, including the historian, through the implications of his life and of his death, because of the importance of his message for human existence and because of the portrayal of his personality witnessed to in each book of the New Testament [. . .]. Nobody can study and present in a totally detached way (*modo prorsus objectivo*) the humanity of Jesus, the drama of his life culminating on the Cross and the message which he left as an inheritance to the human race by means of his words and his disciples and his very own existence. Nevertheless, this historical research is totally necessary in order to avoid two dangers: that of Jesus being considered merely as a mythological hero or that of confession of faith in Him as Messiah and Son of God being left in the hands of an irrational fideism."[15]

It is faith in the incarnation of the Son of God (in the "humanation" of the Word, and all its consequences) that lovingly leads theologians to research the life of Christ. This research is inspired above all by the affirmation that the Word became flesh in the womb of a woman; by the sincerity with which one believes that a particular man, born in Bethlehem and crucified in Jerusalem under Pontius Pilate,[16] is God. The doctrine of the faith not only refers back to history but also contains as an integral part of its make-up certain clearly documented events.

The New Testament makes this very clear; it was written to stir up our faith (cf. Jn 20:21), and conceived as a *narrative* of what Jesus of Nazareth did and taught (cf., e.g., Lk 1:1f; 1 Cor 15:1-8), for it depicts the Apostles first and foremost as *witnesses* of the death and resurrection of our Lord (cf., e.g.,

---

14. International Theological Commission (hereinafter ITC), *Select Questions on Christology* (1979), I.A.1.185. Our quotations are taken from Sharkey, M., *International Theological Commission. Texts and Documents 1969-1985* (San Francisco, 1989).

15. Pontifical Biblical Commission, *Bible et christologie* (Paris 1984), 1.1.3.3., 22.

16. K. Lehmann comments on the article *Crucifixus sub Pontio Pilato*: "That is why the addition of 'he suffered under Pontius Pilate' which introduces a tone of abrupt break, as it were, into the Creed, is indispensable. It underlines in an unavoidable way the specific appearance of God in the midst of the cruelty of history and the infinite seriousness of his compassion towards all creatures": "Souffert sous Ponce Pilate", in various authors, *Je crois*, Paris 1978, 56.

Acts 2:32ff) and only secondarily as bearers of a particular (and sublime) teaching. In this connexion it is interesting to note the form the profession of faith takes in the various *Symbols*. They all focus on the life of Jesus, on his birth and death.[17] The very struggle against the various types of *Docetism* in defence of the fact that our Lord was truly a man of flesh and blood,[18] the tireless insistence on man's salvation being *salus carnis*, salvation of the flesh,[19] is nothing but a consequence (and also a proof) of the fact that the central nucleus of *preaching* is made up of historical events: Jesus of Nazareth (who is asserted to be the Son of God) died according to the Scriptures and rose on the third day according to the Scriptures. This is part of the essential nucleus of the *paradosis*, of the treasure which has to be passed on.[20]

And so theology in every age has meditated at length on the mysteries of the Lord's life, because that life is itself a revelation of God. As the Second Vatican Council teaches, the divine plan "of Revelation is realized by deeds and words, which are intrinsically bound up with each other. As a result, the works performed by God in the history of salvation show forth and bear out the doctrine and realities signified by the words; the words, for their part, proclaim the works, and bring to light the mystery they contain."[21]

As we have pointed out, the purpose of the New Testament is not to provide a cold, detached account of the life of Jesus of Nazareth. It clearly does not aim to provide a biography of Jesus in the twentieth-century sense. The New

17. Our Lord's incarnation and his birth from the Blessed Virgin, his passion and death under Pontius Pilate, his resurrection and ascension into heaven form the core of all the Creeds. Cf., e.g., the so-called *Apostles' Creed*, that of St Epiphanius, the Creed of the First Council of Toledo or the Pseudo-Athanasian Creed (*Quicumque*).

18. Docetism is the name applied to a whole series of sects (especially those with Gnostic, dualist and Manichaean tendencies) which denied the reality of the Saviour's human nature (more specifically, of his body), sufferings and death. They said that this was only *apparent*; hence the name, deriving from *dokein*, to appear. The Church vigorously rejected this distortion of the Gospel. For these heresies the incarnation becomes just a vague epiphany or manifestation of God in the apparent form of a man. The Fathers fought this heresy because, among other reasons, all *soteriology* is based on the *truth* of the flesh, death and resurrection of Christ. If Christ did not die, our faith is vain (cf. 1 Cor 15:14). St Ignatius of Antioch, St Irenaeus of Lyons and Tertullian, to mention but a few, argued along these lines.

19. This is seen very clearly from the stress put on the fact that man's salvation implies resurrection (cf., e.g., 1 Cor 15). As Labriolle points out, the Church had to do battle with all Platonic and Neoplatonic thought, which rejected resurrection (cf. De Labriolle, *La reaction païenne*, Paris, 1934. 223ff). St Irenaeus' theology is very eloquent in this regard; it is a theology of the salvation of the flesh (cf. A. Orbe, *Antropología de San Ireneo*, Madrid, 1979).

20. St Paul emphasizes that he is passing on what he himself received, what was passed on to him: "Now I would remind you, brethren, in what terms I preached to you the Gospel, which you received, in which you stand, by which you are saved, if you hold it fast—unless you believed in vain. For I delivered to you as of first importance what I also received, that Christ died . . ." (1 Cor 15:1-8). As K. Adam points out, what really stands out in early Christian preaching is the human dimension of Jesus, his historical reality, the fact that he *died* and *rose*, thereby proving that he is the expected Messiah (cf. K. Adam, op. cit., 70).

21. Second Vatican Council, Const. *Dei Verbum*, 2.

Testament, and with it the entire Tradition of the Church, bears witness to the Church's faith concerning Jesus as *Christ* (Messiah) and *Kyrios* (Lord). The acknowledgment of Jesus as Christ and Lord implies, among other things, the holy respect with which the witness gives testimony of what his eyes have seen and his hands touched concerning the Word of Life (cf. 1 Jn 1:1-4), Thus, the profession of faith *Jesus is the Lord* refers the believer and Christology back to a totally concrete history (yet one of universal significance), and to the unique destiny of a man who is regarded as a perfect man but not *a mere man*,[22] because he is God.

A theologian needs to have a very balanced and studied approach to this subject, which reflects very acutely the tensions that exist between history and faith. Thus, Jesus insofar as he is the Word Incarnate, that is, to the extent that his reality which transcends humanity becomes involved in our human history, has a dimension (the historical dimension) which is accessible to historico-critical analysis. It is a matter of the same kind of accessibility as that of other personalities of his time, that is, it depends on the sources one uses and their reliability. On the other hand, Jesus Christ, as far as his divine nature is concerned, totally transcends the scope of historical research, or indeed of any human science. Not even his contemporaries—who had physical contact with him, who heard him speak or saw him work miracles—could penetrate the inner mystery of the *Man-God* without a *gift from on high*, and their personal acceptance of that gift—faith.

Therefore, we should always remember that by itself alone historical research is never sufficient to give one knowledge of the mystery of Christ, because true knowledge of Jesus implies believing that he is the Son of God. And, it must also be said, it is impossible to appreciate fully all the events which in principle should be accessible to historical research, if one sets out with the prejudice that Jesus of Nazareth could not be anything more than a *mere* man. That was the mistake of the Pharisees, of Celsus the philosopher and of Rationalist theology's approach to the life of Christ, the miracles he worked, etc.[23]

22. He is a man who *is* Son of God and Lord of history. While stressing that Christ really is a man, the Fathers also emphasize that he is not an ordinary man (*ouk anthropos koinos*, St Gregory of Nyssa says: *Adv. Apollinarem*, 21, PG 45, 1164-5), because his human nature is the human nature of God and therefore it has infinite dignity and is to be given the highest form of adoration, that of *latria* (cf. L.F. Mateo Seco *Estudios sobre la cristología de Gregorio de Nyssa* [Pamplona, 1978], 47ff). At the same time and in view of the Godhead to which it is hypostatically joined, this Humanity has power over life and death. Cf. the importance given to *anakephalaiosis* (Eph 1:10), the "recapitulation" of all things in Christ by, e.g., St Irenaeus of Lyons (cf. *Adv. Haer.* I, 10, 1, PG 7, 549).

23. They all started out from the presupposition that Jesus Christ could not possibly be God and therefore from the need to find "some natural explanation" for the extraordinary events recounted in the Gospels, e.g., the miracles. The scribes, for example, said that he cast out devils by the power of Beelzebub (cf. Mk 3:22), and Celsus attributed his miracles to Jesus'

The Symbols take pains to show the total and indissoluble *oneness* of our Lord, the close connexion between the figure of Jesus of Nazareth (with a particular, limited history) and the mystery of his personal being (eternal, infinite). This "oneness" is the reason why historical study must be done *hand-in-hand* with faith in the fact that Christ transcends this world: although Jesus of Nazareth is *perfectus homo* (perfect man), he is not a mere man, not a *homo vulgaris* (common man). Even his death (he truly was put to death, suffering all the cruelty of human death) was the death of Him who never for a moment ceased to be the Lord of life and death.[24]

Christ's unity or oneness, which is professed in the Creed and given such prominence—directly and indirectly—in the New Testament and in the Tradition of the Church, clearly implies that we must say that Jesus of Nazareth (the Jesus of history) is at the same time the long-awaited Messiah, Lord and God. In this oneness of Christ the core of the Church's faith lies: the *Jesus of history is the Christ of faith*.

3. THE JESUS OF HISTORY AND THE CHRIST OF FAITH

As we know, the distinction between the "Jesus of history" and the "Christ of faith" and the counterposing of these two ideas developed in an environment of strong anti-dogmatic temper. From Reimarus on, this distinction was at the centre of non-Catholic approaches to the subject. "The questions posed by modern non-Catholic theology are based on the rationalistic assumption that the divinity of the Lord, the figure of God made man, is *a priori* impossible and therefore unhistorical, because it contradicts every comparison with experience and destroys the sequence of cause and effect—new, disrupting, miraculous."[25]

Really, what these theologians feared and rejected was the radical and absolute *newness* of Christianity. They simply would not allow the "order of the universe" to be disturbed by the intrusion upon history of the strictly supernatural.

having learned as a child the arts of Egyptian magicians (cf. Origen, *Contra Celsum*, I, 68; M. Borret, *Contre Celse* I, Paris, 1967 [SCh], 120f).

24. In this connexion Patristic exegesis of John 10:18 is particularly insightful: "I have power to lay (my life) down, and I have power to take it up again". St Augustine comments: "His hour had not yet come, nor that in which he would be obliged to die, but that in which he would condescend to be killed [. . .]. He looked forward to that hour not as a fatal one but as opportune and voluntary in such a way that all would be fulfilled which needed to be fulfilled before the Passion. Because, how could he be made subject to the necessity of destiny who elsewhere had said, 'I have power to lay my life down, and I have power to take it up again' (Jn 10:18)": *Tractatus in Johannem*, 9, 1-30 CCL vol. XXXVI, 336f. This exegesis is studied by L.F. Mateo Seco, "Muerte de Cristo y teología de la Cruz" in various authors, *Cristo, Hijo de Dios y Redemptor del hombre* (Pamplona, 1982), 705-11 and "La exegesis de Gregorio de Nisa a Jn 10:18" in *Cistercian Publications* (Kalamazoo, 1987), 483-94.

25. K. Adam, op. cit., 45.

This ideological prejudice (and no other reason) was the decisive factor that led D.F. Strauss (following Reimarus) in his *Life of Jesus* to deny that the *Christ of faith* was the *Jesus of history*. The *Jesus of history*, the "humble dreamer rabbi of Nazareth", the Jesus of events that really happened, had, according to Strauss, very little to do with the Christ *believed in* and preached by the Apostles, the *Christ of faith*, on to whom the messianic expectations of the Apostles had been projected, creating a false picture, a *myth*. Therefore, to discover the *Jesus of history* he must be "rescued" from this mythologizing on the part of his disciples; historical research, these authors say, should suspect the existence of such mythologizing in every event, every word, in the New Testament, that seems to contain anything that goes "beyond the normal", anything supernatural.

Anyone embarking on the study of Christology needs to be aware of this prejudice, which first appeared with Reimarus. It has had great influence on many books and essays, depriving them of that objectivity which good research must have. "In the last few centuries, historical research on Jesus has been directed against the Christological dogma. And yet this antidogmatic sentiment is not a necessary precondition for the appropriate application of the historical-critical method."[26] The *antidogmatic* attitude, which insists on starting out with the indisputable axiom, *Jesus just could not be God*, is simply a prejudice which is incompatible with that sincere search for truth which is the hallmark of the scholar. However, the fact that historical research about Jesus has been influenced by "antidogmatic prejudices" does not mean that rigorous historical research is not "a requirement of the Christian faith".[27]

At any event, ever since *c.*1778, when the problem of the "historical Jesus"[28] first appeared, the distinction between the *Jesus of history* and the *Christ of faith* cannot be ignored by the student of Christology. According to Reimarus' "notes",[29] the Jesus who really existed in Nazareth (*the Jesus of history*) is not the same as the Christ preached by the Gospels: Jesus was a failed political Messiah; all he did was proclaim that the kingdom of God had arrived (a kingdom he understood in a political sense); that was the kind of kingdom the Apostles had been expecting, and when Jesus died (and with him their hope of political power) they invented the story of Jesus' resurrection and along with it a new religion, in a bid to gain a strong religious following. They re-created Jesus' words and deeds, accommodating them to their purpose. And so, for

26. ITC, op. cit., I.A.1.2. (Sharkey, op. cit., 186).
27. Ibid.
28. Until the end of the eighteenth century, the *historical Jesus* was never seen as a problem, given the trustworthiness of the Gosples. The year 1778 is given because that was the year Lessing published the manuscript left by H.S. Reimarus (+1768). Cf. note 29.
29. In these notes Reimarus who harboured a deep resentment towards the Christian religion argued that Jesus was a failed Messiah and that the Gospels were a fraud concocted by his disciples (cf. H.S. Reimarus, *The goal of Jesus and his disciples*, Leiden, 1970).

Reimarus, the Jesus of history and the Christ of faith are not just two different ways of describing one, single reality (Jesus Christ) but two concepts which are mutually incompatible.

Scarcely anyone followed Reimarus completely (his position was too extreme), and even Strauss, his immediate disciple, modified many things he said.[30] However, the distinction between the *Jesus of history* and the *Christ of faith*, which can be interpreted in many different ways, has never managed (not even as a *method*) to free itself from its original radical defect—that of counterposing history and faith, which was Reimarus' problem.[31]

As was to be expected, the Church rejected the distinction between a Christ of faith and a Jesus of history who would only have been a man (a mere man) and would only have been God through the "transfiguration" and "disfiguration" devised by his disciples.[32] And, as is also obvious, from the early Church onwards the Church has always defended the radicalism of the confession of faith, *Jesus Christ = Jesus is the Christ*. However, although Christ's oneness must be defended, the two expressions, *Jesus of history* and *Christ of faith*, do reflect interesting and valid shades of meaning. The first refers to Jesus' humanity and the way he lived and died when he was on earth; the other refers to that God whom the disciples' faith "discovered" beneath the fragility of Jesus' flesh.

The student, therefore, is confronted with a pair of terms (Jesus of history, Christ of faith) referring to two different but not separable things, just as Jesus' humanity and his divinity are distinct but not separable. Therefore, when one uses the expression Jesus of history, if one does so in a theologically correct way one is referring *in recto* (directly) to Christ's human nature as such and the way he displayed his human qualities over the course of his life on earth; and referring *in obliquo* (indirectly) to that God who showed himself *made man* in the day to day actions and words of Jesus, or in his death. And vice versa when speaking of the Christ of faith.

Jesus, who is the same as we are, except for sin (cf. Heb 4:15) lived a real life—and is therefore accessible to historical research. For his contemporaries Jesus was like any other man; he was accessible to them (they could see him, and hear him and touch him); within the same limits as with other personalities from the past he can be studied also by a modern historian.

Research into the Jesus of history, like all historical research, is possible, to a limited extent; but the study of Jesus' life is no ordinary study due to a unique factor: *this man is God*. That means that when a historian looks at Jesus

30. D.F. Strauss (*Das Leben Jesu kritisch bearbeitet*, Tubingen, 1840) replaced the "fraud" theory with one to the effect that the disciples more or less consciously created a myth about Jesus: cf. M. Vigouroux, "Mythique (sens)" in DB, IV, cols 1386-90. Cf. also M.A. Tabet, *David F. Strauss: La vida en Cristo* (Madrid, 1976).

31. Cf. R. Fabris, *Jesús de Nazaret. Historia e interpretation* (Salamanca, 1985), 27.

32. Cf. Decr. of the Holy Office of 3 July 1907 (*Lamentabili*), and Pius X, Enc. *Pascendi* (cf. DS 3427-38 and 3495-8).

he comes up against the same dilemmas Jesus' contemporaries experienced. One example will be sufficient: what is one to make of the expression, "I am the way, and the truth, and the life" (Jn 14:6)? If he accepts that Jesus said this (as the Apostle John claims) there are two things the historian can do: either he accepts that Jesus is the Lord, and, therefore, that he is revealing his divinity; or else he can think that the *Jesus of history* was a megalomaniac. In any event, one cannot totally dissociate historical (merely historical) knowledge of the *Jesus of history* from that *Christ of faith* to whom he is indissolubly united: "The great value of scholarly inquiries on the Jesus of history is beyond doubt. Inquiries of this sort are particularly important for fundamental theology and in exchanges with non-believers. All the same, a truly Christian knowledge of Jesus cannot rest content with these limited perspectives. Our knowledge of the Person and work of Jesus Christ is inadequate as long as we dissociate the Jesus of history from the Christ as proclaimed. We cannot secure a full knowledge of Jesus unless we take into account the living Faith of the Christian community, which sustains this vision of the facts. This applies whether we seek historical knowledge of Jesus, or inquire into the origins of the New Testament, or engage in Christological reflection."[33]

Among the many problems involved in historical research about Jesus, there is one which has special relevance for the theologian—the reliability of the sources, that is, can one trust the New Testament as history? This is not a question that concerns us here; it belongs to Fundamental Theology and the study of Sacred Scripture. It is sufficient to remember that the Christian religion is completely grounded on faith in Chirst, dead and risen, according to the *witness* of the Twelve. Therefore it would go totally against the very nature of theology to begin one's research "suspicious" of the reliability of the Apostles' testimony regarding Jesus.

4. "ASCENDING" AND "DESCENDING" CHRISTOLOGY

The distinction introduced by Reimarus between the Jesus of history and the Christ of faith also has an impact on Christological method, giving rise to "ascending" (*from below*) and "descending" (*from above*) Christology. These are

---

33. ITC, op. cit., I.B.2 (Sharkey, op. cit., 187). As Ratzinger writes, "For the faith of the newly emerging Church it was a basic conviction that, with this interpretation of the figure of Jesus as Messiah and as Son, it was not a question of giving a latter-day theological transfiguration of one of the masters of Israel but of correctly interpreting his personal words and deeds. Therefore, keeping the memory of the words and deeds of Jesus and the itinerary followed by him, especially as regards his Passion, constitutes from the beginning the formative nucleus of the Christian tradition and of its rules. The identity of the earthly Jesus with the risen Jesus is fundamental for the faith of the community and blocks all posterior separation between the historical Jesus and the kerigmatic Jesus": J. Ratzinger, *Dogma e predicazione* (Brescia, 1974), 115; English trs., *Dogma and Preaching* (Chicago, 1985).

simply methods or approaches but they involve deep theological implications.

These two ways into the mystery of Christ began to be described in this way ("ascending", "descending") in the 1950s and are now widely used by scholars. However, it is not at all easy to work out what they mean: every writer seems to have his own definitions.

For some, *descending* Christology simply means "emphasising the rights of Christ's divinity", whereas *ascending* Christology emphasises "those of his humanity".[34] In which case, it is merely a matter of different accents, different emphases. That is why some wished to refer this new distinction right back to the difference in approach of the so-called Alexandrian and Antiochene schools (the former putting the stress on Christ's divinity, the latter on his humanity).

We are very familiar with the problems caused by the theological trends of those two schools[35] — going to prove that extremism (even just in method), unilateralism, reductionism is something to be avoided. For those who understand the distinction between descending and ascending Christology as simply a matter of different emphases, the comparison with the Antiochene and Alexandrian schools would be fairly valid—but only in a certain sense, because the difference between these theologies stems from emphasising Christ's unity of person (Alexandria) or diversity of natures (Antioch), whereas the problem presented by ascending/descending Christologies is quite a different one.[36]

This becomes quite clear the more you analyse other definitions of this ascent/descent distinction—especially those which stress that everything hinges on the application of this distinction to the Jesus of history/Christ of faith binomial initiated by Reimarus. That is the view held by people such as H. Küng, for example, which J.L. Illanes describes as follows: "Descending Christology is that which, in its method, is grounded on and derived from the very beginning from consideration of Christ's divinity; whereas ascending Christology is built up on the man Jesus abstracting from his divinity, which eventually appears only to the extent that it is manifested in his humanity."[37]

---

34. "There is a descending Christology and an ascending Christology—the one stressing the rights of Christ's divinity, the other of his humanity": A. Grillmeier, "La imagen de Cristo . . ." in *Panorámica de la teología católica actual*, Madrid, 1961, 359. This distinction began to circulate from 1954 onwards, in the debate on the Council of Chalcedon.

35. The "Alexandrines" (e.g., Origen, Cyril of Alexandria, Eutyches) by stressing Christ's divinity run the risk of a certain subordinationism or Monophysitism. The main danger in the Antiochene tradition is Nestorianism, because of the difficulty it has in providing a correct theological explanation of the unity of person in Christ. Cf., e.g., J. Liebaert, *L'Incarnation. Des origines au Concile de Chalcédoine* (Paris, 1966), 138-41, 179-81, 221f.

36. The ascending/descending distinction is heavily influenced by the Jesus of history/Christ of faith distinction, a distinction that would be unthinkable for the Fathers (both the Alexandrian and Antiochene "schools" would have rejected it).

37. J.L. Illanes, "Cristología 'desde arriba' y cristología 'desde abajo'", in *Cristo, Hijo de Dios y Redentor del hombre* (see note 34), 146. Here are some phrases from Küng which more than

It is quite obvious that the problems involved here are different from those of the fourth-century controversies.

Between the consideration of the binomial (ascending/descending) as merely a matter of emphasis and the view that Christology is ascending or descending depending on whether one abstracts from the divinity of Christ or not, there is a whole range of views as to what these terms mean, especially among Catholic theologians; the Pontifical Biblical Commission describes the situation as follows: "Among recent researches in Christology those which start out from the historical Jesus are presented, to a certain extent, as Christologies *'from below'*. On the other hand those which place the emphasis on the filial relationship of Jesus with the Father can be called *'Christologies from above'*. Many contemporary projects strive to combine these two points of view demonstrating by means of criticial studies of the texts that the Christology implied in the words and in the human experience of Jesus is in profound continuity with the explicit Christologies to be found in the New Testament."[38]

The synthesis has not yet been achieved and there is as yet no solid definition of the ascending/descending distinction (which as we have seen is not just a matter of methodology). However, most theologians do agree that the distinction must not be absolute: that is, Christology must be both *ascending* and *descending*. In fact, "the validity of the *ascending* approach is at risk to the degree that one proposes it as an exclusive Christological model or as an alternative to the *descending* model on the specious grounds that it is complete and self-sufficient."[39] In other words, an ascending Christology in an exclusivist sense is already, from the very start, clearly reductive of the total mystery of Jesus (the divinity indissolubly united to his humanity), but it is *also* reductive of what actually happened in the humanity of Jesus, because it will only accept as really happening in the Jesus of history those events that human experience is willing to accept. This is certainly the thrust of certain influential publications in recent decades.[40]

---

justify Illanes' description: "Would it not be more in accordance with New Testament testimonies and the markedly historical thinking of contemporary man to start out, like the first disciples, from the true man Jesus, from his message and his historical appearance, from his life and his destiny, from his temporal reality and from his impact on history, in order to inquire as to the relationship of this Jesus-man with God, as to his unity with the Father? In a word: less speculative or dogmatic Christology from above in the classical manner, and more historical Christology from below, that is to say, from the concrete historical Jesus": H. Küng, *Ser cristiano* (Madrid, 1977), 163; English trs., *On Being a Christian* (1991).

38. Pontifical Biblical Commission (see note 15), 1.1.11.1, ed. cit., 42. Authors who are mentioned as seeking this are L. Bouyer, R. Fuller, C.F.D. Moule, I.H. Marshall, B. Rey, C. Duquoc, W. Kasper, M. Hengel, J.D. Dunn.
39. M. Bordoni, *Gesù di Nazaret Signore e Cristo* (Rome, 1982), I, 75.
40. This is true of the Christologies of Schillebeeckx, Küng and Duquoc.

5. CHRISTOLOGY AND JESUOLOGY

Bound up with the distinction between ascending and descending Christology is another distinction made by certain recent writers, particularly in the Latin American world—that between *Christology* and *Jesuology*. *Christology* is used to describe the classical approach to this subject, whereas Jesuology has to do with the study of the *Jesus of history* and, even more specifically, the *Jesus of history* as he appeared to and was understood by his disciples prior to his resurrection. Jesuology seeks "to reflect on the human life, the merely human life, of Jesus Christ. We want to go back to see that Jesus of Nazareth the way his disciples saw him, to understand him as they did . . . when they did not as yet know him as the Lord and the Son of God . . . , when in the eyes of the disciples he was still a man, just a man."[41]

In a sense one can say that *Jesuology* is a particularly radical way of applying the methodology of ascending Christology—not just trying to get back to the *Jesus of history* by abstracting from his divinity but trying to reflect on that Jesus simply and solely as he was "understood" by his disciples before his resurrection; that is, focussing exclusively on the *pre-paschal Jesus* as his disciples saw him. Sometimes this seems not so much a theological approach as an effort to take an evasive detour on the spiritual journey towards a meeting with Christ: "Might it not be that we are determined to accompany the man Jesus, for a large part of the way, in his man's humanity, solely man, as if there were not a divine person in him, instead of wanting to enter straightaway into the secret of his divinity?"[42]

This description of the Jesuology approach indicates the problem it poses for the theologian. The question must be raised: Did a Jesus of Nazareth ever exist who was *solely* a man? Rightly has this approach been charged with taking as its base the idea that you can separate Jesus Christ into *Jesus* and *Christ*, and moreover make a radical distinction between the *pre-paschal* and *post-paschal Jesus*. On the contrary, it has to be said that "The substantive and radical unity between the Jesus of history and the glorified Christ pertains to the very essence of the Gospel message. Should Christological inquiry limit itself to the Jesus 'of history', it would be incompatible with the essence and structure of the New Testament, even before being disavowed from without by a religious authority."[43]

6. THE CHURCH, THE HOME OF FAITH IN JESUS

As we said at the start of this introduction, Christology is in the last analysis

41. J. Comblin, *Jesus of Nazareth* (New York, 1976), 7.
42. Ibid., 19.
43. ITC, op. cit., I.B.2.2 (Sharkey, op. cit., 187).

nothing other than the study in the light of faith of what that faith itself teaches concerning the mystery and the work of Christ. The New Testament is a fruit of that faith and witnesses to it. The writings it comprises originated, by divine inspiration, in the living Church, the Church it is who recognizes their authority and explains their meaning; in the Church, the living Church, these writings reach the men and women of every generation as *living* documents. Thus, the really basic element in Christianity is not the Bible but the living preaching of the Church;[44] it can even be said that "outside the Church, Scripture cannot be understood."[45]

So, the temptation of such "biblicism" which separates off the Bible from the Church must be rejected: "It is clear, therefore, that, in the supremely wise arrangement of God, sacred Tradition, sacred Scripture and the Magisterium of the Church are so connected and associated that one of them cannot stand without the others. Working together, each in its own way under the action of the one Holy Spirit, they all contribute effectively to the salvation of souls."[46]

We can see, on the one hand, that the faith of the early Church is reflected in the New Testament; the wording of its numerous confessions of faith shows the importance given to clear language in professing the main truths concerning the mystery of Christ. "The original and primitive synthesis of the earthly Jesus with the risen Christ surfaces in various 'confessional formulas' and 'homologies', which mention at the same time and with the same particular insistence, both the death and the Resurrection of Jesus. Together with Romans 1:3ff, we can quote, among other texts, 1 Corinthians 15:3-4: 'I handed on to you first of all what I myself received: that Christ died for our sins in accordance with the Scriptures.' These texts posit an authentic connection between the story of a man and the significance of Jesus Christ, which endures forever. In a nutshell, they set forth 'the history of the essence' of Jesus Christ. This synthesis continues to be an example and a model for any genuine Christology to follow."[47]

The New Testament is a faithful reflection of the Apostles' preaching and of the life of the early Christian community. It outlines among other things those homologies through which, in succinct statements, what was considered to be the very essence of the testimony regarding Jesus, was received and transmittted in condensed and binding form. The solemn text just quoted from 1 Corinthians is a good example. By quoting it and referring to the existence in the New Testament of *confessions of faith* the Theological Commission is

---

44. K. Adam, op. cit., 4.
45. J.A. Möhler, *L'unita nella Chiesa. Il principio del Cattolicesimo nello spirito dei Padri della Chiesa dei primi tre secoli* (Rome, 1969), 34. What Möhler says faithfully reflects Patristic tradition: cf., e.g., St Irenaeus, *Adversus haereses*, IV, 33, 8 (PG 7, 1077).
46. Second Vatican Council, Const. *Dei Verbum*, 10.
47. ITC, op. cit. I.B.2.4 (Sharkey, op. cit., 187).

not accepting the idea that there is a canon within the canon;[48] what it is trying to do is to show how these Christological syntheses are the litmus test for distinguishing true and false Christologies.

This document from the Theological Commission is well aware of that "biblicism" and of the attempt of some contemporary scholars to "get back" to the "historical Jesus", to "rescue" his image from the disfigurement it underwent even in the minds of the early Christians.[49] From the theological point of view that approach contains an internal contradiction: it tries to gain access to Jesus Christ taking only what suits (literally "sifting") from the testimony of those whom Jesus himself chose to be his witnesses not only in Jerusalem and for the first few years but to the whole world and for ever. Apostolicity, however, is an essential mark of the Church: " The substantive and radical unity between the Jesus of history and the glorified Christ pertains to the very essence of the Gospel message."[50]

For a Christology to be *authentic*, not only does it have to follow the "example and model" established by the Apostles' testimony but that testimony has to be understood in the way the Church has understood it down the centuries. Just as Christ and his Church cannot be separated (the Head cannot be cut off from his mystical body), by analogy Christology and ecclesiology form a unity. It is not enough to go back to the faith of the primitive community. A valid Christological synthesis needs to comprise not only the confession of faith of the Christian community as a fact of history; it has to show also that the Church (at all periods of history) has been the place to find the truth about Jesus Christ and his work.[51] In other words, "only in the context of the communitarian faith of the Church can one take the Bible literally and believe that what it says is true, that it really happened, that it is history (*Geschichte*).

---

48. We refer to that view (Protestant in origin) which argues that even in Sacred Scripture one must distinguish core writings which have greater authority than others.

49. This is very noticeable in the works of many liberation theologians. Cf. what SCDF, Inst. *Libertatis nuntius* (6 August 1984), X, 5-8 has to say: "The new hermeneutic inherent in the 'theologies of liberation' leads to an essentially political re-reading of the Scriptures [. . .]. Likewise, one places oneself within the perspective of a temporal messianism, which is one of the most radical of the expressions of secularisation of the Kingdom of God and of its absorption into the immanence of human history [. . .]. Moreover, in setting aside the authoritative interpretation of the Church, denounced as classist, one is at the same time departing from tradition. In that way one is robbed of an essential theological criterion of interpretation and, in the vacuum thus created, one welcomes the most radical theses of rationalist exegesis. Without a critical eye, one returns to the opposition of the 'Jesus of history' versus the 'Jesus of faith'." On the methods used to "rescue" the "historical Jesus" cf. L.F. Mateo Seco, "Algunos aspectos de la teología de la liberacion" ScrTh 17 (1985), 265-8; cf. "Boletín de Cristología", ibid., 920-36.

50. ITC, op. cit., I.B.2.2 (Sharkey, op. cit., 187-188).

51. Ibid., I.B.2.5 (op. cit., 187). Cf. Pontifical Biblical Commission, op. cit., 1.1.3, chapter entitled "Christology and historical research" which lists the unsurmountable difficulties that arise when this research is pursued outside the ecclesial context.

This is what gives validity to the dogmatic interpretation of the Bible even
from an historical (*historisch*) point of view: the authoritative source of guidance
for exegesis which the Church is, is the only one that can vouch that the
writings of the Bible are Sacred Scripture and that the Church's own
declarations are true and full of meaning."[52]

7. THE CHRISTOLOGICAL FAITH OF THE EARLY COUNCILS

The *Christological synthesis* which we have been discussing has become more
precise over the course of the Church's history, particularly in the formulations
of the ecumenical councils in the first six centuries—from Nicea (AD 325) to
the Third Council of Constantinople (681). From the point of view of specific
Christological formulations, in a certain sense the highest point is reached with
the Council of Chalcedon (451). For this reason many books and essays in
recent years make a distinction between *Chalcedonian Christologies* and *non-
Chalcedonian Christologies*, depending on whether they accept the teaching of
Chalcedon (with its distinction between *person* and *nature* and its considering
both as included in the order of being); or whether they try to evade that
teaching.[53]

   The debate about Chalcedon[54] implies, in turn, a prior, radical disagreement
on how to view the growing doctrinal *explicitness* which marked the early
centuries of the Church. The question underlying this debate is as follows:
How are we to interpret the evident doctrinal development which took place
in the so-called "Christology Councils"? Is it to be seen as an adding on (of
theological conclusions) to the original, simple Gospel message? Is it simply a
process of *explaining*,[55] a *development* of the Gospel's teaching concerning Jesus
of Nazareth, which could be regarded as simply "one more explanation" (one

52. J. Ratzinger, "Transmisión de la fe y fuentes de la fe", ScrTh 15 (1983), 27.
53. For an analysis of "non-Chalcedonian Christologies" cf. e.g., J. Galot, *Cristo contestato*
    (Florence, 1979), esp. 91-106.
54. The debate begins, oddly enough, in a book written to commemorate that Council (A.
    Grillmeier and H. Bacht, *Das Konzil von Chalkedon. Geschichte und Gegenwart*: Würtzburg,
    1954). The book that in a sense inspires the whole debate is that of K. Rahner, *Chalkedon,
    Ende oder Anfang?* (III, 3-49), where he argues that Chalcedon should be a point of departure
    for new research on key questions of Christology. For an account of the debate cf. B.
    Sesboüé, "Le Procés contemporain de Chalcédoine. Bilan et perspectives", RSR 65 (1977),
    45-80. See also M.V. Leroy, "Le Christ de Chalcédoine", RT 73 (1973), 75-93.
55. We use the word in its etymological sense, of "unfolding" or of "ironing out the creases in
    a garment". What this question asks is whether the doctrinal development which takes place
    in the early councils should be understood as an unfolding made to people who had a
    hellenistic outlook; so that, when that Greek mode of thought had gone out of fashion, the
    whole matter could be folded up again and then subjected to a new unfolding in a sense
    which is more in tune with twentieth-century thinking. In other words, instead of the
    teaching of these councils being taken as a *normative interpretation* of the doctrine of the
    faith, should it not be seen as something temporary and compatible with all sorts of other
    divergent, explanations?

among many) compatible with "other explanations which might well disagree
with it? Indeed, could this "explanation" of Christological dogma by the early
councils not be seen as one of the main effects of a "hellenization" of
Christianity, an influence which sent it off course?[56]

As one can see, the "debate" about Chalcedon, which has led some people
to identify opposite camps (Chalcedonian and non-Chalcedonian) is not a mere
argument about method: it stems from and involves a different view not only
of the main Christological topics (especially, that of the hypostatic union) but
also a different concept of what development of dogma in the Church means,
and a different concept of what the Church herself is. "The theologians who
in our time raise doubts about the divinity of Christ", the International
Theological Commission says, "often argue that this dogma cannot have
emerged from genuine biblical revelation; its origins are traceable to Hellenism.
Deeper historical inquiries show, on the contrary, that the thought pattern of
the Greeks was totally alien to this dogma and that they rejected it with the
utmost vigor."[57]

Basically these writers all espouse one key idea—that the statement *Jesus
is the Lord* (*Kyrios*) is really just one more instance of "divinization" (of
"mythologizing") which would find its parallel model in the "divinizations" of
pagan religions.

What this kind of approach forgets is the vigour with which the writers of
the early centuries asserted that Christ *is not a divinised man*; he is the *Son of
God made flesh*. For example, in the Arian polemic against the Catholic Church,
the "hellenization" lay in Arius' view of the Logos as a *deuteros theos*, or lower
God. "The Arian heresy offers a good illustration of how the dogma of Christ's
divinity would have looked had it truly emerged from the philosophy of
Hellenism and not from God's own revelation. At the Council of Nicaea in
AD 325, the Church defined that the Son is consubstantial (*homoousios*) with
the Father. In so doing, the Church both repudiated the Arian compromise
with Hellenism and deeply altered the shape of Greek, especially Platonist and
neo-Platonist, metaphysics."[58]

---

56. The question of the Hellenization of Christianity was raised by A. von Harnack in his
  Dogmengeschichte, in which he argued that the teaching of the early councils was not a faithful
  unfolding of the content of Revelation, but rather the outcome of a "paganization" of
  Christianity, a betrayal of Revelation.
57. ITC, op. cit., II A.1 (Sharkey, op. cit., 188).
58. Ibid. (II A.2) 189. Here is how Grillmeier sees it: "Nicea is not a 'hellenization' but a
  'dehellenization' or liberation of the Christian image of God further advanced than the
  impasse and the divisions which hellenism gave rise to. So it is not that the Greeks made
  Nicea; rather, Nicea left the Greek philosophers behind", A. Grillmeier, "De Jésus de
  Nazaret dans l'ombre du Fils de Dieu au Christ image de Dieu" in *Comment être chrétien?
  La réponse de Küng*, ed. J.R. Armogathe (Paris, 1979), 128. The same point is made in B.
  Sesboüé, *Jésus-Christ dans la tradition de l'Eglise* (Paris, 1982), 100ff; J. Ortiz de Urbina,
  Nicea y Constantinopla (Vitoria, 1969), 79ff.

Both the early writers and the Council fathers were well aware of the radical newness of Christianity, a newness which prevented its being confused with either Judaism or paganism.[59] "To be sure, 'homoousios', the term used by the Council of Nicaea, is a philosophical and non-biblical term. It is evident all the same that, ultimately, the Fathers of the Council only intended to express the authentic meaning of the New Testament assertions concerning Christ, and to do this in a way that would be uniquivocal and free from all ambiguity."[60] So, we are not dealing here with a later explanation which adds something to the content of Scripture; we are dealing with an *authorised* and *normative interpretation* of the teaching of the New Testament.

And so, for example, by choosing a non-biblical term (*homoousios*), all that the Council of Nicea was trying to do was explain what is meant by the statement that Jesus is the Only-begotten of the Father: it was giving an *authorised reading* of what the New Testament has to say about Jesus' filiation to the Father. Thus, by saying that the Son is of *the same substance as* the Father, all the Magisterium of the Church is doing is pointing out that Jesus' filiation to the Father has to be understood in the fullest sense of the word "filiation"—with all the meaning the Father-Son relationship involves. The teaching of the other Christological councils had exactly the same purpose.[61]

59. Here is an eloquent passage from Gregory of Nyssa (similar to many other fourth-century texts): "So, therefore, he who considers the depth of the mystery with precision, receives in his soul, in a hidden way, a moderate degree of knowledge of the doctrine about God. He cannot, however, explain the ineffable depth of the mystery in words: how it is numbered and yet escapes all counting; it is contemplated as divided and yet considered as one single thing; the fact that it is distinct in hypostasis and yet is not divided in its substance, and, nevertheless, the Word and the Spirit are one and other. But once you have considered its distinction (reflect again on the fact that) its unity of nature does not admit division. So it is that the primacy of the monarchy is not torn asunder in distinct divinities nor is what is being said the same as the Jewish teaching. Therefore the truth passes through the middle between two extremes and purifies both heresies (the Jewish which does not accept the trinity of persons and the Greek which accepts many persons, many gods) and at the same time takes whatever is appropriate from both": *Oratio catechetica magna*, 3: PG 45 17 C-D. For a detailed study of this text, cf. L.F. Mateo Seco, *Estudios sobre la cristología de Gregorio de Nisa*, op. cit., 90-101.

60. ITC, op. cit., II.A.2 (Sharkey, op. cit., 189).

61. St Vincent Lerins rejoices to see that the council Fathers of Ephesus specifically say that they did not want to add anything to what had come down from the Fathers; rather their *only desire was to confirm what had already been received*: "Furthermore we have admired and proclaimed how great the humility and holiness of that council must have been. How such a gathering of priests—Metropolitans, most of them—of such learning and such doctrine that almost all of them could have given a dissertation on dogmas and whom for this reason their very meeting would seem to fill with confidence to say or establish something by themselves, nevertheless, did not innovate anything. They arrogated absolutely nothing for themselves but merely confined themselves to striving by all possible means to ensure that they did not hand on anything that had not been received from the Fathers": *Commonitorium*, 31. Cf. L.F. Mateo Seco, *San Vincente de Lerins: Tratado en defensa de la antigüedad y universalidad de la fe católica* (Pamplona, 1977), 209-211. Cf. B. Sesboüé, op. cit., esp. 100ff; 132-51.

The solemn Christological statements issued by these early councils are not the last word; they do not exhaust the richness of the mystery. They do not put an end to theological study on the subject but invite us to go ever deeper into it. It can be said that the various conciliar definitions arise from the radicalism with which, in line with the Apostles' testimony, the councils confess that Jesus Christ *is* perfect man[62] and at the same time perfect God. That is why, when one examines the long course between the start and the finish of the Christological controversies, one discovers that the final outcome (the conciliar statements ever more precise in their terminology) in no way differ *in content* from the position at the beginning of the process. This shows the limits and the greatness of the work those Councils did: they added nothing to the revealed message, but they prevented it being interpreted in such a way as to drain it of content. "The changes in language did not alter the message; its meaning has not been enhanced or deformed; our understanding and conceptualisation of the message has been strengthened and deepened."[63]

8. CHRISTOLOGY AND THE MYSTERY OF GOD

To say that Jesus Christ is the Only-begotten of the Father, "God from God and light from light" immediately puts the focus on the close links between Christology and the treatise on God. In a sense, it is not possible to know either of these treatises without knowing the other. We will refer now to some of the basic topics.

The New Testament explicitly teaches that the Word existed prior to the moment of the Incarnation.[64] Prior to his self-emptying,[65] it gives another sign of his transcendence over all creation, of his belonging to the sphere of the divine. Jesus Christ, as God, is eternal, immense, infinitely above every other creature. He is infinitely perfect. He is the creator of the universe, as the first

---

62. "The Church confesses thus," the Catechism of the Catholic Church says in completing its account of the christological doctrine of the early Councils, "that Jesus is inseparably true God and true man. He is truly the Son of God who became man, our brother, and this without ceasing to be God, our Lord" (no. 449).

63. M. González Gil, *Cristo, el misterio de Dios*, I (Madrid, 1986), 127.

64. It is enough to recall the prologue of St John's Gospel, the hymn in the Letter to the Philippians, or the opening of the Letter to the Colossians.

65. As the International Theological Commission notes, "Biblical studies have shown how the original datum has evolved through various stages and in different aspects within the limits of the New Testament as the full meaning of the preexistence of Jesus becomes clear: The eternal election and predestination of Jesus Christ (cf. Eph 1:3-7, 10ff; 1 Pet 1:20); The sending of the Son of God into the world and into the flesh (cf. Gal 4:4; Rom 8:38; 1 Tim 3:16; Jn 3:16ff); 'Kenosis', Incarnation, death and glorious Resurrection of Jesus Christ on the Cross, as steps on the way from the Father—all of which show the soteriological and salvific meaning of the event of Jesus Christ (cf. insup. Phil 2:6-11)": *Theology, Christology, Anthropology* (1981), II, A.3 (Sharkey, op. cit., 217-18).

Christian writers stressed, influenced by the prologue of St John's Gospel: "all things were made through him" (Jn 1:3).[66]

In a sense, to discover the truth concerning Jesus Christ one needs to have that preliminary understanding of the divine being who created the universe and conserves its being: "without such a religious prior understanding amounting to man's being open to the meaning of divine transcendence and to God's active presence in human history, it would not be possible for one to accept as historical so singular a figure as that of Jesus of Nazareth, to accept the singular, unique relationship with God which distinguishes him."[67]

At the same time (and the Council of Chalcedon made this very clear), the incarnation of the Word took place without affecting his divine attributes in any way; these attributes reflect the absolute perfection of God and they are identical with the Godhead; therefore, the *kenosis* (emptying) of which St Paul speaks cannot be interpreted as lessening or loss of the perfections of the divine being.[68] In the Son "all things were created, in heaven and on earth, visible and invisible, whether thrones or dominions or principalities or authorities—all things were created through him and for him" (Col 1:16-17). So, "precisely as a confession of Jesus Christ, Christian faith—and in this it is completely loyal to the faith of Abraham—is faith in a living God. The fact that the first article of faith forms the basis of all Christian belief includes, theologically, the basic character of the ontological statements and the indispensability of the metaphysical, that is, of the Creator God who is before all becoming."[69]

But the relationship of Christology to the treatise on God does not derive only from the fact that, if one says that the Son is perfect God, one has to *predicate* of him the *attributes* which are predicated of the Godhead; the connexion goes deeper than that. Not only is Christ said to be God; he is said to be the *Son* of the Father: "Knowledge of Jesus Christ leads to a knowledge of the Trinity and attains its plenitude in the knowledge of the Trinity; on the other hand, there is no knowledge of the Triune God except in knowledge of Jesus Christ himself. It follows that there is no distinction between Theocentrism and Christocentrism; the two terms denote the same reality."[70]

66. When listing the reasons why it was appropriate for the Word to become man, these writers all conclude that it was fitting that man should be sought out by Him who had created him: cf. Irenaeus, Justin, Origen, Gregory of Nyssa, etc.

67. M. Bordoni (see note 39), 137.

68. This was in large measure the mistake of the *theologia crucis*, so much a feature of Lutheran thought and, especially, of the kenotic movements of the nineteenth century. Cf. W. von Loewenich, "Theologia crucis", in *Lexikon für Theologie und Kirche*, vol. 9, col. 60; B. Gherardini, *Theologia crucis. L'eredità di Lutero nell'evoluzione teologica della Riforma* (Rome, 1978); G. Aranda, "La historia de Cristo en la tierra según Fil 2, 6-11", in various authors, *Cristo, Hijo de Dios y Redentor del hombre*, op. cit., 341-58; L.F. Mateo Seco, "Muerte de Cristo y Teología de la Cruz", ibid., 743-7.

69. J. Ratzinger, *Principles of Catholic Theology. Building Stones for a Fundamental Theology* (San Francisco, 1987), 190.

70. ITC, *Theology, Christology, Anthropology*, I.B.1.2. (Sharkey, op. cit., 210).

As St Thomas Aquinas would later point out, although it is the Son and only the Son who becomes man, the incarnation is the initiative of the Trinity, of all three divine Persons.[71] The Son is sent by the Father, because "God so loved the world that he gave his only Son, that whoever believes in him should not perish but have eternal life. For God sent the Son into the world, not to condemn the world, but that the world might be saved through him" (Jn 3:16-17). The Incarnation is, at the same time, the work of the Holy Spirit; to put it correctly, it is the work of the Father *through* the Holy Spirit,[72] as the Angel says at the Annunciation: "The Holy Spirit will come upon you, and the power of the most High will overshadow you" (Lk 1:35).

Although faintly adumbrated in the Old Testament, the Trinitarian mystery (the inner life of God) has been clearly revealed by Jesus Christ. Yahweh is not only a God who saves; he is a God who is Father, Son and Holy Spirit, an infinite inner life of mutual knowledge and love. The salvation which Christ brings consists in fact in sharing in an ineffable way in the intimate inner life of God. Jesus reveals the true face of God.

Jesus reveals to us the Father as Father.[73] Thus, he teaches us to turn to him and say *Our Father* (cf. Mt 6:9; Lk 11:12). We read in the Encyclical *Dives in misericordia*: " 'No one has every seen God,' writes St John (Jn 1:18), in order to stress the truth that 'the only Son, who is in the bosom of the Father, he has made him known.' This 'making known' reveals God in the most profound mystery of his being, one and three, surrounded by 'unapproachable light' (cf. 1 Tim 6:16). Nevertheless, through this 'making known' by Christ we know God above all in his relationship of love for man: in his 'philanthropy' (Tit 3:4). It is precisely here that 'his invisible nature' becomes in a special way 'visible', incomparably more visible than through all the other 'things that have been made': it becomes visible in Christ and through Christ, through his

---

71. Cf. *STh* III, q.2, a.9, esp. ad 2.
72. "For the 'fullness of time' is matched by a particular fullness of the self-communication of the Triune God in the Holy Spirit. 'By the power of the Holy Spirit,' the mystery of the 'hypostatic union' is brought about—that is, the union of the divine nature and the human nature, of the divinity and the humanity in the one Person of the Word-Son [. . .]. The Holy Spirit, who with his power overshadowed the virginal body of Mary, bringing about in her the beginning of her divine Motherhood, at the same time made her heart perfectly obedient to that self- communication of God which surpassed every human idea and faculty": John Paul II, Enc., *Dominum et vivificantem* (18 May 1986), 50-1.
73. "Many religions invoke God as 'Father'. The deity is often considered the 'father of gods and men'. In Israel, God is called 'Father' inasmuch as he is Creator of the world (cf. Dt 32:6; Mal 2:10). Even more, God is Father because of the covenant and the gift of the law to Israel, 'his first-born son' (Ex 4:22). [. . .] Jesus has revealed that God is Father in an unheardof sense: he is Father not only in being Creator; he is eternally Father by his relationship to his only Son who, reciprocally, is Son only in relation to his Father" (CCC, nos. 238 and 240).

actions and through his words and finally through his death on the Cross and his Resurrection."[74]

Jesus not only makes the Father known to us; he shows us that it is he, the Father, who is the goal of our life and our salvation: "This is eternal life, that they know thee the only true God and Jesus Christ whom thou has sent" (Jn 17:3). Jesus reveals and sends the Holy Spirit: "I have yet many things to say to you, but you cannot bear them now. When the Spirit of truth comes, he will guide you into all the truth; for he will not speak on his own authority, but whatever he hears he will speak, and he will declare to you the things that are to come. He will glorify me, for he will take what is mine and declare it to you" (Jn 16:12-14). It is the Holy Spirit who pours love into our hearts: "and hope does not disappoint us, because God's love has been poured into our hearts through the Holy Spirit who has been given to us" (Rom 5:5); through the Spirit we receive adoptive sonship: "For you did not receive the spirit of slavery to fall back into fear, but you have received the spirit of sonship. When we cry, 'Abba! Father!' it is the Spirit himself bearing witness with our spirit that we are children of God" (Rom 8:15-16).

"The Paschal events—the Passion, Death and Resurrection of Christ—," we read in the Encyclical *Dominum et vivificantem*, "are also *the time of the new coming* of the Holy Spirit, as the Paraclete and the Spirit of truth. They are the time of the *new beginning* of the self-communication of the triune God to humanity in the Holy Spirit through the work of Christ the Redeemer. This new beginning is the Redemption of the world: 'God so loved the world that he gave his only Son' (Jn 3:16). Already the *giving* of the Son, *the gift of the Son*, expresses the most profound essence of God who, as Love, is the inexhaustible source of the giving of gifts. The gift *made by the Son* completes the revelation and giving of the eternal love: the Holy Spirit, who in the inscrutable depths of the divinity is a Person-gift, through the work of the Son, that is to say, by means of the Paschal mystery, is given to the Apostles and to the Church in a new way, and through them is given to humanity and the whole world."[75]

---

74. John Paul II, Enc., *Dives in misercordia* (30 November 1980), 2.
75. John Paul II, Enc. *Dominum et vivificantem*, 23.

CHAPTER ONE

The Expected Messiah

Revelation concerning the mystery of Christ covers both his Person and his work of salvation: the two are inseparable. Jesus is not only the Son of God; he is also the promised Messiah, the Saviour man has been expecting. The Church itself speaks in St Peter's confession of faith at Caesarea Philippi saying that Jesus of Nazareth is *the Christ, the Son of the Living God* (Mt 16:16). This states not only the truth of the perfect human nature of Christ and the fact that he is a divine Person but also his essential role as Saviour of mankind. He is, then, by his very nature *mediator between God and man* (1 Tim 2:5). He has been sent into this world "that whoever believes in him should not perish but have eternal life" (Jn 3:16). Messianic truth includes not only the personal history of Jesus of Nazareth and the mystery of his identity but also the history of mankind as a whole, particularly its sinfulness and its need for salvation. The virgin "will bear a son", the angel said to Joseph, "and you shall call his name Jesus, for he will save his people from their sins" (Mt 1:21).

This raises unavoidable questions about the nature of man and the world, and specifically the existence of evil and its presence in the heart of every individual. "Men look to their different religions", the Second Vatican Council points out, "for an answer to the unsolved riddles of human existence. The problems that weigh heavily on the hearts of men are the same today as in the ages past. What is man? What is the meaning and purpose of life? What is upright behaviour, and what is sinful? Where does suffering originate, and what purpose does it serve? . . . And finally, what is the ultimate mystery, beyond human explanation, which embraces our entire existence, from which we take our origin and towards which we tend?"[1] The universality and depth of these questions point to man's need for salvation and show the central place the Saviour of the world occupies in human history. These are questions to which only the Lord of history can give a full answer, for only he is the Saviour of man.

In fact, "it is only in the mystery of the Word made flesh that the mystery of man truly becomes clear."[2] This mystery involves not only man's inner structure and his thirst for the infinite (that irrepressible need in man's heart, expressed in a desire that only God can fill by a totally gratuitous giving of

---

1. Second Vatican Council, Decl. *Nostra aetate*, 1.
2. Second Vatican Council, Const. *Gaudium et spes*, 22.

himself)[3] but also the puzzle of that struggle between good and evil which man experiences within himself.

This tension has its origin in a specific act of rebellion on man's part at the dawn of history and it is reinforced by later sins. This is the reason why man, "when he looks into his own heart, finds that he is drawn towards what is wrong and sunk in many evils which cannot come from his good Creator. . . . Man therefore is divided in himself. As a result, the whole life of man, both individual and social, shows itself to be a struggle, and a dramatic one, between good and evil, between light and darkness. Man finds that he is unable of himself to overcome the assaults of evil successfully, so that everyone feels as though bound by chains. But the Lord himself came to free and strengthen man, renewing him inwardly and casting out the 'prince of this world' (Jn 12:31), who held him in the bondage of sin."[4]

The statement that Jesus is the Christ implies, then, that man needs God and suffers from evils of various kinds. It also implies the idea that man desires salvation and, more specifically a saviour (often, down the centuries, he confesses this need for a saviour). Jesus is the Christ promised by God as far back as *Genesis*, the Christ expected by the people of Israel, to whom the promise had been made. The study of Christology must take into account man's sin: for the Son of God became man in order to redeem man from sin; Christology should also take note of the desires for salvation and for the infinite which God himself has planted in man's heart; for these desires point to the promised Saviour, to him who marks the fulfilment of God's promise of salvation.

The full truth about Christ carries with it definitive enlightenment about who man is and what his destiny is; it also exposes the full meaning of history. The truth about man is, above all, a theological truth, as theological as man's being and goal, made as he is in the image and likeness of God and through Christ's redemption destined to be a son of God in the Son. The following words of John Paul II are in accordance with the unbreakable connection between Christology and anthropology: "How precious man must be in the eyes of the Creator, if he gained so great a Redeemer and if God gave his only

3. This is the desire to see God, which in the present economy of grace is so natural to man that he cannot find happiness outside the vision of God. Man has only one end, a supernatural one—intimate union with God in the beatific vision. As St Augustine so eloquently puts it, "You made us for yourself, O Lord, and our heart is restless until it rests in You" (*Confessions*, I, 1). This desire to see God, which is there prior to any decision on man's part, accords with man's vocation (he is designed for union with God in heaven) and yet exceeds his very nature, because God always transcends everything created. Hence the wording we have used—a desire that only God himself can fill by a total giving of himself whereby he gratuitously fills the human heart. In other words, man's natural, spontaneous desire can only be filled by something which at the same time as it fills him, transcends him. Cf. John Paul II, *Address* to Spanish theologians at the Pontifical University of Salamanca, 1 November 1982.
4. *Gaudium et spes*, 13.

Son, in order that man should not perish but have eternal life (Jn 3:16). In reality, the name for that deep amazement at man's worth and dignity is the Gospel, that is to say, the Good News. It is also called Christianity."[5]

We will now take a brief look at the basic ideas concerning the truth about man and original sin, in order to remind ourselves that it is impossible for man to be his own saviour: he needs a Saviour; and the Incarnation implies salvation; Christ's messiahship is salvific. At the same time, only from Christ does the Revelation about the Beginnings (contained in the first chapters of Genesis) acquire its full perspective; "We must know Christ as the source of grace in order to know Adam as the source of sin. The Spirit-Paraclete, sent by the risen Christ, came 'to convict the world concerning sin' (Jn 16:8), by revealing him who is its Redeemer."[6]

The Saviour is the Only-begotten Son of the Father, he has saved mankind by entering human history, thereby becoming the *alpha* and *omega*: "the Word of God, through whom all things were made, was made flesh, so that as a perfect man he could save all men and sum up all things in himself. The Lord is the goal of human history, the focal point of the desires of history and civilization, the centre of mankind, the joy of all hearts, and the fulfilment of all aspirations."[7] Jesus saves, by virtue of the fact that he is Son of God and Lord of history. We shall conclude this chapter, therefore, with a section on "Christ, the centre and goal of history". Thus, when the Word became man "God entered the history of humanity and, as a man, became *an actor in that history*, one of the thousands of millions of human beings but at the same time unique! Through the Incarnation God gave human life the dimension that he intended man to have from his first beginning; he has granted that dimension definitively—in the way that is peculiar to him alone, in keeping with his eternal love and mercy, with the full freedom of God—and he has granted it also with the bounty that enables us, in considering the original sin and the whole history of the sins of humanity, and in considering the errors of the human intellect, will and heart, to repeat with amazement the words of the sacred Liturgy: '*O happy fault . . . which gained us so great a Redeemer*'."[8]

1. THE ACCOUNT OF THE BEGINNING

The account of the origins of the world and of men, as described (in a special literary form) in the first chapters of Genesis contains events directly connected with the history of salvation. Later books of Scripture often hark back to these events (cf. Rom 5:12ff), particularly to the creation of man in the *image and likeness* of God; *original sin*; and the *promise of a Redeemer*.

5. John Paul II, Enc. *Redemptor hominis*, no. 10.
6. CCC, no. 388.
7. *Gaudium et spes*, 45.
8. John Paul II, Enc. *Redemptor hominis*, no. 1.

a) **Man, made in God's image**   God created man in his own image and put him in the world to be its overlord. This is a key part of Sacred Scripture's teaching about the nature of man. It has the effect of underlining man's dignity: being made in God's "image and likeness" puts him above all other created things of this world; because he is like God, he is endowed with the lordship of creation: "For Sacred Scripture teaches that man was created 'to the image of God', as able to know and love his Creator, and as set by him over all earthly creatures" (cf. Gen 1:26; Wis 2:23).[9]

By describing man as made in God's image, the transcendence of God is highlighted. Scripture does not say that man is equal to God but that he is made "in his image and likeness". This statement also implies that man has a certain capacity to receive further unmerited communications from God: being God's *image* implies that man has an "obediential potency" to be adopted as God's son through grace.[10] So, when Scripture says that man is the image of God, it is also saying that God is not *completely different* from men, he is not some utterly strange being; he is someone to whom man bears some relationship: man is like him in some way.[11] Being the image of an intimately personal God implies being on familiar terms with him, that the Creator loves man as a friend: "endowed with a spiritual soul, with intellect and with free will, the human person is, from conception, ordered to God and destined for eternal beatitude."[12]

If all creatures, simply by virtue of existing and of being "good" (cf. Gen 1:31; 1 Tim 4:4) are vestiges of the Creator and, therefore, to some extent like unto God, who is Being and Goodness in all their fullness, man is the creature in this world who is most like God, for man alone is capable of knowing and loving God. "Man, though made of body and soul, is a unity. Through his very bodily condition he sums up in himself the elements of the material world. . . . Man is not deceived when he regards himself as superior to bodily things and as more than just a speck of nature. . . . When he recognizes in himself a spiritual and immortal soul, he is not being led astray by false imaginings. On the contrary, he grasps what is profoundly true in this matter."[13]

This profound truth lies in the fact that man has been created by God with

9. *Gaudium et spes*, 12.
10. The expression "obediential potency" is used by theology to indicate that man is by his very nature capable of the supernatural (he is in potency with respect to grace), yet this is a capacity which only God can actualize (hence the adjective "obediential").
11. This truth exposes the nonsense of the alternative ("God or me") chanted by the different forms of atheism, some of which fly the flag of humanism (cf. Second Vatican Council, Const. *Gaudium et spes*, 20-1). There is no such alternative: precisely because man is the image of God, there is no "incompatibility" between him and God, as if man, to assert himself, had to reject his Creator. Man's "I" is not realized by denial of God but rather in union with Him in whose image he is made.
12. CCC, no. 1711.
13. *Gaudium et spes*, 14.

a natural structure capable of receiving God's call to friendship, capable of being adopted as a son and being on intimate terms with God. Man is not simply the most perfect of material beings: he is on a special level, because he is a *person*. His special likeness to the Creator has to do particularly with his spirit, that is, with the fact that he has a spiritual and immortal soul capable of intellectual knowledge and possessed of a free will: this permits him to have a loving dialogue with God; but his personal being also includes his body (and not just his soul), that is, it includes his whole self, the two principles (body and soul) which make up his nature.

Man's body-and-soul constitution is a composition, but it is not *dualism*: man is not a soul dwelling in a body. Soul and body, although different things, constitute a single substantial unity, a single essence: to put it more exactly, the soul "informs", imbues, the body, giving it existence and life.[14] Soul and body (matter informed by soul) are co-principles in man; man is the result of the union of those principles. This unity is broken by death, which undoes the human composite, which is "the separation of soul and body".[15] Death ruptures the substantial union of body and soul, that is, it separates man's two co-principles: the soul, because it is spiritual, endures after death, bearing away with it the personal history of the subject; it also retains the capacity to perform personal acts (such as, for example, enjoying the vision of God, being purified in purgatory, interceding for people), whereas the body, deprived of its principle of life, the soul, ceases to be a human body and its tendency is to decompose.[16] St Thomas Aquinas stresses the metaphysical gravity of the rupture of the unity-of-substance when he says that death means that man ceases to be a person.[17] And yet he speaks very clearly about the communion

14. Cf. Council of Vienne, Const. *Fidei Catholicae* (6 May 1312): DZ 902. See, e.g., M. Schmaus, *Katholische Dogmatik* (Munich, 1951-60), II/1 331.
15. The two most common definitions of death are: "Death is the privation of life": St Thomas Aquinas, *STh Suppl.*, q.75, a.3, sed contra; *De anima*, quaest. unica, a.10; "Death occurs in us through the separation of soul from body": St Thomas Aquinas, *In III Sent.*, dist. 21, a.3.
16. The close union between soul and body (the soul is *essentially* the form of the body) makes it very hazardous to describe the state of the "separated soul": cf. J.I. Saranyana, "Sobre la muerte y el alma separada", ScrTh 12 (1980), 593-616. It is clear from Revelation that the soul receives reward or punishment immediately after death; that means that the separated soul is capable of acts of knowing and loving. Yet, given that the natural way of acquiring new knowledge is through the senses, it would seem that we have to say that the soul, in the separated state, is unable of itself to acquire new knowledge; but such knowledge can be given it by God through infused science or in the intuitive vision of the blessed. Here are some expressions from St Thomas Aquinas which highlight how radically we must take the statement that man *is* the union of body and soul: "The soul unites naturally with the body because by its essence it is the form of the body. Consequently it is against the nature of the soul to be without the body [. . .]. For this reason the soul separated from the body is imperfect, in a certain sense, as is any part which is outside the whole, given that the soul is a part of human nature": *Summa c. Gentes*, IV ch. 79.
17. This is philosophical language, which is somewhat different from ordinary language. This

that exists between the blessed and those of us who are still making our pilgrim way on earth.[18]

Because of his spiritual nature, man is not *something*, but *someone*; he is not a mere *object*, but a *person*, capable of acting freely and therefore responsible for his acts. This dignity of man belongs to the entire man—body and soul—because the person is the individual man in his entirety. Therefore, "man may not despise his bodily life. Rather he is obliged to regard his body as good and to hold it in honour since God has created it and will raise it up on the last day."[19]

Man certainly *is* but he also *is becoming*. Thus, the human person can and should be constantly perfecting himself by developing his natural abilities, especially through knowledge and the exercise of his freedom. The high point of this development and perfectioning is to be found in knowledge and love of God.[20]

In his loving plans concerning man, God desires man to know and love his Creator not only through the imperfect knowledge and love his human strength can rise to; but also through supernatural energies, for God "of his infinite goodness has ordained man to a supernatural end, that is, to be the sharer of divine blessings which utterly exceed the intelligence of the human mind."[21] This supernatural goal (which is quite beyond the capacity and needs of any created nature) consists in seeing and loving God as he is, in the Unity of his being and in the Trinity of his divine Persons—Father, Son and Holy Spirit.[22] "For now we see in a mirror dimly," St Paul writes, "but then face to face" (1 Cor 13:12). "We shall see God", says St John, "as he is" (1 Jn 3:2).

It is quite impossible to imagine, even roughly, the greatness of this goal which God has destined for us; nor can we intuit the happiness which man

forceful expression is used because, although the human soul, after death, makes acts of knowing and loving, the word "person" is reserved for the complete subsistent nature and not the soul alone, because it is only *pars humanae specie* (cf. St Thomas Aquinas, *STh* I, q.29, a.1, ad 5). Cf. L.F. Mateo Seco, "El concepto de muerte en la doctrina de S. Tomás de Aquino", ScrTh 6 (1974), 173-208; "Muerte y pecado original en la doctrina de S. Tomás de Aquino", in various authors, *Veritas et Sapientiae* (Pamplona, 1975), 277-313. This not only serves to stress the close unity of man and the importance of the human body, but also the grave evil of death and therefore the importance of the death of Christ. It also underlines the central importance of the resurrection of the dead in Christian teaching and the importance of the Assumption of the Blessed Virgin into heaven. However, these statements obviously do not undervalue the happiness of the blessed or their power of intercession: cf. Second Vatican Council, Const. *Lumen gentium*, 49.

18. Cf. e.g., St Thomas Aquinas, *STh* I, q.89, a.8, in c. and also SCDF, Letter *Communionis notio*, 28 May 1992, no. 6.
19. Second Vatican Council, *Gaudium et spes*, 14.
20. Cf. F. Ocáriz, "Dignidad personal, transcendencia e historicidad del hombre" in *Dios y el hombre* (Pamplona, 1985), 175-95.
21. First Vatican Council, Const. *Dei Filius* (24 April 1870), DS 3005.
22. Council of Florence, *Decr. pro graecis* (6 July 1439), DS 1305.

will experience when he sees God face to face and loves his infinite goodness and beauty. Therefore, St Paul wrote, "no eye has seen, nor ear heard, nor the heart of man conceived, what God has prepared for those who love him" (1 Cor 2:9).

To enable man to know, desire and attain this highest of goals, God gives him, when he is still on earth, *supernatural grace*, which is a new and heightened likeness to God, a sharing in some way in God's own nature. As St Peter writes, "he has granted to us his precious and very great promises that through these you may . . . become partakers of the divine nature" (2 Pet 1:4). This grace, called "sanctifying" because it sanctifies us, that is, makes us more like the Supreme Holiness of God, tranforms the human soul in such a way that, while remaining human, it acquires a divine ("deiform") quality; through grace man is *deified* or *divinized*; he becomes a *son of God*: "see what love the Father has given us, that we should be called children of God; and so we are" (1 Jn 3:1; cf. Jn 1:12; Rom 8:15-16). With grace God gives man supernatural virtues and the gifts of the Holy Spirit, so as to enable the human person to act also in a "deiform" way.[23]

Supernatural life (the life of grace, of faith, hope and charity) brings about a new presence of God in man (the indwelling of the Trinity), to which Jesus referred when he told the Apostles that "If a man loves me, he will keep my word, and my Father will love him, and we will come to him and make our home with him" (Jn 14:23). It is true that God the Creator is present in all created things, but this new presence of God in man, which is called presence in the soul by inhabitation, is in his distinction of persons—as Father, Son and Holy Spirit. *God is present in man* by the mere fact that man is a creature; but through grace *man is present in God*, in the intimacy of the Father and of the Son and of the Holy Spirit: man is a "member of the household of God" (cf. Eph 2:19) as his son, through a mysterious union with and likeness to the eternal Son of the Father. Thus, "through the grace he receives in Baptism, man shares in the eternal birth of the Son of the Father, because he becomes an adoptive son of God—a son in the Son".[24]

The theological theme of man created in the image and likeness of God (so much to the fore in Gen 1:26ff) is set in a new and definitive perspective in the New Testament, in the light of the clear revelation of Christ—the Christological perspective.[25] Thus Christ is "the image of the invisible God,

23. On the supernatural as sharing in the divine nature, cf., F. Ocáriz, *Hijos de Dios en Cristo. Introducción a una teología de la participación sobrenatural* (Pamplona, 1972); M. Sánchez Sorondo, *La gracia como participación de la naturaleza divina según Santo Tomás* (Buenos Aires, Rome, Salamanca, 1979).

24. John Paul II, Homily (23 March 1980), *Insegnamenti*, III, 1 (1980), 682.

25. The expression comes from St Gregory of Nyssa, *De perfectione*, PG 46, 269-72; cf. L.F. Mateo Seco, *Gregorio de Nyssa: Sobre la vocación cristiana* (Madrid, 1992), 67f, nos. 49 and 52. Cf. also R. Leys, *L'image de Dieu chez saint Grégoire de Nysse* (Brussels, 1951).

the first-born of all creation" (Col 1:16), through whom and for whom everything was created (cf. Col 1:16), to the point that the first Adam "was a type of the one who was to come" (Rom 5:14). Christ alone (because he is the Word made man) is the true image of God, in such a way that being the image of God is, in the current economy of Grace, being the image of Christ. Christ, as perfect image of God, is the mediator of all creation; it is he to whom all creation tends. It is he who restores the image of God obscured in man through sin, and it is he who restores to man that original state he lost through sin. Therefore, this restoration does not consist in anything less than "putting on" Christ (cf. Gal 3:27; Eph 4:24), that is, in coming to be "images of the Image".[26]

b) **The destruction of God's image through sin** It is a doctrine of faith that the first man was established by God in a state of justice and holiness.[27] In that state man had *supernatural gifts* (grace, virtues, etc.) and others which are called *praeternatural* gifts because, though not strictly required by human nature, neither, however, do they have to do immediately with the union of man and the Trinity which is the essential feature of the supernatural gifts.[28]

All these gifts, supernatural and praeternatural, were *gifts*, that is, perfections which God gratuitously bestowed on man: they were not in any sense required by human nature for its fulfilment. "With the Council of Trent, we teach that the first man was constituted in holiness and justice. This state of justice was supernatural and absolutely not due to human nature; therefore God could have created man without adorning him with supernatural gifts."[29] However, Adam cut himself off from God through sin, destroyed in himself his supernatural likeness to God, and lessened the perfection of his natural likeness to the Creator. "Set by God in a state of rectitude, man, enticed by the evil one, abused his freedom at the very start of history. He lifted himself up against God, and sought to attain his goal apart from him. Although they had known God, they did not glorify him as God, but their senseless hearts were darkened, and they served the creature rather than the creator (cf. Rom 1:21-25). What Revelation makes known to us is confirmed by our own experience. For when

26. As the Catechism of the Catholic Church (no. 1701) puts it, "It is in Christ, 'the image of the invisible God' (Col 1:15; cf. 2 Cor 4:4), that man has been created 'in the image and likeness' of the Creator. It is in Christ, Redeemer and Saviour, that the divine image, disfigured in man by the first sin, has been restored to its original beauty and ennobled by the grace of God."

27. Cf. Council of Trent, *Decr. de peccato originali* (17 June 1546), DS 1511.

28. On the original state of man, cf. John Paul II, *Address* (3 September 1986), nos. 4-5: *Insegnamenti*, IX, 2 (1986), 525f and M.J. Scheeben, *The Mysteries of Christianity* (London, 1946), 201-39.

29. Council of Cologne (1860), part I, chap. 14 in Mansi, *Sacrorum Conciliorum nova et amplissima collectio*, vol. 48, col. 93; see also Pius V, Bull *Ex omnibus afflictionibus* (1 October 1567), DS 1901-7, against the error of Baius; Pius XII, Enc. *Humani generis* (12 August 1950), DS 3891.

man looks into his own heart he finds that he is drawn towards what is wrong and sunk in many evils which cannot come from his good creator."[30]

The existence of evil in the world is obvious to all; but the origin of evil, particularly that evil which man discovers in his own heart, is something we do not know except through Revelation and by faith.[31] That origin is original sin. The teaching of original sin is "so to speak, the 'reverse side' of Good News that Jesus is the Saviour of the whole human race, that all need salvation and that salvation is offered to all through to Christ. The Church which has the mind of Christ (cf. 1 Cor 2:16), knows very well that we cannot tamper with the revelation of original sin without undermining the mystery of Christ."[32]

At this point we will take a brief look at the Genesis (ch. 3) account of the fall of man.[33] God had given a commandment that man was supposed to freely observe as a sign and expression of his dependence on his Creator. The commandment was a test—not so much in the sense that God wanted to *test man* but because he wanted man to receive the glory of his supernatural goal not as a gratuitous gift but as something *merited* by man himself, through his good actions. In other words, the fact that God put man to the test is a sign of his love for man: he wanted to give him the glory in a way that fully accorded with human freedom.[34]

When woman and man broke the divine commandment (wanting to decide for themselves what was good and what was evil) they committed a sin whose gravity is difficult to comprehend: it involved a radical rebellion against God, whom they knew and with whom they had previously been closely linked by friendship.[35]

The Genesis account spells out the consequences of that first sin. From God's words to the man and the woman, we can deduce, among other things, these consequences of their sin—suffering, fatigue in work, etc. to the point that God tells man, "cursed is the ground because of you" (Gen 3:17). And man loses the praeternatural gift of immortality: "for you are dust, and to dust you shall return" (Gen 3:19). Death is revealed to be punishment for sin in other scriptural passages too (cf. Wis 2:23-24; Rom 5:12-21).[36]

30. Second Vatican Council, Const. *Gaudium et spes*, 13.
31. Cf. A.D. Sertillanges, *Il problema del male*, II (Brescia, 1954), 24-30.
32. CCC, no. 389.
33. As the Catechism of the Catholic Church (no. 390) says, "the account of the fall (Gen 3) uses a language composed of images, but it does set down a primordial event, a happening which took place *at the beginning of the history of man* (cf. *Gaudium et spes*, 13, 1). Revelation provides us with the certainty of faith that the whole of human history is marked by the original sin freely committed by our first parents (cf. Council of Trent: DS 1513; Pius XII: DS 3897; Paul VI: Address, 11 June 1966)".
34. Cf. J. Blinzler, "Pecado original" DTB, 800-7; M. Meinertz, *Teología del Nuevo Testamento*, 2nd ed. (Madrid, 1966), 301-15.
35. Cf. John Paul II, *Address* (10 September 1986), no. 8: *Insegnamenti*, IX, 2 (1986), 588.
36. Among the teachings of the magisterium on original sin these of the Sixteenth Council of

Original sin meant that man *lost* his supernatural likeness to God and suffered a *diminution* in his natural likeness to his Creator, because his human nature deteriorated. Against Luther, who held that human nature was entirely corrupted by original sin and who argued that man was no longer free to do good, the Council of Trent solemnly asserted that after original sin man did not lose his free will nor was it destroyed.[37]

c) Man cannot redeem himself "No one is freed from sin by himself or by his own efforts, no one is raised above himself or completely delivered from his own weakness, solitude or slavery."[38] Man cannot save himself. No one is capable of acquiring grace and salvation by his own efforts.

In the Old Testament Israel saw ever more clearly that man cannot rise above sin by his own efforts: only God can re-establish the holiness destroyed by man's sin. And so we read, for example, "Blessed is he whose transgression is forgiven, whose sin is covered. Blessed is the man to whom the Lord imputes no iniquity, and in whose spirit there is no deceit" (Ps 32:1ff, quoted in Rom 4:7ff: cf. also Ps 65:4ff).[39] This truth is made very plain in the New Testament where the power to forgive sins, which Christ attributes to himself, is (as we shall see later) a sign of his divinity (cf. Mk 2:5-12).

As the Council of Trent teaches "since all men had lost innocence in the transgression of Adam (Rom 5:12; 1 Cor 15:22), having become unclean (Is 64:6) and, as the Apostle says, 'by nature children of wrath' (Eph 2:3), [. . .], they were so far the servants of sin (Rom 6:20) and under the power of the devil and death, that not only the Gentiles by the force of nature, but even the Jews by the very letter of the law of Moses, were unable to be liberated or to rise therefrom, though free will, weakened as it was in its powers and downward bent, was by no means extinguished in them."[40]

We can appreciate why man is incapable of redeeming himself if we bear in mind what sin is and what salvation is. Sin is not just an action of man

---

Carthage (418), Second Council of Orange (529), Council of Florence (1442) and the Trent decree on original sin (1546) are of special importance. Paul VI's *Creed of the People of God* states this truth as follows: "We believe that in Adam all have sinned, which means that the original offence committed by him caused human nature, common to all men, to fall to a state in which it bears the consequences of that offence, and which is not the state in which it was at first in our first parents, established as they were in holiness and justice, and in which man knew neither evil nor death. It is human nature so fallen, stripped of the grace that clothed it, injured in its own natural powers and subjected to the dominion of death, that is transmitted to all men, and it is in this sense that every man is born in sin. We therefore hold, with the Council of Trent, that original sin is transmitted with human nature, 'not by imitation, but by propagation' and that it is thus proper to everyone": op. cit., 16. Cf. also CCC, nos. 397-409.

37. Cf. Council of Trent, Decr. *de justificatione* (13 January 1547) DS 1555.
38. Second Vatican Council, Decr. *Ad gentes*, 8.
39. D. Spada, *L'uomo in faccia a Dio* (Imola, 1983), 170.
40. Council of Trent, Decr. *de justificatione* op. cit (DS 1521).

which, being an *action*, ceases and has no permanence; sin is also the state that man then finds himself in—devoid of supernatural grace and therefore with his will distanced from and opposed to the will of God. Salvation is forgiveness of sin, re-acquisition of grace and the corresponding conversion of the human heart to the love of God.[41]

There is no other way to be: either one is in grace or one is in sin. Since man has been destined by God to *supernatural life*, his existence cannot any longer be confined to the level of nature. Therefore, there is no "natural" salvation attainable by merely natural effort: there is only *supernatural salvation*, which, precisely because it is supernatural, man cannot attain on his own.

Only God can save man, by giving him grace, which destroys sin. God who is almighty can do this; and man is capable of being redeemed: he is not fixed in his decision; he can, with God's help, repent and dispose himself to receive grace.

d) The promise of the Redeemer in the Protogospel After the sin of Adam, God did not abandon man; immediately after the fall of our first parents "he buoyed them up with the hope of salvation, by promising redemption (cf. Gen 3:15); and he has never ceased to take care of the human race. For he wishes to give eternal life to all those who seek salvation by patience in well-doing (cf. Rom 2:6-7). In his own time God called Abraham, and made him into a great nation (cf. Gen 12:2). After the era of the patriarchs, he taught this nation, by Moses and the prophets, to recognize him as the only living and true God, as a provident Father and just judge. He taught them, too, to look for the promised Saviour. And so, throughout the ages, he prepared the way for the Gospel."[42]

The announcement and consequent expectation of the Redeemer began with the words God addressed to the serpent after the sin of Adam and Eve: "I will put enmity between you and the woman, and between your seed and her seed; he shall bruise your head, and you shall bruise his heel" (Gen 3:15). This verse is called "the protoevangelium", because it is the first announcement of salvation to come.[43]

There has been considerable discussion as to whether the reading in this passage of Scripture should be "*he* shall bruise your head" or "*it* shall bruise your head" depending on the meaning of the original pronoun that is used. The most likely meaning is the latter ("it") and so it refers to all Eve's descendants, that is, the human race. But the Greek translation uses the word

41. Cf. M. Schmaus, *Katholishce Dogmatik*, op. cit., II/2, op. cit., 59-67.
42. Second Vatican Council, Const. *Dei Verbum*, 3.
43. J. Coppens, *Le Protoévangile. Un nouvel essai d'exégèse*, ETL 26 (1950) 5-36; B. Rigaux, "La femme et son linage dans Gen 3,15", RB 61 (1954) 321-48; L. Arnaldich, "Protoevangelio", GER, 19, 300-2.

autos, implying reference to a particular, individual descendant of the woman ("he" shall), thereby giving it a more explicitly messianic sense, thus leaving no doubt as to the outcome of the struggle between the woman's offspring and the serpent. The Vulgate has yet another variation, "she shall bruise your head" (*ipsa conteret caput tuum*),[44] understanding the woman referred to to be Mary, the Mother of the Redeemer, and not Eve. But the recent Neo-Vulgate has "he shall bruise your head" (*ipsum conteret*), thus returning to a more literal translation of the Hebrew.

We should remember, however, that in line with Christian tradition Sacred Scripture does not have just one single meaning: often, for example, the word of God refers to a concrete event in order to announce another (future) event. Thus, in the Protogospel the woman has been traditionally interpreted as Eve (in the direct sense) and as Mary (in the full sense); and the woman's offspring refers both the human race and to Christ. Clearly the two interpretations are compatible; they complement one another.

The *Christological* and *Marian* sense of the Protogospel has been affirmed by many Fathers of the Church (St Justin, St Irenaeus, St Cyprian, St Epiphanius, St Leo the Great and others).[45] And Pius IX in the bull *Ineffabilis Deus* (1854), which defined the dogma of the Immaculate Conception, made reference to the Marian interpretation given by the Fathers.[46]

By foretelling that the head of the serpent will be crushed, *Genesis* is announcing and promising that the Evil One will cease to have dominion over man: the human race, the offspring of the woman, will be redeemed.

Even if the text were taken only in its direct, literal, sense (that is, that the descendants of Eve will defeat the Evil One), we would still have not only a general promise of Redemption but also an announcement and promise of the coming of Christ. For, if Redemption will be brought about by man (the descendants of the woman), taking into account that only God can redeem man, then the work of Redemption, victory over the power of the Evil One, will have to be the joint work of God and man. The New Testament shows that this comes true in Christ Jesus.

2. PREPARATION OF ISRAEL

"At all times and in every race, anyone who fears God and does what is right has been acceptable to him (cf. Acts 10:35). He has, however, willed to make men holy and save them, not as individuals, without any bond or link between

44. Cf. D. Spada, *L'uomo in faccia a Dio*, op. cit., 159.
45. Cf. L.F. Mateo Seco, "María Nueva Eva, y su colaboración en la Redención según los Padres", EM, 50 (1985), 51-69.
46. Cf. also John Paul II, *Address*, 17 December 1986, nos. 7-9; *Insegnamenti*, IX, 2 (1986) 1971-2.

them, but rather to make them into a people who might acknowledge him and serve him in holiness. He therefore chose the Israelite race to be his own people and established a covenant with it. He gradually instructed this people—in its history manifesting both himself and the decree of his will—and made it holy unto himself. All these things, however, happened as a preparation and figure of that new and perfect covenant which was to be ratified in Christ, and of the full revelation which was to be given through the Word of God made flesh."[47]

The entire history of Israel is a preparation for and a foretelling of the Incarnation of God. Indeed, what makes this history different from the history of other peoples is the fact that God acts on the Israelites by establishing a special presence among them. This presence becomes perfect and definitive in the Incarnation, when the Word of God becomes flesh and "pitches his tent" among us (cf. Jn 1:14). God's revelation to the people of Israel through the patriarchs and prophets was specially designed to announce and prepare for the coming of Christ. In this Revelation God spoke man's language: this very fact was an announcement of and preparation for the fullness of time, when the Eternal Word of God became man: "In many and various ways God spoke of old to our fathers by the prophets; but in these last days he has spoken to us by a Son, whom he appointed the heir of all things, through whom also he created the world" (Heb 1:1-2).

a) **The Covenant and expectation of the Messiah**   The origin of the Hebrew word *berîth* is unclear, but there is no doubt about its principal meaning: it occurs often in the Old Testament; it means an everlasting alliance, covenant or pact made by two persons in the presence of God through a sacrifice offered to him, a pact which gives rise to rights and duties on both sides.[48]

God himself established an alliance with man: he did so early on with Noah after the flood (cf. Gen 9-10) and particularly with Abraham (cf. Gen 15-17). In this—the Alliance *par excellence*—the initiative was God's: he made the *promise* to give Abraham a huge multitude of descendants and make them a great people; to give them a new land (the promised land) and eventually through this people one day to bless all nations—an announcement and a promise of salvation for all. God laid down as conditions that he be recognized as the only God and that his will be obeyed. He stipulated circumcision as a sign of the Covenant: therefore, it is prophetic sign or "type" of the Christian baptism of the future.

The covenant would be later renewed with Isaac (cf. Gen 26:2-5) and with

---

47. Second Vatican Council, Const. *Lumen gentium*, 9.
48. Cf. J. Galot, *La Rédemption, mystère d'Alliance* (Rome-Bruges, 1965), 31-7; J. Schildenberger, "Alianza", DTB, 32-4.

Jacob (cf. Gen 28:12ff: 35:9-12). Later still, with Moses, it would be given its final form (announced in Exodus 6:2-8 and spelt out in Exodus 19-34).[49] God fulfilled the promise to make a great nation out of Abraham.

It is true that Israel existed before the *Passover* and the *Exodus*, but it was not a real nation, because it was enslaved and was scattered all over Egypt, lacking all sense of nationhood. The *Exodus* makes Israel a people and marks their adoption—really their rebirth—by God.[50] The Passover and Exodus, with all the hardships involved, clearly prefigure the Redemption brought about by Christ which led to the creation of the new people of God. Also, the fact that the establishment of the people of Israel fulfils the promise means that Israel is essentially the *People of the Covenant* in the sense that it was "constituted by and for it" .[51] Moreover, God makes his will known to Moses by giving the Ten Commandments and other instructions—the law of Moses, which St Paul will describe as being "was our custodian until Christ came" (Gal 3:24).[52] "(The law) is not a price God demands as it were to make his promise less gratuitous, or so as to enable man to show his good will and obtain rights 'against' God. What it does is mark the way to life, to full communion with God—joy, happiness, man's route to self-fulfilment."[53] The law itself is a gift from God; it does not oppress man but rather liberates him and fills him with joy (cf. Ps 18:8-9).

Nathan's prophecy (cf. 2 Sam 7) marks another important stage of the covenant. It announces that the Messiah (awaited since the earliest times) will be a descendant of David and will rule not only over Israel but over all nations.[54] Many later prophetic texts will refer to this Messiah, son of David: he will be born in Bethlehem (cf. Mic 5:1); the King-Messiah will belong to the house of David, we are reminded (cf. Is 11:1; Jer 23:5); he will be called Immanuel, that is, *God with us* (cf. Is 7:14), and "Mighty God, Everlasting Father, Prince of Peace" (Is 9:5); etc.[55]

The Covenant prepares the way for the Redemption which Christ will bring about, by establishing a people from whom the Redeemer will come; and it also announces that this Messiah-Redeemer is the son of David (and therefore

---

49. Cf. L. Bouyer, *La Biblia y el Evangelio* (Madrid, 1977), 19-86.
50. Ibid., 67.
51. Ibid., 66.
52. On the theology of the Law in the Old Testament, see P. Grelot, *Sens chrétien de l'Ancien Testament* (Tournai, 1962), 168-94.
53. M. Serentha, *Gesù Cristo ieri, oggi e sempre (saggio di Cristologia)* (Leumann-Turin, 1982), 64.
54. On Israel's awaiting the Messiah, see T. Larriba, "Mesías", GER, 15, 595-602; A. Diez-Macho, *El Mesías anunciado y esperado* (Madrid, 1976); A. Gelin, "Messianisme", DBS, V, 1165-1213.
55. On the fulfilment of the messianic prophecy in Jesus, see also M. Meinertz, *Teología del Nuevo Testamento*, op. cit., 166-87. On names applied to the Messiah in the Old Testament, see the beautiful pages in Fray Luís de León, *The Names of Christ*.

a man); and he is also Mighty God, God with us. But the Covenant is a preparation for and announcement of Christ due to the fact that it is also a *type* (a prophetic figure) of the Incarnation, because by means of the Covenant God establishes a relationship with men similar to that which men have with one another—a very close and in some way a familial relationship. This covenant between man and God is a kind of sonship (Israel is adopted by God as a son: cf. Exodus 4:22; Hosiah 11:1), or a type of marital relationship (cf. Jer 3:19-22; Is 54:5-8).

To sum up: we can say that the Covenant is a prophetic figure (a foretelling and a preparation) of the redemptive Incarnation, because it is precisely in Christ that the most perfect and definitive Covenant is established between God and man: true God and true man in a personal union,[56] Christ establishing in his blood the new and permanent Covenant between God and all mankind (cf. Mt 26:28; 1 Cor 11:25).

b) The poems of the Servant of Yahweh

This is the name given to four fragments contained in the Book of Isaiah which prophetically describe the redemptive mission of the Messiah, who is called *Servant of Yahweh* (*Ebed Yahweh*).[57]

In the first poem (Is 42:1-7) the Servant is depicted as the chosen one of God, in whom God takes delight (reference is made to it in the Baptism and Transfiguration of Christ: cf. Mt 3:17; 17:5). The Servant of Yahweh is a suffering and meek prophet, full of the Spirit of God, who will bring righteousness (holiness) to all nations, not just Israel. God also calls his Servant a "Covenant" between God and the people, and the light of the nations.

In the second poem (Is 49:1-9) the Servant of Yahweh speaks in the first person, identifying himself with the entire people (v.3) but as a single individual destined to gather all the people around God (v.5). This identification implies, therefore, solidarity between the people and the Servant, who, however, reveals the opposition and persecution he will meet from that same people.[58]

The third poem (Is 50:4-9) describes this persecution and opposition in more detail. Particularly noteworthy is what he says to his enemies: "Who will declare me guilty?" (v.9). It is a question of that total innocence which Jesus will, in fact, declare before the Jews (cf. Jn 8:46).

Finally, the fourth poem (Is 52:13 - 53:12) constitutes an impressive prophecy of the passion and death of Christ, of his sacrifice for redemption of

---

56. Cf. J. Schildenberger, "Alianza", art. cit., 38-9.
57. On the exegesis of these texts, see R. Tournai, "Les chants du Serviteur dans la seconde partie d'Isaïe", RB 59 (1952) 355-84; 481-512; F. Spadafora, *Temi di Esègesi* (Rovigo, 1953), 204-17; P. Grelot, *Les poèmes du Serviteur. De la lecture critique a l'herméneutique* (Paris, 1981).
58. On the collective and at the same time personal meaning of the Servant, see M. Bordoni, *Gesù di Nazaret, Signore e Cristo*, II, op. cit., 19-23.

all men: "the figure of the Messiah emerges as *the Prophet* who comes into the world to bear testimony to the truth and who *precisely because of this truth will be rejected by his people*. His death, however, will be the cause of justification for 'many'."[59]

Although a reading of the Old Testament on its own does not easily show this suffering Servant to be the King-Messiah, the New Testament makes it quite clear that he is Jesus Christ (cf., e.g., Mt 27:29-31; Jn 12:38; Acts 8:32-33; etc.). However, a close reading of Isaiah does intimate that the victorious Immanuel (cf. Is 9) and the servant of Yahweh are one and the same, insofar as the ideas of light and eternity are to be found in both cases.[60]

c) The Son of man   The Book of Daniel (belonging to the genre of apocalyptic writing) announces the eschatological coming of God on earth at the end of time, to establish his universal Kingdom. In this context Daniel speaks of the coming of a mysterious personage: "and behold, with the clouds of heaven there came one like a son of man, and he came to the Ancient of Days and was presented before him. And to him was given dominion and glory and kingdom, that all peoples, nations, and languages should serve him; his dominion is an everlasting dominion, which shall not pass away, and his kingdom one that shall not be destroyed" (Dan 7:13-14).

Son of man, both in Hebrew (*ben adam*) and in Aramaic (*bar nascha*) normally means simply *man*, as can be seen from other Old Testament passages (cf. Num 23:19; Ps 8:5; Is 51:12; Job 25:6; etc.).[61] Moreover, God himself calls the prophet Ezekiel (cf. Ezek 2:1) "son of man" to stress the infinite gap between God and the prophet.

In the prophecy of Daniel, on the other hand, we meet a *Son of man*, an outstanding person, a man who mysteriously transcends the human condition and restores the messianic kingdom irreversibly at the end of time. Daniel's vision is very difficult to interpret if one takes into account only the Old Testament, because "son of man" has a collective meaning in Daniel also (cf. Dan 7:18-22) insofar as he is identified with "the saints of the Most High" (Dan 7:27). This collective sense is also messianic; in some way it extends the personal sense, because the Son of man is the head and representative of the people to whom the saints belong.[62]

The importance of this messianic title derives above all from the use Christ made of it: he frequently described himself as the *Son of man*. He certainly does not seem to have adopted this name to emphasize the fact that he is truly man (which all could see) but rather to make the connexion between the glorious

59. John Paul II, *Address* (25 February 1987), no. 7: *Insegnamenti*, X, 1 (1987) 419-20.
60. Cf. H. Cazelles, "Siervo de Yahvé", DTB, 992.
61. Cf. J. Obersteiner, "Hijo del Hombre", DTB 450.
62. Cf. C. Chopin, *El Verbo Encarnado y Redentor* (Barcelona, 1969), 33-4.

messianic figure of the *Son of man* in Daniel's vision and the suffering figure of the Servant foretold by Isaiah, thereby correcting the exclusively eschata-logical-glorious idea of the Messiah so embedded in Hebrew thought. He went so far as to say that "the Son of man will suffer at their hands" (Mt 17:12)—something difficult to understand unless there is identity between the glorious Messiah of Daniel and the servant of Yahweh. This identification is not explicitly stated in the Gospels, but "the doctrinal unity between these two concepts is quite clear: the historical mission of the *Son of man* is the same as that of the *Ebed Yahweh*, who through his passion brings about salvation and the expiation of sins."[63]

d) A saviour, king and priest   As well as depicting the Messiah with features of suffering and glory, the Old Testament also highlights his royalty and his descent from David. In fact, his kingly character is to the fore when the Messiah's coming is foretold. We can see this in Nathan's prophecy (2 Sam 7), which is a promise given to and a pact made with David: through this descendant God guarantees to David the permanence of the rule of his household. It is a matter of an "eternal pact" (cf. 2 Sam 23:5) to which the angel refers in his greeting to Mary (cf. Lk 1:32-33).

Earlier promises which had been becoming ever more concrete are fulfilled in this pact: the promise made to the first parents after they had sinned—the offspring of the woman will crush the head of the serpent (Gen 3:15)—was made concrete in the alliance sealed with Abraham which promised him a countless progeny, to whom he would in turn give the land (Gen 12:1-9; cf. Gen 28:10-16); due to these descendants, the promise to Abraham specifies, all nations will be blessed by him (Gen 12:3). This promise is made more explicit in Jacob's prophetic blessing of Judah: Judah is a lion's whelp, from whom "the sceptre shall not depart", "until he comes to whom it belongs" and to whom the nations shall bear tribute (cf. Gen 49:9-10); and the oracle of Balaam also speaks of a sceptre rising out of Israel, one with dominion, and of a star coming forth out of Jacob (Num 24:15-19).[64]

These prophecies speak of the Messiah as a king; they also say that he will

63. A. Piolanti, *Dio-Uomo* (Rome 1964), 7. On this see also M. Bordoni, *Gesù di Nazaret, Signore e Cristo*, II, op. cit. 391-93; I. de la Potterie, "L'exaltation du Fils de l'homme (Jn 12, 31-36)", Greg 49 (1968) 460-78; J. Caba, *El Jesús de los Evangelios* (Madrid, 1977), 154-86; 253-68; A. Diez Macho, "La cristología del Hijo del hombre y el uso de la tercera persona en vez de la primera", ScrTh 14 (1982), 189-201.

64. "The line begins with the *seed* (*zerà*: seed, and later offspring) of the woman (Gen 3:15), passes through the *seed of Abraham* (Gen 12:7) and extends to the *seed* of David (2 Sam 7:12). This last datum is given by the New Testament, which brings to completion the line begun in Genesis 3:15: the *seed*, simply, on which the promises are bestowed, is Jesus, as Messiah (Gal 3:19), son of David, of Abraham, and of Adam, who for his part was son of God (cf. Lk 3:23-28)": N. Fuglister, "Fundamentos veterotestamentarios de la cristología neotestamentaria" in *Mysterium Salutis*, III, I (Madrid, 1970), 127.

be king of all nations and that it is in fact in this kingdom that all nations will find salvation.[65] In the prophetic books, the salvific and universal perspective is integrally linked with the kingly character of this descendant of David. This perspective is also a feature of the Psalms. For example, in Psalm 2, the key to the universal kingdom is to be found in the fact that the Messiah is the Son of God; in Psalm 109 we can see the kingly character of the Messiah and also the fact that he is "a priest for ever after the order of Melchizedek". The New Testament applies explicitly to Christ, both Psalm 2 (cf. Acts 4:24-28; 13:33; Heb 1:5; 5:5; Rev 2:27; Jn 1:49) and Psalm 109 (cf. Mt 22:44-46; Mk 12:36; Lk 20:42; Acts 2:34; 1 Cor 15:25; Col 3:1; Eph 1:20; Heb 1:3, 13; 5:6, 10; 6:20; 7:17; 10:12-13; Rev 3;21).

The combination in the Anointed (the Messiah) of kingly and priestly power (described so explicitly) means that, strictly speaking, his kingdom cannot be confused with an earthly kingdom: it is a universal kingdom, a kingdom of salvation, which is praised eternally. This is particularly easy to see if Psalm 109 is read along with Psalms 2, 44 and 71; hence the importance given this topic by the New Testament—to the point that the Letter to the Hebrews can even be said to hinge on it: Jesus Christ is a priest according to the order of Melchizedek. The Messiah is a priest in his capacity of successor of King David, since the king also has priestly functions.[66]

This union between the Davidic king and priesthood is further strengthened by the link that exists between the king and the sanctuary of Zion. There is a close connexion between the "house" of David and the "house" of Yahweh, the temple of Jerusalem (cf. 2 Sam 6:7; Ps 132). It is the king who builds the temple and looks after it; the blessing of Yahweh reaches the people through David and through the Holy City: both have been simultaneously the object of Yahweh's choice (cf. 1 Kings 13:32). This link between king and temple is prolonged and fulfilled by the identification of the Messiah with the eschatological temple—a temple "not made with hands" (cf. Mk 14:58; Mt 26:26; Jn 1:14). In the new Jerusalem, there is no temple, because "its temple is the Lord God the Almighty and the Lamb" (Rev 21:22).[67] When Christ talks about the rebuilding of the temple of his body, he makes clear messianic allusions—to his kingly power and his priesthood.

The building of the definitive temple, the kingdom and the enthroning of the Messiah are also interlinked in the New Testament: Jesus' resurrection

---

65. For a detailed study, cf. J. Coppens, *Le messianisme royal. Ses origines, son développement, son accomplissement* (Paris, 1968).

66. The kings, particularly David and Solomon, offer sacrifice as representatives of the people; and also, empowered by God and, in that respect, like the patriarchs, bless the people; in Israel, the king, God's representative on earth, is, thereby, mediator between God and the people (cf. N. Fuglister, op. cit., 152). Cf. also H. Cazelles, *Le Messie de la Bible. Christologie de l'Ancien Testament* (Paris, 1978); A. Amato, *Gesù il Signore. Saggio di cristologia* (Bologna, 1991), 66ff.

67. Cf. M.J. Congar, *Le mystère du Temple* (Paris, 1957).

means not only his glorification and enthronement (cf. Acts 2:22-36) but also the building of the new, definitive Temple, personified in our Lord's human nature. The Letter to the Hebrews stresses that Christ being raised up to the right hand of the Father is also an enthronement as king and marks his entry into the heavenly sanctuary (cf. Heb 7); in doing so it is merely synthesizing a rich, constant theology to do with the Messiah, king and priest, to be found whenever he is referred to as descendant of David (cf. e.g., Is 2:1:4; 4:2-6; 7:14-15; 9:1-7; 11:1-10; 28:16; 35: 1-10).

This is a priestly and kingly messiahship which, during Jesus' life on earth, expresses itself through the Servant's humility and sufferings. Jesus in fact applies Isaiah 61:1-2 to himself in the synagogue at Nazareth: "he has anointed me to preach good news to the poor. He has sent me to proclaim release to the captives . . . to proclaim the acceptable year of the Lord" (Lk 4:18-19). This points up the priestly and transcendent character of his messiahship; and it also highlights the fact that the messianic hopes of Israel are finding fulfilment in his sufferings.[68] The fact that Jesus is the expected Messiah makes it impossible to understand New Testament Christology without constantly referring to the Old Testament.

What is being preached, in fact, is that Jesus of Nazareth is the "Christ" (Mt 16:16), that is, the "anointed" one awaited by Israel. In order to explain to the disciples of Emmaus the saving character of his death, our Lord refers freely to the Scriptures, and calls them "foolish men, and slow of heart to believe all that the prophets have said" (cf. Lk 24:25-27); in a later appearance Jesus "opens the minds" of the disciples and shows them that it was written that the Messiah should suffer and rise on the third day from the dead (cf. Lk 22:44-46).

Our Lord did not come to set aside the Law or the prophets but to bring them to perfection (cf. Mt 5:17); in him the Old Testament reaches its fullness: Christ gave it its full meaning.[69] This fullness is at one and the same time continuity and rupture—continuity with God's promises and with the hopes of the people of Israel; rupture, because those promises are kept through a *New* Testament. Christ is David's descendent, the prophet *par excellence*, the eschatological Saviour, the king-priest and Servant of Yahweh, the one who releases the people from their sins; He is Yahweh who saves.[70]

---

68. Cf. A. Gelin, "Messianisme", DBS, art. cit., 1208.
69. "The Exodus, the Covenant, the Law, the voice of the Prophets, and the spirituality of the *poor of Yahweh* attain their full significance only in Christ. The Church reads the Old Testament in the light of Christ who died and rose for us. She sees herself prefigured in the body of a particular politically and culturally constituted nation, which was inserted into the fabric of history to bear witness to God before the nations": J.M. Casciaro and J.M. Monforte, *Dios, el mundo y el hombre segun la Biblia* (Pamplona, 1992), 623; an English translation is forthcoming from Four Courts Press.
70. "Commenting on the fulfillment, in one person, of these very diverse features of a single

In Christ all these features are to be found fully, in a way which also binds them together and raises them on to a totally new level, in a way no one could have suspected: all these features are to be found in him because he is the descendant of David and the Son-by-nature of the Father. With respect to the Old Testament, there is then in Christ continuity and newness—continuity as regards his features, newness, in the mystery of his Person, particularly. This newness was what disconcerted so many of his contemporaries and made him the stone rejected by the builders of Israel, thereby once more fulfilling the prophecies (cf. Ps 117:22; Is 28:16; Mt 21:42-45).

3. THE PREPARATION OF THE GENTILES

Although God prepared the way for the coming of the Redeemer mainly through his choice of the people of Israel, that does not mean that he turned his back on other nations (the "Gentiles"): "In past generations he allowed all the nations to walk in their own ways; yet he did not leave himself without witness, for he did good and gave you from heaven rains and fruitful seasons, satisfying your hearts with food and gladness" (Acts 14:16-17).

God always takes care of each and every human being. It is true that mankind was under the power of sin, of the Evil One, and of death, as a consequence of original sin. But in the world around them, men always found the way to recognize their Creator (cf. Wis 13:1ff; Rom 1:19-20) and in their heart the desire for and inclination to good (cf. Rom 2:14-15).

Moreover, we must also remember that God's initial revelation to Adam (which included the first promise of Redemption: cf. Gen 3:15) must undoubtedly have influenced the various Gentile religions, even though over the centuries in the course of its transmission from parents to children it became increasingly confused and deformed, with myth and superstition mixed in.

Religion is something universal; it is an expression, in a variety of forms,

---

Messianism, Lagrange writes: "The Old Testament has given several different names to the one who was to bring future salvation. First of all was that of God himself. Very many passages announced that God would come in person to save his people. Israel's salvation, therefore, would be an outstanding theophany, an extraordinary manifestation of the goodness of God towards his people, of his justice against their enemies and of his consuming and purifying holiness. On the other hand, a king was expected, a son of David, who would sit on the throne of his father and who would cause his own nation to rejoice with an unheard of joy. Isaiah had alluded to his miraculous birth and had given divine names to him [. . .]. Isaiah's compilation contained an overall picture of a servant of Yahweh who would convert the peoples to the faith of Israel and whose death would serve as reparation for a multitude. Daniel had said that God would intervene to destroy the persecutors and had portrayed a supernatural being descending from heaven to establish the kingdom of the saints [. . .]. That one person would be able to measure up to all these requirements seemed very difficult, or, rather, it would call for an unheard of miracle whose mystery had not yet been revealed": M.J. Lagrange, *Le messianisme chez les Juifs* (Paris, 1909).

of man's natural religious sense. Every religion has been in some way a religion of salvation, concerned with freeing man from evil and suffering. The hopes that Gentiles harboured in their hearts were basically vestiges of the witness God has always borne of himself through the created world and through man's inclination towards good, set alongside his experience of evil, which is the consequence of sin.

In any event, it is quite clear that divine providence gave the Gentiles a more or less conscious sense of the need for redemption.[71] This awareness later expressed itself in hopes of salvation to come that were sometimes distorted. In primitive and mysterious religions, for example, there is often a mythical redeemer (Osiris, Adonis, Mithras, etc.), who is really only a symbol of the natural cycles of earthly life (animal, vegetable, etc.). In these religions salvation is seen as being at one with the rhythm of nature:[72] this means it is essentially different from the messiahism of Israel and not just different in origin.

However, this vague sense men had of the need for redemption meant that they were to a degree open to the proclamation of true salvation when the Saviour eventually appeared. "Mankind awaited the coming of the Saviour for centuries. The prophets had announced his coming in a thousand ways. Even in the farthest corners of the earth, where a great part of God's revelation to men was perhaps lost through sin or ignorance, the longing for God, the desire to be redeemed, had been kept alive."[73]

4. CHRIST, THE CENTRE AND GOAL OF HISTORY

The Incarnation of God is the central event of human history, and the God-man is also the goal of that history. To explain what this means we will first look at the purpose of the Incarnation.

a) **The purpose of the Incarnation** There are two aspects to this—the actual purpose which the Incarnation had and which it actually attained; and the degree to which the Incarnation and that purpose are interdependent. The first was clearly revealed by God and therefore is a matter of faith. God became man, to save men, and he did in fact save them. The second aspect is not defined (and is open to theological reflection) and therefore the following question may be asked: If man had not sinned, would God still have become man?

In the *Creed* we profess our faith in the Son of God, who "for us men and for our salvation he came down from heaven: by the power of the Holy Spirit he became incarnate from the Virgin Mary, and was made man."[74]

---

71. Cf. E.B. Allo, "Les dieux sauveurs du paganisme gréco-romain" RSPT 15 (1926), 5-34.
72. Cf. M. Schmaus, *Katholische Dogmatik*, II/2, op. cit., 7.
73. Blessed J. Escrivá de Balaguer, *Christ is passing by*, op. cit., 36.
74. First Council of Constantinople, *Symbolum* (DS 150). Cf. also CCC, nos. 457-60.

The same truth is to be found in several places in Scripture. Jesus said of himself that "the Son of man came to seek and to save the lost" (Lk 19:10; cf. Mt 18:11); and in the Gospel of St John we read that "God sent the Son into the world, not to condemn the world, but that the world might be saved through him" (Jn 3:17). Moreover, St Paul wrote to Timothy: "Christ Jesus came into the world to save sinners" (1 Tim 1:15). Many other texts mention the purpose of the Incarnation, referring to the Incarnation or aspects of it—to restore to man his adoption as son of God, to destroy the work of the Evil One, etc. (cf. Gal 4:4-5; 1 Jn 3:5, 8-9). The Fathers of the Church were unanimously of the view that the Incarnation took place to bring salvation to mankind.

Therefore, it is a truth of faith that Christ's mission, that is, the reason why the Word became flesh, was so that "he might in the mysteries of his flesh free man from sin".[75] When we say that the purpose of the Incarnation was to save mankind, that does not mean that Christ is subordinate to man, in the sense that God the Father wanted Jesus to be the *means* by which men were saved, and that he did not love Him in himself and for himself. Rather, Jesus is, in himself, the salvation of man, not a way to bring about salvation. So, it is in Christ that mankind is saved, and each man or woman attains that salvation to the degree that he or she is united to Christ.

But, if Adam had not sinned, would there have been an Incarnation? Revelation gives no clear answer to this question. Yet it is a valid question and has been the subject of much theological debate. Since the Middle Ages there have been two opposite opinions—that of Duns Scotus and that of St Thomas Aquinas, both of whom have their followers.

Scotus said that the Son of God would have become man even if Adam had not sinned. His line of arguing is based principally on the idea that Christ's supreme dignity is not subordinate to sin: it is something willed by God for its own sake as the apex and highest perfection of Creation.[76]

St Thomas said that the Incarnation would not have happened if man had not sinned. His argument is based mainly on the idea that we cannot know God's plans except insofar as he reveals them to us. Revelation in fact constantly tells us not just that the Son of God is our Redeemer but that he became man in order to redeem us.[77] The Fathers of the Church often gave a negative answer to this particular question. For example, St Augustine said: "If man had not sinned, the Son of God would not have come."[78] St Irenaeus, St

---

75. Second Vatican Council, Const. *Lumen gentium*, 55.
76. Cf. Duns Scotus, *Lectura parisiensis*, III, d.7, q.4. Apparently the first to state this thesis was Rupert de Deutz (*d.*1135); cf. *De gloria et honore Filii hominis. Super Matth.*, 1, 13 (PL 168, 1628).
77. Cf. Thomas Aquinas, *STh*, III, q.1, a.3.
78. St Augustine, *Sermo* 174, 2, 2 (PL 38, 940).

Athanasius, St Gregory of Nyssa, St John Chrysostom and St Leo the Great, for example, were of the same view.[79]

The Thomistic opinion, therefore, seems to be the more probable. It should also be noted that the Thomistic thesis manages to skirt the main difficulty which Scotus was trying to avoid, because the fact that the purpose of the Incarnation is the salvation of men does not mean that sin is the *cause* of the Incarnation (it is simply the occasion of it);[80] nor that Christ is subordinate to that salvation: he is Salvation. Some authors, therefore, think that the two opinions can be synthesized.[81] Also, we should remember that God's plans are eternal and therefore, in the order of reality, Christ is part of God's plan from the very beginning of creation (cf. Col 1:16) and not just from the moment when man sinned.

Finally, it might be noted that if one says that the Incarnation would have taken place even if man had not sinned, it should not be presented as something necessary, as the necessary high point of creation. Apart from the fact that it is a truth of faith that the Incarnation was gratuitous (unmerited), it is easy to see that if one claimed any necessity in God with regard to the world, then logically one would be denying his transcendence and would end up in some form of pantheism: God would be nothing more than the self-consciousness of the world and man would become God by taking on this self-consciousness. This in fact happens with some Idealist theories after Hegel.

b) Christ, God's greatest gift to men "In this the love of God was made manifest among us, that God sent his only Son, into the world, so that we might live through him" (1 Jn 4:9; cf. Jn 3:16-17). The Incarnation is the best proof of God's love for men and, since every gift derives from love, the greatest expression of love is the greatest gift.

Christ is God's gift to mankind, also because he is salvation, which is undoubtedly the greatest gift any individual or mankind as a whole can receive. Also, the Incarnation is the greatest gift an individual human nature (that of Jesus) can receive, which is also a benefit to all who share that human nature: "human nature, by the very fact that it was assumed, not absorbed, in him,

---

79. Cf. St Irenaeus, *Adv. haer*, V, 14, 1 (PG 7, 1161); St Athanasius, *Adv. Arian.*, II 56, 6 (PG 26, 268); St Gregory of Nyssa, *Orat. Catech.*, 8 (PG 45, 37); St John Chrysostom, *In. Ep. ad Hebr.*, 5, 1 (PG 63, 47); St Leo the Great, *Sermo*, 77, 2 (PL 54, 412). For a detailed account of the main views on this subject, see J.F. Bonnefoy, "Il primato di Cristo nella teologia contemporanea", in various authors, *Problemi e orientamenti di Teologia Dommatica*, II (Milan, 1957), 123-5; *La Primauté du Christ selon l'Ecriture et la Tradition* (Rome, 1959), where the author adopts the Scotist position.

80. Cf. M. Corvez, "Le motif de l'Incarnation", RT 49 (1949) 109.

81. Cf. B. de Margerie, *Le Christ pour le monde* (Paris, 1971), 28-32; J. Galot, *Gesù Liberatore* (Florence, 1978), 29-31. It is not so much a kind of dialectic synthesis of opposite views, as the insertion into the Thomist position of the basic point in the Scotist stance, that is, the non-subordination of Christ to man's sin.

has been raised in us also to a dignity beyond compare."[82] Jesus Christ is God's greatest gift to men for this reason also—that he is the maximum degree of God's nearness to man; for he is the most understandable and fullest revelation of God to us. But all this presupposes that the Incarnation is gratuitous: something given because nature needs it is never a gift, nor can something done in justice be a gift.

God's will was entirely free to save mankind or not—and above all to decide on the way to go about it. The Incarnation (which was the way he chose) was the outcome of God's free choice: it was in no sense a necessary decision. Indeed, even given God's decision to save mankind, he could have implemented it in many different ways. And if God had decided to save man through Redemption, that Redemption could have been done in many different ways.

When dealing with this aspect of the mystery of Christ, the Fathers of the Church usually confined themselves to the consideration of what in fact happened. As St Peter said, "there is no other name under heaven given among men by which we must be saved" (Acts 4:12). So, it is only in Christ that we are saved. But that does not mean that, if God had so decided, he could not have done it in some other way. As St Augustine taught, "they are mistaken who say: the Divine Wisdom could not redeem mankind except by assuming human nature and being born of a woman and suffering for sinners all that he suffered. To them I reply: he could have done it in the above way, yes, but he could also have followed some other procedure which would be equally disagreeable to your stupidity."[83]

Nor did infinite divine Justice require that, in order to redeem man, satisfaction had to be made which was suited (*ex toto rigore justitiae*—from the total rigour of justice) to the gravity of sin (satisfaction which, as we shall see, could only be made by the God-man), for the Justice of God is also infinite Mercy, and he could forgive sins without requiring any atonement to be done, as the parable of the prodigal son clearly shows (cf. Lk 15:11-32). Firstly, he could have simply forgiven the offence sin implied. That would not have gone against Justice, for, as St Thomas Aquinas argues, the person who suffers an offence can, without injustice, forgive the injury without requiring reparation.[84] Similarly, God could have accepted any satisfaction offered by man or any other creature. Satisfaction is *perfect* when it fully atones for a fault; when the reparation does not equal the injury, satisfaction is *imperfect*, but it can be sufficient if the offended party accepts it. So any man or angel could have made satisfaction for Adam's fault.

However, even though it was not necessary, the Incarnation was the best way to effect Redemption, whether from the point of view of God or from

82. John Paul II, Enc. *Redemptor hominis*, 8.
83. St Augustine, *De agone christiano*, XI, 12 (PL 40, 297).
84. Cf. St Thomas Aquinas, *STh* III, q.46, a.2, ad 3.

that of the nature and needs of man.

Although the Incarnation is a gratuitous gift, and not necessary, if God, in the freedom of his love for man, wanted to give him the grace of being redeemed in the most perfect way, that is, *ex toto genere justitiae* (in the fullest sense of justice), then the Incarnation was indeed necessary. And so we may say that the Incarnation is hypothetically necessary, that is, on the hypothesis that a totally perfect Redemption is desired. Now, a perfect redemption—that is, one effected by perfect atonement on man's part—can be made only by the God-Man. The atonement had to be made by a man, but for it to be perfect (in line with the infinite dignity of God, the offended one) it had to be made by God himself. Therefore, only Christ, true God and true man, could make such atonement: "Only the Man-God could make satisfaction in strict justice."[85]

c) **Christ and time** The Gospels often refer to a particular relationship of Jesus to time, in the sense of the "opportune time" (*kairos*). Jesus speaks of his *hour*, of *his time* not having come yet, etc.[86] We will now take a brief look at the overall relationship between Jesus and *his hour* in the context of human history.

As the Second Vatican Council reminds us, the Church firmly believes that its Lord and Master, Jesus Christ, is "the key, the centre and the purpose of the whole of man's history. The Church also maintains that beneath all that changes there is much that is unchanging, much that has its ultimate foundation in Christ, who is the same yesterday, and today, and forever (cf. Heb 13:8)."[87]

The history of man is not a meaningless succession of unconnected events; it is a history of grace and of sin in which (over and above all the changes) there "are many things that are unchanging"; these include human nature itself and its final goal. So, despite the great diversity of times and cultures, man is always a spiritual and material creature (body and soul), who can attain fulfilment and happiness only through knowing and loving God. In the history of mankind, which is made up of the personal histories of individual men and women, there is one basic point of reference—Jesus Christ, our Lord.

Christ is the centre of human history. The Incarnation took place "when the time had fully come" (Gal 4:4)—not at the start of time, immediately after original sin, nor at the end of history, but when the world was prepared for the coming of the Redeemer. In this sense "when the time had fully come" means when the appropriate time had elapsed; but above all, it was the Incarnation itself which was the cause of that moment being the one in which

---

85. Council of Cologne, AD 1860, part I, chap. 18, in *Mansi*, op. cit., 48, col. 98.
86. Cf. J. Daniélou, *Cristo e noi*, op. cit., 165. This subject has been studied from a non-Catholic perspective by O. Cullmann in particular, in his *Christ et le temps* (Neuchatel, 1966).
87. Second Vatican Council, Const. *Gaudium et spes*, 10.

the time had fully come.[88] It is the most important moment in history, in which the divine eternity of the Word became incarnate in human time and so bestowed on it a transcendent characteristic—that of being the foundation of the whole past, which possesses salvific value solely by means of Christ—and, likewise, being the foundation of the future. Christ is, effectively, the Alpha and the Omega, the beginning and the end (Rev 21:6). With Jesus, "eternity penetrates time, not so as to downgrade itself in time, but to introduce time into eternity."[89]

Therefore, Christ is the centre of human history, not in the strictly chronological sense but qualitatively, insofar as he brings about the division between "the old" and "the new": he brings to fulfilment the Old Testament, which finds its full meaning in him; and he establishes the New Covenant and the new human history, whose foundation he is and to which he gives meaning.[90] Thus, "if anyone is in Christ, he is a new creation; the old has passed away, behold the new has come" (2 Cor 5:17).

Christ is also the goal of human history, not because the Incarnation was the last act of history (clearly it was not) but because the New Covenant in Christ is eternal and permanent (cf. Heb 9:12). That is why "in the spiritual life, there is no new era to come. Everything is already there, in Christ who died and rose again, who lives and stays with us always."[91] Every moment in history after the Incarnation does not look to Christ as something past but as something present. This *contemporaneity* of Christ in all epochs after the Incarnation is not only something that attaches to Christ himself in glory, because he lives for ever: it is also a *salvific contemporaneity* with the mysteries of his life, death and resurrection truly present mysteriously (sacramentally) in the life of the Church.

To say that Christ is the goal of history also means that only in union with him can each man (and through men, the whole material universe) attain his true goal, his fulfilment. God created all things "in him" (cf. Col 1:16) so that at the end of time everything might be united in him (cf. Eph 1:10).[92]

---

88. Cf. St Thomas Aquinas, *STh* III, q.1, aa.5-6; *In Epist. ad Galat.*, c.4, lec. 2.
89. J. Daniélou, *Cristo e noi*, op. cit., 72.
90. Cf. John Paul II, *Address*, 4 February 1987, no. 7: *Insegnamenti*, X, 1 (1987), 260.
91. Blessed Escrivá de Balaguer, *Christ is passing by*, op. cit., no. 104.
92. On *anakefalaiosis* or recapitulation of all things in Christ, according to Eph 1:10, cf. e.g., J.M. Casciaro, *Estudios sobre Cristología del Nuevo Testamento*, op. cit., 308-24.

CHAPTER TWO

The Coming of Christ in the Fullness of Time

Our Lord described his coming to this world as a "mission": "I came from the Father and have come into the world; again, I am leaving the world and going to the Father" (Jn 16:28). He also speaks of his "coming down" (cf. Jn 6:38-41) from heaven to earth. As the Second Vatican Council says, "Wishing in his supreme goodness and wisdom to effect the redemption of the world, 'when the fullness of time came, God sent his Son, born of a woman . . . that we might receive the adoption of sons' (Gal 4:4-5). He for us men, and for our salvation, came down from heaven, and was incarnated by the Holy Spirit from the Virgin Mary (Symbol of Constantinople)."[1]

God's plan of salvation is the fruit of his mercy. To put it into operation, the Father sent into the world the Son who assumed a concrete human nature, making himself like us in all things but sin (cf. Heb 4:15). He is truly *God with us*, the promised Christ or Messiah anointed with the fullness of the Holy Spirit. By sacrificing himself as the suffering Servant, he is the Redeemer of the human race and the Son of man who will at the end of time establish the definitive Kingdom of God.

This chapter is devoted to Christ's entrance into the world, that is, the mystery of the Incarnation. It first looks at the life of Jesus on earth, and goes on to examine the content of the statement that Jesus is perfect God and perfect man. Through the Incarnation one and the same *subject* unites the divine and the human in himself, in the unity of a person. This subject is the Word of God, who "was in the beginning with God", through whom "all things were made" (Jn 1:2-3) and who in the fullness of time "became flesh and dwelt among us" (Jn 1:14). It is a matter, then, of God, in the Person of the Word, uniting himself to a human nature so intimately that the sufferings and joys, all the actions of this nature, are sufferings and joys, actions of God. So, after studying the mystery of the Incarnation in itself, the chapter ends by dealing with complementary questions, which are important insofar as they help us to understand the implications of the basic statement: the Word became flesh.

These questions have to do with the part played by the Blessed Trinity in the Incarnation: although only the Word became man, the Incarnation was a work *ad extra* (towards outside) of the Trinity and in that sense a work of the

---

1. Second Vatican Council, Const. *Lumen gentium*, 52.

whole Trinity; they also touch on the immutability of the Word in the Incarnation, even though there is this new and close relationship between his human nature and the divine Person. Thus, the Incarnation cannot be conceived as a kind of *metamorphosis* of divinity into humanity, but rather as a mysterious assumption of human nature by the Person of the Word—an assumption in which the Word undergoes no change as regards his intimate nature, and yet is truly man. After studying the mystery of the Incarnation, the chapter ends by noting how appropriate the Incarnation was from God's and man's viewpoints, and the fact that it was something totally unmerited by man.

1. JESUS REALLY DID EXIST

That Christ truly lived is an article of faith, as it is that he truly *died* for us and *rose again on the third day*. Faith in Christ is not a belief in a being outside of time whom we have come to know through a mystical experience; even less is it a belief in myth or a symbol of the union of mankind with God. Our faith in Christ is faith in a Person (the eternal Son of the Father) who at a particular point in history "by the power of the Holy Spirit became incarnate from the Virgin Mary, and was made man. For our sake he was crucified under Pontius Pilate; he suffered death and was buried. On the third day he rose again in accordance with the Scriptures; he ascended into heaven and is seated at the right hand of the Father. He will come again in glory to judge the living and the dead."[2] It is therefore faith in a particular, individual man who said of himself, "I am the way, and the truth, and the life" (Jn 14:6).

The life of Jesus on earth is a fact proven by historical research, particularly from analysis of the New Testament, whose historical validity is not in doubt. We might mention, also, non-Christian testimonies to the existence of Jesus. For example, among the Romans, there is Tacitus, who, referring to the reign of Nero, wrote in his Annals (*c*.AD 116) that "Christians take their name from Christ who, in the reign of Tiberias, the proconsul Pontius Pilate condemned to suffer".[3] Seutonius, in his life of Claudius (*c*.120) says that that emperor expelled the Jews from Rome because of the unrest among them "stirred up by Chresto" (Christ).[4] This distorted report seems to contain testimony to the existence of Jesus and to controversy about Christ in Rome (cf. Acts 18:2). Pliny the Younger, proconsul of Bithynia from 111 to 113 in one of his letters to the Emperor Trajan wrote that "the Christians gather at dawn on a fixed

---

2. First Council of Constantinople, AD 381, *Symbolum* (DS 150).
3. Tacitus, *Annales*, XV, 1, 4.
4. Seutonius, *Vita Claudii*, XXV, 4. This testimony ties in with another from the *Vita Neronis*: "the Christians, a class of men belonging to a new and evil-doing superstition" (XVI, 2).

day and sing a hymn to Christ as to a God."[5] Other evidence comes from non-Christian Jewish writers, particularly Flavius Josephus (37-105);[6] although the authenticity of the text that has come down to us is unsure, it is clear that the original text did refer to Jesus Christ.

We will not dwell on this subject, which is usually dealt with in apologetic rather than in dogmatic theology. All we need do here is note that various attempts have been made to deny the historical existence of Jesus, especially in the last century, and to present him as a mythical personage who never really existed. These theories, we know, have no scientific basis and are now quite discredited.[7]

Equally unacceptable is the position of these who, by counterposing the *Jesus of history* and the *Christ of faith* argue that almost everything that the New Testament says about Christ is really the "interpretation of faith" made by Jesus' disciples, not a true, historical account: therefore, we cannot reach the truth about him. This is at odds with the clear intention of numerous texts, which purport not only to pass on a *testimony of faith* but also true historical facts. Thus, we find, particularly in the Gospels, details about the birth, infancy, and activity of Christ, and his passion and death; they even give details about the activities of his disciples.[8] Although the evangelists do not try to write a *biography* of Jesus in the modern sense, they do truthfully repeat "what happened in Jesus of Nazareth", particularly because they are convinced that his words and actions, given the divine authority with which he was invested, are a headline for what we ourselves should do. They repeatedly stress this (cf., e.g., Lk 1:1-4; Jn 20:30-31). We must remember that even if the Gospels were not designed as biographical, they are certainly written as *testimonies* of true eyewitnesses (cf. e.g., Jn 21:24).

5. Pliny the Younger, *Epist.* X, 96.
6. Flavius Josephus, *Antiquitates judaicae*, XVIII, 3, 3; XX, 9, 1.
7. Thus e.g. Voltaire (1697-1778) tries to make out that Jesus was an "unknown and crucified Jew". But the first to deny that Jesus of Nazareth ever existed were the "mythologists", who said he was purely a myth: cf. C.F. Dupuis (1742-1809). Bruno Bauer (1809-82) says that Jesus is the "personification" of the Christian idea, which grew out of a mixture of Graeco-Roman and Jewish elements. A. Kalthoff (1805-1906) says that Jesus is the personification of a certain communistic social tendency to be found in messianic-apocalyptic hopes of the period: cf. L. de Grandmaison, *Jésus dans l'histoire et dans le mystère* (Paris, 1925); M. Lepin, *Le Christ Jésus* (Paris, 1929), 11-135; F.M. Braun, *Où en est le problème de Jésus* (Brussels-Paris, 1932), 159-211; M. Nicolau, "De revelatione christiana (De existencia historica Jesu)", in *Sacrae Theologiae Summa*, I (Madrid, 1955), 282-93; B. Rigaux, "L'historicité de Jésus devant l'exégèse récente", RB 65 (1958), 481-522; R. Fabris, *Jesús de Nazaret. Historia e interpretación* (Salamanca, 1983), 11-50.
8. The *Jesus of the Gospels* and the *historical Jesus* obtained by the use of rigorous historico-critical methods concur with one another": F. Ardusso, *Gesù di Nazaret è Figlio di Dio?* [Turin, 1980], 51). On this subject, see J.M. Casciaro, *Estudios sobre la cristología del Nuevo Testamento* (Pamplona, 1982), 63-111; J. Caba, *De los Evangelios al Jesús histórico. (Introducción a la Cristología)* (Madrid, 1971), C. Skalicky, *Teologia Fundamentale* (Rome, 1979), 193-219.

The Gospels provide us with a true history of Jesus: "Holy Mother Church has firmly and with absolute constancy maintained and continues to maintain, that the four Gospels just named, whose historicity she unhesitatingly affirms, faithfully hand on what Jesus, the Son of God, while he lived among men, really did and taught for their eternal salvation, until the day when he was taken up (cf. Acts 1:1-2)."[9]

To the testimonies in the Gospels as to "what happened in Jesus Christ", must be added the great wealth of information and evidence contained in the Letters and in the Acts of the Apostles, particularly in St Peter's sermons in Acts (which give an account of Christ's death and bear witness to his resurrection) and in what St Paul has to say about the life of Jesus, whom he proposes as the model of virtue.

2. JESUS CHRIST, PERFECT MAN

Jesus showed his contemporaries that he was a true man, just like us. The Gospel tells us many things about Christ's humanity. The Second Vatican Council sums it up in these words: "He worked with human hands, he thought with a human mind. He acted with a human will, and with a human heart he loved. Born of the Virgin Mary, he has truly been made one of us, like to us in all things except sin" (cf. Heb 4:15).[10]

The humanity of Christ can be examined from many aspects. We will concentrate on his conception and birth, on the fact that he had a real body and soul (that he is truly man, as both the early Fathers and the ecclesiastical writers stressed, against the Docetists) and on the fact that he is descended from Adam and is the new Adam.

a) The virginal conception of Jesus   St Mark begins his Gospel with the preaching of John the Baptist, because that marks the beginning of the public proclamation of the coming of the Kingdom, in fulfilment of messianic expectations (Mk 1:1ff); St Matthew and St Luke cover the infancy of Jesus at the start of their accounts because they are conscious that his conception, childhood and adolescence also belong to the *good news*, that is, they too are salvific events. God's definitive intervention in history begins with the coming into the world of the Son: "clearly, the entry into the world of that Jesus who would be raised up by God as Lord and Christ (cf. Acts 2:36) cannot be an event marginal to the history of salvation. This is what led Luke to bring forward the proclamation of these two titles to the moment of (Christ's) birth (Lk 2:11). And the liturgy also celebrates the Nativity and Epiphany of our

9.   Second Vatican Council, Const. *Dei Verbum*, 19. Cf. M.A. Tabet, "Cristología e historicidad de los Evangelios en la Constitución *Dei Verbum*" in *Cristo, Hijo de Dios . . .*, op. cit., 299-324.
10.   Second Vatican Council, Const. *Gaudium et spes*, 22.

Lord as salvific events, and not as mere anniversaries."[11] It was not, therefore, just for anecdotal purposes that Matthew and Luke wrote the *Infancy Gospel*; they give an account of these events because they too are "good news", full of salvific relevance.

These events of the infancy of Jesus are the first that derive from the *mission* of the Son by the Father, for "when the time had fully come, God sent forth his Son, born of woman, born under the law, to redeem those who were under the law, so that we might receive adoption as sons" (Gal 4:4-5). The conception of Jesus is the beginning of the visible mission of the Son.

Here is Matthew's account of the conception of Jesus: "Now the birth of Jesus Christ took place in this way. When his mother Mary had been betrothed to Joseph, before they came together she was found to be with child of the Holy Spirit; and her husband, Joseph, being a just man and unwilling to put her to shame, resolved to send her away quietly. But as he considered this, behold, an angel of the Lord appeared to him in a dream, saying, 'Joseph, son of David, do not fear to take Mary your wife, for that which is conceived in her is of the Holy Spirit; she will bear a son, and you shall call his name Jesus, for he will save his people from their sins.' All this took place to fulfil what the Lord had spoken by the prophet: 'Behold, a virgin shall conceive and bear a son, and his name shall be called Immanuel' (which means, God with us)" (Mt 1:18-23).

Matthew mentions the prophecy of Isaiah (Is 7:14) concerning the Immanuel, saying that it is fulfilled in Christ. Although the Isaiah text does not strictly speak of a virgin, but of a "maiden" (*almah*), it does not exclude the meaning "virgin"; and in fact the Septuagint had already translated the word as *parthenos* (= virgin). But what interests us here is the fact that the Gospel wants to "emphasize" that the conception of Jesus took place in a miraculous way, from a virginal mother, that is, without the involvement of a man.[12]

The virginal conception of Jesus is also vividly reported in the Gospel of Luke: "And the angel said to her, 'The Holy Spirit will come upon you, and the power of the Most High will overshadow you; therefore the child to be born will be called holy, the Son of God" (Lk 1:35). "With God nothing will be impossible", the angel says in conclusion (Lk 1:37), thereby indicating the miraculous nature of the conception of the Messiah: it comes about by the action of the Holy Spirit.

From the beginning, the Church professed to faith in this truth, as we can

11. M. González Gil, *Cristo el misterio de Dios*, op. cit., I, 276.
12. Much has been written on this subject. Cf. e.g., J. Daniélou, *Les évangiles de l'Enfance* (Paris, 1967); S. Muñoz Iglesias, "Midrás y Evangelios de la Infancia", EE 47 (1972) 331-59; J. Galot, "La conception virginale du Christ", Greg 49 (1968), 637-66; M. Schmaus, *Katholische Dogmatik*, II/2, op. cit., 167; C. Pozo, *María en la historia de la salvación* (Madrid, 1974), 265-84 and "La concepción virginal del Señor", SM 1 (1978), 131-56.

see from the early *Symbols* in the various versions: "(Christ) was conceived by the Holy Spirit of the Virgin Mary";[13] or, "by the power of the Holy Spirit he became incarnate from the Virgin Mary and was made man."[14] The *Dogmatic Letter* of Pope Leo I (AD 449), which is even more explicit, says that Jesus "was conceived by the Holy Spirit in the womb of the Virgin mother who bore him without loss of virginity as she conceived him without loss of virginity."[15] We should also mention the Constitution, *Cum quorundam* of Paul IV (1555), which calls to account anyone who says that Jesus "was not conceived of the Holy Spirit according to the flesh in the womb of the most Blessed and ever-virgin Mary, but that his conception is in no way different from the conception of other men, and that he was conceived of the flesh of Joseph"; it also condemns anyone who denies that Mary stayed a perfect virgin "before, while, and forever after she gave birth".[16]

Sacred Scripture speaks of the virginal conception of Christ as primarily a privilege of Christ himself, as something very much in keeping with his filiation to the Father. "Thus", the angel said to Mary that "the child to be born will be called holy, the Son of God" (Lk 1:35). Virginity is also a privilege for Mary. "The entire theological meaning of the Virgin Mary lies in this. By taking flesh within her, the Word has become a true member of the human race. Firstly, through her he has experienced the natural origin of the human being (which forms part of the human nature he has assumed); rising through her from historical humanity (He, who comes from on high) he has been inserted in human history."[17] The Church, at the same time as it asserts that Christ was generated virginally, teaches as unequivocally that Mary is truly the *Mother of God*, *Theotokos* (God bearer). And as the Creed so exquisitely puts it, Jesus Christ *incarnatus est ex Maria virgine*, was truly begotten by a virgin.

Only sin is unworthy of God. Therefore, the Word could have assumed a human nature conceived in a natural way, that is, without the miracle of virginity. But once God chose virginal conception as the route to enter this world, theology has identified how appropriate that choice was.[18]

It points out, that from the Christological angle, it was highly appropriate

---

13. See the different versions of the Apostles' Creed (DS 10ff); Council of the Lateran, ch.3, 31 October 649 (DS 503).
14. First Council of Constantinople, *Symbolum* (DS 150).
15. St Leo the Great, Ep. *Lectis dilectionis tuae*, 13 June 449 (DS 291).
16. Paul IV, Const. *Cum quorundam*, 7 August 1555 (DS 1880). When proclaiming the Blessed Virgin's virginity, the Church has always professed that "Jesus was conceived in the womb of the Virgin Mary solely by the power of the Holy Spirit, affirming in this the corporal aspect of the event too: Jesus was conceived *without seed by the Holy Spirit* (Council of the Lateran, AD 649; DS 503), that is, without a human element by the work of the Holy Spirit" (CCC, no. 496).
17. J.H. Nicolas, *Synthèse dogmatique* (Fribourg and Paris, 1986), 467.
18. Cf. G. Aranda, "Los Evangelios de la infancia de Jesús", ScrTh 10 (1978) 845.

that Jesus who, being one Person, should also in his humanity be the natural son of God the Father (we shall see later what that precisely means), that is, should not have had another, earthly, father.[19] Moreover, "virginal conception, considered as human maternity suited to divine paternity",[20] makes it very plain that *Christ is an exclusive gift from God the Father* to mankind and, in the first instance, to Mary.

Finally, we should add that the miraculous *manner* in which the conception of Christ's humanity took place in no way detracts from the reality of his human nature. As St Leo the Great writes in the Dogmatic Letter just quoted (449), "this marvellously unique and uniquely marvellous generation must not be understood as if by the new mode of creation some property of the (human) race were removed."[21]

b) Christ had a real body   By asserting that Jesus Christ had a true human nature, like ours, we are asserting the truth of the Incarnation. The Church has always professed, ever since the earliest *Symbols*, that the Son of God "took a complete human nature just as it is found in us poor unfortunates, but one that was without sin."[22] And it had to underline this again and again against the Docetist currents of the early centuries.

This truth is clearly and in different ways revealed in the New Testament, where we find the accounts of the conception of Jesus in the womb of a woman; his birth and development; his adult life; his preaching and his death. Not only did Christ *act* as a man: referring to himself, he tells the Jews "but now you seek to kill me, a man who has told you the truth" (Jn 8:40): he *was* man.

The Apostles also speak about the humanity of Christ as an evident fact; for example, St Paul will say that "there is one mediator between God and men, the man Jesus Christ" (1 Tim 2:5; cf. Rom 5:15; 1 Cor 15:21-22). And he says of Christ that he is "born of woman, born under the law" (Gal 4:4).

However, very early on, there began to emerge, in some Christian circles, mistaken ideas about the reality of the human nature taken up by the Son of God, as regards both body and soul.

The Docetists appear in the first century, denying that Christ had a real, material body. *Docetism* was not a clearly defined sect. It was rather a tendency to be found in many sects, particularly Gnostic ones. It simply refused to believe that Christ had a real human body. There were different kinds of Docetists. For some, Christ only apparently had a body (*dokein*, in Greek, means "to

---

19. Cf. Tertullian, *De carne Christi*, 18 (PL 2, 828); St Thomas Aquinas, *STh* III, q.28, a.1.
20. G. Girones, "Cristo objetivo (Apuntes para una cristología objetiva o de recepción)", in *Cristo Hijo de Dios . . .*, op. cit., 671. Cf. also S. Lyonnet, "Le récit de l'Annonciation et la maternité divine de la Sainte Vierge, AC 66 (1956) 33-48.
21. St Leo the Great, Ep. *Lectis dilectionis tuae* (DS 292).
22. Second Vatican Council, Decr. *Ad gentes* 3; Cf. Const. *Gaudium et spes*, 22; John Paul II, Enc. *Redemptor hominis*, 4 March 1979, no. 8.

appear": hence the name Docetists): this was the view of Basilides; for others, (Apelles, Valentinus) this body, though real, was not earthly but heavenly: it was never truly engendered by Mary; rather, being *heavenly*, it *passed* through her, but without being formed *from* (*ex*) her flesh and blood; for others (Marcion), Christ appeared suddenly in Judea without having to be born or grow to adulthood.[23]

These errors (which the Church spent centuries combatting) derive partly from Manichean and Gnostic doctrines which regarded matter and more specifically the human body as something evil and therefore totally inappropriate for God to assume.[24] Another reason for this rejection lay in the profound sense of scandal the mystery of the Incarnation provoked in them: how was it possible that the Eternal, the Almighty, should demean himself by associating with anything so earthly, temporal and carnal?

So the Docetists would never accept that the Only-begotten Son of the Father should have become a true man, born of (*ex*) a woman; a man who grew up slowly, who truly suffered, who experienced hunger and thirst, and died a terrible death. They went to ridiculous extremes to support their theory. Basilides, for example, said that it was Simon of Cyrene who suffered and died on Calvary, taking Christ's place.[25] Anything, rather than simply accept Revelation: "the Word became flesh and dwelt among us" (Jn 1:14).

These heresies tried to bend Scripture to support their case. For example, the Docetists made much of the "likeness of men" in Philippians 2:7, arguing that Jesus was therefore not truly man but only appeared so. However, the likeness to which the inspired text refers does not deny the reality of Christ's

---

23. Cf. J. Lebreton, *History of the Dogma of the Trinity* (New York, 1939), 118; K. Adam, *The Christ of Faith*, op. cit., 28-30; J. Liébaert, *L'incarnation. I. Des origines à Chalcédoine*, op. cit., 13-143; A. Grillmeier, *Gesù il Cristo nella fede della Chiesa* (Brescia, 1982), 249-60; B. Sesboué, *Christ dans la tradition de l'Eglise*, op. cit., 71-80.

24. The Gnostic finds within himself the substance of his own salvation; he does so inevitably because he has been born with it. So, there can be gnosis without a saviour, but no salvation without gnosis, as Cornelius points out (DSp VI, 533). Salvation comes in and through gnosis (through the self-awareness the Gnostic has of himself, not through the saviour, who is only of secondary importance, since he is not the redeemer but merely the bearer of a salvific message whose effectiveness is entirely a function of the nature (depending on whether it is gnostic or not) of the recipient. That is why (against the Fathers, who gave such importance to the Humanity of our Lord) the Gnostics deny the reality of Christ's body (cf. L. Mateo Seco, "Gnosticismo", GER 11, 61-3).

25. This is how St Irenaeus summarizes Basilides' teaching on this point: "He (Christ) appeared on earth, then, as man, to the peoples of those nations and he worked miracles. It was not therefore he himself who suffered death but a certain Simon, a man of Cyrene, who was forced to carry the cross in his place. The latter, transfigured by him in such a way that he could be taken for Jesus, was crucified through ignorance and error, while Jesus, who in the meantime had been transformed into Simon, was there beside him and was laughing at them" (*Adv. haer.* 1, 24, 4). Cf. J. Quasten, *Patrology* (Westminster, 1960), I, 257-8. On the kaleidoscopic world of Gnosticism and its general lines of thought, cf. E. Cornelis, "Gnosticisme", in DSp VI, 523-42; A. Orbe, *Cristología gnóstica*, 2 vols (Madrid, 1986).

human nature; one also speaks of all those who have the same nature as being specifically "like" one another. All one has to do is continue reading the same text to discover how ill-grounded the Docetist exegesis is, because it goes on to say that Christ "became obedient unto death, even death on a cross",—which he could not have done if he did not have a genuine human body.[26]

Valentinus used 1 Corinthians 15:47 in his argument: "The first man was from the earth, a man of dust; the second man is from heaven". To understand this text correctly, St Thomas Aquinas says, one must bear in mind that "Christ is said to have come down from heaven in two ways. First, as regards his divine nature; not that the divine nature ceased to be in heaven, but inasmuch as it began to be here below in a new way. Secondly, as regards his body, not indeed that the very substance of the body of Christ descended from heaven, but that his body was formed by a heavenly power, that is, by the Holy Spirit".[27]

St John the Apostle himself had to combat these errors: "Many deceivers have gone out into the world, men who will not acknowledge the coming of Jesus Christ in the flesh" (2 Jn 7; cf. 1 Jn 4:1-2). In the New Testament there is evidence not only of Christ's true human nature in general, but also of the fact that his body really was made of matter: he needs to eat and drink (cf. Mt 4:2; 11:19; Jn 4:7; 19:28), to sleep (cf. Mt 8:24) and rest (cf. Jn 4:6). He also showed that he was really man by suffering his passion and death. The individual specific characteristics of the body of Christ express the divine person of the Son of God, because he made the features of his body his own to such a point that "belief in the true Incarnation of the Son of God is the distinctive sign of Christian faith".[28]

In the struggle against Docetism, St Ignatius of Antioch[29] and St Irenaeus of Lyons[30] played key roles. Tertullian also wrote a treatise on the true body

---

26. Cf. St Thomas Aquinas, *STh* III, q.5, 1.a, ad 1. On the exegesis of Phil 2:5-11, cf. G. Aranda, "La historia de Cristo en la tierra, ségun Fil, 2, 6-11", ScrTh 14 (1982), 219-36; L.F. Mateo Seco, "Kénosis, exaltación de Cristo y apocatástasis en la exégesis a Filip 2, 5-11 de Gregorio de Nisa", ScrTh 3 (1971), 301-40.

27. *STh* III, q.5, a.2, ad 1.

28. CCC, no. 463; cf. also ibid., no. 477.

29. In his letters, written on the way to his martyrdom, St Ignatius vigorously attacks the Docetists, emphasizing that the *truth* of the Redemption is linked to the *truth* of the Incarnation. Here is an example: "He was of David's line. He was the son of Mary. He was *truly* born, and ate and drank; he was *really* persecuted, in the days of Pontius Pilate, and *truly* crucified and died and arose from the dead": *Ad Trall.* 10; *Ad. Smirn.* 1, 1-2; 7, 8; cf. also *Ad Eph.*, 7, 2.

30. St Irenaeus' fight against Docetism was well grounded on *anakephalaiosis* (the recapitulation of all things in Christ) and on his excellent grasp of the Pauline doctrine of the *two Adams*: "Just as through the disobedience of one man made of vile clay many were made sinners and lost life, so it was necessary that through the obedience of a man born of a virgin woman many should be justified and receive salvation [. . .]. But if he did not in fact suffer truly, then in his not suffering he merited nothing; and then, when we accept true suffering on his behalf, we confess him to be a liar since he exhorts us to suffer and to turn the other cheek without his having truly suffered himself, first. In such a case, he deceived us in

of Christ (*De carne Christi*, between 208 and 211), showing above all that to deny the reality of Christ's body is to deny the reality of Redemption.[31]

c) Christ had a real soul   Those who denied the perfect humanity of Christ included some also who claimed that he did not have a real human soul. The best known authors of this heresy are Arius and Apollinaris of Laodicea "the young". They are both under the influence of the Logos-Sarx approach to Christology which owes its starting point to Origen. This current was interested mainly in emphasizing the unity of Christ. According to them, the Word fulfilled in Jesus the functions of the soul, or at least the intellectual soul. Arius, a priest of Alexandria (+336) taught this and also committed the error of denying that the Word was perfect God. For him the Word was "a second-rate god" (*deuteros theos*), a creature, though the first and most perfect of creatures. In fact it was this error about Christ's divinity which led Arius to deny that he had a human soul, for Arius tried to prove that the Son, in his divinity, was inferior to the Father by using those passages in Scripture which show Christ to have some weakness proper to a true human nature. In order to avoid his arguments being rejected by its being said that these texts referred to Christ's human nature and not to his divine nature, Arius denied that Christ had a soul so that by not being able to attribute to his humanity certain things (such as praying, wondering, obeying), these actions would need to be done by the Word (occupying the place of the soul)—who, therefore, would be inferior to the Father.[32]

The heresy of Apollinaris of Laodicea (+ *c*.390) was similar to Arius': seeking apparently to emphasize Christ's unity (in controversy with Lucian of Antioch and his disciples), he asserted that in Christ there was a body and an animal soul and the Word, who acted as the human spiritual soul. For Apollinaris there is a double problem. On the one hand he thought that two complete *entities* could not constitute one single being. And so, since in Christ there is only one being (*et in unum Dominum Jesum Christum*, we say in the Nicene Creed) and divinity cannot be incomplete, it would follow, acccording to Apollinaris that the humanity of Jesus must be incomplete. The Johannine statement, "the Word became flesh", was taken by Apollinaris to mean that the Logos united himself with the flesh and took the place of the soul. On the other hand, Apollinaris thought that to deny that Jesus had a spiritual soul was the best way to protect his human nature from any trace of sin, because lacking

showing himself to us as something he was not and also when he exhorted us to endure that which he himself did not endure": *Adv. haer.* III, 18, 6-7.

31. "God sent his Son made of a woman. Does he perchance say through a woman or in a woman? What we have here is the most exact possible statement: saying that he was *made* rather than was *born*. Because to say he was *made* confirmed that the Word was made flesh, and restated the truth of the flesh taken from the Virgin": Tertullian, *De carne Christi*, 20, PL 2, 787.

32. Cf. Thomas Aquinas, *Summa contra Gentes*, IV, 32; *Comp. Theologiae*, I, 204.

a human soul, Christ would also lack human freedom. Apollinaris did not realize that if one denied Christ's human freedom, one was also denying that he was capable of obedience and therefore of saving us through Redemption.[33]

In the New Testament, on the other hand, there are many texts which clearly show that Jesus had a true, human spirit, a spiritual soul showing human feelings—feelings, for example, of indignation (cf. Jn 2:15-17; Mk 8:12), of sadness (cf. Mt 26:38; Jn 11:35), of joy (cf. Jn 11:15). This human spirituality is also to be seen in Christ's practice of virtue—his obedience to the Father (cf. Jn 5:30; 6:38ff), humility (cf. Mt 11:29, etc); and also in his prayer (cf. Mt 11:25-26; 14:23; Jn 11:41). Jesus himself referred to his soul or human spirit: "My soul is very sorrowful, even to death" (Mt 26:38); "Father, into thy hands I commit my spirit" (Lk 23:46). Among the many Fathers who combatted Apollinaris' teaching the most outstanding was Gregory of Nyssa.[34]

The Second Vatican Council uses the following expression which was coined in the Patristic era and was the key argument in defending the true humanity of our Lord, his true *incarnation*, a true *humanation*: "what was not assumed was not healed."[35] This aphorism expresses the connexion between the truth of the Incarnation and the truth of the Redemption: if Christ had not been truly man like us (with body and soul) he would not have redeemed us, body and soul.[36]

The Magisterium of the Church condemned the heresies which denied the reality of Christ's body and soul. Arius was condemned by the first Ecumenical Council (Nicea, 325), and Apollinaris' teaching was condemned by the First Council of Constantinople (381) and more specifically by the Council of Rome of 382. Later, at Chalcedon (451), it was defined that Jesus had "a body and rational soul". The same teaching was repeated later when these old heresies appeared again, by the Second Council of Lyons (1274) and the Council of Florence (1442).[37] As the Pseudo-Athanasian Creed (probably 6th century) puts it, "The true faith is: we believe and confess that our Lord Jesus Christ,

---

33. On Apollinaris, cf. J. Quasten, *Patrology* II, (Westminster, 1960), 377-383; A. Grillmeier, *Gesù . . .*, op. cit., 607-26; E. Mühlenberg, *Apollinaris von Laodicea* (Göttingen, 1969); C. Basevi, "La humanidad y la divinidad de Cristo: las controversias cristológicas del s. IV y las cartas sinodales del Papa S. Dámaso (366-377)", ScrTh 11 (1979) 953-99.

34. In the second work Gregory methodically refutes Apollinaris' book *On the incarnation of God in the image of man*, in such a way that the fragments Gregory quotes are the only sections of Apollinaris' work that survive (cf. H. Lietzmann, *Apollinaris von Laodicea und seine Schule* (Tubingen, 1904). Gregory, confident of being immersed in the meaning of tradition, argues that what was not assumed was not healed, and that the Good Shepherd, by taking on himself the sheep (human nature) took not only its skin (the flesh) but also what gives it life and makes it really human—the soul.

35. Second Vatican Council, Decr. *Ad gentes*, 3. The phrase was already used by St Athanasius (*Epist. ad Epictetum*, 7, PG 26, 1060).

36. Cf. St Gregory Nazianzen, *Epist.* 101 (PG 37, 184); St Ambrose, *Epist.* 48, 5 (PL 1202f); J. Tixeront, *Histoire des dogmes dans l'antiquité chrétienne*, II (Paris, 1908), 114ff.

37. Cf. DS 151, 159, 301, 852, 1339-43.

the Son of God, is both God and man. As God he was begotten of the substance of the Father before time; as man he was born in time of the substance of his mother. He is perfect God, and he is perfect man, with a rational soul and human flesh."[38]

d) **Jesus, a man of our race**   Born of the Virgin Mary, Jesus is truly one of us, not only because he has a body and soul like ours, but also because he belongs to our human family, is a descendant of Adam, through Abraham, Isaac and Jacob, and, in the course of the generations, is "descended from David according to the flesh" (Rom 1:3; cf. Lk 1:27). If we look at the two genealogies of Christ (cf. Mt 1:1-17 and Lk 3:28-38), we will notice that "whereas the genealogy of Luke indicates Jesus' connexion with the whole human race, that of Matthew brings out his belonging to the *stock of Abraham*. It is as son of Israel, the people chosen by God in the Old Testament, to whom he belongs directly, that Jesus of Nazareth is by full title a member of the great human family."[39]

Christian faith not only confesses that "the Word became flesh" (Jn 1:14) but that he is descended from David (cf. Lk 1:32; Acts 2:29-31), and is the new Adam (cf. Rom 5) . In other words, our faith teaches that not only is Jesus Christ perfect man; he is a man of our race, descended from Adam, who has been fully inserted into our history, in such a way that he has taken on himself, as the *new Adam*, all mankind. As the Second Vatican Council says, "In fact it is only in the mystery of the Word made flesh that the mystery of man truly becomes clear. For Adam, the first man, was a type of him who was to come (cf. Rom 5:14), Christ the Lord. Christ the new Adam, in the very revelation of the mystery of the Father and of his love, fully reveals man to himself and brings to light his most high calling. . . . By his incarnation, he, the Son of God has in a certain way united himself with each human being."[40]

The close union which exists (due to the Incarnation) between Christ and each man and woman explains how our redemption is brought about. Christ atones for our sins, because there is not a complete otherness between him and us, since we form with him as it were *a mystical person*.[41] This throws into relief a mysterious solidarity among all men and especially between Christ and each of us. The very reason why he became man was to share our human nature so as to redeem us. Therefore, disconnected from the *depth* of the mystery of the Incarnation, soteriology would be deformed.

Jesus' solidarity in history with the human race reveals that divine justice shone in the Redemption by arranging things so that atonement for sin would

38. *Pseudo-Athanasian Creed*, nos. 30-32 (DS 76).
39. John Paul II, *Address*, 4 February 1987, no. 1: *Insegnamenti*, X, 1 (1987) 258.
40. Const. *Gaudium et spes*, 22.
41. Cf. St Thomas Aquinas, *STh* III, q.48, a.2, ad 1.

come from the sinful race itself; moreover, it heightened the dignity of man, because the Evil One was conquered by a member of the race whom he defeated at the dawn of history; and God's omnipotence was revealed because from a weak stock and one wounded by sin he formed the perfect humanity of Jesus and raised it to his dignity.[42]

By assuming human nature, the Son of God chose to take all the natural characteristics of that nature, including the capacity to suffer, and mortality. Although, in us, these things derive from Adam's sin, in themselves they are natural, that is, they stem from the matter/spirit make-up of man. Adam was originally made free from suffering and death by virtue of a *praeternatural* gift from God, a gift he lost through sinning. Christ is absolutely free from sin, so his capacity to suffer and die was not therefore a result of sin but of a nature which he chose to take as a descendant of Adam, without those praeternatural gifts, in order to redeem us through his passion and death.

As St Paul teaches, through one man sin came into the world and, with sin, death; but where sin abounded, grace abounded even more, so that through the righteousness of another man, Jesus Christ, all might be justified; and just as through the disobedience of one man, many became sinners, so also through the obedience of one, many will be justified (cf. Rom 5:12-20). The many different aspects which theology examines in the mystery of the Redemption must be viewed in the light of the solidarity of mankind with Christ and, particularly, the solidarity of Christ with mankind, whereby he is the *new Adam*. "This illuminating principle was not only perceived but clearly formulated by the Fathers of the Church. All of them say in about the same words that Jesus Christ had to become what we are, in order to make us become what he is; that he became incarnate in order that the deliverance should be accomplished by a man; that Christ, as redeemer, comprises and summarizes all humanity."[43]

Even in the self-emptying of his Incarnation, the Word proves his love for men. Not only did he become true man, one equal to us in all things but sin (cf. Heb 4:15), but he is a descendant of Adam, born of woman, under the Law (cf. Gal 4:4). The new Adam is linked to all men: he takes upon himself, therefore, the drama of human history. Christ's sacrificial offering of himself (obedience unto death, death on a cross: cf. Phil 2:8) cannot be properly understood without reference to the implications of the mystery of the Incarnation, to what follows from the fact that Christ, perfect man, is a son of Adam and, by virtue of the hypostatic union, Head of the human race—the new Adam, embracing in mysterious solidarity the being and the history of all mankind.

---

42. Cf. St Augustine, *De Trinitate*, XIII, 18 (PL 42, 1028); St Thomas Aquinas, *STh* III, q.4, a.6.
43. F. Prat, *The Theology on St Paul*, II (London and Dublin, 1945), 201.

e) Human features of Jesus in the Gospels   Being a man like us, Christ has definite human features of his own which were easily recognized by his disciples, even after he had risen from the dead (cf., e.g., Lk 24:30-35). His divinity revealed itself to his contemporaries through his human features, even through his typical Galilean accent.

As regards Jesus' physical appearance the Gospels have not told us anything directly. However, we can deduce that he was physically strong: he could fast for many days, travel long distances by foot, endure the rigours of his passion, etc. There is no reason to think that his divinity strengthened his body abnormally, yet that cannot be totally ruled out.

Some Fathers of the Church, drawing their inspiration from Psalm 45:2 ("You are the fairest of the sons of men") thought that Jesus, being perfect man, had also a perfect physique. This interpretation must be correct, because it is very fitting that the new Adam and head of the renewed human race be physically perfect (the body is an essential part of man), and also the great dignity of the Son of God would also seem to demand it. Some of the earliest Fathers, however, affirmed the opposite, through giving too much importance to the disfigured appearance of the Servant of Yahweh.

However, what are much more important are the spiritual features of Jesus the man. And the Gospels have lots to tell us about these. It is really up to each Christian to discover them for his or herself by contemplating the Gospel in the light of the teaching of the Church. "Besides, this image of the humanity of Jesus, if we were not to see beyond it, would, in fact, be absolutely unfaithful and incomplete, because the documents that portray it for us, always present it as the humanity of the Son of God. As soon as we attempt to isolate it from this root it vanishes to some extent into those pale shadows offered to us by the rationalist historians."[44] It is a matter, then, of discovering in Christ a truly human face, and always remembering that this is the human face of God.

This human face of God has been described to us as one full of understanding and mercy. Jesus is depicted in the Gospels as a man with a perfectly balanced personality, who never loses his self-control, even when he expresses his anger or reveals that his soul is sorrowful unto death; his replies to the Pharisees when they try to catch him in his words are quick, intelligent, direct and, at the same time, are not deceptive. His words are often quite sublime and poetic, as in the Sermon on the Mount or in the parables. "Self-forgetfulness" is one of the marked characteristics of Jesus: his only desire is to bear witness to the Father and do his will saving the lost sheep. Outstanding among the virtues which reveal his holiness is his immense love of the Father and for mankind. This immense, strong love does not distort the

---

44. J. Daniélou, *Cristo e noi* (Alba, 1968), 43; L. Ferreti, "De Christo Deo et Homine pulchritudinis prototypo iuxta doctrinam D. Thomae Aquinatis", in *Xenia Thomistica*, II (Rome, 1925), 318-33.

magnificent harmony of his personality yet it even expresses itself in his feelings, which are strong, deep and visible to all: Jesus cries for Lazarous and for Jerusalem; he is quite often moved, and he candidly expresses his sadness, joy, compassion, his closeness to the weak, his capacity for friendship and for suffering.[45]

f) The Mother of the Redeemer   Jesus is the eternal Son of the Father; according to the eternal plan of salvation he is also the son of Mary. Christology would be incomplete if it did not also focus on the relationship of Son with Mother and Mother with Son, on both the Christological and soteriological levels. When the Church asserts the virginal birth of the Saviour it is referring to an event that has great meaning from both the Mariological and the Christological points of view: it is speaking not only of a quality of the Mother but also of a quality of the Son;[46] this is also true of our Lady's motherhood. When the Coucil of Ephesus applies to Mary the title of *Theotokos*, which had been in the Church since the previous century, it had a primarily Christological (not Mariological) purpose in mind: giving Mary the title of "Mother of God" is simply a necessary consequence of the personal unity with which the Word has taken on human nature for himself.

Mary's motherhood has a profound effect on the *manner* of the Incarnation: the Word becomes flesh not in an abstract way but by sharing with his fellow men the fact of being conceived and born from a woman (and thereby sharing filiation towards a mother). In this connexion both the bulls *Ineffabilis Deus* and *Munificentissimus Deus* and the Second Vatican Council are making an

45. "God does not approach us in power and authority. No, he 'takes the form of a servant, being born in the likeness of man' (Phil 2:7). Jesus is never distant or aloof, although sometimes in his preaching he seems very sad, because he is hurt by the evil men do. However, if we watch him closely, we will note immediately that his anger comes from love. It is a further invitation for us to leave infidelity and sin behind. 'Have I any pleasure in the death of the wicked,' says the Lord God 'and not rather that he should turn from his way and live' (Ezek 18:23). These words explain Christ's whole life. They allow us to understand why he has come to us with a heart made of flesh, a heart like ours. This is a convincing proof of his love and a constant witness to the mystery of divine charity": Blessed J. Escrivá de Balaguer, *Christ is passing by*, op. cit., 162.

46. As we have seen, Mary's virginity in conceiving and giving birth to Jesus is clearly and repeatedly taught by Sacred Scripture and by the Magisterium. It is something taught not because it is a "biological curiosity" but on account of its theological relevance. It is usually seen as showing that Jesus is not just one more individual in the chain of human generation: his conception is a sign that he is the new Adam, whose virginal birth inaugurates a new creation. As Sesboüé writes, "the birth of a child cannot be treated as just one more biological act except in theory. It is a human act, both on the part of the parents and on the part of the child called to life. The carnal aspect of this act necessarily includes biology, but it goes beyond that. One cannot hold that man is body and yet consider that biological matters are not relevant to the human condition. To hold that the coming of the second Adam in the flesh cannot be manifested also in the biological sphere is to set up a dichotomy between the concrete human nature and the gift of God": B. Sesboüé, *Jesus-Christ dans la tradition de l'Eglise*, op. cit., 88.

important point when they say that the Blesssed Virgin was predestined as Mother of God in the original decree of the Incarnation[47]—thus taking it that the Incarnation of the Word and the maternity of Mary are linked.

At the same time, Mary being Mother of God implies that she shares most intimately and intensely in Christ's holiness and in his work of redemption. Thus, Mary throws light on the very essence of the Redemption, just as the Redemption explains the theological essence of her motherhood.[48] When we speak of Mary's motherhood we are, therefore, going much father than simply asserting that she gave birth to Jesus. Mary is rightfully called the Mother of the Redeemer, because it was as such that she conceived Jesus, gave birth to him and was with him right throughout his life. Mary is a mother in the fullest sense of the word: "The daughter of Adam, Mary, consenting to the work of God, became the Mother of Jesus. Committing herself wholeheartedly and impeded by no sin to God's saving will, she devoted herself totally, as a handmaid of the Lord, to the person and word of her Son, under and with him, serving the mystery of Redemption, by the grace of almighty God."[49]

Mary's motherhood not only caused the entry of Jesus into this world: it is also in itself a saving event, a cooperation in the redemption. It is a motherhood in all the physical and spiritual fullness of that concept which, in itself, is already eminently redemptive. Church tradition grasped this very clearly, and expressed it in a beautiful way by calling Mary the "new Eve", thereby seeing her as indissolubly and actively linked to the person and mission of Christ, the new Adam.[50] Her complete Christo-centricity (her vocation and her person have no reason of being other than divine motherhood) allows this motherhood to be described as an "ecclesiological" motherhood, that is, as a relationship of maternity towards the entire mystical body of Christ, because Mary's divine motherhood extends to motherhood of the whole human race.[51]

---

47. "On that account it has been her practice, as well in the ecclesiastical offices as in the sacred liturgy, to apply the very words in which the sacred scriptures speak of the uncreated wisdom and put forward his eternal origin, and to adapt them to the first beginnings of the holy Virgin; beginnings which had been forecast and portrayed in one and the same decree with the Incarnation of the Divine Wisdom": Pius IX, Bull, *Ineffabilis Deus*, 8 December 1854. "Thus from all eternity and by 'one and the same decree' of predestination the august Mother of God is united in a mysterious way with Jesus Christ" (Pius XII, Bull, *Munificentissimus Deus*, 1 November 1960, DS 3902). "The predestination of the Blessed Virgin as mother of God was associated with the incarnation of the divine word: in the designs of divine Providence she was the gracious mother . . .": Second Vatican Council, Const. *Lumen gentium*, 61.

48. Cf. A. Müller, "Puesto de María y su cooperación en el acontecimiento de Cristo", in *Mysterium Salutis*, III/II, op. cit., 429.

49. Second Vatican Council, Const. *Lumen gentium*, 56.

50. The theological meaning of the Eve-Mary parallel is clear: just as Eve cooperated with Adam in our downfall, Mary cooperates with Christ in our salvation. This "Patristic axiom" indicates Mary's association with Christ in the work of redemption, that is, the fact that she is co-redemptrix; cf. see L.F. Mateo Seco, "María, nueva Eva, y su colaboración en la Redención según los Padres", EM 50 (1985) 51-69.

51. The Second Vatican Council, after recalling that Mary's predestination as Mother of God

This motherhood is the work of the Holy Spirit, who "just as he overshadowed the Virgin Mary when he began in her the divine motherhood, in a similar way constantly sustains her solicitude for the brothers and sisters of her Son".[52] This motherhood is closely connected with Mary's fullness of grace, for it is by means of grace that she "understood her own motherhood as a *total gift of self*, a gift of her person to the service of the saving plans of the Most High".[53] This service is a true maternal mediation on behalf of men, which "in no way obscures or diminishes the unique mediation of Christ, but rather shows its power: it is mediation in Christ." It is a matter of a mediation that is "intimately linked with the motherhood" of Mary. This mediation possesses a specifically maternal character—and is therefore distinct from the mediation that other creatures might have—and shows that Christ's triumph involves uniting others with him in a such a way that he causes them to cooperate in the Redemption.[54]

3. JESUS CHRIST, GOD AND SON OF GOD

a) **The Church's belief in the divinity of Christ** From the confession of St Peter ("You are the Christ, the Son of the living God": Mt 16:16) right up to our own days,[55] the Church has never ceased to proclaim that Jesus of Nazareth, born of the Virgin Mary, is true man and at the same time true Son of God—the Only-begotten of the Father. And, also from the beginning and over the centuries, the Church has had to re-assert this fundamental truth, in reply to those who denied or misunderstood the divinity of Jesus Christ.

Even in the first century, the *Ebionites* (Christians of Jewish background and of Judaizing tendency) regarded Christ as a mere man, though the holiest of men. Underlying this ancient heresy is what St Paul called "the stumbling block of the cross" (Gal 5:11; cf. 1 Cor 1:23), that is, the repugnance some Jews felt towards accepting that a divine Person died on the cross and, particularly, the difficulty in accepting the mystery of the Trinity caused by wrong understanding of monotheism. St John may well have had these people

is linked to the plan of the Incarnation, goes on: "She conceived, brought forth, and nourished Christ, she presented him to the Father in the temple, she shared her Son's sufferings as he died on the cross. Thus, in a wholly singular way she cooperated by her obedience, faith, hope and burning charity in the work of the Saviour in restoring supernatural life to souls. For this reason she is a mother to us in the order of grace": Const. *Lumen gentium*, 61.

52. John Paul II, Enc. *Redemptoris Mater*, 25 March 1987, no. 38.
53. Ibid., no. 39. Cf. F. Ocáriz, "María y la Trinidad" in various authors, *Trinidad y salvación. Estudios sobre la trilogía trinitaria de Juan Pablo II* (Pamplona, 1990), 379-405.
54. Cf. John Paul II, op. cit., 38. Cf. J.A. Riestra, "María en la vida de la Iglesia y de los cristianos", ScrTh 19 (1987) 672ff.
55. Second Vatican Council, Const. *Lumen gentium*, 39; John Paul II, Enc. *Redemptor hominis*, nos. 1 and 7.

in mind when he wrote the Fourth Gospel "that you might believe that Jesus is the Christ, the Son of God, and that believing you may have life in his name" (Jn 20:31).[56]

In the second century, there were those who taught that Jesus was the son of God, but only in the sense of adoptive son. This doctrine (known as *Adoptionism*), held particularly by Theodotus of Byzantium and Paul of Samosata, also derived from an error concerning the Trinity. They said that God was only one person (*Monarchianism*), and that Jesus is a man in whom the Word dwelt, but a Word nothing more than the "power" of God. Theodotus was condemned by Pope St Victor I (AD 190), and Paul of Samosata by a council held in Antioch in 268. However, Adoptionism did not disappear; in the fourth century Photinus again said that our Lord had been simply a man, who did not exist before the Virgin Mary; that, thanks to his holy life and acceptance of death he had merited the glory of divinity, which allowed him to be called God not by nature but by grace of adoption. This teaching was condemned by the First Council of Constantinople (381) and a year later by the Council of Rome of 382: "We pronounce anathema against Photinus who, reviving the heresy of Ebion, holds that our Lord Jesus Christ was born of Mary only."[57]

Later, Arius' heresy became widespread (this is referred to above); it denied not only Christ's divinity but also his true humanity. As we have already seen, Arius held that the Word was not a divine Person, but rather the first and most perfect creature, who acted as the spiritual soul of Christ.[58] Arius was condemned by the Council of Nicea (325); and the Symbol of that Council solemnly reaffirmed faith in "one Lord Jesus Christ, Son of God, born only-begotten of the Father, that is, of the substance of the Father, God from God, Light from Light, true God from true God born not made, consubstantial to the Father, and through him were created all things in heaven and on earth, who for our salvation, descended, became incarnate and was made man."[59]

The second ecumenical council (First Constantinople, AD 381) also professed this belief in the *Creed* which we say today at Mass. And subsequent councils (Ephesus, Chalcedon and Second and Third Constantinople) also professed faith in the divinity of Jesus Christ.[60] The Councils of Ephesus and

---

56. It is not possible to give an exact account of the Ebionites' position. The sources are very fragmentary. They considered Jesus to be the prophet foretold by Moses and that he established a new Convenant; but they put him on the same level as Moses. Cf. H.J. Schoeps, "Ebionites", in DGHE 14, 1314-19.

57. Council of Rome, AD 382, *Tomus Damasi*, c, 5 (DS 157).

58. The core of the Arian heresy lies in the notion that the only procession which can take place in God is the Creation. Its error on the Trinity extends therefore into Christology. For further reading, see E. Bellini, *Alessandro e Ario* (Milan, 1974); E. Boularand, *L'heresie d'Arius el la "foi" de Nicee*, 2 vols. (Paris, 1972).

59. First Council of Nicea (DS 130)

60. Since the Council of Nicea the word "consubstantial" is used to indicate that Jesus, in his

Chalcedon were particularly important. Ephesus (431), by asserting that Mary is truly the Mother of God, not only teaches that there was only one person in Christ but also that the Word is divine. Chalcedon (451), by rejecting monophysitism and affirming that there is one person and two natures in Christ, once again stresses the divine transcendence of Jesus.[61]

In spite of these clear definitions, these heresies reappeared later, especially in recent centuries. The sixteenth-century heresy of Laelius and Faustus Socinus (who denied the divinity of Christ, in a similar way to Photinus) said that he was simply a man outstanding for his grace and holiness and that after his death he was raised to such power and dignity that he merited to be called God and to be worshipped, though with a lesser adoration than that due to the true God. These views were condemned by Paul IV in 1555.[62]

In addition to Christological heresies in the sphere of theology, we might mention the denial of Christ's divinity in philosophical circles, especially from eighteenth-century rationalism onwards (Voltaire, Diderot, Reimarus, etc.) and materialist and idealist derivatives which rejected God entirely (this took pantheistic form in idealism). Towards the end of the nineteenth century and the beginning of the twentieth, *Modernism* (at one here with liberal Protestant theology) denied in one way or another the true meaning of Christ's divinity by counterposing the "Jesus of history" with the "Christ of faith", as we have already mentioned. It was typical of Modernism to say that Jesus' divinity had nothing to do with the "Jesus of history" but only with the "Christ of faith": the latter never in fact existed; he was the product of the piety or religious sentiment of the first Christians. This heresy was explicitly condemned by the decree *Lamentabili* issued with Pius X's approval.[63]

In our own day, different philosphical bases have led to conclusions which are really variations of early heresies. The Church, however, does not cease to assert the truth of the Incarnation of God.[64] In 1972 the Congregation for the Doctrine of the Faith declared as opposed to the faith "the doctrines according to which it is neither revealed or known that the Son of God subsists from eternity, in the mystery of God, distinct from the Father and the Holy Spirit;

---

divinity, is "of the same substance as the Father", which means that Jesus had not only a divine nature equal to the divine nature of the Father, but also numerically the same nature, because there cannot be two Gods: cf. I. Ortiz de Urbina, *Nicea y Constantinopla* (Vitoria, 1971), 69-92.

61. By its four adverbs (without confusion, without change, without division, without separation) the Council of Chalcedon excludes the Incarnation having given rise to a state intermediary between divinity and humanity. The dogma teaches that Jesus is perfect God and perfect man.

62. Cf. Paul VI, Const. *Cum quorumdam*, 7 April 1555 (DS 1880).

63. Cf. DS 3423 and 3429.

64. Cf. Second Vatican Council, Const. *Lumen gentium*, 3, 7, 52 and 53; Const. *Dei Verbum*, 2, 3; Const. *Gaudium et spes*, 22; Decr. *Unitatis redintegratio*, 12; Decr. *Christus Dominus*, 1; Decr. *Ad gentes*, 3.

as also the opinions according to which the notion of a single person of Jesus Christ, born of the Father before all ages, as regards his divine nature, and of theVirgin Mary, in time, as regards his human nature, should be abandoned; and finally those assertions which claim that the Humanity of Jesus Christ exists, not as assumed in the eternal person of the Son of God, but rather in itself as a human person, so that consequently the mystery of Jesus Christ would lie in the fact that the revealed God is present in an outstanding way in the human person of Jesus.

"Those who think in this way," the document continues, "have departed from the true faith in Jesus Christ even when they affirm that the unique presence of God in Jesus undoubtedly makes him the supreme and definitive expression of divine Revelation; nor do they reach true faith in the divinity of Jesus Christ by their adding that Jesus can be called God because of the fact that God is fully present in that which they call his human person."[65]

b) **The divinity of Jesus announced in the Old Testament** When discussing the preparation of Israel for the coming of the Messiah, we looked at a number of messianic prophecies. Now we will examine some which hint at the divinity of the Messiah. However, we must remember that the true meaning of these prophecies became clear only in the light of the New Testament. In the Old there is no explicit revelation of the divinity of the promised Messiah: all we have are elements which, containing the truth in a more or less veiled form, help prepare the way for the full manifestation of God in Christ.

First to be mentioned are the prophetic texts attributing divine names to the Messiah. Isaiah announces that the Messiah will be called "Immanuel" (God with us): "Behold, a young woman shall conceive and bear a son, and shall call his name Immanuel" (Is 7:14). The New Testament will explicitly attribute this passage to Christ (cf. Mt 1:22-23). Isaiah himself calls the Messiah "mighty God" (not "power of God", which in Hebrew would have been the more correct term to use to designate a man), and even Everlasting Father: "For to us a child is born, to us a son is given; and the government will be upon his shoulder, and his name will be called Wonderful Counsellor, Mighty God, Everlasting Father, Prince of Peace" (Is 9:6).

Jeremiah not only gives the Messiah a divine name but goes as far as to give him the name of Yahweh: "Behold, the days are coming, says the Lord,

---

65. SCDF Decl. *Mysterium Filii Dei*, 21 February 1972 (ASS 64 [1972] 237-41); cf. J. Ratzinger, "Introduzione" to the commentated edition of this document, op. cit., 9-24. For a critique of the thought of certain writers—P. Schoonenberg, A. Hulsbosch, E. Schillebeeckx, C. Duquoc, J.I. González Faus, J. Sobrino, X. Pikaza, H. Küng, D. Tracy—which fits into the category of the so-called "non-Chalcedonian" Christologies, see. J. Galot, *Cristo contestato* (Florence, 1979).

when I will raise up for David a righteous Branch, and he shall reign as king and deal wisely, and shall execute justice and righteousness in the land. In his days Judah will be saved, and Israel will dwell securely. And this is the name by which he will be called: 'The Lord is our righteousness'" (Jer 23:5-6). Some translations, instead of saying "The Lord, our righteousness" say "Yahweh, our righteousness", which means the same, especially if one remembers that when they read Scripture the Jews refrained from pronouncing the name of Yahweh out of respect, substituting for it *Adonai* (Lord). In any event, this name did not mean for the Jews an explicit revelation of the Messiah's divinity, because it could be interpreted as "revealer of the justice of Yahweh"; also, there was another name Shaddai, which means "Yahweh, my justice" and it certainly was not considered a divine name.[66]

Another way of pre-figuring the divinity of Jesus in the Old Testament is found in texts which attribute divine sonship to the Messiah. We should remember that the title "son of God" is used a number of times to designate not only the Messiah but also the angels (cf. Job 2:1; Ps 88:7), the just (cf. Sir 4:11; Wis 2:13), Israel (cf. Wis 9:7), and kings (2 Sam 7:14).[67] However, when some texts give this name to the Messiah they do so in a way or in a context which prefigures his being the son of God in a pre-eminent way, and in the light of the New Testament it becomes clear that this title means divinity in the proper sense of the word. For example, in Psalm 2 we read, "[the Lord] said to me, You are my son, today I have begotten you" (Ps 2:7).

It is God who says this to the Messiah (the Son of God, therefore), who is "begotten this day" by the Father (a veiled hint at the eternal origin of the Son of God).[68] This Psalm will be applied explicitly to Christ in the Epistle to the Hebrews (cf. Heb 1:5). Psalm 10 also has this meaning: "The Lord says to my Lord: 'Sit at my right hand, till I make your enemies your footstool.' The Lord sends forth from Zion your mighty sceptre. Rule in the midst of your foes! Your people will offer themselves freely on the day you lead your host upon the holy mountains. From the womb of the morning like dew your youth will come to you." This Psalm is applied to Christ in Mt 22:42-45.

It is possible also to interpret in this sense certain Old Testament texts which speak about God descending among men, especially those which refer to divine Wisdom—as distinct from God (the Father) and yet divine and proceeding from God; divine Wisdom which "appeared upon earth and lived among men" (Bar 3:38; Prov 8:22-31). In fact, Wisdom in the Old Testament is, in the direct sense, God himself in his relationships with the world. It is

66. Cf. J. Galot, *Chi sei tu, o Cristo?* (Florence, 1977), 53.
67. Cf. J. Blinzler, "Filiación", DTB, 405f.
68. In this verse the "today" can also be interpreted as a prophetic reference to the moment of Christ's Resurrection and entry into glory: cf. J. Dupont, "'Filius meus es tu'. L'interpretation du Ps II, 7 dans le Nouveau Testament", RSR 35 (1948), 522; R. Schnackenburg, "Cristologia del Nuovo Testamento", MS V, 334f.

not just a literary device, personification of a divine attribute, nor a name applied directly to the Second Person of the Blessed Trinity. However, "this explanation of God's action in the world under the image of Wisdom has great theological importance and not just literary importance: the hagiographers of the Old Testament have smoothed the way to the revelation of Christ in the New Testament by using the figure of divine Wisdom."[69] St Paul calls Christ "Wisdom of God" (1 Cor 1:24-30) and applies to him numerous expressions which the Old Testament uses to refer to divine Wisdom: "image of the invisible God" (Col 1:15; cf. Wis 7:26); "the first-born of all creation" (Col 1:15; cf. Prov 8:22; Sir 1:1, 4); his role in creation and in the conservation of the world (cf. 1 Cor 8:6; Col 1:17; cf. Wis 8:1; 9:1ff), etc. And St John's Gospel clearly shows the connexion between the Logos and Wisdom (cf. Prov 8:22; Wis 7:22, 25-30; 8:1; Sir 24:6-8).

In this context of the descent of God to earth, we might also mention the prophecies of Daniel concerning the Son of Man (cf. Dan 7:13-14); a man of mystery, who is superhuman and who comes down from heaven.

c) The divinity of Jesus in the Synoptic Gospels Jesus revealed his divinity gradually; this pedagogical method fitted in very well with the strong monotheistic sensitivities of the people of Israel, who would have found it difficult to accept Christ's divinity had they not been conditioned gradually for the revelation of the supreme mystery of the Blessed Trinity: *that* revelation was a prerequisite for understanding (to the limited extent that we can understand it) the mystery of the Incarnation of the Son of God. The entire New Testament is an impressive testimony to the divinity of our Lord Jesus Christ.

We shall begin by considering the evidence in the Synoptic Gospels, dealing first with the divine nature of the *Son of man*. We have already referred to the origin of this messianic title, which Jesus was so fond of using. In the Synoptic Gospels we find many passages in which he uses this title to describe himself, claiming to possess divine dignity and power.

The *Son of Man* attributes to himself the power *to forgive sins*. In the scene described in Mark 2:5-12, Jesus says to the paralytic: "'My son, your sins are forgiven.' Now some of the scribes were sitting there, questioning in their hearts, 'Why does this man speak thus? It is blasphemy! Who can forgive sins but God alone?' And immediately Jesus, perceiving in his spirit that they thus questioned within themselves, said to them, 'Why do you question thus in your hearts? Which is easier, to say to the paralytic, 'Your sins are forgiven,' or to say, 'Rise, take up your pallet and walk'? But that you may know that the Son of man has authority on earth to forgive sins'—he said to the

69. G. Zeiner, "Sabiduría", DTB, 943.

paralytic—'I say to you, rise, take up your pallet and go home.' And he rose, and immediately took up the pallet and went out before them all".

Christ does not reject the scribes' thesis: only God can forgive sins. In fact, he shows his divinity by performing a miracle (the cure of the paralytic) which, again, is something only God can do.

The *Son of man* presents himself as Son of God equal to God when the Sanhedrin questions him about his Messiahship and divine filiation and he replies that he is the Messiah, the Son of God, and adds, "You will see the Son of man sitting at the right hand of Power, and coming with the clouds of heaven" (Mk 14:62). Then "they all condemned him as deserving death" (v.64). The expression used by Jesus—"Son of man sitting at the right hand of Power [God]"—gave to the statement of his divine filiation the precise meaning of being God equal in divinity (in Omnipotence) to God the Father, and it was on this account that they said that he deserved to die. That would not have happened if his statement about being *Son of God* could have been taken in a general or moral sense (as meaning "just man" or "God's chosen one"). It should be pointed out, therefore, that in this passage the key thing is not that Jesus said 'Yes' when asked about his divinity and divine filiation (which could have been taken in a broad sense), but that he does so identifying himself with the *Son of man* of Daniel, seated, besides, at the right hand of the Almighty: that is why Caiaphas realized that Jesus was claiming to be God and why he was accused of blasphemy (cf. also Lk 22:66-71).[70] The equality with God shown in "sitting at the right hand of God" was also manifested by Jesus when he announced that the *Son of man* will come as judge and universal Lord at the end of time *in the glory of his Father* (Mt 16:27; 25:31).

The *Son of man* states that he has a completely unique dignity: he declares that he is greater than the Temple (cf. Mt 12:6), the kings (cf. Lk 10:24) and specifically David (cf. Mt 22:43-45), the prophets (cf. Mt 11:11ff), the Law (cf. Mt 5:21-22), the Sabbath (cf. Mt 12:8), etc.[71]

Jesus, as the *Son of man*, presents himself as the object of an absolute, unconditional election which is due to God only. He says that anyone who accepts the *Son of man* will be saved, and that he who rejects him will be lost (cf. Mt 16:24-25); he requires his disciples to give their lives for him (cf. Mk 8:34-38) and to love him more than they love their parents and children (cf. Mt 10:37).

Another important feature of the testimony of the Synoptics concerning the divinity of Jesus is the title of *Son of God*, and in general the attributions of divine sonship to Christ.

As already pointed out, the title *Son of God* can have (and in fact does have)

---

70. Cf. L. Bouyer, *La Biblia y el Evangelio*, op. cit., 241f.
71. Cf. J. Daniélou, *Cristo e noi*, op. cit., 47-52.

in the Old Testament a general and moral meaning (angels, the just, etc. are sons of God). There are some passages in the Synoptics in which *Son of God* can be interpreted in this sense (cf. Mt 5:9; Mk 3:11).

In other passages, however, the expression *Son of God*, or simply *the Son*, refers to divine sonship in the full and proper sense, that is, the true divinity of Jesus Christ. In addition to the passages mentioned, in which the *Son of man* says that he is the Messiah, Son of God, in a context which clearly refers to his divinity, we will look at other passages which are particularly clear.

The most noteworthy are those in which Christ himself addresses God—in prayer—as *Father* or *My Father* (cf. Mt 11:25-26; 26:39, 42; Mk 14:36; Lk 22:42; 23:34, 46). The Aramaic term used by Jesus seems in all cases to have been *abba* (that is, even when the Gospels do not themselves use *abba*). Analysis of this usage by Jesus (a usage absolutely unknown in the prayers of Jews) shows that "he is not a man who already existed prior to his election as son: his entire concrete being is indissolubly bound up with his relationship with the Father. In everything he proceeds from the Father and, therefore, he has with the Father that relationship of intimacy which is inconceivable in others."[72] Therefore, we must say that "the *abba* reveals that Jesus' intimacy with God is such that it excludes the distance between creature and Creator: only a Son-God can speak in such terms to a God-Father."[73]

We can also take into consideration a passage in St Matthew which is very like the type of language in St John: "All things have been delivered to me by my Father; and no one knows the Son except the Father, and no one knows the Father except the Son and anyone to whom the Son chooses to reveal him" (Mt 11:27).

Jesus is showing that he has a special and unique relationship with the Father. Notice the symmetry in the passage; it very clearly expresses the equality between Father and Son in the Godhead. Christ himself stresses the type of divine mystery involved in his relationship with the Father. Finally, we can notice that this mutual *knowing one another* between Father and Son refers not only to intellectual knowledge; it also points to a relationship of mutual possession, knowledge and love.[74]

The Father himself bears witness to the Son, when Jesus is baptised (cf. Mk 1:11) and when he is transfigured (cf. Mk 9:7), calling him "my beloved Son", which also suggests the idea of only Son.[75]

Other evidence in the Synoptics of the divinity of Jesus is to be found in the account of Peter's confession of faith at Caesarea Philippi: "You are the Christ, the Son of the Living God" (Mt 16:16), which is completed by Jesus's

72. M. Bordoni, *Gesù di Nazaret, Signore e Cristo* II, op. cit., 268.
73. Ibid., 267.
74. Cf. M. Meinertz, *Teología del Nuevo Testamento*, op. cit., 208-10.
75. Cf. J.M. Voste, *De Baptismo, Tentatione et Transfiguratione Jesu* (Rome, 1934), 12-126.

reply: "Blessed are you, Simon Bar-Jona! For flesh and blood have not revealed this to you, but my Father who is in heaven" (v.17). Christ—"in an unusually solemn way"[76]—accepts being called Son of the living God, and emphasizes that this is a mystery revealed to Peter by the Father: therefore, it is not simply a matter of the kind of divine sonship known in the Old Testament, which applies to angels and to the righteous,[77] but something more.

d) The divinity of Jesus in St Paul

In the Pauline epistles we find many testimonies to the divinity of Jesus. Let us look first at the very clear passage in the Letter to the Philippians, a text which has been subject to the most detailed exegesis: "Have this mind among yourselves, which was in Christ Jesus, who, though he was in the form of God, did not count equality with God a thing to be grasped, but emptied himself, taking the form of a servant, being born in the likeness of men. And being found in human form he humbled himself and became obedient unto death, even death on a cross. Therefore God has highly exalted him and bestowed on him the name which is above every name, that at the name of Jesus every knee should bow, in heaven and on earth and under the earth, and every tongue confess that Jesus Christ is Lord, to the glory of God the Father" (Phil 2:5-11).[78]

This Christological hymn sums up the whole mystery of Christ: from the eternal pre-existence of the Word (having the form of God) prior to the Incarnation, up to his glorification as man, raised to the glory of the Father and established as Lord of all (the *name* which is above every other name is *Kyrios*, that is, Lord); this is a glory he reaches through *kenosis* or voluntary self-emptying. We will examine later what this *kenosis* means. The fact that Christ is God and man is underlined by the words "in the form of God" and "taking the form of a servant".

The pre-existence of Christ, as God, is vigorously asserted by St Paul in the Epistle to the Colossians: "He is the image of the invisible God, the first-born of all creation, for in him all things were created (. . .). He is before all things, and in him all things hold together" (Col 1:15-17). Not only does he exist before any other creature as *the image of God*, that is, as Word of God, but he is begotten by the Father: therefore, he is Son of God, and he exercises over all creation a role that belongs solely to God: he creates all things and conserves them in being.[79]

In the same epistle the Apostle writes that in Christ "the whole fullness of

---

76. John Paul II, *Address*, 13 May 1987, no. 8: *Insegnamenti*, X, 2 (1987), 1670.
77. The parallel text (Mk 8:29) transcribes only the words *You are the Christ* as Peter's confession (cf. also Lk 9:20).
78. See A. Feuillet, "L'hymne christologique aux Philippiens" (II, 6, 11), RB 71/72 (1965) 352-80, 481-507; L. Cerfaux, *Cristo nella Teologia di San Paolo* (Rome, 1979), 315-32.
79. Cf. F. Prat, *The Theology of St Paul*, I (London and Dublin, 1945), 287-92; L. Cerfaux, *Cristo nella Teologia di San Paulo*, op. cit., 332-5; P. Rossano, "Vangelo e culture a Efeso e

deity dwells bodily" (Col 2:9). This text seems to refer more directly to the glorification (divinization) of Jesus' body after the Resurrection,[80] but it also indicates that his divinity is not simply God dwelling in a man, but God living bodily, in other words, the Incarnation of God.[81]

Finally, we will recall some of the doxologies contained in the Pauline epistles where Christ is called God: "to them belong the patriarchs, and of their race, according to the flesh, is the Christ, who is God over all, blessed for ever" (Rom 9:5). Exegesis traditionally indicates that this passage should be read as shown, rather than in another way which by altering the position of a comma in the original gives a different reading thus: "is the Christ, who is overall, God (be) blessed for ever." That is to say, the word *God* is applied to Christ.[82] A similar passage is to be found in the Epistle to Titus: "awaiting our blessed hope, the appearing of the glory of our great God and Saviour, Jesus Christ" (Tit 2:13). This is clearly the correct reading, because in the original Greek there is only one article common to great God and Saviour Jesus Christ ; in other words, that Saviour Jesus Christ and great God apply to the same person. Moreover, the "awaiting" referred to in the passage is the "awaiting" for the second coming of Christ at the end of time.[83]

So, there does not appear to be sufficient grounds for saying that "St Paul probably never gave Jesus Christ the name of God,"[84] although it is true that he does normally assert the divinity of Jesus by calling him Lord, reserving the name of God for the Father (cf. 1 Cor 8:6).[85]

e) Christ, the Word and Son of God in St John   As we have already noticed, the whole Gospel of St John is designed to display the divinity of Christ (cf. Jn 20:31). In the Prologue (Jn 1:1-18), St John sketches the basic features of the mystery of Christ, which he goes on to develop over the course of his Gospel both in the words and deeds of Jesus himself and in his (the evangelist's) words.

The Prologue begins with the revelation of the eternal pre-existence of Christ as Word of God: "In the beginning was the Word, and the Word was

nella Provincia d'Asia al tempo de S. Paolo e di S. Giovanni", *Civiltà Classica e Cristiana* 1 (1980) 278-88.
80. Cf. L. Cerfaux, *La théologie de l'Eglise suivant saint Paul* (Paris, 1942).
81. Cf. St Augustine, *Epist.* 187, 39 (PL 33, 847f).
82. However, the interpretation of this doxology is debated. Cf. L. Cerfaux, *Cristo nella teologia di San Paolo,* op. cit., 434-6.
83. Cf. V. Loi, *San Paolo e l'interpretazione teologica del messaggio di Gesù* (L'Aquila, 1980), 95f. On this interpretation of Titus 2:13 (on which the Fathers can be said to be unanimous), cf. e.g. Athanasius, *Epist. ad Adelphium,* 7 (PG 26, 1079); St Augustine, *Contra Maximinum arianorum episcopum,* 13-14 (PL 42, 718-21).
84. J. Galot, *Chi seu tu, o Cristo?,* op. cit., 79.
85. Cf. ibid., p. 81. In the Acts of the Apostles the divinity of Jesus is indicated mainly by the title *Kyrios* (cf. A. Polanti, *Dio Uomo,* op. cit., 18-23).

with God and the Word was God" (Jn 1:1). The *Word* of God is also, therefore, God. The Greek term *Logos* may have been taken by St John (under the influence of divine inspiration) either from Greek culture or from Judaism, which as we know was familiar with the expression *Word of God* (*Debar Yahweh*). At any event, it is quite clear that we have here a revelation of the persons of the Father and the Son. Thus, a little further on the Word will be called *the Only Son from the Father* (Jn 1:14). This Word of God became man: "And the Word became flesh and dwelt among us" (Jn 1:14); he is the one who has been *beheld* (ibid.) by the disciples of Jesus; he it is to whom the Baptist bore witness (cf. Jn 1:15). This Word of God made man is, therefore, Jesus of Nazareth.

Jesus in fact attributes eternal pre-existence to himself: "before Abraham was, I am" (Jn 8:58; cf. 17:5, 24). St Gregory the Great comments: " 'Before' indicates an earlier time. 'I am' indicates the present. God has neither past nor future, he always simply *is*. That is why the Lord does not say: Before Abraham, I was; rather he says, *Before Abraham, I am*."[86] The expression *I am* (Gk: *ego eimi*), which Jesus often used, had a very powerful meaning for the Jews, because it was the name for God revealed to Moses; the name the Jews avoided saying, out of reverence:[87] "with this expression Jesus indicates that he is the true God".[88] Therefore, "the apex of Revelation was reached at that point where the Word was able to cause to reverberate in human flesh the eternal 'I am' of God."[89] Just as it was proper to the Word prior to the Incarnation to be light and life for men (cf. Jn 1:4-5), so too the incarnate Word, Jesus, declares that he is *the light of the World* (Jn 8:12) and that he is Life (Jn 14:6) and the source of life: "For as the Father raised the dead and gives them life, so also the Son gives life to whom he will" (Jn 5:21). So, we can see that "through the words of Christ in St John's Gospel the close link between what Christ is and what he does is revealed."[90] The actions of Christ manifest that he is the Son of God, God's equal.

"The only Son from the Father" (Jn 1:14) is a title St John often attributes to Jesus and which Jesus also uses of himself, as equivalent to "the Son", "the Son of God" or "Son of the Father". Although it is true that sometimes in the Fourth Gospel, *Son of God* is used in a broad sense (in the way that angels and the righteous are sons of God), on many other occasions the words undoubtedly refer to Christ's divinity. Jesus' words in chapter 10 of St John's Gospel are particularly explicit: "I and the Father are one (. . .) the Father is

86. St Gregory the Great, *Homiliae in Evangelia* XVIII, 3 (PL 76, 1152d).
87. Cf. D. Mollat, "La divinité du Christ d'aprés saint Jean", LV 9 (1953) 127.
88. John Paul II, *Address*, 26 August 1987, no. 7: *Insegnamenti*, X, 3 (1987), 249f. See also A. Feuillet, "Les *ego eimi* christologiques du quatrième évangile" RSR 54 (1966) 5-22, 213-40.
89. D. Spada, "L'importanza dell'evento pentecostale nel processo di riconoscimento della divinità di Gesù", ED 33 (1980), 269.
90. J. Daniélou, *Cristo e noi*, op. cit., 67.

in me and I am in the Father" (Jn 10:30, 38). Christ, therefore, does not just call God "Father": he says that he "and the Father are one"; that is, that his being Son of God means that he is God.

Jesus proved the truth of his assertion of his divinity by performing, on his own authority, works which only God can do, particularly miracles, of which the most outstanding was that of his own Resurrection, which gave rise to that impressive profession of faith: "My Lord and my God" (Jn 20:28).

Some passages, which at first sight might appear to go against the divinity of Christ, do not, in fact, present difficulties for exegesis. For example, when Jesus said that his Father was "greater" than he (cf. Jn 14:28), it is obvious that he was referring to God being superior to his (Christ's) human nature.[91]

Finally, the full revelation of Christ's divinity (as also the definitive achievement of his redemptive action) takes place at Pentecost, because, by sending the Holy Spirit (Spirit of the Father and the Son) in visible and verifiable form, Jesus shows the truth of what he said about being "one" with the Father (cf. Jn 10:30).

f) **The testimony of the Fathers of the Church**   This has been discussed above in connexion with the reaffirmation of the Church's faith in Jesus' divinity in reaction to heresies which denied it (the climax being the solemn declaration of the Council of Nicea).

There is certainly in the writings of the post-Nicean Fathers a clear, unanimous affirmation of this fundamental truth of faith. But the same unanimity also existed among the Fathers who lived before that Council, although (naturally) they expressed themselves in less theologically developed language. St Athanasius in the fourth century could well challenge the Arians to produce one piece of evidence from any early Father in support of the teaching of Arius: "you will never be able to quote for me a single one who is learned and reasonable."[92]

In the writings of the Fathers and other ecclesiastical writers prior to Nicea we find firm, unanimous profession of faith in the divinity of Jesus Christ, and this is true of texts which date from immediately after the New Testament writings. The *Didache*, written around the year 90 or 100, and therefore contemporaneous with the Gospel of St John, calls Jesus "God of David".

St Clement of Rome (pope from 92 to 101), in his Letter to the Corinthians, written between 96 and 98, says that Jesus is "the sceptre of God's majesty".

91. As St Augustine writes, "Since Christ is God and man [. . .] one must consider both things in him when one speaks, or when Scripture speaks about him, and one must bear in mind what is being said about what. For just as body and soul make one man, so Word and man are one Christ. Therefore, as the Word, Christ is the creator: 'all things were made through him' (Jn 1:3); as man, Christ is created: 'he was descended from David according to the flesh' (Rom 1:3), 'being born in the likeness of man' (Phil 2:7)": St Augustine, *Epist.* 187, 8, PL 33, 835.

92. St Athanasius, *Epist. de Decr. Nicaen. Synod.*, 27 (PG 25, 465).

A few years later St Ignatius of Antioch will say that Jesus is "God living in the flesh" (Letter to the Ephesians). "The only Son of God", and "our God" (Letter to the Romans). St Polycarp of Smyrna, a disciple of St John, wrote *c*.107 that Christ is "God the Son" (Letter to the Philippians).

After the Apostolic Fathers, the Apologists also show their unanimity in professing the divinity of Jesus. For example, St Justin, in his *First Apology* (written between 150 and 155) affirms that "Christ is the Word" and that "as First-born of God, he is God." Similar testimonies are found in Aristides (*Apology*, *c*.140), and in Melitus of Sardis (+ *c*.194). St Irenaeus of Lyons, in *Adversus haereses* says that Jesus is "our Lord, God, Saviour and King." Tertullian, in his *Apologeticum* (AD 197) calls Jesus "God who proceeds from God". Finally, we might mention Origen who was apparently the first to use the expression God-Man to describe Christ (*De principiis*, *c*.230).

There is no doubt therefore, not only from the point of view of the faith but also from historical analysis, that when the Council of Nicea solemnly defined the divinity of Christ, it was providing not a "new interpretation" of the New Testament, or opting for one among many early Christologies; rather, it was reaffirming the faith the Church had held since the beginning.[93]

4. THE INCARNATION, THE WORK OF THE TRINITY

Jesus Christ is God made man; more exactly, he is the Son, the Word, who has made himself one of us. That is what the New Testament repeatedly tells us, and it is what we profess in the Creed. The Incarnation was the mission to the world given by God the Father to his Son to become man and redeem us. Therefore, the Incarnation of God is the Incarnation of the Son, not of the Father, not of the Holy Spirit. However, the Incarnation was an action of all the Trinity.

In Sacred Scripture the action which resulted in the Incarnation of the Son is sometimes attributed to the Father; for example, the Epistle to the Hebrews has Jesus addressing the Father in these words: "a body thou hast prepared for me" (Heb 10:5); and St Paul says that "God sent forth his Son" (Gal 4:4): in this text it is clear that the word *God* means God the Father.

In other New Testament passages the act of Incarnation is attributed to the Son himself: for example, when it is said that the Son emptied himself, taking up a human nature (cf. Phil 2:7).

And indeed there are passages in which the work of Incarnation is attributed to the Holy Spirit: "The Holy Spirit will come upon you," Gabriel announces to Mary, "and the power of the Most High will overshadow you" (Lk 1:35;

93. On the testimony of the pre-Nicean Fathers concerning the divinity of Jesus, see e.g. L. Liébaert, *L'Incarnation. Des origines au Concile de Chalcédoine* (Paris 1966); F. Trissoglio, *Cristo nei Padri: i cristiani delle origini dinanzi a Gesù. Antologia di testi* (Brescia, 1982).

in this text it is attributed to the Father also—the Most High). There are also the words addressed to St Joseph: "Do not fear to take Mary your wife, for that which is conceived in her is of the Holy Spirit" (Mt 1:20).

This triple attribution to the Father, the Son and the Holy Spirit makes it particularly clear that the work of Incarnation was one single action, common to the three divine Persons. "The fact that Mary should conceive and give birth", St Augustine wrote, "was the work of the Trinity, for the actions of the Trinity are inseparable."[94] The Eleventh Council of Toledo gave the same teaching.[95] Later, in the Fourth Lateran Council, it was reaffirmed that "the only-begotten Son of God, Jesus Christ, was made incarnate by a common action of the Holy Trinity."[96]

In fact, divine actions *ad extra* (that is, actions whose effects are "outside God", in other words, on creatures) are the joint (or "common") work of the three Persons together, for the divine Being is one only and unique; it is the infinite power of God. On the other hand, the real distinction between Father, Son and Holy Spirit belongs to the inner life of God. This does not mean that divine actions *ad extra* are the work of "God One" as distinct from "God Triune". In every divine action, Father, Son and Holy Spirit act, through the omnipotence common to them.

So, the creation of Jesus' human soul and the formation of his body in the womb of Mary, as also the assumption of that soul and that body joining them to the Person of the Word only, was the action of the Father, Son and Holy Spirit.

In all this there is an ineffable mystery, also because the act of Incarnation, since it is an action *ad extra*, has its terminus *ad intra* (= "inside" the Trinity), since Jesus' humanity is assumed ("introduced") into the Trinity as the humanity of the Son, and not of the Father or the Holy Spirit: the Father sends the Son to mankind, and the Holy Spirit is the perfect Anointing of the humanity of the Son.[97]

5. THE IMMUTABILITY OF GOD, AND INCARNATION

When we read in the Prologue of St John's Gospel that "the Word became flesh" (Jn 1:14), or in St Paul's Epistle to the Galatians that "God sent forth his Son, born of woman" (Gal 4:4), or in many other similar passages, it might

---

94. St Augustine, *De Trinitate*, II, V, 9 (PL 42, 850).
95. Eleventh Council of Toledo, 7 November 675 (DS 535).
96. Fourth Lateran Council, 30 November 1215 (DS 801).
97. See F. Marinelli, "Dimensione trinitaria dell'Incarnazione", Div 13 (1969) 271-343; "L'Incarnazione del Logos e lo Spirito Santo", Div 13 (1969) 497-556. On the appropriateness of its being the Son and not another member of the Trinity who became man, see pp. 83-5 below.

seem that, in the Incarnation, God underwent a change, a mutation, given that in a sense he began to be what he was not before: he began to be a man. In fact, that is not so. Our faith teaches us that God is immutable: "we firmly believe and simply confess that there is only one true God, eternal, immense, unchangeable."[98]

This immutability of God (precisely because of immutability) does not cease with the Incarnation, because the Word in himself did not acquire any perfection. Using classical language, we can say that in the Incarnation the only newness occurs in the assumed human nature, which at the Incarnation begins to exist and to be humanity, the divinity experiences no change.

For us this is a great mystery, which we express by asserting that prior to the Incarnation the Word was not man; that the Word is man from the moment of Incarnation on, but that nothing has changed in the Word himself. It is a mystery similar to the more general mystery of the relationship between God and creatures: creation, like the Incarnation, involved no change in God.

This is classically explained in the following way: all relations between the creature and God are real in the creature; but for God they represent only a relation in reason. Thus, the human nature of Jesus has a real relationship of belonging with respect to the Word, whereas in the Word there is a relationship of reason towards his humanity. These relationships (of God to the world, of the Word to the human nature of Jesus) are regarded as *relations of reason* (that is, as thought by us on the basis of the reality of Creation and the Incarnation, but they have no real existence in God, that is, do not really change him),[99] whereas on the part of the world to God or Christ's humanity to the Word the *relationship* is a *real* one.

This terminology, taken from classical theology is accurate but not very refined (given the limitations of our language), and one has to understand it properly; otherwise we will fall into making statements like these: "the things of this world are really creatures of God, but God is not really the creator of the world", or, "Jesus' human nature is really the humanity of the Word, but the Word does not in reality have a humanity united to him." Clearly, such statements would be heretical. In other words, when one says that the relationship of the Word with the humanity of Jesus is only one of reason, whereas the relationship of this humanity with the Word is real, one simply means that the Incarnation does not undermine God's immutability, and that it adds no new perfection to God, who is infinitely perfect, and, therefore, that the Incarnation is totally gratuitous and, in the same way as Creation, involved no change in God, whereas that would have happened if due to the Incarnation God had acquired a real relationship, for the acquisition of a real relationship, which did not previously exist does involve a kind of change. It is really a

---

98. Fourth Lateran Council (DS 800).
99. Cf. C. Chopin, *El Verbo Encarnado y Redentor*, op. cit., 115-16.

matter of affirmation of divine transcendence[100] and of the *gratuitous character* of both Creation and Incarnation.

We are dealing here with a (strictly supernatural) manifestation of the mystery of the relationships between the finite and the infinite, between the relative and the Absolute, between what is temporal and what is Eternal; relationships which the human mind cannot fully grasp. Moreover, we should not forget that the great mystery is God himself. His immutability (like everything divine) is something we cannot directly grasp; we can only know it by analogy. Thus, divine immutability means that it is impossible for there to be any kind of change in God; which is true, as a denial of what we know through the concept of "change". But the positive meaning of this immutability remains a mystery, because in no way does it mean what we might take it as meaning—absence of activity and of life: it is the immutability which is proper to Life in its fullest form.

In other words, God is immutable, not because of absence of activity, but because of his infinite activity, infinite dynamism. Infinity of activity and of life which (precisely because it is infinite) is identical (paradoxically, to our minds) with maximum tranquillity, because infinite activity excludes any kind of passivity, and passivity is the very pre-requisite for any type of change.

It is in the context of God's immutability that we must also view the *kenosis* of the Word. The term and meaning of *kenosis* are taken from this well-known passage in St Paul: "have this mind among yourselves, which was in Christ Jesus, who, though he was in the form of God, did not count equality with God a thing to be grasped, but emptied himself, taking the form of a servant, being born in the likeness of men. And being found in human form he humbled himself and became obedient unto death, even death on a cross" (Phil 2:5-8).

Many interpretations have been given of this passage (which we have already looked at), with special attention to the expression "he emptied himself", that is, the self-emptying or *kenosis* of the Word. Some of these are at odds with the doctrine of the faith: for example, the so-called *kenotic theories* (clearly Lutheran at source) whose first exponents were sixteenth- and seventeenth-century Protestants; their influence is also noticeable in some Orthodox theologians—for example, Serge Bulgakof—and are also to be found in the writings of some Catholics in recent years.[101] Although the theories vary they

---

100. Cf. J.H. Nicolas, "Jesucristo, Hijo de Dios", in *Cristo, Hijo de Dios . . .*, op. cit., 424ff.
101. See L. Iammarrone, "La teoria chenotica e il testo di Fil 2, 6-7", DT 82 (1979) 341-73, for an analysis of the various interpretations. See also G. Aranda, "La historia de Cristo en la tierra, según Fil 2, 6-11", in *Cristo Hijo de Dios*, op. cit., 341-58. On the interpretation of *kenosis* in the Patristic era, cf. P. Henry, "Kénose", DBS, 56-135. See also ITC (International Theological Commission), *Theology, Christology, Anthropology* (1981) in Sharkey, op. cit., 207-23; cf. J. Jeremias, "Zu Phil 2, 7; eauton ekenosen" NovT 6 (1963) 182-8; J. Coppens, "Phil 2, 7 et Is 53, 12. Le problème de la kénose", ETL 41 (1965), 147-50; A. Feuillet, "L'hymne christologique de l'Epitre aux Philippiens, (II, 6-11)", RB 72 (1965) 352-80; 481-507.

have a common element in that they start off from the premise that *kenosis* meant a change in God: the Godhead would change into humanity, while retaining some divine properties; or even, in the Incarnation would have ceased to be God and been changed into a man; according to others the Incarnation would be a kind of limitation of the divine in the human, a *kenotic condition* of divinity prior to the exaltation of Christ after the resurrection.

Although these theories differ from one another in details, they all deny the immutability of God. The less radical versions are Christologically Monophysite, with a Monophysitism akin to that already rejected by the Council of Chalcedon fifteen centuries ago.[102]

What is the true meaning of *kenosis*, of the Son of God's self-emptying in the Incarnation? We can distinguish two dimensions in *kenosis*. Firstly, that God assumed a non-divine nature, manifesting himself to the world through a human nature, while at the same time both revealing and hiding his divinity. Secondly, the Son of God renounced, in his human nature, the glory due to it as *God's* humanity. He who, even in his humanity, is Lord and Head of mankind, chose to be a suffering servant, dying on the cross, obeying the Father's plan.[103] This second aspect of *kenosis* has to do with the way in which the Incarnation came about, not with the Incarnation as such, because, for human nature, to become the humanity of God represents the highest possible perfection. Jesus is in fact perfect man and his human nature is supernaturally joined to God in the most intimate way.

6. THE APPROPRIATENESS OF THE INCARNATION

Love is the deepest reason behind every action of God; this is true principally of the Incarnation, the greatest communication of God. It also bears out the well-known adage: *Bonum est diffusivum sui*, Goodness spreads itself. Every action of God *ad extra* is simply a communication of his goodness and of his perfection. We can distinguish three stages in this communication: a) through *creation*, whereby God gives being to creatures in the form of a certain imitation (God is the *efficient* and *exemplar* cause of every created being), so that the whole of creation is a reflection of God's goodness and perfections; b) through *grace*, by means of which God communicates himself in a new and more intimate way, because grace makes man, in Christ, a son of God and heir to heaven; c) finally, through the Incarnation, whereby God communicates himself

102. Cf. A. Gaudel, "Kénose", in DTC, VIII, 2339-42. Cf. also Pius XII, Enc. *Sempiternus Rex*, 8 September 1951 (AAS 43 [1951] 637f).
103. St Paul's text considers *kenosis* with reference mainly not to the Incarnation itself but to the conditions under which it came about: cf. A. Feuillet, "L'Homme-Dieu considéré dans sa condition terrestre de Serviteur et de Rédempteur", RB 51 (1942) 58-79; J. Dupont, "Jésus-Christ dans son abaissement et son exaltation", RSR 37 (1950) 500-14; L. Iammarrone, *La teoria chenotica . . .*, op. cit., 358-9.

to the creature *substantially*, in such a way that he joins the creature to himself in a unity of person. In the Incarnation he reveals in a new and definitive way what he already manifested by creating the world—his infinite goodness, and generosity.[104]

It is customary, at the beginning of Christology, to highlight the way the mystery of the Incarnation fits in not only with men's needs (the need of a Saviour) but also with the goodness and fatherhood of God; to stress the wonderful insight it gives us into God himself.[105]

a) The Incarnation and the divine perfections   Reflecting on the mercy God showed by becoming man, St Paul called the Incarnation "self-emptying" (*kenosis*) (cf. Phil 2:5-11). This self-emptying implied by becoming man and taking all human history on his shoulders, making himself obedient unto death, the death on the cross, in no way contradicts the perfections inherent in the divine nature of the Word. "Everything that pertains to it by its very nature," writes St Thomas Aquinas, "is suited to a being [. . .]. God's nature is goodness. Therefore, everything that pertains to the notion of good is suited to God. Communicating oneself to others pertains to the notion of good [. . .]. Consequently it pertains to the notion of the highest good to communicate oneself to the creature in a supreme way."[106] And the supreme communication to the creature is nothing less than God uniting the creature to himself in a unity of person.

The Incarnation is a manifestation of God's infinite love for man, of his inexhaustible mercy, of his great kindness: "God so loved the world that he gave his only Son, that whoever believes in him should not perish but have eternal life" (Jn 3:16). Love is something that belongs to the divine essence itself, because "God is Love" (1 Jn 3:8). As John Paul II writes, in Jesus Christ, "the God of creation is revealed as the God of redemption, as the God who is 'faithful to himself' (1 Thess 5:24), and faithful to his love for man and the world, which he revealed on the day of creation [. . .]. Above all, love is greater than sin, than weakness, than the 'futility of creation' (cf. Rom 8:20), it is stronger than death, it is a love always ready to raise up and forgive, always ready to go to meet the prodigal son (cf. Lk 15:11-32), always looking for 'the revealing of the sons of God' (cf. Rom 8:19), who are called to the glory that is to be revealed (cf. Rom 8:18). This revelation of love is also described as

104. "The Redeemer of the world! In him has been revealed in a new and more wonderful way the fundamental truth concerning creation to which the Book of Genesis gives witness when it repeats several times 'God saw that it was good' (cf. Gen 1)": John Paul II, Enc. *Redemptor hominis*, no. 8.

105. Cf. e.g., St Thomas Aquinas, *Summa contra Gentes*, IV, 40; *STh* III, q.1, a.1. Cf. A. Michel, "Incarnation", DTC, VII, esp. 1462-82 and its bibiography; also J.H. Nicolas, *Synthèse Dogmatique*, op. cit., 446ff.

106. *STh* III, q.1, a.1, in c.

mercy (cf. STh III, q.46, a.1, ad 3); and in man's history this revelation of love and mercy has taken a form and a name: that of Jesus Christ."[107]

The Incarnation also manifests God's infinite power, his infinite capacity to communicate. Against the pagan philosophers who said it was not possible for God to communicate himself in this way (because they thought that it went against the infinite transcendence of God), the Fathers argued that the reason for God's ability to communicate himself without harming his transcendence lies in that very transcendence.[108] This omnipotence is manifested (as St Leo the Great pointed out) in the fact that the glory of Godhead did not obliterate the human nature the Word took on, and, in turn, the assumption of human nature did not *lessen* the glory of the Godhead.[109]

As we shall see in more detail, the Word became man in order to save mankind by the Redemption. This way of saving man shows the indissoluble linking of divine justice, mercy and wisdom. "Indeed this redemption," writes John Paul II, "is the ultimate and definitive revelation of the holiness of God, who is the absolute fullness of perfection: fullness of justice and of love, since justice is based on love, flows from it and tends towards it."[110]

Here we can see one reason for the appropriateness of the Incarnation put forward by St Thomas Aquinas; it shows the infinite wisdom with which God, in his actions, accommodates himself to the nature of things: "since friendship consists of a certain equality, it seems that there cannot be a friendly union between things that are very unequal. Consequently, in order to have a more familiar friendship between God and man, it was appropriate for the latter that God should become man. In this way knowing God visibly we should feel ourselves 'caught up in love of the God we cannot see' (preface of Christmas I)."[111]

b) The appropriateness of the Incarnation from the point of view of the Word   It is the Word who becomes man. And so theology reflects not only on the appropriateness of God becoming man, but also on the reasons why it was appropriate that it should have been the Son, the second Person of the Trinity who did so; those reasons which make it fitting that God, who spoke often and in many ways through the ministry of prophets, should eventually speak to us through his Son (cf. Heb 1:1-2) made man.

107. John Paul II, Enc. *Redemptor hominis*, no. 9.
108. Cf. e.g., St Gregory of Nyssa, *Oratio catechetica magna*, 24 (PG 45, 63); St Basil the Great, *In psalmum 44, n. 5* (PG 29, 399). Cf. L.F. Mateo Seco, *Estudios sobre la cristología de Gregorio de Nisa*, op. cit., esp. 101-27.
109. Cf. St Leo the Great, *Sermo 21 de Nativitate Domini*, 2 (PL 44, 191-2). Cf. *Tomus ad Flavianum* (DS 290-95).
110. John Paul II, Enc. *Dives in misercordia*, no. 7. Cf. St John Damascene, *De fide orthodoxa*, III, 1 (PG 94, 983); St Leo the Great, loc. cit., ch. 3; St Augustine, *De agone christiano*, 21 (PL 40, 297); St Thomas Aquinas, *Summa contra Gentes*, IV, 54; *STh* III, q.46, a.3.
111. *Summa contra Gentes*, IV, 54.

The Incarnation of the Word is also described as the *visible mission* of the Son.[112] The New Testament often states that the Father sent the Son into the world (cf., e.g., Jn 3:17, 5:37; 8:16) and that the Son and the Father will send the Holy Spirit (cf., e.g., Jn 14:26). The Son is the *envoy*, who has come down from heaven to do not his own will but that of him who *sent him* (cf. Jn 6:38). The Incarnation is the result of the desire of the Holy Trinity, and of their love for men; but insofar as it is *the Son's mission* the Incarnation is evidence particularly of the Father's love.[113]

From early on the following reasons have been suggested for the appropriateness of its being the Word-Son who should become man, who should make *manifest* to men the invisible God:

a) It was fitting that it should be the Son, "through whom all things were made" (Jn 1:3), who should restore human nature which had fallen due to sin; it was right that he, who is the Wisdom of God, should make good the crimes committed by the folly of man.[114]

b) The Word is the *image* (likeness) and radiation of the glory of the Father (cf. Heb 1:3); it was fitting that it should be he who restored the *image* of God in man, which had been deformed by sin.[115]

c) The Word is the *natural* Son of the Father, he is of the same *substance* as the Father, and men are saved by being made adoptive sons of God. "God sent forth his Son (. . .) so that we might receive adoption as sons" (Gal 4:4-5). This is a thought much loved by the entire Latin Tradition.[116] "It was

112. "Mission can be applied to a divine person therefore, insofar as it includes, on the one hand, a relationship of origin with regard to the one who sends him and, on the other, a new way of being present for any one of them. Thus the Son is said to have been sent by the Father into the world—even though he *was* already *in the world* (cf. Jn 1:10)—because he began to be in the world in a visible way by taking flesh": St Thomas Aquinas, *STh* I, q.43, a.1 in c. On the theology of the missions, cf. M.J. Scheeben, *The Mysteries of Christianity*, op. cit., 149-80.

113. Cf. J.H. Nicolas, *Synthèse Dogmatique*, op. cit. 253.

114. "In the effable unity of the Trinty" says St Leo the Great, "whose works and judgments are common (to all three Persons) in all things, it was the Person of the Son who really took upon himself the reparation for the human race. This was so since he, being the one *through whom all things were made and without whom was not anything made that was made* (cf. Jn 1:3) and who gave life to man formed from the mud of the earth, with the breath of life, was the one to restore our nature, that had been cast out of the fortress of immortality, to its original dignity and who was the reformer of that of which he had been the maker": *Sermo* 64, 13, 2 PL 54, 358. Cf. also St Irenaeus, *Adv. Haer.*, V, 1, 3 (PG 7, 1120, 1123); St Gregory of Nyssa, *Orat. catech. magna*, 8 (PG 45, 40).

115. "It was not appropriate that the one who had been made—the image of God—should perish. What was appropriate for God to do then? What else but to renew that likeness according to which men had been made—the image of God, so that through it men could come to know God again? Who would be the one to do this only the very image of God, our Saviour Jesus Christ?": St Athanasius, *Orat. de incarnatione Verbi*, 13, PG 25, 119.

116. "God was born of men", writes St Augustine, "so that men should be born of God. Because Christ is God and Christ was born of men [. . .]; born of God he through whom we were to be made, born of woman he through whom we were to be remade. Do not be

appropriate that man should obtain a participated likeness in divine filiation," writes St Thomas reflecting this tradition, "through Him who is the natural Son, according to the expression of the Apostle: 'for those whom he foreknew he also predestined to be conformed to the image of his Son' (Rom 8:29)."[117] Only he, who is Son, can have adoptive brothers and sisters.

c) **The appropriateness of the Incarnation from the point of view of human nature** This subject has been dealt with by theology from different viewpoints: from the angle of human nature considered in itself (whether it is fitting for a human nature to be *assumed* in a divine Person); from the angle of fallen mankind and its need for salvation; from the perspective of the circumstances of time and place in which it occurred; from the viewpoint of the glory and beauty of the universe, of the perfection of every created being.[118] In fact, the correct answering of these questions calls for a prior knowledge of all Christology, because only from the very nature of the hypostatic union and its effects on the human nature of Christ can one say whether it was fitting for this human nature to be *assumed* by the Word.

The effect of the Incarnation is that the Word of God becomes man; vice versa, it makes it possible to say that *this man*—Jesus—is God. Is it *fitting* that a human nature should be *elevated* in this way? The Church solemnly and ceaselessly professes that Christ is *perfectus Deus, perfectus homo*. The *assumption* of human nature harms in no way the perfections of human nature, "denaturalizes" it in no way. God who as, efficient and exemplary cause, gives everything its being and its goodness, and fills it with the perfections

surprised then, O man, that you have been made a son of God through grace because you are born of God according to his Word": *In Joh, tract* 2, 15, PL 35, 1395. St Augustine insists frequently on this thought (cf. also *De Trin*, 2, 5, 7,; 4, 20, 27; 13, 19, 24, PL 42, 248, 906, 1033).

117. *STh* III, q.3, a.8, in c. In this article St Thomas gives the reasons which make it *exceedingly appropriate* that it should be the Word that became man to save man. St Thomas argues, as one must when dealing with reasons of appropriateness, in the framework of the *divine economy* regarding the salvation of men through a *redemption* via obedience and through the sanctification of man in adoptive filiation. From this angle, the case is unanswerable, for, given the infinite wisdom and goodness of God, the arguments concerning appropriateness should not be taken as weak reasoning. Earlier (*STh* III, 3, 5), St Thomas, following a recognized theological tradition, says that the Father and the Holy Spirit could also have become man. This is what one finds stated in textbooks. K. Rahner severely criticized this statement in his *Theological Investigations*, arguing that only the Logos, *by virtue of his immanent relationship to the divine Persons is capable of assuming hypostatically something created and of being the essential and irreplaceable revealer* of God. Rahner here exaggerates the reasons for appropriateness to the point of introducing a need into the bosom of the Trinity, or, at least, establishes a distinction in the *nature* of the three divine Persons, since only one of them (the Second) would be capable of uniting a created nature to himself hypostatically. For a more detailed outline of Rahner's position and its ambiguity, cf. J.H. Nicolas, *Synthèse Dogmatique*, op. cit., 170f and 254ff; F. Marinelli, "Dimensione trinitaria dell'Incarnazione", Div 13 (1969) 271-343.

118. Cf. e.g., A. Michel, "Incarnation", DTC, art. cit., 1467ff.

appropriate to its nature, cannot harm human nature in what is, in fact, the most intimate communication he can make to a created being—uniting it to himself in a unity of person.

It must also be said in this connexion that this union is an *absolutely* unmerited elevation of any nature: it is gratuitous. No created nature possesses a positive *capacity* (a natural potency) to be *assumed* by God in the sense that if it were not assumed it would be left with this capacity unfulfilled. Therefore, when we say that the hypostatic union is the closest *union* that God can bestow on a created nature, this simply means that that nature merely has a *non-repugnance* for the hypostatic union; it has only an *obediential potency* to be assumed in the hypostatic union.[119] The reason for this is quite simple: if one regarded the capacity to be *assumed* by God in a hypostatic union as a *positive* capacity of human nature (not as simply a *non-impossibility*), that would inevitably lead to the following assertions: except for Jesus, every other man and woman would in the same sense be *incomplete* in their human nature; on the other hand, Christ would be *more* man than other men, on account of having this potentiality activated. That is why the Church, as the Council of Chalcedon made quite clear, has stressed that neither the divine nor the human nature changed through the hypostatic union. St Leo the Great puts it this way, God is born in the complete and perfect nature of a true man, *totus in suis, totus in nostris* (complete in what is his, complete in what is ours).[120]

The Incarnation is also appropriate in the light of man's need of salvation; as Tertullian put it, *Homo perierat, hominem restitui oportebat* (man had perished, it was necessary that man be restored).[121] Many authorities, naturally, can be cited in this connexion. A good summary of the reasons most frequently suggested to show that the Incarnation of the Word was the most *fitting* method of saving us is to be found in St Thomas' *Summa Theologiae* (III, q.1, a. 2). St Paul is the model of this type of argument, when he shows how the entire *economy of salvation* fits together: cf. for example, Romans 5:12ff, which contrasts the *two Adams*: "As one man's trespass led to condemnation for all men, so one man's act of righteousness leads to acquittal and life for all men."

This vision of the symmetry of the divine plan of salvation, this conviction about the profound wisdom of the mode chosen to save man (the mode most *appropriate* to his nature) is to be found in the writers of every century. It was fitting that Christ should be born of the race of Adam, as St Irenaeus puts it,

119. As Cardinal Cajetan writes, "Because, though in all truth one denies the suitability of any creature for personal union with God as also all natural potency for same, it would be false to deduce from this a repugnance or incompatibilty towards such union. Neither (suitability or natural potency) belongs to the creature of himself: this is so because the creature, in accordance with the circumstances of his nature, has nothing which would entitle him to lay claim to either. The complete ordering of the creature with regard to this union belongs to the excellence of the goodness and power of God. Therefore in that regard it has an obediential potency only": Cajetan, *In I partem STh*, q.1, a.1, n.9.

120. *Epist* 28 (*Tomus ad Flavianum*), of 13 June 449 (DS 293).

121. *De carne Christi*, 14 (PL 2, 777).

so that man would be saved by one of his own kind, by a new Adam who would recapitulate in himself the whole human race.[122] God could, St Augustine agrees, have chosen to save mankind by a man not of the race of Adam (who enchained the human race through his sin). But he judged it more appropriate to conquer the enemy of the human race by a man taken from the same conquered race.[123] And St Thomas develops this line of thought: "First, because it would seem to belong to justice that he who sinned should make amends; and therefore it was logical that he who was going to make satisfaction for the whole of nature should belong to that same nature corrupted by sin. Secondly, to invest man with a greater dignity it was appropriate that the conqueror of the devil should spring from the same stock conquered by the devil. Thirdly, because God's power is thereby made more manifest: he took from a corrupt and weakened nature that which was raised to such might and glory."[124]

d) God's freedom as regards the Incarnation   Sacred Scripture shows us in many passages that the work of salvation by means of the Incarnation of the Word stemmed from the mercy of God. "God, who is rich in mercy, out of the great love with which he loved us, even when we were dead through our trespasses, made us alive together with Christ" (Eph 2:4-5; cf. 2 Tim 1:9; Tit 2:11).

In creating our parents in holiness and righteousness, God showed his gratuitous benevolence; in restoring man to the state of grace, he reveals even more clearly the breadth of his goodness and mercy. Like creation, the Incarnation is a most free initiative of the divine will.

Over the course of history there have been many authors who, in one way or another, have failed to grasp how totally free God was when creating man or *restoring* him through the Incarnation; their failure was often due to their pushing arguments for appropriateness too far. These arguments (as their name suggests) are designed simply to show how fitting, not how necessary, the Incarnation was. All they do is highlight the great wisdom and consistency in everything God does. The Magisterium of the Church has on occasion had to counter those who claimed that the Incarnation was necessary, not just appropriate.

This was the case with those theologians who argued that once creation had happened there was a *metaphysical* need for the Incarnation. These are usually described as *optimists*, because they say that once creation was projected God necessarily had to create the best of all possible worlds and to fill it with every possible perfection. So, for example, according to Ramón Lull (1235-1316),

---

122. Cf. *Adv. haer.*, 3, 21, 10 (PG 7, 955).
123. Cf. *De Trinitate*, 13, 18 (PL 42, 1032).
124. *STh* III, q.4, a.6, in c.

God could not decide on creation without at the same time deciding on the Incarnation, because he was obliged to produce the best and most perfect kind of creation, that is, a creation which included union of a created nature with an uncreated Person.[125] Malebranche (1638-1715) spoke of a *metaphysical necessity* in God: he argued that creation and Incarnation form an indivisible whole, because Incarnation is the best way to crown creation.[126] Leibnitz (1646-1716) thought along the same lines starting out from the basic thesis of his *Theodicy*: God was *required* by his wisdom and goodness to create the best of all possible worlds, and, therefore, to crown creation with every perfection including the Incarnation.[127] A somewhat softer position (attributed to Rosmini, 1797-1855), which speaks of a *moral necessity* only, was rejected by the Magisterium as incompatible with the faith.[128] A moral necessity, in an infinitely holy being, *would in fact* be really the same as a metaphysical necesssity, and, therefore, would be incompatible with God's transcendence over all creation and with his infinite freedom. The highest form of divine communication—union with a created nature in a personal unity—is a work of the infinite mercy and freedom of God.

The reasons of appropriateness adduced for this communication by God should not be taken as mere metaphors, but as genuine reasons underlying God's free choice. The work of Incarnation is not only the effect of God's infinite mercy, but also and at the same time the effect of his infinite wisdom. To say that God is infinitely free is not the same as to say that his choices are arbitrary,[129] nor to deny that love is what guides all his actions. As John Paul

125. Cf. *Ars magna*, 8: cf. B. Nicolau Tor, "El primado absoluto de Cristo en el pensamiento Luliano", EL 2 (1958), 297-313.

126. Cf. *Entretiens sur la métaphysique et la religion*, ent. 9, 5; *Traité de la nature et de la grâce*, diss. 1, 2, 3. Cf. M. Gueroult, *Malebranche, II-III: Les cinq abîmes de la providence* (Paris, 1959), 114-36.

127. Cf. H. Hirschberger, *Historia de la Filosofia*, II (Barcelona, 1962), 59f.

128. Here is proposition 18, rejected by the Holy Office in its decree of 14 December 1987: "The love with which God is loved in creatures and which is the reason for which the decision to create is taken, constitutes a moral necessity, which in a totally perfect being is always put into effect. It is only in the case of imperfect beings that a necessity of this kind leaves their freedom unaffected" (DS 3218).

129. Some scholastic theologians are so impressed by the reasons of appropriateness usually given when it comes to speaking of motives for the Incarnation and so desirous at the same time to "protect" the freedom of God and the *gratuitous* nature of grace and of the Incarnation, that they speak of "a moral necessity in a broad or metaphorical sense." Here is a typical way this is put: "There is in God a tendency or moral necessity towards what is best and therefore towards putting the Incarnation into effect. This necessity, through, is really only a metaphorical one since it does not represent a real difficulty against the opposite view; it only provides foundation for a prudent opinion as regards the best being done and makes it imprudent and unacceptable to think it was not done": Viva, *De incarnatione*, disp. I, q.II, a.2. Other authors who go along with this include Ruiz (*De voluntate Dei*, IX) and Granados (*De voluntate Dei*, III). Although we know what they mean, it seems wiser not to use this sort of language, because it does tend to take from God's absolute freedom. Cf. A. Michel, *Incarnation*, op. cit., DTC 1474.

II writes, *"the divine dimension of the redemption* enables us, I would say, in the most empirical and *historical* way, to uncover the depth of that love which does not recoil before the extraordinary sacrifice of the Son, in order to satisfy the fidelity of the Creator and Father towards human beings created in his image and chosen from the beginning, in this Son, for grace and glory."[130]

From Hegel onwards, and particularly after the *kenotic* theories of the nineteenth century,[131] there have been authors, particularly those associated with the more radical trend of *theologia crucis*, who have tried to argue that the need for Incarnation came from the very nature of God: it did not have to do with salvation of man or the perfection of the universe; no, they say, Incarnation is a need internal to God himself, who attains his own perfection by a process of *alienation* and *recovery*.[132] In other words, the Incarnation would give God a new perfection, or would be a further step towards God's own *fulfilment* (God, they said, is not absolutely perfect and immutable but is in the *process* of developing). From this point of view, Incarnation would be a necessity, because it would stem from a real *need* for Incarnation within God's own nature.[133]

Traditional theology, on the other hand, has consistently pointed out that the Incarnation, as also creation, in no way adds to either God's glory or his perfections. God is not in *need* of Incarnation. Infinite goodness which, by its very nature *tends to communicate itself*, implies absolute freedom in giving—on the part of infinitely pure love, precisely because it flows from that Being who is infinitely perfect and infinitely happy in his own interpersonal unity.[134] The Incarnation of the Word, the supreme work of the mercy and generosity of God is, at the same time, the work of the supreme and absolute liberty of God—an absolutely gratuitous gift from every point of view.

---

130. Enc. *Dives in misericordia*, no. 7.
131. Cf. A. Gaudel, "Kénose", in DTC, VIII, 2339-42; L. Iammarrone, "La teoria chenotica e il testo di Fil 2, 6-7", DT 82 (1979) 341-73.
132. "Hegel", says the International Theological Commission, "was the first to postulate that, for the idea of God to be comprehensible, it has to include 'the suffering of the negative', that is, the 'hardship of abandonment' ('die Haerte der Gottlosigkeit'). In him there is a fundamental ambiguity: Does God have or not a real need of the world?": ITC, *Theology, Christology, Anthropology*, II, B.1.1. (Sharkey, op. cit., 220). Cf. E. Brito, *La Christologie du Hegel, Verbum crucis* (Paris 1983).
133. On this subject see L.F. Mateo-Seco, "Muerte de Cristo y Teología de la Cruz", in various authors, *Cristo, Hijo de Dios y Redentor del hombre*, op. cit., 739-42. Cf. also, P. Sequeri, "Cristologie nel quadro della mutabilità e passibilità di Dio", SC, 1977, 114-51.
134. Cf. J.H. Nicolas, "Aimante et bienhereuse Trinité", RT, 78 (1978), 271-92. "Since the goodness of God is perfect'" writes St Thomas Aquinas, "and can exist without all the other beings, which are not able to add any perfection to him, it follows that it is not absolutely necessary that he should want things distinct from himself": *STh* I, q.19, a.3 in c.

CHAPTER THREE

The Person of Christ

Christ Jesus is God and he is Man; he is *one* subject, *one* person, existing in two natures, divine and human. He who is God is Man. This oneness in Jesus has always been a presupposition in the Church's faith regarding the humanity and divinity of our Lord. We find this oneness clearly expressed as early on as Peter's confession of faith at Caesarea Philippi: "You are the Christ, the Son of the living God" (Mt 16:16). The very man—Jesus, the Christ or Messiah—that Peter had before him is the Son of the living God. This same unity (of divine and human) is emphasized by the early Symbols when they profess faith *in unum Dominum Jesus Christum*, in one Lord Jesus Christ.

In the controversies following the Council of Nicea, the main thing at issue was how divine nature and human nature combined in Christ. On this aspect of the mystery there were two main heretical positions—one which (in order to explain the unity of Christ) did not distinguish the two natures clearly enough, and the other which did the opposite and ended up denying the unity of Christ. These errors led the Magisterium to use increasingly more exact language to proclaim the true faith.

This chapter deals with the hypostatic union as such. It begins with sections on the unicity of person and distinction of natures in Christ, and goes on to examine his ontological and psychological unity, that is, questions to do with his being and his I. Within the limited space available, special attention is given to the notion of person and to the theories relevant to directly explaining the hypostatic union. The chapter ends by looking at some matters inherent in the hypostatic union, specifically Jesus filial relationship with the Father, and the adoration due to his humanity.

1. THE UNICITY OF CHRIST'S PERSON

a) **Nestorianism and the Council of Ephesus**   Nestorius, who became patriarch of Constantinople in 428 and died in 451, had been trained in theology at the school of Antioch in Syria, which was heavily influenced by the ideas of Diodorus of Tarsus (+392) and Theodore of Mopsuestia (+429), who were in the forefront of the defence of the faith against Apollinarianism, but who understood the union of the human and the divine in Christ in a somewhat confused and superficial way.

Nestorius espoused their position and when he became patriarch of

Constantinople he recommended that the famous and much used title of our Lady, Mother of God (*Theotokos*) should be dropped and that of Mother of Christ (*Christotokos*) be used in its stead. Although it is not easy, from the documents of the period, to be quite sure what Nestorius' thinking was, there is no doubt that an error in Christology was the cause of his error about Mary.[1]

The principal points (at least implicit) in Nestorius' thought can be summed up as follows: there are two natures (nature = *physis*) in Christ, *two subjects* each subsistent in itself (subject = *hypostasis*) and two physical persons (person = *prosopon*). In other words, there is in Christ, according to Nestorius, a divine person (the Word) and a human person (Jesus the man), but these are so closely linked to one another that in practice it is as if there were only one person: they constitute a kind of union person (a union *prosopon*). It is not a matter of there being just a man in whom God dwells, but something between that and a physical and substantial union.

Nestorius seems to have thought that every nature (*physis*) necessarily constitutes a subject (*hypostasis*) and a person (*prosopon*). It logically leads to denying Mary the title of "Mother of God", because she would only be the mother of a man, a human person, though one specially united ("assumed") by the union person (union *prosopon*) to the divine person of the Word.

St Cyril of Alexandria (+444) reacted immediately to this teaching: see, especially, his Second Letter to Nestorius, written around January/February 430. In the same year Cyril called a synod at Alexandria and sent Nestorius a third letter, containing twelve anathemas in which the Nestorian propositions were condemned. Nestorius, however, replied with another dozen counter-anathemas, accusing Cyril of being Apollinarian.

The controversy between the two patriarchs caused a lot of confusion in the Church, and the emperor Theodosius II called the Council of Ephesus (431), at which St Cyril presided. Because of its importance the Second Letter, which was read and approved by the Council, is reproduced below with only a few omissions: "Cyril to his colleague, the most reverend and most religious Nestorius, health in the Lord [. . .]. The great and holy Council [Nicea] said that the Only-begotten Son was begotten by God the Father according to nature, true God from true God, light from light, through whom the Father made all things; that he descended, he became flesh, he became man, he suffered, he rose on the third day and ascended into heaven. It is necessary that we should adhere to these words and teachings and consider what it is they mean: that the Word of God became incarnate and became man. We do

---

1. Cf. A. Amann, "Nestorius et sa doctrine", DTC XI, 76-157; M. Jugie, *Nestorius et la controverse nestorienne* (Paris, 1912); J. Liebaert, *L'Incarnation*, I, op. cit., 187-207; A. D'Ales, *Le dogme d'Ephèse* (Paris, 1931); A. Grillmeier, *Gesù il Cristo nella fede della Chiesa*, op. cit., 823-81; M. Agnes, *La professione di fede nei concili ecumenici di Efeso e di Calcedonia* (Casino, 1983), 17-65.

not say that the nature of the Word, having changed, became flesh, nor that it became transformed into a complete (composite) man of body and soul; rather, we say that the Word, having united itself according to hypostasis to a flesh animated by a rational soul, became man in an ineffable and incomprehensible way, and was called Son of Man. This union is not due to will alone or to pleasure nor did it happen by the assumption of a person [*prosopon*], and even though the two natures united by a true union are distinct, from them both there arises a single Christ and Son; not as if the union were to suppress the difference of the natures, but because the divinity and the humanity constitute for us a single Lord Christ and Son, by their ineffable and mysterious coming together.

"Thus it is said that he subsists before all the ages and that he was begotten by the Father, that he was begotten by a woman according to the flesh, not that his divine nature started its existence in the holy Virgin [. . .]. Because an ordinary man was not, first of all, born of the holy Virgin and the Word descended upon him afterwards, but what we say is that, united to the flesh, from his mother's womb, he submitted to a carnal birth, claiming that birth as his own.

"In this sense we say that he suffered and rose again, not because the God Word suffered in his own nature, the wounds, the holes made by nails and the other wounds (the divinity is impassible, because it is non-corporeal); but rather, given that the body, which he had made his own, suffered these wounds, it is said once again that he (the Word) suffered for us: that which was impassible was in a passible body.

"We have the same way of thinking regarding his death. The Word of God is by nature immortal, incorruptible, living, vivifying. But, in addition, he has his own body, by the grace of God. He tasted death for the good of all, as St Paul says (Heb 2:9); what is said is that he suffered death for the good of all of us. This does not mean that he experienced death in that which regards his own nature (it would be madness to say this or to think it), but that, as I have said a short while ago, his flesh tasted death [. . .]. Thus we confess one single Christ, one single Lord, not adoring a man with the Word so as not to introduce the idea of division by the use of the word 'with'; rather we adore one single and same (Christ), because the body of the Word is not apart from him and it is with it that he is now seated with the Father. There are not two sons seated with the Father but one only on account of the union in his own flesh.

"All that is meant by saying that the Word became flesh is the following: he participated like us in flesh and blood (Heb 2:14); He made our body his own and came into the world as man born of woman; he did not abandon his divine being nor his generation from the Father God but remained what he was while, at the same time, taking on flesh.

"Here you have all that is taught by orthodox faith everywhere; that is how we will find it in the teaching of the Fathers. In this way, they [the Fathers] did not hesitate to call the holy Virgin, Mother of God [*Theotokos*], not because the nature of the Word or his divinity had taken from the holy Virgin the principle of his existence, but because, once the holy body animated by a rational soul to which the Word was united according to hypostasis was born of her, it is to be said that the Word was begotten according to the flesh."[2]

St Cyril's twelve anathemas against Nestorius were also read out at Ephesus, but they do not form part of the acts of the council.

Nestorius was deposed with the approval of Pope Celestine who had sent his legates to the council. For this reason the Church has ever since then regarded the doctrine content of Cyril's anathemas as the Christological teaching of the Council of Ephesus.[3]

These are the main points of this teaching: Christ is one subject only (*hypostasis*) and one person only (*prosopon*); he who is God is also man, through a union of a divine *physis* (nature) and a human nature. Therefore, Mary is truly Mother of God, because she gave birth according to the flesh to the Word of God made flesh; Christ is the Son of God and it is wrong to say that Jesus the man is a divinised man and an adoptive son of God; Christ's flesh is life-giving (an implicit reference to the Eucharist), because it is the flesh of the Word; Christ should be worshipped with *one* adoration, and not worshipped as God and separately worshipped as man; to the Person of the Word should be attributed not only the divine actions but also the human actions and passions of Jesus.[4]

The terminology which St Cyril used was still somewhat inexact. For example, in addition to very clear statements, he also used the expression "a single nature (*mia physis*) of the Incarnate Word". But this did not, for him, mean denying that Jesus had two natures (divine and human): it was simply a terminologically inexact way of underlining the intimate union of the two natures in the one Person of the Word incarnate. Also, St Cyril seems to have used this expression because it occurred in a text attributed to St Athanasius, who enjoyed great authority, but the text was later shown to have been tampered with by an Apollinarian writer.

The controversy between Antioch and Alexandria continued after the Council of Ephesus. And so, two years later (in 433), in the reign of Sixtus III, a *Formula of Union* (between Antioch and Alexandria) was devised which was accepted by both parties (the key figures being John of Antioch and St

---

2. St Cyril of Alexandria, *Second Letter to Nestorius* (AD 430), approved at the Council of Ephesus (431).
3. Cf. T. Camelot, *Efeso y Calcedonia* (Vitoria, 1971), 72.
4. Cf. DS 252-63. As the Catechism of the Catholic Church says, when commenting on the rejection of Nestorianism by the Council of Ephesus, "The humanity of Christ has no other subject than that of the divine person of the Son of God who assumed it and made it his own from his conception" (no. 466).

Cyril himself). The *Formula of Union* expresses Christological dogma in these words: "Jesus Christ is perfect God and perfect man. . . . Consubstantial with the Father in divinity and consubstantial with us in humanity. Given that the union was made of the two natures . . . union without confusion."[5] As we shall see this formula prepared the way for the dogmatic formula of the Council of Chalcedon.

b) The testimony of the New Testament   The New Testament does not give us a literal statement of the unity of Person of Jesus Christ, but it does carry the content of that unity, to such an extent that "we can take it as an essential characteristic of New Testament Christology that one finds both divine and human assertions predicated of the one same subject."[6]

In the testimony already examined in connexion with the true humanity and the true divinity of Jesus, we can clearly see that He who is man is the same (person) as He who is God: Jesus is a single subject or person.

But there are passages which are particularly important to this question. First, the Prologue of St John: "The Word became flesh" (Jn 1:14); so, it is the Word, who is God (cf. Jn 1:1-2), who has become flesh, not because the Godhead has changed into humanity (which would be impossible) but because that flesh is the flesh of the Word; therefore, divinity and humanity belong to the one subject or person—the Word incarnate.

Christ says to Nicodemus: "No one has ascended into heaven but he who descended from heaven"(Jn 3:13); therefore, he who ascends is the same one as descends and who is in heaven; he who ascends as man is the same one as has descended as God.[7]

A similar testimony is contained in the following prayer of Jesus: "And now, Father, glorify thou me in thy own presence with the glory which I had with thee before the world was made" (Jn 17:5). Obviously, the *me* and the *I* here indicate the same Person; the *me*, referring to the human nature to be glorified, and *I* meaning the glorious divinity in eternity, that is, before the creation of the world.

We should also note in this connexion the well-known passage in St Paul's Letter to the Philippians: "who [Christ Jesus], though he was in the form of God [. . .], emptied himself, taking the form of a servant" (Phil 2:6); the very Person who had the form of God (divine nature) is the same Person as he who later took the form of a servant (human nature).

And the following text of Paul recalls the words of Jesus (Jn 3:13) already

5.   DS 272.
6.   W. Kasper, *Jesus the Christ*, op. cit., 233. On Kasper's Christology, which contains interesting ideas but also some controversial points, see L.F. Mateo Seco, "W. Kasper: Jesús el Cristo", ScrTh 11 (1979) 269-93.
7.   Cf. St Augustine, *Sermo* 263, 3 (PL 38, 1211); *Sermo* 294, 9 (PL 38, 1340-1).

quoted: "He (Christ) who descended is he who also ascended far above all the heavens" (Eph 4:10). This passage is sometimes used to show Christ's oneness of Person, but in fact "descended" here refers to the burial of Jesus (to his descent into hell); and "ascended" to his resurrection and ascension (cf. Eph 4:9): therefore, this text does not mean the same as John 3:13.

c) **The testimony of the Fathers** The Fathers prior to St Cyril of Alexandria, when asserting the divinity and humanity of Jesus Christ, always spoke of Jesus himself as of one who is God and man; that is, they spoke of the unity of Christ.

Even before the Council of Ephesus, we find very clear terminology being used. For example, Tertullian (+223) used a formula similar to that later used by the Council of Chalcedon: "(in Christ) we see two states (= natures) with no confusion, but, rather, united in one person, God and man, Jesus."[8] Among the Eastern Fathers the statement of St Gregory Nazianzen (+390) is especially noteworthy: "Although he (Christ) had two natures, God and man, and the man is body and soul, they are not however two Sons or two gods. . . . So, in the Saviour there are two different things, but not two individuals."[9]

Finally, St Augustine (+430) will use a very precise expression: "the same one who is God, is man; and the same who is man, is God; not through the confusion of the natures but through the unity of the person."[10]

In the writings of other Fathers we find the same teaching, sometimes with less exact terminology. It will not be until after the Council of Chalcedon that the language becomes fixed and enters into general use. St Ephraim of Antioch (+545) and St Leontius of Byzantium (+543) and, among the Latins, Severinus Boethius (+525) were particularly influential in honing the language of Christology.[11]

2. UNION AND DISTINCTION OF JESUS' HUMANITY AND DIVINITY

The expression *hypostatic union* is used to show that the union of the human nature and divine nature in Christ is a union in the *hypostasis* in the Person. That is, the union is not in the nature (the two natures are not mixed together); there is a union of natures, because both belong to the same Person.

a) **Monophysitism and the Council of Chalcedon** In the struggle against Nestorianism (which denied the personal unity of Jesus Christ), some writers

---

8. Tertullian, *Adversus Praxeam*, 27 (PL 2, 215).
9. St Gregory Nazianzen, *Epist. 101 ad Cledonium*, I, 3 (PG 36, 285); cf. *Oratio* 40 (PG 36, 424).
10. St Augustine, *Sermo* 186, 1, 1 (PL 38, 999).
11. In section 3a below we deal at greater length with this honing of terminology.

fell into the opposite error—that of saying that there is only one nature (*mono-physis*) in Jesus. One brand of Monophystism thought that the human nature, when assumed by the divine nature, was completely absorbed by it and therefore annihilated. Others thought that the union of the two natures gave rise to a new and special *divine-human* nature exclusive to Christ. Finally, another type of Monophysitism was the old one of Apollinaris which held that the divinity entered into a *composition* with Christ's body, functioning in it as its spiritual soul.[12]

The main representatives of the Monophysite heresy were Eutyches, archimandrite of a monastery in Constantinople, and Dioscorus, patriarch of Alexandria after St Cyril. Their brand of Monophysitism was of the first type mentioned above; so, they asserted that Christ is a person of two natures (prior to their union) but not in two natures (after their union). They intended to follow the teaching of St Cyril, who had used the expression "one single nature of the Incarnate Word"; however, they interpreted this expression incorrectly, in a different way from St Cyril.

In fact, as we have already pointed out, during the period of the Nestorian heresy the terminology had not yet been worked out exactly. Some expressions used by the Fathers which were clear in the overall context of their positions, could be misinterpreted when taken out of context (by context we mean not just the writings but the theological environment and language of the period).

These texts were used by Eutyches in his Monophysite interpretations. The formulae used by St Cyril (and correctly interpreted up to Eutyches) were approved a century later by the Second Council of Constantinople, removing any doubt as to their true meaning: "If anyone [. . .] speaking of one single nature of the Word of God incarnate (*unam naturam Dei Verbi incarnatam*) does not understand this as the Fathers taught, that a hypostatic union having been made of divine nature and human nature, one Christ came into being, but proposes to introduce by these expressions one nature or substance of the divinity and flesh of Christ: let such a one be anathema."[13]

The Monophysite theses of Eutyches were condemned by Flavian, patriarch of Constantinople, who deposed Eutyches in 448. Pope St Leo I approved Flavian's actions and sent him the Dogmatic Letter *Lectis dilectionis tuae* (449), also known as the Tome of St Leo. In his letter, the pope reaffirmed the true doctrine concerning the hypostatic union, teaching that in Christ there is only one Person and two natures, which are united while remaining distinct and not confused: "with the character of both natures unimpaired, therefore, coming together in one person, humility was assumed by majesty, weakness

---

12. Cf. M. Jugie, *Monophisisme*, DTC X, 2216-51; J. Liébaert, op. cit., 209-21; A. Grillmeier, op. cit., 607-29.

13. Second Council of Constantinople (AD 533), *Anathematisms of the Three Chapters*, c.8 (DS 429).

by strength, mortality by eternity, and in order to wipe out our guilt the inviolable nature was joined to the nature subject to suffering so that, as our salvation demanded, one and the same 'mediator of God and man, the man Christ Jesus' (1 Tim 2:5) could from one element be able to die and from the other not. The true God therefore was born in the complete and perfect nature of man, complete in his (nature) and complete in ours."[14]

For his part, Dioscorus persuaded the emperor Theodosius to call a new council at Ephesus, presided over by Dioscorus himself, which rehabilitated Eutyches and rejected the Dogmatic Letter of Leo. This Council, later called the *Latrocinium of Ephesus*, has no doctrinal authority, because only followers of Dioscorus attended and the pope did not approve it but disowned it.

At last, in 451, a genuine ecumenical council was held at Chalcedon, which solemnly defined the hypostatic union. We quote this important definition in full: "Following therefore the holy Fathers we unanimously teach that the Son, our Lord Jesus Christ, is one and the same, the same perfect in divinity, the same perfect in humanity, true God and true man, consisting of a rational soul and a body, consubstantial with the Father in divinity and consubstantial with us in humanity, 'in all things like as we are, without sin' (Heb 4:15), born of the Father before all time as to his divinity, born in recent times for us and for our salvation from the Virgin Mary, Mother of God, as to his humanity.

"We confess one and the same Christ, the Son, the Lord, the Only-begotten, in two natures unconfused, unchangeable, undivided and inseparable. The difference of natures will never be abolished by their being united, but rather the properties of each remain unimpaired, both coming together in one person (*prosopon*) and substance (*hypostasis*), not parted or divided among two persons (*prosopa*), but in one and the same Only-begotten Son, the divine Word, the Lord Jesus Christ, as previously the prophets and Jesus Christ himself taught us and the Creed of the Fathers handed down to us. The above having been considered with all and every care and diligence, this Holy Ecumenical Council has defined that no one may advance any other belief or inscribe, compose, hold or teach it in any other way."[15]

Although this dogmatic text was particularly aimed at the Monophysite heresy, it contains a wider and more complete exposition which excludes the principle previous errors (Arianism, Apollinarianism, Nestorianism) also. It is important to notice also how this dogmatic definition asserted not only the distinction of the two natures of Christ, but also the direct consequence of that distinction: the hypostatic union was formed "while preserving intact the property of both natures". That is to say, after the union, each nature retains

14. St Leo the Great, *Ep. Lectis dilectionis tuae*, op. cit (DS 293). See also M.J. Nicolas, "La doctrine christologique de saint Léon le Grand", RT 51 (1951) 609-60.
15. Council of Chalcedon, *Definitio* (DS 301-2). Cf. T. Camelot, op. cit., 115-73; A. de Halleux, "La définition christologique à Chalcédoine", RTL 7 (1976) 3-23; 115-70.

its own characteristics; they are not confused. So, for example, Jesus Christ is eternal, almighty, etc., in respect of his divinity, while at the same time he is born in time, has a limited potency, etc., as far as his humanity is concerned; he is equal to God in his divinity, but inferior to the Father in his humanity.

This consequence has special importance as regards everything to do with Christ's spiritual faculties. So, he has two intellects (divine and human), and also two wills (divine and human). These aspects of the mystery of Christ are clearly revealed in the New Testament: there, Jesus himself shows his human will to be distinct from the will of the Father (which is the same divine will as the Son's): "I have come down from heaven, not to do my own will, but the will of him who sent me" (Jn 6:38). The human will of Jesus is most clearly to be seen at Gethsemani: "My Father, if it be possible, let this cup pass from me; nevertheless, not as I will, but as thou wilt" (Mt 26:39). Through this human will, "in Gethsemani the humanity of Jesus is seen more clearly than at any other time."[16]

The distinction between Christ's human and divine actions is also clearly expressed in the New Testament, when we are shown Jesus working, speaking, walking, etc. as true man, and also doing things proper to God alone (forgiving sins, etc.), as we have discussed already in connexion with the humanity and divinity of Christ.

The perfect integrity of Jesus' human nature is manifested not only in his human actions but also in his passions, which are not in themselves "defects" of that nature but, rather, natural consequences clearly aimed towards good. In addition to purely bodily passions (such as physical pain), Christ also had emotions, proper to his sensibility, and spiritual passions, proper to his will.[17] The Gospel gives us numerous examples: for example, his sadness (cf. Mt 26:38), wonder (cf. Mt 8:10), anger (cf. Jn 2:15; Mt 23:13-33), joy (cf. Jn 15:11), affective love (cf. Jn 11:36), etc.

However, in addition to Jesus' not having passions derived from imperfection, it is worth noting that the perfection of him who is perfect Man gives his passions certain characteristics of their own. Specifically, whereas in other men and women these passions often rebel in a disordered way, that is not the case in Christ. On other occasions they forestall the judgments of reason, whereas in Christ all his emotions are perfectly controlled by reason. Moreover, our Lord (contrary to what sometimes happens in the case of other men) held the natural motions proper to his sensible humanity under control in the area of the senses in such a way that they never obstructed the use of reason. Therefore, Christ's passions are usually termed *propasiones*, to show that they were always motions kept within the sphere of sensibility.[18]

16. A. Feuillet, *L'Agonie de Gethsèmani* (Paris, 1977), 190.
17. Cf. St Thomas Aquinas, *STh* III, q. 15, a. 4.
18. Ibid.

In the light of faith, we know that Christ chose to take our nature with all its passions; he did so to teach us that they are good in themselves and become evil only through sin; and also, so as the better to redeem us from that disorder. Passions are not bad in themselves; on the contrary, when they are controlled by reason, through a firm will and directed to their right end, they are a great help in doing good. Also, by choosing to have them, our Lord healed them in us, thereby enabling man not only to control his passions but to re-order them in the service of God, and to love God passionately, with all his heart.

The fact that he has two natures should not, however, cause us to forget that there is only one subject in Christ. After Chalcedon, some conceived Christ's human nature as a kind of personal subject. Against these, the Second Council of Constantinople (553) affirmed that there is in Christ "only one hypostasis".[18a] Therefore, "everything in Christ's human nature is to be attributed to his divine person as to its proper subject".[18b]

b) Monothelism and the Third Council of Constantinople

In spite of the solemn definition of Chalcedon, Monophysitism continued to receive more or less open support, particularly in the East. To put an end to the controversy, Sergius, patriarch of Constantinople from 610 to 638, tried to steer a middle course by proposing the thesis that there are indeed two unconfused natures in Jesus but only one type of operation (*monoenergeia*; hence the name *Monoenergetism*), and he ended up also attributing to Jesus only one will (*Monothelism*), because the human will of Jesus would be moved by the divine will in such a way that the human will would be completely passive and never produce a genuine human desire.[19]

The Monothelists justified their thesis by saying that the Fathers taught that, in Christ, the human nature was the instrument of the divinity. Since an instrument is not moved by its own will but by the will of the user, they concluded that Christ did not have a human will. It is true that it is proper to an instrument to be moved by the principal agent; but each instrument is moved in a different way, according to its mode of being. Therefore, there is no contradiction involved in saying that Christ's humanity was an instrument of the Godhead while being moved through the medium of its own will.[20]

Against Monothelism (which was in open opposition to the faith defined by Chalcedon) the main combatants were St Sophronius (+638), a Palestinian monk who became patriarch of Jerusalem, and St Maximus the Confessor

---

18a. Cf. Second Council of Constantinople, *Anathematisms of the Three Chapters*, c.4 (DS 424).
18b. CCC, no. 468.
19. Cf. M. Jugie, "Monothélisme", DTC XI, 2307-23; F.X. Murphy and P. Sherwood, *Constantinople II et III* (Paris, 1973).
20. Cf. St Thomas Aquinas, *STh* III, q. 18, a. 1, ad 2.

(+662).[21] The history of this controversy was quite turbulent, due particularly to the fact that Pope Honorius (621–638) did not express himself as clearly as he ought.[22]

The strife ended only with the Third Council of Constantinople (680–681), which was confirmed by Pope Agatho. This council condemned Monothelism and solemnly defined that "two natural wills and two natural active principles inseparably, unchangeably, undividedly and unconfusedly in him (Christ). And two natural wills, not opposing each other [. . .], but his human will following without resistance or reluctance being, subject rather to his divine and omnipotent will."[23]

In this definition, the Third Council of Constantinople applied to the wills and operations of Jesus, the terminology ("inseparably, unchangeably, undividedly and unconfusedly") which the Council of Chalcedon had applied to the two natures—as was only logical, since will and operations are proper to natures. In fact, a human nature without an effective human will (which was the Monothelist position) would be a severely truncated nature; Christ would not, then, have been perfect man. This was the understanding of the Fathers of the Church from the earliest times. For example, St Athanasius, commenting on Matthew 26:39, wrote: "Jesus there shows two wills, the human will which is that of the flesh and the divine will which is that of God; the human will, on account of the weakness of the flesh, appeals for the removal of the suffering; the divine will, however, is ready to accept it."[24]

As St John Damascene put it, "there are in our Lord Jesus Christ, in accordance with the diverse natures, two wills that are not opposed to each other. Neither the natural will, nor the natural faculty of wanting, nor things which are naturally subject, nor the natural exercise of the will itself, are contrary to the divine will. The divine will created all the things of nature. Only that which is contrary to nature is contrary also to the divine will, such as sin, for example, which Jesus Christ did not take on. Further still, because the person of Jesus Christ is one and Jesus Christ himself is one, he who wills by means of either of the two natures is one also."[25]

St Thomas explains that, in our Lord his *voluntas ut natura* (human will insofar as it was influenced by human feelings) and his human feelings sometimes demured from the divine will, but were entirely subject to it through the *voluntas ut ratio* (human will insofar as it was influenced by human reason). It was God's will that Christ should undergo his passion and death; God did

21. See F.M. Léthel, *Théologie de l'agonie du Christ: La liberté humaine du Fils de Dieu et son importance sotériologique mises en lumiére par Saint Maxime Confesseur* (Paris, 1979).
22. Cf. A. Amann, "Honorius I", DTC VII, 93–132. Cf. also H.G. Beck, "La primitiva Iglesia bizantina" in H. Jedin, *Historia de la Iglesia*, II (Barcelona, 1980), 625ff.
23. Third Council of Constantinople, Session of 16 September 681 (DS 556).
24. St Athanasius, *De Incarnatione Dei Verbi*, 21 (PG 26, 1021)
25. St John Damascene, *De duabus in Christi volunt.*, 25 (PG 95, 157).

not desire them for their own sake, but as the means to an end—to save mankind. Therefore, there is no doubt but that Christ with his feelings and his *voluntas ut natura* could want something different from what God wanted, as one can see from his prayer: "My Father, if it be possible, let this cup pass from me" (Mt 26:39). However, with his *voluntas ut ratio*, he always wanted the same as God, as is evident when he says: "not as I will, but as thou wilt" (ibid.).[26]

There was, therefore, no clash of wills in Christ. Clash of wills occurs only when there is opposition both as regards the same object and for the same reason. This did not happen in Christ, because his *voluntas ut natura* rejected death as something repulsive to human nature, whereas his *voluntas ut ratio* and the divine will did desire death for a different reason, the salvation of men. And not only was there no opposition: the very movements of his feelings and of his *voluntas ut natura* which shrank from death and suffering, were willed by Christ with his *voluntas ut ratio* and were perfectly submissive through that will to the divine will.[27]

c) **The human actions of God in Christ**   The mistake of Monoenergetism (which gave rise to Monothelism) was to speak of divine-human (*theandric*) actions of Jesus, in the sense of these actions not being regarded as divine and human but as a new "intermediary", "divine-human" type of action.

However, since all Jesus' actions are actions of the divine Person, all his human actions can and should be called actions of God—actions which can properly therefore be called divine-human (*theandric*). For example, when Jesus spoke (a human action) it was God speaking, because Jesus is God; his speech was divine and human (divine, because it was a divine Person speaking; human, because he spoke through his human nature).

So, there is a correct sense in which to take the expression "divine-human (*theandric*) actions of Jesus Christ": all his human actions, insofar as they are actions of the divine Person, are divine-human.

It became quite frequent for Catholic theologians to speak of theandric actions of Jesus (not in the Monothelistic sense) this occurred mainly due to the authority given to the writings of an unknown author who for long was thought to be the Dionysius who was a disciple of St Paul (cf. Acts 17:34), although later he was found to be a sixth-century writer; which is why is he called *Pseudo-Dionysius*. He wrote that Jesus Christ "did not act as God does, which is divine, nor as man does, which is human, but he showed us a new way of acting, the theandric action."[28] This text could be interpreted in a

26. Cf. St Thomas Aquinas, *STh* III, q. 18, a. 5.
27. Ibid., a. 6.
28. Pseudo-Dionysius, *Epist.* 4 (PG 3, 1072).

Monothelist and even in a Monophysite sense: but it was also correctly interpreted, particularly by St Thomas Aquinas.[29]

To sum up, we are saying that in Christ's activity there are exclusively divine actions (all those performed by God; these are common to the three divine Persons), and human actions. The latter, because they are performed by the divine Person through his human nature, can (all of them) be termed theandric. However, this term is usually reserved for those human actions of Jesus which are an *instrument* of his divine activity to produce effects which surpass human capacity. For example, the conservation in existence of all creation (cf. Heb 1:3) is a divine action of Jesus; his speaking, walking etc. are human actions; his theandric actions are the miracles, in which through his human action (speaking, etc.), his divinity produces an effect which only God can bring about (for example, raising a dead person to life).

However, it is important, when considering the ordinary human actions of Jesus, to bear in mind that "All this human behaviour is the behaviour of God. 'For in him dwells *all* the fullness of the godhead bodily' (Col 2:9). Christ is God become man a complete, perfect man. And through his human nature, he shows us what his divine nature is [. . .]. Everything Christ did has a transcendental value. It shows us the nature of God."[30]

d) The inception of the Incarnation and its permanence   Faith in the Incarnation includes the belief that the hypostatic union happened the very moment the humanity of Jesus Christ was conceived, and that this union never ceased and never will cease. As St Gregory of Nyssa wrote: "From the beginning and for ever the divinity was united to the body and soul (of Christ)."[31]

Therefore, it was not that first a man was conceived and then later on he was assumed by the Word, but that the conception of the humanity (creation of the soul in the body formed in the womb of the Blessed Virgin) and the assumption of this humanity by the Word were simultaneous. So it is professed in the symbols of the faith, when we affirm that the Son of God was conceived as a man of Mary through the action of the Holy Spirit. If that had not been so, Mary would not be the Mother of God, as in fact she is.

We might also mention here the error of Origen, who thought that human souls exist before their bodies do. And so, according to him, the soul of Jesus would have existed before being united to the Word, and then the Word and the soul would have been united to the body. This error was condemned by a synod held in Constantinople in 543.

The man Jesus had no existence of his own prior to being the humanity of

29. Cf. St Thomas Aquinas, *Compendium Theologiae*, I, 212.
30. Blessed J. Escrivá de Balaguer, *Christ is passing by*, op. cit., no. 109.
31. St Gregory of Nyssa, *Adversus Apollinarium*, 55 (PG 45, 1257).

God; Jesus' human nature "was not assumed in the sense of being created beforehand and then assumed; it was created in the very act of being assumed."[32]

The hypostatic union *never ceased*, not even at the passion and death of Jesus. The faith teaches us (as can be seen from the dogmatic definition of the Council of Chalcedon) that, after the union, the divine and human natures remain *inseparable*. There are also the words St Peter addressed to the Jews: "[you] killed the Author of life" (Acts 3:15) and a similar statement of St Paul's: "[they] crucifed the Lord of glory" (1 Cor 2:8), which clearly show that the hypostatic union continued during the Passion. When Christ, on the cross, said, "My God, my God, why hast thou forsaken me?" (Mt 27:46), repeating the words of Psalm 21, he was fulfilling that prophecy of the Passion. In any event, those words do not imply an interruption in the hypostatic union (as Cerinthus wrongly claimed in the first century); they mean that his divinity did not protect Christ's humanity from death. They are, then, a kind of human prayer of Jesus', rather like his prayer in Gethsemani (cf. Mt 26:39), which shows very emphatically the human suffering of God in Christ.[33]

The Incarnation is something definitive: it remains for ever. As we profess in the Creed, repeating the words of the Annunciation to Mary: Jesus' kingdom "will have no end". And in the Epistle to the Hebrews, we read that Christ "holds his priesthood permanently, because he continues for ever" (Heb 7:24) and that "Jesus Christ is the same yesterday and today and for ever" (Heb 13:8).

In the sixth century there was an error that gained some credence which held that at the end of time the Word would shed his human nature; this error had been previously proposed by Marcellus of Ancyra (+374) and condemned by the First Council of Constantinople.[34]

Absolutely speaking, if God had so wished the hypostatic union could come to an end, but it is his design (as we have seen) that Jesus Christ, God-Man, should remain forever. We can see how appropriate this is, if we remember that Jesus is God's greatest gift to mankind and that "the gifts and the call of God are irrevocable" (Rom 11:29). This is in line with the classic theological argument: God never takes back his gifts unless the recipient is at fault; and in Jesus there is no sin.[35]

The fact that the Incarnation will last forever helps us see that Jesus is not just a "device" for the salvation of mankind: he *is* salvation. It also helps us to

---

32. St Leo the Great, *Epist.* 33, 3 (PL 54, 807).
33. Cf. L.F. Mateo Seco, "Muerte de Cristo y Teología de la Cruz", en *Cristo, Hijo de Dios . . .*, op. cit., 713.
34. Cf. First Council of Constantinople, AD 381 (DS 151).
35. Cf. St Gregory of Nyssa, *Adversus Apollinarium*, 54 (PG 45, 1255); St Thomas Aquinas, *STh* III, q. 50, a. 2.

appreciate the great dignity of man, which is sourced in God's love for him, for us, and especially the love of the Father for Him who, even as man, is his beloved Son (cf. Lk 3:22).

3. THE ONTOLOGICAL UNITY OF THE PERSON: CHRIST'S BEING

The Incarnation is a mystery we can never fully understand. It is true that we know a great deal through Revelation, which the Church, by will of Christ, has a mission to safeguard and to interpret authentically and infallibly. But this does not mean that we can totally penetrate the mystery by means of dogmatic formulae, however accurate and exact. As St Cyril of Alexandria puts it, we should always recognize that the hypostatic union "is a mystery that surpasses reason; our mind cannot grasp how the Incarnation came about."[36]

That said, theological reflection is a help in deepening our knowledge of the mystery of Christ. That reflection starts out from the truth of faith and it must always keep that faith as its point of reference. The Church has always proclaimed that Jesus Christ's humanity was fully real and it has also had occasion often to point to the fact that he is one single subject—that is, that this human nature "belongs, as his own, to the divine person of the Son of God who assumed it. Everything that Christ is and does in this nature derives from 'one of the Trinity'. The Son of God therefore communicates to his humanity his own personal mode of existence in the Trinity. In his soul as in his body, Christ thus expresses humanly the divine ways of the Trinity (cf. Jn 14:9-10)."[36a]

In studying the hypostatic union, we cannot avoid using the concepts of nature and person to designate two distinct things: nature gives us the answer to the question *what* a thing is (*quid*), while person tells us *who* he or she is (*quis*). At the same time it should be remembered that the Christian faith confesses that in the Blessed Trinity there is one nature and three persons (*mia ousia, treis hypostaseis*), and that in Jesus Christ there is one person in two natures (*mia hypostasis en duo phusesin*).

In theology the concepts of nature and person must be used, obviously, analogically when referring to God or to created beings. Classical theology defined person in God as "subsistent relationship",[37] while it kept to Boethius' definition—*rationalis naturae individua substantia* (an individual substance of a rational nature)—when using it in Christology.

Prior to the Council of Chalcedon there was no generally accepted use and meaning attaching to the terms "person" and "nature".[38] We know that,

36. St Cyril of Alexandria, *Homilia Paschalis* XVIII, 3 (PG 77, 782).
36a. CCC, no. 470.
37. See, for example, *STh* I, q. 29, a. 4.
38. For a detailed history of the terms and of the evolution of the concept, cf. A. Michel,

originally, the term *prosopon* or person (from the Latin *per-sonare*) meant the face and also the mask of the actor in a theatre, and later the personage represented. This initially involved a certain ambiguity: it meant that one might think that, when referring to the three Persons of the Trinity, one meant them in a Sabellian sense as three different *representations* of the one divine substance (like three different ways of presenting itself). However, it may have been the best term available. In fact, as early as the Septuagint translation of the Bible, for example, it was used to designate the face of God—which is the language which will be imposed at Chalcedon.

a) **The terms "hypostasis", "substance" and "person" in the Patristic period up to the Council of Chalcedon** The term *hypostasis* underwent considerable evolution prior to obtaining its final theological meaning. Etymologically, *hypostasis* means that which underlies, the foundation. The New Testament sometimes uses it to designate something that has consistency, something real and objective, as opposed to subjective (cf. 2 Cor 9:4; Heb 1:3; 3:14; 11:1). That is how it is used in the Council of Nicea, when it rejects the Arian position which said that the Son is "of a different *hypostasis* or *ousia*" from the Father,[39] using both terms in the sense of substance or nature or essence. St Athanasius later commented that the Council of Nicea had done well to use both terms as synonyms, because "these two words are used to signify everything that is most real in a being."[40]

The term *hypostasis* is also used to designate the divine Persons to show their distinction from one another and when this happens the meaning comes to be the opposite of that of *ousia*. For example, although he still uses *ousia* and *hypostasis* sometimes as meaning the same, Origen avoids using *ousia* to describe the three divine Persons; he uses *hypostasis* instead.[41] Dionysius of Alexandria already speaks of three *hypostasis* in the unity of the Godhead,[42] and St Dionysius of Rome condemns those who say that in the Godhead the three *hypostasis* are separated from each other.[43] Prior to the year 362, the word *hypostasis* continued to mean the objective reality and, when applied to the

"Hypostase", DTC VII, 370-437; and "Hypostatique (union)" ibid., 437-568; M. Nedoncelle, "Prosopon et persona dans l'antiquité classique", RevSR, 22 (1948) 277-99; E. Lohse, " πρόσωπον ", in *ThWNT* VI, 769-81; J. Ratzinger in *Dogma and preaching*, op. cit.; H. Doerrie, *Hypostasis, Wort und Bedeutungsgeschichte* (Göttingen, 1955); E. Forment, *Ser y persona* (Barcelona, 1983); J.A. Sayés, *Jesucristo, ser y persona* (Burgos, 1984).

39. "Ex heteras hupostaseos e ousias" (DS 126).
40. St Athanasius, *Epist. ad Afros*, 2, 4 (PG 26, 1036). Athanasius uses *hypostasis* and *ousia* without distinguishing between them: cf., e.g., *De decretis Nicenae synodi*, 27 (PG 25, 465); *Epist. ad Serapionem*, no. 4 (PG 25, 641); *De synodis*, nos. 45, 48 (PG 35, 772-3).
41. Cf. A. Michel, "Hypostase", art. cit., 374.
42. Cf. cited by St Basil, *De Spiritu Sancto*, 29, 72 (PG 32, 201).
43. St Denis of Rome, *Epist. contra Tritheistas et Sabellianos, c.*AD 260 (DS 112).

divine essence, it could mean the same as *ousia*, but when applied to the divine Persons considered in themselves it acquired the more exact meaning of complete "substance", that is, an independent subject counterposed to *ousia*.[44]

In the Latin world, Tertullian already distinguished *substance* and *person*. He is the first to speak of *one substance and three persons* in the Trinity, and of two *substances* and one *person* in Christ,[45] using *person* as distinct from *substance*; whereas he regarded *hypostasis* as the equivalent to essence or substance.[46] This terminological confusion between Latins and Greeks thus became an additional complication in the already difficult Trinitarian and Christological questions of the period. In his *Epistola ad Damasum* (376), St Jerome took the situation in hand: "I beg of you to take a decision on the matter, if you have no objections; I would have no qualms about speaking about *three hypostasis*. Give orders for a new post-Nicea formula of faith to be composed, a faith which orthodox and Arians may confess in the same terms."[47] The same meaning is to be found in St Gregory Nazianzen, who also was trying to fix the terminology.[48]

The three great Cappadocians played an outstanding role in this attempt to get the language right—St Basil, St Gregory of Nyssa and St Gregory Nazianzen. Here is a very relevant passage from a letter Basil sent his brother Gregory: "the *ousia* is that which is common to individuals of the same species, that which they all possess equally and which makes it possible for them all to be designated by the same word without distinguishing any one in particular. But this *ousia* cannot exist really unless under the condition that it be completed by the individuating characteristics that determine it."[49] The basic reason for the confusion and also for the differences in meaning is the fact that *hypostasis* means *ousia* insofar as it is individualized, that is, insofar as it is distinguished from those that share with it in the same ousia. This distinction comes about through what St Basil calls the properties, the *idiomata*. Thus, in God, that which is related to the *ousia* (goodness, divinity) is common to all three

44. Cf. A. Michel, art. cit., 375.
45. Cf. Tertullian, *Adversus Praxeam*, chaps. 11, 13, 18, 21, 24, 27, 31 (PL 2, 166-7, 168-9, 173-5, 177, 179-81, 186-7, 190-2, 196).
46. Cf. Tertullian, *Adv. Praxeam*, 7 (PL, 2, 162). It is also used in this sense by St Hilary, *De synodis*, 12, 29, 32 (PL 10, 490, 503, 504); St Augustine, *De Trinitate*, V, 8, 9; VII, 4, 8 (PL 42, 917, 918, 941); St Isidore, *Etymologiae*, VII, 4, 11 and 12 (PL 82, 271, 272).
47. St Jerome, *Ad Damasum, Epist*. 15, 3 (PL 22, 356).
48. "We, the Greeks, say religiously that there is only one *ousia* and three *hypostases*. The first word reveals the nature of the divinity, the second the triple-ness of the individuating properties. The Latins think the same, but because of the limitations of their language and their shortage of words they were not able to distinguish *hypostasis* and *ousia*, and so they used the word *person* to avoid people thinking in terms of three *ousias*. What happened? Something which would be quite comic were it not so lamentable. It was thought that a difference in faith was involved, when in fact it was simply a confusion of terms. Sabellianism was seen in the *three persons*, Arianism in the *three hypostases*—pure fantasies caused by the spirit of criticism": St Gregory of Nazianzen, *Oratio*, 21, 35 (PG 35, 1124-5).
49. St Basil, *Epistula* 38, 1-2 (PG 32, 325-6).

hypostasis, which are distinguished from each other only by the character of fatherhood, of sonship or of sanctifying power.[50] St Gregory of Nyssa follows his brother in the use of these terms, bringing the meaning of *hypostasis* closer to that of *person*, and keeping the distinction between *hypostasis* and *ousia*, because he understands *hypostasis* as a specification of the *ousia*, the *ousia* being distinguished from all others by virtue of its propertites, its *idiomata*.[51]

The use of the term *hypostasis* as synonymous with person begins in trinitarian doctrine and later extends into Christology. Apollinaris of Laodicea seems to have been the first to use it in Christology. In Apollinaris' thought, Christ is *one*, because in him there is a vital synthesis, making him to be a single *physis*, a single *ousia*. This synthesis occurs precisely because the Word acts as the intellectual soul of Christ.[52] We might say that Apollinaris' problem had resulted from his inability to make a distinction between nature and person. For him, every complete nature would necessarily have to be an hypostasis. That was why he preferred to alter the humanity of Christ rather than say that there are two *hypostasis* in him. St Gregory of Nyssa's reaction in defence of the completeness of Christ's humanity could not have been more effective or devastating.

The School of Antioch holds the opposite position, which takes its starting point from the fact that there are two complete natures in Christ. That is the position of Diodorus of Tarsus, who has been accused of defending the existence in Christ of two *hypostasis*[53] and of Theodore of Mopsuestia who, after defending the two complete natures, finds real difficulty in doing the same for the unity of person.[54] Theodore's view can be described as a search

---

50. Cf. St Basil, *Epistula* 209, 4; 189, 6, 7 and 8 (PG 32, 789 and 692-6).

51. Cf. St Gregory of Nyssa, *Contra Eunomium*, I (PG 45, 320); *De communibus notionibus* (PG 45, 182); *Oratio catechetica magna* 1 (PG 45, 13). Cf. J. Ibáñez and F. Mendoza, "El valor terminológico del término *hypóstasis* en el libro I del *Contra Eunomio* de Gregorio de Nisa" in L.F. Mateo Seco (ed.), *El Contra Eunomium I en la producción literaria de Gregorio de Nisa. Actas del VI Coloquio Internacional sobre Gregorio de Nisa* (Pamplona, 1988), 329-39; cf. also B. Studer, "Der geschichtliche Hintergrund des ersten Buches *Contra Eunomium* Gregors von Nyssa", ibid., 139-72; cf. also M. Richard, "L'introduction du mot *hypostase* dans la théologie de l'incarnation", MSR, 2 (1945), 5-32, 243-70.

52. Here is how St Epiphanius describes Apollinaris' thinking: "Man is an *hypostasis* by virtue of the *nous* which is the principle of life. His animal soul (*psyche*) and his body have their *hypostasis* in and by means of this *nous*. Therefore, if the Word as divine *nous* and divine *pneuma* assumed a human *nous*, there would be two *hypostases* in Christ—which is impossible. If, on the contrary, he has assumed simply a body and an animal soul, these are necessarily found in him hypostasized, and so Christ is but a single hypostasis": St Epiphanius, *Ancoratus*, 77-8 (PG 43, 161 B-164 C).

53. Cf. A. Richard, "L'introduction du mot *hypostase*", art. cit., 17.

54. Cf. R. Devreesse, *Essai sur Thédore de Mopsueste* (Vatican City, 1948). Here is a paragraph from Theodore of Mopsuestia in which this difficulty is clear to see: "This means that (the Logos) on coming to dwell (among us) has joined Himself to the assumed man so as to form a single whole and has caused him to share with Himself all the dignity in which He, being the Son by nature, shares, to the point of being taken as a single *prosopon* by virtue of the

for the unity of Christ starting out from the clear defence of the two complete natures. This is what leads him to conceive the union as if the Word had *assumed the man Jesus* after his creation and had united him intimately to himself in such a way as to form only a single person. Be that as it may, because he does not have a fixed and clear concept of person, Theodore seems to point to the unity of person as a matter of the intimate union of natures,[55] that is, without conceiving it as something distinct from the natures.

Nestorius had similar though deeper problems.[56] He did not accept the *communication of properties* in Christ (predicating divine and human attributes of the one subject) precisely because he does not grasp the notion of a subject who unites the two natures in himself, the divine and the human, and therefore thinks that, in the event of a union between the two, it would have to be a kind of mixture of both. Nestorius does not distinguish nature and person and therefore he conceives the union of the two natures as a union of two subjects, of two persons. In order to keep each nature complete, Nestorius could do nothing else but conceive their union as a moral union—not a unity but a joining-up of two complete subjects.[57]

Cyril of Alexandria, on the other hand, accepted the communication of properties and all its implications: divine and human attributes are predicated of one single subject or person. The key phrase in Cyril (which in due course gave rise to muddled thinking) is the oft-cited "one nature of God-Logos become flesh" (*mia physis tou Theou Logou sesarkomene*), a form of words which comes from Apollinaris of Laodicea and which Cyril accepts because he thinks it is St Athanasius',[58] but he gives it a correct meaning.[59] St Cyril insists, also, that the union of the human and the divine in Christ is a physical union (*enosis physice*), meaning that it is a real union, which takes place on the ontological

union with Him and of sharing all His power with Him; and, so, he does everything in Him, just as he will exercise through Him judgment over all things and will bring us the second coming. And here, one can see, the difference between the features proper to each nature is not eliminated": H.B. Swete, *Theodori Mopsuesteni in Epistolas B. Pauli Commentarii*, II (Cambridge, 1882), 300.

55. Cf. J.A. Sayés, *Jesucristo, Ser y Persona*, op. cit. 26.

56. On the thought of Nestorius, cf., for example, A. Grillmeier, *Gesù il Cristo nella fede della Chiesa*, op. cit., 823-81.

57. The distinction of two levels of *prosopon* (*prosopon* designating the hypostasis in the sense of person, and *prosopon unionis* designating the special moral union of the two natures) and the rejection of the Blessed Virgin being the *Theotokos* in the full meaning of that word, shows that one cannot approach the mystery of the hypostatic union without accepting the distinction between subject and nature: cf. M. Jugie, *Nestorius et la controverse nestorienne* (Paris, 1912); A. Michel, "Hypostase", art. cit., 387-8.

58. Cf. A. Michel, "Hypostase", art. cit., 388.

59. A careful reading of St Cyril's *Second Letter* to Nestorius, read and approved by the Council of Ephesus (DS 250), which affirms the distinction of natures, makes it plain that Cyril keeps the duality of natures and, therefore, does not conceive the hypostatic union as a fusion of natures. On the correct interpretation of the key phrase referred to, cf. Second Council of Constantinople (DS 429). Cf. also Pius XII, Enc. *Sempiternus Rex*, AAS 43 (1951) 636.

level—beyond that of intentionality. Cyril also speaks in the same sense of a *kat'-hypostasin* union,[60] according to the *hypostasis*.

So, from the time the Council of Ephesus accepted the expression *kat-hypostasin*, the hypostatic union comes to be understood as a union in the person (rather than in the natures). In Christ divine and human attributes are predicated of one and the same subject, that is, there is a perfect exchange of properties (*communicatio idiomatum*) in Christ, because in him divine nature and human nature are united in a true union, in such a way that the human nature *physically* belongs to the Word. The formula of union between St Cyril and the Antiochene bishops (433) insists on there being one and the same subject to whom are attributed both consubstantiality with the Father and consubstantiality with man.[61]

With the Council of Chalcedon the distinction between person and nature became firmly established; also the hypostatic union was recognized as something real, that is, belonging to the objective order of being. This was very clearly expressed in the Tome of St Leo to Flavian (449), which was read out and approved at the Council.[62] The Chalcedon definition says that we are to confess "one and the same Christ the Lord and Only-begotten Son in two

---

60. "For we do not say that the nature of the Word became flesh by being changed, nor that it was transformed into a whole man consisting of body and soul, but we do say that the Word united himself in his Person in an inexplicable and incomprehensible way with the flesh animated by a rational soul and thus became man and is called the Son of Man, not solely by his will nor solely by the assumption of a person. And although the natures are different, they truly come together in union to make one Christ and Son for us" (DS 250). Grillmeier comments: "The expression *kenosis kath hupostasin* (union in accordance with the hypostasis) contained in the letter clearly creates a certain precedent for Chalcedon and eases the way to the definitive acceptance of the term *hupostasis* in the proclamation of the Christian faith. But we certainly should not seek a philosophical definition in this expression, which appears for the first time in Cyril as a Christological formula. The phrase 'union in accordance with the hypostasis' is simply designed to convey the reality of the union in Christ as distinct from a purely moral and accidental interpretation, which, the synod judged, would be the teaching of the other party; it should then be opposed to a *henosis kata thelesin monen* (a unity according to a single will) or *kat eudokian* (for the sake of good appearance) or to a unity which is brought about only by the assumption of the external mode of appearance of another prosopon": A. Grillmeier, *Gesù il Cristo nella fede della Chiesa*, op. cit., 880.

61. "We confess, therefore, our Lord Jesus Christ only-begotten Son of God, perfect God and perfect man, composed of body and soul, begotten by the Father before the ages according to his divinity, the same who in these latter days, for our salvation, was begotten of Mary according to his humanity; the same one who is consubstantial to the Father according to divinity and consubstantial to us according to humanity": *Formula unionis inter S. Cyrillum ep. Alex. et episcopos Eccl. antiochenae: DS* 272.

62. "Hence, the proper character of each nature and substance was kept inviolate, and together they were united in one person. This was lowliness assumed by majesty, weakness by power [. . .]. In the full and perfect nature of true man, therefore, the true God was born—perfect in every characteristic proper to us as well as in every one proper to himself": *Ep.* Lectis dilectionis tuae *ad Flavianum*", 13 June 449: PL 54, 763Aff DS 392.

natures, without confusion, change, division or separation, the difference of
the two natures being in no way suppressed by their union, but the proper
nature of existence of each being safeguarded, while each nature is united with
the other in one person (*prosopon*) and in one subsistence (*hypostasis*) not
separated or divided among two persons (*prosopa*)."[63]

Clearly, the close union that exists in Christ should not be sought in the
idea of nature; it must come from something different, since the two natures
remain unchanged after the union. Jesus is not a subject who has emerged *from*
two subjects, but a subject existing in two natures: it is the subject, not the
natures, that confers the unity. The four famous adverbs (*asugchutos, atreptos,
adiairetos, achoristos*) try to achieve a balance between the distinction (without
confusion, without change) and the union (without division, without separation).[64] It is always beyond the human mind to grasp this balance, because it
has to do with the mystery of the Word made flesh. This is the ontological
aspect of the *Mediation* of the one and only Mediator, Christ Jesus. And so
Chalcedon points to this equilibrium in negative form—*without* confusion,
without change, *without* division, *without* separation. This negative form,
however, is at the service of the assertion of a union (the hypostatic union)
that is unique and ineffable. Anyway, the unity between the difference of
natures is given by the person, the *hypostasis*, the *prosopon*.

As pointed out in the Introduction to this book, the Councils (Nicea,
Ephesus, Chalcedon etc.) have been accused of *adapting* biblical teaching to
Greek philosophy by using "Greek philosophical notions of person and
nature"—a kind of hellenization of Christianity.[65] That is not in fact the case,
for the very reason that the words *nature* and *person*, in the formulae of the
Councils, are simply notions common to all genuine human knowledge. In fact,
in the formulation of faith concerning the mystery of Christ, the Councils had
to part company with Greek philosophy, because the latter could not accept a
human nature which did not constitute at the same time a corresponding human
person. It was Nestorianism that stayed fixed in that philosophy, by asserting

---

63. DS 301-2.
64. As Sesboüé writes: "duality is depicted in Christ by the expression *in two natures*. The
    Fathers debated at length on the term *in*, which some wanted to reduce to an *of* (*ex*). The
    preposition 'in' is very important and unfortunately it is very often forgotten. Chalcedon
    does not say: one hypostasis and two natures; it says: one Christ *in* two natures. So, his
    concrete unity remains complex and composed. There is something in his structure which
    resists total identity. Faith recognizes in him a real otherness, based on the otherness of
    God himself and man. In two natures means that the union of the Word to his humanity
    sets in place an otherness which is maintained . . . in the interior of the unity of one single
    subject": B. Sesboüé, *Jésus-Christ dans la tradition del'Eglise*, op. cit., 140-1.
65. In addition to A. von Harnack, cf., *Lehrbuch der Dogmengeschichte*, 5th edition (Tubingen,
    1931), p. 20, this thesis has also been defended by certain modern scholars who have parted
    company with the true faith of the Church (see a critique of their views in J. Galot, *Cristo
    contestato*, op. cit., 75ff).

that the human nature of Jesus also constituted a human person. The Monophysites, too, tried to hellenize Christianity, insofar as they also were anchored on the mistaken idea that an individual nature had to equal a person. On the contrary, "the painstaking elaboration of Christological dogma constructed by the Fathers and by the Councils always lead us back to the mystery of the one Christ, the Word who became incarnate for our salvation just as he is made known to us through Revelation."[66]

b) Being, person and nature according to St Thomas Aquinas The Church infallibly affirms that in Jesus there is one single human nature but not a human person. This immediately gives rise to the question: What was lacking to Jesus' human nature in order to constitute a human person? Or, to put it more generally: What is the constituent proper to the human person?; in ordinary human beings, what is it that makes a human nature a human person? These are still open questions, philosophically and theologically, because the Church Magisterium has not adopted any particular philosophy. Chalcedon, for example, uses a concept of person which it does not define metaphysically; to refer to the distinction in the unity of Christ it limits itself to appealing to universal human experience, which has always distinguished between the individual and its nature.[67] It used the concept of person basing itself on the universal and intuitive opinion with regard to the concept of *subject* as being the possessor of a nature. However, the concept and indeed the distinction between person and nature were laden with implications which philosophers and theologians would tease out over the course of the centuries.

Many different explanations have been put forward, varying with the philosophical positions taken. Certainly, like all theological speculation, exploring the mystery of Christ calls for a metaphysical and ontological perspective, given the subject in question. "Such a metaphysical (ontological) alignment of theology is not, as we have long feared, a betrayal of salvation history. On the contrary, if theology will remain true to its historical beginnings, to the salvation event in Christ to which the Bible bears witness, it must transcend history and speak ultimately to God himself."[68]

It is the Church's wish that theological teaching should follow the basic points in the thought of St Thomas Aquinas,[69] because on these points (in addition to his profundity) he is the author who is most clearly in line with the ordinary notions of person and nature used by the Church to define dogmatic truth concerning the mystery of Christ.[70] Naturally, this does not

66.   John Paul II, *Address*, 9 March 1988, no. 11: *Insegnamenti*, XI, 1 (1988) 598.
67.   A. Grillmeier, *Gesù il Cristo . . .*, op. cit., 969-81.
68.   J. Ratzinger, *Principles of Catholic Theology*, op. cit., 320.
69.   Cf. Second Vatican Council, Decr. *Optatam totius*, 16; Decl. *Gravissimum educationis*, 10.
70.   On continuity between spontaneous knowledge and philosophy, so that the latter may be a

mean restricting oneself to repeating St Thomas, but there is no getting away from the fact that for Christology (as for theology in general) metaphysical and ontological reflection "centred on the intuition of being in a Thomistic perspective is absolutely irreplaceable today".[71]

We will very briefly go over some points of this Thomistic perspective on being. In every single created thing there is a metaphysical composition of two basic elements—*essence* and *the act of being*. It is not a matter of two separable physical parts, but of two constituent metaphysical co-principles. *Essence* is that which in the singular thing makes it to be what it is (thus, the essence of an individual man is what makes him to be properly a man, and not something else); whereas the *act of being* (or simply *being*) is what makes a thing exist, makes it really be.[72]

By analogy: just as *running* is the act which makes the runner run, so *being* is the act which makes anything *be* or exist. Therefore, one can say that the act of being is what constitutes something in real existence. But this act of being (or simply being) is not existence: existence is the *fact* of being or existing, the *result* of having the *act* of being. Therefore, the act of being is not a formal act (a form), it does not have "formal content": it is the act of all the other (formal) acts, which makes them really be. To put it another way, "Thomist being expresses the fullness of the act which is possessed by essence (God) or which rests (*quiescit*) at the base of every being as the primordial participated energy which sustains it above nothingness."[73]

The concrete essence of something can also be called *nature*. In man this essence or nature is in turn made up of matter and spirit. In addition to essence and the act of being, there are what are called *accidents*, which are secondary modes of being in which the essence (the primary or fundamental mode of being) *is made to be this particular existing being*. So, in an individual man, his

valid instrument in theology, cf. C. Cardona, *Metafísica de la opción intelectual*, 2nd ed. (Madrid, 1973), 261-83.

71. John Paul II, *Address*, 10 December 1982: *Insegnamenti* V-3 (1982) 1572. As regards the contemporary relevance of St Thomas's Christology, see D. Ols, "Reflexions sur l'actualité de la christologie de Saint Thomas", DC 34 (1981) 58-71.

72. Here we shall simply refer briefly to the more important aspects, without going into the proof, which is a matter for metaphysics. We do point out, however, that on these matters (which only *seem* to be simple and elementary) not all St Thomas' followers are in agreement; in fact, for a considerable time now the originality of St Thomas thought on being as the act of being has been obscured; this has led to a certain essentialization of metaphysics with subsequent negative effects which have had much to do with the disdain for and ignorance of metaphysics in modern philosophical and theological spheres. C. Fabro has done very important work on this whole subject: see, particularly, his *La nozione metafisica di partecipazione* (Turin, 1950); *Partecipazione e causalità* (Turin, 1950); *Introduzione a San Tommaso* (Milan, 1983). For a synthesis of St Thomas' thought and method, the recent history of Thomism, the relevance of St Thomas in the response to the challenge of modern thought, see A. Livi, C. Fabro, F. Ocáriz, C. Vansteenkiste, *Le Ragioni del tomismo* (Milan, 1979).

73. C. Fabro, *Partecipazione e causalità*, op. cit., 40.

nature has many accidents, which are determinations, such as colour, a certain degree of wisdom in his mind, etc.

St Thomas will use basically the Boethian notion of person—*rationalis naturae individua substantia* (an individual substance of a rational nature),[74] which underlines what personality implies in terms of particularity and individuality as well as something which is inseparable from it—its intellectual character. The person is, then, a concrete individual, an active subject, master of and responsible for his own actions. "'Substance' as used in the definition of person stands for 'first substance', namely *hypostasis*. However, to add 'individual' is not superfluous. For what is excluded by the word *hypostasis* or 'primary substance' is both the idea of the universal and of the partial [. . .]; by adding 'individual' we rule out from the notion of person that which is taken up by another. Thus the human nature of Christ is not a person since it is taken up by a greater being, namely the Word of God."[75] And so, St Thomas will define person as "a complete substance subsisting of itself and separate from all else."[76]

The word *subsistence* becomes in this way a key concept for understanding the Thomistic notion of person. The person is a person because, being a complete substance, he subsists on his own, separate from other substances. The term *subsistence*, initially, was used as a synonym for *hypostasis*. It was, then, a concrete noun which meant subsistent being, a substance which exists on its own.[77] But even in St Thomas the word *subsistence* is often used abstractly, that is, as no longer meaning the concrete subsistent being in itself, but the reason or formality of that subsistence.[78] The question, then, of the metaphysical constituent of the person is identical with the question of how to interpret the notion of *subsistence*.

St Thomas does not directly pose the question of the formal constituent of the person. But his commentators do, trying to keep to the spirit of his

74. S. Boethius, *Liber de persona et de duabus naturis*, 3 (PL 64, 1343). Cf. A. Lobato, *La persona, I. Historia. Perspectiva metafísica* (Rome, 1973), 162ff; J.A. Sayés, *Jesucristo. Ser y Persona*, op. cit. 43-8.

75. St Thomas Aquinas, *STh* I, q. 29, a. 1, ad. 2.

76. *STh* III, q. 16, a. 12, ad 2. Richard of St Victor had already stressed that person is *naturae intellectualis incommunicabilis existentia*, the incommunicable existence of an intellectual nature, showing that *person* is what is most perfect on the level of being. All the Scholastics go along with this. And so *person* is defined as including within itself the dimension of completeness, wholeness, perfection, being-for-itself. That is, the concept of *person* implies unity, incommunicability, uniqueness, dignity. Cf. Richard of St Victor, *De Trinitate*, 4, 22, 24 (PL 196, 945-7); St Albert the Great, *In IV Sent.* III, dist. 5, a. 14; Alexander of Hales, *Summa Theologica*, I, inq. II, tract. un. q. II; cf. ibid, III, inq. un. tract I, q. IV, tit. II. Cf. E. Schiltz, "La notion de personne d'après St. Thomas", *ETL* 10 (1933) 409-26; U. Degl'Innocenti, *Il problema della persona nel pensiero di S. Tommaso* (Rome, 1967).

77. St Thomas uses it in this sense; cf. e.g. *STh* III, q. 2. a 3; q. 29, a. 2; *De potentia*, q. 9, a. 1.

78. *STh* III, q. 6, a. 3.

thought. All agree in affirming that person implies the *subsistence* of the complete nature.

From this angle, it becomes quite clear that human nature, and its accidents, equals person (that is, the whole man) when it has the act of being and through that act exists really. "From this metaphysical base, the consideration of the person leads on to other perspectives; in particular, to the phenomonological-psychological perspective, which grasps the personal character of a man whereby he is an *I* open to a *thou*; an I who attains his highest expression and grandeur in the relationship of knowing and loving the divine Thou."[79] The richness of *personal being* is not exhausted on the metaphysical level, but this level needs to be taken account of, particularly in Christology, because it is on this level that we can best grasp (to the limited degree that it is possible for us to understand a mystery) how Christ, while being a perfect man, is not a human person.

c) Being and person in Christ Every individual human nature constitutes a human person, unless the case occurred of a human nature which existed by virtue not of its proportionate act of being but by virtue of the being of another person. We could, of course, not even have imagined such a situation, if we had not known the mystery of Christ, whose human nature, though lacking nothing as such, is not a human person.

In fact, the human nature of Jesus is perfect, but it does not constitute a human person because it does not exist by virtue of a proper and proportionate act of being of its own, but by virtue of the divine being of the Word.[80] Of course, we must not confuse *esse ut actus essendi* (act of being) and *esse formale*. So whereas we do not predicate of Christ's human nature its own finite act of being, we certainly should predicate of it an *esse formale* of its own, that is, the *esse humanae naturae*.[81]

The fact that the Person of the Word is what makes the human nature of Jesus exist, without being thereby limited or circumscribed, is certainly a great

---

79. F. Ocáriz, "Dignidad personal, transcendencia e historicidad del hombre", in various authors, *Dios y el hombre*, op. cit., 178.

80. Cf. St Thomas Aquinas, *STh* III, q. 17, a. 3. However, elsewhere St Thomas is not totally clear, which is why Thomists have different views on this point. Specifically, he seems to have different things in two texts from almost the same period—the *Summa Theologiae* and the *Quaestio disputata de unione Verbi incarnati*. See A. Patfoort, *L'unité d'être dans le Christ d'après St Thomas* (Paris-Tournai, 1964); J.H. Nicolas, "L'unité d'être dans le Christ d'après St Thomas", RT 65 (1965) 229-60; J.I. Saranyana, "La doctrina sobre el 'esse' de Christo en los teólogos de la segunda mitad del siglo XIII", in *Cristo Hijo de Dios*, op. cit., 637-47; M.V. Leroy, "L'union selon l'hypostase d'après S. Thomas d'Aquin", RT 74 (1974) 205-43; A. Patfoort, "L'enseignement de Saint Thomas sur l'esse du Christ", in H. Bouessé and J.J. Latour, *Problèmes actuels de christologie* (Paris, 1965), 101-28. For a select bibliography of the debate on what St Thomas' thinking on this subject really was, cf. J.A. Sayés, *Jesucristo, ser y persona*, op. cit., 53.

81. St Thomas Aquinas, *De unione Verbi Incarnati*, a. 4, ad 1; *STh* III, q. 17, a. 2, ad 4.

mystery, but it is not something impossible to almighty God; and it does not mean that the divine being enters into composition with human nature (which would be a peculiar form of Monophysitism).[82]

On the other hand, it seems logical that the union between humanity and divinity in Christ would involve that, in some way, there should be *something* in common between the divine Person and the human nature: if that were not the case, we would not have Incarnation but simply an indwelling of God in man. This *something in common* is precisely divine Being which, however, does not form part of the human nature: it is the energy (act) which causes it to exist. Consequently, it is the Word who gives existence to the human nature of Jesus; that is, the humanity of Christ does not exist on its own (it is not subsistent), but rather exists in the divine Person. Therefore, the human nature of Christ is complete and perfect in itself and yet it is not a human person; because the subsistence which constitutes it as a person is really distinct from the nature. In Jesus, it is the Word who causes the human nature to subsist in himself.[83]

---

82. In his famous article "Actuation créee par l'Act incrée" (*RSR* 18 [1928] 253-68) De la Taille distinguishes between *actuation* and *information* to try to avoid confusion arising between the fact that the Word *actuates* the human nature of Christ and the unacceptable theory that the Godhead enters into a composition with human nature as *form* does with *matter*. "In this case," he writes, "actuation does take place, but without there being information in the sense defined. It is impossible for uncreated Act to depend on anything to do with any creature. It gives itself and receives nothing. So, there will be no material causality on the part of the creature and therefore there will not be formal causality strictly speaking on the part of (uncreated) Act . . .": art. cit., 260. The point that De la Taille makes shows how thorny this question is (and it is one he does not solve). For, to say that there is "no formal causality strictly speaking" means that there is formal causality *loosely speaking*. Grillmeier is justified in calling this causality *quasi-formal* (*L'Image du Christ dans la theologie d'aujourdui*, op. cit., 108) and J.H. Nicolas (cf. *Synthèse Dogmatique*, op. cit., 316f) has shown it to be a somewhat desperate attempt to solve this problem. For, either the *quasi* absorbs the *formal*, and then we find we cannot talk about *actuation*, or the *formal* overpowers the *quasi* and then we find that we have a genuine formal causality euphemistically termed *quasi-formal*. However, a more profound notion of *being as act* (distinct, therefore, from the *fact* of existing or existence) does not raise this problem of a *quasi-formal* causality, because the act of being is not a form.

83. Capreolus understands *subsistence* as belonging to the sphere of *esse*, or the act of being: "The suppositum is the same as the substantial individual which has *esse per se*" (*In IV Sent.*, 1. III, d. 5, q. 3, a. 3). This allows *person* to be defined as rational nature insofar as it is under its own being (*ut est sub suo esse*). Therefore, according to Capreolus, precisely because the Word makes the human nature subsist in his own act of being and not in that which would belong to the human nature, the latter is not a human person but is, rather, the human nature of the Word, that is, it is hypostasized in the person of the Word. And so, according to Capreolus, it is existence by itself alone that causes something to subsist and that constitutes nature as a person. In the Incarnation, Christ's human nature is not a person, because it has does not have existence of its own but exists with the existence of the Word: cf. G. Fraile, "El constitutivo formal de la persona humana según Capreolo", CT 67 (1944) 129-99; F.P. Muniz, "El constitutivo formal de la persona creada en la tradición tomista", CT, 68-9 (1945) 5-89; 70-1 (1946) 201-93; D. Quarello, "Il problema scolastico della persona nel Gaetano e nel Capreolo", DT, 55 (1952) 34-5. Capreolus' interpretation is close to the

The fact that Jesus' human nature has no *subsistence* of its own in no way diminishes its dignity, because it is more worthy to exist in something more noble than to have existence of one's own. Therefore, in fact, human nature enjoys greater excellence in Christ than in other men or women.[84]

All this helps us to a better (though always limited) understanding of the truth of faith which teaches that *the union* does not come about in the nature (that would be Monophysitism, which is something impossible because of God's absolute transcendence and immutability), nor is it an *accidental union* (which would be Nestorianism).

When the Athanasian Symbol affirms that *sicut anima rationalis et caro unus est homo, ita Deus et homo unus est Christus* (for as the rational soul and the body are one man, so God and man are one in Christ), the analogy is not meant in a full sense, since soul and body form, in man, a double unity (of nature and of person), whereas divinity and humanity form in Christ only a unity of person. Insofar as it is said that the unity in Christ is not accidental, it is worth noting that some Fathers sometimes used expressions like "putting on" a human nature, but this should not be taken to mean that they regard the union as accidental. Christ's human nature is compared to a garment or clothing, not to imply that there is an accidental union of the two natures, but to explain that Christ becomes visible through his human nature, as analogously a man expresses himself by his dress. And also because just as the dress changes, moulding itself to the shape of the person who wears it without that person changing his nature, so the Word has assumed humanity without undergoing any change as far as his divinity is concerned.[85]

If the union had been accidental, the Word would not have become man. It is important to remember also that to equiparate the hypostatic union to the union with God which results from his indwelling through grace, would be to deny the truth of the Incarnation because "for the Word of God to dwell in man it is not necessary for the Word of God to become incarnate. The Word of God and God himself dwelt in all the saints from the beginning of the world [. . .] and, nonetheless, this indwelling cannot be called incarnation; otherwise God would have become incarnate frequently from the beginning of the world. Nor is it sufficient to constitute incarnation that the Word of God or God should dwell in a man with more abundant grace because the greater or less (abundance) does not change the species of the union."[86]

Why is it that the human nature cannot be accidentally united to the Word?

---

one we have opted for, but its inadequate distinction between act of being and existence introduces an element of confusion.

84. Cf. St Thomas Aquinas, *STh* III, q. 2, a. 2, ad 2.
85. Cf. ibid., a. 6, ad 2.
86. St Thomas Aquinas, *Summa contra Gentes*, IV, c. 34.

Because the union which a *suppositum* has with its own nature is never accidental, because if it were accidental it would not *subsist* in it. Now, the Word subsists as man, since he truly is man. This (being man) is conferred on him by a substantial formal act, the nature assumed, an act which the accidents cannot communicate because it is beyond their proper sphere, that of accidental formal acts. The fact that Christ pre-exists from all eternity "does not imply that the human nature was united accidentally to him afterwards, for he assumed it in such a way that he is truly man. To be a man is a substantial mode of being. Since the hypostasis of the Word is man in virtue of the human nature, the latter did not come to him accidentally because accidents do not confer a substantial formal act."[87] In conclusion, the union occurred in the Person, leaving the natures not confused but united, precisely because they belong to the same person.[88]

When speaking of the Person of Christ, we cannot avoid referring to Trinitarian theology. The divine Person of Jesus is identical with the divine Nature and divine Being, but he is really distinct from the Person of the Father and the Person of the Holy Spirit insofar as they are opposed relations. This makes the mystery of Christ even more inaccessible to us. We are not dealing only with the Incarnation of the divine Being, but with the Incarnation of the sole Person of the Son of God, who is relation with the Father (one of the opposed relations mentioned above).

Whereas in the case of ordinary men the human person is not ontologically a relationship (although he has multiple relationships, with God, with other men, with the world); *in Christ the Person is the subsistent relationship* with the Father (Filiation). Therefore, Jesus' human nature, because it does not subsist in itself but exists through and in the Being of the Son, has no relationship of its own with the Father; rather, the whole Christ (God and man) is the natural Son of the Father.

Finally, it is useful to consider that Jesus' human nature is not impersonal: it has a personality, a divine one;[89] there can be no existing rational nature which is not a person, that is, which is not *hypostasised* in some subject. This is what Leontius of Byzantium shows when he says that what is proper to a person is to *be for himself*, in that independence with which he subsists in himself;[90] and he makes us see that the humanity of Christ is not *ahypostatic*

87. Ibid., c. 49.
88. Cf. St Thomas Aquinas, *STh* III, q. 2, aa. 1-3.
89. Cf. St Thomas Aquinas, *In III Sent.*, d. 5, q. 1, a. 3, ad 1; cf. A. Miralles, "Precisiones terminológicas en torno al misterio de Cristo sugeridas por la lectura de los Concilios I y III de Constantinopla", in *Cristo, Hijo de Dios . . .*, op. cit., 605.
90. He was the first to formulate the distinction between *hypostasized* (*enupostaton*) and *non-hypostasized* (*anupostaton*): Leontius of Byzantium, *Libri tres contra nestorianos et eutichianos*, I (PG 86, 1280 A); *Capita triginta contra Severum* (ibid., 1901-6); *Solutio argumentorum a Severo objectorum* (ibid., 1917 D). The *enhypostasized* nature, Michel comments, is not an *hypostasis*, because it does not exist in itself. Yet it is not an accident,

(that is, does not lack a subject in which it rests), but is *hypostasised* in the person of the Word.[91] The humanity of Christ lacks nothing, as regards human nature; it needs nothing for it to be able to be constituted a human person: it is a perfect humanity. If God were to substitute the direct activity of his Being on the humanity of Jesus with a created act of being, the hypostatic union would be interrupted and the human nature of Jesus would begin to constitute a human person.[92] Of course, that will never happen, but the idea helps us understand better that, although he is not a human person, Jesus is complete and perfect man.

This way of looking at the hypostatic union has clear advantages: it underlines the ontological unity of Christ, and, therefore, it explains why the Word is the subject of the actions of Jesus' human nature, that is, why the actions of his human nature are actions of the Word, who is the subject responsible for them.[93]

Other ways of conceiving the hypostatic union give less emphasis to this ontological unity. This is true of the positions held by Duns Scotus and by Typhanus, to mention the most outstanding writers who take an approach different to Aquinas'.[94]

because it is a nature, a substance. It would be more correct, therefore, to speak of "heterupostaton", hypostasized-in-another (A. Michel, "Hypostase", art. cit., 392).

91. According to Leontius, Christ's humanity is not ahypostatic, that is, it does not exist without a subject in which it resides, but neither is it *idiohypostatic*, that is, it is not sustained in itself, in a person of the same nature as itself. It is not sustained in a human person, but in a non-human person. Cf. Leontius Byzantium, *Adv. Nestorianos*, II, 10 (PG 86, 1, 1556 A).

92. "The human nature, while it is united to the Word and does not therefore, exist by itself, does not have a supposition or hypostasis of its own apart from the person of the Word. But if it were to be separated from the Word, it would have not only an hypostasis or suppositum of its own but also a person of its own given that it would then be existing by itself": St Thomas Aquinas, *De unione verbi incarnati*, a. 2, ad 10..

93. As it well known, among commentators on St Thomas and other Scholastic and Classical writers a variety of interpretations exist as regards the formal constituent of person and therefore on the hypostatic union. Thus Cajetan, who intially held the position of Capreolus referred to above (Cajetan, *De ente et essentia*, ch. 5, no. 84; *In I*, q. 3, a. 3-7), later placed the formal constituent of the hypostatic union in a *substantial mode*, that is, in something which modifies substance and confers *incommunicability* on it. The chief objection to Cajetan's position is that this *substantial mode*, which is nothing more than a termination, seems to be superfluous: cf. L. Billot, *De Verbo Incarnato* (Rome, 1927), 88. Nor does Cajetan have a sufficient grasp of being as *act*, distinct from the *fact* of being or existence.

94. For Duns Scotus what would formally constitute a person [referring to the human nature of Christ, to explain why it is not in fact a person: translators' note] lies in nothing other than a double negation—denying that it is assumed by a divine person, and denying that it can be assumed by a divine person [neither of these applies to the human nature of Christ and therefore it is not a person: translators' note]. What Scotus is really doing is pushing to its limits the feature of *incommunicability* to which Richard of St Victor had already given some standing. The main reason why he says this is that, by locating the formal constituent of person in a mere negation he avoids having to say that the human nature assumed by the Word lacks something positive (though only a substantial mode) which completes the perfection of other human beings, because he thinks that if Christ were to lack something

4. THE PSYCHOLOGICAL UNITY OF THE PERSON: CHRIST'S I

That Christ has two natures and one Person is an ontological fact (to do with being and the modes of being). As we know, the duality of natures brings with it duality of the spiritual activity of knowing and loving, while the unity of person means that all Jesus' activity, human as well as divine, is activity of the divine Person.

In the particular case of intellectual activity, the nature is the source of that knowledge, self-knowledge, which involves *psychological awareness* or *self-consciousness*, later expressed by the word "I". In fact the I is an expression of the entire Person; when we say "I", we are referring to our whole person; the fact that we know ourselves is what makes it possible for us to do this.

Looking at the duality of natures and intellects in Christ, one might expect him to have two I's (divine and human) because he has two self-consciousnesses (divine and human). And yet to the extent that the I is expressive of the Person, it would seem that because Jesus is only one Person, then he should have only one I.

positive which other human beings have in their nature, he would not be a man like us (D. Scotus, *In III Sent.*, d. 1, q. 1, no. 55ff, and d. 5, q. 2, nos. 4 and 5). The main objection to this position is that it seems contradictory to say that that which constitutes the most perfect being (which person is) consists in something negative (this is the criticism made by Cajetan and John of St Thomas: cf. Cajetan, *In III*, q. 4, a. 2, nos. 3, 13, 15; John of St Thomas, *Cursus philosophicus. Philosophia naturalis*, q. 7, a. 1). F. Suárez tries to find a middle way between Scotus and St Thomas. For one thing, he locates the metaphysical constituent of person in something positive (not negative as Scotus does)—a substantial mode which makes the human nature incommunicable. Christ's human nature is not a person, because it does not have this *substantial mode* which would make it incommunicable and, therefore, a person (F. Suárez, *Disp. Metaphys*, disp. 34, sect. 1-2, nos. 9ff; *De Incarnatione*, disp. 11, sect. 3). Suarez' position seems very similar to Cajetan's, but the different notion Suárez has about the distinction between essence and existence *vis-à-vis* Cajetan leads him to hold a position quite distinct from Cajetan's: cf. A. Michel, "Hypostase", art. cit., 418-21; and also J.I. Alcorta, *La teoría de los modos en Suarez* (Madrid, 1949); J. Solano, "De Verbo Incarnato", in *Sacrae Theologiae Summa*, III, Madrid, 1953, 42-53. One of the most serious objections to the Suarezian position is that, because for him *existence* is the ultimate actualization of substance, something which is added to the complete substance already constituted in being, can only do so as an accident, as something added on. But the hypostatic union cannot be conceived as something accidental (this is how L. Billot, op. cit., 90f argues). What lies at the root of these complications is inadequate metaphysical understanding of the act of being, and, in the case of Suárez, that essentialism which comes from denying the real distinction between being and essence.

Typhanus comes even closer to Scotus, although, for him, *subsistence* cannot be understood as something merely negative, but as something positive, because it confers that ultimate perfection which makes a complete nature a person. This perfection is substantial *totality* and *integrity* (C. Typhanus, *De hypostasi et persona*, Paris, 1880, chap. 23). Typhanus' problem lies in the fact that what he calls *totality* is completely the same as *incommunicability*, that is, *non*-assumption by another; or (as is the same thing) it is equivalent to something negative (which is Scotus' position). That is why many scholars see his position as being just a variant of Scotus': that is the view, e.g., of A. Michel, "Hypostase", art. cit., 414f; P. Galtier, *L'unité du Christ. Etre-Personne-Conscience* (Paris, 1939), 232.

We are here confronting the mystery of the psychology of Christ, which has only in recent times been studied by theology. Various theories have been put forward in this connexion.

To approach this aspect of the mystery of Christ correctly, one must never forget that he has a complete human nature, with its own activity, and one must also bear in mind the profundity of the hypostatic union. Also, it is very important not to confuse the Person with the I: the I in fact is not the Person; it is the expression of his self-consciousness. In an ordinary man, since the act of self-awareness is an intellectual act and he has only one intellect, there is only one I, and therefore the human person, when he says "I", is referring to himself. But as has just been pointed out, the fact that Christ has two intellects raises questions about whether he has one or two I's.

a) The theory of the "assumptus homo"   One of the best-known attempts to explain Jesus' psychology theologically is that of Déodat de Basly (+1937). Using as his base the completeness of Christ's human nature, he asserted that he has *two I's*—one divine (which, according to him, would be common to the three divine Persons) and the other human.

Christ, as man, would be the *assumptus homo* (assumed man), an expression Patristic in origin,[95] but taken in the sense that Jesus' humanity would constitute an individual human being distinct from the Word, though joined ontologically to Him in such a way that, while forming one person with the Word, Jesus' humanity would be in itself an autonomous subject, with the same autonomy as any human subject has. This autonomy would have a corresponding human I (not just the corresponding human consciousness of the I of Christ), as counterposed to divine consciousness.[96] Thus, Jesus, according to L. Seiller, a radical supporter of this theory, would have a genuine *human psychological personality*.

This does not expressly deny the defined teaching of the Church, but it

---

95. Cf., e.g., St Augustine, *De agone christiano*, 11 (PL 40, 297). Although the expression was originally quite valid, it was soon dropped because its meaning in practice moved dangerously towards Nestorianism: to say that Christ was an "assumed man" causes one to think in terms of a man already constituted in being which the Word then took over in a moral sense. "The word 'man'," Aquinas says, "signifies human nature in the concrete, inasmuch as it is in a suppositum; and therefore, just as we cannot say the suppositum was assumed, so we cannot say the man was assumed": *STh* III, q. 4, a. 3, ad 2.

96. Cf. Deodat de Basly, "Le Moi de Jésus-Christ", in *La France franciscainé* 12 (1929) 125-60; 325-52; "L'Assumptus Homo", ibid., 11 (1928) 265-313; "Inopérantes offensives contre l'Assumptus Homo", ibid., 17 (1934) 419-73; "Inopérantes offensives contre l'Assumptus Homo", *Supplèment à la France franciscaine* (Paris, 1935). See also H. Diepen, "La critique du baslisme selon Saint Thomas", RT 50 (1950), 82-118; 290-329; "La psychologie humaine du Christ selon Saint Thomas d'Aquin", RT 50 (1950) 515-62; "L'assumptus homo patristique", RT 63 (1963) 225-45; 363-88; 64 (1964) 32-52, 364-86. Cf. J.H. Nicolas, *Synthèse Dogmatique*, op. cit., 322-7.

does assert a psychological division of the Person, which is difficult to reconcile with the truth of faith concerning the unity of Christ.[97]

Really, this theory has as its basis the distinction between individual and person already rejected by St Thomas.[98] It conceives the hypostatic union as the union of two perfectly defined autonomies, that is, as the union of two autonomous individuals in a single person. What it tries to do is to point up the consistency of Jesus' humanity, but it does so at the cost of his unity. However much Déodat may say that there is unity of person in Christ, this insistence seems purely verbal, because the union of *two autonomous subjects* cannot be conceived in any way other than as a moral union.

This is clearly to be seen in the way in which Déodat applies *communication of properties* to Christ.[99] He accepts this predication only *in obliquo* (indirectly). This happens, for example, with the statement that Jesus is God. According to Déodat, this can be said of Jesus only *in obliquo*: Jesus the individual is God, because he is joined to the Word. The same happens with Mary's divine motherhood: she can be said to be Mother of God only in the sense that she is the Mother of an individual (Jesus) who is ineffably joined to the Word. This really amounts to saying that she is not the Mother of God, because the Word was not really born of her; only Jesus the individual was.[100]

Déodat's position is encapsulated in this statement: a creature, be it a body or a spirit, cannot enter into unity of being with the Absolute, that is, cannot subsist in the subsistence of the Word. As against the Thomistic unity of *esse*, Déodat de Basly presents what he calls "deifying subjunction" as a guarantee of the perfect transcendence of God and the perfect autonomy of the assumed man. The assumed man is, according to Déodat, perfectly autonomous as an agent, in such a way that the Word exercises no influence on his activity.[101] In this way he tries to defend the humanity of Christ; but what he in fact does,

---

97. For this reason L. Seiller's article, "La psychologie humaine du Christ et l'unité de persone", FS 31 (1949) 49-76, 246-74, was put in the Index of prohibited books issued by the Holy See; cf. AAS 43 (1951) 4-12.

98. "Some conceded one person in Christ, but maintained two hypostases in him or two supposita, because according to them, a man, composed of body and soul, was assumed by the Word from the beginning of his conception. And this is the first opinion set down by the Master of the Sentences. [. . .] Both of these opinions fall into the heresy of Nestorius, the first because to maintain two hypostases or supposita in Christ is the same as to maintain two persons. . . ." (*STh* III, q. 2, a. 6 in c.).

99. The subject of communication of properties is also dealt with further on at section 5c of this chapter.

100. Cf. J.H. Nicolas, *Synthèse Dogmatique*, op. cit., 325.

101. What Déodat really does is turn the classical teaching on its head. As against the notion that it is the person of the Word who acts through his humanity and therefore is the subject of attribution of his actions, Déodat's position is that what is really autonomous is Jesus' humanity, that is, that the centre of gravity of Christ's autonomy is the I of Christ's humanity, not the Word. Cf. A. Grillmeier, "L'image du Christ dans la théologie d'aujourdui", in various authors, *Questions théologiques d'aujourdui*, op. cit., II, 111-5.

by following this route, is to make Jesus an individual distinct from the Word.[102] The problem lies in that (apparently impossible) distinction between suppositum and person, already rejected by St Thomas. By saying that Christ's humanity has a suppositum distinct from the Word, what is really being said is that there are two persons in Christ. And, of course, it is impossible to conceive that actions over which he exercises no influence can be attributed to the Word. The Magisterium's rejection of the theory of Seiller (a follower of Déodat) shows that this extreme theology of a *Homo assumptus* is simply not viable.

In 1951, Pius XII, in the encyclical *Sempiternus Rex*, made the following point: "Although there is nothing to prevent Christ's humanity from being more profoundly studied, even by psychological methods, there are some who in difficult studies of this kind go unreasonably far from old ideas in order to introduce new ones and who make use of the authority and definitions of the Council of Chalcedon to support their views. These people put the special state and condition of Christ's human nature so much to the fore as to set it up almost as a *'subiectum sui iuris'*, as though it did not subsist in the Person of the Word himself. Now the Council of Chalcedon, in agreement with that of Ephesus, clearly lays down that both natures of our Redeemer come together 'in one person and subsistence' and forbids the positing of two individuals in Christ as if some autonomous *'homo assumptus'* were attached to the Word."[103]

This intervention by the Pope amounted to a rejection of the theory of the "*assumptus homo*" as Déodat de Basly understood the term. However, obviously it made no definition on the subject, which remains an open one from many other aspects.

b) **Theories concerning the I of Christ**   The Galtier-Parente debate in the 1950s on the I of Christ helped to explore this matter of Christ's self-consciousness. The debate hinged on the question of how to explain that Christ's humanity has the Word as its I.[104]

Galtier asserted that in Jesus, there are two I's as well as two intellects: divine and human; however, the human I of Christ (which expresses the selfconsciousness of his humanity) knows that it is not an expression of a human person; it is the human I of the divine Person, because from the moment of the Incarnation Jesus the man had the beatific vision (that is, the direct

---

102. As J.H. Nicolas writes, "Classical (and Catholic) theology in no way diminishes the truth of Christ's humanity. That humanity is concrete and living, subsistent, personalized, the agent and master of its actions. But the Person who exists and acts *through this nature is not someone distinct from the Word; he is* the Word" (*Synthèse Dogmatique*, op. cit., 326).

103. Pius XII, Enc. *Sempiternus Rex*, op. cit. (DS 3905).

104. A lucid summary of the debate is given in B. Xiberta, *El Yo de Jesucristo. Un conflicto entre dos cristologías* (Barcelona, 1954); cf. also M. Cuervo, "El Yo de Jesucristo", CT (1955) 123ff.

knowledge of the Godhead proper to cèlestial glory). According to Galtier, Jesus' human intellect would see in the divinity that it properly belonged to the Son of God.[105]

Parente, on the other hand, putting the emphasis on the hypostatic union, says that there is only one I in Christ: the divine I of the Word, which is known both by the divine intellect and by the human mind of Jesus. How can a human mind express divine selfconsciousness? According to Parente, this is made possible by the hypostatic union itself, and it is reinforced by the beatific union which Christ's human soul enjoyed.[106]

More recently, J. Galot has also argued that in Jesus there is only one I: the Person of Christ has a psychological unity corresponding to his ontological unity. But he differs from Parente in that he thinks that the divine I is known by the human mind and not through the hypostatic union solely, not through the beatific union, but through a particular mystical experience which God gave Jesus' humanity to cause him to know, for certain, that it was personally united to the Word; that it was the humanity of God.[107]

Without going into the details, all these theories certainly have things in their favour, but they also have points which are not so clear. At any event, Galtier's interpretation seems as though it should be left to one side, because it establishes a division in the Person (though only on the psychological level), which has no basis in the Gospels, where the use Jesus makes of the pronoun "I" seems to refer to a highly unitarian intimacy. It must however be said that Galtier's position, although it does stress the psychological autonomy of Christ's humanity, is quite different from those of Deodat and Seiller—precisely because it allows for only one *subsistence* in Christ.[108]

c) **Christ has only one I**   There are passages in the New Testament where we read that Jesus speaking as "I" expresses his personal unity as God-man. Take, for example, this prayer he makes: And now, Father, glorify thou me in thy own presence with the glory which I had with thee before the world was made" (Jn 17:5).

105. Cf. P. Galtier, *L'unité du Christ, Etre-Personne-conscience* (Paris, 1939), 350, 371; "La conscience humaine du Christ", Greg 32 (1951) 525-68 and Greg 35 (1954) 225-46.
106. Cf. P. Parente, *L'Io di Cristo*, 3rd ed. (Rovigo, 1981). In this edition the author provides a useful up-dating appendix (pp. 409-60).
107. Cf. J. Galot, *Chi sei tu, o Cristo?*, op. cit. 308-14; *La conscienza di Gesù* (Assisi, 1971), 136-51.
108. As Grillmeier notes, "the text of *Sempiternus Rex* published on 13 September 1951 in *L'Osservatore Romano*, said the following: *Hi humanae naturae statum et conditionem ita provehunt ut eadem saltem psychologice reputari videatur subjectum quoddam sui juris, quasi in ipsius Verbi persona non subsistat.* But in the official, definitive, edition the words *saltem psychologice* were suppressed. So the question of Christ's human consciousness is still open. All that has happened is that the old Nestorian theory of the two *ontological subjects* has been once again condemned": A. Grillmeier, *L'image du Christ dans la théologie d'aujourdui*, op. cit., II, 116 and 118).

There is no doubt that the *me* refers to Jesus in his humanity (because, in him, that was all that was yet to be glorified), and that the *I* refers to Jesus in his divinity (because he existed before the world began). Now, to say that the *me* and the *I* are not the same would be plain distortion of the text. The very words Jesus used (*I am*) point to his having one I—a divine one.[109]

It might be pointed out, moreover, that Paul VI, speaking about the Christological dogma defined by the first councils, said that in Jesus "there is but one Person, but one I, alive and operative in a double nature, human and divine."[110]

We do not know for certain how Christ's human mind, in the act of psychological consciousness, expresses the divine I of the Word. This aspect of the mystery of Jesus has not been revealed to us, and theology does not appear to have provided a satisfactory explanation. However, what seems more and more certain is that Christ has only one I—that psychological unity follows on from the ontological unity of his Person.

5. OTHER THEORIES ABOUT PERSON AND ITS REPERCUSSIONS IN CHRISTOLOGY

a) The Cartesian twist. Anton Günther and Antonio Rosmini   With the inversion given by Descartes to philosophical thinking, an entirely different perspective is also created on the concept of person. If "person" had previously been defined from the objective standpoint (substance, the act of being), from Descartes onwards the trend is to try to define it in terms of subjectivity—self-consciousness of the I, capacity to relate to a thou, openness to transcendence. It is certainly true that exploring all these aspects of person has led to a fuller understanding of the richness of human personality. But the problem arises when one forgets that rational nature is the substratum on which person is built and focuses one's attention on the person's spiritual actions as if these were the basis of personal being?[111] It can be said that "with Descartes a new concept of person begins to develop: it is no longer defined in terms of

109. Cf. A. Feuillet, "Les 'ego eimi' christologiques du quatrième évangile", art. cit., 221.
110. Paul VI, *Address*, 10 February 1971: *Insegnamenti di Paolo VI*, IX (1971) 100.
111. On the permanent value of the notions of person and nature and their decisive importance in Christology *vis-à-vis* the difficulties raised in modern philosophy, cf. John Paul II, *Address*, 13 April 1988: *Insegnamenti*, IX, 1 (1988) 877-80. This address is entitled, "Le definizioni christologiche dei Concilii e la fede della Chiesa d'oggi", and among other things it points out that in using the concepts of nature and person these Councils are simply penetrating more deeply into the mystery of unity and diversity in Christ. They do this by using "concepts and terms taken from ordinary language, which was the natural expression of people's way of knowing and thinking prior to any conceptualization devised by a philosophical or theological school. This search for understanding, this reflection and a desire to perfect terminology is found among the Fathers and would go on in succeeding centuries of the Church, when the terms used in Christology (particularly the term 'person') would be given greater depth and exactness (to the benefit even of progress in human

autonomy of being, but in terms of self-consciousness. Man has a guarantee of being himself, of really existing, of not being a pure dream, because he thinks on himself. *Cogito ergo sum!* (I think, therefore I am.) The I consists in self-consciousness. *This* is what makes man different.[112]

For Descartes the person is identical with the thinking I or, better said, the conscious I.[113] His anthropology leads him to place the essence of the person in the soul *qua* thinking being, without extension and in contradistinction to the body. Descartes still conceives the soul as something, as *res cogitans* (a thinking thing), as a substance having no extension. And so, initially, it is not easy to recognize the twist he gives to the concept of person—which came to have such an influence on most of modern and contemporary thought.

In the question that concerns us, the full effect of this twist will be seen more clearly when Locke argues that substance has no metaphysical reality and that therefore it makes no sense to speak of the soul as a substance. Now the I comes to be seen as mere awareness of one's identity, as demonstrated by memory or as a collection of internal phenomena, or as a series of sensations, or as the link between events, or as an ever-changing product of vital phenomena.[114]

Rationality, and therefore self-consciousness, always formed part of the definition of person—as can clearly be seen from the Boethian definition itself, *rationalis naturae individua substantia* (an individual substance of a rational nature). Self-consciousness forms part of the person, because in it is manifested the fullness of being in oneself, the self-possession of being. But the act of knowing shows the *quality* of self-possession, the perfection of the nature in which it is sustained, and not vice versa. That is why Boethius says that *praeter naturam non potest esse persona* (apart from nature there cannot be a person).[115]

> thought). But their meaning when applied to the articulation of revealed truth was not linked to or conditioned by particular authors or schools: it was something which could be gathered from the ordinary language of both the learned and the unlettered of every age." And, after pointing out that the modern mind should not be regarded as incapable of absorbing preaching of the truth regarding Jesus Christ, he says, "From this too it follows that it is possible for there to be a discourse well-grounded and loyal on the Christ of the Gospels and of history, formulated in the knowledge of the mystery, and therefore almost stammering—but this cannot happen without the clarity provided by concepts worked out with the help of the Holy Spirit and of the Fathers and passed on to us by the Church."

112. B. Mondin, "Il concetto di persona nella filosofia contemporanea", in *Incontri Culturali* 7 (1974) 176; cf. also his "La persona umana e il suo destino in San Tommaso e nel pensiero moderno", in *Aquin* 17 (1974) 366-402.

113. For Descartes, thought is "everything that happens within us in such a way that we immediately perceive it by ourselves. Therefore, not only to understand, to want, to imagine, but also to feel, is the same thing as to think": R. Descartes, *Les principes de la philosophie*, I, no. 9: cf. A. Bridoux, *Descartes. Oeuvres et Lettres* (Paris, 1952), 574. For a critical analysis of the Cartesian approach to philosophy, cf., e.g., C. Cardona, *René Descartes. Discurso del método* (Madrid, 1975).

114. Cf. A. Michel, "Hypostase", art. cit., 429-31.

115. S. Boethius, *De persona* . . ., op. cit., 2 (PL 64, 1342 C).

Anton Günther (+1863) was the first to try to incorporate this notion of person into Christology; he saw person as self-consciousnessness (*Selbstbewust-sein*).[116] This caused difficulties immediately. For, if what constitutes the person is its self-consciousness, and in Christ there are two intellects (human and divine), he must be given as many persons as intellects in order to be self-conscious; or, on the contrary, if one starts out from the position that he is only one person, one has to posit that, by some means or other, he has only one act of understanding. Günther is inclined towards a dynamic unity of consciousness in Christ, so that it would be this unity which brings about the hypostatic union. That is why his critics have put him close to Nestorianism.[117] Pius IX issued a general condemnation on the Günther approach to the hypostatic union, without specifying what its underlying defect was.[118]

A. Rosmini (+1855) raises similar difficulties with his idea that the I and openness to being are what constitutes the person. Rosmini starts out from the premise that the idea of being is innate. This idea is simply openness to objective Being, that is, to God. To put it another way, in the first intuition of being which every man has, he intuits something of the Word;[119] this already means

116. Günther writes: "Personality—is it anything other than self-awareness? And is this awareness not the essential form of the spirit? And can one speak of a genuine human nature that excludes this essential form, that is, enclosing in a corporeal wrapping a spirit reduced by half because it has no form": *Vorschule zur spekulativen Theologie*, II (Vienna, 1882), 260. So, self-consciousness is what gives form to the spirit, to the point of turning it into a subject. And a little further on, commenting on why he calls self-consciousness the *essential form* of the spirit, he writes: "In each person, one needs to distinguish essence and form. The first is the being in itself, substance-principle; the second is the thought this being thinks, when it has itself for its content. That is why self-consciousness is that whereby the being re-takes possession of itself, becomes a spiritual substance, an I" (ibid., 296). Cf. A. Michel, "Hypostase", art. cit., 431-2.

117. Cf. J. Kleutgen, *Die Theologie der Vorzeit*, III (Münster, 1870), 136-52; L. Orban, "Theologia Güntheriana et Concilium Vaticanum", *Analecta Gregoriana*, 50 (Rome, 1949), 2, 60-110; R. Garrigou-Lagrange, *De Verbo Incarnato* (Rome, 1946), 99-100; J. Solano, *De Verbo Incarnato*, op. cit., 33-4.

118. "We hold it to be quite clear that the things which are said (in the writings of Gunther) concerning the mystery of the Word incarnate and the unity of the divine person of the Word in the two natures, divine and human, are not better or more perceptive (than those said concerning the three divine Persons)"; Pius XII, *Eximiam tuam*, 15 June 1857, DS 2828.

119. Rosmini belongs among the ontologists, that is, those who conceive of God not only as the *primum ontologicum* but also as the *primum logicum*. Consequently, intuitive and confused knowledge of the divine being is prior to every other kind of human knowledge and, in turn, the openness to being which man has in his very first intuition of being is already openness to God, to the Word. This is plain to see in these propositions in the decree of the Holy Office *Post obitum* (14 December 1887), taken from his book *Teosofia*: "1. In the order of created things something divine manifests itself directly to the human understanding. . . . 4. That indeterminate being which, without doubt, is known to all understandings, is that something divine which is manifested to man in nature. . . . 5. The being (*esse*) which man sees must necessarily have something of the necessary, eternal Being (*Ens*) of the creating, determining and perfecting cause of all contingent beings

a real openness to divinity. In Christ this openness is such that it is identical with the Word. Here is how his thinking is described in proposition 27 of the Holy Office's condemnatory decree: "in the humanity of Christ the human will was so carried away by the Holy Spirit to adhere to the objective Being, that is, to the Word, that it yielded the control of the man totally to him, and the Word assumed it personally, thus uniting himself to human nature. Hence it is that the human will ceased to be personal in the man (in the case of Christ) and, even though it is a person in the case of the rest of men, in Christ it remains the nature."[120] The hypostatic union has been interpreted here in terms of action, not in terms of being; therefore, it will never be more than a moral union of wills (with the problems inherent in the Nestorian approach). In Günther and Rosmini we see a theological attempt to speak of the hypostatic union using the concept of person that results from the subjectivist twist given to philosophy. Their stabs at a new theory were open to misinterpretation, and they failed because they did not manage to explore adequately the relationship between being and consciousness.[121] The main reason they failed was because they proposed a concept of person that depended on its spiritual acts (knowing or loving), forgetting that these acts are not what make the person: they proceed from the already constituted person. Therefore, the union in Christ of the human and the divine, produces (in these theories) a union on the moral level, on the level of action, but not on the level of being and of substance. From this point of view, one could say that Christ is God (though it would be an abuse of language) because God *acts* in Christ in such a special way as to have *taken possession* of his human personality; it could not be said, however, that Christ *is* God with the full power of identity implied in the verb to *be*.

b) Karl Rahner's theory   In Rahner we find a further attempt to incorporate into theology the concept of self-consciousness as the nucleus of the notion of person. And, given that there is human consciousness in Christ, Rahner will speak of two centres of consciousness, the divine and the human, and therefore of two subjectivities. This might seem to locate Rahner as extending the route taken by Galtier. But, naturally, Rahner's approach is within the framework of his transcendental philosophy and of his entire theology.

His transcendental Christology, specifically, starts out from an anthropology in which man is seen "as the being who in the exercise of his intellect is characterized by a tendency towards the infinite which goes beyond the data of experience."[122] In this tendency towards the infinite, as an inalienable feature

(*entes*). . . . 7. The indeterminate being of intuition, the initial being, is something of the Word. . . ." (DS 3201, 3204, 3205, 3207).

120. Decr. *Post obitum*, op. cit. (DS 3227). The proposition is taken from Rosmini's *Introduzione del Vangelo secondo Giovanni commentata* (Turin, 1882), lec. 85.
121. Cf. W. Kasper, *Jesus the Christ*, op. cit., 243.
122. Cf. K. Rahner and W. Thüsing, *Cristología. Estudio teológico y exegético* (Madrid, 1975), 21. The words quoted are from J.A. Sayés, *Jesucristo, ser y persona*, op. cit., 81.

of the personal centre of consciousness, we find the Rahnerian concept of the person. The person is constituted by the *a priori* opening of human consciousness to being in general, an opening which is basically an opening to the infinite, that is, to God.[123] And going a stage further, he adds that this opening to God is an *obediential potency* to self-giving to God, an obediental potency to be fulfilled when God responds to this opening by communicating himself.[124]

In Christ, given that there are two centres of consciousness, there are two subjects—the divine and the human. Jesus' human subjectivity is distinct from that of the Word and, at the same time, precisely because in Him, in Jesus, there is a *total* openness to the infinite, this subjectivity can receive the total self-giving of God. "With regard to the Father", Rahner writes, "the man Jesus is situated in a unity of will which dominates *a priori* and totally his whole being and in an *obedience* from which derives his whole human reality. Jesus is, *par excellence*, the one who constantly receives his being from the Father and who lives surrendered to the Father always and without reserve in all the dimensions of his existence. In this surrender he can achieve from within God that which we could never ever achieve. Jesus is he whose *fundamental situation* is identical with his full and complete proceeding from God and with his total surrender to him."[125]

Consistent with his intention to import the modern concept of person into

123. Cf. J.A. Sayés, ibid. As one can see this chain of statements contains two inferences which are far from clear. Rahner infers that the openness to *being in general*, which characterizes the intellect according to classical thought on this subject, is the *same* as openness to the infinite. And he adds that this aprioristic openness to being is equivalent to openness to God. In a sense, this statement is close to Rosmini. On the Rahnerian concept of person, cf. also G. Lafont, *Peut-on connaître Dieu en Jésus-Christ?* (Paris, 1969), 198ff.

124. If earlier we said that Rahner seems to be going along the route opened by Galtier (two I's in Christ), it is worth noting here the problem raised by his concept of *obediential potency*. Now, the classics speak of obediential potency to show that God does not do impossible things, that is, that if God gives a grace to human nature it is because that nature is capable of receiving it, that is, has a capacity to be elevated by that grace. This is termed *obediential potency* to distinguish it from every other type of potentiality. *Obediential potency* is defined as *mere non-repugnance*, a definition designed to avoid its being conceived as something more, as a positive capacity, thereby forcing the theologian to admit that this capacity *ought* to be filled and, therefore, to prevent God's free gift from being seen as not absolutely gratuitous. When Rahner defines obediential potency as a *tendency to self-giving*, he must face up to two problems: 1. those of us who have not received the hypostatic union have not totally actualized our obediential potency, that is, our tendency to self-giving, and 2. Christ is not a man like us; rather he has realized the human ideal on a quite different level. "If one examines the notion of obediential potency used by Rahner," J.H. Nicolas writes, "this objection can be rigorously formulated. For him, obediential potency is something positive, a tendency to shed oneself for the benefit of the absolute God (in the ontological and not only in the moral sense), a readiness to go out of oneself [. . .]. It would seem more correct to say that obediential potency is the essence itself, considered not as a positive ordination to that act with respect to which it is said to be in potency, but rather as being able, without contradiction, to be actuated in this way by the omnipotent power of God": *Synthèse Dogmatique*, op. cit., 322f.

125. K. Rahner and W. Thüsing, *Cristología. Estudio teológico y exegético*, op. cit., 67.

theology, Rahner tries to show in Jesus an original unity of being and consciousness, which seems to be inspired by Plotinus' definition of God: Jesus is conscious of what he is, and he is what he is conscious of. That has to be what he means by such statements as: "the *man* Jesus is situated in a union of will which dominates *a priori* his entire being and in an *obedience* from which *derives his entire human reality*."

If this is taken rigorously, it means that it is the unity of will that so dominates Christ's being, that it actually constitutes it. This seems to be what he means when he says that his *human* reality derives from his obedience. It seems fair to say that "by positing two subjects, Rahner can only reach unity on the level of action. When two subjects are put facing one another, the union between them will simply be a union of action, a love-relationship, in which case we cannot say that Jesus is God."[126] In the last analysis, the same old problem arises: what makes the human person a person? His actions, or his being which is given to him together with his nature? In the case of the hypostatic union, one has to add, also, that it is the Word who takes upon himself—*assumes*—human nature, without human *obedience* being what the *entire human reality* of Jesus derives from.

It can be said that, from here on, what the scholar will find are more or less complex variants of this same problem and of some of the solutions already listed: how can it be that there are two natures and one person in Christ, if one starts out by defining "person" as "centre of consciousness". The Rahner example is typical of attempts made to incorporate into Christology the concept of person resulting from philosophy's plunge into subjectivity—and typical too of the questions those attempts leave unsolved and of the new doctrinal difficulties they raise.

c) "Non-Chalcedonian" Christologies   These very problems are the reason why some authors have tried to develop a Christology which marginalizes or contradicts the Council of Chalcedon definition (hence "non-Chalce-donian").[127] Thus, for example, for Schillebeeckx, Jesus is a human person, "for no one is man if he is not a human person."[128] Clearly Schillebeeckx's *a priori* is unjustified, because in fact human nature is not man unless it is a person; but the human nature of Christ is man, because it is a person; and it is a person because it subsists (is hypostatized) in the Person of the Word. It is then the Person of the Word that makes Jesus a man.

For Schillebeeckx, on the other hand, Jesus is a human person, a human person so full *of God* that we can say there is a *hypostatic identification* in him.

126. J.A. Sayés, *Jesucristo, ser y persona*, op. cit., 87.
127. On the impact of Rahner's thought on these Christologies, cf. J. Galot, *Cristo contestato*, op. cit., 101 and 153.
128. E. Schillebeeckx, *Jesús, la historia de un viviente* (Madrid, 1981), 615.

Schillebeeckx seems to have chosen his words carefully, to avoid ever having to make a clear assertion that Jesus is God. Jesus is a human being in whom the supreme revelation of God took place; but he goes no further than that. Here is an eloquent phrase from Schillebeeckx: "in the man Jesus the revelation of the divinity and the opening out of a true human being, good and genuinely different (really the supreme human possibility) overlap completely in one unique and identical person."[129] That is not to say that Jesus is God, or that he is the natural Son of God. All he is saying is that in the *one* person of Jesus the Godhead is revealed and the human opens up to the divine. Which simply means that Jesus is outstandingly holy—and that's all.

One can see why the Congregation for the Doctrine of the Faith felt (in 1972) called on to say, apropos mainly of the views of the non-Chalcedonians: "The opinions according to which it has not been revealed and made known to us that the Son of God subsists from all eternity in the mystery of the Godhead, distinct from the Father and the Holy Spirit, are in open conflict with this belief; likewise the opinions according to which the notion is to be abandoned of the one person of Jesus Christ begotten in his divinity of the Father before all the ages and begotten in his humanity of the Virgin Mary in time; and lastly the assertion that the humanity of Christ existed not as being assumed into the eternal person of the Son of God but existed rather of itself as a person, and therefore that the mystery of Jesus Christ consists only in the fact that God, in revealing himself, was present in the highest degree in the human person Jesus."[130]

To end this section, we can do no better than quote these words of Karl Adam from a book on that subject: "the multiplicity of theories by which theology has tried to approach the mystery of the incarnation is a fresh testimony to the truth that the incarnation is a *mysterium stricte dictum* (mystery in the strict sense) that cannot be solved, even after revelation."[131]

6. OTHER ASPECTS OF THE PERSONAL UNITY OF CHRIST

From the union without confusion of divine nature and human nature in the one Person of the Son of God incarnate, other important consequences arise in addition to the distinction of two wills and operations in Christ. These are worth considering in order to have a deeper knowledge of the mystery of Christ.[132] We shall look firstly at the unity of the filial relationship of Christ to the Father; that is, the unity of his divine sonship. We shall then go on to the relationship of men with Christ, that is, the one adoration due to Jesus.

---

129. E. Schillebeeckx, *En torno al problema de Jesús. Claves de una cristología* (Madrid, 1983), 174-5. On Schillebeeckx' explanation to the Congregation for the Doctrine of the Faith, cf. "Letter of SCDF to Fr. E. Schillebeeckx", 20 November 1980, in SCDF, *Documenta inde a Concilio Vaticano secundo expleto edita* (1966-85), (Rome, 1985), 194-202, and Cardinal Seper's note annexed.

130. SCDF, Decl. *Mysterium Filii Dei*, 21 February 1972, no. 3 (AAS, 64 [1972] 238).

131. K. Adam, *The Christ of Faith*, op. cit., 202.

132. Cf. L. Guillon, "La notion de conséquence de l'union hypostatique", Ang 15 (1938) 17-34.

Finally, we shall examine certain matters that the personal unity of Christ gives rise to in regard to human language about the mystery of the Incarnation.

a) Jesus' filial relationship to the Father   In the eighth century, in Spain, Migetius, proposed an erroneous (modalist-type) interpretation of the Trinity: God is *one* Person, who manifested himself as Father in David, as Son in Jesus and as the Holy Spirit in St Paul. Elipandus, archbishop of Toledo, and Felix, bishop of Urgel, defended the traditional teaching: the Son of God is a Person distinct from the Father, and Jesus, as God, is the natural and Only-begotten Son of the Father; but they went wrong when they said that Jesus himself, as man, is an adoptive son of God, like all just men are by virtue of grace.

This error is called Adoptionism (not to be confused with the original Adoptionism, defended by Theodore of Byzantium, Paul of Samosata and later, Photinus). It was condemned by Adrian I in 785, in a letter to the bishops of Spain, in which he said that this error was nothing but a form of the Nestorianism condemned by the Council of Ephesus. Adrian reaffirmed this in a letter (793) to the bishops of Spain and France, where the heresy had won some supporters. The true doctrine was also reaffirmed by provincial and other councils, particularly Ratisbon in 792, Frankfurt in 794 and Cividale (Friuli) in 796. Finally the Second Ecumenical Council of Lyons (1274) also reaffirmed that Jesus had only one form of divine filiation: "We believe in the very Son of God, the Word of God, eternally born of the Father, consubstantial, co-omnipotent, and in all things equal to the Father in his divinity, born in time of the Holy Spirit and the ever-Virgin Mary; having a rational soul; having two births, one an eternal birth from the Father, the other a temporal birth from his mother; true God and true man, proper and perfect in both natures. He is not the adopted son, nor an apparent son, but the one and only Son of God, in two natures and of two natures, that is, a divine nature and a human nature in the singleness of one person."[133]

Early, clear, evidence of this truth of faith is to be found in the New Testament. Thus, he who was born eternally of the Father and he who was born in time in the womb of the Blessed Virgin is called "Son of God, Son of the Most High" (cf. Lk 1:32-35), "beloved Son" of the Father (cf. Lk 3:22), his "own son" (cf. Rom 8:32). It is, then, perfectly clear that there are not two relationships of divine filiation in Jesus (one natural and one adoptive). Our Lord himself distinguishes between our adoptive filiation and his natural filiation when, for example, he says to Mary Magdalen: "Go to my brethren and say to them, I am ascending to my Father and your Father, to my God and your God" (Jn 20:17). But at the same time we can see from this passage that although Jesus is the Father's Son in a different way from that in which

133. Second Council of Lyons, 6 July 1274 (DS 852).

men are sons of God, the Father is the same in both cases;[134] in fact, the disciples' divine filiation is "a kind of participation in the filiation of the Word".[135]

The Fathers of the Church also speak of Jesus as being an only Son of God. For example, St Augustine said: "Reading Scripture, you will never find it said of Christ that he is Son of God by adoption."[136]

To say that Jesus is (even as man) the natural Son of God does not in any way mean that his humanity has a divine property (natural divine filiation): that would be a form of Monophysitism. For the very reason that it does not make him a human person, Jesus' human nature does not have any filiation, because filiation is a relationship of person to person.[137] It is the Only-begotten Son of God who has a human nature, and therefore this man (Christ as subject or Person) is God and eternal Son of God. For exactly the same reason, Mary is not only mother of a man but truly Mother of God, as the Council of Ephesus teaches. Being a son is something (a relationship) which belongs to the person, not to the nature.

To put it another way, as Adrian I declared, to say that Christ as man is an adoptive son of God would be the same as saying that his human nature constituted a human person—which would be Nestorianism.

b) **Man's relationship of adoration to Christ**   Adoration (or the cult of latria) is the act of rendering the greatest honour and respect to God on account of his infinite perfection and his transcendence over all created beings. It is therefore different from the mere veneration (or the cult of dulia) that is given saints, and it is also different from the cult of hyperdulia or maximum veneration due to the Blessed Virgin on account of her divine motherhood.

As will be remembered, Nestorius said that a dual honour was due to Jesus—adoration in the strict sense, to be given to Christ-God, and appropriate veneration to be given to Jesus-man.

In reproving the Nestorian heresy, the Council of Ephesus taught that Jesus should be worshipped through one, single form of worship.[138] Later, the Second Council of Constantinople (553) defined that "If any one say Christ is adored in two natures whereby two separate adorations are meant, one for the divine Word and one for the man; or in order to do away with the flesh, or

---

134. Cf. D. Spada, *L'uomo in faccia a Dio*, op. cit., 146.
135. Cf. St Thomas Aquinas, *In Ioan. Ev.*, c. I, lec. 8, II; *STh* III, q. 3, a. 5, obj. 2; *In Ep. ad Hebr*, c. II, lec. 3; etc. See also F. Ocáriz, *Hijos de Dios en Cristo*, op. cit., 93-111, 119-27.
136. St Augustine, *Contra Secundinum manichaeum*, 5 (PL 42, 581) and cf. his *Sermo* 214, 6 (PL 38, 1069); St Hilary of Poitiers, *De Trinitate*, 3, 11 (PL 10, 82). St Jerome, *In Epist. ad Ephesios*, 4, 9-10 (PL 26, 531); St Gregory Nazianzen, *Oratio* 37, 2 (PG 36, 285).
137. Cf. St Thomas Aquinas, *STh* III, q. 23, a. 4.
138. Cf. Council of Ephesus (DS 259); St Cyril of Alexandria, *Epist. I ad Nestorium* (PG 77, 18).

to fuse divinity and humanity, falsely speaks of one nature or substance of (the natures) which come together, and thus adores Christ, not adoring with *one adoration* the incarnate Word of God together with his flesh, as was handed down to the Church of God from the beginning, let such a one be anathema."[139]

It is important to note how this definition, by affirming that only one form of adoration is to be rendered to Jesus Christ, is excluding both dual worship (Nestorianism) and a mistaken idea (Monophysitism) of the reason for this one worship. It is also stressed that Christ's very flesh should be adored, not for its own sake or in the abstract, as if it were independent of the divine Person: it should be adored when the whole Christ is adored.[140]

Therefore, adoration is due to the Person with everything belonging to him—divinity and humanity. Christ's humanity, so, is adored insofar as it is God's humanity. As St Athanasius wrote, the reason for this undivided adoration due to Christ is that his flesh "became God's body".[141]

It is in this context that devotion to the Sacred Heart of Jesus, to his wounds etc. should be understood. Specifically, devotion to the Sacred Heart is not directed to his physical heart in itself considered as something independent of his hypostatic union with the divine Word; it is always borne in mind that the Heart of Christ is the heart of a divine Person, that is, of the Word incarnate and therefore, represents all the love God had and has for us.[142] In fact, "when Holy Scripture refers to the heart, it does not refer to some fleeting sentiment of joy or tears. By heart it means the personality which directs its whole being, soul and body, to what it considers its good, as Jesus himself indicated: 'for where your treasure is, there will your heart be also' (Mt 6:21). So when we talk about the heart of Jesus, we stress the certainty of God's love and the truth of his commitment to us."[143] This devotion asks man to put his heart into it when worshipping God, that is, to be involved personally, body and

139. Second Council of Constantinople, 2 June 533 (DS 431).
140. Cf. St Thomas Aquinas, *STh* III, q. 25, aa. 1-2; M. Schmaus, *Katholische Dogmatik*, op. cit., II, 2, 275.
141. St Athanasius, *Epist. ad Adelphium*, 3 (PG 26, 1073). Cf. Didymus, *Expositio in Psalmos*, 131, 7 (PG 39, 1589); St Epiphanius, *Ancoratus*, 51 (PG 43, 105); Pius VI, Bull *Auctorem fidei*, 28 August 1794 (DS 2661).
142. Cf. Pius XII, Enc. *Haurietis aquas*, 15 May 1956 (DS 3922-5). "The heart of Jesus, therefore, from the very moment of his Incarnation, has been and will always be united to the Person of the Word of God. Through the union of the Heart of Jesus to the Person of the Word of God we can say that, in Jesus, God loves humanly, suffers in a human manner and rejoices in a human way. And vice versa, in Jesus, human love, human suffering, and human glory acquire a divine intensity and power": John Paul II, *Address*, 9 July 1989, no. 2: *Insegnamenti*, XII, 2 (1989) 60-61. In this heart are found the sources of salvation: "Lifted high on the cross, Christ gave his life for us, so much did he love us. From his wounded side flowed blood and water, the fountain of sacramental life in the Church. To his open heart the Saviour invites all men, to drink in joy from the springs of salvation" (Roman Missal, Solemnity of the Sacred Heart, preface).
143. Blessed J. Escrivá de Balaguer, *Christ is passing by*, op. cit., no. 164.

soul: "when we recommend devotion to the Sacred Heart, we are recommending that we should give our whole self to Jesus, to the whole Jesus—our soul, our feelings and thoughts, our words and actions, our joys."[144]

c) Human language on the mystery of Christ   Among the many things that can be said about theological language, in Christology there is one of special importance which is a direct consequence of the Incarnation: the communicability and the reciprocal interchange of Christ's divine and human properties (*communicatio idiomatum*—exchange of properties—in the traditional phrase, taken from the Greek).

Because Jesus Christ is God and man, his Person can be spoken of in words which refer to each nature. He can be called Son of God, Word, God; but he can also be called Jesus of Nazareth, Son of David, etc. Therefore human attributes can be attributed to the Person, called by a divine name, and, vice versa, divine attributes can be attrituted to him, even when referring to him by a human name. For example, we can say that God died on the cross, that the Son of David is almighty, etc.

This has always been the practice; even the New Testament gives us examples of "exchange of properties". For example, when St Peter, addressing the Jews, said, "[You] killed the Author of life" (Acts 3:15), he was attributing something human (being killed) to Jesus, referred to through his divinity (Author of life). We can also find statements of this type on our Lord's lips: for example, when he tells Nicodemus that "No one has ascended into heaven but he who descended from heaven" (Jn 3:13); here Jesus is attributing something human (ascending to heaven) to himself, referred to through his divinity (descending from heaven). Cf. also Acts 20:28; Rom 8:32; 1 Cor 2:8; 1 Jn 3:16.

The Fathers, too, often speak in this way, especially when referring to Christ's passion as the suffering of God, so as to emphasize the value attaching to the passion and death of Jesus. St John Damascene (+ before 754) explained the basis for speaking in this way as follows: "Since the properties of his holy humanity are his, the Word claims these human properties for himself and causes the humanity to share his (divine) properties by a mutual exchange."[145] Before him, other Fathers had taught along the same lines (St Ambrose, St Augustine, St Cyril of Alexandria, etc.).

Exchange of properties must not be done arbitrarily but only in a way that respects the truth of the Incarnation. For example, while one can say (referring to Jesus) that "God has died", one cannot say that "divinity has died"; because Christ is God, it is true to say that God died; but since he died only in his

144. Ibid.
145. St John Damascene, *De fide orthodoxa*, 3, 3 (PG 94, 993).

humanity, it is wrong to say that divinity died (it cannot). Similarly, it is quite correct to say of Christ, "this man is God"; but it is heretical to say, "The Humanity of Christ is God."

Theology, reflecting on this Christological language, lays down exact rules for exchange of properties.[146] The main ones given by St Thomas[147] are:

(1) Concrete names of one nature and its properties may be predicated in Christ of the concrete names of the other nature and its properties, in affirmative but not in negative statements. For example, one can say (in relation to Christ) God is man and the man is God; the Almighty suffered. But one cannot say: the Son of God was not born (negative statement). This rule cannot be applied if the meaning is restricted with some reduplicative expression (one cannot say: Christ as man is God), or if the meaning is modified by some term or expression (one cannot say: Christ is man only).

(2) The abstract names of one nature cannot be predicated of the abstract names of the other nature and its properties. For example, it is false to say the deity is the humanity.

(3) The concrete names—of a nature and its properties—cannot normally be predicated of abstract things. So it cannot be said, for example: the deity is passible, the humanity is eternal, God is the humanity, the divinity is human.

(4) The abstract names of the divine nature can be predicated of the concrete names of the human nature because of a real identity even though the expression may not be grammatically correct. This applies to the statement: this man—Christ—is the deity, the Omnipotence etc.

(5) The abstract names of the human nature cannot be predicated of the concrete names of the divine nature. It is not lawful to say: the Son of God is the humanity.

(6) The adjectives of the divine nature cannot be predicated of the concrete names of the human nature, although the adjectives of the human nature can be predicated of the concrete names of the divine nature. For example, it cannot be said that Christ is a deified man since he is already God by essence. But it can be said that Christ is the Word humanized.

(7) Statements which express the *fieri* or beginning to be, applied to Christ, have to be used with great caution."

So, the proposition *God became man* is true; the proposition *Man became God* is ambiguous (it can be right or wrong, depending on how you understand it). The statement "*This man* [Christ] began *to exist*" is false because *this man* refers to the Person, who is eternal.

More important than learning these rules (which are easy to forget) the

---

146. Leontius of Byzantium, in the sixth century, seems to have been the first to have laid down these rules; cf. V. Grumel, "Léonce de Byzance", DTC IX, 416-8.

147. Cf. St Thomas Aquinas, *STh* III, q. 16; cf. M. Cuervo, "Introducción a la cuestión 16", in *Suma Teológica*, XI (Madrid, 1960), 580-3.

point to always bear in mind when speaking about the mystery of Christ is the reality of the hypostatic union as defined by the Council of Chalcedon. This helps one see immediately that it would be wrong to say, "The Son of God did not die" and (on the contrary), it is quite correct to say, "The Son of God insofar as he is God did not die", etc.

As one can readily see, exchange of properties is not a marginal or unimportant question, because it helps to articulate our faith concerning the mystery of Christ, whereas if we did not try to get the terminology right we could easily distort revealed truth.

CHAPTER FOUR

Christ: Way, Truth and Life

"God who 'wills that all men be saved and come to the knowledge of the truth' (1 Tim 2:4), 'who in many times and various ways spoke of old to the fathers through the prophets' (Heb 1:1), when the fullness of time had come sent his Son, the Word made flesh, anointed by the Holy Spirit, to preach the Gospel to the poor, to heal the contrite of heart (cf. Is 61:1; Lk 4:18), to be a bodily and spiritual medicine (cf. St Ignatius of Antioch: *Ad Ephesios*, 7:2)—the Mediator between God and man (cf. 1 Tim 2:5). For his humanity united with the Person of the Word was the instrument of our salvation."[1]

Our Lord works our salvation; in fact, he *is* our salvation. He is "the way, and the truth, and the life" (Jn 14:6). It is perfectly true to say that Christ is the way, because not only is he the way to God, he is also the goal, because he himself is God; he is the way to life, because he is Life: "Christ described himself as the way united to its terminating point, because he is the termination, which contains in itself all that can be desired, that is to say, subsistent Truth and Life."[2] Salvation comes to us through incorporation into Christ, through our participating in the mysteries of his life, becoming intimately attached to him, the way parts of the body participate in the life of the head. As St Paul wrote, "We were buried therefore with him by baptism into death, so that as Christ was raised from the dead by the glory of the Father, we too might walk in newness of life. For if we have been united with him in a death like his, we shall certainly be united with him in a resurrection like his" (Rom 6:4-5).

For the very reason that Christ is Life, he saves us by incorporating us into himself, passing on his life to us, as the vine does to the branches (cf. Jn 15:1-8). It is not just his example or his teaching which lead us to salvation; what makes us "a new creation" (cf. 2 Cor 5:17), is his very life that he communicates to us. This is something we should keep very much in mind in these chapters on the personal mystery of Christ and on his redemptive work, for Jesus saves us through the very events of his life, particularly his death and resurrection. This is beautifully put by St Bernard: "not only will I give you my conception, Jesus replies to me, but also my life and that in all the degrees of age, of infancy, of childhood, of adolescence and of youth; I will give you everything, he goes on, giving you my death as well, my resurrection, my ascension and the coming of the Holy Spirit. And all this so that my conception may purify

1. Second Vatican Council, Const. *Sacrosanctum Concilium*, 5.
2. St Thomas Aquinas, *Super ev. S. Joannis lectura*, 14, 3.

yours, my life instruct yours, my death destroy yours, my resurrection precede yours. . . ."[3]

We must not settle for (seriously reductive) approaches which limit Christ's work (Christ's contribution to mankind) to his preaching or his example, ignoring the redemptive value of his death and resurrection, or the salvific causality of his humanity operating through the sacraments. This mistake was made, for example, by the Gnostics of the first centuries. They were the first to reduce Christ's role in salvation to being a mere revealer, someone who simply "alerted" the Gnostic; the latter would save himself through self-awareness.[4] This approach appears again and again over the course of history, whenever Gnosticism raises its head.

The Pelagians arrived at a similar notion by a different route: by not accepting that original sin was passed on from one generation to the next and by defending the idea that man could, on his own, defeat the evil tendencies in his own heart, they really reduced Christ's work to good example. The same happened in the case of Abelard: he held that the Word took on our nature in order to show us how to live a virtuous life. According to Socinus, who denied that Christ was God, Jesus saves us simply by setting us an example and interceding for us in heaven. Liberal Protestants (Ritschl, Sabatier, Harnack) had a similar theory; they too, did not accept that Christ was God; all he did was set us an example that encourages us to love God and detest sin.

However, the work of Christ is much wider than the holy "model" of his life; it covers everything. Our Lord not only enlightens minds by preaching the truth and attracting us by the wonderful example of his life: he redeems us by atoning for our sins, healing our hearts with his grace and sanctifying us by his power. He glorifies his saints.

By giving us his Son, "in whom are hid all treasures of wisdom and knowledge" (Col 2:3), God has given us everything: he has given us the Truth, the Way and the Life. Christ's work, then, is so rich and all-embracing that it re-creates us. That is why the notion of Christ the Mediator is such a key idea in both Christology and soteriology. In fact, both Christology and soteriology can be synthesized perfectly in terms of mediation, that is, by considering Christ *qua* mediator and by examining the various aspects of his mediation.

We can see this in the title given to this chapter—"Christ: Way, Truth

3. St Bernard, *Sermones de tiempo*, 2, 8.
4. The Gnostic finds *within himself* the stuff of his own salvation, and he cannot but find it, because he is born with it. Hence salvation reaches him *in* and *through* gnosis, not through the saviour; the saviour is only someone secondary, only the bearer of a salvific message, but is not he who really saves. One can see how, in those movements, worship of the word is on a higher plane than worship of Christ; they take very little interest in the fact that Christ was really part of our history—hence their lack of appreciation of the visible Church and of the sacraments (cf. E. Cornelis, "Gnosticisme", DSp VI, 533).

and Life." These three words taken from John 14:6 express not only Christ's mediation but also the unique and particular manner in which he exercised that mediation. It is not the kind of mediation that would correspond to an intermediate entity positioned between two extremes (like a step, which leads one to the top when one goes beyond it); it is the mediation exercised by one who, being perfect God and perfect man, unites God and man in himself. It follows that Christ's mediation is entirely a function of his being. Mediator and mediation are, consequently, inseparable: it is his ontological make-up that constitutes Christ a mediator and, at the same time, mediation necessarily follows from and is dependent on his divine-human reality.

We begin this chapter with a brief study of the features and ontological basis of Christ's mediation and then go on to analyze in more detail the ministeries through which the Mediator exercises his mediation: we study Christ as King and Shepherd, as Prophet and Teacher, and as Priest. We also examine two hightly important matters—Christ's knowledge and holiness. In other treatises these matters are studied in the context of the human perfections assumed by the Word when he became man, and are thus viewed in an ontological and static context;[4a] here knowledge and holiness are more directly related to the ministeries of the Mediator and therefore are examined from a dynamic viewpoint, that is, in their relationship to Christ insofar as he exercised his mediation by being Way, Truth and Life. The chapter ends by studying the ascending and descending aspects of Christ's mediation.

1. CHRIST, MEDIATOR BETWEEN GOD AND MEN

"There is only one God, and there is one mediator between God and men, the man Christ Jesus" (1 Tim 2:5; cf. Gal 3:19-20; Heb 8:6). When referring to Christ's mediation, the Magisterium of the Church has often cited these words of St Paul, either explicitly or implicitly—for example, in the *Dogmatic Letter* of St Leo to Flavian (449), at the Council of Florence (1442), at the Council of Trent (*Decree on Original Sin*, 1546),[5] and a number of times in the documents of Vatican II.

A mediator is one who brings about union between people who are separated from one another. In a sense there is no separation between God and men, because God's presence in man is so intimate that (as St Paul says) "in him we live and move and have our being" (Acts 17:28). But, in another sense, sin

---

4a. This is, for example, the way St Thomas structures them as he begins to discuss Christ's holiness: "It is now time to consider these things assumed by the Son of God in the human nature by way of concomitance. First, those things which affect the perfection must be considered and then those which affect the defectibilty. With regard to the former here are three points (for consideration): first, the grace of Christ, second, his knowledge and, finally, his power": *STh*, III, q. 7.

5. Cf. DS 293, 1347, 1513; see also John Paul II, Enc. *Redemptor hominis*, op. cit., 8.

completely cuts man off from that intimacy with God to which he was raised by grace. God could have restored this union in a direct way, without the intervention of a mediator, but he chose to repair the damage done by sin and re-establish man as a son of God, through the incarnation of his Only-begotten Son. Therefore, "there is no other name under heaven given among men by which we must be saved" (Acts 4:12).

Christ in fact said that he was the only mediator between God and men: "No one comes to the Father, but by me" (Jn 14:6). Jesus, therefore, is not only the Pontifex (the bridge-builder between God and men): he is the Bridge itself;[6] a bridge which is, at the same time, the goal of the journey; he is not only the way to the new life: he himself is our new life; just as he is not only the Master who teaches us the truth: he is Truth itself: "I am the way, and the truth, and the life" (Jn 14:6).

This shows how perfect Christ's mediation is, for it is the *most direct mediation possible*. "In Christ the mediator, God is immediately present to us. Christ reveals himself as the true mediator precisely by the fact that he leads to immediacy, or, rather, that he is himself that immediacy."[7]

The fact that Jesus is the only mediator between God and men does not mean that there are no other subordinate mediators. In fact, the angels, the saints, and, above all, Mary, cooperate with Christ in leading men to union with God. And, indeed, any Christian in this world can and should be a mediator between God and other men, because all Christians are called to identify themselves with Christ the Redeemer: "our Christian vocation, this calling which our Lord makes to each of us personally, leads us to become identified with him. But we should not forget that he came on earth to redeem everyone."[8] Therefore, every Christian can and should cooperate with Christ in his work of uniting men to God. Also, those Christians who have received priestly ordination are, in a particular way, mediators between God and men. But all these types of mediation exist as a participation in the unique mediation of Christ Jesus.

Christ's mediation is grounded on the hypostatic union. The Fathers of the Church teach in various ways that Jesus is able to bring about reconciliation of men with God *because* he is God and man. "Just as he is united to the Father and the Father is united to him by identity of nature, so we are united to him and he to us because he became man. Through him, as mediator, we are united to the Father."[9]

---

6. Cf. M. Schmaus, *Katholische Dogmatik*, op. cit., vol. II/2, 281.
7. J. Ratzinger, *Principles of Catholic Theology*, op. cit., 272.
8. Blessed J. Escrivá de Balaguer, *Friends of God* (Dublin, 1982), no. 259.
9. St Cyril of Alexandria, *In Ioannem*, 6 (PG 73, 1045); cf. St Augustine, *Sermo 47*, 21 (PL 38, 310); St John Chrysostom, *Homiliae in Epist. I ad Timotheum*, 7, 2 (PG 62, 536-7); St Epiphanius, *Ancoratus*, 44 (PG 43, 97).

To put it another way, Jesus Christ is the mediator between God and men because he is God and man, but he mediates through his humanity. It is not his divinity but his human nature (because it is united to God in the Person of the Word) that stands in the middle, as the bridge linking God and man. And so, St Paul says, in the passage quoted, that there is only one mediator between God and men—the man Christ Jesus (cf. 1 Tim 2:5). As St Augustine explains, "between the Trinity and the weakness of man with his iniquity, a man was made mediator, not iniquitous but weak so that through his non-iniquity he should unite you with God and through his weakness draw close to you, and so, to be mediator between man and God, the Word became flesh."[10] That is to say, Jesus' humanity is also in the middle (between men and God) insofar as, in addition to its union *secundum personam* (in regard to person) with the Godhead, in itself it has no need for reconciliation with God, because in it there is no sin.[11]

Christ's mediation, therefore, is effected through his human actions, which, because they are human actions of God, have a salvific value for men.[12]

Christ's mediation operates in two directions—*upwards*, insofar as he offers God worship, thanksgiving, expiation of sins and prayer on behalf of men; and *downwards*, insofar as Jesus himself causes all the divine gifts, all the graces of salvation, to reach men.

We can also distinguish in Jesus' mediation what are called the three *munera Christi*—three basic dimensions which can be glimpsed in Christ's words when he says, "I am the way, and the truth, and the life" (Jn 14:6). They are the pastoral (or royal), prophetic (or teaching) and priestly offices of Christ.[13] So, "God has spoken to us by a Son, whom he appointed the heir of all things" (cf. Heb 1:2), to make him Teacher, King and Priest of all, the Head of the new and all-embracing people of the family of God.[14] These three roles are not separate functions; rather, they are expressions or, better, fruits, of one and the same root, the Incarnation. In his each and every action and word, Christ exercises his Teaching Authority, his Priesthood and his Kingship; but each of these aspects is expressed in a special way at particular moments during Jesus' life.

2. CHRIST, KING AND SHEPHERD

The Church affirms its belief that "of his [Christ's] kingdom there will be no end,"[15] thereby repeating the announcement made to Mary: "He will be called

10. St Augustine, *Enarrationes in Psalmos*, 29, 1 (PG 36, 216).
11. Cf. St Thomas Aquinas, *In III Sent.*, d.19, q.1, a.5, sol. 2 ad 1.
12. Cf. St Thomas Aquinas, *STh* III, q.26, aa.1-2.
13. Cf. C. Spicq, "Mediación, DTB, 629-30.
14. Cf. Second Vatican Council, Const. *Lumen gentium*, 13.

the Son of the Most High; and the Lord God will give to him the throne of his father David, and he will reign over the house of Jacob forever; and of his kingdom there will be no end" (Lk 1:32-33). Many liturgical texts also manifest the Church's belief in our Lord's sovereignty—the Advent antiphons *O Rex gentium* and *O Emmanuel, rex et legifer noster*; the office and Mass of Christ the King, established by Pius XI in the encyclical *Quas primas* (11 November 1925), etc.

The kingly divinity of Christ was already proclaimed in the Old Testament (cf. Ps 2:6; Is 9:6; 11:1-9; Dan 7:14; Mic 4:7; etc.) and equiparated to the status of Shepherd of the people, a people who are regarded as his flock (cf. Is 4:9-11; Ps 78:52; Mic 2:12-13; Jer 3:15; etc.).

Jesus' contemporaries were familiar with the idea of the Messiah as King. For example, the Magi on their arrival in Jerusalem asked, "Where is he who has been born the king of the Jews" (Mt 2:2); and Nathaniel, recognizing Jesus as the Messiah, says, "Rabbi, you are the Son of God! You are the King of Israel!" (Jn 1:49).

In fact, it was precisely because so many Jews had such a material and earthbound idea of the messianic Kingdom, that Jesus did not make much reference to his kingship; for example, when the people in their amazement over the multiplication of the loaves, wanted to proclaim him king, he "withdrew from them" (cf. Jn 6:15).[16] But at a particularly solemn juncture, replying to Pilate's question, he affirmed, "You say that I am a king" (Jn 18:37). In the New Testament we find many other evidences of Christ's kingship, especially in the statement that Christ is the Lord (cf. Acts 2:36; Phil 2:11; Rom 10:9; 1 Cor 12:3; etc.). Finally, St John, in the Book of Revelation, sees Jesus in glory wearing a robe of royalty: "On his robe and on his thigh he has a name inscribed, King of kings and Lord of lords" (Rev 19:16).

a) **The nature of Christ's kingship**   To say that Jesus is King is not to use a metaphor or attribute a mere title of honour. Christ's kingship is a fact, deriving from his being God-Man. "His kingship is based on that marvellous union called 'hypostatic'."[17] He is also King by acquired right, that is, by virtue of the Redemption: "Christ is our King by acquired, as well as by natural right, for he is our Redeemer."[18] We have been bought at a great price (cf. 1 Cor 6:20), "not with perishable things such as silver or gold, but with the precious blood of Christ, like that of a lamb without blemish or spot" (1 Pet 1:18-19).

Christ exercises his royal function in the establishing of his kingdom through actions proper to the Lord—gathering his people together and establishing the

15. First Council of Constantinople, *Symbolum* (DS 150).
16. Cf. St Augustine, *In Ioannis Evangelium*, tract. XXV, 2 (PL 35, 1596-7).
17. Pius XI, Enc. *Quas primas*, 11 December 1925 (DS 3676).
18. Ibid., AAS 17 (1925), p. 599.

laws of the kingdom, whose supreme judge he declares himself to be. In fact, it is a matter of defined faith that Christ is our Lawgiver: "If anyone should say that Christ Jesus was given by God to men as a redeemer in whom to trust and not also a legislator to obey—anathema sit."[19] The Gospels tell us that Christ laid down laws—for example, in the Sermon on the Mount; by instituting the Church and the sacraments; and by promulgating the New Law of love (cf. Jn 13:34-35). He is the "new lawgiver" who abrogated the Mosaic law and established an "eternal law and a new testament".[20] It is also a matter of faith that Christ is our Judge: "He shall come to judge the living and dead."[21] He himself taught that "the Father judges no one, but has given all judgment to the Son" (Jn 5:22), and he ordered the Apostles "to preach to the people, and to testify that he is the one ordained by God to be judge of the living and the dead" (Acts 10:42). "In this power is included the right of rewarding and punishing all men living, for this right is inseparable from that of judging. Executive power too, belongs to Christ, for all must obey his commands; none may escape them, nor the sanctions he has imposed."[22]

Christ is, then, Judge, Lawgiver and Lord (cf. Is 33:22). But this power of judging should not be seen as something marginal to the salvific will of God: "since the power of judgment is profoundly united to the will to salvation, as can be inferred from the Gospel, it is a new revelation of the God of the Alliance *who comes* towards men as the Immanuel, to *free us from the slavery* of evil. It is the Christian revelation of the God who is Love."[23] Jesus does not come as a new King to an already existing kingdom; he establishes his Kingdom himself. "does that mean, then, that he who feared to be proclaimed king was not a king already? Yes, he was, but not a king proclaimed by men; rather, he was the king who had granted a kingdom to men."[24] In fact, Christ begins his preaching by proclaiming the arrival of the Kingdom of God (cf. Mk 1:15), and "brings about the kingdom of God throughout the whole development of his mission so that the kingdom is born and expands here in time, as a seed sown in the history of man and of the world. This bringing the kingdom into being is done through the word of the Gospel and the whole earthly life of the Son of man which had its crowning moment in the paschal mystery of the Cross and Resurrection."[25]

This Kingdom, which is the Kingdom of God, is a Kingdom which "*is not from the world*" (Jn 18:36); a Kingdom which is "the kingdom of heaven" (cf.

---

19. Council of Trent, Decr. *De iustificatione*, c.21 (DS 1571).
20. St Justin, *Dial. cum Triphone Iudeo*, 18, 43 (PG 6, 515 and 567).
21. Apostle's Creed (DS 12).
22. Pius XI, Enc. *Quas primas*, op. cit., p. 599; cf. the announcement of the last judgment in which Christ depicts himself as Judge (Mt 25:31ff).
23. John Paul II, *Address*, 30 September 1987, 8: *Insegnamenti*, X, 3 (1987) 776.
24. St Augustine, *In Ioannis Evangelium*, tract. XXXV, 2 (PL 1596).
25. John Paul II, *Address*, 27 April 1988, 2: *Insegnamenti*, XI, 1 (1988) 1043-4.

Mt 5:20; 7:21); an essentially spiritual Kingdom, in men's hearts: "the kingdom of God is within you" (Lk 17:21); but insofar as it is made up of men, it is also something visible, a people: it is the Church, which makes its way on earth towards the eschatological fullness of the Kingdom at the end of time.[26]

The eminently spiritual and supernatural character of the Kingdom means that Christ's rule consists in serving: "I am among you" he tells the Apostles, "as one who serves" (Lk 22:27), because the Son of man "came not to be served but to serve, and to give his life as a ransom for many" (Mt 20:28). For this very reason, Jesus prefers to show himself to his followers as a Shepherd rather than a King: "I am the good shepherd. The good shepherd lays down his life for the sheep" (Jn 10:11).[27] Christ's role consists in this: giving his life to establish the new people of God who live his very own life, thereby forming a "kingdom of holiness and grace, a kingdom of justice, of love and of peace."[28] The Kingdom, as the Kingdom of Justice, is proclaimed particularly in the Beatitudes (cf. Mt 5:3-12; Lk 6:20-23).

Therefore, being King is, in Christ Jesus, the same as being Saviour; being under Christ's sway is being saved, whereas to reject his kingdom (like those people in the parable: "We do not want this man to reign over us": Lk 19:14) is to perish: it means rejecting salvation.

b) **The universality of Christ's Kingdom**   The Kingdom of Christ is universal; it can be said to cover all creation. However, this Kingdom is established in a gradual way; it began with the Incarnation and will reach its fullness only at the end of time.

"To carry out the will of the Father, Christ inaugurated the kingdom of heaven on earth and revealed to us his mystery; by his obedience he brought about our redemption. The Church—that is, the kingdom of Christ—already present in mystery, grows visibly through the power of God in the world. The origin and growth of the Church are symbolized by the blood and water which flowed from the open side of the crucified Jesus (cf. Jn 19:34), and are foretold

---

26. Cf. Second Vatican Council, Const. *Lumen gentium*, 3 and 9. On the Kingdom of God proclaimed and inaugurated by Jesus, see M. Meinertz, *Teología del Nuevo Testamento*, op. cit., 27-81; R. Schnackenburg, "Reino de Dios", DTB, 888-907; M. Schmaus, *Katholische Dogmatik*, III/1, op. cit., 653-88. On the connexion between the Kingdom of God and the Church, cf. ITC, *Select Themes of Ecclesiology* (1984) (Sharkey, op. cit., pp. 267-304).

27. Cf. J.M. Bover, "El símil del Buen Pastor", EB 14 (1955) 197-208.

28. Roman Missal, *Solemnity of Christ the King*, preface. This text underlines the fact that Christ is at the same time king and priest, and therefore it points up the priestly nature of his eternal kingdom: "You anointed Jesus Christ, your only Son, with the oil of gladness, as the eternal priest and universal king. As priest he offered his life on the altar of the cross and redeemed the human race by this one perfect sacrifice of peace. As king he claims dominion over all creation, that he may present to you, his almighty Father, an eternal and universal kingdom, a kingdom of truth and life, a kingdom of holiness and grace, a kingdom of justice, love and peace."

in the words of the Lord referring to his death on the cross: 'And I, if I be lifted up from the earth, will draw all men to myself' (Jn 12:32)".[29] The parables of the Kingdom (cf. Mt 13:24-50) also tell us that Christ's reign will be established in a gradual way.[30]

In fact, just as Christ is not only the author of our salvation but *is* our very salvation, by analogy Christ not only establishes the Kingdom, but in a certain sense *is* the Kingdom,[31] because the Church is the whole Christ of which Jesus is the Head: "he has put all things under his feet and has made him the head over all things for the church, which is his body, the fullness of him who fills all in all" (Eph 1:22-23).

Christ's kingly rule extends to all creation—from the material world to the angelic spirits. "It would be a grave error, on the other hand, to say that Christ has no authority whatever in civil affairs, since, by virtue of the absolute empire over all creatures committed to him by the Father, all things are in his power."[32] This is a direct power, which derives ultimately from the hypostatic union, on which the perfection of his kingship is based.

Although Jesus had this lordship over all things from the very moment of the Incarnation, he did not exercise it to the full until, after his death, he was glorified by the Father through the Resurrection and the Ascension (cf. Phil 2:9-11). But in the period between his ascension and the end of the world, he does not impose himself with all his power, because he wants men to "merit" salvation by freely opting for him. And so he teaches us to ask the Father that his Kingdom "may come" (Mt 6:10; Lk 11:2). It will be at the end of time, when death is no more, that Christ will extend his rule over all creation in a permanent way, and will offer the Father his Kingdom, now perfect and complete (cf. 1 Cor 15:24-28).[33]

c) **Christ's power** Jesus has shown that his humanity has an operative potency, a power, which surpasses the natural abilities of man, particularly when he performs miracles—calming storms, multiplying loaves, raising the dead to life, etc. For this reason it is normal to distinguish in Christ, in addition to his infinite divine power, a double human potency—the natural potency proper to his humanity as such, and an instrumental potency.

That Christ has natural human potency, through which he can do everything that can be done by a man in the fullness of his strength, follows from the fact that he has a perfect human nature.

---

29. Second Vatican Council, Const. *Lumen gentium*, 3.
30. Cf. M. Bordoni, *Gesu de Nazaret, Signore e Cristo*, op. cit., II, 122-32.
31. Cf. Origen, *In Matth.*, 14 (PG 13, 1197).
32. Pius XI, Enc. *Quas primas*, op. cit., p. 600.
33. Cf. J. Sancho, "Realeza de Cristo y 'Anakefalaiosis' ", in *Cristo, Hijo de Dios y Redentor del Hombre*, op. cit., 951.

The instrumental potency is that which Jesus' humanity has to do things which are beyond the natural power of man; in fact, some of these things only God can do (raising the dead, forgiving sins, etc.). These latter are what are called "theandric" actions. This instrumental power of Jesus' humanity is not something transitory (limited to the moment at which he worked the miracles) but permanent, because the Incarnation—which makes Jesus' humanity the humanity of God, an instrument joined to the Godhead—is permanent and definitive.[34]

The permanent character of Christ's instrumental power can be seen from the way he works miracles: he does not ask God to do them, he does them himself, using direct, imperative words which produce the desired result. In no part of the Gospel do we ever see him asking God to work a miracle; sometimes he does pray, but it is a prayer of thanksgiving, not petition (cf. Jn 11:41-42), clearly meant to teach the disciples. But it is genuine prayer: thanksgiving for gifts received is true prayer, and the hypostatic union and the instrumental potency which follows on from it are a divine gift to Christ's human nature. It is worth pointing out that the power of Christ-Man is not almighty: omnipotence is an attribute exclusive to and incommunicable of the Godhead. That is, Jesus is Almighty through his divinity, not through his humanity.

In addition to Christ's thanksgiving prayer, the Gospel also shows him praying to God the Father to give him things. This is genuine prayer of petition: "I do not pray that thou shouldst take them out of the world, but that thou shouldst keep them from the evil one" (Jn 17:15).

Jesus used his superhuman power (when forgiving sins and working miracles) to establish the Kingdom, but never to dominate men, rather to save them. The Kingdom will be manifested "in power" only at the end of time (cf. Mt 24:30; 25:31; Lk 21:27).

3. CHRIST, PROPHET AND TEACHER

a) **Christ, the fullness of God's Revelation** "In many and various ways God spoke to our fathers by the prophets; but in these last days he has spoken to us by a Son" (Heb 1:1-2).

A prophet is someone who speaks to men words which God has personally revealed to him for passing on to others. There were many prophets in the Old Testament, and the Messiah himself was also foretold as a great Prophet. So, for example, we read in Deuteronomy: "I will raise up for them a prophet like you from among their brethren; and I will put my words in his mouth, and he shall speak to them all that I command him" (Dt 18:18).

34. Cf. Thomas Aquinas, *STh* III, q.13, a.2; D. van Meergeren, *De causalitate instrumentale humanitatis Christi iuxta D. Thomae docrinam* (Venlo, 1939).

Jesus' contemporaries were expecting a Messiah who would also be "the Prophet" (cf. Jn 1:21, 25), and he did in fact apply to himself Isaiah's words: "The Spirit of the Lord God is upon me, because the Lord has anointed me to bring good tidings to the afflicted; he has sent me to bind up the brokenhearted, to proclaim liberty to the captives, and the opening of the prison to those who are bound; to proclaim the year of the Lord's favour" (Is 61:1-2; cf. Lk 4:18-19). Jesus proclaims the Gospel, the Good News, of the Kingdom of God (cf. Mk 1:15).

Jesus is, then, Prophet. He is the Envoy sent by the Father to bring men the Word of God; his teaching therefore has divine authority; the Father himself requires us to listen to the word of Jesus (cf. Mt 17:5). But Christ is more than Prophet; he is the Master, that is, he who teaches on his own authority (Mt 7:29): thus he is acknowledged and called Master by his disciples, and he accepts this title; he is not one master among many, but the absolute and only Master of the New Testament: "You", he tells the Apostles, "call me Teacher and Lord, and you are right, for so I am" (Jn 13:13). This personal authority with which he teaches, which the evangelists themselves bear witness to, made them "surprised to see him teaching everywhere and at all times, teaching in a manner and with an authority previously unknown;"[35] it comes across very strongly in the words "I tell you" (cf. Mt 5:22; Jn 8:51; etc.).[36] And when Jesus quotes passages from the Old Testament, not only does he expound his teaching in the light of the sacred text but he also, and in a particular way, explains the sacred text in the light of himself.[37]

Only Jesus Christ is the perfect revealer of God: "No one knows the Son except the Father, and no one knows the Father except the Son and any one to whom the Son chooses to reveal him" (Mt 11:27). Therefore, his teaching is the fullness of divine revelation: "The most intimate truth which this revelation gives us about God and the salvation of man shines forth in Christ, who is himself both the mediator and the sum total of Revelation."[38] Whereas the prophets proclaimed what had been revealed to them, Christ speaks of what he sees and knows: "We speak of what we know, and bear witness to what we have seen" (Jn 3:11). "Jesus *reveals* God in the most authentic way, because it is based on the only absolutely sure and undoubted source—the essence of God. Christ's testimony therefore possesses the value of absolute truth."[39]

The supreme and definitive character of Jesus' teachings derives from the fact that he is God-Man; this makes his human words to be in the fullest sense

---

35. John Paul II, Apos. Exhort. *Catechesi tradendae*, 7.
36. Cf. J. Daniélou, *Cristo e noi*, op. cit., 55-6.
37. Cf. M. Bordoni, *Gesu de Nazaret, Signore e Cristo*, op. cit., II, 159-60.
38. Second Vatican Council, Const. *Dei Verbum*, 2.
39. John Paul II, *Address*, 1 June 1988, 2: *Insegnamenti*, XI, 2 (1988) 1718.

human words of God.[40] But we can say even more: Jesus does not only teach the truth; he is the Truth (cf. Jn 14:6), because he is the Word, the eternal and perfect Word of the Father made visible in the flesh. He is, at one and the same time, the Master who teaches and the Truth that is taught.[41] Therefore, Christ is in himself the Revelation of God, not just through the words he uses but through everything he does—"by his words and deeds (*verba et gesta*)."[42] It follows that to see Jesus is to see the Father (cf. Jn 12:45; 14:9). Therefore, "everything Christ did has a transcendental value. It shows us the way of being of God."[43]

It is a matter, then, of the revelation of God in a most immediate way, because the one who is revealing the Father is the immanent Word of the Father, his perfect Image, his Son, begotten in an eternal "today", identical in nature to the Father: he and the Father constitute one single God. Jesus' words, "He who has seen me has seen the Father" (Jn 14:9; 12:45) must be taken at full value—referring also to his revelatory ministry. Christ is not only the teacher of truth: he is the mysterious Wisdom pre-existent in God (cf. Prov 8; Wis 7; Eccles 4-6); in him Truth and Life are identified with each other (cf. Jn 14:6) to the point that man only knows the truth if he lives in Him, and he cannot live in Him without identifying himself with the truth: in the Word "was life, and the life was the light of men. The light shines in the darkness" (Jn 1:4-5).

It follows that Christ has to be accepted as a teacher on a different level from all others; strictly speaking, he is the only teacher: "you are not to be called rabbi; for you have one teacher, and you are all brethren" (Mt 23:8). Not only must one learn what he teaches, that is, accept his message, but one must identify with him to the point of being able to say with St Paul, "it is no longer who live, but Christ who lives in me" (Gal 2:2). Only through this personal identification can one come to full knowledge of the truth. Really, revelation and salvation are two interchangeable terms, when understood in all their richness: to know does not mean just a mere act of the reason; it is an existential action which affects a person's entire being, an action which requires commitment from a person in the area of his love and of his freedom and which fills him with joy. That is why seeing God face to face is called the "beatific vision"—and why our Lord describes eternal life as "knowledge": "this is eternal life, that they know thee the only true God, and Jesus Christ whom thou hast sent" (Jn 17:3). This is so, because Truth and Life are

40. To use St Thomas' words: "in Cristo Deus docet immediate" (*In Epist. ad Galat.* c.1, lec. 2).
41. On various aspects of the intimate connexion between Incarnation and Revelation, cf. R. Latourelle, *Theology of Revelation* (Cork, 1968), 359-76.
42. Second Vatican Council, Const. *Dei Verbum*, 2.
43. Blessed J. Escrivá de Balaguer, *Christ is passing by*, op. cit., 109.

identified with each other and with him who is the Son and Word of the Father: "the Word became flesh and dwelt among us, full of grace and truth; we have beheld his glory, glory as of the only Son from the Father" (Jn 1:14).

The majesty of Christ the Teacher and the unique consistency and persuasiveness of his teaching can only be explained by the fact that his words, his parables and his arguments are never separable from his life and his very being. Accordingly, the whole of Christ's life was a continual teaching: his silences, his miracles, his gestures, his prayers, his love for people, his special affection for the little and the poor, his acceptance of the total sacrifice on the Cross for the redemption of the world, and his Resurrection are the actualization of his word and the fulfilment of revelation."[44]

Finally, it should be stressed that Christ's teaching is definitive, also in the sense that it marks the culmination of God's revelation to mankind in this world. So, "the Christian economy, since it is the new and definitive covenant, will never pass away; and no new public revelation is to be expected before the glorious manifestation of our Lord, Jesus Christ."[45] Therefore, although it is possible (and always will be) for men to obtain a deeper knowledge of God and to grow in fidelity to Christian truth, Christian progress is progress in identification with Christ, in living in accordance with the teaching he as Master has given us, and progress in drawing on the life which he has given us as our Shepherd. Therefore, "in the spiritual life, there is no new era to come. Everything is already there, in Christ who died and who rose again, who lives and stays with us always. But we have to join him through faith, letting his life show forth in ours to such an extent that it can be said that each Christian is not simply *alter Christus*, another Christ, but *ipse Christus*, Christ himself."[46]

b) Christ's human knowledge   By saying that there are two perfect natures in Christ, one divine and one human, and therefore two operations, one divine and one human, one is by implication saying that there are in Christ two modes of knowledge, one divine (common to the three Persons of the Trinity) and the other human, in Christ's human intellect;[47] and this means that Christ has genuine human knowledge, knowledge which is the basis for his free human decisions and consequently of his capacity to merit salvation for us.

It was the very fear of Christ's human freedom that led Apollinaris of

---

44. John Paul II, Apos. Exhort. *Catechesi tradendae*, op. cit., 9.
45. Second Vatican Council, Const. *Dei Verbum*, 4.
46. Blessed J. Escrivá de Balaguer, *Christ is passing by*, op. cit., no. 104.
47. On Christ's human knowledge see, in addition to the text books already cited, the following: F. Vigué, "Quelques précisions concernant l'objet de la science acquise du Christ", RSR 10 (1920), 1-27; S. Szabo, *De scientia beata Christi* (Rome 1925); J. Lebreton, *History of the Dogma of the Trinity* (New York, 1939); A. Michel, "Science de Jésus Christ", DTC XIV, 1626-65; A. Durand, "La science du Christ", NRT, 71 (1949) 497-503; J. Galot, "Science et conscience de Jésus", NRT 82 (1960), 113-31.

Laodicea to deny that Christ had an intellectual soul.[48] The Church condemned the Apollinarian teaching, thereby defending the completeness of Jesus' human nature and the genuineness of his human operations. So, Christ has a human mind, corresponding to his rational soul. This mind, in turn, is not deprived of the activity proper to it, as is clear from the teaching of the Third Council of Constantinople.[49] And although the Magisterium has never directly said anything about the existence of human knowledge in Christ, this truth is implicitly defined when it states that he has a rational soul,[50] and that each of his natures acts in a way proper to it.[51]

The New Testament makes it quite plain that Christ has human knowledge. St Luke tells us that Jesus grew in wisdom and grace before God and men (cf. Lk 2:52). As the Second Vatican Council underlines, the Son of God "worked with human hands, he thought with a human mind, he acted with a human will, and with a human heart he loved."[52]

In studying Christ's human knowledge, theologians since the Middle Ages have sought to identify in Christ, during his life on earth, the three modes of knowledge for which the mind has at least an obediential potency. They have looked for *acquired knowledge, infused knowledge* and the *knowledge of the blessed* or the *science of vision*. We shall therefore look at these three modes and what they involve, and then go on to the qualities of Christ's knowledge, especially its infallibility.

i) *Acquired knowledge*   By acquired knowledge we mean those things a man comes to know through his own efforts, starting with sense knowledge; this is the knowledge which St Luke, for example, speaks about when he shows us the young Jesus growing up "in wisdom and in stature, and in favour with God and man" (cf. Lk 2:52). It is a type of experiential knowledge, which develops through effort and experience as time goes on. When we say that Christ had this kind of knowledge (and that he therefore gradually became more knowledgeable), it simply follows from accepting the Incarnation of Christ as a real fact and from the assertion that he has assumed a true human nature (and therefore a nature with limitations).

Great theologians like St Bonaventure, Scotus and Suárez and even St Thomas in his earlier works, denied that Christ had genuinely acquired knowledge, because they thought that it was more befitting the dignity of the Word made flesh to say that his humanity had all this sort of knowledge from

---

48. Apollinaris thought that human freedom necessarily includes the capacity to sin.
49. Cf. DS 151. Cf. St Damasus, *Epist. ad Episcopos orientales* (*c*.378), DS 149.
50. Second Council of Constantinople, Const., DS 250, Council of Florence, DS 1343.
51. Cf. ibid., DS 556ff.
52. Const. *Gaudium et spes*, 22.

the very beginning, as something infused.[53] "There was a time when I thought differently," St Thomas says towards the end of his life, "but it must be said that in Christ there was acquired knowledge, which is properly knowledge in a human fashion, as regards both the subject receiving and the active cause; for such knowledge springs from Christ's agent intellect, which is natural to the human soul."[54]

In denying that Christ had acquired knowledge (which is the normal way men come to know anything, because at the start of human life the mind is "tamquam tabula rasa in qua nihil neque fictum neque pictum" (as a blank writing tablet on which there is nothing moulded or painted), the main thing these writers were concerned about was the dignity of the Word, the Truth and the Life, a dignity which they thought incompatible with the fact that his soul could initially have been (like that of any other man) in a state of pure potency, *tamquam tabula rasa*, and would have had to learn things in the laborious way other men do. However, St Thomas, in his maturity, in order not to lessen in any way the radicalness with which the Word became man, states that Christ did have genuine acquired knowledge, with all its characteristics, especially the fact that it is attained gradually.[55] Despite this, St Thomas was reluctant to accept that Christ was ever really taught anything by anyone.[56] So, he plays down those passages in the New Testament in which the Lord asks questions, shows amazement, etc., following the exegesis of Origen, according to which Jesus would have asked questions, for example, not in order to learn something, but "to teach by asking".[57] Although in some of these instances Jesus (as is quite common in human language) enquires without really looking for information (cf., e.g., Mt 8:26; 9:4), and in others the evangelist himself actually says that Jesus does not ask to get information but with a pedagogical purpose (cf., e.g. Jn 6:5), in other texts (e.g. Mk 6:38; 11:13; Lk 8:30) we can see that he is asking in order to learn something. To deny to Christ the man, to Jesus the child, the possibility of being taught something in a genuine way really amounts to denying that he learned things from his Mother, as other children—how to speak, the customs of his people, etc.

Many theologians, including St Thomas, have taught that Christ's acquired knowledge extended to "all that can be known by the activity of the agent

---

53. Cf. St Thomas Aquinas, *In Sent* III, d.14, q.5, a.3, ad 3; d.18, q.1, a.3, ad 5; St Bonaventure, *In III Sent.*, d.14, a.3, q.2; J. Duns Scotus, *In III Sent.*, d.14, q.3; F. Suarez, d.30, s.2. Cf. H. Santiago-Otero, *El conocimiento de Cristo en cuanto hombre en la teología de la primera mitad del siglo XII* (Pamplona, 1970); J.T. Ernst, *Die Lehre der hochmittelalterlichen Theologen von der vollkommenen Erkenntnis Christi* (Fribourg, 1971).
54. *STh* III, q.9, a.4 in c.
55. *STh* III, q.12, a.2.
56. *STh* III, q.12, a.3.
57. Ibid., ad 1.

intellect".[58] If that were so, it would be unlimited. Christ would have been ignorant of nothing in any sphere of human knowledge. A statement like that seems incompatible with the realism of an *acquired* knowledge which Christ obtains by applying his senses and powers and learning in a progressive way like other men. The experience available to Christ was, obviously, limited and circumscribed by his time and place: "the knowledge acquired by the Saviour always had (error having been excluded) the perfection appropriate to his age, the time he lived in, the places he knew, and was in keeping with the people he conversed with and the designs of wisdom intended for the glory of God and the salvation of the world."[59]

ii) *Infused knowledge*   Infused knowledge is the name given to knowledge which is not acquired directly by the application of reason, but is infused into the human mind directly by God—for example, prophetic knowledge, which is not prognostication but genuine, definite knowledge of the future.

Most theologians from the Middle Ages on teach that Christ had infused knowledge.[60] This conviction is based on the *principle of perfection* with which they approach the study of Christ's human knowledge: the created intellect of Christ (they say) could not have been in an imperfect state, because it is appropriate that a nature united hypostatically to the Person of the Word should have an unlimited perfection. Therefore, Christ's intellect could not have had any potentiality which was not actualized, and therefore, given that it was capable of receiving infused knowledge, it must indeed have received it.[61]

Sacred Scripture does not provide us with any texts which clearly demonstrate that Christ had infused knowledge. Those which theologians normally use to support their view that he did possess this knowledge (Jn 1:14; Heb 10:5-7) are not incontrovertible, yet they do not rule out the existence of infused knowledge in Christ. And, obviously, the universality of Christ's knowledge should not be limited *a priori*, apart from those cases which are clearly in accordance with the limits inherent in human nature.[62]

However, we should not underrate those passages of the New Testament which point to Christ having supernatural knowledge, a knowledge which can be attributed to the gift of prophecy to do with things which Jesus could not have known simply by recourse to his human intelligence. For example, the

58. *STh* III, q.12, a.1, in c.
59. F. Vigué, *Quelques précisions . . .* , op. cit., 27.
60. Cf. G. de Gier, *La science infuse du Christ d'après S. Thomas d'Aquin*, Diss. P.U.G., Tilburg 1941; J.C. Murray, *The infused knowledge of Christ in the theology of the 12th and 13th centuries*, Diss. P.A. Angelicum, Windsor 1960.
61. Cf. e.g., St Thomas Aquinas, *STh* III, q.9, a.3 and q.11, a.1.
62. Cf. *Decr. S. Officii* of 5 June 1918 in which the following is rejected: "The opinion of certain innovators about the limited knowledge of Christ's soul is no less to be received in Catholic schools than the view of the ancients on his universal knowledge" (DS 3647).

—

Gospels show us the knowledge Jesus had of hearts and of events, not only of present events but also of future ones. Even at their first meeting Jesus knows what is in Nathaniel's heart (Jn 1:47-49), in the Samaritan woman's background (Jn 4:17-18); he knows what the disciples are arguing about behind his back (Mk 9:33-35); he knows for certain that Lazarus is dead (Jn 11:14); he predicts Peter's denial and the disciples' defection (Mk 14:18-21, 27-31; Lk 22:31-39); he foretells his death and resurrection (cf., e.g., Mt 12:39-41; Lk 11:29-32); he announces the end of the world and the destruction of Jerusalem (Mt 24:1ff; Mk 13:5ff; Lk 21:8ff). The Gospels clearly mean to emphasize Jesus' supernatural knowledge, the absolute certainty and authority with which he speaks, the fact that the source of his knowledge on these occasions transcends the normal source of human kind. Jesus *sees* beyond what the eyes of his flesh can see (cf., e.g., Jn 1:48-50).

The dignity of Christ's humanity (united hypostatically to the Word) makes it very fitting that he should have grace in the highest degree, including gifts and charisms. The Holy Spirit reposes in Christ with all his gifts and in all his fullness (cf. Is 11:1-3). There is therefore no reason to deny that Christ has infused knowledge. Moreover, he is the Head of men and of angels; "from his fullness have we all received, grace upon grace" (Jn 1:16), and it seems appropriate for the Head to have all the graces which will be given to the members (including infused knowledge).

iii) *Science of vision*   Along with acquired knowledge and infused knowledge, the great majority of theologians agree that, from the first moment of his conception, Christ had the knowledge of the blessed (called "the science of vision"), that intuitive vision of the Godhead which St Paul refers to as "to see God face to face" (cf. 1 Cor 13:12), and St John when he says that we shall know God "as he is" (cf. 1 Jn 3:3).

When dealing with this topic it is usual to cite those passages of Sacred Scripture which speak of the Son having seen the Father, the Son bearing witness to the Father. Most of these occur in St John's Gospel: "No one has ever seen God; the only Son, who is in the bosom of the Father, he has made him known" (Jn 1:18; cf. Jn 3:11). "Not that anyone has seen the Father except him who is from God; he has seen the Father" (Jn 6:46; cf. Jn 8:55; 3:32). "Truly, truly, I say to you, we speak of what we know, and bear witness to what we have seen" (Jn 3:11). Similar expressions occur in St Matthew: "All things have been delivered to me by my Father, and no one knows the Son except the Father, and no one knows the Father except the Son and any one to whom the Son chooses to reveal him" (Mt 11:27).

It is worth stressing that these and similar passages put it beyond doubt that the revelatory power of Christ originated not in a revelation made to him, nor in his *faith*, but in the direct knowledge he has of the Father. He, Jesus, bears witness in the strict sense: he testifies to what he has seen. At the same time, Scripture is notably silent about what Jesus would have needed if he did not have vision of God—faith. Jesus, who is the faithful High Priest (cf. Heb 3:2), is never depicted as a believer, as someone who walks in the obscurity of faith, but as someone who knows God intimately and directly.[63]

If it is true that the first patristic text which seems to affirm that Christ had science of vision comes from St Augustine, it is also clear that at no time do the Fathers speak of Christ as a *believer* or as one who walks in the chiaroscuro of faith. On the contrary: writers of the early centuries vigorously asserted our Lord's wisdom, his infallibility, even though the question had not yet arisen as to the source of his knowledge.[64]

From the middle ages up to the Second Vatican Council theologians almost unanimously held that Christ had science of vision; they did so not on the basis of any particular text, but by drawing on the ensemble of biblical and patristic sources.[65] From the point of view of argumentation, the reasons adduced are reasons of appropriateness connected with the perfection befitting Christ's human nature, the fact that he is Head, and his fullness of holiness. As St Thomas puts it, linking the first two arguments: "what is in potency is actualized by what is in act [. . .]. Man is in potency to attain the knowledge of the blessed, which consists in the vision of God; and is ordained to it as to an end, since the rational creature is capable of that blessed knowledge inasmuch as he is made in the image of God. Men are brought to this end of beatitude by the humanity of Christ, according to Hebrews 2:10 [. . .]. So, it was necessary

63. Cf. J.H. Nicolas, *Synthèse Dogmatique*, op. cit., 385. For exegesis of the scriptural texts quoted, cf. A. Feuillet, "Le prologue de IVe évangile" DDB (Paris, 1973), 123-36. Cf. also M.J. Lagrange, *Evangile selon Saint Jean* (Paris, 1925); B. de Margerie, art. cit., 5-15.

64. Here is what St Augustine says: "After this life all veils will be taken away so that we may be able to see face to face. How great is the difference between that man who was borne along by divine Wisdom (Jesus) and by whom we were freed, and the rest of men, can be understood by this. Lazarus was not unbound until after he had come from the tomb. That is to say that even the soul which is reborn cannot be free from all sin and all ignorance except after the dissolution of the body. In the meantime it sees the Lord, as it were, in a mirror, in an enigma. But the linens and the shroud of him who did not sin, of him who is not ignorant of anything, were found in the tomb. He alone was not oppressed in the flesh in the tomb as if at last sin came to be found in him, nor was he wrapped in linens as if anything could be hidden from him": *De diversis quaestionibus*, LXXXIII, q.65, PL 40, 60. This text of St Augustine cannot be regarded as apodictic. For its study, cf. P. Galtier, "L'Enseignement des Pères sur la vision béatifique dans le Christ", RSR 15 (1925), 54-62; A. Caron, "La science de Christ dans saint Augustin et saint Thomas", Ang 7 (1930), 501ff; A.M. Dubarle, "La connaissance humane du Christ d'après saint Augustin", ETL 18 (1941), 5-25. The following text of St Fulgentius of Rome is undoubtedly clearer: "It is a very hard thing and totally at variance with rectitude of faith to say that the soul of Christ did not have full knowledge of his divinity since with this we believe that he is one person [. . .]. We can affirm in all certainty that the soul of Christ had full knowledge of the Trinity": *Epist*. XIV, 3, 31, PL 65, 420.

65. Cf. J.A. Riestra, "La scienza di Cristo nel Concilio Vaticano II: Ebrei 4, 15 nella constituzione dogmatica *Dei Verbum*", AnTh 2 (1988), 99-119.

that Christ-Man should pre-eminently have the beatific knowledge which consists in the vision of God, since the cause ought always to be more perfect than its effects."[66]

At first sight the argument seems to be inconsistent, because the objection can be made, firstly, that the causality of Christ's humanity which St Thomas refers to is an instrumental causality, and, as we know, there is nothing to prevent an instrumental cause producing an effect above its proper capacity, by virtue of the principal cause operating through it (in this case our Lord's divinity); secondly, this argument would seem to require that Christ had the beatific vision only after his death and resurrection, because it is from that point onwards that Christ's humanity effectively leads men to heaven. However, this line of argument acquires its true value when it is put in the context of Christ's *mediation*. "He is the *Mediator*, the one who unites men to God; and the beatific vision is the climax of this union, the last touch. It cannot be allowed that he, as man, needed to be united to God, for he would have needed mediation, but he is the first and only mediator."[67]

Christ's fullness of holiness and grace seems to demand that he also has science of vision. Intuitive vision of God face to face is not an accidental gift added to and separable from the maximum degree of grace; it is in itself grace at its fullest, the apex of the union of the soul with God. Therefore, to deny Christ science of vision implies necessarily denying his soul the absolute fullness of grace and union with the Trinity.

Many contemporary theologians, therefore, add as an argument the difficulty involved in conceiving how Jesus could have acted if his human mind did not have direct vision of the Godhead. It is enough to recall the absolute sureness with which Christ bears testimony not only to the existence of God, but also to the divine intimacy, to the nature of the paternal heart of God, as to how he pardons etc. Christ always conveys absolute sureness. Attempts have been made to explain this feature of Christ's behaviour without having recourse to his science of vision, but the difficulties that arise are even greater than those that are avoided by denying him this knowledge during his earthly life.[68]

Through the science of vision, the blessed contemplate the divine essence, the inner life of God, and in so doing (because everything is contained in God as in its cause) they also know many other things, especially those which affect them directly. Therefore, when we say that Christ has science of vision, this raises the question as to the object and extension of that knowledge. Obviously, given that God is infinite and our Lord's human intellect is limited, this

---

66. *STh* III, q.9, a.2. Cf. L. Iammarrone, "La visione beatifica di Cristo viatore nel pensiero di San Tommaso", DC 36 (1983) 287-330.
67. J.H. Nicolas, *Synthèse Dogmatique*, op. cit., 388.
68. Cf. F. Dreyfus, *Did Jesus know he was God?* (Chicago, 1989); J. Galot, *Chi sei tu, o Christo?* op. cit., 323-7 and his *La coscienza di Gesù*, op. cit., 165-225.

knowledge cannot take in the divine mysteries or embrace God totally: God is beyond the grasp of any created intellect. Nor can Christ's science of vision embrace everything God could have created, that is, the infinite world of *possible being*. Those theologians who accept that Christ has science of vision agree in saying that it enables him to know all the past, present and future, because all these things affect him as King of the universe and Redeemer of mankind.[69]

The Magisterium of the Church has seldom intervened in connexion with this subject; when it has done so, it asserts that Christ does have science of vision, thereby echoing the common opinion of theologians. When, at the beginning of this century, some Catholic authors, Schell[70] among them, denied that Christ had science of vision prior to the Resurrection, the Holy Office in a decree of 5 June 1918 declared that "this thesis cannot be taught with safety."[71] Later, Pius XII in the encyclicals *Mystici corporis* (1943) and *Haurietis aquas* (1956) explicitly mentioned Christ as having the beatific vision prior to the Resurrection.[72] More recently John Paul II has taught that Christ "in his condition as pilgrim on the roads of our earth (*viator* = wayfarer), was already in possession of the goal (*comprehensor* = one who has already grasped) to which he would lead all others."[73]

iv) Jesus, viator and comprehensor   The main difficulty the existence of science of vision in Christ involves stems from the fact that it also means admitting that during his life on earth he was at one and the same time *viator* and *comprehensor*, that is, both a wayfarer (with all the features that status implies—capacity to merit, etc.) and one who had arrived at the goal of his human destiny, the vision of God. This seems to be self-contradictory. Certainly, it cannot be denied that in his life on earth Christ followed the path trodden by his contemporaries. The Gospels make that clear. It was by sharing in our human lot that he was able to redeem us. As is true for any other man, Christ's time for meriting ends with his death.[74] After his death he will cause

---

69. Cf. St Thomas Aquinas, *STh* III, q.10, a.2.
70. Cf. A. Michel, "Science de Jésus-Christ", DTC XIV, 1660ff.
71. Cf. DS 3645.
72. In *Mystici corporis*, Pius XII wants to make it quite clear that Christ was perfectly aware of his mission as Redeemer and head of the mystical Body prior to his Resurrection. "By means of the Beatific Vision, which he enjoyed from the time when he was received into the womb of the Mother of God, he has forever and continuously had present to him all the members of his Mystical Body, and embraced them with his saving love" (DS 3812). We find similar expressions in the Encyclical *Haurietis aquas*, when Pius XII explains that the Heart of Christ is the symbol and indicator of the love of the Redeemer for God and for men. This Heart is a symbol of "the ardent charity which infuse into his soul, ennobles his human will, a charity whose activity is enlightened and directed by his twofold perfect knowledge, namely the beatific and the endowed or infused" (DS 3924).
73. John Paul II, *Address*, 4 May 1980: *Insegnamenti*, III-1 (1980) 1128.
74. Cf. St Thomas Aquinas, *STh* III, q.50, a.6, in c.

our redemption *per modum efficientiae* (by way of effective causality), but not *per modum meriti* (by way of merit).[75]

So, the combination in one Person of two states as distinct as those of *viator* and *comprehensor* creates serious problems for the theologian, or, to put it better, confronts him with a mystery which he cannot plumb. Moreover, a *comprehensor* is necessarily supremely happy—which seems to be incompatible with the pain Christ experienced in his passion and death.[76]

A third objection usually raised against Christ having science of vision is connected with the nature of intellectual work: how could Christ have had genuine acquired knowledge if he had science of vision; if he already sees everything, how could he be like us and learn in a gradual way? How could the total knowledge implied by science of vision be compatible with the partial knowledge inherent in human growth in knowledge?

St Thomas repeatedly says that the state of *viator* and that of *comprehensor* coexist in Christ.[77] And the whole scholastic tradition agrees with him. On this subject he writes: "A wayfarer is so called from tending towards beatitude, and a comprehensor is so called from having already obtained beatitude [. . .]. Now before his passion Christ's soul saw God fully, and therefore he had beatitude as far as it regards what is proper to the soul; but he was missing

75. Christ is said to "merit" our redemption because, by atoning for our disobedience with his obedience, he obtains from the Father not only his own glorification but also our forgiveness. It is in this sense that one speaks, for example, of Christ "ransoming" us or "buying" us at a high price, the price of his blood. Christ is said to be the efficient cause of our salvation (he causes our salvation *per modum efficientiae*) because it is he himself who causes our sanctification, who imbues us with grace he has merited through his Passion. That is why St Thomas writes: "The death of Christ considered *in facto esse* (as already occurred), though it did not effect our salvation by way of merit, did so by way of efficiency as has been said above" (ibid., ad 2). This question will be studied in more detail in Chapter 6, 2b and 2c.

76. Some scholars, to avoid this dilemma, hold that Jesus enjoyed the beatific vision from the beginning but then voluntarily gave up that state so as to be capable of suffering. Here is how K. Adam puts it: "If the vision of God of Jesus' humanity had been absolutely unconfined, it would set certain limits to the sovereign freedom, for it would have imposed an inner compulsion upon Jesus' human volition [. . .]. On the other hand, it would have poured such an abundant measure of bliss upon the emotional life of Jesus that his soul would have lost all sensitivity to human suffering, and he could never have been the Lamb of God who gave his life for our sake. His suffering would be only the appearance of suffering, and the heresy of Docetism would not be far to seek. And so the vision of God of Jesus's humanity must be restricted even with regard to his volition and his feeling, it must be a *visio partialis*, never extending so far as to effect Jesus' moral freedom or his capability of suffering. Where scholasticism did not follow Duns Scotus, it overlooked both restrictions upon Jesus' vision of God": K. Adam, *The Christ of Faith*, op. cit., pp. 269-70. Adam has expressed very beautifully the great difficulty that arises from the coexistence of supreme pain and supreme joy in Christ. The proposed solution, however, does not seem convincing. In fact, if the whole life of Christ was affected by its redemptive character it is not logical to accept the beatific vision for certain moments only and to deny it for others. A similar position is held by G. Gironés in "Uno de nosotros es Hijo de Dios", *Anales del Seminario Metropolitan* (Valencia, 1971), p. 114f.

77. Cf. e.g., *STh* III, q.7, a.8 in c; q.8, a.4 ad 2; q.11, a.1, ad 2; q.15, a.10; q.18, A.5, ad 3; q.19, a.3; q.19, a.3, ad 1; q.30, a.2 ad 1.

other elements which are integral to beatitude, since his soul was passible, and his body both passible and mortal, as we have already said. Hence he was at once blessed, inasmuch as he had the beatitude proper to the soul, and, at the same time, wayfarer, inasmuch as he was tending towards those elements still wanting to his beatitude."[78]

As we can see, St Thomas tries to solve this dilemma while still maintaining that "It is impossible to be moving towards one's goal and resting at one's goal, in the same respect, at the same time."[79] So, he points out that Christ is a *viator* insofar as his body and soul are passible and a *comprehensor* insofar as, in the depths of his soul, he is already at the end of his journey. So, there is no contradiction. And although at first sight it might appear that St Thomas is making too subtle a distinction, in fact what he is doing is accepting the mystery. And in fact, while on the one hand the Gospels show Jesus to be a travelling companion with us on this earth (with his life taking its course until it ends at death: he is a wayfarer), on the other hand, because he is the Only-begotten of the Father also in his humanity, it is quite clear that he is a *comprehensor*. For, if being a *comprehensor* is nothing other than being definitively united to the Godhead, there is no closer or more irreversible union possible than the hypostatic union. It follows that in one way or another one has to accept that Jesus on earth enjoyed the status of both *viator* and *comprehensor*. Therefore, in the strict sense, Christ did not have the virtue of hope directed to its proper object (possession of God); he had hope only as regards those things he did not yet possess, for example, the glorification of his body and soul.[80] "If St Thomas teaches that Christ as he made his way on earth was both *viator* (that is, in a state of making his way) and *comprehensor* (that is, already at his goal), he is very careful to point out that this is so from two different points of view, that is, *in relation to two formally different goals*: on the one hand, beatitude insofar as it concerned just his soul (insofar as it is spiritual: essential beatitude); on the other hand, insofar as it affected his bodily existence (the good things which make up beatitude)."[81]

The question can also be looked at from another point of view: how is it possible that the joy of the *comprehensor* (enjoyment of God) does not redound to the benefit of his soul and body, and that the glory of his soul does not benefit his body? To put it another way: is it possible for there to be in the same subject the supreme happiness of heaven and the atrocious pains of the Passion? St Thomas returns to this subject a little later, asking whether

78. *STh* III, q.15, a.10.
79. Ibid., ad 1.
80. "From the first moment of his conception, Christ enjoyed the full possesion of God, and hence he did not have the virtue of hope. Nevertheless he had hope as regards some things he did not yet possess, although nothing could be an object of faith for him": St Thomas Aquinas, *STh* III, q.7, a.4, in c.
81. J.H. Nicolas, *Synthèse Dogmatique*, op. cit., 372.

"Christ's entire soul enjoyed the joy of the blessed during the Passion." The answer he gives is similar to that given to the objection about the impossibility of Christ being both *viator* and *comprehensor* at the same time: "There is nothing to prevent two contrary things coexisting in the same subject if they are there under different formalities."[82]

While Christ was *viator*, the glory in the depths of his soul did not flow over the lower part of his soul or body; and vice versa, the pain and sorrow of the lower part of the man did not deprive his soul of the fruition of God.[83]

The theologian is up against a great mystery here—that of Jesus' inner life when he was on earth, something the Gospels reveal very little about. Jesus is Son of God and Servant of Yahweh, a man of sorrows. In a sense, the dilemma is inescapable and parallel to this other one: how is it possible that the glory of the Word did not redound on the entire human nature of Jesus from the very first moment? One can understand why the Lutheran kenotic movements thought that the Word was in a state of "exinanition" from the moment of the Incarnation to the moment of Christ's glorification. What we have is the same problem (the co-existence in Christ during his life on earth of radical opposites) seen the other way round and from an incorrect understanding of communication of properties:[84] whereas some theologians asked how come the glory of the Word did not immediately make for the glory of Christ's humanity, the Lutheran kenotic thinkers asked how could the Word possibly stay glorious while Jesus' humanity was suffering. St Thomas' solution, widely followed by Catholic theologians, keeps the two extremes of the problem—the joy, and the sorrow, of our Lord's humanity during his life on earth. The co-existence of both extremes seems to be the clear message in the Gospels.

Finally, we come to the difficulty involved in reconciling in Christ the man, total, clear and certain knowledge (intuitive and direct knowledge of the divine essence), with acquired knowledge (which develops gradually, is not total and does not have the clarity of science of vision). The solution lies in the very fact that there are two distinct kinds of knowledge; whereas natural knowledge is acquired through the senses via images or *species*, the science of vision involves no images or *species*, because it is communicated directly by God, who causes the soul to know in a manner absolutely beyond that of human knowledge.[85]

---

82. *STh* III, q.46, a.8, ad 1.
83. Cf. ibid., in c.
84. Cf. L.F. Mateo Seco, "Muerte de Cristo y teología de la cruz", in *Cristo, Hijo de Dios . . .*, op. cit. 741ff.
85. As St Thomas stresses, because of God's infinite simplicity and his absolute transcendence over all created things, it is not possible to know him in himself adequately through any created likeness, and, consequently, it is impossible for the human mind to know him "as he is" (cf. 1 Jn 3:2) through any kind of *species* devised by itself. Therefore, the knowledge of science of vision (intuitive, face to face knowledge) exceeds every type of natural knowledge and is therefore quite different from acquired knowledge. "Only to the divine intellect is subsistent existence itself connatural. This means it is beyond the natural capacity of any

We are talking about two different kinds of knowledge, which are on different levels and have different features but which co-exist without contradicting or cancelling out each other.

Jesus' mission (to be the Revealer of the Father) is another argument for the appropriateness of his having these different kinds of knowledge. He is prophet, on a much higher level than the other prophets. He is the Son who reveals and bears witness to what he sees in the bosom of the Father (cf. Mt 11:25-27; Lk 10:22; Jn 3:31-32). "No one has ever seen God; the only Son, who is in the bosom of the Father, he has made him known" (Jn 1:18). "He is the Revealer because the transcendent and ineffable divine Truth, which he grasps in all its transcendence by direct vision, is refracted, in his mind and sensibility, in a human language (made up of concepts, images and words)—in a language through which he communicates it to men."[86] Science of vision and acquired knowledge work together in the revelatory mission; of the Son, who bears witness to what he has seen (cf. Jn 3:11-14)

v) Jesus' faith   Because Christ has science of vision, theology has usually denied the existence of the virtue of faith in him out of consistency with the essential features of that science. Whereas science of vision is a clear, direct knowledge of the divine essence, faith is indirect and obscure knowledge, because it means believing what one does not see (cf. Heb 11:1): it is incompatible with clear vision. And so, following St Paul (cf. 1 Cor 13:9-13) when speaking of the blessed we say that their faith has been fulfilled in vision or been displaced by it. Therefore, in the strict theological sense of the word "faith", we must say that Christ did not have faith; he had vision.[87]

Some scholars, while accepting that he had science of vision, like to speak of Christ having faith, either because they use the term "faith" in a loose sense (as fidelity) or because they use it in an analogous sense, as if science of vision meant faith consummated, or because they liken science of vision to some special kind of intuitive knowledge.[88] Those also, as is obvious, who deny that

created understanding. Hence no created mind can see the essence of God unless he by his grace joins himself to that mind as an object of knowledge": *STh* I, q.12, a.4, in c. The same happens with knowledge of created things on contemplating the divine essence: "To know things through their own likenesses is to know them in themselves; but to know them through their likenesses pre-existing in God is to see them in God. These two knowledges are different. Hence when things are seen in God by those who see his essence, they are not seen through any likeness extraneous to God but through his very essence present to the mind by which they are actually seeing God" (ibid., a.9, in c).

86. J.H. Nicolas, *Synthèse Dogmatique*, op. cit., 392.

87. Cf. St Thomas Aquinas, *STh* III, q.7, a.3, in c.

88. "It is our view," writes González Gil, "that the theory of *science of vision* is simply saying that Christ's knowledge is not reducible to other, inferior, kinds of knowledge. In that sense, we accept it completely. But we are afraid of not being able to avoid attributing to Christ a science of objects, thematic and conceptual or conceptualizable, static, incapable of development; in fact, it seems impossible to do so": M. González Gil, *Cristo, el misterio de*

he possessed the science of vision, speak of the existence of faith in Christ. In fact, one way of denying science of vision to Christ is to say that he did have faith (because the two, strictly speaking, are incompatible). In any event, as St Thomas observed, although Christ did not have the virtue of faith, he did have the merit of faith: "the merit of faith lies in the assent which man renders by voluntary obedience to God to that which he does not see [. . .]. Christ, in fact, was perfectly obedient in regard to God. Therefore it is that Christ did not teach anything related to the merit of faith which he himself had not already practised in a more excellent manner."[89]

It is not only the fact that Christ is the Revealer of the Father that makes it very fitting that he should have science of vision and therefore absence of faith; the very nature of the virtue of faith leads one to the same conclusion. Faith is not direct and immediate knowledge of the object; it is a *mediated* knowledge, that is, it needs the *mediation* of the authority of the witness. One believes on the word of the witness, and not because one sees with one's own eyes the evidence of the thing believed in. It does not seem fitting or possible that He who is the sole mediator by virtue of the directness of his union with the Word (the hypostatic union) should need any other mediation in order to know and speak about the inner life of God. The best evidence for Jesus not having faith is the fact that he speaks on his own authority (cf., for example, the Sermon on the Mount), without referring to his faith; and the New Testament never mentions his having faith.

c) **Jesus' infallibility; were there things he did not know?** When proposing himself to his disciples as their Master, Jesus says of himself: "I am the way, and the truth, and the life" (Jn 14:6). In Christ man meets the Truth. Therefore, He is the only Master: "Neither be called masters, for you have

---

Dios, op. cit., I, 420. The intuitive vision of God, the science of vision, does not grow, does not develop. Speaking of a science of vision which develops is to use this expression in a way that is contrary to its usual meaning in theology. González Gil likens it to a special connatural knowledge. "The science of Jesus surpasses all these modes of science which are merely mediated ways of knowing God: his is primarily and above all the perception of his immediate link with God. Even better: it is this very immediacy as the connaturalness, the base, the fountain and the origin of all his intellectual human activity in relation to divine things" (ibid.). The same kind of fluctuation is found in regard to the faith of Jesus: "Only in this sense is it possible to speak of faith in Jesus, a faith, as we have just written, analogical to ours. Because it is not a knowledge mediated by another prophet but immediately received in the dialogue of intimate union with the Father. But it is faith insofar as it is an attitude of receptivity, submission and total surrender, and insofar as there are included in its object border areas that are somewhat hazy and that are only gradually clarified by virtue of connaturalness with divine things": M. González Gil, loc. cit., 423. A similar use of terminology is found, e.g. in J. Guillet, *La foi de Jésus-Christ* (Paris, 1979). Cf. also L. Malevez, "Le Christ et la foi", NRT 88 (1966) 1009-43. On this subject see J.A. Riestra, "Cristo e la fede nella cristologia recente" in various authors, *Antropologia e Cristologia ieri e oggi* (Rome, 1987), 101-17.

89. *STh* III, q.17, a.3, ad 2.

one master, the Christ" (Mt 23:10). This is how Christians in all ages have regarded Christ; trusting in his word, they have followed him taking his teaching as the word of God.

It was not until after the critique initiated by Reimarus (1694-1768) that in non-Catholic circles the idea began to spread that Christ was subject to error about the date of the end of the world and about the very nature of his messiahship. Among Catholics the Modernists (specifically Tyrrell, Loisy and Schnitzer)[90] were the first to speak about Christ being wrong about the end of the world. They based their argument mainly on the well-known passages of the *Eschatological Discourse* (Mt 24; Mk 13 and Lk 21), in which our Lord seems to announce the end of the world as being imminent, and on other isolated verses such as Matthew 16:27-28, Mark 14:62 and par.[91] This error would have led Jesus as a result to preach a provisional morality (not valid for all time), because it would have been a temporary morality, and it would have led him also not to wish to institute the Eucharist or found the Church; the Church would have been founded by the Apostles once they realized that the end of the world was not coming.[92]

This is not the place to enter into the detailed exegesis of those particular parts in Sacred Scripture with which, naturally, the Fathers were familiar, (as all theologians have been) and which need to be interpreted in the light of the totality of our Lord's teaching. Thus, for example, the parables of the Kingdom always depict a Kingdom which grows gradually, like the seed sown in the field or the dough being leavened, and therefore do not seem to be compatible with the statement that the world is going to end very soon. Also, it does not seem to make sense for our Lord to say that "of that day and hour no one knows, not even the angels of heaven, nor the Son, but the Father only" (Mt 24:26), and exhort his disciples to be vigilant "for you do not know on what day your Lord is coming" (Mt 24:42), and interpret his words in the very same chapter ("this generation will not pass away till all these things take place": Mt 24:34) as if he meant that the end of the world was nigh.[93]

The views of the Modernists were condemned by St Pius X in the Decree *Lamentabili* (8 July 1907) and in the Encyclical *Pascendi* (8 September 1907).[94]

From the Christological viewpoint, it must be said that if Christ was wrong,

90. G. Tyrrell, *Christianity at the Cross-Roads* (1910); A. Loisy, *L'Evangile et l'Eglise* (1902); *Autour d'un petit livre* (1903); J. Schnitzer, *Hat Jesus das Papsttum gestiftet? Das Papsttum eine Stiftung Jesus?* (1910).

91. More generally, the authors belonging to the trend known as "consequent eschatologism" take this position. Cf. P.F. Ceupens, *Theologia Biblica*, II (Rome, 1930), 121-41; M. Schmaus, *Katholische Dogmatik*, IV/2, op. cit., 136-60. See also L.F. Mateo Seco, "Fin del mundo", GER, IX, 442-9.

92. Cf. K. Adam, *The Christ of Faith*, op. cit., 276-84.

93. Cf. A. Michel, "Science de Jésus-Christ", art. cit., DTC, XIV, 1631ff.

94. Cf. DS 3432-4 and 3412.

particularly in something to do with his mission and his teaching, that would imply he was not God. For it would be the Person of the Word who would be making a mistake in his human words: even a mistake made by his human intellect would be imputable to the Person of the Word. Therefore, most theologians say that that it is a matter of faith that not only did Christ not make a mistake but that he was infallible—that because of the hypostatic union it was metaphysically impossible for him to err.

The New Testament contains some passages which seem to indicate that there were certain things Jesus did not know. He asks questions, looking for an answer (cf., e.g., Mk 5:9; Lk 8:30; Mk 9:16, 32; Lk 8:45; etc.); certain things he says suggest ignorance (cf. Mt 26:39; Mk 15:34) and he sometimes shows surprise and amazement (cf., e.g., Lk 7:9). The most important text is the one mentioned earlier where he says he does not know the day or the hour of the judgment (Mt 24:36).

As regards Matthew 24:36, some Fathers read it literally as meaning that Christ did not know things about the judgment (they include, for example, St Irenaeus,[95] Origen,[96], St Athanasius,[97] St Basil,[98] St Gregory of Nyssa[99]). Many of these patristic texts were part of the polemic against the Arians or against Apollinaris of Laodicea, and were written in an attempt to show that Jesus really was a man; they used his "ignorance" about the judgment day as proof that he did have a human mind and human knowledge. However, in spite of such prominent witnesses in favour of Christ's ignorance, there are also many Fathers who think that Christ, even as man, did know about the day of judgment (we might mention Didymus the Blind,[100] St John Chrysostom,[101] St Ambrose,[102] and St Jerome[103]). St Augustine, who often commented on Mark 13:32,[104] always argued that Christ did know when the world would end. His interpretation (with minor variations) was followed by the Scholastics: Christ said that he did not know the day, not because he did not in fact know it, but because he did not want to or could not reveal it.[105] This is also the solution given by St Gregory the Great: Christ, even as man, knew the day of

95. *Adv. Haer.*, II, 28, 6-8 (PG 7, 808-11).
96. *In Matth.*, 13 (PG 13, 1686f).
97. *Ad Serapionem*, 9 (PG 26, 621-4).
98. *Epist.* 8, 6-7 (PG 32, 256-7).
99. *Adv. Apollinarem*, 24 (PG 45, 1173-6); ibid., 28 (PG 45, 1185).
100. *De Trinitate*, III, 33 (PG 39, 916-21).
101. *In Matth.*, 77, 2 (PG 58, 703).
102. *In Lucam.*, VIII, 34-36 (PL 15, 1775).
103. *In Matth.*, IV, 24-36 (PL 26, 188f).
104. Thus, e.g., *De diversis quaest.*, 83, 9 (PL 40, 48); *Serm.*, 97 (PL 38, 589); *De Trinitate*, I, 12, 23, (PL 42, 837); *De Genesi ad litt.*, I, 22, 34 (PL 34, 190).
105. A very complete dossier of the patristic texts is to be found in A. Michel, *Science de Jésus-Christ*, op. cit., 1639-47.

judgment, but he did not know it through his natural powers.[106] St Thomas
gives a similar solution, based on Chrysostom: "(Christ) does 'not know the
day or the hour' meaning that he will not make it known, since on being asked
by the apostles he was unwilling to reveal it [. . .]. The Son knows the day of
judgment, not merely in his divine nature, but also in his human nature. As
Chrysostom argues: 'If it is given to Christ as man to know how to
judge—which is a greater matter—much more is it given to him to know the
less, that is, the time of judgment'."[107]

In any event, one must make a distinction between error, ignorance and
not-knowing. Error means regarding something false as true, or vice versa;
ignorance means not knowing something one ought to know (a lack of due
perfection); not-knowing is not knowing something one does not need to know.
In this sense, error and ignorance have no place in Christ. They would go
against the dignity of his Person and against divine Providence itself, for not
endowing Christ's human nature as befitted his mission as Teacher. But it is
correct to say that there were things Christ did not know and did not need to
know: as we have seen, his mind was not omniscient. It might be argued that
when the Son of God took on human nature he also assumed the defect of
ignorance as he took on passibility; but that theory should probably be rejected.
Although not in a formal way, the Magisterium has at various times rejected
the theory which says that Jesus was ignorant of certain things, including the
day of judgment.[108] Ignorance (unlike the capacity to suffer pain) was not
necessary to the redemptive mission of the Son of God.

4. JESUS CHRIST, PRIEST OF THE NEW COVENANT

In the Letter to the Hebrews, Christ is depicted as the High Priest of the New
Covenant. In fact it is particularly as priest that we see him "seated" to the
right of his Father: "The point in what we are saying is this: we have such a
high priest, one who is seated at the right hand of the throne of the Majesty
in heaven" (Heb 8:1).[109] His, therefore, is a *priestly kingship* and a *royal
priesthood*.

---

106. ". . . the incarnate Only-begotten, made man for us, in the nature of his humanity knew
the day and the hour of the judgment, but, nevertheless, he did not know this from the
nature of humanity" (Epist. *Sicut aqua frigida*, PL 77, 1097: DS 474-6).
107. *STh* III, q.10, a.2, ad 1.
108. Cf. St Gregory the Great, *Epist. ad Eulogium* AD 600 (DS 474-6); Council of the Lateran
(AD 649), c. 18 (DS 518ff); Third Council of Constantinople (cf. Mansi, XI, 441, 501,
635, 683).
109. On the subject of the Priesthood of Christ, the following works could usefully be consulted
in addition to relevant sections of textbooks and dictionaries: J. Bonsirven, "Le Sacerdoce
et le sacrifice de Jésus-Christ d'après l'épître aux Hébreux", NRT (1939) 641-60; 769-86;
J. Tournay, "Les chants du Serviteur de Yahvé dans la seconde partie du libre d'Isaïe",
RB 59 (1952) 355-84, 481-512; J. de Fraine, *L'aspect religieuse de la Royauté israélitique*

Jesus never called himself a priest; nor do the Evangelists give him that title. But the priesthood of Christ is the central theme of the Letter to the Hebrews. However, Christ's priesthood cannot be regarded as a subject dealt with there for the first time; Hebrews collects and synthesizes an already venerable scriptural tradition found in both the Old and New Testament, and one to which the very earliest Fathers have recourse. Thus, St Clement of Rome speaks of Christ as "high priest of our oblations".[110] Polycarp of Smyrna calls him "eternal high priest,"[111] and St Ignatius of Antioch calls him "high/supreme priest."[112]

a) **The Messiah, priest and king** As early as Psalm 110 the Messiah is described as a king-priest: "The Lord says to my Lord: 'Sit at my right hand, till I make your enemies your footstool' [. . .]. The Lord has sworn, and will not change his mind, 'You are a priest for ever after the order of Melchizedek'" (vv. 1 and 4). In the New Testament this Psalm is frequently quoted as being a messianic prophecy (cf. Mk 12:36; Mt 22:44; Lk 20:42; Acts 2:34-35; Rom 8:34; 1 Cor 15:27-28; Eph 1:20-22; Heb 5:6, 10; 6:20; 7:1-10). So, Hebrews not only refers to Psalm 110 to underline its teaching about the priesthood of the Messiah; in doing so it is extending an already established New Testament tradition of quoting from this Psalm.

As well as Psalm 110, with its clear prophecy about the priestly character of the Messiah, we should also bear in mind the clear affirmation in the Old Testament to the effect that the Messiah would save his people through suffering: we might mention particularly the poems of the Servant of Yahweh (Is 42:1-7; 49:1-9; 50:4-11; 52:12 - 53:12), which had great influence on the way the New Testament describes the messiahship of Jesus (cf., e.g., Mk 1:11; 10:45; Lk 22:37; 24:25-26; Acts 3:13-18; 8:26-36; 1 Cor 15:3; 2 Cor 5:21; Phil 2:7; Heb 9:28).

To say that the people are saved through the sufferings of the Messiah means that his death is redemptive, is a sacrifice in the strict sense of the word.

(Rome, 1954), 309-41; J. Coppens, "La portée messianique du Psaume CX", in *Analecta Lovaniensia biblica et orientalia*, III, 15-23; H. Cazelles, "Les Poémes du Serviteur", RSR 43 (1955) 5-55; J. Coppens, "Le Serviteur de Yahvé. Vers la solution d'un énigme", in *Sacra Pagina*, I (Gembloux, 1959), 434-54; A. González Nuñez, *Profetas, sacerdotes y reyes en el antiguo Israel* (Madrid, 1962); A. Navarro, *El sacerdocio redentor de Cristo* (Salamanca, 1960); J.R. Shaefer, "The Relationship between Priestly and Servant Messianism in the Epistle to the Hebrews", CBQ 30 (1968) 359-85; A. Vanhoye, "Le Christ, grand-prêtre selon Héb 2, 17-18", NRT 91 (1969) 449-74; "Situation du Christ. Hébreux 1-2", in *Lectio Divina* (Paris, 1969) and *Textus de Sacerdotio Christi in epistula ad Hebraeos* (Rome, 1969). These commentaries on the Epistle to the Hebrews are particularly interesting: F. Prat, *The Theology of St Paul*, II (London and Dublin, 1945); C. Spicq, *L'Epître aux Hébreux*, I-II (Paris, 1952).
110. St Clement of Rome, *Epistola ad Corinthios*, 36, 1 (PG 1, 272).
111. St Polycarp, *Epistola ad Philipenses* (PG 5, 704).
112. St Ignatius of Antioch, *Epistola ad Philadelphios*, 9, 1 (PG 5, 1016).

It is enough to recall what Jesus says at the Last Supper when he refers to his death as the sacrifice of the New Covenant, which he offers for the forgiveness of sins (cf. Mk 14:24; Mt 26:28; Lk 22:20; 1 Cor 11:24-25). The fact that Christ himself regarded his death as a sacrifice implies that he is a priest: the offering of sacrifice is the act proper to priesthood. So, the assertion that the Messiah is a priest is to be found not only in those places where he is called a priest but also, though implicitly, in other statements about his giving himself voluntarily for men when he makes himself an offering for sin (Is 53:10), contained in both the Old Testament and the New Testament.

The author of the Letter to the Hebrews not only makes our Lord's priesthood the central theme of his message, but depicts the entire messianic work of Christ as a "priestly mediation", describing him as the great priest of the New Alliance.[113] Our Lord himself spoke at the Last Supper about his blood being poured out like "blood of the covenant" (Mk 14:24). The underlying argument of the Letter can be summed up in this way: the covenant implies sacrifice, and therefore a mediator with priestly functions. When Hebrews speaks, therefore, about a new covenant it also has to speak of a new priesthood.

The very nature of the covenant (called new, to distinguish it from the old) created a need to examine in what sense Jesus Christ continued the Old Covenant and in what sense he superseded it. Jesus had fulfilled and exceeded the priesthood the Messiah was foretold to have, as also his kingship (cf. Acts 3:20-23; 2:36). It was logical, then, to ask whether the Old Testament priesthood had not also found its pre-eminent fulfilment in Christ.

If the death of Christ was a sacrifice which superseded the old sacrifices, and it was prophesied that the Messiah would be priest and king, his priesthood must similarly have superseded the Levitical priesthood. The fact that the Old Testament speaks of the priesthood of Melchizedek shows that the Levitical priesthood was not the only one, and so, although Jesus was not of the tribe of Levi, it must be said of him (as Psalm 110 does) that he is a priest; indeed, that his is the only priesthood, superseding all others, just as his sacrifice is unique and supersedes all others. He is priest after the order of Melchizedek, a priest forever.

b) The notion of priesthood. Priest after the order of Melchizedek   The Letter to the Hebrews expressly propounds a concept of priesthood in two passages, each time in connexion with sacrifice (Heb 5:1-2 and 8:3): "Every high priest chosen from among men is appointed to act on behalf of men in relation to God, to offer gifts and sacrifices for sins" (5:1). It is essential for

---

113. Cf. J. Alfaro, "Las funciones salvíficas de Cristo como Revelador, Señor y Sacerdote", in *MS* III/1, op. cit., 700.

the priest to belong to the human family ("chosen from among men") and to have been chosen and established by God to offer gifts and sacrifices for sins. The Letter emphasizes that all these features (real man, divine calling, consecration, connexion with sacrifice) are to be found fully present in Christ (cf. Heb 2:11-18; 9:26; 10:5-10).

In this sense it brings together and goes deeper into everything earlier New Testament books said about Christ's mediation (cf. 1 Tim 2:5). That mediation is much more effective and on a different level from that of the prophets (Heb 1:1), the angels (1:4-6), and Moses (3:2-3): "Christ has obtained a ministry which is as much more excellent than the old as the covenant he mediates is better, since it is enacted on better promises" (Heb 8:6). See also Hebrews 9:15 and 12:24, where Christ's mediation is linked up with his redemptive death.

This priestly mediation includes (Hebrews stresses) the fact that Jesus shares our flesh and blood and has also partaken of our suffering and death (2:11-18). He partakes of everything that is ours—with the exception of sin (4:15), because it was fitting that our High Priest should be holy and spotless so that, not needing to offer sacrifices for himself, he could offer for all the people the sacrifice of his own body and blood (7:26). He is a mediator who does not stand in need of anyone else's mediation; his is a perfect priesthood.

The Letter refers to Christ as priest with the following titles—a priest (*hiereus*) after the order of Melchizedek (5:6; 6:20; 7:11 and 17); a high priest (*archiereus*: 5:10); a merciful and faithful high priest (2:17); the high priest of our confession (3:1); a great high priest (4:14); a high priest, holy, blameless and unstained (7:26); a high priest of the good things to come (9:11).

The Letter to the Hebrews, when quoting Psalm 110:4, says that Jesus Christ is a priest after the order of Melchizedek, emphasizing that there are three reasons for describing him in this way: a) because Melchizedek means king of righteousness, and king of Salem means king of peace, and the kingdom of the Messiah will be the kingdom of peace and righteousness (7:1-2); b) because Melchizedek is "without father or mother or genealogy and has neither beginning of days nor end of life, but resembling the Son of God he continues a priest for ever" (7:3); c) because it was he, Melchizedek, who blessed Abraham and who received tithes from him, which showed that Melchizedek was higher than Abraham, and therefore showed the superiority of Him (Christ), of whom Melchizedek was a type (7:4-10).[114] These references to Melchizedek show that the priesthood does not come to Christ through physical inheritance (he is not of the tribe of Levi, but that of Judah), and they also show that the Aaronic priesthood has been abolished by the new priesthood of Christ (7:11-19).

---

114. Cf. A. Michel, "Jésus-Christ", art. cit., 1238.

Christ's priesthood (already prefigured by Melchizedek, *without father or mother, or genealogy* (7:3) is an *eternal* priesthood, one which lasts *for ever* (5:6; 6:20; 7:17 and 21; 7:3; 7:25). Jesus, "because he continues for ever holds his priesthood permanently" (7:24); "he always lives to make intercesssion for them" (7:25). However, his priestly sacrifice, his immolation, was *once for all* (9:11-14 and 26-28). And through his death, with his blood, he sealed the New Testament; therefore, he is the mediator of the New Covenant (9:15).[115]

c) Priest and victim   As we have seen, one of the strongest arguments for asserting the priesthood of Christ is the sacrificial nature of Christ's death (Heb 2:14-18; 5:7-9; 7:26-28; 9:11-28; 10:11-18). This sacrifice is also described as being very superior to all the old sacrifices, which were simply its figure and which in fact received their value because of their orientation to him. The superiority of Christ's sacrifice derives not only from the priest who offers it but from the victim offered (a victim of infinite value), and also from the perfection whereby the priest who offers and the victim who is offered are united in one and the same subject, who is none other than the priest himself, who offered "himself without blemish to God" (Heb 9:14) and "entered once for all into the Holy Place . . . thus securing an eternal redemption" (Heb 9:12).

This perfect identity between the priest who offers and the victim offered makes for perfect unity between interior sacrifice and exterior sacrifice, adoration of God, "in spirit and truth" (cf. Jn 4:23), which is always the purpose of the highest form of worship (sacrifice) when it is offered sincerely.

This is the same as what the Gospels[116] and other New Testament books[117] say about the meaning of Christ's death. Thus, Jesus speaks of his body being offered as food, and of his blood as the blood of the covenant which is poured out for many for the forgiveness of sins (cf. Mt 26:26-28; Mk 14:22-25; Lk 22:19-20; 1 Cor 11:23-26). We find that the same language of sacrifice in St

115. His mediation is both priestly and royal. "The paschal events unveiled the true meaning of the Messiah-king and of the king-priest according to the order of Melchesidech which, already present in the Old Testament, reached its fulfilment in the mission of Jesus of Nazareth. It is significant that during his trial before the Sanhedrin, in answering the high priest who asked him, 'Are you the Christ, the Son of God?', Jesus replied: 'you have said so. But I tell you, hereafter you will see the Son of man seated at the right hand of power.' This is a clear reference to the messianic psalm (Ps 110) in which the tradition of the king-priest is expressed. It must be said, however, that the complete manifestation of this truth is to be found only in the Letter to the Hebrews which deals directly with the question of the relationships between the levitic priesthood and that of Christ": John Paul II, *Address*, 18 November 1987, 5-6: *Insegnamenti*, X, 1 (1987) 364.

116. Cf., e.g., A. Feuillet, "Les trois grandes prophéties de la Passion et de la Résurrection", RT 68 (1968) 41-75.

117. Cf., e.g., L. Sabourin, *Rédemption sacrificielle. Une enquête exégétique* (Paris, 1961). Cf. also the commentaries on the Epistle to the Hebrews cited earlier.

Paul: Christ, our paschal lamb, has been sacrificed (cf. 1 Cor 5:7), he gave himself up for us, a fragrant offering and sacrifice to God (cf. Eph 5:2), as a victim for sin (cf. 2 Cor 5:21); he is an expiation (cf. Rom 3:25). Similar expressions connecting the death of Christ with sacrifice are to be found in 1 Peter 1:18-19, and in the Book of Revelation, for example, the reference to Jesus as the slain Lamb (cf. Rev 5).[118]

Patristic teaching is very much in line with this. As an example, this eloquent passage from St Gregory of Nyssa should suffice: "Jesus is the great High Priest who sacrificed his own lamb, that is, his own body, for the sin of the world [. . .]; he emptied himself taking the form of a servant and offered gifts and sacrifice for us. He was the priest after the order of Melchizedek coming many centuries later."[119]

"Christ, says Divine Scripture," the Council of Ephesus teaches, "is 'the apostle and high priest of our confession' (Heb 3:1) and 'hath delivered himself for us, an oblation and a sacrifice to God for an odour of sweetness' (Eph 5:2) and to the Father."[120] And the Council of Trent (when it is stressing that the Mass is a sacrifice, in fact) says that Jesus Christ "declaring himself constituted 'a priest forever according to the order of Melchisedech' (Ps 109:4), offered up to God the Father his own body and blood under the form of bread and wine."[121]

Some authors have raised the objection (against the sacrificial character of Christ's death) that that death did not have a cult-like character (or, to put it more accurately, lacked the external rite of an act of cult); others (defending the idea that Christ's death was a sacrifice) have sought that *ritual character* in the interior offering Christ made of himself on the cross.[122] This objection and the reply to it are based on a too narrow concept of sacrifice and ritual worship.[123] It is true that Christ's death does not have the trappings of a liturgical ceremony, but it is also clear that Jesus dies offering his life to the Father as a supreme act of love and obedience. And that is the greatest act of worship the Mediator could offer. Therefore, it can be categorically stated that Christ's death is *cult-like without being liturgical*; it is also the origin, the source and the centre of all liturgy.

The unity in the sacrificial act between what is offered and the offerer brings to its fullness what is, in a sense, the universal law of all sacrifice.

---

118. Cf. P. Parente, "Sacerdozio di Cristo", in *Enciclopedia Cattolica*, 1540-3.
119. St Gregory of Nyssa, *Contra Eunomium I* (PG 45, 177 B-C). Cf. L.F. Mateo Seco, "Sacerdocio de Cristo y sacerdocio ministerial en los tres grandes Capadocios", in *Teología del Sacerdocio*, IV (Burgos, 1972), 175-201.
120. Council of Ephesus, *Anathematismi Cyrilli*, 10 (DS 261).
121. Council of Trent, Decr. *De SS. Missae sacrificio*, chap. 1 (DS 1740).
122. Cf. A. Michel, "La messe chez les théologiens postérieurs au Concile de Trente. Essence et efficacité", DTC X, 1192ff.
123. Cf. J.H. Nicolas, *Synthèse Dogmatique*, op. cit., 537-8.

External sacrifice has meaning and value to the extent that it is the expression of the *interior* sacrifice by which the victim is offered to God for sin or as a sacrifice of praise. The fact that Christ's death, as viewed from the outside, happened as a sentence of punishment issued by a wicked process of law and not as a liturgical ceremony, brings to mind something which is quite obvious and which our Lord insisted on strenuously—the importance of interior sacrifice; the fact that external sacrifice is meritorious to the extent that it is the expression of interior sacrifice. So it is no argument to say that Christ's death was not sacrificial simply because it did not take a liturgical form. And at the same time, the fact that the exercise of Christ's priesthood, in his sacrificial offering, presented Christ himself as the victim, shows that his is a perfect priesthood, in which priest and victim are so perfectly identical and interior and external sacrifice coincide exactly.

Moreover, it is worth noting that in Hebrews 9:14, where it points out that Christ offered himself to the Father "through the eternal Spirit", we can see an implicit reference to liturgical sacrifice; just as in the Old Testament sacrifices the victim was offered by means of fire, the sacrifice of the New Covenant was carried out by Christ through the High Spirit, the fire of infininte Love. In fact, the content of this verse (Heb 9:14) becomes the central point of Hebrews 10.

Speaking of the perfect nature of Christ's sacrifice, St Augustine stressed the close unity of priest and victim; and also the close unity in Christ's mediation: Christ, who is the only true Mediator, reconciled us to God through the sacrifice of peace, remaining one with Him to whom he offers the sacrifice and also in solidarity with those for whom he offers it; and the offerer and what he offers are one and the same.[124]

d) **Christ's priesthood, one and eternal** Christ's sacrifice is unique, one of a kind. The sacrifices of the Old Covenant refer to this sacrifice, of which they were only the figure. Also Christ's priesthood is unique, one of a kind. This is made very clear by the author of the Letter to the Hebrews. Christ has no successors in his priesthood. Just as he is the only victim, he is the only priest.

All other priesthood—the priesthood of the New Covenant—is nothing but a *participation* in this unique priesthood of Jesus Christ, by means of *assimilation* to Christ, *identification* with Christ, *putting on* Christ by means of the sacraments. This happens in the *priesthood of the faithful*, which is conferred

---

124. ". . . since there are four things to be considered in every sacrifice, namely, to whom it is being offered, by whom it is offered, what is being offered and for whom it is being offered; similarly here. He who is the sole and true mediator reconciles us with God by means of the sacrifice of peace, remaining one with him to whom he offers it and making those for whom he offers it one with himself; and he is one and the same who offers and what is offered": St Augustine, *De Trinitate*, IV, 14, PL 42, 901.

in the sacrament of baptism, and in the *ministerial priesthood*, which is received through the sacrament of Order.[125]

So, neither the priesthood of the faithful nor the ministerial priesthood follows on from or is added on to Christ's priesthood: they are a participation in that priesthood. They are not successors, because Christ's priesthood is for ever: he "holds his priesthood for ever, because he continues for ever. Consequently he is able for all time to save those who draw near to God through him since he always lives to make intecession for them" (Heb 7:24-25). They are not added to Christ's priesthood, because it is not possible to add either another offering or another victim to the sacrifice which was already made on Calvary. That sacrifice is renewed in the Eucharist, without adding anything essential to what happened at Calvary. It is Christ the Priest himself who, in the eucharistic celebration, offers himself to the Father through the ministry of priests as an unbloody offering.[126] In this context these words of the Second Vatican Council take on a special force: "priests by the anointing of the Holy Spirit are signed with a special character and so are configured to Christ the priest in such a way that they are able to act in the person of Christ the head."[127] It is in this configuration of the ministerial priesthood to Christ the priest and in their acting *in persona Christi Capitis* (in the person of Christ the Head) when renewing the unique sacrifice of Calvary that the unicity of Christ's priesthood is most irrefutably manifested. This explains why it is Christ himself who, present in the liturgical action, carries out the act of worshipping the Father and surrenders his body to men.

125. It is the entire Church that is a priestly people; in the Church the common priesthood of the faithful and the ministerial priesthood, which are different from each other essentially and not just in grade, are ordained to each other: "Christ the Lord, high priest taken from among men (cf. Heb 5:1-5), made the new people 'a kingdom of priests to God, their Father' (Rev 1:6; cf. 5:9-10). The baptized, by regeneration and the anointing of the Holy Spirit, are consecrated to be a spiritual house and a holy priesthood, that through all the works of Christian men and women they may offer spiritual sacrifices and proclaim the perfection of him who has called them out of darkness into his marvellous light (cf. 1 Pet 2:4-10)": Second Vatican Council, Const. *Lumen gentium*, 10. Consequently, Christian spirituality has priestly features, for all Christ's disciples "should present themselves as a sacrifice, living, holy and pleasing to God (cf. Rom 12:1). They should everywhere on earth bear witness to Christ and give an answer to everyone who asks a reason for the hope of an eternal life which is theirs (cf. 1 Pet 3:15)" (ibid.).

126. Council of Trent, *Doctrina de ss. Missae sacrificio*, chap. 2 (DS 1743).

127. Second Vatican Council, Decr. *Presbyterorum ordinis*, 2. We could also say that this outlines the role of priestly ministry in the *oeconomia salutis*. As Mgr. A. del Portillo writes, commenting on this text: "Christ the shepherd is present in the priest so as continually to actualize the universal call to conversion and repentance which prepares for the coming of the kingdom of heaven (cf. Mt 4:17). He is present in order to make men understand that forgiveness of sins, the reconciliation of the soul in God, is not the result of a monologue, no matter how keen a person's capacity for reflection and self-criticism. He reminds us that no one alone, can calm his own conscience; that the contrite heart must submit its sins to the Church-institution, the the man-priest, permanent historical witness, in the sacrament of penance, of that radical need which fallen humanity has of the man-God, the only Just One, the only Justifier": *On Priesthood* (Dublin and Chicago, 1974), 62.

Only from Christ does salvation come, and only in conformity to and in conformation with Christ is salvation to be found. It is he who by means of his Church and the actions of his ministers renders acceptable worship to God and offers salvation to men. The phrase *in persona Christ Capitis* shows the greatness of ministerial priesthood but what it shows above all is the unicity of Christ's mediation and priesthood. As St Paul writes, "there is one God, and there is one mediator between God and men, the man Christ Jesus, who gave himself as a ransom for all" (1 Tim 2:4-5).

The unicity of Christ's priesthood is very closely linked to one of the features on which Hebrews puts so much emphasis (citing Psalm 110): Jesus is a priest for ever: "You are a priest for ever, after the order of Melchizedek" (Ps 110:4; Heb 5:6)—Melchizedek, who appears in Scripture "without father or mother or genealogy, and has neither beginning of days nor end of life, but resembling the Son of God he continues a priest for ever" (Heb 7:3). Christ's is a priesthood which began at the Incarnation and will never have an end.[128] It is also said to be for ever because its effects (the glorification of God and the salvation of men) extend over all time and will endure for ever.[129]

However, the *event* of the sacrifice offered by Christ on the cross is not eternal: it happened *only once*: Christ, when he "had offered for all time a single sacrifice for sins, sat down at the right hand of God" (Heb 10:12; cf. also Heb 7:27; 9:12, 26, 28). He cannot sacrifice himself again in heaven. The Letter to the Hebrews is very clear about this: "he entered once for all into the Holy Place . . . thus securing an eternal redemption" (Heb 9:12).

Although it is true to say that Christ's sacrifice happened *once for all*, that does not mean that Christ does not for ever continue to exercise his priesthood. Christ's priestly role did not cease with his death; it remains for ever: glorified, he is seated at the right hand of God the Father as Lord of the universe and High Priest of the new Covenant. The Letter to the Hebrews depicts him as exercising his mediation in heaven on our behalf (Heb 7:25; 9:24). This permanent intercession is connected with the sacrifice offered on the cross;

---

128. "He, therefore, our God and Lord, though he was by his death about to offer himself once upon the altar of the cross [. . .] so that his priesthood might not come to an end with his death (Heb 7:24 and 27), at the last supper on the night he was betrayed, so that he might leave to his beloved spouse the Church a visible sacrifice [. . .] declaring himself constituted 'a priest forever according to the order of Melchisedech' (Ps 109:4), offered up to God the Father his own body and blood under the form of bread and wine, and under the forms of those same things gave to the Apostles, whom he then made priests of the New Testament, that they might partake. . . ."; Council of Trent, Decr. *De SS Missae sacrificio* (DS 1739).

129. Cf. St Thomas Aquinas, *STh* III, q.22, a.5. "Speaking of the bodily presence of the Word, he said: *He who is faithful to him who made him an apostle* (cf. Heb 3:12-2). With these words he highlights the fact that Jesus Christ, in his humanity also, is the same today as yesterday, and will remain forever. And in the same way as the apostle recalls his incarnation by way of his priesthood, so also he speaks of his divinity"; St Athanasius, *Oratio II contra Arianos*, 10 (PG 26, 167); Cf. also St John Chrysostom, *In Epist. ad Hebr. Hom.* 13, 2 (PG 63, 105).

Christ enters the sanctuary through the sacrifice of his own life (Heb 9:12, 22, 24, 25). St John, also, describes Christ's exercise of his priesthood in heaven as intercession on men's behalf, an intercession whose effectiveness derives from the sacrifice offered at Calvary: "We have an advocate with the Father, Jesus Christ the righteous; and he is the expiation for our sins, and not for our sins only but also for the sins of the whole world" (1 Jn 2:1-2). Here again we see Christ's intercession linked to his self-offering, his sacrifice, which is renewed (not repeated) in the Eucharist.

By his Incarnation, the Son is established as mediator-priest for ever. All Christ's work is directed to the salvation of man and it contains three basic stages—his incarnation (cf. Heb 2:10-18; 10:5-9), his death on the cross (Heb 2:26-28) and his eternal glorification (Heb 10:11-15). The entire mystery and work of Christ is priestly, because he is essentially a priest. And, in heaven, seated at the right hand of the Father he continues to exercise this priesthood and will go on doing so for eternity, for ever giving glory to the Father as Head of the Church.

e) Christ is priest as man. The essential constituent of his priesthood
Jesus Christ is priest *as man*. As pointed out in the Letter to the Hebrews, every high priest is "chosen from among men" and "appointed to act on behalf of men" (Heb 5:1). This priesthood is the reason why he came on earth: Christ, therefore, "had to be made like his brethren in every respect, so that he might become a merciful and faithful high priest in the service of God, to make expiation for the sins of the people" (Heb 2:17).

It is proper to a priest to be a mediator, with a descending and an ascending mediation. And this mediation is found in Christ, precisely through his humanity *insofar* as it is united hypostatically to the Word, because on the one hand offering sacrifice and praying are acts of man and not of God, and on the other the infinite value of this mediation comes to Christ's humanity through its union in unity of person with the Word. Hebrews also identifies two other characteristics of priesthood (specifically the priesthood of Christ): divine calling—"one does not take the honour upon himself, but he is called by God, just as Aaron was" (Heb 5:4)—and consecration (constitution, appointment)—"chosen from among men (and) appointed" (5:1). Christ's priestly vocation comes across very clearly in Hebrews: "So also Christ did not exalt himself to be made a high priest, but was appointed by him who said to him, 'Thou art my Son, today I have begotten thee'" (5:5); however, the Letter does not say how he is constituted a priest.

In the passage we have just quoted, it seems to be implied that his consecration as priest lies in his being the Son. It is often held that Christ's anointing as a priest, his consecration, is nothing other than the hypostatic union itself, by which the Humanity of Christ is truly constituted as mediation between God and men. However, opinions, are divided as to what exactly is the essence of this priestly consecration.

The most common opinion has it that his priestly consecration is the very grace of union insofar as it brings with it habitual grace and capital grace.[130] The main reasons given are: a) it is the hypostatic union itself that ontologically constitutes Christ as mediator between God and man, capable of offering his own life in sacrifice; b) but if one views Christ's priesthood not only in ontological terms but in terms of its dynamic (that is insofar as it is the real *cause* of men's sanctification) it would seem necessary to include as essential to that priesthood—(i) Christ's habitual grace by which, on giving himself freely *ex infinita caritate et obedientia*, he merits salvation, and (ii) his capital grace whereby he sanctifies us.[131] For this reason the grace of union is regarded as the constitutive element of Christ's priesthood insofar as it brings with it habitual grace and capital grace. "Christ is, then, substantially a priest since he is substantially the *anointed one* and the *holy one* by virtue of the hypostatic union."[132]

There are other writers who say that capital grace is the metaphysical constituent of the hypostatic union.[133] Here are the main reasons they give: a) if what constitutes Christ's priesthood is located in the hypostatic union, that would mean that his priesthood (on its own) would express all the richness of the Incarnation, because it would be one and the same thing with it; b) if (as is self-evident) the hypostatic union cannot be participated in, Christ's priesthood could not be shared by anyone, but that is clearly wrong. Therefore they conclude, "it must be said that it is created grace, which in Christ derives from the (hypostatic) union but is distinct from it, that makes Christ a priest. It is this grace, with its priestly dimension, that he communicates to his Church."[134]

With regard to the first reason given, it can be said that "limiting it formally to his created grace"[135] involves reducing the greatness of Christ's priesthood. Thus, while for those who think Christ's priesthood is essentially constituted by the hypostatic union, everything Christ does is seen as priestly activity, for the second group of writers the royal and prophetic functions of Christ seem to be more independent of each other, and his priesthood is reduced to functions of worship.[136]

---

130. Cf. M. Cuervo, in *Suma Teologica* (Introduction to q.22), op. cit., 760.
131. Among those who hold this view are Cajetan, Scheeben, Franzelin, Michel, Garrigou-Lagrange, H. Boüessé.
132. A. Michel, "Jésus-Christ", art. cit., 1338.
133. They include John of St Thomas, Charles Journet, J.H. Nicolas.
134. J.H. Nicolas, *Synthèse Dogmatique*, op. cit., 537.
135. Cf. H. Boüessé, *Le Sauveur du monde. II. Le mystère de l'Incarnation* (Chambery, 1953), 634.
136. This is what happens, for example, in the position adopted by J.H. Nicolas. Here is how

The next reason (the hypostatic union cannot be participated in, and so would render the priesthood of Christ incapable of being participated in) does not seem sufficient for not locating the essence of Christ's priesthood in the hypostatic union. The term "participation" does not mean that in order to be a priest one has to participate in the hypostatic union as such; what it means is that, by being incorporated in Christ through the sacraments, man is sacramentally configured to him, who is essentially a priest, and in this sense one can say that he participates in Christ's priesthood.[137]

To sum up: we can say that, in Jesus, priestly consecration is the hypostatic union itself, because it is through that union that his humanity is constituted the humanity of God and, therefore, has been established as a *bridge* and a perfect mediation between God and man. This perspective makes it easier to understand the characteristics we have identified in Christ's priesthood: Jesus is a priest from the first moment of his conception, a priest for ever; in Jesus the fullness of priesthood resides; and finally, Christ's priesthood is infinitely superior to every other priesthood just as the grace of union is infinitely superior to every other grace.

5. JESUS CHRIST'S HOLINESS

The work of the Mediator consists in reconciling men with God. This reconciliation takes place, in fact, in and through the holiness of the Mediator. "The redemption of the world—this tremendous mystery of love in which creation is renewed—is, at its deepest root, the fullness of justice in a human Heart—the Heart of the First-born Son—in order that it may become justice in the hearts of many human beings, predestined from eternity in the First-born Son to be children of God and called to grace, called to love."[137a] And so, having studied the ministries of the Mediator, we shall move on now to consider his holiness.

> he puts it: "Just as Christianity can never be reduced to the *cult of the Christian religion*, so Christ cannot be confined to the notion of the *High Priest of the New Alliance*. In particular, one can never confuse the essential revealing function of Christ, which, as we have seen, forms an integral part of the mission of the Word, with his priestly function. One can never identify his royal function with his priestly function through they are closely linked to each other; the royal (pastoral) function of Christ is a matter of leading to God the people whom he ransomed by his blood": *Synthèse Dogmatique*, op. cit., 536. This position seems contrary to what is said in Hebrews. As we have seen, the royal function of Christ is here described with truly priestly characteristics. In fact, it is the hypostatic union which effectively constitutes Christ as king, teacher and priest. The habitual grace and the capital grace—which follow such great dignity—harmonize the human nature of Christ with such an end and with such a function, but do not constitute it in this priesthood or in that royal dignity.

137. Famous among the different opinions concerning the formal constituent of Christ's priesthood is that of the Salamanca school (cf. *Cursus theologicus*, d.31, dub. 1, nos. 16ff), who place it *radically* in the grace of union and *formally* in his habitual grace. The reasons pro and con are in fact the same as apply regarding the opinions of Journet or J.H. Nicolas.

137a. John Paul II, Enc. *Redemptor hominis*, op. cit., 9.

Holiness is an attribute proper to God. When applied to God particularly, the notion of holiness is easier to intuit than to define. Holiness is a word which designates God's transcendence, his perfection, his majesty, his infinite goodness as the ultimate Good, to whom the rational creature owes worship and love in recognition of his righteousness and mercy. Holiness has to do with God's ontological transcendence, his superiority over all created things. God is completely holy, because he is subsistent Goodness itself. He is subsistent Holiness. Therefore all his works are holy.[138] His is a holiness which fills one with veneration, love, respect, holy trembling and fear (cf., e.g., Ex 3 and 20).

When places, things and people are described as being "holy" it is because of a special relationship they have to God, a special union with him. Thus, the sabbath is called "holy" because it is dedicated to God (Ex 35:2); the temple is holy because it is used exclusively for divine worship (cf., e.g., Mt 24:15; Acts 6:13; 1 Cor 3:17; Heb 8:2-3; the city of Jerusalem is holy for the same reason (cf., e.g., Mt 4:5; 27:53), as is the heavenly Jerusalem (Rev 21:2, 10).

On a different level one speaks of the holiness of rational creatures, both angels (cf. Mk 8:38; Lk 9:26) and men. God's holiness communicates itself to men, and should also be reflected in their lives. Thus, for example, the priests and levites had to sanctify themselves and be holy, because Yahweh is holy (cf., e.g., Lev 11:44; 20:26; 21:8). This *sanctification*, in the case of the high priest, is effected through the anointing and consecration which makes him a priest (Lev 21:10-15). Sometimes, the adjective "holy" is applied to all the people of Israel, because they are God's own people (Deut 7:6; 14:2).

Christians constitute the *holy* people of God (cf. 1 Pet 1:15-16); indeed, they are "a chosen race, a royal priesthood, a holy nation, God's own people" (1 Pet 2:9). This *holiness* also requires that their works be holy, "since it is written, 'You shall be holy, for I am holy'" (1 Pet 1:16; Lev 11:44). And those who serve God during their life are called "holy", they are "saints" (Mt 27:52).

"Clearly this communication of God's life and goodness can only come about through grace: it is a gift which raises the person to a higher level than that on which his own nature puts him, the level of the divine operations. Holiness is, then, a gift of grace."[139] This participation in the divine life (for that is what the life of grace is) reaches its plenitude in heaven, where "we shall be like him [God], for we shall see him as he is" (1 Jn 3:2). This *divinization* of man, this transformation into God, this communication which God makes to man of his own inner life, involves adoptive filiation, that is, God loving man with a fatherly love and making him his son. As St John writes, "See

138. Cf. G. Kittel, *Theologisches, Wörterbuch zum Neuen Testament* (Stuttgart, 1932), 1, 88.98; P. van Imschoot, "La Sainteté de Dieu dans l'A.T.", VS (1946) 30-44; L. Scheffczyk, "La santidad de Dios, fin y forma de la vida cristiana", ScrTh 11 (1979) 1021-35.

139. J.H. Nicolas, *Synthèse Dogmatique*, op. cit., 363.

what love the Father has given us, that we should be called children of God; and so we are" (1 Jn 3:1).

a) **The Holy Mediator** The entire meaning of Christ's mediation lies in uniting men to God, that is, sanctifying them. He is the holy Mediator who, by uniting men to himself, sanctifies them by communicating his own life to them. The grace of union which makes Christ a mediator is at the same same time the source of his holiness.[140] The ministeries through which he exercises his mediation are dependent on his holiness and, in turn, sanctify men. This intrinsic and indissoluble relationship between the Mediator's holiness and his sanctifying efficacy are particularly clear to see when he is viewed in his capacity as priest and victim. Christ is the High Priest "holy, blameless, unstained" (Heb 7:26); "he knew no sin" (2 Cor 5:21). In fact, he is "the Lamb of God, who takes away, the sins of the world" (Jn 1:29).

Sacred Scripture speaks very clearly and insistently of Christ's holiness. The Spirit of Yahweh shall rest upon him (Is 11:1-5); when announcing his conception, the angel tells the Mother of Jesus: "The Holy Spirit will come upon you, and the power of the Most High will overshadow you; therefore the child to be born will be called holy, the Son of God" (Lk 1:35). He is "the Holy and Righteous One" (Acts 3:14); he is the one "whom the Father consecrated and sent into the world" (Jn 10:36); he is "full of grace and truth" (Jn 1:14).

In speaking of Christ's holiness, we are not of course referring to the holiness of the Word, for he is essentially holy because he is one with the Father and the Holy Spirt. The Word has that absolute and total holiness which belongs to the Godhead. When discussing Christ's holiness, we are referring exclusively to Jesus Christ as man, that is, we are dealing with the divinization of his human nature. We are studying how the holiness of God is communicated to Jesus' human nature, which is joined to the Word in unity of person.

A triple grace is to be found in Christ—the grace of union (that is, the hypostatic union viewed as a gift or grace to the humanity of Jesus), habitual grace (so-called sanctifying grace), and capital grace, that is, the grace he has as head of the human race.

Why is it necessary to speak of Christ having habitual grace if he already has the grace of union? Because the hypostatic union changes nothing in his human nature; therefore, it is open to be raised to the supernatural order by

---

140. On the subject of Christ's holiness, the following may usefully be consulted in addition to the relevant sections of textbooks and dictionaries: A. Michel, "Jésus-Christ", in DTC, art. cit., 1274-1312; J.H. Nicolas, *Synthèse Dogmatique*, op. cit., 361-75; E. Hugon, *Le Mystère de l'Incarnation* (Tegui, 1913); R. Garrigou Lagrange, *Le Sauveur* (1933); J. Rohof, *La sainteté substantielle du Christ dans la théologie scolastique* (Fribourg, Switzerland, 1952); H Boüessé, *Le mystère de l'Incarnation*, op. cit., 225-97; K. Adam, *The Christ of Faith*, op. cit., 244-60; E. Bailleux, "L'impecable liberté du Christ", RT 67 (1967) 5-28. J. Auer, *Curso de Teología Dogmática*, VI.1, *Jesucristo hijo de Dios e hijo de María* (Barcelona, 1989), 469-85.

habitual grace and the infusion of the supernatural virtues and the gifts of the Holy Spirit. Looked at in this way, the distinction of natures is highlighted and also, as the Council of Chalcedon taught, the fact that "the difference of natures will never be abolished by their being united, but rather the properties of each remain unimpaired."[141] Despite the hypostatic union, whereby the Word is so intimately united to Christ's human nature, that nature is not changed in its qualities and therefore it needs to be raised to the supernatural order through grace.

But it must be remembered that the *subject* of that accidental sanctification by grace is the Word (that is, infinite holiness) in his human nature. So, although we are speaking of the sanctification and sanctity of that humanity, we should not forget that that humanity should not be considered in isolation but rather as *hypostasized* by the Word. In other words, he who is *holy* and *sanctified* is *that man*, Jesus, whose human nature is *hypostasized, personalized*, by and in the Word. The Word, is the *subject*, then, of this sanctification of his human nature.

b) The grace of union and "substantial holiness"   Holiness, in man, is belonging to God, union with God, relating to him, sharing in the holiness of the infinite Good, sharing in the inner life of God; through that sharing man is raised to the dignity of a son.[142]

Through the incarnation, the human nature of Christ was raised to the greatest possible degree—that of union with the Godhead, with the Person of the Word. So, the grace of union is for Christ the greatest gift he could receive. An infinite grace with the very infiniteness of the Word to which his human nature is ontologically and permanently joined.[143] And by this union, the *man Jesus* (Jesus' human nature hypostasized in the Word), by being a person *in* and *by* the Word, does not receive adoptive filiation: he is the natural Son of the Father.

Therefore, there is in Christ only one filiation with the Father. This is natural, not adoptive, filiation.[144] He is the Son, the Only-begotten, of whom

---

141. Council of Chalcedon, *Symbolum* (DS 302).
142. "Grace", St Thomas writes, "is a certain partaking of the Godhead by the rational creative, according to 2 Peter 1:4: 'he has granted to us his precious and very great promises, that through these you may [. . .] become partakers of the divine nature' ": *STh* III, q.7, a.1, obj. 1. Cf. F. Ocáriz, *Hijos de Dios en Cristo*, op. cit., 69-92.
143. "The grace of union is the personal being that is given through divine grace to the human nature in the Person of the Word, and it is the terminus of its assumption": *STh* III, q.6, a.6 in c.
144. "In Christ", St Thomas writes, "there is no other person or hypostasis than the uncreated one, to whom it belongs by nature to be the Son. As we have already said, adoptive sonship is a participated likeness of natural sonship; and a thing cannot be said to participate in what it has essentially. Therefore Christ, who is the natural Son of God, can in no way be called an adopted son": *STh* III, q.23, a.4 in c.

the voice from heaven says: "This is my beloved Son, with whom I am well pleased" (Mt 3:17; Mk 1:11). There can be no greater union with God than this; and therefore no greater holiness.

To describe this holiness, the term "substantial holiness" is normally used. For no one can be more united to God, or belong more to him, than as a natural son. If Scripture is called holy because it contains the word of God, and priests are called holy because of their consecration to God, Jesus (the Son of God by nature) is substantially holy also in his *human* nature. His Humanity is holy, because it is the humanity of the Word. And for the same reason Jesus is to be worshipped also in his Humanity: that Humanity is substantially holy with the holiness of God.

This *substantial holiness* is also described (especially by writers of the early centuries) as *Anointing* or *Unction*, which sanctifies and consecrates Christ as priest. That was how the Fathers usually speak of the anointing of the incarnate Word: although obviously not using the technical language employed later by Scholasticism, they linked grace of union with the ontological holiness of Christ. "[The Son] is the Anointed [Christos] because of his divinity; the latter is, in effect, the anointing of his humanity; sanctified not by some operation as in the case of others who are anointed, but by the total presence of him who anoints."[145] And Cyril of Alexandria: "Holy by essence insofar as he is God, he sanctifies himself in regard to his humanity."[146] And St Augustine writes: "Holy from the beginning of his existence, when the Word became man he sanctified himself in himself: that is to say, himself as being man, in himself as being the Word."[147]

This holiness, which the Word gives the human nature when assuming it in unity of person, is called *substantial*, simply because the human nature is not united to the Word accidentally but *substantially*.[148] And in the same way as there can be no greater union than this union between the Word and his human nature, neither can there by any greater holiness than that with which our Lord's human nature is sanctified substantially or essentially by the grace

---

145. St Gregory Nazianzen, *Or.* 30, 21 (PG 36, 133).
146. St Cyril of Alexandria, *De sancta consubstantiali Trinitate dialogi* (6 PG 75, 1017). Cf. J.M. Odero, "La unción de Cristo y el bautismo de Cristo en S. Cirilo de Alejandría", in *Cristo, Hijo Dios y Redentor del hombre*, op. cit., 519-40.
147. St Augustine, *In Johannis evangelium tractatus* 108, 5 (PL 35, 1910).
148. "As we have seen previously", Chopin writes, "the hypostatic union is a substantial union of human nature and divine nature in the pre-existing person of the Word. It follows that the Godhead penetrates the human nature and the human nature is consecrated to the Godhead. This consecration is substantial: the human nature finds itself immediately united to the person of the Word through its whole substance. And so this consecration can be compared to an anointing, to show the intimate penetration of the humanity by the divinity. The hypostatic union, which confers this substantial holiness, is something entirely supernatural. It is a grace, the grace of union": C. Chopin. *El Verbo encarnado y redentor*, op. cit., 135.

of union:[149] through this union not only does Christ's soul *belong* and be intimately and indissolubly united to the Word: but also his body is united to the Word substantially.

We might refer to an area of dispute between Thomists and Scotists in order to explore what is meant by "substantial" as distinct from accidental holiness. Both graces as we shall see are closely linked—the grace of union (which makes Christ's humanity "substantially holy") involves the need for habitual grace (which sanctifies accidentally) and for glory as the ultimate perfection of operative union with God.[150]

Durandus had defended the hypothetical idea that if the soul of Christ had not received sanctifying grace, it would have been fallible in spite of the hypostatic union and could have committed sin.[151] This theory logically implies that habitual grace is absolutely necessary for the sanctification of Christ, and the reason adduced in its defence is the point that, as the Council of Chalcedon teaches, neither nature (the human or the divine) is changed by the hypostatic union, and that therefore Christ could not have acted in a holy way unless he had habitual grace. The main problem with the Durandus approach stems from the fact that if, according to the celebrated axiom *actiones sunt suppositorum*, it is the person who is responsible for his acts, and the Person of the Word is incapable of sinning, one cannot see how in order to render his human nature so holy that it is incapable of sinning, his own personal—substantial—union with this nature is not enough, but that it should be absolutely necessary that it be given this impeccability through an *accidental* gift, which is what habitual grace is.[152]

But the debate was sparked off. The Scotists defend the notion that the hypostatic union sanctifies Christ's humanity only in the sense that it is the basis, source and root of Christ's habitual grace, in such a way that it makes necessary the gift of this grace to Christ. In other words, the grace of union would not formally sanctify Christ's humanity; it would just be its source insofar as it would require habitual grace for this to happen.

According to the Thomists, Christ's humanity is sanctified by the grace of union not only *radicaliter* but also *formaliter*. The term *formaliter* is used here with a very precise meaning—as opposed to *radicaliter*. Therefore, when the

---

149. This grace, therefore, can be said to be in some way infinite, through the union with the Word, essentially holy, in a unity of person, although obviously we cannot say that Christ's human nature is holy with the essential holiness of God himself. Thus, the Word gives his human nature its *subsistence*, but he does not give it his divine attributes, because each nature continues to possess its own attributes, as the Council of Chalcedon says.

150. Cf. J. Rohof, *La sainteté substantielle du Christ dans le Théologie scholastique. Histoire du problème*, op. cit., 59ff.

151. Cf. Durandus, *In IV Sent.*, 1. III, dist. XIII, q.II, no. 7; A. Michel, "Jésus-Christ", art. cit., 1275-9.

152. Cf. e.g., Mastrius, *De incarnatione*, disp. II, q.1, no. 16.

question is raised as to whether Christ's humanity is sanctified *formaliter* by the grace of union, the question being asked is: Is the grace of union alone sufficient to make the humanity of Christ holy in itself independently of habitual grace, or, to put it another way, is the grace of union alone what gives Christ impeccability. Thomists and, with them, most theologians say that it is.[153] Their view is that, if holiness is nothing other than a union with God so solid as to exclude all sin,[154] then that indissoluble bonding to God is something Christ has already through the grace of union; no other grace is called for.

So holiness in the strict meaning of the word—1) involves participation in the divine nature (*consortium divinae naturae*), a sharing or *consortium* which cannot be greater than that of union in unity of person; 2) confers divine filiation, whereby the just man is made an adoptive son of God: this filiation is so close a relationship in the case of Christ, thanks to the hypostatic union, that it is not adoptive but natural; 3) makes one pleasing to God, and the humanity of Christ is incomparably pleasing to God for the simple reason that it is the humanity of the Son. All this argues in favour of the view that the grace of union, on its own, (that is *formaliter*) sanctifies Christ; it is not just the source of his sanctification. As Garrigou-Lagrange notes, St Thomas never calls Christ's habitual grace "sanctifying grace", because Christ's sanctification comes from the grace of union.[155] In any event, it is clear that while habitual grace can give Christ's soul the gift of avoiding sin, only the grace of union gives him his absolute impeccability. That is why most theologians are of the view that the grace of union sanctifies Christ's human nature properly and formally, because from it his absolute impeccability derives.

c) Habitual grace, the infused virtues and the gifts of the Holy Spirit

Christ's humanity is substantially holy because it has been assumed by the Word in unity of person. Because it is the humanity of the Word, it is very appropriate that it should be endowed in the highest degree with habitual grace, the infused virtues and the gifts of the Holy Spirit. Although through the hypostatic union Christ's humanity is the humanity of the Word and has been sanctified by that union, if it did not have habitual grace it would remain simply human, without being "divinized" through that accidental transformation

---

153. Karl Adam takes a Scotist position. He seems to misunderstand the manner in which Thomists understand the word *substantialiter* by giving it the same meaning as *formaliter*. "They maintain that because our Lord's human nature is united in one person with the self of the Logos, Jesus' human soul possesses *in substantia*, in his entire substance, the sanctity of God. Even if Jesus's human soul were conceived of as denuded of all created sanctity and all sanctifying grace, it would still be bound to give forth infinite joy on account of its union in one person with the substantial sanctity of God's Logos. The Scotists contest this, and rightly so": K. Adam, *The Christ of faith*, op. cit., 255.

154. Cf. St Thomas Aquinas, *STh* II-II, q.81, a.8.

155. Cf. R. Garrigou-Lagrange, *Christ the Saviour* (St Louis and London, 1950), 251.

which raises the nature and operations of the soul onto the level of the inner life of God.[156]

Very few authors have argued against Christ having habitual grace.[157] Obviously, no Christian author has denied that Christ was holy. The few who have said that Christ's soul was not adorned with habitual grace, have held that view because they thought he had no need of it, given that everything to do with Christ was substantially and formally holy through the grace of union.

Three reasons are usually put forward in favour of Christ having habitual grace—a) the closeness of Christ's humanity to the source of grace (the Word), made it very fitting that he should receive the influence of grace; b) Christ's soul, because it is so close to the Word, should attain to God as intimately as possible through its actions of knowing and loving, and therefore it needed to be elevated by grace; c) Christ, as man, is the mediator between God and men and head of all the saints; his headship is such as to effect what is said in John 1:16: "From his fullness have we all received, grace upon grace." To do this he has to have grace which would overflow on others.

It is the common opinion of theologians that, in Christ, habitual grace follows the grace of union as something *morally* required by the grace of union itself, that is, as a *deification* of the essence of his soul and its powers consistent with their belonging ontologically to the humanity of the Word. However, it can also be argued that the hypostatic union necessarily brings with it the *deification* of Jesus' human nature through the fullness of habitual grace, without this in any way threatening the non-confusion of natures in Christ.[158]

As in our own case, so also in Christ the supernatural elevation of the human nature is needed in order for him to carry out supernatural actions. Therefore, after speaking of Christ's habitual grace, it is appropriate to consider the infused virtues and the gifts of the Holy Spirit. Christ had all the virtues in the manner befitting his perfection as Son and his mission as Redeemer. There is a close link between these virtues and the fullness of grace proper to Christ. Some of these virtues, notably his faithfulness and obedience to the Father, his charity and his mercy, have been graphically described in the New Testament.

Other virtues (those which have exclusively to do with the *status viatoris*, such as faith and hope, or those which involve imperfection—such as

156. Here is Thomas Aquinas' solution to this objection: "Christ is true God by his person and by his divine nature. But since the distinction of the natures remains in the unity of person, the soul of Christ is not divine in its essence. Therefore it is necessary that it should come to be so through participation. And this is an effect of grace": *STh* III, q.7, a.1, ad 1.

157. Cassian is usually included among these authors (cf. A. Grillmeier, *Gesù il Christo . . .*, op. cit., 852-58, as are some medieval authors according to Petrus de Palude (*In IV Sent.*, 1. III, dist. 13, q.2) and, among contemporaries, Malmberg: cf. F. Malmberg, *Über den Gottmenschen* (Fribourg, 1960), 71-88.

158. Cf. F. Ocáriz, *Hijos de Dios en Cristo*, op. cit., 133.

penance—are not found formally in Christ, but any element of perfection which is found in them is found in Him, raised to a higher level of perfection. This is true of the virtue of faith, as discussed earlier.[159] Those who speak of Christ having faith do so, either because they hold that he did not have *science of vision* while he was still on earth, or because they understand the virtue of faith not in its usual meaning (believing what one does not see, trusting in the authority of God revealing) but in some way in the sense of fidelity.[160]

A similar difficulty has to do with the existence in Christ of the virtue of hope, the idea of which includes not having what one hopes for: it includes the *not yet* so characteristic of yearning. Because he is the Incarnate Word, Christ cannot hope for his humanity something it already naturally has—union with God. But he does hope for everything which he does not possess during the course of his life on earth, for example, the glorification of his body.[161] Christ did not *formally* have the virtue of penance, because due to his sinlessness he did not have what is proper to that virtue (contrition for one's own sins), even though, in solidarity with mankind, he made satisfaction for our sins.[162]

All the gifts and fruits of the Holy Spirit (cf. Is 11:2 and Gal 5:22) are to be found in Christ in the highest degree; including the gift of the fear of Yahweh, as Isaiah described it, that is, the sense of the majesty and grandeur of God, reverence for the Father, which elicits his instant and indignant reply: "You shall worship the Lord your God and him only shall you serve" (Mt 4:10).

The gifts of the Holy Spirit bring the virtues to their highest perfection, uniting them in the higher unity of supreme perfection.[163] That is why they should be in Christ—to make for the complete perfection of all his virtues. We are repeatedly told in the Gospels that "Jesus was full of the Holy Spirit" and "was led by the Spirit") (cf., e.g., Lk 4:1). "The work of the divine Spirit accomplished not only the conception of Christ, but also accomplished the sanctification of his soul, which in the Scriptures is called the 'anointing' (Acts

159. Remember St Thomas Aquinas' reasoning: "If we maintain that the divine reality was not inevident, we exclude the very essence of faith. Now from the first moment of his conception Christ saw God's essence fully. Hence there could be no faith in him": *STh* III, q.7, a.3 in c.

160. Cf. section 3(v) of this chapter.

161. St Thomas Aquinas, *STh* III, q.7, a.4 in c.

162. To avoid misunderstanding, the Holy Office on 15 July 1893 prohibited the use of the term "penitent" with reference to the Heart of Jesus, even if it were to be used in the form of *poenitens pro nobis*. As González Gil notes, "if we turn our eyes to Jesus Christ himself, we notice that even though he has a very profound sense of the holiness of God, and has a very high notion of the ideal of virtue, he never manifests any trace of remorse for sin, never experiences the need to ask for forgiveness of his sins; on the contrary, he can claim with calm assurance that he 'always does what is pleasing to his Father' (cf. Jn 8:29)": *Cristo, el misterio de Dios*, I, op. cit., 338f.

163. Cf. J.A. de Aldama, "Los dones del Espíritu Santo. Problemas y controversias en la actual teología de los dones", RET 9 (1949) 3-30.

10:38). Furthermore, every action of Christ, especially the sacrifice of himself, was done, with the Holy Spirit present. 'Through the eternal Spirit, he offered himself without blemish to God' (Heb 9:14) ."[164]

Christ also had all the graces *gratis data* (gratuitously given) and all the charisms, as befitted "the first and principal teacher of the faith."[165] The reason most generally given was expressed by St Augustine in these words: "In the same way as all the senses are in the head, so in Christ all the graces are to be found." For all graces come from the fullness of the grace of Christ.[166] Some of these graces, such as that of prophecy, were predicted of him (cf. Dt 18:15), and Jesus applied to himself the title of prophet (Jn 4:44). Clearly, Christ is not only a prophet; he is more than a prophet. But, although in him the gift of prophecy lacks the imperfection (obscureness and limitation) inherent in other prophets, nevertheless,"he can be considered to be a prophet in that he knows and announces things that are beyond the knowledge of the rest of human wayfarers. Therefore he is said to have the gift of prophecy."[167]

d) Gratia capitis Christ is the new Adam, who has a relationship with th' redeemed like that of the vine with its branches. One can bear fruit only if one stays united to him, in the same sort of way as the branch is attached to the vine. It is from the vine that the branch receives the sap, its life (cf. Jn 15:1-8). This allegory throws light on what John 1:16 says: "from his fullness have we all received, grace upon grace". Christ is also the Head of the Church, as St Paul so often stressed:[168] "Grace was given to each of us according to the measure of Christ's gift" (Eph 4:7).

Christ has been given grace not only because of his dignity as Son, but also with a view to his mission as the new Adam and Head of the Church, to sanctify it. As Pius XII says, "Christ is the author and efficient cause of holiness; for there can be no salutary act which does not proceed from him as from its supernatural source. [. . .] From him flows into the Body of the Church all the light which divinely illuminates those who believe, and all the grace which makes them holy as he himself is holy. [. . .] His inexhaustible fullness is the fount of grace and glory."[169]

164. Leo XIII, Enc. *Divinum illud munus*, 9 May 1897 (DS 3327).
165. Cf. St Thomas Aquinas, *STh* III, q.7, a.7 in c.
166. St Augustine, *Epist ad Dardanum*, 13 (PL 33, 847).
167. St Thomas Aquinas, *STh* III, q.7, a.9 in c. And in the ad 2, he writes: "Faith has as its object such things as are unseen by him who believes; and hope, too, is of such things as are not possessed by the one who hopes. But prophecy has regard to such things as are beyond the ordinary knowledge of men, with whom the prophet shares the condition of wayfarer. Hence faith and hope are repugnant to the perfection of Christ's beatitude; but prophecy is not."
168. Cf. especially Rom 8:29; 12:3-8; 1 Cor 15:45; Eph 1:22-24; 4:7-16; 5:22, 27, 29; Col 1:18-20; Tit 3:6; Heb 5:9.
169. Pius XII, Enc. *Mystici corporis*, op. cit., AAS 35 (1943) 193-248.

We are not, then, talking about a grace distinct from the personal grace of our Lord's humanity, but about an aspect of that grace, about Christ being Head, about his sanctifying causality.[170] That habitual grace that Christ has as source and cause of all the grace men receive is termed capital grace (*gratia capitis*). All grace comes to us from him and through him. This explains the vigour of St Paul's language when he speaks of our salvation and sanctification being *in* the Son; of *putting on* Christ, of dying and rising *with* Christ, of being made one body *with* him.[171] We are made Sons of God *in* Christ through the Holy Spirit.[172] He is the source and cause of every gift that is given to men, including the gift of the resurrection of the body.[173] That is why the Fathers call Christ's body *caro vivifica*, the flesh that gives life.[174] This does not mean, obviously, that the grace that is given to man is *materially* Christ's own habitual grace, "like the transfusion of something physical,"[175] but that we are loved by God in Christ, that all the grace we receive is given in him and by him; that he is the instrumental cause (*instrumentum conjunctum*) of all sanctification.[176]

e) The fullness of grace in Christ   Very often, when citing Sacred Scripture we have met the statement that in Christ there is fullness of grace: Jesus was "full of grace and truth; from his fullness have we all received, grace upon grace" (Jn 1:14 and 16). God gave Him the Spirit without measure (cf. Jn 3:34). The entire Christian tradition has it that not only is Christ holy but he has the fullness of grace. Chrysostom puts it in this way: "All grace was poured out

170. "Christ's soul", Aquinas explains, "possessed grace in all its fullness. This pre-eminence of grace is what enables Christ to bestow his grace on others; that in fact is what capital grace consists in. Hence the personal grace whereby the soul of Christ is justified is essentially the same as the grace which is his as head of the Church and with which he justifies others; there is merely a distinction of reason between these (two graces)": *STh* III, q.8, a.5 in c.

171. L. Cerfaux, *Le Christ dans la théologie de saint Paul* (Paris 1951), especially 315-28; F. Prat, *The Theology of St Paul*, II, op. cit., 283-99. Ch. Journet, *Teología de la Iglesia* (Pamplona, 1962), 41-54; E. Sauras, *El cuerpo místico de Cristo* (Madrid, 1956), 182-482.

172. Cf. F. Ocáriz, *Hijos de Dios en Cristo*, op. cit., 93-115.

173. Thomas Aquinas, in line with all tradition, teaches that the risen body of Christ is the efficient cause and exemplary cause of the resurrection of the just (cf. *STh* III, q.56, aa. 1 and 2. Cf. L.F. Mateo Seco, "Eucaristía e Resurreceiçao dos corpos", *Theologica* 8 (1973) 1-19.

174. Cf. e.g., St Gregory of Nyssa, *Oratio catechetica magna*, 37 (PG 45, 93-7).

175. In the words of J.H. Nicolas; cf. *Synthèse Dogmatique*, op. cit., 375.

176. This doctrine is set forth with precision at the Sixth Session of the Council of Trent (13 January 1547): "Finally, the single formal cause is the justice of God, *not that by which he himself is just but that by which he makes us just* (canons 10 and 11), that, namely, whereby being endowed with it by him, we are renewed in the spirit of our mind, and not only are we reputed but are truly called and are just, receiving justice within us, each one according to his own measure, which *the Holy Spirit distributes to everyone as he wills* (1 Cor 12:11), and according to each one's disposition and co-operation" (DS 1529). Regarding participation in the capital grace of Christ, cf., e.g., F. Ocáriz, "La elevación sobrenatural como re-creación en Cristo, in *Atti dell'VIII Congresso Tomistico Internazionale* (Vatican City, 1981), 281-92.

upon that temple [Christ's humanity]; for he was not given a measured quantity of grace. And we all have received grace from his fullness. But that temple received it wholly and completely."[177]

There are two aspects to this fullness of grace: Christ's fullness of grace was *intensive* (this refers to its perfection) and it was *extensive* (this refers to the gifts and graces it includes). The reasons in favour of this double fullness are the same as those we gave when speaking about Jesus' holiness: this fullness is due to Christ's human nature by virtue of its union in unity of person with the Word, and in view also of his mission as Head of the human race. In him reside, as St Paul tells us, all the treasures of wisdom and knowledge (cf. Col 2:3). This fact poses the question whether Christ had this grace to an infinite degree. That is, whether Christ was infinitely holy, not only through the grace of union but also through habitual grace.

St Thomas replies in the affirmative but with nuances, basing what he says mainly on two passages of Scripture: John 3:34 ("It is not by measure that (God) gives [him] the Spirit") and Ephesians 4:7 ("Grace was given to each of us according to the measure of Christ's gift"), where there seems to be a clear contrast between the grace Christ has (unlimited, no measure) and our grace, which is measured out to us. The rational arguments used in support of this position are the same as those adduced in favour of the fullness of grace in Christ. Given that it is created grace that is in question (in the case of both the created entity of grace and the created entity of Christ's soul), it must be said (this is St Thomas' view) that from this point of view Christ's grace cannot be described as infinite. However, it can be called infinite if it is grace itself we are considering. In this sense Christ does have infinite grace "since he has everything which pertains to the concept of grace, without any limitation", because "it is bestowed on Christ's soul as a universal principle for bestowing grace on human nature."[178]

These statements about Christ's grace being infinite are based on factors valid for any point in our Lord's life—the hypostatic union and Jesus' position as head of the human race. Therefore, generally, theology considers that Jesus Christ does have this fullness of grace from the very first moment of his conception, because already then he was the natural Son of God and the new Adam.[179] However, two things follow from this, which are explicitly accepted

---

177. St John Chrysostom, *In Ps 44*, 2 (PG 55, 185).

178. St Thomas Aquinas, *STh* III, q.7, a.11 in c. The example which St Thomas then employs shows that he is speaking of a relative infinity: "Similarly we can say that the light of the sun is infinite, not as regards its being but insofar as it is light, because it has whatever pertains to the nature of light." For this reason, this affirmation is generally understood as expressing an infinity not in the *entitative* sense (considered as a reality) but in the *formal* sense (considered as a grace).

179. Cf. e.g., A. Michel, "Jésus-Christ", art. cit., 1283f. In this sense Christ's fullness of grace is quite different from the Blessed Virgin's. When we refer to her as being "full of grace",

by those who support the theory of Christ having infinite grace, that is, all classical theologians: (a) Christ had the beatific vision from the first moment of his conception; b) Christ could not grow in grace over the course of his life.

The first consequence is obvious. The consummation of grace (the highest degree of grace) is produced by the beatific vision. To say that Christ has infinite grace intensively and extensively is the same as saying that he has it in the highest degree and therefore that he enjoys the beatific vision.

The second consequence is also obvious. If one argues that Christ had infinite grace, this implies that he could not grow in grace, since he already had maximum grace from the very first moment.[180] If one says that Christ did grow in grace, that is the same as saying that he did not have grace to an infinite degree.[181] And vice versa, if one denies that Christ has the beatific vision, one must say that he did not have grace to an infinite degree and that during his life he grew in grace like any other *viator*.

The classical doctrine's view is it does not seem logical that he who is already God should *walk* towards God (that is the position of the *viator*) and that, therefore, it is better to face the difficulties of having to explain how during his earthly life Christ was both *viator* and *comprehensor* than to say he did not have infinite grace. Even on the human level, that is, in his human heart, Christ has infinite charity, bears his cross with infinite love and obedience,[182] because that infinite charity is necessarily linked to infinite grace.

The difficulty this position involves is usually put as follows: if Christ is truly man, and men during their life on earth are wayfarers and can grow in grace, if one says Christ could not grow in this way, then that seems to mean he was not truly human; therefore, one must take it that Christ grew in grace over the course of his life on earth. In support of this, the passage in Luke 2:52 is usually cited: "And Jesus increased in wisdom and in stature, and in

we mean that at every moment of her life she had all the grace appropriate to God's will in her regard and that yet she continually grew in grace.

180. St Thomas Aquinas is a good example of this approach for he not only defends Christ's possessing grace in an infinite degree but also his having it thus from the very first moment of his conception so that he could not grow in regard to grace. Grace could not grow in Christ, he writes, "because Christ as man was from the very first moment of his conception truly and fully blessed. Therefore grace could not increase in him, nor could it do so in the rest of the blessed because they are in a terminus state are not open to growth." (*STh* III, q.7, a.12, in c.). The logic followed here is obvious: the reasons for saying that Christ possessed grace in an infinite degree are the same as for saying that he had this grace from the first moment of his conception. In fact, he was then already united hypostatically to the Word and was Head of the human race and of the Church. This being so, defending Christ's possession of grace in an infinite degree is the same as defending his having it to a supreme degree and his having, also, the beatific vision, that is to say, his being in a terminus state. And both of these reasons—the infinity and the state of terminus—are incompatible with growth in grace.

181. Cf. J.A. Riestra, "Historicidad y santidad en Cristo según Santo Tomás" in *Cristo, Hijo de Dios y Redentor del hombre*, op. cit., 893-907.

182. Cf. St Thomas Aquinas, *STh* III, q.48, aa.1-3.

favour with God and man". St Thomas' commentary on this text is very illuminating: "Someone can grow in wisdom and grace in two ways—first, because the very habits of wisdom and grace grow, and in that sense Christ did not grow; secondly, as regards the effects, that is, in as much as they produce wiser and greater works; and in this way Christ grew in wisdom and grace just as he grew in age, since in the course of time he did more perfect works, to show that he was a true man, both in the things of God and in the things of man."[183] Christ, as the patristic tradition emphasized so much, is perfect man, but he is not an ordinary man, a *vulgaris homo*; he is a man who is, at the same time, God.[184] Therefore, to require that Jesus and other men be totally the same, while also holding that he is God, is simply impossible: so, for example, with regard to impeccability, even during his life on earth, Christ was metaphysically incapable of sin, as we shall go on to see.

f) Christ is incapable of sin, and he is free A consequence of the hypostatic union and of Christ's substantial holiness and infinite habitual grace is the unanimous assertion about there being no sin in Christ (his *impeccancy*) and his inability to sin, his impeccability.

Sacred Scripture explicitly states that Christ did not commit sin: "Which of you convicts me of sin?" (Jn 8:46). He is the spotless Lamb (cf. 1 Pet 1:19); who "takes away the sin of the world" (Jn 1:29). He is the holy priest, like us in every respect, "yet without sinning" (Heb 4:15), who offered himself "without blemish to God" (Heb 9:14). "For our sake he (God) made him to be sin who knew no sin, so that in him we might become the righteousness of God" (2 Cor 5:21; cf. also 1 Pet 2:22; 1 Jn 3:5).

Given the unanimity on this matter, the Magisterium has intervened very seldom, and has limited itself to saying that there was no sin in Christ. Jesus, because he knew no sin, "did not need to offer any offering on his own behalf";[185] "he was conceived without sin, was born without sin, and died without sin."[186] The absence of sin in Christ follows from three basic things—the hypostatic union, Christ's holiness, and his mission as Redeemer. Persons are those who are responsible for the actions they do through their own nature; if Christ had committed sin, it would have been the Person of the Word who sinned through his human nature. And Christ's infinite holiness is incompatible with any shadow of sin. Finally his mission as Redeemer (this is the argument we have seen the Council of Ephesus use) was completely at

---

183. *STh* III, q.7, a.12, ad 3.
184. Cf. e.g., St Gregory of Nyssa, *Adv. Apoll.*, 21 (PG, 1164f), where he says that Christ is not an ordinary man (*homo vulgaris* is the usual Latin translation, *ou dia panton koinos anthropos*, in Greek).
185. Cr. *Anathematismi Cyrilli Alexandrini*, 10; Council of Ephesus (DS 261).
186. Eleventh Council of Toledo, AD 675 (DS 539). The same words are found in the Council of Florence, *Decr. pro Jacobitis* (DS 1347).

odds with commission of sin. He is the holy priest who does not need to offer victims and sacrifices for himself, but only for his brethren, and he could not have been their perfect model if there had been sin in him.[187]

Although Catholic authors agree in saying that Christ was incapable of sinning, they differ in the way they explain the scope and basis of this impeccability.

Peter Lombard,[188] St Bonaventure,[189] St Thomas,[190] and Suarez[191] think that Christ has this impeccability through the hypostatic union itself and that it is therefore absolute and antecedent to every other grace. Thus, they argue that it is the person who is responsible for his actions, because the person expresses himself and performs actions through his nature. So, to say that Christ could sin is the same as saying that God could sin, because it would be the Word who was expressing himself in the sin committed by his human nature. Therefore, Christ must be impeccable by virtue of the impeccability of the Word.

Scotus, consistent with the way he differs on the subject of Christ's substantial holiness, sees Christ as impeccable but not by virtue of the hypostatic union; rather, by virtue of divine Providence and the beatific vision, which he also says Christ has from the first moment of his conception.[192] So, Christ would be impeccable not because he is the Word made flesh but because of an external grace. Clearly Scotus (who also accepts that the Word is impeccable) locates the basis of Christ's impeccabilty in an external grace for the simple reason that, in one way or another, he conceives the relationship of the human nature to the Person of the Word as one of autonomy with actions that are not the direct responsibility of the Person of the Word.[193]

To say that Christ was incapable of sinning, and particularly to do so in the way St Thomas does, inevitably brings up the question of his freedom. How can one say that Christ was absolutely impeccable by virtue of his very Person and that he had at the same time genuine human freedom. St Thomas was aware of the problem, and he draws attention to something which it is very important to remember: "The reality of human nature is not proved by sin, since sin does not belong to human nature, whereof God is the cause;

---

187. Cf. St Thomas Aquinas, *STh* III, q.15, a.1.
188. *Sententiarum Liber* III, d.12.
189. *In III Sent.* d.12.
190. *In II Sent.* d.12; *STh* III, q.15, a.1.
191. *Disp* 33, sect. 2
192. "The nature which he (Christ) assumed could in itself commit sin because it was not blessed by reason of the union, and it did have free will so that it could turn to one side or to the other. But through blessedness it was confirmed from the very first moment in such a way as to be incapable of sin, as the Blessed are also impeccable": Duns Scotus, *In III Sent.*, disp. 13, q.1, ad 2.
193. Among the few authors who have denied the impeccability of Christ are Günther and Farrar, who say that if Christ did not sin that was purely because he chose not to, but he was not really impeccable (cf. A. Michel, "Jésus-Christ", art. cit., 1291).

rather, sin has been introduced against nature, by a seed of the devil, as Damascene says."[194]

It is a matter of faith that Christ was free, among other reasons because the Gospels show him to be free, and because without liberty he would not have been able to obey. Therefore, as proof that Christ was free (with a meritorious freedom like other men during their time on earth), theology has interpreted those texts which speak of his obedience (e.g., Phil 2:5-11),[195] and those others in which Jesus says that he does not do his own will but that of the Father who has sent him (cf., e.g., Jn 5:30).

The question as to how liberty and impeccability combined in Christ is usually studied apropos of his obedient freedom in his passion and death: if Christ was impeccable, how could he disobey his Father; and if he obeyed him not being able to do otherwise, how can it be said he died of his own free will?

Many distinguished theologians have found the question so difficult to answer that they have avoided it. However, it needs to be approached with the humility of one who knows that there is a mystery here, and also with the conviction that Christ's freedom *and* impeccability are matters of faith. These are some of the solutions suggested over the centuries: Christ did not have the beatific vision during his passion or at least it was suspended; or else the beatific vision did not make Christ's soul intrinsically impeccable and therefore it did not take away his freedom (Scotists); Christ was not given a strict commandment to undergo death: he was simply given advice which he was free to follow or not (Franzelin); Christ was given a strict commandment to undergo death but he was free when it came to choosing the circumstances of his death (Lugo, Vazquez); Christ was given a genuine commandment to die, a commandment which he obeyed with impeccable freedom (Thomists, School of Salamanca, Bellarmine).[196]

This last position, though it may at first seem difficult to hold, is probably the most reasonable. For, defending the idea that Christ was obedient and at the same time free even though he could not disobey, seems to fit in better with the teaching of Scripture, which speaks of Christ's obedience (especially at his death) and of his impeccability, and which locates in Christ's obedience (and there can be no obedience where there is no freedom) the reason why his sacrifice was pleasing to God: Christ made himself obedient unto death on a

---

194. St Thomas Aquinas, *STh* III, q.15, a.1, in c. Cf. A. Durand, "La liberté du Christ dans son rapport a l'impecabilite", NRT 70 (1948) 821f.

195. As did St Maximus the Confessor in his struggle against Monothelism. Cf. F.M. Lethel, *Théologie de l'agonie du Christ*, op. cit., 76f. Cf. A.C. Chacon, "La libertad meritoria de Cristo y nuestra libertad" in *Cristo, Hijo de Dios y Redentor del hombre*, op. cit., 875-92.

196. Cf. Charles Pesch, *De Verbo Incarnato* (Fribourg, 1909), 179-80; A. Michel, "Jésus-Christ", art. cit. 1297-309; J. Stohr, "Reflexiones teológicas en torna a la libertad de Cristo en su Pasión y Muerte", in *Cristo, Hijo Dios y Redentor del hombre*, op. cit., 809-49.

cross and for that reason God exalted him and gave him a name that is above every other name (cf. Phil 2:8-9).

Freely obedient acceptance of death by Christ is all the more remarkable given the severity of his death; however, the difficulty of understanding how he could be free *and* impeccable applies to his whole life and not just his last hours. Christ was free and impeccable whenever he had to obey God's commandments and even the natural law over the course of his life on earth: freedom and obedience at the time of his death are just one more part of the mystery of how the divine and the human combined forces in Christ throughout his life.[197]

The solution to this apparent dilemma is to be found, first, in the quotation we have just given from St Thomas: sin is not native to, is not intrinsic to, human nature; it is anti-nature. Just as error neither perfects the intellect nor is in agreement with it, though it is a sign of the existence of the intellect, so too sin neither perfects man's freedom nor is in line with the nature of freedom, though it does show that man has freedom.[198] Choice is a sign of freedom, but choice as such is not essential to the free act, especially choice between good and evil. The essence of freedom lies in the *manner of willing*: in willing without the will being moved by anything other than itself, as St Thomas says, giving a somewhat different meaning to Aristotle's dictum: *Liberum est quod causa sui est* (That which is free is that which is its own cause).[199] The will is free because it is the cause of its own act, because it is not moved of necessity, either by the intellect or by any other external or internal factor. Since the good is the proper object of the will, there is no contradiction between being free and not being able to choose evil; what there is is in fact freedom in its most perfect form.

g) The temptations of Christ By virtue of the hypostatic union Christ was essentially impeccable. And also by virtue of that union and of his own lack of sin, Christ did not have the *fomes peccati*, that is, the disorder occurring in

---

197. As J. Auer writes, "given that every sin reaches the personal core of man, which in Jesus is the divine *Logos*, and given that moreover the divine nature completely penetrates Christ's human nature through grace, it must be said of Jesus first and foremost that he is *essentially impeccable* by virtue of the hypostatic union; in other words, that he could not sin, even though his human nature was (in the abstract) sinful": J. Auer, *Jesucristo, Hijo de Dios e Hijo de María*, op. cit., 478. This last phrase, "nature (in the abstract) sinful" is not very happy, for various reasons, including the fact that Christ's human nature "in the abstract" does not exist; also, in any man, human nature "in the abstract" is neither sinful nor non-sinful; it can only be described as "sinful" due to original sin; every other attribution of the idea of "sinful" refers to persons (personal sin), not to their nature. On freedom and sin, cf. L.F. Mateo Seco, *Martín Lutero: Sobre la libertad esclava* (Madrid, 1978), 59-79.

198. Cf. St Thomas Aquinas, *De Veritate*, q.22, a.6, in c.

199. St Thomas Aquinas, *De Veritate*, q.24, a.1. Cf. C. Fabro, *Riflessioni sulla libertà* (Rimini, 1983), especially 22-5.

man as a result of original sin.[200] Therefore, Christ did not experience temptation *ab intrinseco*, from within. All theologians agree on this, with the exception of Theodore of Mopsuestia who did say that Christ had disordered passions and the concupiscence of the flesh.[201] We have already often referred to the theological reasons which underpin this unanimity—the infinite holiness of Christ and the fact that he had no sin of any kind, not even original sin.[202]

This does not mean that Christ's soul and body did not have an appetite for things which were good for them and a distaste for harmful things, or that Christ did not have human passions. To say that Christ did not experience the disorder of concupiscence is not the same as saying that he had no feelings. On the contrary, he was a person of great feeling, as can be seen from his reactions, and in his preaching and parables. Jesus feels hunger and wants to eat; he is thirsty and sleepy and feels the need to drink and rest; he becomes indignant with a holy anger; he knows the joy of friendship; he weeps with a heartfelt human sorrow; he feels "sorrowful and troubled" when faced with death (cf. Mt 26:37-38). We have already, when discussing Christ's will, made the distinction between *voluntas ut ratio* (the will as a free and reasonable act) and *voluntas ut natura* (the will as a natural tendency towards good). Christ shows this, for example, in the agony in the garden, when he says to the Father, "not my will, but thine, be done" (Lk 22:42). His human nature, which is holy and orientated in the right way, rejects anything which will harm it, such as pain and death, but there is nothing wrong about that—on the contrary. That same human nature, acting with freedom, and in obedience to the Father, controls the revulsion it feels at the prospect of the pain and torment that awaits him. As St Thomas writes, Christ suffered "(at the thought of) the loss of his bodily life, which is naturally horrible to human nature".[203] Here we can see Christ's freedom at work as also his impeccability: neither the Father's commandment, nor the loving infallibility with which he obeys that command-

---

200. Cf. e.g., Paul VI, *Creed of the People of God*, 30 June 1968, no. 10.
201. He was condemned in the eighth session of the Third Council of Constantinople (2 June 553) for saying, among other things, in line with his idea there were two subjects in Christ, that "one was God the Word and the other Christ, who was troubled by passions of soul and desires of the flesh, and who therefore gradually became a better man by virtue of his works"(DS 434).
202. St Thomas notes, moreover, that it was not appropriate for Christ to take on this defect of human nature, because "instead of helping to make satisfaction for sin, it does the opposite" (St Thomas Aquinas, *STh* III q.15, a.2, in c.).
203. St Thomas Aquinas, *STh* III, q.46, a.6 in c. And in ad 4, he continues this point in an enlightening manner, showing that the revulsion which Christ feels in regard to death comes precisely from his holiness: "The bodily life of Christ was of such great dignity especially due to its union with the divinity that he had to be hurt by its loss even if it was only for an hour [. . .]. Hence the Philosopher says in III Ethics that the virtuous man loves his life all the more that he is aware of his being better and, nevertheless, he is prepared to risk it for the good of virtue. In the same way, Christ put his life at stake, a life which he loved in supreme fashion, for the good of charity."

ment causes Christ to be attracted directly and inevitably to that death, which he continues to find repugnant.[204]

Sacred Scripture gives prominence to temptations Christ experienced, particular the temptation in the wilderness reported by the Synoptics just after his baptism (Mt 4:1-11; Mk 1:12-13; Lk 4:1-13). Christ did experience temptation. It was not temptation *ab intrinseco* (which stems from one's inner disorder) but a temptation *ab extrinseco*, from outside. But this does not mean that Christ did not experience genuine temptation. Christ felt the devil bearing down on him, and also pressure from people and pressure of events, all pushing him to be untrue to his mission, to debase his messiahship. These were real temptations, which do no imply interior stress in the person who experiences them, but they do call for fortitude if they are to be rejected: "we have not a high priest who is unable to sympathize with our weaknesses, but one who in every respect has been tempted as we are, yet without sinning" (Heb 4:15).

This is not the place to make an exegesis of the scriptural passages which report the temptations of Christ.[205] All we need do here is remember that Christ's temptations have to be set into the broader framework of his struggle with Satan, which is something the Gospels put a lot of stress on. Satan attacks Jesus with all the weapons at his disposal, but he is always defeated.

From the point of view of their content, the three temptations reported in the Synoptics point towards Christ's messiahship, and they are in close parallel to the earthly interpretation of the Messiah prevalent among the Jews: Satan tempts Jesus to turn his messiahship to his own advantage and opposite to the will of his Father. And, throughout his life Jesus had to reject pressure from the people around him, his disciples included,[206] which went counter to the Father's plan. Even when he was on the cross, the same temptation was put to him: "If you are the Son of God, come down from the cross" (Mt 27:41-43; Mk 15:27-32).

So, Jesus was truly tempted at many times and consistently rejected these temptations, setting a genuine example of how to struggle against evil. Satan was the main tempter, but temptation also came from his enemies, his environment, and even his own disciples. For the experience of temptation to be real, and victory also to be real, a man's heart does not necessarily have to

204. The following example may be useful by way of analogy. The more a mother loves her small child the more unfailingly will she get up in the middle of the night if the child needs her. This does not mean that she does not have freedom but only that she has more love. But no matter how much love she has, her body will always want to rest more than to get up at an untimely hour.

205. Cf., e.g., R. Schnackenburg, "Der Sinn der Versuchung Jesu bei den Synoptikern" TQ (1952) 297-326; J. Dupont, *Les tentations de Jésus au désert* (Bruges, 1968).

206. Take, for example, the scene where Peter tries to dissuade Jesus from entering his Passion and Jesus replies, "Get behind me, Satan! You are a hindrance to me; for you are not on the side of God, but of men" (Mt 16:23).

be inclined to evil, nor does he need to have the *fomes peccati*. Christ never dialogues with evil: the "law of sin" (cf. Rom 7:21-25) has no control over him. But he is truly tempted. And he gives a real example of how to defeat the Evil One. His victories over these temptations are part of his victory over the "ruler of this world" (cf. Jn 12:31; 14:30; 16:11).

In God's plan, the temptations which Christ undergoes do not simply have a pedagogical purpose: they are part and parcel of his struggle against and victory over the Evil One. Jesus defeats the attacks of Satan, which "recapitulate the temptations of Adam in Paradise and those in Israel in the desert". This victory "anticipates the victory at the Passion, the supreme act of obedience of his filial love for the Father".[207] As St Hilary writes, commenting on Matthew 12:29: "Christ publicly acknowledges that all the power of the devil was wiped out by him in the first temptation, given that nobody can enter a strong man's house and take away his property from him unless he had first tied him up. And it is clear that whoever can do that to a strong man has to be stronger still than he is. Satan became tied up when our Lord called him by his name; the public declaration of his evil nature served to chain him. Once he had thus tied him up he deprived him of his arms and of his house, that is to say, of us who were his arms previously. He restored us to the ranks of the military in his kingdom and made us into a house evacuated by the one who was conquered and enchained."[208] Christ's victory over the devil reaches its climax on the cross; but it began (very definitely) much earlier on. The temptations he experienced were significant moments in his struggle and his victory.

6. DESCENDING AND ASCENDING MEDIATION

Jesus Christ is the cornerstone (cf. Mt 21:42; Acts 4:11), because he is one and universal Mediator (cf. 1 Tim 2:5); in no one else is salvation to be found, for "there is no other name under heaven given among men by which we must be saved" (Acts 4:12). He is the Mediator of the New and eternal Covenant (cf. Heb 8:6; 9:15; 12:24). It is worth stressing that the notion of mediation used here is not an abstract one; mediation has an endearing name—Jesus Christ. He is not only the mediator: he is also mediation, because the mediation takes place in him: "He is before all things, and in him all things hold together. He is the head of the body, the church; he is the beginning, the first-born from the dead, that in everything he might be pre-eminent. For in him all the fullness of God was pleased to dwell, and through him to reconcile to himself all things, whether on earth or in heaven, making peace by the blood of his cross" (Col 1:17-2).

207. CCC, nos. 538f.
208. St Hilary, *Commentarius in Mt* (PL 9, 988).

This identity of the Person of the mediator with his mediation means that the mediation has a total immediacy,[209] that is, the mediation on men's behalf takes place precisely through their incorporation in the Mediator, whereby they become virtually linked to him as "branches and vine" (cf. Jn 15:1ff). And for the very reason that Christ's mediation happens with total immediacy (he is the intimate Word of the Father and at the same time the first-born of many brethren) this mediation endures forever, because it is in the person of the mediator that the union of men with God occurs—in heaven as well as in this life.

Christ's mediation is, therefore, universal and unique. Universal, because it extends to all men and to all nations: Jesus Christ is the new Adam, who recapitulates in himself the whole human race (cf. Rom 5:15-21; 1 Cor 15:45-49); unique, because any other mediator is but an instrument of Christ's unique mediation, thereby showing the effectiveness of this universal mediation.[210] Because it is universal and unique, this mediation is absolutely necessary: "there is salvation in no one else" (Acts 4:12). Our Lord himself makes that very clear: "no one comes to the Father, but by me" (Jn 14:6); "no one knows the Father except the Son, and anyone to whom the Son chooses to reveal him" (Mt 11:27).

As we have seen, Christ exercises this mediation in the first place in a "descending" manner. He himself is, before all else, the Father's gift to men who comes down from heaven, Immanuel, God with us, for "God so loved the world that he gave his only Son" (cf. Jn 3:16); he is "the Lamb of God [the lamb whom God hands over to mankind] who takes away the sin of the world" (cf. Jn 1:29). This descending aspect of Christ's mediation is prior to its ascending aspect—a very important theological point, because it focusses light on the fact that salvation is, first and foremost, a divine initiative and shows that this initiative is entirely gratuitous on God's part: "God shows his love for us in that while we were yet sinners Christ died for us" (Rom 5:8).

The ministry of Christ as revealer has its setting in this descending mediation: he is the one who bears witness to the Father, the one who brings light into the world by giving it the truth that sets men free (cf. Jn 8:12-30), that is, the one who gives a knowledge which is life and salvation. He speaks in the name of the Father; his teaching is not his own, but belongs to the one who has sent him (cf. Jn 7:16); he causes our sanctification and liberation,[211]

---

209. Cf. M. González Gil, *Cristo, el misterio de Dios*, II, op. cit., 600-3.

210. Apropos of Mary's maternal mediation, John Paul II writes: "The Church knows and teaches with St Paul *that there is only one mediator* (cf. 1 Tim 2:5-6) [. . .]. The teaching of the Second Vatican Council presents the truth of Mary's mediation as *a sharing in the one unique source that is the mediation of Christ himself*" (John Paul II, Enc. *Redemptoris Mater*, 25 March 1987, no. 38). Cf. Second Vatican Council, Const. *Lumen gentium*, 62; cf. also F. Ocáriz, *María y la Trinidad*, op. cit., especially 787-94.

211. As Sesboüé writes, "it can never be said often enough that this doctrine of justification

or, to put it better, it is the Father who is reconciling us in Him (cf. Col 1:20). This sanctification takes place through our sharing in the divine life as adoptive children, that is, through our insertion into Christ. He sends the Holy Spirit, who is the fruit of the cross.[212] Even the resurrection of the body ("the redemption of our bodies": (Rom 8:23) is caused efficiently and effectively by the risen Redeemer, the effective Mediator of our resurrection.[213]

By being truly man and the head of the human race, Jesus constitutes the gift which men offer to God. He is the complete "amen" spoken to the Father, the "faithful and true witness" (Rev 3:14). His obedience unto death, which expiated for and destroyed the effects of Adam's disobedience (cf. Rom 5:12-19), is both a loving surrender of his human freedom, and atonement for mankind. The Mediator, as our head, offers his life to the Father: he does not "stand in" for us, nor is he just our representative: he really acts as the new Adam who recapitulates mankind in himself, forming with us, as it were, a mystical person".[214]

Ascending mediation consists in making a gift of men to God, in uniting them to God, in offering them to him. The gift which God makes to men is his loving gift of self; the acceptance of this gift, in its turn, can only take the form of the loving gift of man to God: "in either case, the gift cannot be external to the giver: if God gives himself man must give himself in a love which Scripture describes as nuptial".[215] At the very core of this ascending mediation is the sacrifice Christ offers the Father on the cross, as also the offering which Christ makes, along with himself, of his entire Church—worship, thanksgiving, expiation of sins and the prayer of all men and on behalf of all men. In union with Christ, immersed in his sacrifice like a drop of water in the wine, men offer God perfect homage, or, rather, the Mediator offers it by joining them to himself.

So, we can say that in the movement of ascending mediation man loves God unto death, for in Christ's sacrifice we find total adoration and total self-giving. Jesus' self-surrender as head of the human race makes it possible for each and every human being to make his personal self-surrender. We are touching here on a key dimension of Christ's mediation which is the basis of Christian moral optimism: the effectiveness of descending mediation lies in the fact that it makes ascending mediation possible; that is, it makes it possible for Christ, as head of mankind, to offer the Father the love and self-surrender of

[he is referring particularly to the teaching of the sixth session of the Council of Trent] has to do with the descending movement: it refers to that action of God which justifies man, not to the action of man which does right by God": B. Sesboüé, *Jesucristo el único mediador*, (Salamanca, 1990), 121.

212. Cf. Blessed J. Escrivá de Balaguer, *Christ is passing by*, op. cit., no. 137.
213. Cf. e.g., St Thomas Aquinas, *STh* III, q.56, aa. 1-2.
214. The expression is St Thomas': cf. e.g., *STh* III, q.48, a. 2.
215. B. Sesboüé, *Jesucristo el único mediador*, op. cit., 121.

his brother men—genuine self-surrender and love which has been made possible only because of our incorporation in Christ, because we truly are justified (justification is not merely imputed to us). By incorporating us into himself the Mediator truly sanctifies us and so, because we are inserted into him, he can present us to the Father as a spiritual sacrifice, pure and holy.

We must remember that the distinction between ascending and descending mediation is only a distinction; they are never two separate things: they are simply aspects of one, unique mediation. They are simply ways of speaking— valid only in a limited way and always inadequate to express the unfathomable mystery of the Person and work of Jesus Christ, the Redemption. We can see very clearly how these two aspects coalesce in the light of another key concept in soteriology—that of reconciliation. "The Father was pleased through him to reconcile to himself all things" (cf. Col 1:19-20); it is the Father who, in Christ, reconciles man to himself; but this reconciliation calls for reciprocal action on man's part: reconciliation cannot take place if man does not accept the gift of God, that is, if man does not let himself be reconciled. It is the Mediator who makes the this *synergia* possible, this collaboration between man and God: his mediation is, at one the same time, descending and ascending.

This mediation continues eternally in heaven as both an ascending and a descending movement. Thus, the elect not only give glory to God for all eternity in and through Christ (as we can see in great visions of the Book of Revelation (cf., for example, Revelation 7), but they also enjoy intuitive vision of God in the revelation of the Word.[216]

---

216. As J.H. Nicolas writes: "revelation culminates in the beatific vision, where God unveils himself in the fulness of light. All revelation tends towards this, finding here its finish and terminus. Should we say that Christ contrives even here to mediate, or should we say that his mediation disappears at this moment? The Catholic Church, on the basis of what St Paul and St John say, teaches as belonging to faith that in the beyond, the elect see the face of God directly [. . .]. This direct vision is possible and it takes place thanks to the supreme gift of grace, the *lumen gloriae*: it is called light because through it the Trinity makes itself visible to man's spirit; but it is not a matter of an objective light, that is, of a light which would illuminate the object (because the Trinity is light in itself), but of a subjective light, which makes the human spirit able to see what it is incapable of seeing not because it is dark but because it is too bright. The ultimate source of this light is clearly God himself (*God makes himself seen*), but the immediate source is the created spirit of Jesus enriched with the light of glory, of unique elevation and intensity. Thus, while the Greeks seem to understand Jesus' mediation in the vision of the elect as a mediation on the part of the object (the elect would see the divine nature in the splendour of the face of Jesus), the Latins, without denying or minimizing that mediation, place it in the subjective order: the elect see God directly, but the gift of grace by virtue of which they can see God comes to them from Jesus. That is truly how they see the Trinity in Him": J.H. Nicolas, *Synthèse Dogmatique*, op. cit., 549-50. Cf. J.A. Riestra, "El influjo de Cristo en la gloria de los santos", in *Atti del VIII Congresso Tomistico Internazionale, IV Prospettive teologiche moderne* (Vatican City, 1981), especially 232-40.

CHAPTER FIVE

The Redemption (I)

Right throughout his life on earth Christ exercised his triple role of mediation (as king, prophet and priest) re-establishing unity between men and God; and he continues to act as a mediator in heaven. Every human action of Jesus, because it is a human action of God, is of transcendent value for our salvation and redemption.[1] Even the apparently insignificant actions of Jesus are effective as mediation between God and men. He is essentially the Mediator and the new Adam. And all his actions (each of them of infinite value) combine to work our redemption. Jesus' entire life on earth is orientated towards the paschal mystery of his Death, Resurrection and Ascension. These are the highpoints of his life and they illuminate and explain it.

The salvation brought about by Christ involves two things which are indissolubly linked—man's liberation from sin and its consequences, and his reconciliation with God. The *causal relationship* between the mysteries of Christ's life and the good effects of salvation on man is many-faceted. By his life, death and glorification, Jesus, out of love and obedience, rendered satisfaction to the Father which more than compensated for our disaffection and disobedience; he *atoned* for our sins; he *merited* for us the grace of forgiveness and reconciliation with God; he was the *efficient cause* in us of that same salvific grace. All these things together constitute the *mode* in which Christ brought about the salvation of mankind, for which the best term is "Redemption", because it was a salvation he "bought" at the cost of his blood. Since all these aspects of the Redemption are present in different ways at different points and in different actions in Christ's life, it is not easy to deal very systematically with the subject of soteriology (Church teaching on

---

1. It should be noted that the Creed places everything referring to the mysteries of Christ's life (from the Incarnation to his Ascension into heaven and his second coming) under the words "For us men and for our salvation . . ."—articulating something which is to the forefront of the Church's mind. The Gospels in fact are primarily an account of the life of our Lord as Saviour of men. And his birth and infancy are described because they are the birth and infancy of the Messiah and form part of his work of salvation. The central role of the mysteries of Christ's life in the life of the Church can be seen particularly in the celebration of the Liturgy and in the liturgical year itself, where everything is built around the life of Christ. Theology too gives a great deal of attention to the life of Christ; cf., e.g., St Thomas Aquinas, *STh* III, qq. 31-48; I. Biffi, *I misteri della vita di Cristo in S. Tommaso d'Aquino* (Varese, 1972). On the importance of reflection on the mysteries of Christ's life in the history of Christian theology and piety, cf. A. Grillmeier, "Los misterios de la vida de Jesús", in *MS*, III/II (Madrid, 1969), 21-39.

salvation); we will therefore explain why we have chosen to follow the order we do.

In this chapter we shall discuss Christ's life, death and resurrection, in reply to the question: What did Jesus do to save us, to redeem us? Chapter 6 will deal with the *content of this salvation* (liberation from evil and reconciliation with God) and the *mode* in which Jesus brought it about (making satisfaction to the Father, atoning for sins, meriting grace, being the efficient cause of grace); in other words, chapter 6 examines that salvation in more depth and the form it took, which we discover when we look at the life of Christ (in chapter 5) from the time he is sent by the Father into the world up until he returns to the Father: "I came from the Father and have come into the world; again, I am leaving the world, and going to the Father" (Jn 16:28).

1. THE LIFE OF CHRIST

As we have just pointed out, every single human action of Jesus, on its own, could be sufficient to redeem all mankind, being an action of the God-Man, who is the perfect mediator between God and men.[2] But God so willed that the Redemption should come about through the death and glorification of Christ: "The Son of man must suffer many things, and be rejected by the elders and chief priests and scribes, and be killed, and on the third day be raised" (Lk 9:22). This "must suffer" implies that the Father had a plan and that the Son made man obeyed that plan, so that his entire life on earth was a preparation for, a journey towards, the Cross and the Resurrection.

However, starting with the Incarnation, the mysteries of Christ's life are not merely preparation for the Redemption: they are themselves the Redemption, because they combine with the Paschal Mystery to form one single salvific continuum.[3] The very act of the Incarnation already had a redemptive meaning

2. This was something very much emphasized in the Middle Ages, due to the fact that the subject of the Redemption was usually approached from the viewpoint of a justice of God which exacted *due* satisfaction for sins. A good example of this is to be found in Clement VI's Bull *Unigenitus Dei Filius* (27 January 1343) which states that on the Cross Christ "shed not just not one drop of his blood—which on account of the union with the Word would have sufficed for the redemption of the entire human race—but poured it out in abundance" (DS 1025). This point is not the result of dispensing with a global consideration of the life and death of the Lord but, rather, is an attempt above all to highlight the Lord's immense generosity in the sufferings which he freely assumed for our redemption, since he wished to take on "such quantity of suffering as would be proportional to the magnitude of the fruit which was going to flow from it": St Thomas Aquinas, *STh* III, q.46, a.6 in c. The same point is made in the Patristic era: "we shall go on to consider the question and dogma which is so often passed over in silence", St Gregory Nazianzen writes, "and that is the very reason why I am going to examine it so closely: this glorious and precious blood of God that is shed for us: . . . why and for what purpose was so high a price paid?": St Gregory Nazianzen, *Or .45*, 22 PG 36, 653 A.

3. Cf. St Thomas Aquinas, *Compendium Theologiae*, I, 239. This salvific unity of Jesus' entire life is something which the Fathers already emphasized. Cf. e.g., P. Alvés de Sousa, "El

and made for our salvation. As we read in the Epistle to the Hebrews: "Consequently, when he [Christ] came into the world, he said, 'Sacrifices and offerings thou hast not desired, but a body hast thou prepared for me; in burnt offerings and sin offerings thou hast taken no pleasure. Then I said, "Lo, I have come to do thy will, O God" [. . .].' And by that will we have been sanctified through the offering of the body of Jesus Christ once for all" (Heb 10:5-7, 10).

The essence of the redemptive act is the Son of God's love expressed as an offering of his Humanity to the Father for the salvation of men. This love is to be seen in his obedience to the Father, freely submitting his will to the Father's plan (a submission which is permanent and unwavering): "My food," says Jesus, "is to do the will of him who sent me, and to accomplish his work" (Jn 4:34); and also, "He who sent me is with me [. . .], for I always do what is pleasing to him" (Jn 8:29). Therefore, all Jesus' life forms a unity with the paschal mystery in the plan of salvation and in obedience to the Father.

Everything in Jesus' life is a sign of the mystery of his Person and his mission. "His humanity appeared as the 'sacrament', that is, the sign and the instrument of his divinity and of the salvation he brings: what was visible in his earthly life leads to the invisible mystery of his divine sonship and redemptive mission."[3a] The whole life of Jesus, his words and his deeds, his silences and his sufferings, are at the same time Revelation of the Father (cf. Jn 14:9) and mystery of redemption and of Recapitulation, because "all Jesus did, said and suffered had for its aim restoring fallen man in his original vocation."[3b]

a) **The Incarnation** If the essence of the redemptive act lies in Christ's infinite charity and obedience, the reason why we can receive the saving benefits of his life stems from his being the Mediator and especially from his being one with us. The better we appreciate what the Incarnation of the Word involves, the better will we understand Christian teaching concerning the Redemption. Thus, at the Incarnation, the Word does not just become man: he becomes one of us, "born of woman, born under the law" (Gal 4:4), that is, he takes on himself our history; he is part of it, it is not foreign to him.

St Paul puts this very well when he points to Christ as the "new Adam": "Then as one man's trespass led to condemnation for all men, so one man's act of righteousness leads to acquittal and life for all men" (Rom 5:18). The Redemption will come about through the obedience of the new Adam (Christ), who will erase the disobedience of the first Adam (cf. Rom 5:12 and 19).

So, the Incarnation already marks the beginning of salvation, because by

concepto de 'sotería' en el 'De Incarnatione Verbi' de San Atanasio", ScrTh 10 (1978) 14-17; L.F. Mateo Seco, *Estudios sobre la cristología de San Gregorio de Nisa*, op. cit., especially 101-67.

3a. CCC, no. 515.
3b. CCC. nos. 516-18.

taking flesh the Word takes on mankind itself [4] and, in a sense, becomes linked to every man and every woman.[5]

This "solidarity" with all mankind, resulting from the act of Incarnation itself is what enables the "satisfaction" Christ offers the Father to be satisfaction for all the sins of mankind. As St Thomas Aquinas wrote, in reply to the objection that only the offender (and therefore only the sinner himself) can offer satisfaction, "the head and members form as it were a single mystical person. Christ's satisfaction therefore belongs to all the faithful as to his members".[6] This union between Christ (as the new Adam) and all men simply through the fact of the Incarnation is, in itself, a salvific union: in fact, in Mariology it will come to be said that the Blessed Virgin begins to be the mother of men the very moment she becomes Mother of Christ, the Head of mankind.[7]

The origin of Jesus, as St Ignatius of Antioch says, belongs to the mystery which occurred in the clamorous silence of God.[8] "Jesus came from Nazareth. But do we know his true origin if we know the geographical place of his birth? The Fourth Gospel takes pains to stress that the real origin of Jesus is *the Father*, from whom he proceeds totally and in a different way from any other divine messenger. The 'infancy gospels'of Matthew and Luke show us Jesus coming from the *unknowable* mystery of God, not to dispel the mystery but to confirm it."[9]

4. Cf., e.g., in this regard the rich patristic exegesis of the parable of the lost sheep, from St Irenaeus onwards: the Word takes all mankind on his shoulders, that is, he puts on humanity and recapitulates it in himself: cf., A. Orbe, *Parábolas evangélicas de San Ireneo*, II (Madrid, 1972), 117-77.

5. The Second Vatican Council puts this very eloquently: "Christ, the new Adam, in the very revelation of the mystery of the Father and of his love, fully reveals man to himself and brings to light his most high calling [. . .]. Human nature, by the very fact that it was assumed, not absorbed, in him, has been raised in us also to a dignity beyond compare. For, by his incarnation, he, the Son of God, has in a certain way united himself with each man": Const. *Gaudium et spes*, 22.

6. St Thomas Aquinas, *STh* III, q. 48, a. 3 ad. 1. J.H. Nicolas, referring to this statement, comments that mystical inclusion presupposes an ontological inclusion: it is a dynamic inclusion: "Man is profoundly ordained to God, to union with God, and, in this dynamic ordination, human individuals communicate: in Jesus, the Man-God, this dynamic tendency common to all mankind finds its absolute realization, in such a way that the communion which all men have with each other by their very nature is now a communion in Christ. This communion, adumbrated only in the beginning of every human life, needs to be actualized in each man/woman as they freely make their way (by faith and sacraments)": J.H. Nicolas, *Synthèse dogmatique*, op. cit., 441. Chapter 6 will go further into the subject of men's solidarity with Christ and sanctification.

7. "This motherhood of Mary," the Second Vatican Council teaches, "in the order of grace continues uninterruptedly from the consent which she loyally gave at the Annunciation and which she sustained without wavering beneath the Cross, until the eternal fulfilment of the elect" (Const. *Lumen gentium*, 62).

8. St Ignatius of Antioch, *Epistola ad Ephesios*, chap. 19. See T. Camelot, *Ignace d'Antioquie, Polycarpe de Smyrne: Lettres*, SCh (Paris, 1969), 74-5, nts. 1-4.

9. J. Ratzinger, *Introduction to Christianity* (New York, 1980), 205f.

This mystery is first and foremost the mystery of his divine origin—he is the Son of the Father, begotten by the Father in an eternal "today" (cf. Ps 2:8)—and it is also the mystery of the intratrinitarian plan for the Incarnation. When broaching the subject of the Redemption, that is something that needs to be stressed once again: the Incarnation of the Word (the key to the economy of salvation) is firstly an initiative of the Father. The Son is *sent* to this world, his food is to do the will of him who sent him (cf. 17:8ff; 4:34). In this context Hebrews 10:5-7, which we have just quoted, becomes more explicit: the Incarnation is not only a preparation for the Redemption; it is also a salvific fulfilment of the Father's will.[10]

Jesus' repeated references to his "mission", that is, to the fact that he has been *sent* to this world, point to the saving design of the Father who sent him, and therefore to the mysterious origin of his redemptive mission, which lies, above all, in the Father's faithful love for men, "created in his image and chosen from 'the beginning', in this Son, for grace and glory,"[11] the Father's faithfulness to his fatherhood.

The mystery of Jesus' origin also includes the virginity of his Mother, that is, an inseparable pneumatological dimension,[12] which also involves that mysterious solidarity Jesus has with every man and woman because he is the Head, the *caput* of the human race.[13] This explains why St Paul insists so much about our being saved *in* Christ, through being made *like into* Christ, by dying and rising *with* him: "For the love of Christ controls us, because we are convinced that one has died for all; therefore all have died. And he died for all, that those who live might live no longer for themselves but for him who for their sake died and was raised" (2 Cor 5:14-15).[14]

10. The Incarnation is already "an act of redemption" through which "God entered the history of humanity and, as a man, became an actor in that history, one of the thousands of millions of human beings but at the same time Unique!": John Paul II, Enc. *Redemptor hominis*, op. cit., 1.

11. Cf. John Paul II, Enc. *Dives in misericordia*, op. cit., 7.

12. "The conception and birth of Jesus Christ", John Paul II says, "are in fact the greatest work accomplished by the Holy Spirit in the history of creation and salvation: the supreme grace—'the grace of union', source of every other grace, as Saint Thomas explains [. . .]. 'By the power of the Holy Spirit,' the mystery of the hypostatic union is brought about—that is, the union of the divine nature and the human nature, of the divinity and the humanity in the one Person of the Word-Son": John Paul II, Enc. *Dominum et vivificantem*, op. cit., 50.

13. In the same place Pope John Paul II writes: "The Incarnation of God the Son signifies the taking up into unity with God not only of human nature, but in this human nature, *in a sense of everything that is flesh*: the whole of humanity, the entire visible and material world. The Incarnation, then, also has a cosmic significance, a cosmic dimension. The *first born of all creation* (Col 1:15), becoming incarnate in the individual humanity of Christ, unites himself in some way with the entire reality of man, which is also *flesh*—and in this reality with all *flesh*, with the whole of creation."

14. Here is a truly meaningful comment on this text from Prat: "The theory of penal substitution would force us to conclude: If one died for all, then all have no more to die. St Paul reaches the very opposite conclusion: *if one died for all, then all died* ideally and mystically in him.

St Luke sums up in these words the longest period in our Lord's life, the years of his "hidden life": "He went down with them and came to Nazareth, and was obedient to them. [. . .] Jesus increased in wisdom and in years, and in favour with God and man" (Lk 2:51-52). These years of hidden life in Nazareth allow "everyone to enter into fellowship with Jesus by the most ordinary events of daily life."[14a] Jesus is in no hurry; he shares with his brother men "a daily life without any apparent importance, a life of manual work. His religious life was that of a Jew obedient to the law of God (cf. Gal 4:4), a life in the community."[14b] Jesus' obedience to his parents is an earthly reflection of his filial obedience to his heavenly Father and a foretaste of his silent self-giving on Holy Thursday. His obedience in Nazareth inaugurates his work of restoring what Adam's disobedience had destroyed.[14c]

It follows that the years of *Christ's hidden life* were not just a preparation for his public ministry: they too were genuine redemptive actions, orientated towards the climax of his life, the paschal mystery. "Through his annihilation, through his simplicity and obedience, by divinizing the everyday, common life of men, the Son of God conquered."[15] The eternal Word, by not only taking on human nature but also living an ordinary life, has redeemed and sanctified all the noble things which go to make the fabric of everyday life—family life and social relationships, children's games and adults' challenges, fatigue and rest. . . . During these years of hidden life Jesus set us an example, but he was also carrying out our redemption through the love and obedience with which he imbued his every action, offering it up to the Father to atone for the sins of the world.

Jesus also wins our redemption during his years of ordinary work, doing what the Creator commands man to do on earth—to work the land (cf. Gen 2:15). His job was a modest one, that of a tradesman, and in solidarity with the rest of men he used it to direct creation towards its goal. By the work of his hands he cooperated in the work of the Creator, thereby giving work all its divine meaning in the history of salvation.[16] "Therefore, one can say that in the history of salvation *human work has come to re-discover in the life of Christ the dignity it had at the very beginning*, so desired by the Creator; it was even raised to the dignity of being an essential occupation of the Word incarnate

This is because he starts from the principle of solidarity which makes the death of Christ our death and the life of Christ our life": F. Prat, *The Theology of St Paul*, II, op. cit. 202.

14a. CCC, no. 533.

14b. CCC, no. 531.

14c. Cf. CCC, no. 532.

15. Blessed J. Escrivá de Balaguer, *Christ is passing by*, op. cit., no. 21; cf. no. 20.

16. "When men and women provide for themselves and their families in such a way as to be of service to the community as well, they can rightly look upon their work as a proclamation of the work of the Creator, a service to their fellow men, and their personal contribution to the fulfilment in history of the divine plan": Second Vatican Council, Const. *Gaudium et spes*, 34.

during his long years in Nazareth."[17] So, union with Christ also implies love for work as part of love for one's Christian vocation, because "since Christ took it into his hands, work has become for us a redeemed and redemptive reality. Not only is it the background of man's life, it is a means and path of holiness. It is something to be sanctified and something which sanctifies."[18]

The same holds for everything else to do with our Lord's hidden life; thus, family life finds its full divine meaning in Christ.

b) Christ's public life   It is of course much easier to appreciate the salvific virtue of Jesus's *public life*—his preaching, which proclaims the kingdom of God, calls men to conversion, and frees consciences from error;[19] and his miracles (already a proof that the Kingdom had come), which confirmed his message of salvation and strengthened his disciples' faith. Christ's ability to redeem is to be seen, above all, when he forgives sins and casts out devils: "But if it is by the Spirit of God that I cast out demons, then the kingdom of God has come upon you" (Mt 12:28).

Some points in Jesus' public life show very clearly that his whole life is orientated towards the paschal mystery. For example, his *baptism* in the Jordan (cf. Mk 1:9-11; Mt 3:13-17; Lk 3:21-22; cf. Jn 1:32-34 and Acts 1:22 and 10:38) marks the start of his public ministry in such a way that in the election of Matthias, according to the words of St Peter, a man was sought who had "accompanied us during all the time that the Lord Jesus went in and out among us beginning from the baptism of John until the day when he was taken up from us—one of these men must become with us a witness to his resurrection" (cf. Acts 1:21-22).

In fact, the words "baptism", to "be baptized", are used by Jesus on two later occasions (cf. Mk 10:38-39; Lk 12:50) to refer to his death—thereby showing clearly the baptism/paschal mystery connection,[20] and St Paul connects Christian baptism with the mystery of the death, burial and resurrection of our Lord (Rom 6:3-4). At Baptism Jesus associates himself with sinners (his brothers), taking their crimes upon himself as prophesied of the

---

17. J.M. Aubert, "La santificación del trabajo", in various authors, *Mons. J. Escrivá de Balaguer y el Opus Dei* (Pamplona, 1982), 204.

18. Blessed J. Escrivá de Balaguer, *Christ is passing by*, op. cit., 47. The spirituality of Opus Dei hinges on the sanctification of work. On this subject and on the influence of contemplation of our Lord's hidden life on the teaching of Mgr. Escrivá de Balaguer, cf. J.L. Illanes, *On the Theology of Work* (Dublin and Chicago, 1967). The relevant bibliography on this is surveyed in L.F. Mateo Seco, "Obras de Mons. Escrivá de Balaguer y estudios sobre el Opus Dei", in various authors, *Mons. J. Escrivá de Balaguer y el Opus Dei*, op. cit., 375-460.

19. Cf. K. Adam, *The Christ of Faith*, op. cit., 296-302; L. Malevez, "Le message de Jésus et l'histoire du salut", NRT 89 (1967) 420-33; R. Schnackenburg, *Reino y reinado de Dios* (Madrid, 1970); J. Coppens, *Le messianisme et sa relève prophetique* (Gembloux, 1974), 219ff; M. Bordoni, *Gesù di Nazaret*, II, op. cit., 77-154.

20. Cf. A. Feuillet, "Le coupe et le baptême de la Passion", RB 74 (1967) 356-91.

Servant of Yahweh, in Isaiah 42:1-9, and joins them in doing penance to reconcile them with God.[21] He is baptized along with sinners, just as later he will die along with transgressors (cf. Mk 15:27).[21a] So it is no accident that the Baptist describes him as "the Lamb of God, who takes away the sin of the world" (Jn 1:29)—clearly a reference to the fact that his whole life is orientated towards the sacrifice on Calvary.[22] The word "Lamb" is full of allusions to sacrifice—from the Servant of Yahweh (compared to a Lamb who suffers in silence: Is 53:7) to the paschal lamb itself. The phrase *Lamb of God* is particularly meaningful, because it involves the idea of the Lamb offered to God as a gift, and recalls the sacrifice of Isaac (Gen 22:1) and the lamb God provided in place of Isaac.[23]

Jesus' baptism, therefore, was not simply a *preparation* for his public life; it was something which contributed to his work of salvation, linked as it was with his cross and resurrection: Christ submitted to the baptism of John in order to save us.[24] His baptism was one of the events which revealed his relationship to the Holy Spirit and to holiness: as his very name (Messiah) implies, he is the Anointed.[25] The Fathers of the Church, to illustrate the effects of Christ's baptism, used to say that it marked the point when he conferred on water the capacity to be the matter of Christian baptism, the new baptism which would truly forgive sins. "The Lord", St Ambrose says, for example, "was baptized not to be purified but to purify the waters: cleansed by his flesh which knew no sin, the waters were empowered to perform the work of salvation."[26]

21. Cf. A. Legault, "Le baptême de Jésus et la doctrine du Serviteur souffrant", ScEccl 13 (1961) 156ff.

21a. "The baptism of Jesus is on his part the acceptance and the inauguration of his mission as God's suffering Servant. He allows himself to be numbered among sinners (cf. Is 53:12); he is already 'the Lamb of God who takes away the sin of the world' (Jn 1:19). Already he is anticipating the 'baptism' of his bloody death (cf. Mk 10:38; Lk 12:50)" (CCC, no. 536).

22. Cf. A. Feuillet, "Le symbolisme de la Colombe dans les récits évangeliques du Baptême", RSR 46 (1958) 524-44; "Le baptême de Jésus", RB 71 (1964) 321-52; "Le personalité de Jésus à partir de sa soumission au rite de repentance du précurseur", ibid., 77 (1970) 30-49.

23. Cf. M. González Gil, *Cristo, el misterio de Dios*, II, op. cit., 313-14.

24. As the antiphon of second vespers for the feast of the Epiphany puts it, "today Christ wished to be baptized by John in the Jordan, that he might save us."

25. "When he had occasion to speak in the synagogue, he opened the Book of Isaiah and found the passage where it was written: 'The Spirit of the Lord is upon me, because he has anointed me'; and having read this passage he said to those present: *Today this scripture has been fulfilled in your hearing*. In this way he confessed and proclaimed that he was the Messiah, the one in whom the Holy Spirit dwells as the gift of God himself, the one who possesses the fullness of this Spirit, the one who marks the 'new beginning' of the gift which God makes to humanity in the Spirit" (John Paul II, Enc. *Dominum et vivificantem*, op. cit., no. 18). On the Spirit's anointing at Christ's baptism, cf. among others, I. de la Potterie, "L'Onction du Christ", NRT 80 (1958) 225-52; A. Orbe, *La unción del Verbo* (Rome, 1961); J.M. Odero, "La Unción y el Bautismo de Cristo en San Cirilo de Alejandría", in various authors, *Cristo, Hijo de Dios y Redentor del hombre*, op. cit., 519-40; A. Aranda, "Cristología y pneumatología", ibid., 649-70.

26. St Ambrose, *Expositio Evangelii secundum Lucam*, 2, 83 (PL 15, 1583). Jesus "was baptized

Jesus' baptism is the model of Christian baptism which, in turn, derives its saving effectiveness from the fact that it is orientated and essentially related to the death and resurrection of Christ: "Do you not know that all of us who have been baptized into Christ Jesus were baptized into his death? We were buried therefore with him by baptism into death, so that as Christ was raised from the dead by the glory of the Father, we too might walk in newness of life" (Rom 6:3-4). This death-resurrection idea is also to be found in the symbolism of the baptism of Jesus; just as the death on the Cross was followed by the Resurrection, so Jesus' humiliation (entering the waters to receive John's baptism) was followed by his glorification by the Father: "and lo, a voice from heaven, saying, 'This is my beloved Son, with whom I am well pleased'" (Mt 3:17).

The very same words are said in the theophany at the Transfiguration: "This is my beloved Son, listen to him" (Mk 9:7). St Luke, instead of "beloved" uses "chosen" (Lk 9:35); St Matthew adds "with whom I am well pleased" (17:5): both phrases occur in the first of the songs of the Servant of Yahweh (Is 42:1). St Mark points out that the Transfiguration takes place six days after the announcement of the Passion (9:2), perhaps to imply that there is a connexion between the two episodes, and to show that Christ is on the way to his death.[27] Thomas Aquinas comments that with the Transfiguration our Lord, who had already told his disciples about his Passion, is encouraging them to follow him even in that.[28] And St Luke spells out the paschal content of this theophany, when he tells us that "two men talked with him, Moses and Elijah, who appeared in glory and spoke of his departure, which he was to accomplish at Jerusalem" (Lk 9:31-32).

Also, the miracles worked by Jesus when taken together, and even in a way every single one of them, are very much in the nature of *signs*, which contain a *polivalency* of salvific meaning and effectiveness, linked to the mystery of his death and resurrection.[29]

Firstly, the miracles can be seen as *marks of divine love*, insofar as they are actions which come from Jesus' human love (the human love of God), which is compassionate towards human suffering and deprivation (cf. Mt 11:28); Mk 6:34; Lk 7:13; etc.).

They are also *signs of the coming of the messianic Kingdom*, for, as had been

in order to cleanse water" (St Ignatius of Antioch, *Ad Ephesios* 18, 2); *Baptizato enim Christo, id est sanctificatione aquas in suo baptismate . . .* (Tertullian, *Adv. Judaeos*, 8). St Gregory of Nyssa talks of "the great mystery of the Jordan" in a detailed exegesis in *Or. de baptismo* (PG 46, 419-22).

27. Cf. A. Feuillet, "Les perspectives propres a chaque évangeliste dans les récits de la Transfiguration", BL 39 (1958), 284ff.

28. St Thomas Aquinas, *STh*, q.45, a.1 in c.

29. R. Latourelle, *Theology of Revelation*, op. cit., 390-405; M. Meinertz, *Teología del Nuevo Testamento*, op. cit., 198-203.

foretold (cf. Is 35:5-6; 26:19; 29:18), Christ gives sight to the blind, makes the dumb speak and the deaf hear, raises the dead to life, and casts out demons (cf. Lk 4:16-22; Mt 12:28; etc.).

Another aspect of the miracles, as already pointed out, is that they are *signs* of the truth of Jesus' teaching, in the sense that they confirm that he comes from God (cf. Mk 16:20; Jn 2:23; 3:2; 9:33; etc.), in the same sort of way as miracles in the Old Testament were signs of the divine mission of Moses (cf. Ex 3:12; 4:1-9; 14:31 and of the prophets (cf., e.g., the case of Elijah: 1 Kings 18:36-39), and as miracles bore out the truth of the Apostles' preaching (cf. Acts 14:3).

In fact, Christ's miracles are depicted not only as signs that he was sent by God, but also as a *revelation of his divinity*, specifically of his unique relationship with God the Father, because what one does the other does, and vice versa (cf. Jn 14:10-11). "He who reveals God as Father Creator and Lord of creation, reveals himself as Son consubstantial with the Father and equal to him in his mastery over creation, when he does those miracles by his own power."[30]

Nor can we forget that our Lord's miracles contain a *proclamation of the sacramental nature* of the Christian economy, through their connexion with grace, which sets man free from sin (cf. Mk 2:9), and because they prefigure the sacraments of the Church: cf., for example, the multiplication of the loaves just prior to the promise of the Eucharist (Jn 6).[31]

In addition to being signs, Jesus' miracles are *already in themselves salvific things*, because salvation includes (at least in its definitive eschatological stage) total liberation from all evil and suffering: cf. Rev 21:4: in a limited form a miracle, being an event of the Kingdom, anticipates that ultimate, total liberation.

Finally, it is worth stressing that Jesus Christ's public life (like his hidden life) was not something unconnected with the paschal mystery: its fullest meaning and effectiveness lay in the fact that it was orientated towards his (imminent) death and glorification and formed a continuum with them. The miracles are signs which anticipate *the* sign and miracle—the resurrection of Jesus; and, on the other hand, once the resurrection has taken place the full meaning of his miracles becomes clearer. In Sacred Scripture Christ's miracle-working is so much part of his life as to be inseparable from it, so much so that a Jesus who did not work miracles could not be the Jesus of the Gospels. Like the resurrection (to which they point) the miracles are also a manifestation of the mystery of Christ—of his divinity and of his mission as Redeemer.

---

30. John Paul II, *Address*, 2 December 1987, no. 1: *Insegnamenti*, X, 3 (1987) 1254.
31. Cf. ibid., no. 3, p. 1255.

c) **The passion and death of Jesus**   Jesus' death, therefore, was not just one of a number of possible ways his life on earth could have ended: it was the foreseen *goal*, which *completed* his redemptive work—foreseen by God and desired also by Jesus' human will. As he himself told his disciples in reference to his death: "I have a baptism to be baptized with; and how I am constrained until it is accomplished" (Lk 12:50).

The New Testament accounts and the symbols of the faith present the cross, first and foremost, as an historical event: *He was crucified under Pontius Pilate*, the Creed declares. And St Paul, stressing that he is passing on what he himself has received, spells out for the Corinthians what he sees as the core of the Gospel: "For I delivered to you as of first importance what I also received, that Christ died for our sins in accordance with the Scriptures, that he was buried, that he was raised on the third day in accordance with the Scriptures, and that he appeared to Cephas, then to the Twelve" (1 Cor 15:3-5).[32]

The Gospels give us a full account of the final hours of Jesus' life, from the Last Supper to his death on the cross. As an indication of how important the evangelists saw these hours, we have only to remember that the Passion takes up a third of St Mark's Gospel. We shall not stop to list here all the various events involved;[33] however, before studying their redemptive dimension (how and why they bring us salvation) we shall examine some questions to do with the events themselves which will help to elucidate Christian teaching on Redemption.

i) *Jesus foretells his death*   As we have seen, St Paul makes the point that Christ died "in accordance with the Scriptures": he sees the events of the paschal mystery as fulfilling the prophecies and figures of the Old Testament. It is not possible to read even a few lines of the New Testament account of Christ's

---

32. John Paul II expresses the centrality of the mystery of the Redemption in these words: "The Church never ceases to relive his death on the Cross and his Resurrection, which constitute the content of the Church's daily life. Indeed, it is by the command of Christ himself, her Master, that the Church unceasingly celebrates the Eucharist, finding in it the '*fountain of life and holiness*', the efficacious sign of the life and grace and reconciliation with God, and the pledge of eternal life. The Church lives his mystery, draws unwearyingly from it and continually seeks ways of bringing this mystery of her Master and Lord to humanity—to the peoples, the nations, the succeeding generations, and every individual human being—as if she were ever repeating, as the Apostle did: '*For I decided to know nothing among you except Jesus Christ and him crucified*' (1 Cor 2:2). The Church stays within the sphere of the mystery of the Redemption, which has become the fundamental principle of her life and mission": John Paul II, Enc. *Redemptor hominis*, op. cit., no. 7.

33. For an account of these events, among other *Lives of Jesus*, see L. de Grandmaison, *Jesus Christ: His Person, His Message, His Credentials* (New York, 1930); F. Prat, *Jésus-Christ* (Paris, 1933); F.M. Willam, *The Life of Jesus Christ in the land of Israel and among its people* (London, 1940); M.J. Lagrange, *The Gospel of Jesus Christ* (Westminster, 1938); R. Guardini, *The Lord* (Cleveland, 1969); L.C. Fillion, *The Life of Christ* (St Louis and London, 1928); E. Lohse, *La storia della passione e morte di Gesù Cristo* (Brescia, 1975).

death without immediately meeting allusions to and explicit quotations from Old Testament texts, which are fulfilled to the letter during his passion. In the account of his appearance to the disciples of Emmaus, Jesus himself (now risen) tells them: "'O foolish men, and slow of heart to believe all that the prophets have spoken! Was it not necessary that the Christ should suffer these things and enter into his glory?' And beginning with Moses and all the prophets, he interpreted to them in all the Scriptures the things concerning himself" (Lk 24:25-26).[34]

In addition to these prophecies, the Gospels contain our Lord's own explicit predictions of the Passion[35]—in the Synoptics, the first, on the occasion of Peter's confession of faith at Caesarea (Mt 16:21-23; Mk 8:31-33; Lk 9:22); the second, after the Transfiguration (Mt 17:22-23; Mk 9:31; Lk 9:44); the third, the last time Christ goes up to Jerusalem (Mt 20:17-19; Mk 10:33-34; Lk 18:31-44). The predictions became more and more explicit, more detailed, the closer we get to our Lord's death. The Gospel of St John also contains three predictions of the Passion from Jesus' own lips—the first, in his conversation with Nicodemus when he uses the symbolism of the bronze serpent (Jn 3:14); the second, when he compares himself to the Good Shepherd who gives up his life for his sheep (Jn 10:17-18); the third, when he makes the comparison about the grain of wheat which remains unfruitful unless it dies (Jn 12:24). Whereas the predictions in the Synoptics put the focus on the cross as something humiliating and shameful, the predictions in St John stress the glory of the cross: "'Now is the judgment of this world, now shall the ruler of this world be cast out; and I, when I am lifted up from the earth, will draw all men to myself.' He said this to show by what death he was to die" (Jn 12:31-33). He calls the death on the cross a "lifting up", using as the key image the action of the crucified being "raised on high".

Along with these explicit predictions, the Gospels also contain more or less veiled references by Christ to his passion and death. For example, his reference to the fact that the "bridegroom" will be taken from the disciples and then

34. As P. Grelot writes, commenting on 1 Corinthians 15:4 ("Christ died for our sins in accordance with the scriptures"), "the reference to the Scriptures includes the *sacred history* which they evoke in various forms, *the promises* they contain, the *wisdom of life* which they proclaim. This reference is constant in the sacred writers who, in order to proclaim the Gospel, present the content of Christology in different ways. This reference also serves to explain the *saving mediation* which Jesus effected during his life, which he consummated by the act of his death, which he continues to effect in his glorious mastery to the extent of revealing *the mystery of his personal relationship with God*, a relationship which provides the basis for his redemptive mediation [. . .]. The principle of the unity of the two testaments is then something essential to christology, as it is, also, in all areas of theological reflection": P. Grelot, "Pour une étude scripturiare de la christologie", in Pontifical Biblical Commission, *Bible et christologie*, op. cit., 128.

35. Cf. A. Feuillet, "Les trois grandes prophéties de la Passion et de la Résurection des évangiles synoptiques", RT 67 (1967), 533-60; 68 (1968) 41-74; J. Guillet, *Jésus devant sa vie et sa mort* (Paris, 1971).

they will fast (cf. Mt 9:15; Mk 2:19-20; Lk 5:34-35); the announcement of the "chalice" of which he is to drink (Mt 20:22; Mk 10:38); the way he compares the anointing at Bethany to embalming (Mt 26:6-13; Mk 14:3-9; Jn 12:1-8); the parable of the wicked vinedressers, who kill the owner's son (Mt 21:33-46; Mk 12:1-12; Lk 20:9-19).[36]

Obviously, the words our Lord says over the bread and wine at the Last Supper are particularly relevant; he speaks of his body being given up and of the blood of the New Covenant being poured out for the forgiveness of sins (Mt 26:26-29; Mk 14:22-25; Lk 22:19-20; cf. 1 Cor 11:23-25)[37]—words which show that he was fully aware of his imminent death and its redemptive meaning.[38]

ii) *The Father's initiative* Jesus' passion is first and foremost an iniative of the Father. In Christ, "God was reconciling the world to himself" (2 Cor 5:19). "God so loved the world that he gave his only Son, that whoever believes in him should not perish but have eternal life. For God sent the Son into the world, not to condemn the world, but that the world might be saved through him" (Jn 3:16-17). We must not forget that the cross is, above all, God's gift to mankind, the initiative of the Father who sends his Son to the world.[39]

Jesus speaks very clearly about his having been *sent* by the Father to the world (cf., e.g., Jn 20:21). But not only is his *mission* the Father's initiative; so too his fidelity unto death. Jesus also speaks of his *obedience* to the Father when the time comes to accept the cross—for example, during the agony in the garden, when he asks that the chalice of the passion pass from him, and then submits to *the will* of the Father (cf. Lk 22:42).

This conviction runs right through the New Testament—that the passion and death of Jesus is first and foremost the Father's initiative. It is God who

36. On Christ's own statements about his death, it is very useful to read what K. Adam has to say in *The Christ of Faith*, op. cit., 304-9. See also M. Bordoni, II, op. cit., 435-40.

37. Cf. H. Schürmann, "Palabras y acciones de Jesús en la última Cena", Conc 40 (1968) 629-40; and his *Cómo entendió y vivió Jesús su muerte?* (Salamanca, 1982), especially 19-72.

38. Rightly the International Theological Commission in speaking of the messiahship of Jesus refers to Mark's version of these events so as to demonstrate briefly the Lord's clear consciousness of his mission: "Jesus was aware of the purpose of his mission: to announce the Kingdom of God and make it present in his own Person, in his actions, and in his words, so that the world would become reconciled with God and renewed. He freely accepted the Father's will: to give his own life for the salvation of mankind. He knew the Father had sent him to serve and to give his life 'for many' (Mk 14:24)": ITC, *The Consciousness of Christ Concerning Himself and His Mission* (1985), 2nd proposition, in Sharkey, op. cit., 309.

39. "The Cross appears primarily as a movement from above to below. It does not stand there as the work of expiation which mankind offers to the wrathful God, but as the expression of that foolish love of God's which gives itself away to the point of humiliation in order thus to save man; it is his approach to us, not the other way about. With this twist in the idea of expiation, and thus in the whole axis of religion, worship too, man's whole existence, acquires in Christianity a new direction": J. Ratzinger, *Introduction to Christianity*, op. cit., 215.

directs the history of salvation. "This Jesus," Peter says in his first address, "delivered up according to the definite plan and foreknowledge of God, you crucified and killed by the hands of lawless men" (Acts 2:23). We often find the Gospel saying that "it is necessary", it is "fitting", that Christ should suffer (cf., e.g., Mk 8:31; Lk 17:25; 22:37; 24:7, 26, 44; Jn 3:14; 20:9), to show Providence at work in Jesus' life.

This initiative of the Father in regard to redemption through the death of Christ is described as a real commandment (*entole*) given to Jesus, a commandment requiring obedience. Jesus refers to his preaching as being in response to a commandment (cf. Jn 12:49-50); the Father has given him the commandment to sacrifice his own life (Jn 10:18). And there are explicit passages referring to the fact that Jesus was obedient (*upekoos*) to God (cf. Phil 2:8).

The fact that the Father actually imposed a commandment on the life of Jesus is something that some theologians find very hard to take, because that commandment in one way or another implied that Christ was obliged to accept death. The main problem raised has to do with trying to work out how Christ's human freedom (which he had to have, if he was to carry out the redemption) was compatible with his impeccability (which meant that he could not sin and therefore could not disobey). Some in fact have tried to solve the problem by eliminating it, that is, by saying that no real commandment from the Father was ever given Jesus concerning his death—no commandment that morally bound his conscience.[40]

However, the New Testament texts are unambiguous in this regard. As we have seen, Jesus refers to it on many occasions, by saying things like "it is necessary", "it is fitting", and also harking back to the fact that it "was written", that is, it was prophesied, as clearly part of God's plan. St John's Gospel refers especially to "the Father's commandment" concerning Christ's mission, that is, concerning his preaching and even his death (cf. Jn 12:49-50; 10:17-18; 14:31; 15:10).

This commandment is parallelled by the Son's obedience, an "obedience

---

40. Various positions were taken: thus, Franzelin and Billot said that Christ was given no real commandment by the Father regarding his death; Vazquez, Lugo and Lessius thought that he was given a directive only as regards the substance of his death but no circumstances were specified, and Tournely says that Christ could have obtained a dispensation from this precept (cf. R. Garrigou-Lagrange, *Christ the Saviour*, op. cit., 448f). The texts of Scripture regarding the Father's commandment and Christ's obedience in death are fairly clear; the fact that theologians so eminent on other subjects should try to "soften" its content despite the clear meaning of the texts shows how they felt the need to combine, in Christ, impeccability with free obedience. Be that as it may, the solutions they offer are unacceptable for two basic reasons: 1. because they contradict the obvious meaning of those texts that speak of Christ's obedience: and 2. because in one way or another they imply that Christ was not truly free when it came to obeying other precepts, e.g., those of the natural law. Cf. chapter 4, section 5(f) above. More generally on the freedom, impeccability and obedience of Christ, cf. J. Stohr, "Das Miteinander von Freiheit, Unsündlichkeit und Gehorsam in der Erlösungstat Christi", DC 22 (1969) 57-81, 225-41, 365-80.

unto death, even death on a cross" (cf. Phil 2:8). This means real obedience, which would have been impossible had there been no real commandment to die—and impossible too if Christ had not had human freedom. St Paul gives special importance to Christ's obedience and actually sets it in the framework of the history of salvation: "For as by one man's disobedience many were made sinners, so by one man's obedience many will be made righteous" (Rom 5:19).[41] Obedience is necessary to the redemptive work of Christ, who recapitulates in himself the history of mankind, healing through his obedience the disobedience of Adam.

We are in the presence here of a great mystery concerning the divine will—the choice of the Son's obedience unto death as the route to man's salvation.[42] There is a "commandment to die"—and this has to be balanced off with other passages of Scripture which say that God does not desire death: "God did not make death, and he does not delight in the death of the living" (Wis 1:13). This commandment to die cannot be read as a direct, positive, desire for Christ's death, as if it actually pleased the Father that he should die: in that sense the Father does not desire Christ's death, just as he does not desire injustice or evildoing.

On the other hand, the Father does want the Good Shepherd to give up his life for the sheep (cf. Jn 10:10-18), by preaching without ambiguity and holding to that preaching, accepting the death to which this fidelity leads, death that is imposed by the malice of men who rise up against God; Jesus is asked to be like the Good Shepherd—not to run away when the wolf comes to scatter the sheep but to give his life in their defence (cf. Jn 10:11-13).[43] In a similar way one can say that God does not desire the martyr's death and yet he does desire that the martyr be faithful unto death.

So, when referring to the agents of the Passion one can say with Romans 8:32 that the Father did give Christ up to his passion: "He did not spare his own Son but gave him up for us all." St Thomas sees three aspects to this "giving him up"—1) preordaining the liberation of the human race through the passion of Christ; 2) imbuing him with a love that enabled him to accept

41. St Gregory of Nyssa makes the following comments: "Given that death came in through the disobedience of the first man, for this reason, it is cast out through the obedience of a second man. That is why he became obedient unto death so that the evil arising from disobedience should be cured by obedience and so that the death which came along with disobedience should be annihilated by resurrection from the dead. For annihilation of death is a matter of the resurrection of man from the dead": St Gregory of Nyssa, *Adv. Apollin.*, 21, PG 45, 1165 B. The consideration of the relationship between the obedience of Christ and Adam's disobedience and its consequent essential position in the work of salvation is a subject that is very much developed in the Fathers, particularly from St Irenaeus on. It does not make sense, then, to undermine that obedience by undermining the mandate of the Father which makes it possible: if there is genuine obedience it is because there is a genuine mandate.

42. Cf. John Paul II, *Address*, 7 September 1988, no. 8; *Insegnamenti*, XI, 3 (1988) 613f.

43. Cf. M. González Gil, *Cristo, el misterio de Dios*, II, op. cit., 40-3.

the cross; 3) not protecting him from his persecutors.[44] These three aspects are linked, and are in a certain sense inseparable. The second aspect is of great importance; because even the love and the freedom with which Christ accepts the cross are a gift from God to Christ's humanity, proceeding from the charity infused into his heart by the Holy Spirit.

iii) *Jesus being "abandoned"*   The death of Jesus is related in Sacred Scripture with the fact that he was "betrayed" (cf. 1 Cor 11:23). He was "betrayed" by Judas to the leaders of the Jews (Mt 10:4); "delivered up" by Pilate to the Jews (Lk 23:25). He (en)trusted himself (1 Pet 2:23). All these derive from the "delivering-up" which the Father made of him to men. This "delivering-up" should be read as something very definite, and not at all vague. Christian tradition was right to see Isaac as prefiguring Jesus: the only difference was that on Calvary something happened that Abraham did not need to do on the mountain of Moriah (Gen 22:2): as always, the "reality" goes further than the "figure". The expression "Lamb of God" evokes the lamb which was sacrificed instead of Isaac. The Father "delivers up" the Son to his destiny to die; he "abandons" him to the forces of evil; he does not prevent his enemies from overpowering him.

When they were watching Jesus die, people present said, "He trusts in God; let God deliver him now, if he desires him" (Mt 27:43). Here we have a theological interpretation of the Passion; they want to send Christ to his grave as the one "rejected" by God, arguing that God has "abandoned" him, thereby showing that his claim to be the Messiah was spurious. In this hostile setting Jesus cries out: "My God, my God, why has thou forsaken me?" (Mt 27:46; Mk 15:34). These words carry a direct, obvious meaning: God, whose providence directs the course of history, neither "protects" him from his enemies nor accepts his prayer to have the bitter chalice set aside: the Son, then, can rightly claim that he feels "abandoned" into the hands of his enemies.[45]

These words are also a quotation from Psalm 21. Jesus's cry, therefore, is a prayer. He uses them to express his feelings at that moment—pain; trust in God; details of the form his passion takes; a conviction that he will triumph

---

44. St Thomas Aquinas, *STh* III, q.47, a.3 in c.

45. A writer of the Patristic era understood these words to mean the dissolution of the hypostatic union; so shocked was he to think that God should die that he argued that for Christ to die he should first be separated from the Godhead. The same view was, logically, held by those who thought that the hypostatic union was what gave Christ his human life; consequently, they had to see his death as a dissolution of the hypostatic union. As St Thomas notes, the abandonment Christ refers to cannot be interpreted in that sense: "This abandonment (*derelictio*) does not refer to a dissolution of the personal union, but to the fact that God the Father exposed Christ to his passion. Hence, 'abandon' simply means that he did not protect him from his persecutors. Or, Jesus declared himself abandoned, having in mind his own prayer, 'Father, if it is possible, let this cup pass from me' " (*STh* III, q.50, a.2 , ad 1).

in the end. St Matthew "had a special reason for recording this saying of Jesus. It comes from a Psalm and means that the situation described in the Psalm is verified in Jesus' situation. In both cases, the abandonment is not rejection, much less reproval. Thus, the just man never ceases to call God his God: his cry is one of trust rather than of reproach. God abandons him into the hands of his enemies in line with a mysterious design which will have a victorious outcome—as in the Psalm, so in the resurrection recorded in the Gospels."[46]

But, in addition to having this meaning, do these words refer to a deeper kind of abandonment? Is this a reference to a last (and most severe) temptation of Christ? Do they refer to spiritual pain; as if in some sense Christ was himself feeling that God was far away, experiencing that separation from God which sin involves? The evangelists report the bold fact: they simply tell us what Jesus said, without adding any kind of commentary or explanation, perhaps because they think that there was no need for explanation. Jesus' words were sufficiently clear, because the reader would recognize in them the prayer of the suffering just man.[47]

Some writers think that at this "hour of darkness", Christ said the words "My God, my God, why hast thou forsaken me", because he was experiencing again the kind of spiritual desolation he felt in the garden;[48] and that this was the bitterest moment of all[49]—as if he were undergoing a test similar to what mystical writers call the "night of the soul",[50] a veritable interior crucifixion.[51]

---

46. M.J. Lagrange, *Evangile selon saint Matthieu* (Paris, 1927), 530f. And in *Evangile selon saint Marc* (Paris, 1966, 434), he writes: "It must not be forgotten that these words are taken from a Psalm. By repeating them, the Saviour invites us to consider that his soul had the sentiments stressed by the psalmist. The situations are the same, and yet, in the midst of sufferings, the psalmist looks forward to liberation and salvation (Ps 22:25); does it not make sense to attribute to Jesus these same—and even more perfect—elevated thoughts?"

47. From the beginning these words naturally attracted the attention of theologians, and they have a long exegetical history. Cf., e.g., G. Jouassard, "L'abandon du Christ en Croix chez S. Agustin", RSPT 13 (1924), 316-26, "L'abandon du Christ en Croiz dans la tradition grecque", RSPT 14 (1925) 633ff, and "L'abandon du Christ en Croix dans la tradition", RSR 25 (1924) 310ff, 26 (1925) 609ff; B. Botte, "Deus meus, Deus meus, ut quid dereliquisti me", QLP 11 (1926), 105ff.

48. Cf. R. Cornely, *Cursus Scripturae Sacrae. Commentarius in Evangelium secundum Mattheum* (Paris, 1922), 542.

49. Cf. M.J. Lagrange, *The Gospel of Jesus Christ* (Westminster, 1938), II, 271.

50. "To explain this, it has been suggested that the least unworthy comparison might be made with the experience of the great mystics [. . .]. But really Christ's experience cannot be compared with anyone else's": M. González Gil, *Cristo, el misterio de Dios*, II, op. cit., 86.

51. "In the last analysis pain is the product and expression of Jesus Christ's being stretched out from being in God right down to the hell of 'My God, why hast thou forsake me?' Anyone who has stretched his existence so wide that he is simultaneously immersed in God and in the depths of the God-forsaken creature is bound to be torn asunder, as it were; such a one is truly 'crucified'. But this process of being torn apart is identical with love; it is its realization to the extreme (Jn 13:1) and the concrete expression of the breadth which it creates": J. Ratzinger, *Introduction to Christianity*, op. cit., 221.

Many argue that Christ had to suffer this "passive purification" (which he had no *need* to suffer), in order to provide a headline for the sufferings his disciples, his members, would have to experience.[52]

This theology of the cross and, especially, the ever more sombre interpretation of Jesus' feelings at this moment as a tremendous mystical test, (stressed particularly by Renanist mysticism),[53] influenced the rigid interpretation Luther gave to these words and to the whole mystery of the cross. For Luther what happens on the cross is that Christ takes our place in a total, absolute sense; Christ not only takes our sins on himself as head of the human race: he actually becomes sin and malediction. What he felt was not only spiritual desolation, in an act of self-abandonment; he actually *was* abandoned by the Father. This would mean a total "substitution" of us by Christ (paralleled by the way, in Lutheran doctrine, our own justification comes about through Christ taking our place: man is justified extrinsically and legally by reference to Christ's merits); Christ on the cross is covered with our sins so much so that he becomes sin and malediction.[54] Luther seems to see this cry of Christ's as meaning that Christ felt totally abandoned by God; and this led some of Luther's followers to interpret it as a cry of despair: Jesus would have suffered the same rejection and the same despair as someone condemned to hell. This would be the reverse of the well-known expression *simul justus et peccator* (just man and sinner at the same time) applied to Christ: he too would have been *simul justus et peccator*.

This interpretation of Luther's continues to have influence in certain circles. However, it is clearly unacceptable: it goes far beyond what the sacred text says; it is inconsistent with the other words Jesus said on the cross which show his total trust in the Father and a great sureness about his own mission; and it derives from Lutheran prejudices about the relationship between the sinner and God. Particularly it stems from his idea of God as an arbitrary God.[55]

---

52. Others completely reject the understanding of these words as an interior desolation. One example is that of Carra de Vaux Saint Cyr who writes: "the abandonment that is in question here has nothing to do with a mystical trial, it is the distress of a just man delivered up to the persecutions of his enemies [. . .] whom God apparently ignores because he no longer protects him": "L'abandon du Christ en la Croix", in H. Bouessé and J.J. Latour, *Problemes actuels du Christologie* (Bruges, 1965), 305.

53. Cf. L. Mahieu, "L'abandon du Christ sur la Croix", MSR 2 (1945) 209-42.

54. Luther becomes ever more radically committed to this position with the passing of the years. Here is one of his phrases from the year 1535: "And this is something which all the Prophets saw, that Christ would be the greatest robber, murderer, adulterer, thief, blasphemer, etc. of all, so much so that there was never any worse in the world": M. Luther, *In epistolam S. Pauli ad Galatas Commentarius* (1531), ed. WA40/1, 433, 26-7. Cf. B.A. Willams, "Soteriologia. Desde la Reforma hasta el presente", in various authors, *Historia de los dogmas*, III/2c (Madrid, 1975), 10-12.

55. As González Gil writes: "a feeling of condemnation would only have been possible in Jesus either through consciousness of sin or through the denial of the goodness and even the justice of God [. . .]. It is completely lamentable that a certain form of oratory, sentimental

These words of Christ on the cross are not a cry of despair but rather a sign of his suffering and his trust, a prayer in which he makes his own the sentiments expressed in the Psalm he quotes.[56]

"Jesus did not experience reprobation as if he himself had committed sin (cf. Jn 8:46). But in the redeeming love that always united him to the Father (cf. Jn 8:29), he assumed us in the state of our waywardness of sin, to the point that he could say in our name from the cross: 'My God, my God, why hast thou forsaken me?' (Mk 15:34; Ps 22:2)."[56a]

In conclusion, "if Jesus experiences a feeling of being abandoned by his Father he knows, nevertheless, that that is absolutely not the case. He himself said: 'I and the Father are one' (Jn 10:30), and speaking of his future passion: 'I am not alone, because the Father is with me' (Jn 16:32). At the loftiest point of his spirit, Jesus has a totally clear vision of God and certainty of his union with the Father. But in those areas bordering on sensibility and, therefore, more subject to impressions, emotions and repercussions of painful internal and external experiences, the human soul of Jesus is reduced to a desert, and he does not then feel the presence of the Father, but, rather, suffers the tragic experience of the most complete desolation."[57]

In the interrogative form of the words, "My God, my God, why hast thou forsaken me"?, we can see a question which is given no answer, because God's designs are far beyond the grasp of any human mind; but this also throws into sharper relief Jesus' supreme love, obedience and trust when he says, "Father, into your hands I commit my spirit" (Lk 23:46).

iv) *The glory of the cross*   Christ is perfect man, but he is not, however, an ordinary man, he is not just a man. The Fathers always kept this aspect of his humanity in mind, by repeatedly asserting that Jesus is a perfect man but not a common man (*koinos*).[58] His body and soul are body and soul of God. This fact also has to be kept in mind when studying the events of the death and burial of Jesus: he who dies and is buried is the lord of life and death. The metaphysical gravity which death involves (by dying Christ ceases to be a man in the sense that he can only be called a *dead man*)[59] and the essential passivity

rather than theological, should have attempted to move the hearts of Christians by presenting the infernal torments of Jesus for their consideration. These, they say, he would have had to taste in all their bitterness, to free us from the pain of hell which our sins deserved. It is high time that there should be a reaction against these exaggerations, at first sight pious, but deep down blasphemous against God and against the Lord. Jesus could not have felt himself to be a sinner nor could God ever have treated him as such": *Christo, el misterio de Dios II*, op. cit., 83.

56. Cf. M. Bordoni, *Gesù de Nazaret. Signore e Cristo*, II, op. cit., 494-6.
56a. CCC, no. 603.
57. John Paul II, *Address*, 30 November 1988, no. 4: *Insegnamenti*, XI, 4 (1988) 1, 1694.
58. Cf., e.g., St Gregory of Nyssa, *Adv. Apoll.*, 21 (PG 45, 1164 D–1165 A).
59. Answers to the question *Utrum Christus in triduo mortis fuerit homo* are very enlightening. Cf., e.g., St Thomas Aquinas, *STh* III, q.50, a.4.

of death[60] happen alongside Christ's absolute dominion over his bodily life.[61]

This conviction is often found in the patristic tradition, which interprets the following words of our Lord as having strong force: "The Father loves me, because I lay down my life, that I may take it again. No one takes it from me, but I lay it down of my own accord. I have power to lay it down, and I have power to take it again" (Jn 10:17-18). Jesus is making it quite clear that no one takes his life away: he alone will do so.[62] These words bring us right into what happens on the cross, right into the agonized heart of Jesus.[63] The humiliation, pain and shame of the cross must not make us forget the power of the One who is dying there; and yet Christ's omnipotence does not lessen the depth of his *abandonment*.[64]

Jesus himself, as we can see especially in St John, alludes to this glory of the cross when he refers to it as "raising up"[65]: the saviour is lifted up on the cross like the serpent in the desert (Jn 3:14); when he is lifted up above the earth, he will draw all things to himself (Jn 12:32-34): "when you have lifted up the Son of man, then you will know that I am he", we are told in John 8:28—a clear reference to the "I am" of Exodus 3:14.[66] Christ's death on the cross is also the consummation of his life on earth: through it, as priest and victim he consummates his redemptive sacrifice: "It was fitting that he, for whom and by whom all things exist, in bringing many sons to glory, should make the pioneer of their salvation perfect through suffering" (Heb 2:10).[67]

60. Cf. St Thomas Aquinas, *In III Sent.*, dist. 30, q.1, a.1, sed. c. 1.

61. Cf. L.F. Mateo Seco, "Muerte de Cristo y teologia de la cruz", in various authors, *Cristo, Hijo de Dios. . . .* op. cit., 701-11.

62. St Augustine comments: "his hour had not yet come, not meaning the one in which he should be obliged to die, but that in which he should deign to allow himself to be killed [. . .]. He was awaiting this hour, not one that would be fatal, but opportune and voluntary in such a way that all those things would be fulfilled which needed to be fulfilled before his Passion. Because how could it be possible to subject to the necessity of destiny that One who said elsewhere, *I have power to lay down my life and I have power to take it up again*"?: *Tract. in Joh.*, XXXVII, 9, 1-30, CCL, 336-7.

63. "From the start" writes Lagrange, "absolute freedom of Christ because he has received the fullness of life from his Father. *Exousia* indicates not only the right but also the power even to give his life, for without his consent no one can ever take it from him": M.J. Lagrange, *Evangile selon saint Jean* (Paris, 1936), 283.

64. Cardinal Cajetan makes the point that the voluntareity of Christ on the cross was not only one of acceptance; it *caused* his death, in line with what is said in John 10:18: Cajetan, *In III*, q.17, ed. Leon., XI, 455.

65. Cf. L. Malevez, "La gloire de la Croix", NRT (1973), 1058ff.

66. "From the cross, where his universal kingship is proclaimed to all men, the king Messiah draws all to himself, revealing the mystery of his Person, the meaning of his work of salvation and the Father's love (cf. Jn 3:14-16; 8:28). The response that he expects of men is belief. Through this faith in Christ 'raised up', men are made into the new people of God, the community of believers": I. de la Potterie, *La verdad de Jesús* (Madrid, 1979), 102f.

67. Suffering and death "perfect" Christ as saviour of men, in as much as they give him something extra, "because they allow him to perform the essential act of the Great Priest [. . .]. Suffering is the means whereby Christ is 'perfected' because it enables him to bring his work as Saviour to a conclusion": C. Spicq, *L'Epitre aux Hébreux*, II (Paris, 1953), 39-40.

2. THE SALVIFIC MEANING OF CHRIST'S PASSION AND DEATH

Christ is the Good Shepherd who gives his life for his sheep (cf. Jn 10:1-21). In him is our salvation (cf. Acts 4:12). Developing this, the Second Vatican Council says: "As an innocent lamb Christ merited life for us by his blood which he freely shed. In him God reconciled us to himself and to one another (cf. 2 Cor 5:18- 19; Col 1:20-22), freeing us from the bondage of the devil and of sin, so that each one of us could say with the Apostle: the Son of God 'loved me and gave himself for me' (Gal 2:20). By suffering for us he not only gave us an example so that we might follow in his footsteps (cf. 1 Pet 2:21; Mt 16:24; Lk 14:27), but he also opened up a way. If we follow this path, life and death are made holy and acquire a new meaning."[68] Salvation comes to us from Jesus Christ, not only through his example, not only through his word, but also and primordially through his own life, through his death and resurrection. His sufferings have reconciled us to God, setting us free from the power of the devil, from sin and from death. By this "dying for us", Jesus fulfils "what was spoken by the prophets" (cf. Lk 24:25-27).

a) **The sacrificial character of Christ's death**   For theology, Christ's death is set principally in a religious context, which considers the relationships between God, who is holy, and man, who is a sinner. In other words, this death is directly connected to human sin (cf. Rom 5:12-17), and to reconciliation with God (cf. 2 Cor 5:18-19). The New Testament vigorously and persistently draws our attention to the fact that Christ's death is a true sacrifice, that is, a supreme act of worship to be rendered to God alone. And it sets this sacrifice against the background of the Old Testament sacrifices; but it is much greater than they were, as reality is so much greater than figure (cf. Heb 9:9-14).[69] According to the New Testament, Christ's death is closely connected to three key sacrifices in the Old Testament—the sacrifice of the Covenant (Ex 24:4-8), that of the passover lamb (Ex 12:1-14, 21-27, 46-47); and that of the Day of Atonement (Lev 16:1-34).[69a]

Reference to the sacrifice of the Covenant is to be found in the words our Lord says over the chalice, calling his blood the "blood of the covenant" (cf. Mt 26:28; Mk 14:24; Lk 22:20). St Paul reminds us of this when he passes on

---

68. Second Vatican Council, *Gaudium et spes*, 22.

69. "One can say," Sabourin says, "that the sacrifices of the Old Testament have in a general way found their fulfilment in Christ's sacrifice, because it has achieved the purposes for which they were offered, the expiation of sin": L. Sabourin, "Sacrifice", DB Supl. X, 1513.

69a. "Christ's death is both the Paschal sacrifice that accomplishes the definitive redemption of men, through 'the Lamb of God, who takes away the sin of the world' (Jn 1:29; cf. 8:34-36; 1 Cor 5:7; 1 Pet 1:19) and the *sacrifice of the new Covenant*, which restores man to communion with God by reconciling him to God through the 'blood of the covenant, which was poured out for many for the forgiveness of sins' (Mt 26:28: cf. Ex 24:8; Lev 16:15-16; 1 Cor 11:25)": CCC, no. 613.

the tradition he has received about the Eucharist (cf. 1 Cor 11:23-27). That is why Hebrews stresses so much that Christ is the mediator of a New Testament (cf. Heb 7:22), that is, of a new and everlasting covenant.

The Passover and the sacrifice of the paschal lamb are referred to by the Baptist when he introduces our Lord as "the Lamb of God, who takes away the sin of the world" (Jn 1:29). The Last Supper takes place in an obvious passover setting, and the evangelists emphasize this, pointing to Christ's death as a sacrifice which seals the new Covenant. The words used at the institution of the Eucharist also allude to the passover sacrifice, when they include the instruction to renew the sacrifice of the bread and wine as a "memorial" of our Lord's death (cf. 1 Cor 11:24 and 26), thereby connecting it with an essential feature of the Jewish passover—the fact that it is a commemoration of God's liberation of the Hebrews from slavery in Egypt (cf. Ex 12:14). In St John there are many allusions linking Christ's death to the passover sacrifice— for example, when he calls attention to the fact that "they did not break his legs", thereby fulfilling the regulation that not a bone be broken of the passover lamb (cf. Jn 19:33-36; Ex 12:46; Num 9:12). Also the Lamb (sacrificed and glorified) in the Book of Revelation is evocative of the passover lamb (cf. Rev 5:6, 9; 12:4; 15:3).[70] And St Paul, in a clear reference to the passover meal, exhorts the faithful of Corinth to get rid of the old leaven and become "a new lump", that is, "unleavened because Christ, our paschal lamb, has been sacrificed" (1 Cor 5:7).[71]

The sacrifice on the Day of Atonement, for the blotting out of the faults of the people, was a particularly solemn one. This was the only day in the year when the high priest could enter the holy of holies to sprinkle the blood of sacrificial victims on the Propitiatory, set upon the Ark of the Covenant (cf. Lev 16:1-34). The Letter to the Hebrews makes a lengthy comparison between this sacrifice and the death of Christ and his entry into the sanctuary (cf. Heb 9:1-7).[72] St John is probably referring to this sacrifice when he says of Christ that he is "the expiation for our sins" (1 Jn 2:2) and that God "sent his Son to be the expiation of our sins" (1 Jn 4:10), and when he says that "the blood

---

70. On the different exegetical interpretation of the title and its sacrificial meaning, cf., A. Garcia Moreno, "Jesucristo, Cordero de Dios", in various authors, *Cristo, Hijo de Dios . . .*, op. cit., 269-97; S. Virgulin, "Recent Discussions of the Title *Lamb of God*", Scr 13 (1980) 74-80.
71. Cf. L. Pirot, "Agneau Pascal", DB Supl. I, 158f.
72. Cf. A. Medebielle, *Expiation*, DB Supl. II, 1-263. "That blood", says Pope John Paul II, "represented the life of the people, and its sprinkling in the most holy place of the Presence of God proclaimed an irrevocable will to adhere to Him and to enter into communion with Him, thus overcoming the separation and distancing caused by sin. Above all, the author of the *Letter to the Hebrews*, with the help of this ritual, has interpreted the death of Christ on the Cross and specially noted the outstanding effectiveness of the Sacrifice of Christ who 'entered once for all into the Holy Place, taking not the blood of goats and calves but his own blood, thus securing an eternal redemption": John Paul II, Address, 21 September 1983: *Insegnamenti*, VI/2 (1983), 596.

of Jesus cleanses us from all sin" (1 Jn 1:7). The propitiatory character of Christ's death is spelt out particularly clearly in Romans 3:23-25: "since all have sinned and fall short of the glory of God, they are justified by his grace as a gift, through the redemption which is in Christ Jesus, whom God put forward as an expiation by his blood, to be received by faith. This was to show God's righteousness, because in his divine forbearance he had passed over former sins."[73] It is worth pointing out that the text has God as the subject: it is God who makes Christ Jesus a sacrifice of propitiation, thereby manifesting his salvific justice by the destruction of sin.[74]

The New Testament also contains numerous references to Christ's death being a sacrifice, without their being necessarily allusions to the three types of sacrifice we have mentioned. Indeed, the entire New Testament is imbued with the idea that Christ's life and death has a sacrificial meaning.[75] This comes across very clearly in the songs of the Servant of Yahweh, which are echoed, for example, in the hymn in Philippians 2:5-11. Jesus "emptied himself unto death" out of obedience, because the Father had commanded him to give up his life for his sheep (cf. Jn 10:18; 14:31). St Paul repeatedly says that Christ gave his life for us, out of love of us: "Christ loved the church and gave himself up for her" (Eph 5:25); "he died for all" (2 Cor 5:14); one died for all (cf., e.g., Rom 5:6, 8; 8:32; 14:15; 1 Cor 11:24; Gal 2:20; 1 Tim 2:6; Tit 2:14); "Christ loved us and gave himself up for us, a fragrant offering and sacrifice to God" (Eph 5:2). In Hebrews, Christ's death, of greater value than all sacrifices, replaces them; it, on its own, suffices to purify the consciences of all men (cf. Heb 9:11-28).[76]

There are many more passages which speak of Christ's death being a sacrifice.[77] In fact all these statements are already to be found in the earliest New Testament writings and are linked to what Jesus says about giving up his

---

73. Prat commented: "Whatever may be the precise meaning of *hilasterion*—victim of propitiation, instrument of propitiation, or even mercy-seat—it follows inevitably from this text that the sacrifice of the cross is for Christians and carried out in a more excellent manner what the solemn day of *Kippurim*, the annual sacrifice of expiation or propitiation, was for the Jews": F. Prat, *The Theology of Saint Paul*, II, op. cit., 184. Cf. S. Lyonnet, *De notione expiationis*, VD 38 (1960), 241-61.

74. As González Gil, writes, "in the Old Testament the action of *propitiating* does not usually have God in the accusative case as its object, but rather sin; propitiating is performing the rite by which sin is blotted out or suppressed; propitiating is causing sin to disappear. Following this line of thought, what Paul says will be interpreted as meaning that Jesus was the propitiatory or expiatory victim who was able to blot out our sins": *Cristo, el Misterio de Dios*, II, op. cit., 181.

75. Cf. M. Meinertz, *Teologia del Nuevo Testamento*, op. cit., 145-53; L. Sabourin, "Sacrifice", DBS, art. cit., 1512-42.

76. Cf. L. Cerfaux, *Cristo nella teologia di San Paolo*, op. cit., 124-6; V. Loi, *San Paolo e l'interpretazione teologica del messagio di Gesù*, op. cit., 113-23.

77. Cf. L. Sabourin, *Rédemption sacrificielle. Une enquête exégètique* (Paris-Tournai, 1961), esp. 302ff.

life, when applying to himself the sufferings of the Servant; they are connected, particularly, to what he said when instituting the Eucharist.[78] It is not surprising, therefore, that the teaching of the Fathers is unvarying on this point. One only needs to recall the *Paschal homilies*, from that of Melitus of Sardis in the second century to those of the end of the seventh century, which deal with this subject directly. And it would be impossible to list the passages where the Fathers depict Christ's death as a sacrifice, often using technical, exact, sacrificial terminology.[79]

The Magisterium of the Church solemnly teaches that Jesus Christ offered himself on the cross as a true and proper sacrifice for the salvation of mankind. In the anathemas of St Cyril of Alexandria, included in the texts of the Council of Ephesus, it is said that Jesus "gave himslf up for us, a fragrant offering and sacrifice to God (Eph 5:2)."[80] And the Council of Trent, in its teaching on the sacrifice of the Mass, clearly takes for granted the sacrificial character of Christ's death on the cross, of which the Mass is a sacramental renewal.[81] The Second Vatican Council, in the text quoted above, reiterates this teaching.[82]

As pointed out earlier, Christ's death cannot be regarded as one of a number of possible ways his mortal life could have ended, or as an outcome which took him by surprise; rather, it was an ending foreseen in God's plan and also accepted by Jesus' free human will (cf. Lk 12:50).[82a] "From its earliest

---

78. According to the Modernists, "the teaching about the expiatory death of Christ is not evangelic but only Pauline" (cf. Decr. *Lamentabili*, 3 July 1907, prop. 38, DS 3438). In addition to its having been rejected by the Magisterium this proposition is unacceptable even from the study of history alone. This is so because texts such as the narration of the institution of the Eucharist with its reference to the sacrifice of the alliance (1 Cor 11:23-25), the affirmation that Christ died for our sins *in accordance with the scriptures* (1 Cor 15:3), the christological hymn with the relationship between Christ and the Servant of Yahweh, humbled unto death (Phil 2:6-11), are all pre-Pauline.

79. Our Lord, Origen (+253-5) writes, "led to death like a lamb and offered in the Sacrifice of the Altar, has obtained forgiveness of sins for the whole world": *In Num. Hom.* XXIV, 1 (PG 12, 757); and St Basil (+379): "The Son of God gave life to the world when he offered himself to God as a victim for our sins" (*In Ps.* 28, 5: PG 36, 1165). St Gregory of Nyssa (+385): "Christ, our Pasch, was immolated for us; the same Christ, the priest, offered himself as a sacrifice" (*De perfect.*, PG 46, 264A): cf. L.F. Mateo Seco, "Sacerdocio de Cristo y sacerdocio ministerial en los tres grandes Capadocios", in various authors, *Teología del Sacerdocio*, IV (Burgos, 1972), 177-201. The Latin Fathers speak in exactly the same terms, cf. e.g., St Augustine, *De Trin.*, 4, 13 (PL 42, 899)

80. Cf. *Anathematismi Cyrilli Alexandrini* (DS 261).

81. Council of Trent, sess. XXII, chaps. 1 and 2 (DS 1739-43).

82. Second Vatican Council, Const. *Gaudium et spes*, 22. Cf. also Paul VI, *Creed of the People of God*, 30 June 1968, no. 17, AAS 60 (1968) 438; John Paul II, Enc. *Redemptor hominis*, op. cit., no. 20.

82a. "Jesus' violent death was not the result of chance in an unfortunate coincidence of circumstances, but is part of the mystery of God's plan, as St Peter explains to the Jews of Jerusalem in his first sermon on Pentecost: 'This Jesus [was] delivered up according to the definite plan and foreknowledge of God' (Acts 2:23). This biblical language does not mean that those who handed him over were merely passive players in a scenario written in advance by God (cf. Acts 3:13)": CCC, no. 599.

formulation the apostolic preaching involves the conviction that 'Christ died for our sins according to the Scriptures' (1 Cor 15:3), that 'he gave himself for our sins' (Gal 1:4), and this was according to the will of God the Father, who 'delivered him to death for our sins' (Rom 4:25; Is 53:6), 'for us all' (Rom 8:32), 'to redeem us' (Gal 4:4), who 'desires all men to be saved' (1 Tim 2:4), excludes no one from his plan of salvation, which Christ embraces with all his being .The entire life of Christ, from 'his entrance into the world' (Heb 10:5) to the giving of his life, is a single and unique gift 'for us'. And that precisely is what the Church has preached from the very outset (Rom 5:8; 1 Thess 5:10; 2 Cor 5:15; 1 Pet 2:21; 3:18, etc.)."[83]

"This sacrifice of Christ is unique; it completes and surpasses all other sacrifices (cf. Heb 10:10). First, it is a gift from God the Father himself, for the Father handed his Sin over to sinners in order to reconcile us with himself. At the same time it is the offering of the Son of God made made man, who in freedom and love offered his life to his Father through the Holy Spirit in reparation for our disobedience."[83a]

b) Christ, the offerer of his own sacrifice   Christ's death is a sacrifice in which he himself is the offerer and the offering, the Priest and the Victim: "Jesus Christ is both priest and sacrifice."[84] It is a question then of a single sacrifice, among other reasons because of the perfect identity of priest and victim. This identity does not, obviously, imply that Jesus "killed himself";[85] but it does mean that his offering of his own life was a voluntary one; that he was humanly free to accept his own death.

The events of Christ's passion and death constitute what one might term

83. ITC, *The Consciousness of Christ*, op. cit., 4.1 (Sharkey, op. cit., 314).
83a. CCC, no. 614.
84. Council of the Lateran, chap. 1, *De fide catholica* (DS 802).
85. Patristic exegesis gave special prominence to the text of Jn 10:18, where Christ says that nobody has power to take away his life from him but that he himself lays it down and will take it up again, highlighting the fact that Christ is referring here to a specific voluntariety. St Thomas deals with this question in several places (cf. *Quodl.* I, q.2, a.3; *In Jn* II, lect, 3; X, lect. 4; *Comp. Theol.*, chap. 230; *STh* III, q.47, a.1) striving to express himself in ever clearer language each time. Here is how he puts it in the *Compendium Theologiae*: "The death of Christ was the same as ours in that which belongs to the very nature of death, that is to say, in the fact that the soul is separated from the body. Nevertheless there is some difference between the death of Christ and ours. We die as being subject to death by necessity of nature or from whatever violence is inflicted on us; Christ died, not of necessity, but of his own will in accordance with what he said (cf. Jn 10:18) [. . .]. It should not be said that the Jews did not kill the Lord, or that Christ killed himself. Because that person who inflicts the cause of death on somebody is said to kill him; death, however, does not follow until the cause of death overcomes the nature that is preserving that life. Well, in this case, it was in Christ's power that the nature could yield to the cause which would destroy it or could resist it as much as he wanted to. Therefore Christ himself died voluntarily and, nevertheless, the Jews killed him" (chap. 230). Cf. L.F. Mateo Seco, "La muerte de Cristo. La thanatología de Santo Tomás a la luz de sus precisiones en torno a la muerte de Cristo", EscV 12 (1982) 523-45.

his *external sacrifice*, while his *interior sacrifice* lies in his obedience and love for his Father. In this obedience and love are to be found the innermost essence of Christ's sacrifice: Jesus suffered and died out of love for the Father (cf. Jn 14:31) and out of love for men, which means that every man and woman can say with St Paul that he *"loved me and gave himself up for me"* (Gal 2:20). Christ's crucifixion cannot be put on the level of the ritual sacrifices of the Old Testament, which were only its figure. Looked at from the point of view of those who perpetrated the deed, Christ's death is an act of profanity, the unjust killing of an innocent man, a grave sin; seen from the point of view of Christ himself, who offers his life out of love and obedience, his death is his supreme act of self-giving and worship of the Father: as the new Adam, established as mediator and chosen priest, in solidarity with the whole family of man, he manifests his interior attitudes of submission to and love for the Father by accepting suffering and death, thereby irrevocably consecrating his entire existence to God by the irreversibility of death, and wiping out Adam's disobedience *by his obedience* (cf. Rom 12:5 and 17).

The clarity and frequency with which the New Testament uses the setting and language of sacrifice when speaking of Christ's death make it plain that it is not speaking metaphorically. In fact this is already clearly hinted at in the Old Testament when it depicts the Messiah as saving the people *through his suffering*. This real sacrifice is much greater than all the sacrifices which came before it; they in fact had value only through their orientation to this unique and real sacrifice, and at the same time the new sacrifice is very much in line with the old ones.[86] Jesus, in effect, offers himself as Priest and Victim of the new and eternal Covenant.[87]

3. THE DEATH AND BURIAL OF OUR LORD

The Gospels give a brief and vivid account of the death of Jesus. "He breathed his last," we are told in Mk 15:37; Lk 23:46 and Mt 27:50; and Jn 19:30 says "he gave up his spirit." It is a matter of faith that Christ truly died, that he was really dead (was buried and "descended into hell"), and on the third day rose from the dead.

Therefore, in Christ's death are verified the essential features of every human death.[88] These include the separation of body and soul;[89] that is, the

---

86. Cf. St Thomas Aquinas, *STh* III, q.48, a.3, ad 1.
87. On this, cf. also what is said above in Chapter 4, section 4(c).
88. St Cyril puts a lot of emphasis on this: "If anyone fails to confess that the Word of God suffered in the flesh and was crucified in the flesh, and experienced death in the flesh and became the first-born from among the dead, according to which as God he is life and life-giving, let him be anathema": *Epist.* 17 *Ad Nestorium*, anath. 12, PG 77, 121; DS 263.
89. Death tends to be defined in two ways, on the basis of observation: *Mors est privatio vitae* (cf. St Thomas Aquinas, *De anima*, q.un. art. 10); *mors est secundum separationem animae a corpore* (St Thomas Aquinas, *Comp. Theol.*, chap. 229).

body is rendered lifeless, it loses its vital operations. To say that Jesus truly died, therefore, is the same as saying that his body became lifeless, it had no vital operations. This is also the same as saying that during the days he was dead, in a sense he ceased to be a man; because man is a union of body and soul; neither body nor soul on its own constitutes a man.[90]

Jesus, then, "tasted death", that is to say, he experienced "the condition of death, the separation of his soul from his body, between the time he expired on the cross and the time he was raised from the dead. The state of the dead Christ is the mystery of the tomb and the descent into hell."[90a]

a) **The indissolubility of the hypostatic union** Christ's death, then, means that in him as in other dead persons, the vital connexion between body and soul was broken; however, Christ's body and soul stayed united to the Word even during the three days after his death. This is the common doctrine of the Fathers and of later theologians,[91] who rely on what Scripture says about Christ's priesthood being eternal and his kingdom having no end (cf., e.g., Heb 7:24; 13:8; Lk 1:33; Jn 12:34).

Those who thought that during these three days the Divinity was separated from Christ's body and who therefore denied that the hypostatic union was indissoluble included Marcellus of Ancyra, who also denied the everlasting nature of Christ's kingdom,[92] and the Apollinarists who, because they thought that the Word acted as the soul of Christ's body, logically said that Christ could not have died unless the divinity was separated from his body.[93]

The Magisterium has always consistently asserted that the hypostatic union is indissoluble. The two natures are united in Christ inseparably, says the Council of Chalcedon, and similar wording is used by Pope Agatho,[94] the Third

---

90. St Thomas has an article on this topic which is particularly eloquent in regard to the importance which must be given to the union of body and soul as components of man (cf. *STh* III, q.50, a.4), where he states without hesitation: "It belongs to the truth of the death of a man or of an animal that through death it ceases to be a man or an animal. This is so because the death of a man or of an animal arises from the separation of the soul which completes the notion of animal or of man. Therefore, to say that, during the triduum of his death, Christ was a man, is, speaking simply and absolutely, erroneous."

90a. CCC, no. 624.

91. Cf. A. Michel, "Hypostatique (Union)", DTC, art. cit., 536-9, which provides extensive coverage on this subject.

92. Cf. M.D. Chenu, "Marcel d'Ancyre", DTC IX, 1993-8. St Cyril of Jerusalem replies to him: "If you happen to hear someone say that the kingdom of Christ will come to an end, reject that heresy; it is another head of the dragon that has appeared recently in Galatia": *Cathequeses*, 15, 22, PG 33, 910.

93. Cf. St Athanasius, *Scriptum contra Apollinarium* (PG 26, 1160); *De salutari adventu Christi*, 14 (PG 26, 1154).

94. "For we know that our one and same Lord Jesus Christ, only begotten Son of God, subsists of two substances and in two substances, unconfused, unchanged, undivided and inseparable": Ep. dogm. synodalis, *Omnium bonorum spes*, 27 March 680, DS 548.

Council of Constantinople,[95] and the Eleventh Council of Toledo: "we believe that there are two natures in the Son of God, one divine and one human, which so united themselves in the one person of Christ that the divinity can never be separated from the humanity nor the humanity from the divinity."[96]

In the same (fourth) century we also find clear statements to this effect in the writings of the Fathers: St Vincent of Lerins says that "in Christ there remains the singularity of one unique, same person and there also remains for ever the particular properties of each of the natures;"[97] and St Leo the Great: "the natures which were united will never be separated, nor ever have an end;"[98] and St Gregory of Nyssa: "Although it is true that (the Word) permitted that on (Christ's) death, the soul should separate from the body, the divinity was never separated from the body or from the soul;"[99] and St John Damascene teaches that, although the soul was separated from the body, "the divinity was never separated from either of the two, that is, was never in any way separated from the soul or from the body. Since the body and the soul had at the same time and from the beginning existence in the Word, and although at death they were separated, each of them subsisted in the hypostasis of the Word. So, the hypostasis of the Word was itself the hypostasis of the soul and of the body. Neither the soul nor the body ever had a hypostasis of their own outside the hypostasis of the Word."[100]

Therefore, there is no reason to think that either Christ's body or his soul was broken off from the hypostatic union. In addition to the reasons already given (the eternal nature of Christ's priesthood and kingdom), theology has added another which it regards as very important. Here is how St Thomas formulates it: "whatever is granted through grace will never be taken away, unless for a fault, according to the saying, 'the gifts and the call of God are irrevocable' (Rom 11:29). This being so, the grace of union by which the divinity is united to the flesh of Christ in the unity of a single person, is much greater than the grace of adoption, by which others are sanctified. Also, it is more permanent by its very nature because this grace is ordered to personal union, while the grace of adoption is ordered to a certain affective union only. But we see that the grace of adoption is not lost unless it is for a fault. Therefore, since there was no sin whatever in Christ, it was impossible that the union of the divinity with the flesh should be broken."[101]

95. ". . . one and same Christ only begotten Son of God to be acknowledged in two natures unconfused, unconverted, inseparable and undivided": Third Council of Constantinople, sess. 18, 16 September 681, DS 554.
96. Eleventh Council of Toledo XI, *Symbolum* (DS 534).
97. St Vincent of Lerins, *Commonitorium*, 13 (PL 50, 656).
98. St Leo the Great, *Sermo 30*, 6 (PL 54, 233).
99. St Gregory of Nyssa, *Epist.* 3 (PG 46, 1021).
100. St John Damascene, *De fide orthodoxa*, 3, 27 (PG 94, 1098).
101. St Thomas Aquinas, *STh*, q.50, a.2.

Consequently it can be said that God, in his humanity, experienced death in a particularly intense way; that is, he experienced what it was like for the soul to be separated from the body, and also what it was like to be a body without life (which is not the case when a human person dies, because the dead body is not something of the person). In the unique case of Jesus, the fact that the hypostatic union continues even with his lifeless body, gives his death an especially full sacrificial character even after the moment of death itself.[102]

So, although Christ's death was a real death in the sense that it put an end to his earthly life, "because of the union his body retained with the person of the Son, his was not a mortal corpse like others, for 'divine power preserved the body of Christ from corruption' (cf. St Thomas Aquinas' *STh III*, q.51, a.3). Both of these statements can be made of Christ: 'He was cut off out of the land of the living' (Is 53:8); and 'My flesh will dwell in hope. For you will not abandon my soul to Hades, nor let your Holy One see corruption' (Acts 2:26-27; cf. Ps 16:9-10)."[102a]

b) Christ's burial Joseph of Arimathea asks Pilate for permission to give Jesus' body a dignified burial; and the very people who were responsible for having Jesus condemned ask Pilate to mount a guard at his tomb. The Gospel accounts of the Passion include a detailed description of Jesus' burial (cf. Mt 27:57-61; Mk 15:42-47; Lk 23:50-56; Jn 19:38-42). We find the same explicit mention of it in Acts 13:29 and in St Paul's summary in 1 Corinthians 15:4.

We do know that Jesus' burial was a basic element in early baptismal catechesis (cf. Rom 6:4; Col 2:12). St Thomas comments: "the baptized, who through the death of Christ die to sin, come to be buried, as it were, with Christ through immersion, according to what is said in Romans 6:4: 'we were buried therefore with him by baptism into death'."[103]

Through baptism the mysteries of Christ's death, resurrection and ascension are mystically re-enacted in the person being baptized;[104] real salvation is caused in the baptized, for, as St Cyril of Jerusalem writes, "In Christ's case, death was something real, and his burial was real. . . . To you, however, has been given a semblance of that death and of those sufferings; but your salvation, on the contrary, is not a semblance; it is real."[105]

Finally, it should be noted that the dead body of Christ did not suffer corruption (in accordance with Acts 2:22-31): "(David) foresaw and spoke of

102. Cf. F. Ocáriz, "La Resurrection de Jesucristo", in various authors, *Cristo, Hijo de Dios y Redentor del hombre*, op. cit., 751f.
102a. CCC, no. 627.
103. St Thomas Aquinas, *STh* III, q.51, a.1.
104. Cf. St Basil, *De Spiritu Sancto*, 15 (PG 32, 127-34).
105. St Cyril of Jerusalem, *Catech. Myst.*, 2, 7 (PG 33, 1084).

the resurrection of Christ, that he was not abandoned in Hades, nor did his flesh see corruption."[106] Christ's burial is the consequence and complement of his death and is therefore also something salvific. Christ is sown in the tomb, like the grain of wheat, which falls into the furrow and yields abundant fruit (cf. Jn 12:24). From this event onwards, at the burial of those who have died with Christ through Baptism, what St Paul says come true: "what is sown is perishable, what is raised is imperishable [. . .]. It is sown in weakness; it is raised in power;" a body of flesh is sown and a spiritual body is raised (cf. 1 Cor 15:42-44).

c) **The descent into hell** The words "he descended into hell" were not added to the Creed until the end of the fourth century. The first reference to its addition is found in Rufinus of Aquileia,[107] and it gradually found its way into the various symbols.[108] In the thirteenth century two ecumenical councils made solemn mention of the "descent into hell"—the Fourth Council of the Lateran, which specifies that "he went down in the soul and was raised in the flesh,"[109] and the Second Council of Lyon.[110] From then onwards this article of faith was including in all catechisms.[111]

The few passages in Sacred Scripture which do speak of the descent into hell are not easy to interpret. The key text occurs in Acts 2:27-31; here St Peter quotes Psalm 15:10 ("thou wilt not abandon my soul to Hades"), referring to the fact that Christ's body did not suffer corruption in the tomb and that his soul was not left abandoned during its stay in the underworld (cf. also 1 Pet 3:18-20; Rom 10:6-7).

On the other hand, from St Ignatius of Antioch onwards there are ancient and very numerous references in the Fathers to Christ's descent into hell,[112] but they differ as to why this happened and what its effects were. Some of the

---

106. Cf. St Gregory of Nyssa, *Adversus Apollinarem*, 17 (PG 45, 1156); St John Damascene, *De fide orthodoxa*, 3, 28 (PG 94, 1100); St Thomas Aquinas, *STh* III, q.51, a.3.

107. Tirannus Rufinus, *Expositio in Symbolum* (PL 21, 335-81, DS 16). Cf. also DS 23, 27, 29, 30, 76.

108. A detailed history is given in H. Quilliet, "Descente de Jésus aux enfers", DTC IV, 567-73.

109. "He suffered on the wood of the cross for the salvation of mankind and died, descended into hell, rose from the dead, and ascended into heaven: but he descended in the soul and rose in the body; but ascended equally in both": Fourth Council of the Lateran, chap. 1, *De fide catholica*, DS 801.

110. ". . . he died and was buried, and descended into hell, and the third day rose again from the dead in a true resurrection of the body": *Second Council of Lyons*, Sess. IV, DS 852.

111. Here is how the Trent catechism puts it: "we are not to imagine that his power and virtue alone, and not also his soul, descended into hell; but we are firmly to believe that his soul itself, really and substantially, descended thither, according to this conclusive testimony of David: 'thou wilt not leave my soul in hell' (Ps 15:10)": *Catech. ad parochos*, I, 6, 4.

112. Cf. St Ignatius of Antioch, *Ad Magnesios*, 9, 2; St Justin, *Diál. with Trypho*, 72 (PG 6, 645); St Irenaeus, *Adv. Haer.*, III, 20, 4; ibid., IV, 22, 1 (PG 7, 945; 1046).

Greek Fathers tend to the view that Christ preached to everyone who was in hell,[113] and some mistakenly think that this preaching invited the dead to be converted.[114] This led St John Chrysostom to remind people that conversion is impossible after death,[115] and St Gregory the Great (asserting that Christ freed only those who had died in the grace of God) called the notion of conversion after death "heretical".[116]

One could argue that the descent into hell or *Sheol* is contained in the statement that Christ "was buried". For, just as burial identifies the condition of Christ's lifeless body, the descent into hell shows that Christ's soul had truly entered upon that mystery which is referred to by the expression "kingdom of the dead". Jesus was really dead during the three days: death affected all of his human nature (body and soul) just as it affects every human being who dies.[117] So during those days Jesus found himself "among the dead". Often when referring to the resurrection of our Lord, the New Testament will use the formula "raised *from (among)* the dead"[118] (cf., e.g., Acts 3:15; 13:30; 17:3). As St Irenaeus stresses, "the Lord observed the laws of death so as to become the first-born of the dead."[119] So, the descent into hell has an initial and obvious meaning: Jesus shares death with those who have died, he fulfils "the laws" of death, so that it can truly be said that he rises *from among* the dead. But if one examines biblical and theological tradition more closely, the *descent* into hell is a sign of Christ's kingly sovereignty over death and over the dead. That is why theology generally regards this *descent* as meaning that Jesus brings redemption to the just who have already died, that is, applies redemption to them by going down into hell.[120]

There is little else that can be safely said about the meaning of the statement that Jesus "descended into hell". Every age has imagined this "descent" in line with its anthropological deductions and its ideas about the Beyond and the state of the separated soul. Clearly, when submitting to the laws of death, when truly dying, Jesus continues to be the Lord of life and of death. Exegesis has traditionally interpreted the "descent into hell" as designed to liberate the souls

113. Such as St Irenaeus, consciously drawing on an old tradition. Cf. *Adv. Haer.*, IV, 27, 1-2 (PG 7, 1056-58); St John Damascene, *De fide orthodoxa*, III, 29 (PG 94, 1101).
114. Cf. Clement of Alexandria, *Stromata* VI, 27, 2 (PG 9, 265ff); Origen, *Contra Celsum*, II, 43 (PG 11, 864).
115. Cf. St John Chrysostom, *In Mat. Hom.* 36, 3 (PG 57, 417).
116. St Gregory the Great, *Ep.* 7, 15 (PL 77, 869).
117. The Church confesses that the human soul is immortal, that is to say, that the human spirit lives on after death; it does not mean to say, however, that death does not gravely affect the soul, also. It must even be said, in classical language, that separated from the body of which it is essentially its form, the soul remains in a state that is *contra naturam*": cf. e.g., St Thomas Aquinas, *Contra gentes*, IV, 79.
118. The Greek expression "ek nekron" implicitly contains the idea of place from which proceeds.
119. St Irenaeus, *Adv. Haer.*, V, 31 (PG 7, 1209).
120. Cf. K. Adam, *The Christ of Faith*, op. cit., 338-43.

of the just, who were eagerly awaiting this holy visit,[121] following the difficult text of 1 Peter 3:18-19. The Fathers stress that Jesus' soul descended voluntarily;[122] death could not prevent it from doing so.[123] St Thomas says that one of the reasons why it was so fitting that Jesus should descend into hell was "so that having conquered the Evil One by his Passion, he might wrest from him the prisoners he had detained in hell" and so that "just as he showed on earth his power to live and to die, so also he would show it in hell by visiting and enlightening it [. . .]. And so at the name of Jesus 'every knee should bow, in heaven and on earth and under the earth' (cf. Phil 2:10)."[124]

So, following traditions which go back to Judaeo-Christian theology, exegesis has normally said that, during the three days when he was dead, Christ's soul acted in a salvific way by announcing to the just the advent of Redemption and their liberation; however, many contemporary authors prefer to stress the fact that this "descent" implies submission by Christ to the laws of death, that is, they emphasize his passivity and his solidarity with the dead; they do not, of course, say that this descent into the kingdom of the dead was not "for our salvation", but they put the salvific effect not so much in any one action as in the self-emptying dimension of being dead,[125] in his sharing in death (the final consequence of his redemptive obedience) with the salvific effect proper to a victim already sacrificed.

"The descent into hell brings the Gospel message of salvation to complete fulfilment. This is the last phase of Jesus' messianic mission, a phrase which is condensed in time but vast in its real significance: the spread of the Christ's redemptive work to all men of all times and of all places because all who are saved have been made sharers in the redemption."[125a]

4. CHRIST'S EXALTATION

Apostolic preaching about the death of Christ does not stop there; it immediately goes on to speak of his exaltation. "Let all the house of Isaiah therefore know assuredly that God has made him both Lord and Christ, this Jesus whom you crucified," St Peter says in his address on the day of Pentecost (Acts 2:36); referring to this event as the "exaltation" of the Messiah. This "exaltation" comprises his resurrection from the dead, his ascension to the right

---

121. Cf. St Thomas Aquinas, *STh* III, q. 52; H. Kürzinger, "Descenso de Cristo a los infiernos", DTB, 259-64.

122. Cf. e.g., St Cyril of Jerusalem, *Catech.* 14, 19 (PG 33, 847).

123. Cf. e.g., St Athanasius, *De incarnat. Dom.*, 13 (PG 26, 1117). And St Thomas Aquinas says that he descended "not as if he were owing a debt of punishment, but to free those who were" (*STh* III, q.52, a.1, ad 1).

124. St Thomas Aquinas, *STh* III, q.52, a.1.

125. Cf., e.g., J. Ratzinger, *Introduction to Christianity*, op. cit., 223.

125a. CCC, no. 634.

hand of the Father, and the sending of the Holy Spirit (cf. Acts 2:32-33). The glorification of Christ after his death should not be understood as something which happened to Jesus *after* he accomplished our redemption: it is an integral part of that redemption.[126]

Christ's glorification began immediately after his death, in the descent into hell. "If death involves the separation of soul and body, it follows that in Christ too there was, on the one hand, the body in the state of a corpse, and on the other, *the heavenly glorification of his soul from the moment of death*. The First Letter of St Peter speaks of this dual aspect when, referring to the death of Christ for sin, it says of him: 'being put to death in the flesh but made alive in the spirit' (1 Pet 3:18)."[127] Christ's soul, united *secundum Personam* (according to the Person) to the Word, already has in the fullest degree the glory deriving from the beatific vision (the saints receive it immediately after death),[128] but the complete glorification of Christ, as *God-Man*, takes place through his resurrection and ascension into heaven.

a) Our Lord's resurrection   The resurrection of Jesus is the central theme of apostolic preaching and is inseparable from his crucifixion and death. "God has made (this Jesus) Lord and Christ," St Peter says in the address just quoted (Acts 2:32, 36). We find a similar statement in the discourses of St Paul: "We bring you," he says in the synagogue of Antioch, "the good news that what God promised to the Fathers, this he has fulfilled to us their children by raising Jesus; as also it is written in the second psalm, 'Thou art my son, today I have begotten thee'" (Acts 13:32-33).

The resurrection of our Lord is also to be found in all the symbols[129] and professions of faith,[130] because they faithfully follow the nucleus of apostolic preaching. Some of these professions of faith have additions which state in the most explicit manner possible that it was a true resurrection (this, to avoid Docetism); hence their reference to his having eaten and drunk after the resurrection.[131] In some texts it is stated that our Lord rose by his own power.[132]

---

126. Cf. M.J. Scheeben, *The Mysteries of Christianity*, op. cit., 436.
127. John Paul II, *Address*, 11 January 1989, no. 5, *Insegnamenti*, XII, 1 (1989) 77.
128. *Mox post mortem*: cf. Benedict XII, Const. *Benedictus Deus*, 25 April 1342, DS 530.
129. Cf., e.g., DS 11, 12, 13, 14, 15, 16, 17, etc.
130. Cf., e.g., DS 791, 801, 852, 1338, 1862, 2529.
131. "Suffered for us for our salvation with a true passion of his flesh and was buried, and rose from the dead on the third day with a true resurrection of the flesh; for the purpose of confirming this he ate with the disciples, not because he needed food but from his sole will and power": Leo IX, *Professio fidei*, DS 681. "He died with a true death of his body and rose with a true resurrection of his flesh and a true reuniting of his soul to his body: in which, afterwards, he ate and drank": Innocent III, *Professio fidei Walensibus praescripta*, DS 791. St Pius X similarly takes issue with the "dehistoricizing" of the Resurrection of Jesus, as practised by the Modernists (cf. Decr. *Lamentabili*, propos. 37 and 38, DS 3437 and 3438).
132. "And on the third day, raised up by his own power, he rose from the tomb" (Eleventh

These professions of faith in the Resurrection also mention that he rose on the third day; in the Latin symbols this is usually done by simply stating that "he rose on the third day", whereas in the Greek Symbols, such as the Nicene-Constantinopolitan, it is more usual to find the words "he arose on the third day in accordance with the Scriptures" So, the creeds are simply keeping very close to what the New Testament says (the wording is the same, for example, as in 1 Corinthians 15:4). And St Peter uses Psalm 15:10 ("For thou dost not give me up to Sheol, or let thy godly one see the pit") as a prophetic text referring to our Lord's resurrection (cf. Acts 2:24ff). St Paul does the same (cf. Acts 13:35ff).[133]

The Resurrection is, first and foremost, the glorification of Christ himself, who had become "obedient unto death, even death on a cross. Therefore, God has highly exalted him and bestowed on him the name which is above every name" (Phil 2:8-9). This glorification, which is his right because he is the Son,[134] is also something Christ has won (merited), as the passage from Philippians spells out: God exalted him *because* he was obedient unto death on a cross; that is, Christ, by obeying, merited to be raised on high. This exaltation was also for Christ an object of hope,[135] and something he prayed for, as we

Council of Toledo, *Symbolum*, DS 539). "By his own power he rose": (Paul VI, *Creed of the People of God*, 30 June 68, no. 12: in AAS 60 (1968) 438. Sacred Scripture sometimes attributes the resurrection of the Lord to the Father (cf., for example, Acts 2:24ff; 3:13ff; Gal 1:1), and at other times it uses the expression he rose, on its own, thus seeming to attribute the resurrection to the Lord himself. In fact, he had declared expressly: *no one takes (my life) from me, but I lay it down of my own accord. I have power to lay it down, and I have power to take it again* (Jn 10:18). This power by which Christ rose again is that of the Divinity, whether it be attributed to the Father, or to the Son himself, or to the Father in the power of the Holy Spirit. Through the power of the divinity united to his body and his soul, St Thomas Aquinas writes, "the body of Christ took up once more his soul which he had laid down, and his soul reassumed the body which it had left [. . .]. If we consider, however, the body and soul of Christ in death according to the power of his created nature, these two could not be united of themselves but had to be raised by God." And, he concludes, the principal cause of the Resurrection is the Trinity, because "the divine power and activity of Father and Son are the same": *STh* III, q.53, a.4.

133. Cf. M.J. Lagrange, "Le Messianisme dans les Psaumes", RB 14 (1905) 192. Cf. also L. Cerfaux, *Cristo nello teologia di S. Paolo*, op. cit., 66-8.

134. Reflection on the perfect unity of Person in Christ has led the Fathers and theologians to the conviction that Christ's exaltation is nothing other than the Godhead causing his humanity to share in his own glory insofar as human nature can (cf., e.g., St Gregory of Nyssa, *Adv. Apollin.* 21: PG 45, 1165; *Ad Theophilum*: PG 45, 1276 A; cf. L.F. Mateo Seco, *Estudios sobre la cristología de San Gregorio de Nisa*, op. cit., 56-61). Hence it seemed to them perfectly "natural" that so close a unity should bring Christ's human nature to share the attributes of divinity (immortality etc.) in such a way that its capacity to suffer is due to *permission* given by the divine will, a positive wish of God's with a view to the redemption: "it pleased the divine will to *permit* him to suffer in the flesh" (St John Damascene, *De fide orthodoxa*, III, 19 PG 94, 1080), that is, total participation of the humanity in the glory of the Word was as it were impeded. Cf. *STh* III, q.14, a.1.

135. "From the first moment of his conception," St Thomas writes, "Christ enjoyed the full possession of God, and therefore he did not have the virtue of hope. However, he had

can see, for example, from John 17:1 and 5: "Father, the hour has come; glorify thy Son, that the Son may glorify thee [. . .]. Now, Father, glorify thou me in thy own presence with the glory which I had with thee before the world was made."[136] The raising up of Christ, therefore, marks the crowning point of his life and work: the resurrection ushers in not only a new form of existence for Jesus of Nazareth (the life of glory), but also a new form (in power) of his activity as Messiah, as St Paul says, "designated Son of God in power according to the Spirit of holiness by his resurrection from the dead" (Rom 1:4).

In a sense, this new form (in power) is also present even in the humiliation of the passion and death, which is why theology always sees these events as interconnected. As we have seen, St John is stressing this when he describes the crucifixion as a lifting up;[137] the resurrection and the crucifixion are also inseparable because he who is raised up is the Crucified, who still bears the wounds of the cross (cf., e.g., Jn 20:26-29). It is all one and the same mystery—the mystery of the Passover of the Lord,[138] in which there is an indissoluble continuity between the Crucified Jesus and the Risen Jesus.

In this mystery is manifested the intimate nature of Jesus' Lordship: "if you confess with your lips that Jesus is Lord and believe in your heart that God raised him from the dead, you will be saved," St Paul writes to show that belief in Jesus as Lord depends on the supreme event whereby he is revealed—the resurrection (cf. Rom 10:9). The same idea is to be found in St Peters' discourses reported in Acts (cf. Acts 2:32, 36; 3:13-26). Jesus resurrection, therefore, has an indisputable soteriological dimension. By the resurrection of Jesus, God fulfils his promise of a Saviour-Messiah (cf. Acts 13:30, 32-37). The connexion between Jesus' resurrection and our salvation is so close, that St Paul goes so far as to say, "If Christ has not been raised, then our preaching

> hope as regards such things as he did not possess [. . .]; he did not as yet fully possess all that pertained to his perfection, such as immortality and the glorification of the body, which he could hope for" (*STh* III, q.7, a.4).

136. In this prayer, Christ not only recognizes the Father as the author of his glorification but also in some sense prays for us, as St Thomas observes: "The very glory which Christ sought for himself in prayer was relevant to the salvation of others: 'He rose again for our justification' (Rom 4:25). Consequently, even the prayer which he uttered for himself was in some degree for the benefit of others. The same is true of any person who asks a gift of God so that he may use it to help others; he prays not simply for himself but also for others":*STh* III, q.21, ad 3.

137. "When the evangelist causes Christ's glorification and his Passion to overlap (Jn 12:23; 13:31), this means that the Passion must not be seen as separate from the Resurrection. The connexion between the two events is extremely close; they are united by the same 'hour'. The Passion is already under the sign of the Resurrection; it marks the beginning of Christ's glorification. In the suffering of the Passion John already sees Christ glorified, Christ whom God is glorifying": J. Dupont, *La christologie de Saint Jean* (Bruges, 1951), 261.

138. It is worth emphasizing, as Bordoni does, that a Christianity which in order to "focus on the conquering power of the Christian message in terms of life and victory puts brackets round the proclamation of Christ crucified and the shedding of his blood, would run the

is in vain, and your faith is in vain [. . .]. If Christ has not been raised, your faith is futile and you are still in your sins" (1 Cor 15:14 and 17).

It is worth pointing out that these statements are made in the context of a soteriological view of the Resurrection, and not from a mainly apologetic viewpoint. What we are studying here is not so much the fact that the Resurrection bears out the truth of Jesus' words (an apologetic perspective)[139] as that it marks the definite victory over death,[140] a victory which is an essential part of our resurrection and in which we share through our union with him: "Christ has been raised from the dead, the first fruits of those who have fallen asleep. For as by a man came death, by a man has come also the resurrection of the dead" (1 Cor 15:20-21).

Finally, Jesus' resurrection can be considered from the apologetic point of view, that is, focussing on the *miracle* of the resurrection, which confirms our Lord's holiness, the truth of his words, and the legitimacy of his messianic claims: that is, the fact that God raised him from the dead confirms Jesus' *credibility*. During his life on earth Jesus himself appealed to his miracles as reasons for believing in him (cf. Jn 10:38) and spoke of his resurrection as a sign for the generation who were listening to him (cf. Mt 12:39-40), that is, he referred to his resurrection as proof that he was the true Messiah.[141]

i) *The testimony of the New Testament*   The New Testament contains very many references to our Lord's resurrection, even in those writings which do not report to any great extent on events in his life. One senses an urgency running through the New Testament to bear witness to the resurrection of the Lord not only in the four Gospels but also in the missionary discourses of St Peter and St Paul reported in Acts, in the Pauline letters and in the other apostolic writings.

risk of losing a substantial part of its identity and the true sense of its historicity": *Gesù di Nazaret*, II, op. cit., 520.

139. This perspective also has importance. The Resurrection is a divine seal marking the authenticity of Jesus' mission and the truth of his message. But although Jesus' Resurrection must be seen as an "historical" event (we shall go on to see what exactly that means in this context) it is also an object of faith. Thus, accepting the Resurrection involves also accepting its supernatural character and, above all, accepting Christ's divinity. Cf. F, Ardusso, *Gesù di Nazaret è Figlio di Dio?*, op. cit., 103-28; H. Schlier, *Das Ostergeheimnis* (Einsiedeln, 1976); M.J. Nicolas, *Théologie de la résurrection* (Paris, 1982); S. Pié i Ninot, *Tratado de teología fundamental* (Salamanca, 1989), 250-91.

140. As the Second Vatican Council says, death confronts man with a probing question about the very meaning of life, because the seed of eternity which he bears within him rebels against death (cf. Const. *Gaudium et spes*, 18). It is worth pointing out here that Christianity has never tried to solve the question posed by death by appealing exclusively to the immortality of the soul; rather, it appeals to the Resurrection, that is, to the victory over death which Jesus' Resurrection involves. By reason of his resurrection he is rightly described as "victor over death".

141. Theology has traditionally focussed on this aspect of our Lord's Resurrection; it does so in treatises on Fundamental Theology, and therefore we shall not go into it in detail here. For further information and bibliography, cf., among others, A. Lang, *Teología Funda-*

All the New Testament writings speak about Jesus' resurrection. In some cases (such as the Gospels) the narrative is extensive; others contain direct expositions and theological applications (such as Acts or chapter 15 of 1 Corinthians); elsewhere the references are in the form of statements in hymns, or short confessions of faith. It is fair to say that all these testimonies point to an essential dimension of apostolic ministry—testifying to Jesus' resurrection, in keeping with St Peter's words: "God raised him from the dead. To this we are witnesses" (Acts 3:15). It is noteworthy that the condition stipulated for the choice of someone to take Judas' place was that he should have lived with the Lord and been a witness to his resurrection (cf. Acts 1:21-22).

The resurrection of Jesus is the centrepoint of apostolic preaching, as can be seen from the discourses of St Peter and St Paul, even those addressed to pagans and those delivered to audiences not at all well-disposed to the idea of resurrection, as was the case in St Paul's speech in the Areopagus (cf. Acts 17:31), because conversion to Christianity necessarily involves belief in the resurrection of Jesus. Hence the explicit statements in the early New Testament writings, which in turn refer to a received *paradosis* (tradition) which, it is realized, must be passed on in its entirety. That is to say, they refer to the earliest preaching, some of which is recorded in Acts.

This is the case with the well known passage of 1 Corinthians 15:3-8, written between AD 53 and 57, where the solemn opening warns us that we are being told the essentials of the *paradosis*: "For I have delivered to you as of first importance what I also received, that Christ [. . .] was raised on the third day in accordance with the scriptures, and that he appeared to Cephas, then to the twelve. Then he appeared to more than five hundred brethren at one time, most of whom are still alive, though some have fallen asleep. Then he appeared to James, then to all the apostles. Last of all, as to one untimely born, he appeared also to me." It is easy to see the solemnity with which the resurrection of the Lord is being proclaimed, and also St Paul's desire to emphasize that it really happened, that is, his desire to make it very clear that it is not a subjective conviction of the disciples. We can see this desire, for example, in the fact that he gives a list of Jesus' appearances (expressly mentioning that many of those "more than five hundred brethren" were still alive) as events which guarantee the objective reality of the Lord's resurrection.[142]

In this connexion, it is usual to stress the importance given to the apparitions of the risen Christ and the force conveyed by the verb used in their regard—*ophthe*, he was seen—because this verb stresses that the vision was objective, that it is Jesus himself who was seen,[143] that he made himself

---

mental, I (Madrid, 1966), 297-316; S. Pié i Ninot, *Tratado de Teología Fundamental*, op. cit., 250-92; J.A. Sayés, *Cristología fundamental* (Madrid, 1985), 303-89.

142. The appearance to Peter is also hinted at in Mark 16:7 and is mentioned in Luke 24:34, when on the return to the upper room of the disciples of Emmaus, they are received with the greeting, "The Lord has risen indeed, and has appeared to Simon!"

143. "There can be no doubt", Díez Macho writes, "that *ophthe* means a real appearance, an

visible,[144] that is, it is Christ himself who reveals himself by himself and from himself,[145] to the point of coming out to meet the disciples; the verb *ophthe* indicates that it is he who appears, he who takes the initiative. This is something which is linked to other details in the accounts of the apparitions: they always begin with the Risen One and are not an effect of the apostles' faith or hope or desire to see him. He comes to meet them, he makes himself present.

1 Corinthians 15:3-8 is a text which is very Semitic in character, its language, containing expressions not normally used in St Paul, shows how faithfully he is trying to pass on the words given to him. It is a text from the earliest tradition "expressed in such a way that certain words confirm the next: he died, *therefore* he was buried; he was buried, *but* rose; he was risen, *therefore* he appeared.[146]

These short statements constitute the very earliest expressions of preaching and of belief in the resurrection of Jesus, as if they were formulae which were crystallizing. Compare, for example, in addition to 1 Corinthians 15:3-8, Romans 10:9 ("Jesus is the Lord"; "God raised him from the dead"), Acts 2:23ff; 3:15; 4:10: 5:30-31; 10:37-40; 13:27-31; 1 Peter 3:18ff; etc. Only later does the resurrection of Jesus come to be spoken of in narrative forms, that is, in the Gospel accounts of the apparitions and the empty tomb. These accounts, obviously, are closely dependent on belief, firmly held from the beginning, in the resurrection of Jesus: they derive from what is the essential statement: "The Lord has risen indeed" (Lk 24:34).[147]

objective manifestation which imposes itself from outside, if we examine the meaning of the verb in parallel passages of the Gospel: Lk 24:34; Acts 9:17; 13:31. This active "appearing" of Jesus is the fulfilment of the promise made to his disciples in the accounts of the empty tomb when they are told that he "will appear", to them in Galilee: Mk 16:7; Mt 28:7, 10; Jn 20:18, 25, 29; Acts 9:27; 22:18; Lk 24:37, 39": A. Diez Macho, *La resurrección de Jesucristo y la del hombre en la Biblia* (Madrid 1977), 272.

144. This is how Bordoni translates *ophthe*: "Il Cristo si è fatto vedere: *óphthe*": M. Bordoni, *Gesù di Nazaret*, II, op. cit., 535.

145. Outstanding among the features of the Apostles' "paschal certainty" is the fact that this certainty is common to all accounts and results from the fact that "the Risen Christ has *let himself be seen or has shown himself*." We have here "an expression which, in the New Testament is as it were a point on which there is a convergence between the two basic groups of data through which the mystery of the Risen One is proclaimed. This convergence, which we cannot fail to notice, is shown in the use of the verb *ophthe*, a passive aorist whose literary construction should not be translated as *was seen* (putting the accent on the act of the seeing or experiencing subject) but rather in the sense of *made himself seen*, thereby stressing that the initiative is with the Risen One. In this way, via the appearances (of Christ), (the disciples') experience of the Resurrection is seen to have an objective character, being experience of someone who imposed himself by his real presence and with respect to which the *seeing* by the disciples is something passive": M. Bordoni, *Gesù di Nazaret*, op. cit., 537.

146. A. Diez Macho, *La resurrección de Jesucristo y la del hombre*, op. cit., 265-73.

147. From very early on, the Fathers were aware of the difficulty that existed in harmonizing some details of the accounts in these pericopes, for example, in regard to the location where the appearances took place, the angels seen by the women, etc., and they tried to harmonize them without complete success. The difficulty arose, H. Schlier notes, because there was felt to be no need to present the facts in chronological succession, or to harmonize

These narratives are to be found in all four Gospels, taking up the final chapters (Mk 16; Mt 28; Lk 24; Jn 20-21) and in Acts 1:1-11. They are written in a very unemotional style. They all speak of appearances of Jesus, but in none is it said that anyone saw Jesus rise; they testify simply to the fact that the risen Christ has appeared to them. It is quite clear that no one claims to have witnessed the actual resurrection. The resurrection is borne witness to by evidence of meeting the already risen Christ.

One thing very noticeable in these accounts is the "continuity" between the crucified and the risen Jesus. It is the same Jesus who is *recognized* when he appears. He is recognized, for example, in his speech (Jn 20:16), and in the breaking of the bread (cf. Lk 24:31). Sometimes the fact that it is Christ himself is stressed by actual physical contact. For example, Jesus invites people to check, by touching him, that it is really he, to show that he has a real body (cf. Lk 24:39), and, showing them his wounded hands and pierced side, he insists that this is the same body as was crucified (Jn 20:27).

In this connexion the fact of the empty tomb has great importance. All four Gospels in fact begin their account of the resurrection by mentioning the discovery of the empty tomb. It is not that the empty tomb as such is the main proof of the resurrection; the definitive proof is our Lord's appearances, especially to the Eleven. But the fact of the empty tomb is essential, for there to have been a resurrection.[148] The accounts speak of a continuity between the buried body and the risen body—which would not have been possible had the tomb not been empty. The empty tomb points to resurrection and, especially, to the fact that the Risen One had a real body. Jesus is not in the tomb, for he has risen: whoever wants to find him must look for him among the living, not among the dead. This is the message the angels gave to the holy women: "He is not here; for he has risen, as he said" (Mt 28:6); "You seek Jesus of Nazareth who was crucified. He has risen, he is not here" (Mk 16:6); "Why do you seek the living among the dead? He is not here, but has risen" (Lk 24:5-6).

Although the empty tomb is not in itself a direct proof of the Resurrection, it has become for all an essential indication. St John says that, on entering the empty tomb and discovering " 'the linen cloths lying there' (Jn 20:6) 'he saw and believed' (Jn 20:8). This suggests that he realized from the empty tomb's condition (cf. Jn 20:5-7) that the absence of Jesus' body could not have been

them, because the very event of the Resurrection is regarded as not subject to doubt": cf. H. Schlier, *La Résurrection de Jésus Christ* (Mulhouse, 1969), 11-16.

148. In the earliest preaching, the empty tomb occupies a discreet, secondary place. The oldest account of the empty tomb is that of Mark 16:1-8, which passes on an earlier tradition. It should be remembered that this tradition centres on an exact, specific place in Jerusalem and mentions facts and names, such as, for example, that of Joseph of Arimathea, which if they were false could easily have been refuted. On this matter, cf., A. Diez Macho, *La resurrection de Jesucristo y la del hombre*, op. cit., 279-82.

of human doing and that Jesus had not simply returned to earthly life as had been in the case with Lazarus."[148a]

So, there is no doubt about the importance the vacant tomb had in the minds of the disciples when it came to speaking about the resurrection and distinguishing it from the mere survival of something "spiritual". This is the underlying argument in Peter's discourse when he speaks about the resurrection of Jesus: "Brethren, I may say to you confidently of the patriarch David that he both died and was buried, and his tomb is with us to this day. Being therefore a prophet, [. . .] he spoke of the resurrection of the Christ, that he was not abandoned to Hades, nor did his flesh see corruption" (Acts 2:29-31).[149] This form of argument presupposes not only that Jesus' body is no longer in the tomb, but that it is known not to be in the tomb, that is, that it is a known fact that the tomb was found to be empty. These words, spoken in Jerusalem, imply, moreover, the conviction, the confidence, that no one (no opponent) can prove the contrary.

At the same time as they point up the fact that the buried body and the risen body are one and the same, the accounts of the resurrection also bear witness to the fact that the body is now in a higher state, one in which it is free from the normal laws of physics. This can be seen from the form the appararitions take: Jesus enters the upper room when its doors are closed (cf. Lk 24:36; Jn 20:19-26). In 1 Corinthians 15 St Paul will speak of the glorious resurrection having in mind the glory which is given off by the risen body of Jesus: it is raised imperishable, in power and in glory. It is a case, then, of a physical body raised to its greatest possible degree of glorification. St Paul himself will term the glorious body *soma pneumatikon*, a spiritual body (1 Cor 15:44), to highlight the difference there is between it and the earthly body.[150]

This difference is to be found in the very nature of the apparitions. Although it is true that they are real apparitions (it is Jesus who "is showing" himself to the disciples), in order for these apparitions to be fully accepted for what they are, faith is needed on the part of the apostles. Jesus' body no longer belongs to this world; it may be said to have a "supernatural" character. The Gospel accounts draw attention to the doubts even some disciples have when they see Jesus (cf. Mt 28:7). They truly did see him and yet this sight is a gift of grace.[151] St Thomas Aquinas puts it very incisively: "The Apostles could

---

148a. CCC, no. 640.

149. The incorrupt condition of Christ's body in the tomb is also implied in those passages (such as 1 Cor 15:4) in which it is emphasized that he rose on the third day, which was when the Jews thought that bodies began to corrupt.

150. On the glorification of the body as "deification of matter", cf. John Paul II, *Address*, 9 December 1981: *Insegnamenti*, IV, 2 (1981) 880-3; M.J. Scheeben, *The Mysteries of Christianity*, op. cit., 666f; F. Ocáriz, *La Resurrección de Jesucristo*, op. cit., 756-61.

151. "So what the disciples beheld and witnessed", says K. Adam, "was not a purely natural perception, apprehended through the senses. It was also a supernatural experience, not

testify to the resurrection of Christ *de viso* ('by sight'), also, because, after the resurrection, they saw the living Christ (whom they knew to be dead) *oculata fide*", with a faith that has eyes", that is, "with the eyes of faith."[152] Jesus' new life is now inaccessible to the common perception of men. He shows himself to the apostles, who see him *oculata fidei*, with the eyes of faith. Because they see him, they can bear witness with a unique type of testimony;[153] and yet this vision is a gift of grace which, in its turn, they have to accept through faith. Jesus says to Thomas: "Have you believed because you have seen me? Blessed are those who have not seen and yet believe" (Jn 20:29). It is a matter of a true seeing, but it can bear fruit only if it is accepted in faith. To put it another way, the character and the supernatural implications of the Resurrection are such that the apostles, in order to accept it with full certainty, still needed faith even when they had physical sight of the Risen One.

ii) *The resurrection of Jesus—a matter of history or of faith?*   Clearly the assertion that Jesus has risen from the dead is a radically original one. There are no precedents. What is said of the risen Christ is something unique: his body is no longer in the tomb, because it has come back to life; not to the life which it had prior to death, but to a very different life: it has been *transformed* in the glory of God. The Risen One no longer belongs to the mode of physical existence with which we are familiar and which we can verify. In the resurrection of Jesus there is an analogy with the resurrection of dead people reported in the Gospels, for example, the raising of Lazarus or the widow of Nain's son (cf. Jn 11:33-44; Lk 7:11-17); in other words, Jesus comes back to life; his body becomes alive again. But having said that, there are differences; because Jesus not only rises again but his material body enters a new form of life, which cannot be grasped from where we are.[154] Even those "chosen by

unlike the experience of Christ known to many of the saints. Moreover, it was brought about because the person of the Resurrected One wrought upon the spirit and senses of the disciples. It was inspiration, it was Grace in the same sense as St Paul's vision of Christ on the road to Damascus was Grace. It was not natural sight, but one endowed by Grace. And thus the foundation and the blissful content of their faith in the resurrection was not so much the resurrection as an historical event, as the presence of the Resurrected One himself": *The Christ of Faith*, op. cit., 353.

152. St Thomas Aquinas, *STh* III, q.55, a.2, ad 1. Cf. H. Bouillard, *Sur la Resurrection de Jésus. Le point théologique* (Paris, 1972), 45ff.

153. In the New Testament a clear distinction is made between visions of Jesus which other Christians could have had (e.g. that of Ananias, reported in Acts 9:10) from appearances as such of the Risen One, which are placed on a different level. "The experience of which they tell us is, in their view, a completely *sui generis* experience, different from any other mystical experiences which may be repeated indefinitely, and even more different from other phenomena of religious enthusiasm, which can be caused at will": M. González Gil, *Cristo, el misterio de Dios*, II, op. cit., 308.

154. Theologians usually list the following characteristics of our Lord's Resurrection, to show that it is not a matter of his coming back to his previous life. The main ones are: *true*,

God as witnesses" (Acts 10:41) to testify to the resurrection of the Lord can fully accept him only *oculata fide*, with the eyes of faith.

This fact and the restriction of the term "historical" to events whose causes and effects lie within the confines of history have led some contemporary authors to describe the resurrection of Jesus as "non-historical" or "metahistorical". They try to employ a language inherited from the Enlightenment, with its own special concepts of what pertains to human history. And indeed, if one accepts as historical only things which pertain to the intraterrestrial (as far as causes and effects are concerned) and which fit within the limits of the "historically likely", that is, into a context of events with which we are familiar, then clearly the Lord's resurrection cannot be described as "historical", for there are no events to compare it with (it is something totally new) and the life of the Risen One is not subject to our intraterrestrial laws.

However, if one uses this language, one clearly runs the risk of *dehistoricizing* and of *spiritualizing* the Easter message, "The Lord has risen indeed, and has appeared to Simon!" (Lk 24:34).

For, according to normal usage, what cannot be called "historical" cannot be said to have really happened—for what makes something historical is the fact that it really happened and we can come to know it because we have heard it from reliable witnesses. In other words, the accent falls not on whether it can be checked experimentally by us but on the reliability of the witness.[155]

because what died comes back to life; *perfect*, because it constitutes a definitive victory over death, since Christ's body comes back to an immortal life; *glorious*, because *deification* affects the very body in which the glory (clarity, impassibility, etc.) of his soul is manifested. Cf. St Thomas Aquinas, *STh* III, qq. 53-4; P. Rodriguez, "La Resurrection de Cristo en el pensamiento teológico de Santo Tomás de Aquino", in various authors, *Veritas el Sapientia* (Pamplona, 1975), 327-36; M.J. Scheeben, *The Mysteries of Christianity*, op. cit., 666-73; F. Ocáriz, *La resurrección de Jesucristo*, op. cit., 756-61.

155. This, logically, implied the non-acceptance of the narrow meaning of "historical" proposed by the Enlightenment outlook and, consequently, giving back to the word its ordinary meaning. Here are some of the reasons put forward: "Is it certain that the historical as a reality enters into the experience of its spatio-temporal dimension? [. . .]. Is it certain that the historical is always something we have to experience for ourselves? [. . .]. When or how does a document from the past become converted for us into a testimony of an historical event? Only when some actual contemporaries of the event convert this document into a testimony for us on the basis of their experiential knowledge. Thus historicity does not depend primarily for us on the physical account in space and time; what really determines the quality and certainty of the historical account is the narrators themselves: if they take something as historical and transmit it to us as such, it is then historical for us also [. . .]. Therefore we as Christians can and should say, without any doubt (since we have to draw our knowledge regarding the historical events as content of our faith from the testimony of Scripture): the biblical account of the *empty tomb* and of the appearances of Jesus to his apostles and of the relationships of the apostles with the Risen One, are understood and recounted by the narrators of Scripture—the evangelists—as historical events without any shadow of doubt. Even further, it is by the quality of the historical that those biblical accounts acquire their true content of faith; without such quality these accounts would have been, even for the narrators themselves, mere myths or fables. Therefore, those who today question or deny the historicity of the resurrection of Jesus

In this sense it follows that the resurrection of Jesus is an historical fact, because we have been told about it by reliable witnesses. Of course it is a unique historical fact (it can never have an equal), reported by witnesses who can give testimony because they have seen, not the fact, the event, of resurrection, but the Risen One. But their testimony is valid,[156] and the existence of this testimony as also the discovery of the empty tomb are things which can be checked in the normal way past events are checked, that is, by examination of documents. But just as the witnesses on seeing the Risen Christ needed faith to accept the resurrection fully (they didn't see the resurrection, only the Risen One, so they needed faith to accept 'it' fully), so too we need faith in order to accept their testimony, which reaches us through the life and preaching of the Church. In a certain sense, today, too, Christian faith *should* scandalize every mind that is closed to the supernatural, that is bound by the power of science, because what the Church is proclaiming is that Christ has risen—a statement based not on scientific reasons or the opinion of scholars, but on the testimony of the Apostles, that is, on the word of a few fishermen.

This testimony justifies calling the event "historical" in the sense that there are sufficient *signs* to enable one to say that it really did happen.[157] That is why some writers prefer to say that Jesus' resurrection is a fact that is "in a certain way" historical, because although, when Jesus' body rose, it was changed into a "glorious body" (Phil 3:21), "it was manifested in different effects and signs;"[158] and they propose that, if one decides to regard as "historical events" only those which can be verified by historico–critical research, then Jesus'

must also, on the same account, question or deny the faith of the hagiographers in this event. Are we not becoming more clearly aware nowadays that our modern language regarding such events, inspired by the Enlightenment or born of a purely scientific notion of the world, is not compatible with our faith in this reality?": J. Auer, *Curso de Teología Dogmática*, IV/2, *Jesucristo Salvador del mundo*, op. cit., 356-8.

156. As González Gil writes, "Nowadays an historical fact is measured more in terms of its influence on the course of history than on the bare precise material content of it: the epithet 'historical' is used (or abused) to designate an event which has had important historical results": *Cristo, el misterio de Dios*, II, op. cit., 339. In this sense at least, the testimony borne by the Apostles must be described as historical given its impact on history. But that alone is insufficient to express everything contained in the Christian assertion that Jesus has risen, for Christians, on the testimony borne by the Apostles, believe that Jesus has truly risen.

157. As Latourelle puts it, "we have the vestiges of a mysterious reality, the object of faith. What history can reach is those *vestiges*, those *signs*, which theological research seeks to interpret. The historico-theological method consists in deducing the reality of the Resurrection to be the only coherent explanation of a whole series of facts constantly attested to": R. Latourelle, "L'Istanza storica in Teologia Fundamentale", in various authors, *Istanze della teologia fondamentale oggi* (Bologna, 1982), 81; cf. S. Pié i Ninot, *Tratado de Teología Fundamental*, op. cit., 257, nt. 124 and p. 273, nt. 146.

158. That is how Pié i Ninot puts it; he goes on: "1. The Resurrection in fact made Jesus' body *disappear* from the *tomb*, thereby causing a proximate sign, albeit one that is purely negative of itself. 2. And at the same time the Risen One in his *mysterious encounters* with his witnesses left *signs* of his new life, such as the Eucharist, the Spirit, the Church, the

resurrection should be called an "indirectly historical event," because it is manifested by historical signs.[159]

Other scholars, whose views we share, prefer to describe the event of Christ's resurrection as "historical".[160]

In any case, the importance of this event for the Christian faith is quite clear. St Paul puts it very forcefully: "If Christ has not been raised, then our preaching is in vain and your faith is in vain. We are even found to be misrepresenting God, because we testified of God that he raised Christ [.. .]. If for this life only we have hoped in Christ, we are of all men most to be pitied" (1 Cor 15:14 and 19). So, then, anyone who accepts Christian teaching cannot "dehistorize" our Lord's resurrection, interpreting it in a Docetist sense, that is, depriving it of realness. The insistence with which the Fathers assert that Jesus *truly* rose parallels their insistence that he was *truly* born of the Virgin Mary, and *truly* died,[161] and it is a testimony also to the importance the reality of Christ's body and the facts of his life have for the Christian faith. The repeated use of the adverb "truly" is an intentional rejection of Docetism and also of a Docetist view of the events of Jesus' life, which, for example, when it comes to talking about the resurrection of Jesus, reduces it to a mere "living on", for example, in memory (the view of the Gnostics of the second

'burning' heart (Lk 24:32), peace (Jn 20:26) . . .": *Tratado de Teología Fundamental*, op. cit., 272-3.

159. "In effect", argues Pié i Ninot, "through direct historical research we know both the *empty tomb* and the testimonies concerning the *appearances*; these two facts, together with the death of Jesus, the situation the disciples were in, the burial, the first report of the women, the reassembled community, its subsequent missions . . . *suggest* a common motive and by their joint force constitute a *motive* for accepting the Resurrection as the transcendent explanation": *Tratado de Teología Fundamental*, op. cit., 273.

160. Díez Macho is one of these; he writes: "The act itself of Jesus' Resurrection, certainly, does not fall under the monitor of history, because it is of its nature transcendental. As J. Delorme graphically puts it, a witness, enclosed in Jesus' tomb, could have attested to the disappearance or volatilization of the body, but not to the Resurrection, as our faith understands it. But the historical fact of Christ having risen, that certainly is something that falls within the scope of historical experience: if Jesus, having died, then makes his appearance, if he has been seen by witnesses, the reason is that Christ has risen": *La resurrección de Jesúcristo*, op. cit., 265f. That is also the position J. Auer takes: "The biblical account of the *empty tomb* and of Jesus' appearances to his apostles and of the apostles' contact with the Risen One, are understood and reported by the narrators of Scripture, the evangelists, as historical events not in any way open to doubt": J. Auer, *Jesucristo, salvador del mundo*, op. cit., 357.

161. "Close your ears," St Ignatius of Antioch writes, "if anyone preaches to you without speaking of Jesus Christ. Christ was of David's line. He was the son of Mary; he was *indeed* born, and ate and drank. He was *truly* persecuted in the days of Pontius Pilate, he was truly crucified [. . .], he was also *truly* raised up again from the dead": *Ad Trall*, 9, 1. This echoes similar formulae from Ignatius elsewhere (cf., e.g., *Ad Magn.* 11; *Ad Smyrn.*, 1, 1-2) and in the writings of many other Fathers, such as St Justin (I *Apol.*, 21, 1; 31, 7; *Dial.*, 85, 2). They echo very ancient professions of faith, whose language we find already fixed in 1 Cor 15:3ff and which were used in the liturgy of baptism and of the Eucharist. The use of the adjective *alethos* (truly, really, verily,) so vigorously emphasized by Ignatius of Antioch, clearly shows that the birth, life, death and resurrection of Christ are not mere

century) or an event which takes place exclusively in the faith of the Apostles,[162] so that it is possible to "demythologize" it, removing from it the features of being a real event, independent of and prior to the faith of the Apostles.

In conclusion "we can see the Resurrection as an historical event, above all. In fact, it occurred in a *very definite setting of time and of place* [. . .]. But even though it is an event that can be thus chronologically and spatially determined, nevertheless, *the Resurrection transcends and is above history.*"[163]

Our Lord's resurrection is, then, an actual event which transcends history, but which had "manifestations that were historically verified, as the New Testament bears witness".[163a] "Given all the testimonies, Christ's Resurrection cannot be interpreted as something outside the physical order, and it is impossible not to acknowledge it as an historical fact".[163b] And, at the same time, this "historical event that could be verified by the sign of the empty tomb and by the reality of the Apostles' encounters with the risen Christ" belongs to "the very heart of the mystery of faith as something that transcends and surpasses history."[163c]

iii) *The soteriological value of Christ's Resurrection* Jesus' glorification is not simply the reward for his obedience; it is an essential part of our redemption. As the Symbol of Nicea declares, Jesus has risen "for us and for our salvation": "Blessed be the God and Father of our Lord Jesus Christ," writes St Peter. "By his great mercy we have been born anew to a living hope through the resurrection of Jesus Christ from the dead, and to an inheritance which is imperishable" (1 Pet 1:3-4). He is clearly saying that the resurrection of Jesus affects us so much that through it we have *"been born again to an inheritance that is imperishable."* Not in vain is Jesus' resurrection his triumph over death. The Resurrection is at the very centre of the redemption: it and Jesus' death constitute one, unique, saving mystery. St Augustine will say, therefore, that we would have gained no advantage from the dead Christ if he had not risen from the dead,[164]—not only because the Resurrection confirms the truth of what Jesus had said but also because it is through it that salvation reaches us.

St Paul keeps making this point in all sorts of ways. In raising Jesus from the dead and not permitting his body to see corruption in the tomb, the Father

appearances (as the Docetists would have it) but solid reality: cf. T. Camelot, *Ignace d'Antioche, Polycarpe de Smyrne: Lettres*, SCh, (Paris, 1969), 25 and 100.

162. To stay true to apostolic preaching, it is not enough, then, to say that Jesus has risen, because he continues to live in the kerygma or in the Apostles' faith. "Is it Jesus' resurrection," Fabris writes, "that engenders faith in him, or is it faith in Jesus that creates his Resurrection? In the latter proposition, although that is to put it too simply, one can see R. Bultmann and those inspired by him, particularly W. Marxsen": R. Fabris, *Jesús de Nazaret*, op. cit., 267f.

163. John Paul II, *Address*, 11 March 1989, nos. 2 and 3: *Insegnamentii*, XII, 1 (1989) 456f.

163a. CCC, no. 639.   163b. CCC, no. 643.   163c. CCC, no. 647.

164. "The dead Christ would be of no benefit to us unless he had risen from the dead": St Augustine, *Sermo* 246: 2 PL 38, 1154.

has kept the messianic promises he made to the Patriarchs (cf. Acts 13:32-37), that is, his promises to save mankind. This salvation involves not only the justification of souls, that is, liberation from sin, but also "the redemption of our bodies" (Rom 8:23), that is, victory over death through resurrection. Both aspects of salvation depend on Jesus' resurrection. Our Lord "was put to death for our trespasses and raised for our justification" (Rom 4:25);[165] the resurrection of our bodies is dependent on the resurrection of Jesus (1 Cor 15:12-28).

We need to apply here, rigorously, what has been said about Christ's solidarity with every man and woman, his role as head of mankind. He is the new Adam: "Christ has been raised from the dead, the first fruits of those who have fallen asleep. For as by a man came death, by a man has come also the resurrection of the dead. For as in Adam all die, so also in Christ shall all be made alive" (1 Cor 15:20-23).

First fruits of those who are asleep; the new Adam in whom we receive new life—the two phrases point to something essential in Christianity: salvation reaches us through Christ, in Christ, through union with Christ. St Peter's statement—"we have been born anew [. . .] through the resurrection of Jesus Christ from the dead, and to an inheritance which is imperishable" (1 Pet 1:3-4)—has to be taken quite literally. The Father acts primarily in Christ, and in him, with him and through him he acts in us.

This is the same type of thinking as we find in Paul: Jesus is "the first fruits of those who have fallen asleep" (1 Cor 15:20), "the beginning, the first-born from the dead, that in everything he might be pre-eminent" (Col 1:18). These expressions indicate that Jesus' resurrection causes our resurrection: just as according to Jewish law the "first fruits" are specially for God and are offered to him in petition for a good harvest, so Jesus, on rising from the dead, is the "first fruits" which guarantee the resurrection of the dead; in him, who is the "first-born from the dead" the divine blessings are ear-marked for the entire human family.

These statements acquire a further meaning if they are read in the light of the fact that Jesus Christ is the new Adam who communicates life to us; this is the perspective to which St Paul refers immediately after saying that Jesus is the "first fruits of those who have fallen asleep". Through the old Adam death comes to us; through the new, resurrection from the dead. Like the first Adam—who passed his death on to us—but in a much more intimate way, the new Adam gives us his victory over death through resurrection.

"Christ can be called first-born of those who rise from the dead," writes St Thomas Aquinas, "not only in the temporal sense [. . .] but also in the

---

165. Prat comments: "Jesus Christ did not come to this earth simply to die; he came to unite us with him and to associate us with his triumph. It was not therefore sufficient for him to die for us; he had also to rise again for us": *The Theology of St Paul*, II, op. cit., 210.

causal sense, because his resurrection is the cause of that of others and also from the point of view of dignity, because he rose in a more glorious way than all others."[166] This is a double kind of causality—efficient and exemplary. That is to say, the resurrection of the dead is intimately linked to that of Jesus, as effect to cause; moreover, in the "resurrection for life" (Jn 5:29), that is to say, in the resurrection of the just, Jesus Christ "will change our lowly body to be like his glorious body, by the power which enables him even to subject all things to himself" (Phil 3:21).

The first cause of our resurrection is God, but the resurrection of Jesus works our resurrection, truly and effectively, as an instrumental cause, that is, as an instrument connected with the Godhead: "the Word of God first gives immortal life to the body which is united to him naturally, and then by means of it causes resurrection in all others."[167] Some authors ask whether the efficient cause of our resurrection will be the *risen* Christ or the resurrection itself, that is, Christ *rising from the dead* (*Christus resurgens*),[168] because some Pauline texts, especially those which spoke of baptism as a "dying (along) with" and "rising along with" Christ seem to attribute our resurrection to Christ's resurrection.[169]

The difficulty about saying that it is Christ's resurrection itself which is the cause of the resurrection of the dead has to do with conceiving how a past event can be an efficient cause (even if only an instrumental efficient cause) of a future effect. St Thomas says that: "the resurrection of Christ is the efficient cause of our resurrection by divine power, to which it belongs to give life to the dead. And this divine power reaches *praesentialiter* (by mode of presence) all places and all times."[170] And although this is applicable to all the events of Christ's life, in the case of the resurrection it is doubly so: to reach *praesentialiter* all places and times belongs not only to *divine power*, but also to the *power* of the human reality of Jesus, fully deified in soul and body, which has entered into the participated eternity of glory. This perhaps explains why

166. St Thomas Aquinas, *Comp. Theol.* I, chap. 239.
167. St Thomas Aquinas, *STh* III, q.56, a.1, in c.
168. For a more detailed study, cf. F. Ocáriz, *La resurrección de Jesucristo*, op. cit., 764-7. On St Thomas' thought on this subject, cf. F. Holtz, "La valeur sotériologique de la résurrection du Christ selon saint Thomas", ETL 29 (1953) 616-27; A. Piolanti, *Dio-Uomo*, op. cit., 577-88.
169. Thus it says in Romans 6:2-7: "Do you not know that all of us who have been baptized into Christ Jesus were baptized into his death? We were buried therefore with him by baptism into death, so that as Christ was raised from the dead by the glory of the Father, we too might walk in newness of life. For if we have been united with him in a death like his, we shall certainly be united with him in a resurrection like his." Cf. also Col 2:12. Prat comments: "To be baptized into the death of Christ is to be baptized into the dying Christ—that is, to be incorporated with Christ in the very act by which he saves us, to die mystically with him who suffered death in the name and for the benefit of all": *The Theology of St Paul*, II, op. cit., 257. If "to be baptized into the death of Christ is equivalent to being baptized into the dying Christ, the parallelism seems to imply that the resurrection also that is signified in baptism is a resurrection in 'the rising Christ'."
170. St Thomas Aquinas, *STh* III, q.56, a.1, ad 3.

St Thomas sometimes says that the efficient cause of our resurrection is Christ risen, and at other times Christ's rising.

The resurrection of Christ is also the cause of our spriritual resurrection—an efficient cause and an exemplary cause of our passage from the state of sin to that of grace. The Pauline texts on baptism already cited show this very clearly.[171] From the point of view of efficient causality, the life, death and resurrection of Christ form one single causal thing, effecting both the resurrection of souls and the resurrection of bodies. But from the point of view of exemplary causality, Christ's death is the exemplary cause of our death to sin and to the old life, whereas the Resurrection is the exemplary cause of the new life of grace, and of immortality (cf. Rom 4:25).[172]

Finally, the resurrection of Christ also affects all of creation in some mysterious way, by giving it a share in the freedom of the glory of the children of God, for "we know that the whole creation has been groaning in travail together until now; and not only the creation, but we ourselves, who have the first fruits of the Spirit, groan inwardly as we wait for adoption as sons, the redemption of our bodies" (Rom 8:22-23). The redemption brings about "the time for establishing all" (Acts 3:21), when, in the words of the Second Vatican Council, "together with the human race, the entire universe, which is so closely related to man and which attains its destiny through him, will be perfectly re-established in Christ",[173] thereby achieving the final "recapitulation" of all things in Christ (cf. Eph 1:10).[174]

b) The Ascension and Pentecost   The Ascension of the Lord is an article of faith, to be found in the earliest symbols[175] as an essential part of Christ's exaltation. It serves to show Jesus' lordship, his fulness of life and power, his

---

171. Cf. also St Thomas Aquinas, *STh* III, q.56, a.2.
172. Cf. F. Ocáriz, "Estudio de la Resurrección de Cristo en cuanto causa de la resurrección de los hombres, según la doctrina de Santo Tomás de Aquino", in various authors, *Cristo, Hijo de Dios y Redentor del hombre*, op. cit., especially 980f.
173. Second Vatican Council, Const. *Lumen gentium*, 48.
174. On "recapitulation" (*anakefalaiosis*) in Eph 1:10, cf. J.M. Casciaro, *Estudios sobre la Cristología del Nuevo Testamento*, op. cit., 308-24.
175. The formulas always have the same chain of components: ascension—being seated at the right hand of the Father—he will come to judge; they also are drawn up in almost identical literary style; Credimus . . . in deiformem ascensionem in sessionem ad dexteram Patris, in terribilem (et gloriosum) adventum (We believe . . . in a God-like ascension, a sitting at the right hand of the Father, an awesome (and glorious) coming) (DS 6); Credis in Christum Jesum . . . qui . . . et ascendit in caelis et sedit ad dexteram Patris, venturus iudicare vivos et mortuos? (Do you believe in Jesus Christ who ascended into heaven and was seated at the right hand of the Father and will come to judge the living and the dead?) (DS 10); ascendit in caelis, sedet ad dexteram Patris, unde venturus est iudicare vivos et mortuos (he ascended into heaven, sits at the right hand of the Father, from thence he shall come to judge the living and the dead (DS 12, 13, 14, 15, 16, 17, 18, 19, 23, 25, 26, 28, etc.).

authority as King of the universe.[176] We can say that the essential core of the Ascension lies in the fact that he *sits at the right hand of the Father*—that he shares in the sovereignty of the Father,[177] who has given him "all authority in heaven and on earth" (Mt 28:18). Also, the Ascension (like the other mysteries of Christ's life), is positioned in the Symbol of Nicea under the eloquent observation that it was "for us and for our salvation", that is, the Ascension affects not only Christ's exaltation as such but also his messianic activity.[178] As the Second Vatican Council says, "The wonderful works of God among the people of the Old Testament were but a prelude to the work of Christ our Lord in redeeming mankind and giving perfect glory to God. He achieved his task principally by the paschal mystery of his blessed passion, resurrection from the dead, and glorious ascension, whereby 'dying, he destroyed our death, and rising, restored our life'."[179]

The Ascension is recounted twice by St Luke (Lk 24:50-53 and Acts 1:9-14) and at the end of St Mark's Gospel (Mk 16:19). St Peter presents it in his first discourse as the end of the period during which "the Lord Jesus went in and out among us, beginning from the baptism of John until the day when he was taken up from us" (Acts 1:21-22).

There are many other allusions to the Ascension in the New Testament, either as predictions (cf. Mt 26:64; Lk 24:25-26; Jn 6:62; 14:2; 16:28; 20:17), or as references after the event (cf. Acts 2:34; Eph 4:10; 1 Tim 3:16; Heb 4:14; 6:19-20; 7:26; 9:24; 1 Pet 3:22).[180]

The accounts of the Ascension in Mark 16:19, Luke 24:50-53 and Acts 1:9-14, give it special relevance by linking it with the last appearance of the Risen Christ, bringing to a close the period in which the disciples shared Jesus' life. A new era now begins—the era of the Church—in which we live in hope of the Lord's coming again. This coming will take place at the end of the world. Until then, one may perhaps be able to speak of "visions" of Jesus, but not of apparitions in the exact sense given to that word—experiences which constitute people witnesses of the Resurrection, people who had seen Jesus in

---

176. The Ascension occupies a close relationship with the exaltation of Christ on the cross: " 'I, when I am lifted up from the earth, will draw all men to myself' (Jn 12:32). The lifting up of Jesus on the cross signifies and announces his lifting up by his Ascension into heaven, and indeed begins it": CCC, no. 662.

177. Cf. K. Adam, *The Christ of Faith*, op. cit., 356.

178. This is beautifully expressed in the Preface for the Solemnity of the Ascension: "The Lord Jesus, the king of glory, the conqueror of sin and death, ascended to heaven [. . .]. Christ, the mediator between God and man, judge of the world and Lord of all, has passed beyond our sight, not to abandon us but to be our hope. Christ is the beginning, the head of the Church; where he has gone we hope to follow": *Roman Missal*, preface.

179. Second Vatican Council, Const. *Sacrosanctum Concilium*, 5.

180. After listing the places in Scripture where there is reference to the Ascension, Lebreton comments that it makes no sense to say that the historicity of the Ascension rests, ultimately, on one text only: "on the contrary, it is supported by an ensemble of testimonies which represent the entire apostolic tradition": J. Lebreton, "L'Ascension", DBS I, 1070.

the flesh:[181] those apparitions which the Apostles refer to ended with the Ascension.

The Ascension can be described as the other side of the coin of the Resurrection. As such it has fundamental importance for future salvific events; it is a necessary condition for the *parousia* or second coming. It is the basis of that *interim* of the Church, because of its connexion with the sending of the Holy Spirit.[182] It is also a manifestation of Jesus' entering into his glory, "his entry into the heavenly sanctuary", where "seated at the right hand of God" he lives forever "to intercede on our behalf", thereby exercising in heaven his kingly and priestly power.

By his glorious Ascension Jesus fully completes his redemptive sacrifice and from then on intercedes for us as our advocate before God the Father. In other words, not only did he intercede for us here on earth, when "in the days of his flesh (he) offered up prayers and supplications, with loud cries and tears . . . becoming the source of eternal salvation to all who obey him" (cf. Heb 5:7ff), but he also continues to intercede for us in heaven, showing the Father his human nature marked with the glorious signs of his Passion and expressing the great desire of his soul to obtain out salvation.[182a] The Church therefore, in directing its prayers to God the Father, relies on this fact ("per Christum Dominum nostrum")—seeking protection in the intercession of Him who is the only mediator between God and man, the man Christ Jesus (1 Tim 2:5). Once the pilgrim Church has been entirely changed into the heavenly Church, this intercessory action of Christ will cease, giving way to the eternal hymn of the "total Christ" in praise of the Blessed Trinity.[182b]

What does the Ascension add to the glory of the risen Christ? In what way does it make for our salvation? A first answer might be as follows: the Ascension did not add anything to the glory of the Risen One or to his work of redemption; it simply manifested Jesus' glory to his disciples and marked the end of his visible presence on earth. This is a possible reply.[183]

This reply, however, does not seem to do justice to the importance given to the Ascension in Sacred Scripture and in the Tradition of the Church, including its liturgy. Although in essence, for Jesus Christ, the Ascension

---

181. The only one that is similar to the primitive appearances is the appearance to St Paul on the road to Damascus referred to in 1 Cor 15:4-8.

182. Cf. H. Schlier, *Problemas exegéticos fundamentales del Nuevo Testamento* (Madrid, 1970), 315-6.

182a. St Thomas Aquinas, *STh* III, q.57, a.6; cf. also *In Epist. ad Hebr.*, VII, 4 (Marietti, 417).

182b. H.M. Esteve, *De caelesti mediatione sacerdotali Christi juxta Hebr 8, 3-4.* (Madrid, 1949), 166; J.H. Nicolas, *Synthèse Dogmatique*, op. cit., 543ff and 932ff.

183. Thus, e.g., P. Benoit, "L'Ascension", RB 56 (1949) 201; R. Koch, "Ascensión del Señor", DTB 113, says that "one can only attribute to the Ascension a secondary importance or meaning".

coincides with his resurrection and in this sense adds nothing to his glorification, it does have importance, however, in salvation history. Our Lord alludes to this when he says: "It is to your advantage that I go away, for if I do not go away, the Counsellor will not come to you; but if I go, I will send him to you" (Jn 16:7). God wanted the mission of the Holy Spirit in the Church and in the world to be carried out through the humanity of Jesus, making it for us the source of every good thing, of every divine gift and, above all, of the gift par excellence, the Holy Spirit.[184] And "by bestowing the Holy Spirit, Christ becomes Saviour in the deepest sense of the word. He can make himself present to all men with all his salvific force."[185]

Like the Resurrection, the Ascension is also an efficient cause of our salvation, as St Thomas argues, because through it "first of all, he prepared the way for us to heaven, as he himself said, 'I am going to prepare a place for you' [. . .]. Since Christ is our head, it is necessary that we as members of his body should follow him to the place where he went before us, and so he adds 'so that where I am you may be also' (Jn 14:2-3) [. . .]. Secondly, [. . .] the presence of his human nature in heaven is itself an intercession for us. [. . .] Thirdly, enthroned in heaven as God and Lord, Christ from above showers upon men his divine gifts."[186]

During the forty days between the Resurrection and the Ascension, our Lord eats and drinks in the company of his disciples (cf. Acts 10:41) and teaches them about the kingdom (cf. Acts 1:3); his glory continued to be veiled under the appearance of an ordinary man (cf. Mk 16:12; Lk 24:15; Jn 20:14-15; 21:4). "The veiled character of the glory of the Risen One during this time is intimated in his mysterious words to Mary Magdalene: 'I have not yet ascended to the Father; but go to my brethren and say to them, I am ascending to my Fahter and your Father, to my God and your God' (Jn 20:17). This indicates a difference in manifestation between the glory of the risen Christ and that of the Christ exalted to the Father's right hand, a transition marked by the historical and transcendent event of the Ascension."[187]

Linked with the Ascension is what Sacred Scripture describes as "being seated at the right hand of the Father", an ancient biblical expression (cf. Ps 109:1) which refers to the royal authority and the priesthood of the Messiah. In New Testament language, "being seated at the right hand of the Father" is the expression and complement of what we are told when we are told that the Ascension took place: "When he had made purification of sins, (Jesus) sat

184. Cf. A. Aranda, "Christología y pneumatología", in *Cristo Hijo de Dios y Redentor del hombre*, op. cit., 667-9; B. de Margerie, *Le Christ pour le monde*, op. cit., 392-5.
185. F. Ardusso, *Gesù di Nazaret è Figlio di Dio?*, op. cit., 125. More generally, cf. also M. Bordoni, "Cristología e pneumatología. L'evento pasquale come atto del Cristo e dello Spirito", Lat 47 (1981), 432-92.
186. St Thomas Aquinas, *STh* III, q.57, a.6, c.
187. CCC, no. 660.

down at the right hand of the Majesty on high, having become as much superior to angels as the name he has obtained is more excellent than theirs" (Heb 1:3-4).

Through the Ascension, Christ's humanity is given *effective* authority over all creation, sharing ineffably in God's own power, as Lord and Judge of all the world: "It is he whom the Father raised from the dead, exalted and placed at his right hand, constituting him judge of the living and the dead."[188]

"All authority in heaven and on earth has been given to me," Jesus says when taking final leave of his Apostles (Mt 28:18). Although this authority is something he already had by virtue of being the Son, the effective exercise of this authority over the whole universe is only given to him when he is raised on high (and it is given too as a reward for his self-emptying and obedience unto death: cf. Phil 2:6-11). From this point of view it is necessary to give the fullest importance to the exaltation of Christ referred to in the texts. It is a genuine exaltation which marks the climax of the life of Christ, who "enters heaven" as Son of God with the power of the Holy Spirit (Rom 1:4; 1 Tim 3:16), with a sovereignty that extends over the entire cosmos (cf. Phil 2:9-11; Eph 1:20-21; Col 2:15), and which will be revealed definitively at the Second Coming (1 Thess 1:10; Phil 3:20).

In fact it is through the exercise of this universal power that salvation becomes effective for us. By this power we are re-born, made a "new creation in Christ"; through this power we will also receive resurrection and glory. So, we are saved in the exaltation of the Son of man, to the point that St Paul can say that we have been "raised up with him and made sit with him" (cf. Eph 2:6). Ever since Jesus went up into heaven, "our commonwealth is in heaven, and from it we await a Saviour, the Lord Jesus Christ, who will change our lowly body to be like his glorious body, by the power which enables him even to subject all things to himself" (Phil 3:20-21).

So, to the question as to what the Ascension adds to the Resurrection, a fuller answer might be this: the Ascension adds nothing to the Resurrection as far as the glorification of Christ is concerned, but it does add his *being seated at the right hand of the Father*. That expression not only means that he is in heaven; it includes the full exercise of his universal dominion as *Kyrios* (Lord). "Being seated at the Father's right hand signifies the inauguration of the Messiah's kingdom, the fulfilment of the prophet Daniel's vision concerning the Son of man (cf. Dan 7:14)."[189] And it is the exercise of that power that causes our salvation. The Lord, "having entered the sanctuary of heaven once and for all, intercedes constantly for us as the mediator who assures us of the permanent outpouring of the Holy Spirit".[190]

188. Second Vatican Council, Const. *Gaudium et spes*, 45.
189. CCC, no. 664.
190. CCC, no. 667.

In the New Testament the relationship between Jesus and the Spirit is indicated as having two aspects, like two converging lines.[191] In the first place Jesus appears as the fruit of the Spirit. His conception is attributed to the Spirit, who will "overshadow" the Blessed Virgin, and on that account the fruit of her womb will be called blessed (cf. Mt 1:18, 20; Lk 1:35); he descends on Jesus in his baptism (Mt 3:16; Mk 1:10; Lk 3:22; Jn 1:32-33); the Spirit leads Jesus into the desert (cf., e.g., Mt 4:1; Mk 1:12; Lk 4:1); he also has a role in the resurrection, for Christ was "put to death in the flesh but made alive in the spirit" (1 Pet 3:18).

The Spirit also appears in the New Testament as a gift from Jesus. Jesus is not only "he who comes through the Holy Spirit; he is the one who *brings* the Holy Spirit"; "he brings him as a gift proper to his own Person, in order to distribute that gift by means of his humanity."[192] The Messiah not only possesses the fulness of the Spirit of God; he also mediates the bestowing of this Spirit on all the people.[193]

Our Lord repeatedly refers to this aspect of his messiahship. He prays asking the Father to send the Holy Spirit to the disciples (cf. Jn 14:16-17); only if he leaves this world will the Spirit come (cf. Jn 16:7; 14:26). Jesus gives the Spirit to his Apostles on the day of the Resurrection (cf. Jn 20:22). At his last appearance, he promises his disciples that they will be given the power of the Spirit, who will come upon them, and they will be his witnesses unto the ends of the earth (Acts 1:8). Finally, after the Ascension (when the day of Pentecost arrives, as St Luke stresses: cf. Acts 2:1), the Apostles receive the Holy Spirit.

The Holy Spirit, John Paul II writes, "through the work of the Son, that is to say, by means of the Paschal Mystery, is given to the Apostles and to the Church in a new way, and through them is given to mankind and the whole world."[194] In the economy of salvation, the coming of the Holy Spirit is linked

191. Cf. J.A. Dominguez Asensio, "La teología del Espíritu Santo", in various authors, *Trinidad y salvación* (Pamplona, 1990), especially 206-19. Cf. also I. De La Potterie, "Christologie et Pneumatologie", in Pontifical Biblical Commission, *Bible et Christologie* (Paris, 1984), 271-87.

192. John Paul II, Enc. *Dominum et vivificantem*, op. cit., nos. 19 and 22.

193. "The confession of faith 'Jesus the Christ' sums up Jesus' significance for salvation. This credo means first, that the person of Jesus is himself salvation; therefore it expresses the unique and irreplaceable character of the Christian gospel. Secondly, it contains Jesus' universal and public claim and thereby excludes any false idea that salvation is only interior and private. Finally, it says how Jesus is the salvation of the world; he is filled with the Holy Spirit and we share in this plenitude in the Spirit. Salvation is therefore participation through the Holy Spirit in the life of God revealed in Jesus Christ": W. Kasper, op. cit., 253.

194. John Paul II, Enc. *Dominum et vivificantem*, op. cit., 23. Domínguez Asensio comments: "From the resurrection of Christ onwards, the Spirit—the same Spirit who acted in creation and spoke by the prophets—is given in a new way. He is not *novus sed nove datus* (new but newly given). This newness to which the Encyclical refers so insistently is rooted in the intervention of the Risen One. The Spirit is now not only the Spirit of God, but also the *Spirit of Christ*. (Rom 8:9; Phil 1:19; 2 Cor 3:17; Gal 4:6). His bestowal is no longer

to the paschal mystery.[195] "Being therefore exalted at the right hand of God, and having received from the Father the promise of the Holy Spirit, (Jesus) has poured out this which you see and hear" (Acts 2:33). it is the gift of the Spirit that creates the Church and gives it life.

In his Gospel St John refers to this gift as dependent on Christ's exaltation. Jesus promises that rivers of living water will flow from whoever believes in him. And St John adds: "Now this he said about the Spirit, which those who believed in him were to receive; for as yet the Spirit had not been given, because Jesus was not yet glorified" (Jn 7:39). Clearly the words "the Spirit had not yet been given" do not refer to the Spirit's non-existence but to a form of presence which will only begin when the Spirit is sent at Pentecost, that is, after the exaltation of Christ. This presence of the Spirit will build up the Church and give it unity,[196] since it is "by one Spirit we were all baptized into one body [. . .] and all were made to drink of one Spirit" (1 Cor 12:13).[197] Pentecost, then, will inaugurate the age of the Church and round off the Redemption.[198]

c) **Christ, Head of the Church** The Father raised Christ from the dead, made him sit at his right hand in heaven, and "has put all things under his feet and has made him the head over all things for the church, which is his body, the fullness of him who fills all in all" (Eph 1:22-23).[199] This is the continued exercise of his priesthood in heaven which Hebrews 7:20-28 speaks about; it also marks the fulfilment of the promise made by Jesus himself to his Apostles: "I am with you always, to the close of the age" (Mt 28:20). His presence in the Church forms part of his "being seated at the right hand of the Father".

just a bestowal of the Holy Spirit, in general, but insofar as he is the Spirit of Christ. Therefore, from the resurrection onwards, the mission of the Holy Spirit appears always in constant reference to the work of Jesus": J.A. Domínguez Asensio, *La teología del Espíritu Santo*, op. cit., 218.

195. The coming of the Holy Spirit is the fruit of Christ's victory, a victory which involves both his immolation on the cross (that is why it is said to be the fruit of the cross) and of his exaltation; and at the same time the coming of the Holy Spirit shows how great Christ's triumph is. Cf. Blessed J. Escrivá de Balaguer, *Christ is passing by*, op. cit., 127-38.

196. The Church "has its origin in the mission of the Son and the Holy Spirit according to the plan of the Father": Second Vatican Council, Decr. *Ad gentes*, 2.

197. Cf. M. González Gil, *Cristo, el misterio de Dios*, II, op. cit., 486-88.

198. "Today you sent the Holy Spirit on those marked to be your children by sharing the life of your only Son, and so you brought the paschal mystery to its completion": *Roman Missal*, Pentecost, Preface.

199. The meaning of this passage can be established by this linking: '1. God fills Christ, who, thereby, is the *fullness of God* (Col 1:19; 2:9; Eph 3:19); 2. Christ fills the Church, which, thereby, is the fullness of Christ (Eph 1:22-23); 3. The Church is filling the faithful, who become united to Christ in the Church and by the Church (Eph 4:11-13): cf. J. Leal, "Carta a los Efesios", in various authors, *La Sagrada Escritura, Nuevo Testamento: Texto y Comentarios*, II (Madrid, 1961), 687; J.A. Riestra, *Cristo y la plenitud del Cuerpo Místico* (Pamplona, 1985), 155ff.

This presence is a presence which gives life to his mystical body, just as the vine does to the branch that is joined to it (cf. Jn 15:1-8). Therefore, when we say that the mystery of Christ is "prolonged" in the mystery of the Church we are not using a metaphor; we are referring to something that actually happens. The Church is the *pleroma* (fulness) of Christ precisely because the Risen One is constantly giving it life through the continuous working of his "capital" grace.[200] The Church exists as the fruit of the saving effectiveness of the paschal mystery. It is called the *pleroma* of Christ because it grows by sharing in the fulness of Christ's grace. Therefore it is quite correct to say that the Church (which flows from the wounded side of Christ on the Cross) exists as the Church of Christ by virtue of that exaltation by which he is "made Lord" (Acts 2:36). The exaltation of Christ and the pouring out of the Holy Spirit are intimately connected with her.

The pouring out of the Holy Spirit is designed to "Christify" men, to make them like the image of the Son, to make them children of God in the Son (cf. Rom 8:14-17). We are children of God in Christ through the Holy Spirit.[201] "That new life, which involves the bodily glorification of the crucified Christ", we read in the Encyclical *Redemptor hominis*, "became an efficacious sign of the new gift granted to humanity, the gift that is the Holy Spirit, through whom the divine life that the Father has in himself and gives to his Son (cf. Jn 5:26; 1 Jn 5:11) is communicated to all men who are united with Christ."[202]

The "Christification" the Fathers refer to with such richness of language[203] is a real and mysterious identification with Christ, which will only reach its fulness in the glory of the future resurrection, when he himself "will change our lowly body to be like his glorious body, by the power which enables him even to subject all things to himself" (Phil 3:21). Therefore, with St Paul we can say in hope and as a beginning of something that is to come, that God has raised us up and has seated us in the heavenly places, not only with Christ but also in Christ (cf. Eph 2:6).

This identification with Christ actually comes about due to the fact that as soon as he ascended into heaven, he sent us his own Spirit: "in order that we might be unceasingly renewed in him (cf. Eph 4;23), he has shared with us his Spirit who, being one and the same in head and members, gives life to, unifies and activates the whole body. Consequently, his work could be compared by the Fathers to the role that the principle of life, the soul, plays in the human body."[204]

200. Cf. J.F. Bonnefoy, *La Primauté du Christ* (Rome, 1959), 244-54.
201. Cf. F. Ocáriz, "La elevación sobrenatural como re-creación en Cristo", in *Atti del'VIII Congresso Tomistico Internazionale* (Rome, 1981), IV, 281-92 and *Hijos de Dios en Cristo*, op. cit., especially 129-37.
202. John Paul II, Enc. *Redemptor hominis*, op. cit., no. 20.
203. Cf. J.H. Nicolas, *Les profondeurs de la grâce* (Paris, 1969), 61-3.
204. Second Vatican Council, Const. *Lumen gentium*, 7.

d) Judge of the living and the dead   After proclaiming that the Lord ascended into heaven and is seated at the right hand of the Father, the symbols state that "from thence he shall come to judge the living and the dead."[205] In some (for example, the Symbol of Nicea) this all comes under the very relevant heading which covers all the Christological part of the Creed—"for us and for our salvation . . .". This power to judge and the judgment itself are, then, understood as having to do with the Redemption.[206]

Our Lord himself often refers to this judgment, using language akin to the description of the Ascension, for he says that he will come "on the clouds of heaven with power and great glory" (cf. Mt 24:30-31; Mk 13:26-27; Lk 21:27). At the Ascension, the angels tell the apostles, who have seen Jesus go up into heaven, "This Jesus, who was taken up from you into heaven, will come in the same way as you saw him go into heaven" (Acts 1:11). Jesus says that he has received from the Father "authority to execute judgment, because he is the Son of man" (Jn 5:27; cf. 8:26; 9:39; 12:48).

It is very fitting that Christ should have judicial power not only as God but also as man. The Church confesses that, at the end of time, Christ will judge men in the same nature as he himself assumed: "with that same flesh he will come to judge the living and the dead."[207] Christ as man is the head of the Church; and as man he has been raised above all creation; to him, then, also as man, belongs the power of judgment.[208] He will come "in glory" to judge the living and the dead; at his first coming he came in flesh which could suffer and was mortal, but "his second manifestation to us will be glorious and truly divine; then, he will come not to suffer but to give to all the fruits of his own cross, that is, resurrection and incorruptibility. He will not be judged; instead, he will judge all."[209]

It was prophesied of the Son of man that he would receive dominion, glory and kingdom over all the nations (cf. Dan 7:13-14); the Baptist speaks of the messianic times as a time of salvation and also of judgment (cf. Mt 3:1-12). This judgment is an integral part of the Messiah's victory over evil and, therefore, is part of his salvific activity. It is an essential part of the *kerygma* (the first apostolic preaching), as St Peter says: "He commanded us to preach to the people, and to testify that he is the one ordained by God to be judge of the living and the dead" (Acts 10:42; cf. 17:31; 2 Tim 4:1; 1 Pet 4:5).

This judgment is linked to the glorious coming of the Lord. In the New

---

205. Cf. e.g., DS 11, 12, 30, 41, 44, 76 etc.
206. This is not the place to go into the subject of the Judgment; which is dealt with in Eschatology. As far as the present work is concerned, all that need be done is point out the connexion between the general judgment and the exaltation of Christ and the Redemption. See also Chapter 4, section 2a.
207. Innocent III, *Profession of faith*, 18 November 1208 (DS 791).
208. Cf. St Thomas Aquinas, *STh* III, q.59, aa. 2 and 3.
209. St Athanasius, *De Incarnatione Verbi*, 56 (PG 25, 195).

Testament this is called the *"parousia"* (cf. 1 Cor 15:23; 1 Thess 2:19; 3:13; etc.) and sometimes "epiphany" (cf., e.g., 2 Thess 2:8; 1 Tim 6;14; etc.), both of which words indicate the solemn, public character of the Lord's return, as a king making his formal entry into his city. The time has come for the full and definitive revelation of Christ's triumph over evil. For that reason the Parousia is something to hope for and pray for: "Come, Lord Jesus!" (Rev 22:20)—*Maranatha*. After the victory, "when all things are subjected to him, then the Son himself will also be subjected to him who put all things under him, that God may be everything to every one" (1 Cor 15:28).

CHAPTER SIX

The Redemption (II)

The Incarnation, the mysteries of the life of Christ and particularly those of his death and resurrection, took place, as the Symbol of Nicea proclaims, "for us men and for our salvation." In the previous chapter we studied the salvific value of Christ's life and especially of his death and glorification: our salvation has been won by our Lord at the cost of his blood; that is why it is called "Redemption".[1] Two great questions concern us in this last chapter—the nature and content of this salvation wrought by Christ, and the manner in which it was brought about. We shall study, then, all the many dimensions of the Redemption and also analyze in more detail than in the previous chapter, how the life, death and resurrection of the Lord are the cause of our salvation.

As a first approximation to the meaning of the word "salvation", it should be noted that it indicates being set free from some evil, whether physical or moral: one is saved from danger, from grave illness, from slavery, etc. Therefore, salvation has to do with as many aspects and levels of evil as man can or does suffer from.

The notion of salvation is also connected with two kindred notions—health (in Latin, the same word *salus* is used for salvation and health), and liberation. In the synagogue of Nazareth our Lord applies to himself some words of Isaiah which show the connexion between salvation, health and liberation: "The Spirit of the Lord is upon me, because he has anointed me to preach good news to the poor. He has sent me to proclaim release to the captives and recovering of sight to the blind, to set at liberty those who are oppressed" (Lk 4:18-19).

Our Lord sets these words in a universal framework, which transcends the purely temporal. The salvation which he brings to men is all-embracing; it affects them through and through, at every level of their existence. He was to be given the name of Jesus (Saviour), the angel told Joseph, because "he will save his people from their sins" (Mt 1:21). The word "salvation" is given a marked religious meaning in the New Testament. It comprises, on the one

---

1. St Thomas put it like this, ". . . there is a difference between liberation and redemption. Redemption occurs on payment of a just price but liberation can be caused in any other way. Therefore, it is said that the human race could not be redeemed in any other way but that of the incarnation and passion of a divine person because, otherwise, there could not have been a just price, that is, a condign satisfaction": *In III Sent.*, d. 20, q.1, a.3. Any other way of saving mankind—God could have saved it in many other ways—"would not have fallen in with the meaning of redemption, but only with that of liberation, because liberation would have been attained, but without the paying of a price": ibid. a.4.

hand, liberation from sin; and on the other (like the other side of the same coin) the blessings of God which include, in their final eschatological form, liberation from every type of slavery.

Considered dynamically, the salvation wrought by Christ can be described as the changeover from death (the state of sin and its consequences) to life (the state of grace and ultimately the state of glory). It is a matter, then, of a transition, a transformation, which starts out from the situation from which we are liberated and ends up at the new life to which man is born again as "a new creation in Christ" (cf. 2 Cor 5:17).[2] And, as liberation from sin, salvation necessarily involves man's *reconciliation* with God.

1. THE REDEMPTION AS LIBERATION AND RECONCILIATION

Jesus proclaims that his work is a form of liberation: "If the Son makes you free, you will be free indeed" (Jn 8:36). The Jews who hear these words interpret them as meaning physical liberation; Jesus insists that he is referring to a liberation which affects man in the deepest possible way—a liberation from error and sin, since "everyone who commits sin is a slave to sin" (Jn 8:34). The freedom Jesus speaks of is a deep, all-embracing freedom which affects every aspect of man reaching his very core, and one which makes him "free indeed" (cf. Jn 8:31-36).

The ancient concept of freedom (*eleutheria* in Greek) does not have to do directly with the interior freedom of the person, but with his *state* or situation, that is, with being free as distinct from being a slave. In the New Testament this term (*eleutheria*) goes further, referring above all to the condition of children as distinct from that of slaves or servants, and more specifically, the condition of *children of God*. So, New Testament freedom is not simply an external, legal, state or situation, but a condition of *being*: it is "the freedom of the sons of God", as St Paul repeatedly says in his Letter to the Galatians (cf. Gal 4:1, 5, 21-31; 5:13).[3]

It is a matter, then, of a religious liberation, not because it does not affect every aspect of men's lives but because its primary impact is on the root of all the evils which beset man—sin (cf. Gen 3; Rom 5:12ff). Christ's work, we find, has to do both with the origins (sin committed at the dawn of history) and with what lies beyond human history, when the last enemy (death) will eventually be defeated by the resurrection (cf. 1 Cor 15:26).

Jesus himself revealed his messianism to belong to the sphere of religion (that is, of man's relationships with God), and he did everything he could to avoid its being confused with political messianism. He came to save men primarily from their estrangement from God; he came to free them from sin.

2. Cf. C. Spicq, "Salvación", GER XX, 741-3.
3. Cf. J. Ratzinger, *Chiesa, ecumenismo e politica* (Rome, 1987), 183-7.

He preaches the Kingdom of God. Or, rather, he ushers in the Kingdom of God. That is why he began his preaching with a message of penance: "The time is fulfilled, and the kingdom of God is at hand; repent and believe in the Gospel" (Mk 1:15).

a) Liberation from sin When the Pharisees are surprised that Jesus is "the friend of sinners", our Lord declares that he has "not come to call the righteous, but sinners to repentance" (Lk 5:32). This *call to penance* was not just an exhortation to conversion; it involved the actual forgiving of sins. Our Lord shows very clearly and energetically that he has the power to forgive sins, and he does in fact forgive them. Indeed, more than once he performs a miracle to show that sin has been forgiven (cf., e.g., Mt 9:2; Lk 5:20; 7:48). After rising from the dead, by the infusion of the Holy Spirit he gives the Apostles the power to forgive sins (cf. Jn 20:23). The forgiving of sins is so central to his mission that he identifies this forgiveness as the reason for his offering up his body and blood (cf. Mt 26:28).

Thus, St Paul writes to Timothy: "The saying is sure and worthy of full acceptance, that Christ Jesus came into the world to save sinners" (1 Tim 1:15; cf. Eph 1:7). This salvation from sin is a genuine liberation: "Thanks be to God, that you who were once slaves of sin [. . .] having been set free from sin, have become slaves of righteousness" (Rom 6:17-18).[4]

The way St Paul contrasts and parallels Christ and Adam (Rom 5:12-21)— Adam as the cause of sin and Christ as the cause of liberation from sin—also shows the central position liberation from sin has in Christ's work of salvation.[5] The Church has always recognized the importance of forgiveness of sins, making it even an article of the Creed.

Our Lord's victory over sin is total. And he gives us a share in it. In his preaching he exposes sin; he shows it for the evil it is, and he condemns it for what it is—enmity of God, a diabolical expression of selfishness. By his obedience he cures our disobedience and by his justice we are justified (cf. Rom 5:12-21). Not only does he atone for sin superabundantly (he is "the expiation for our sins" (1 Jn 4:16), but he has the power to restore man to grace, to cause him to be born again. When he says, "Your sins are forgiven you", it is not simply a legal non-imputing of them, but a genuine cure; not just an external covering-over but a genuine interior transformation—a veritable annihilation of sin.

Sacred Scripture contains eloquent passages which praise God's faithfulness and his victory over the evil which comes from the human heart and in some way affects all creation (cf. Rom 8:19-24). Neither God's faithfulness nor

4. Cf. L. Cerfaux, *Cristo nella teologia di San Paolo*, op. cit., 114-19.
5. On the Adam-Christ antithesis, cf. F. Prat, *The Theology of St Paul*, II, op. cit., 171-7; L. Cerfaux, *Cristo nella teologia di San Paolo*, op. cit., 193-208.

Christ's victory on the cross would befit divine omnipotence if they only affected the external part of man, if they only brought about an extrinsic justification (merely covering him over with the merits of Christ) and did not re-make man, did not restore him to the justice and holiness in which he was created.[6]

Christ's victory over sin involves its annihilation in us. This includes God's forgiveness; it also includes uprooting evil from man's heart. In Christ the Redeemer "man finds again the greatness, dignity and value that belong to his humanity. In the mystery of the Redemption man becomes newly 'expressed' and, in a way, is newly created. He is newly created!"[7] Liberation from sin consists precisely in making sinful man just, that is, truly holy. It is in a way a kind of creation: it involves making man a *new creature* in Christ (cf. Eph 4:24; Col 3:10).

Liberation from sin is not just liberation from the faults one has committed—purification from the disfiguring stains on one's heart. It also means that man can (with the grace of God) defeat sin's power over him, that is, the tendencies towards evil which rise up within him due to the disorder in his nature caused by the original sin and by his own personal sins.

This disorder is so severe that one can say that human nature is wounded[8] (the mind inclined towards error, and the will attracted to evil), and it is part of the Church's faith that unless we have the grace of God (which God refuses no one), we cannot for long keep even the natural law.[9] Christ's victory over sin means that with his grace man can defeat the sin which festers in his heart. " The divine dimension of redemption is put into effect not only by bringing justice to bear upon sin, but also by restoring to love that creative power in man thanks to which he once more has access to the fullness of life and holiness that comes from God."[10]

---

6. Paradigmatic in this respect is Luther's position regarding the corruption of man and, as a result of that, regarding justification. According to Luther man is intrinsically corrupted and therefore his "justification" consists in his sins not being imputed to him on account of Christ's merits: cf. J. Paquier, "Luther", DTC IX, esp. 1206ff; J. Lortz, *Historia de la Reforma*, II (Madrid, 1964); C. Boyer, *Lutero: su doctrina* (Barcelona, 1973); L.F. Mateo Seco, *Lutero: Sobre la libertad esclava*, op. cit., especially 57-9. The Council of Trent takes up this matter in its sixth session when its teaches that the grace of God truly *justifies* man, making us truly just (cf. Council of Trent, Decr. *De justificatione*, chap. 7: DS 1529).

7. John Paul II, Enc. *Redemptor hominis*, op. cit., no. 10.

8. "We believe that in Adam all have sinned" says the Credo of Paul VI, "which means that the original offence committed by him caused human nature, common to all men, to fall to a state in which it bears the consequences of that offence [. . .]. It is human nature so fallen, stripped of the grace that clothed it, injured in its own natural powers and subjected to the dominion of death, that is transmitted to all men" (op. cit., no. 16).

9. Cf. Council of Trent, Sess. VI, chap. 13 and canon 22 (DS 1541 and 1572).

10. John Paul II, Enc. *Dives in misericordia*, op. cit., no. 7. Cf. P. Giglioni, "La misercordia di Dio e la catechesi", in various authors, *Dives in misericordia. Commento all'Enciclica di Giovanni Paolo II* (Rome-Brescia, 1981), 263.

Liberation from sin involves, finally, liberation from the punishment due to sin. When explaining this point, St Thomas says that, when man sinned, he incurred eternal and temporal penalties—which implies a kind of captivity, because it is proper to a free man to do whatever he wants, whereas to have to suffer something one does not want is a form of bondage.[11] "There is therefore now no condemnation for those who are in Christ Jesus. For the law of the Spirit of life in Christ Jesus has set me free from the law of sin and death" (Rom 8:1-2).

The fact that Christ has destroyed sin and reconciled us to God does not mean that we are no longer capable of sinning. When we say that Christ has destroyed sin, we are saying that he has established a universal cause of forgiveness of sins, whereby all sins can be forgiven if ever they are committed. But, for forgiveness to take effect, this universal cause needs to be applied to the individual (and, in the case of someone who has reached the use of reason, he or she must cooperate in its application); this comes about particularly through the sacraments of baptism and penance. The classic comparison made in this connexion is that of the doctor who has prepared a medicine that can cure any ailment: for it to work, the patient must take the medicine.[12]

In liberating man from sin, Jesus Christ also liberates him from other consequences of sin, particularly error, the power of Satan and the dominion of death. Mainly through the teaching of religious truth, Jesus liberates man from the slavery of ignorance and error. It is a true liberation, also because knowledge of the truth is a necessary condition for the use of freedom (cf. Jn 8:32), since love (the free choice of good) is the proper act of freedom, and knowledge of the truth is what enables us to know what is truly good.

b) Liberation from the power of the devil   To the extent that man is the slave of sin he is also under the sway of the devil, not because Satan as a "right" over the sinner but because he is very able to influence him to do evil. The Council of Trent taught that, after original sin, man falls "into the hands of 'him who has the power of death, that is, the devil' (Heb 2:14)."[13]

From the beginning Jesus made it plain that part of his mission was to defeat Satan and destroy his power over the world. The coming of the kingdom of God implies the destruction of the devil's tyranny. He is the tempter, who induced man to sin, thereby bringing death into the world (cf. Gen 3:15); "that ancient serpent, who is called the Devil and Satan, the deceiver of the whole world" (Rev 12:9). He uses his power against the kingdom of God by means of deception and seduction, for he is "a liar and the father of lies" (cf. Jn 8:44).

11. Cf. St Thomas Aquinas, *STh* III, q.48, a.4.
12. Ibid. III, q.49, a.1, ad 3 and 4.
13. Council of Trent, Decr. *De peccato originali*, op. cit. (DS 1511); cf. St Thomas Aquinas, *STh* III, q.49, a.2.

By seducing man the devil becomes the master of the world, to the point that he can be called "ruler of this world" (cf. Jn 12:31; 14:30; 16:11).

Jesus conquers Satan from early on by overcoming the temptations (cf. Mt 4:1-11; Mk 1:12-13; Lk 4:1-13); he expels demons, demonstrating his power over them and giving a sign of the liberating character of his messianic role (cf. Mk 1:21-27; 5:1-20; 7:24-30; 9:14-29; Mt 17:17-18; Lk 4:35; 11:20; etc.). The Gospels, particularly St Mark's, focus on the fact that these expulsions are part of Christ's struggle against the devil.[14] In reaction to the Pharisees who say that he expels devils "by the power of Beelzebul", Jesus himself says that he performs these cures by the power of God, and that they are a sign that the kingdom of God has come: "But if it is by the finger of God that I cast out demons, then the kingdom of God has come upon you" (Lk 11:14-27; cf. Mt 12:22-29),[15] and he sometimes sums up the nature of his work of salvation as a victory over the devil, whose dominion over the world will be destroyed: "Now is the judgment of this world, now shall the ruler of this world be cast out" (Jn 12:31).

Christ's victory over Satan is seen to be a thorough one, because he defeats him without having recourse to his kind of weapons. He does not expel devils through magic or the use of earthly power, but by the "finger of God" (Lk 11:20); he defeats lies not with lies but with the simplicity of truth; the power of the devil he overcomes only by divine power, the power of holiness and truth.

The kingdom of God made manifest in Christ is not a political regime, nor is it based on earthly power; it is the revelation and establishment of the law of love and of the truth of God. Jesus overcomes Satan (as is shown in his victory when he is tempted) because he does not seek worship or self-glorification, but only the worship of God (cf. Mt 4:1-11),[16] thereby showing us the way and enabling us to struggle against the devil. This victory over the devil is already something real, even though he has not been stripped of all power to tempt man. However, the devil is truly defeated, because he cannot gain the final victory, nor ever again hope to control the world; in a veiled but effective way the kingdom of God has come among us, and the Church "even on earth, is endowed with a holiness that is real though imperfect."[17]

Early Christian writings sometimes refer to the devil's "rights" over man. The question these writings raised may be summed up as follows: by going away from God men have submitted to the yoke of the devil; does the devil not have some sort of right of conquest over them which God, when the time

---

14. "What have you to do with us, Jesus of Nazareth? Have you come to destroy us? I know who you are, the Holy One of God": Mk 1:24. These words are a veritable exegesis of Jesus' action.
15. Cf. John Paul II, *Address*, 3 August 1988, nos. 3-4: *Insegnamenti*, XI, 3 (1988), 206f.
16. Cf. M. Schmaus, *Katholische Dogmatik*, IV/2, op. cit., 94.
17. Second Vatican Council, Const. *Lumen gentium*, 48.

to redeem man comes, should take account of and in some way respect?[18]

St Irenaeus posed this question very early on. The devil, he said, had to be overcome by just means, "and our enemy would not have been conquered by just means, if he who overcame him had not been a man born of woman."[19] St Irenaeus also says, very clearly, that we owed the devil nothing; we were in debt to God alone.[20]

Origen takes up this idea, exaggerating man's captivity to the devil; he says that by sinning "we have sold ourselves to the devil; the devil has bought us by means of our sins; his coin (the coin that bears his effigy) is murder, adultery, and every kind of sin. He has purchased us with this coin and has acquired property rights over us."[21] Clearly, he is using words designed mainly to win his listeners' attention (he is preaching), by underlining that through sinning man makes himself the devil's slave. It is worth remembering that, as Origen sees it, we are rescued from the devil's power by Christ's death, which is a sacrifice offered to God and not to Satan; however, sometimes he wrongly says that Christ's blood was a ransom paid to the devil to win our release.[22]

St Basil and St Gregory of Nyssa also echo this way of explaining how we are liberated from the power of the devil as part of the salvation brought by Christ.[23] It is easy to see the almost irreverent extremes this kind of language could lead to. Heretics (for example, Migetius the Marcionite) actually pushed this theory to grotesque extremes. And the theory itself, even in the milder form that Origen gave it, was widely rejected—for example, in the *De recta in Deum fide* (Concerning right faith in God).[24] And St Gregory Nazianzen, who was very close to St Basil and St Gregory of Nyssa, reacted strongly against it.[25]

The theory of the "devil's rights" is linked in these same writers to another called the "theory of the devil's fraud" or the "theory of the abuse of the devil's power." This theory has it that the devil has a certain right over sinners; by

18. For extensive coverage of this subject, cf. J. Rivière, *Le dogme de la Rédemption. Essai d'étude historique* (Paris, 1905), 373-94 and "Redemption", DTC XIII, 1939f.
19. St Irenaeus, *Adv. Haer.*, V, 1 (PG 7, 1121); and ibid., III, 18, 7 (PG 7, 937-8).
20. Cf. St Irenaeus, *Adv. Haer.*, V, 16, 3 and 17, 1 (PG 7, 1168-9).
21. Origen, *In Exod.*, VI (PG 12, 338 A-C).
22. Cf. Origen, *In Rom.*, II 13 (PG 14, 991 C-D).
23. Cf. St Basil, *Hom. in Psalm.* 48, 3 (PG 29, 437); St Gregory of Nyssa, *Orat. Cat.*, 18 (PG 45, 53). Cf. L.F. Mateo Seco, *Estudios sobre la cristologia de San Gregorio de Nisa*, op. cit., 127-56.
24. Adamantius, *De recta in Deum fide*, sect. I (among the works of Origen, PG 11, 1736-7).
25. "We were prisoners of the devil because we sold ourselves to sin and had given up our right to happiness. If (the blood of Christ) is not offered as a ransom to him who holds us prisoner, to whom then (I ask) has the blood of Jesus Christ been offered and to what purpose? If you say it has been offered to the devil, what a perverse thing to say! How could you think that the devil receives from God not just a ransom but God himself as ransom, with the idea that there is offered to his tyranny such superabundant payment that (the devil) in justice cannot but set us free": St Gregory of Nazianzen, *Or.*, 45, 22; PG 36, 653.

engineering Christ's death (which he does, some of these writers say, because he is not aware of all the consequences of that death) the devil abused his power and therefore justly merited being deprived of it. Through his death, Christ tolerated the devil's abuse of his power and so rescued us "justly" from the power the devil had obtained over us by getting us to submit to him through sin.

Some Latin Father, such as St Ambrose, St Augustine and St Fulgentius, use similar language: "By a certain justice on God's part," St Augustine says, "the human race was given over to the power of the devil—not of course by God's command but by just permission. God wanted to conquer the devil not by power but by justice [. . .]. What justice is it that has conquered the devil, if not that of Jesus Christ? How was the devil overpowered? By the killing of Christ when there was nothing in him that deserved death. It was right, then, that the debtors he held prisoner should be set free, those who believe in Him who was not a debtor and yet was condemned to death."[26] St John Chrysostom, St Cyril of Alexandria and St Gregory the Great write in similar vein.[27]

St Anselm, rejecting this interpretation of liberation from the power of the devil, says that "the devil's right to punish was null; indeed, his behaviour in this was all the more unjust given that what motivated him was not love of justice, but hatred."[28] The devil has no right over men: "the devil had no right to prevent God from using force against him and setting man free."[29]

From that point on, theology gave up this sort of language to explain man's captivity by the devil, although it continued to recall St Augustine's phrase quoted above "to draw out its implications more clearly".[30] "The Redemption", writes St Thomas, "was required for the liberation of man in regard to what concerns God, not for that which concerns the devil, because the ransom had to be paid to God, not to the devil."[31]

Our Lord frees us from the power of the devil, precisely by freeing us from the power of sin, which is the instrument of his dominion over man. As the Second Vatican Council teaches, "the Lord himself came to free and strengthen man, renewing him inwardly and casting out the 'prince of this world' (Jn 12:31), who held him in the bondage of sin."[32]

c) **Liberation from death**   Death and all the pain and frustration it involves, is punishment for sin: "sin came into the world through one man and death

---

26. St Augustine, *De Trinitate*, 13, 12, 16-18 (PL 42, 1026-8).
27. St John Chrysostom, *In Rom. Hom.*: 13, 5 (PG 60, 514); St Cyril of Alexandria, *In Joan.*, 6, 8, 44 (PG 73, 894); St Gregory the Great, *Moralia*, II, 22, 41 (PL 75, 575ff).
28. St Anselm, *Cur Deus Homo?*, 1 (PL 158; cf. ibid., 567).
29. Ibid.
30. Cf. e.g., St Thomas Aquinas, *STh* III, q.49, 2, in c.
31. *STh* III, q.48, a.4, ad 3.
32. Second Vatican Council, Const. *Gaudium et spes*, 13.

through sin, and so death spread to all men because all men sinned" (Rom 5:12; cf. Gen 2:17; 3:17ff).[33] Liberation from sin, then, involves liberation from death, because "with sin destroyed, death which proceeds from sin is also annihilated. If the root be dead, how can the branches survive? If sin be gone, why should we have to die?"[34]

The victory over death is the resurrection of the dead. Jesus Christ conquered death by his resurrection; but he can also be said to have conquered death by his own death, since he thereby atoned for our faults and merited his resurrection and our own: "Through his death the Saviour has freed us from death; by giving himself up to death, he kills death; he receives death and hangs death on the Cross. In Christ's death, death itself has been mortally wounded; life, by dying, has killed death; the fullness of life has absorbed death."[35]

This victory of Christ's has a double meaning as far as our death is concerned. Above all, it means our future resurrection (cf. Rom 8:10-11; 1 Cor 15:20-28); but it also means liberation, in this life, from the *fear of death*, Christ came "that through death he might destroy him who has the power of death, that is, the devil, and deliver all those who through fear of death were subject to lifelong bondage" (Heb 2:14-15). If it is true that God did not want the Redemption to give us back immortality immediately, but instead wanted us to make our way to eternal life through the pains and anguish proper to physical death, that death already has a new meaning for those who believe in Christ: it means stepping into life, and that rids death of its basic horror; we have been set free from the fear of death and, at the end of time, we will be freed from death itself: death will be totally overthrown: "The last enemy to be destroyed is death [. . .]. When the perishable puts on the imperishable, and the mortal puts on immortality, then shall come to pass the saying that is written: 'Death is swallowed up in victory.' O death, where is thy victory? O death, where is thy sting?" (1 Cor 15:26, 54-55).

Christ's victory over pain and death also involves, so to speak, that its meaning changes: it has become something positive; it is no longer something negative.[36] For one who becomes a member of Christ through faith and the

---

33. Cf. Sixteenth Council of Carthage, *De peccato originali*, canon 1 (DS 222); Second Council of Orange, *De peccato originali*, cn. 1 (DS 371). Cf. also Council of Trent, Sess. V. Decr. *De peccato originali* (DS 1511f); Second Vatican Council, Const. *Gaudium et spes*, 13-14. Cf. L.F. Mateo Seco, "Muerte y pecado original en Santo Tomás de Aquino" in various authors, *Veritas et Sapientia* (Pamplona, 1975), 277-315.

34. St Cyril of Alexandria, *In Joan.*, I, 29 (PG 73, 192).

35. St Augustine, *In Joan. Tract.*, XII, 10-11 (PL 35, 1489f).

36. This conviction (and not more or less philantropic sentimentalism) is the source of the Church's appreciation for those who suffer from any of the countless trials which dog mankind; in them particularly she sees the face of Christ; they are a treasure for mankind. This can be seen, for example, in the works of Blessed J. Escrivá who on the one hand shows his Christian appreciation of suffering as radically as this: "Blessed be pain. Sanctified

sacraments, pain, failure and death are no longer the negation of human fulfilment: they mark the real, transcendental fulfilment of one who, by being joined to Christ, co-redeems with him. Death and the negativity of human limitation become thereby cooperation in the redemption of mankind; death "has lost its sting, it has been swallowed up in [Christ's] victory" (cf. 1 Cor 15:55), a victory in which we share. Thanks to that victory, "life and death are made holy and acquire a new meaning"[37]—the possibility of becoming identified with Christ and of cooperating with him (through pain and failure, among other things) in the salvation of the world (cf. Col 1:24). United to Christ, our suffering and our death acquire the same meaning as that of the suffering and death of the Redeemer; in them, too, the kingdom of God is present, and so we are "heirs with Christ, provided we suffer with him in order that we may also be glorified with him" (Rom 8:17).[38]

d) Liberation from the Old Law Jesus Christ came not "to abolish the law but to filfil it" (cf. Mt 5:17); but he also speaks of his blood as being the blood of a "new covenant" (cf. Lk 22:20), and like a new Moses he speaks words which bring the Old Covenant to its ultimate perfection, a perfection which at the same time transcends it. Therefore, while it "gives fulfilment to the law", it sets us free from the regime of the Mosaic Law.[39] St Paul is emphatic that Christ's victory over sin also brings freedom from the Old Law. The Law was in itself holy, just and good (cf. Rom 7:12). but it was in some way an occasion of sin; firstly, because the detailed knowledge it gave of the natural law and of what was sinful meant that sin was something people were more aware of and they could sin more gravely. The Apostle points this out when he says: "If it had not been for the law, I should not have known sin. I should not have known what it is to covet if the law had not said, 'You shall not covet' " (Rom 7:7).[40] Secondly, because once the Law was promulgated, sin became a transgression of a positive law of God. That does not mean that

be pain . . . Glorified be pain!" (*The Way*, no. 208). On the other hand, he shows his freedom in regard to fear of suffering or of failure: "You say you've failed! We never fail. You placed your confidence wholly in God. Nor did you neglect any human means. Convince yourself of this truth: your success—this time, in this—was to fail. Give thanks to our Lord . . . and begin again!": *The Way*, no. 404; finally, he expresses his appreciation for those who suffer, considering them nor as frustrated individuals but as special bearers of Christ: "Children. The Sick—as you write these words don't you feel tempted to use capitals? The reason is that in children and in the sick a soul in love sees Him!": *The Way*, no. 419.

37. Second Vatican Council, Const. *Gaudium et spes*, 22.
38. Cf. St Thomas Aquinas, *STh* III, q.43, a.3, ad 3. On the Christian meaning of pain, cf. John Paul II, Ep. Apost. *Salvifici doloris*, 11 February 1984.
39. On Jesus' attitude to the Law and the legal institutions of Israel, cf. R. Banks, *Jesus and the Law in the Synoptic Tradition* (Cambridge, 1975); M. Hubaut, "Jésus et la Loi de Moïse", RTL 7 (1976) 410-25; R. Fabris, *Jesús de Nazaret*, op. cit., 115-28.
40. Cf. St Thomas Aquinas, *In Epist. ad Rom.*, c. V, lect. 6; *In II Epist. ad Cor.*, chap. III, lect. 2.

there were no sins before the Law came (the natural law, impressed on men's hearts, made them responsible for their actions); it means that sin acquired a new dimension, one which only Adam's sin had before that—transgression of a positive divine law. This explains why St Paul could say that "Christ redeemed us from the curse of the law" (Gal 3:13).

Our need for Christ to set us free from the Mosaic Law was all the greater given that the Law itself did not provide man with the grace to fight successfully against sin and temptation. Under the New Law, established by Christ, man is given easy access to the sources of grace to equip him to fight against sin.[41] This does not mean that in the Old Testament there were no just people, by the grace of God: grace they did receive, through faith in the future Messiah and in anticipation of his merits. In that economy faith in Christ found its expression in fulfilment of the Mosaic Law.

Once God sent his Son "to redeem those who were under the law" (Gal 4:5), the Christian is no longer under the letter of the Law. The old legal precepts are no longer in force, and the rites of that Law have no longer any meaning (as signalled by the rending of the veil of the Temple when Christ died on the cross: cf. Mt 27:51). However, the moral precepts of the Law remain in force, not because they are part of the Mosaic Law, but because all that law did was to spell out the natural law.[42] By virtue of the Passion of Christ, the New Law confers the grace needed to keep its commandments.[43] And so St Paul can write that we are "not under the law but under grace" (Rom 6:14). Grace always brings with it charity, whereby we share in the Holy Spirit who is infinite Love, and since the new Law is summed up in the precept of charity, the obligatory nature of this law does not force our freedom, because one cannot love unless one is free. The New Law is, then, "the perfect law of liberty" (Jas 1:25).[44] According to Pauline teaching, the Old Law "disappears naturally with the coming of Christ, who is its end, when it has no more reason for existence, and when the promises which are irreconcilable with it are realized. But even though it should retain its validity in principle, the Christian, by the fact of baptism, is released from its empire."[45]

e) The reconciliation of men with God The *terminus a quo* (starting-off point) of Redemption involves liberation from sin, from the power of the devil and from death; considered positively (in the light of its *terminus ad quem*—finishing point) the Redemption is something quite new, which the New

41. Cf. St Thomas Aquinas, *STh* I-II, q.103, a.3, ad 2; III, q.47, a.2, ad 1.
42. Ibid., q.100, a.1.
43. Ibid., q.107, a.2.
44. Cf. F. Ocáriz, "Lo Spirito Santo e la libertà dei figli di Dio", in *Atti del Congresso Internazionale di Pneumatologia* (Rome, 1982), 1239-51.
45. F. Prat, *The Theology of St Paul*, II, op. cit., 23.

Testament often describes as reconciliation with God: "while we were enemies we were reconciled to God by the death of his Son" (Rom 5:10). It is a reconciliation in which God is the one who takes the initiative: "It pleased (the Father) that in him (Christ) all fullness should dwell, and through him to reconcile to himself all things, whether on earth or in heaven, making peace by the blood of his cross" (Col 1:19-20).

This reconciliation implies forgiveness of sins, which had made men enemies of God: "God was in Christ reconciling the world to himself, not counting their trespasses against them" (2 Cor 5:19). Forgiveness actually annihilates sin, to the point that man is changed so profoundly by supernatural grace that he becomes a "new man", a "new creature": "If any one is in Christ, he is a new creation; the old has passed away, behold, the new has come. All this is from God, who through Christ reconciled us to himself" ((2 Cor 5:17-19; cf. Gal 6:15). Therefore, to be reconciled with God does not simply mean something external or legal (not being charged with the fault); rather, one is radically renewed in the core of one's being.[46] That is what the Fathers in the early centuries mean when they describe the redemption wrought by Christ as being "reconciliation with God". "In the first Adam," says St Irenaeus, "we had offended God by not observing his command; in the second Adam we have been reconciled when He became obedient unto death."[47] Origin speaks frequently of Christ as the high priest who reconciles us with the Father and as the victim of a sacrifice of reconciliation.[48] This is the same language as the Council of Trent will use much later on: Christ "who reconciled us to God by his blood, 'made unto us [. . .] justice and sanctification and redemption'."[49]

The reconciliation of the world and of men with God is not simply a re-establishing of the primitive state of things in which man found himself before original sin. Through the Redemption, man recovers God's friendship, and grace, and the state of being a son of God; but he does not recover the praeternatural gifts proper to the state of original justice; after his reconciliation with God he continues to have an inclination to evil (concupiscence) and to error; he still experiences suffering and death. But these wounds of human nature acquire a new meaning and value through the redemption: they become a means of cooperating with Christ in his work of redemption. Man finds himself in a transitional situation (as a wayfarer, during his life on earth) which will eventually end when Christ comes again in glory and God wipes away our

---

46. Cf. M. Schmaus, *Katholische Dogmatik*, III, op. cit., 344.
47. St Irenaeus, *Adv. Haer.*, V, 16, 3 (PG 7, 1168).
48. Cf. Origen, *In Levit. Hom.*, 9, 10 (PG 12, 523); *In Joan.*, 1, 37 and 6, 33 (PG 14, 85 and 292).
49. Council of Trent, Decr. *De peccato originali* (DS 1513). Cf. Second Vatican Council, Const. *Gaudium et spes*, 78. Cf. also St Thomas Aquinas, *STh* III, q.49, a.4.

tears and "death shall be no more, neither shall there be mourning nor crying nor pain any more, for the former things have passed away" (Rev 21:4).

There is another difference between the state of original justice and the position of redeemed man, who has received the fruits of redemption: the reconciliation of God and men brought about by Christ puts man in a state of union with God more intimate than that of Adam, because Jesus Christ himself is the "place" of our reconciliation: "Jesus Christ, son of the living God, has become our reconciliation with the Father" (cf. Rom 5:11; Gal 1:20);[50] for, "God was in Christ reconciling the world to himself" (2 Cor 5:19), and no more intimate union is possible, no closer Alliance between God and man than that forged in Christ, who is true God and true man. It is in Christ that we are reconciled with God—through our spiritual union and identification with Jesus. Therefore, it is right to say, with all that it implies, that he is our reconciliation with the Father.[51]

f) Christian freedom and human liberation Christian freedom is the "freedom of the children of God" (cf. Rom 8:21); it is the freedom with which "Christ has set us free" (Gal 5:1); it is, above all, something inside man, for it consists first and foremost in man's friendship with God and in liberation from sin. Of course, that is not to say that that inner freedom cannot expand outwards, cannot tend to liberate all human things (family, society, etc.), even purifying social structures from the effects of sin, error, the devil and death. "The work of Christ's redemption concerns essentially the salvation of men; it takes in also, however, the renewal of the whole temporal order."[52]

There is, then, nothing human that can be considered marginal to the Redemption and that should not be freed from the influence of sin. But it should not be forgotten that sin itself is the radical cause of all the tragedies that mark the history of freedom, and that the course of human history has a kind of mysterious link with sin. So, the only place where true freedom can begin and where it can fully develop is in the heart of man.[53] This liberation, then, begins in man's heart, freeing him from the slavery to the various idols he has fashioned, for "when man attributes to creatures an infinite importance, he loses the meaning of his created being. He claims to find his centre and his unity in himself. Disordered love of self is the other side of contempt for God.

---

50. John Paul II, Enc. *Redemptor hominis*, op. cit., no. 9.
51. Cf. M.J. Scheeben, *The Mysteries of Christianity*, op. cit., 625-30; L. Cerfaux, *Cristo nella teologia di San Paolo*, op. cit., 119-22.
52. Second Vatican Council, Decr., *Apostolicam actuositatem*, 5.
53. "As the kernel and centre of his Good News, Christ proclaims salvation, this great gift of God which is liberation from everything that oppresses man but which is above all liberation from sin and the Evil One": Paul VI, Apos. Exhort. *Evangelii nuntiandi*, 8 December 1975, no. 9; cf. also no. 18. Cf. also C. Basevi, "Promoción humana y salvación cristiana en la Declaración de la Comisión Teológica Internacional" (September 1977), ScrTh 10 (1978), 673-713.

Man then tries to rely on himself alone; he wishes to achieve fulfilment by himself and to be self-sufficient in his own immanence."[54]

Freeing man from the error of being turned in on himself implies healing his heart, setting it free for love. Freedom finds its meaning in love. Our Lord's exhortations about everyone taking up his cross and following him, about whoever wants to be greatest having to become the servant of all, show that this is the case. "Nowadays it is sometimes held, though wrongfully, that freedom is an end in itself, that each human being is free when he makes use of freedom as he wishes, and that this must be our aim in the lives of individuals and societies. In reality, freedom is a great gift only when we know how to use it consciously for everything that is our true good. Christ teaches us that the best use of freedom is charity, which takes concrete form in self-giving and in service. For this 'freedom Christ has set us free' (Gal 5:1, 13)."[55]

The connexion between freedom and charity is basic to Christian thought, because man is made in the likeness of God, who is Love (cf. 1 Jn 4:8). This indissoluble connexion between freedom and love has been stressed right down the Christian centuries. As St Augustine writes, "freedom belongs to love";[56] and St Thomas Aquinas: "the more love one has, the freer one is."[57] The reason why freedom belongs to charity has to do with the inner nature of freedom, which is a capacity to choose and love what is truly good, a capacity which is filled only by loving God: "freedom finds its true meaning when it is put to the service of the truth which redeems, when it is spent in seeking God's infinite Love which liberates us from all forms of slavery."[58]

g) **Presuppositions for a theology of liberation** The originality of Christian freedom is to be seen in its very nature (founded as it is on charity and grace); it has nothing to do with selfishness or violence, but only with love, a love that is the fruit of the Redemption.

The deepest questions to do with freedom and human liberation are essentially theological, for, as the Second Vatican Council says, "in reality it is only in the mystery of the Word made flesh that the mystery of man truly becomes clear."[59] It is Christ who definitively reveals to man his dignity and destiny and who, by redeeming him, gives love back to him and with it the sense of freedom. Hence it may be said that "truth, beginning with the truth about redemption, which is at the heart of the mystery of faith, is thus the root

---

54. Congregation for the Doctrine of the Faith, Instr. *Libertatis conscientia*, 22 March 1986, no. 41.
55. John Paul II, Enc. *Redemptor hominis*, op. cit., 21; cf. *Inaugural Discourse at the Third General Conference of the Latin American Episcopate*, 28 January 1979, in AAS 71 (1979) 202f.
56. "Libertas est caritatis": St Augustine, *De natura et gratia*, 65, 78 (PL 44, 286).
57. St Thomas Aquinas, *In III Sent.*, d.29, q. unica, a.8, q. 1a. 3, s.c.
58. Blessed J. Escrivá de Balaguer, *Friends of God*, op. cit., no. 27.
59. Second Vatican Council, Const. *Gaudium et spes*, 22.

and the rule of freedom, the foundation and the measure of all liberating action,"[60] and, as John Paul II stresses, "the theology of liberation should, above all, be faithful to the whole truth concerning man, in order to show clearly, not only in Latin America but everywhere, what this freedom is 'for which Christ set us free'."[61]

Christ's salvific work makes the liberation of man central to the Church's work and to theology. In this connexion there began in 1968 a theological current called "theology of liberation", which rapidly gained a following. This broadly based movement[62] began in Latin America and has been very influential in many countries around the world. Human liberation is its central theme, and some of its main proponents have adopted rather Marxist positions (even as regards key concepts like being, truth, and the good).

Obviously not every discussion about the liberation of man is automatically a theological discussion. To be truly theological, it must begin with Revelation, that is, Sacred Scripture and Tradition as proposed by the Magisterium, and work outwards from there; moreover (and recent history has proved this), error, even philosophical error, not only fails to set man free: it enslaves him. This explains why the hierarchies of many countries and the Sacred Congregation for the Doctrine of the Faithful have felt obliged to intervene in this matter.[63]

The fact that the Church rejects certain approaches to the subject which were wrong because the methodology was wrong, do not mean that there is no room for theological reflection on liberation, or that the liberation agenda has no place in the Christian context. However, it should not be forgotten that only if one bears in mind the deeper side of man (which is theological) can one speak of liberation in the full sense, given that complete freedom can only be attained through identification with Christ.

"The Church feels the duty", John Paul II teaches, "to proclaim the liberation of millions of human beings, the duty to help this liberation become firmly established (cf. Paul IV, *Evangelization of Peoples*–EN–30); but she also

---

60. Instr. *Libertatis conscientia*, op. cit., no. 3. Cf. L.F. Mateo Seco, "Libertad y liberación" ScrTh 13 (1986) 873-89.
61. John Paul II, *Address*, 21 February 1979: *Insegnamenti*, II, 1 (1979) 431.
62. For a survey of this movement and its doctrinal content, cf., among others, A. Bandera, *La Iglesia ante el proceso de liberación* (Madrid, 1975); B. Mondin, *I teologi della liberazione* (Rome, 1977); A. Lopez Trujillo, "La cristología, perspectivas actuales" in various authors, *Cristo, Hijo de Dios . . .*, op. cit., 55-77; L.F. Mateo Seco. G. Gutiérrez, H. Assmann, R. Alvés: *Teología de la Liberación* (Madrid, 1981); "Teología de la liberación", GER 25, 1139-46; "El futuro de la teologia de la liberación", ScrTh 22 (1990) 195-211.
63. In this connection, special attention should be given to the Instruction *Libertatis nuntius* of the Congregation for the Doctrine of the Faith, which was issued to "draw attention [. . .] to the deviations, and risks of deviation, damaging to the faith and to Christian living, that are brought about by certain forms of liberation theology which use, in an insufficiently critical manner, concepts borrowed from various currents of marxist thought": Inst. *Libertatis nuntius*, 3 September 1984, no. 3. Cf. L.F. Mateo Seco, "Algunos aspectos de la teología de la liberación", ScrTh 17 (1985) 225-71.

feels the corresponding duty to proclaim liberation in its internal and profound meaning, as Jesus proclaimed and realized it (EN, 31). Liberation from everything that oppresses man but which is above all liberation from sin and the evil one in the joy of knowing God and being known by him (EN, 9). Liberation made up of reconciliation and forgiveness. Liberation springing from the reality of being children of God [. . .] which makes us recognize in every man a brother of ours, capable of being transformed in his heart through God's mercy. Liberation that, with the energy of love, urges us towards fellowship, the summit of fullness which we find in the Lord. Liberation as the overcoming of the various forms of slavery and man-made idols, and as the growth of the new man. Liberation that in the framework of the Church's proper mission is not reduced to the simple and narrow economic, political, social or cultural dimension, and is not sacrificed to the demands of any strategy, practice or short-term solution (EN, 33)."[64]

So, there are close, indissoluble links between the Gospel and liberation: it is not posible to follow the Gospel seriously without that having a profound impact on social structures and on even the way society is structured; and at the same time it is not possible to have a full liberation of man unless that liberation is firmly grounded on the truth of the Gospel. It follows that, although it may be useful to distinguish earthly progress from the growth of the Kingdom, since they do not belong to the same order, this distinction does not mean a separation; "because the distinction between the supernatural order of salvation and the temporal order of human life must be seen in the context of God's singular plan to recapitulate all things in Christ."[65] And so, the Church "takes great care to maintain clearly and firmly both the unity and the distinction between evangelization and human advancement—unity, because she seeks the good of the whole person; distinction, because these two tasks enter, in different ways, into her mission."[66]

So, although the political management of society is not a direct part of the Church's mission ("this task belongs to the laity to work in this sphere according to their own vocation") the Church should resist attempts to confine its mission to the "private" sphere, because its teaching "extends to the whole moral order and notably to the justice which must regulate human relations". Therefore, "when the Church speaks about the promotion of justice in human societies, or when she urges the faithful laity to work in this sphere according to their own vocation, she is not going beyond her mission."[67]

True, the fullness of this human liberation is eschatological, because death

---

64. John Paul II, *Inaugural Discourse at the Third General Conference of the Latin American Episcopate*, op. cit., III.
65. Instr. *Libertatis conscientia*, op. cit., no. 80.
66. Ibid., no. 64.
67. Ibid., nos. 61-4.

and suffering will not disappear until the end of time (cf. 1 Cor 15:26; Rev 21:4). But, in the meantime, human liberation (which does form part of the salvation won by Christ) is actually at work in history ; firstly, because Christ has already delivered us from the fear of death (cf. Heb 2:15) and from the fear of suffering, by giving suffering and death a new meaning (that of being able to be associated with his redemptive suffering: cf. Mt 10:38; Jn 16:33); secondly, because human liberation is also at work in history insofar as it is the goal and duty of Christians, to whom Christ has given the supreme commandment to love all men—a love which presupposes (but transcends) simple justice (cf. Jn 13:34; 1 Jn 3:17), because it is governed by the message of the beatitudes.[68]

2. SATISFACTION, MERIT AND EFFICIENT CAUSALITY OF CHRIST IN THE WORK OF REDEMPTION

The Redemption is essentially destruction of sin, and reconciliation with God. It is, then, something theologically very rich, something many-faceted, and a mystery beyond our grasp. Sacred Scripture uses different names and analogies to describe the *manner* in which Christ's life, death and glorification have brought about our redemption. The Redemption has as many angles to it as liberation from sin has: if sin is a fall, redemption is raising up the fallen person; if sin is illness, redemption is a cure; if sin is a debt, redemption is payment, purchase, ransom; if sin is a fault, redemption is atonement; if sin is slavery, redemption is liberation; if sin is an offence against God, redemption is satisfaction, propitiation, reconciliation with God.[69]

Three of these aspects of redemption call for special study—satisfaction, merit and efficacy. Christ has *made satisfaction* for our sins, he has *merited* new life for us and as the *efficient cause* of that life he has given us this new life of grace and glory. These are not three disconnnected things: they are simply three aspects of one and the same mystery. Christ's life and death is not only a victory over sin, devil and death; it is also true expiation and satisfaction for sin; Christ has conquered evil by dying and he died to atone for man's sin.

68. Cf. F. Ocáriz, "Presupuestos para una válida Teología de la liberación" in various authors, *Portare Cristo all'uomo* (Rome, 1985), 743-53.
69. Cf. F. Prat, *The Theology of St Paul*, II, op. cit., 200f. This is the same language as used by the Fathers to refer to the mystery of our redemption. "Our nature, so sickly," St Gregory of Nyssa writes, "had need of a physician; man, who had fallen, had need of someone to lift him up; he who had cut himself off from life needed one to give him life; he who had separated himself from goodness needed someone who would lead him back again to goodness; he who had fallen into darkness needed the presence of light. The captive sought a redeemer; the vanquished, someone to help him to fight; he who was under the yoke of slavery sought a liberator": *Or. Cat. Magn.*, 15: PG 45, 48.

a) **Satisfaction for sin**   The expiatory value of Christ's life and death is, perhaps, the aspect of the Redemption where one should make most effort to speak with precision, in order to avoid deforming its theological content. "Satisfaction value" is the term used in relation to Christ's death to show what his death does to make up to God for the offence committed by mankind, that is, by reparation and atonement for sins. That is what "satisfaction" means in a theological context—making good the offence implied by sin through offering God a love and an obedience unto death where Christ "wipes out" the offence, the injustice, the disgrace that sin implies (cf. Rom 5:12-21).[70]

It is very clear from Sacred Scripture that the salvation the Messiah brings is connected with men's sins. The Messiah will be called *Jesus*, "for he will save his people from their sins" (Mt 1:21). As the Old Testament develops we begin to see more and more clearly the redemptive value of the pain and death of the just man as also his *solidarity* with the people. For the very reason that he is friendly with God the sufferings of the just man draw divine blessings down upon himself and on all the people.

So, for example, God confirms his blessings to Abraham and his offspring in response to Abraham's heroic obedience. This thought finds perhaps its most eloquent expression in the fourth poem of the Servant of Yahweh (Is 52:13 - 53:12), which speaks of the redemptive value of the sufferings of the Servant, who "has borne our griefs and carried our sorrows [. . .]. He was wounded for our transgressions, he was bruised for our iniquities [. . .], he made himself an offering for sin." St Peter refers to this prophecy, when he reminds us that Christ suffered for us: "He committed no sin; no guile was found on his lips. When he was reviled, he did not revile in return; when he suffered, he did not threaten; but he trusted to him who judges justly. He himself bore our sins in his body on the tree, that we might die to sin and live to righteousness. By his wounds you have been healed" (1 Pet 2:22-24). This same idea (the redemptive value of suffering) is also very plain to see in the passages about sacrifice. The two theological lines (the expiatory value of the just man's sufferings; and that of sacrifice) converge in the figure of Christ, the just man who suffers, and whose suffering is not only atonement for the sins of the people but also a redemptive sacrifice offered to God, who turns his poured-out blood into blood which seals the "new covenant" (Lk 22:20).[71]

In the New Testament, from the very earliest writings the death of the

---

70. *Expiation* is properly the fulfilment of the punishment due for a fault, and therefore it has the quality of satisfaction; but satisfaction does not necessarily involve expiation, since it is possible to give satisfaction for an offence by offering something which recompenses the offended party, and this could happen without having to undergo punishment. The satisfaction made by Christ is rooted in his love and obedience towards the Father; and the fact that (especially in his Passion and death) this love and obedience includes the acceptance of suffering, means that his *satisfaction for sins in fact included expiation for those sins.*

71. Cf. A. Medebielle, "Expiation", DBS, III, 253f.

Messiah is linked to the sins of men: Christ "died for our sins" (cf. 1 Cor 15:3; Rom 4:25; Gal 1:4), he "died for the ungodly" (Rom 5:6), "he gave himself for us to redeem us from all iniquity" (Tit 2:14), "he died for sins once for all, the righteous for the unrighteous" (1 Pet 3:18), etc.

Although Sacred Scripture does not use the term "satisfaction" in connexion with Christ's death, it does use similar words or ones which involve the idea of satisfaction. For example, Jesus' dying on behalf of the evildoers or sinners means that it is *in* Christ's death that the reconciliation of sinners with God is brought about, so that his death becomes ransom (*lutron*), propitiation (*ilasmos*), and atonement (*ilasterion*) for our sins. "The Son of man came not to be served but to serve, and to give his life as a ransom for many" (Mt 20:28); God "loved us and sent his Son to be the expiation for our sins" (1 Jn 4:10).

When referring to Christ's death as satisfaction for our sins, we should not forget that Christ's self-surrender—and Christ himself—is God's gift to mankind. So the satisfaction in point is not primarily something made by man; it is a divine initiative. In this context Romans 3:21-27 is a key text: "The righteousness of God has been manifested apart from law [. . .]; since all have sinned and fall short of the glory of God, they are justified by his grace as a gift, through the redemption which is in Christ Jesus, whom God put forward as an expiation by his blood [. . .]. This was to show God's righteousness, because in his divine forbearance he had passed over former sins; it was to prove at the present time that he himself is righteous and that he justifies him who has faith in Jesus."

In this passage the key idea which establishes the scope of the theological concept of satisfaction is that of "the righteousness of God". What St Paul is referring to is the holiness of God which reveals itself by causing the salvation and sanctification of men.[72] Given that all have sinned and therefore been deprived of the glory of God, this righteousness is manifested in the fact that it is God himself who has put forward Christ as a sacrifice of expiation and to justify all those who believe in him. This means that it is precisely Christ's death that makes it possible for the righteousness of God to act, by removing the obstacle of sin. So, when speaking of Christ's death as satisfaction for sins, one must remember that the initiative comes from the offended party, God; hence the need to use analogy when talking of satisfaction as restoring God's "honour", and when one speaks about God's "anger". And, of course, Christ is offered by the holiness of God as a propitiatory victim; at no point is it said

---

72. The expression "righteousness of God" has a very rich meaning in St Paul: sometimes it refers to justice in the sense of rendering to each person according to his deeds; sometimes (as in the passage we are dealing with) it refers to God's own holiness. "The 'justice of God' is presented by St Paul under two distinct but not incongruous aspects: the justice which is in God and the justice which comes from God. The intrinsic justice of God is not merely a vindictive or distributive justice, it is also—and sometimes chiefly—redemptive justice": F. Prat, *The Theology of St Paul*, II, op. cit., 246.

that he was put forward to be *punished* for our sins. The idea of undergoing a penal sentence on another's behalf appears nowhere in the text.[73]

The Father's initiative in the redemption is highlighted again by St Paul a little further on: "God shows his love for us in that while we were yet sinners Christ died for us. Since, therefore, we are now justified by his blood, much more shall we be saved by him from the wrath of God. For, if while we were enemies we were reconciled to God by the death of his Son, much more, now that we are reconciled, shall we be saved by his life. Not only so, but we also rejoice in God through our Lord Jesus Christ, through whom we have now received our reconciliation" (Rom 5:8-11).

As in the passage quoted earlier, St Paul speaks of two states—one in which we are under the wrath of God (that is, under sin) and the new state (reconciliation with God). The cause of the new state is the death of the Son which, for this reason, has to be seen as redemption and propitiation for our sins. So, Christ's death is what takes away God's anger from the sinner, and therefore it is that death that offers something to God which brings about the sinner's reconciliation. This something comes from God himself; he it is who has taken the initiative to reconcile us to himself in Christ (cf. 2 Cor 5:18-22).

The same elements occur again in Romans 5:12 and 17-21, when Christ and Adam are contrasted. Here St Paul focusses on the personal element in Adam's sin and Christ's satisfaction: disobedience is met by obedience unto death; an obedience whereby Christ renders the Father a supreme act of worship, indisputably more valuable and more fruitful than Adam's disobedience was the reverse. What wipes out Adam's disobedience is not a *punishment* laid on Christ's shoulders thereby *satisfying* God's *anger*, but a moral act of infinite value performed by Christ who, as head of mankind and in solidarity with his brothers and sisters, renders God a homage of total adoration, thereby wiping out Adam's disobedience. That is to say, the essence of satisfaction is not atonement, although Christ's death was also an atonement, an expiation.

This obedience unto death was *painful*. So Christ is the expiatory victim for the sins of men: "he is the expiation for our sins" (1 Jn 2:2); God has put him forward "as an expiation by his blood" (Rom 3:25). This allows St Paul to say, outspokenly, that "for our sake he made him to be sin who knew no sin, so that in him we might become the righteousness of God."[74] So, although

---

73. "If we suppose that St Paul really had in mind the theory of substitution, how come it that he never formulated it? Why does he always say that Christ was crucified *for* us (*huper* and occasionally *peri*), *for* all men, for sinners, that he went to death *for* us, that he was made a curse *for* us, that he was made sin *for* us, and that he gave himself up *for* our sins; and why does he *never* say that Christ died *in our place* (*anti*), which logically would dispense us from dying": F. Prat, *The Theology of St Paul*, II, op. cit., 197.

74. "This cannot mean that God made Christ *sin* [. . .] or a *sinner* [. . .], first, because in the very same line it has just been said that Jesus was *innocent of any sin*; secondly, because sin is a vital, free and personal act, which cannot be imposed from without; thirdly, because

we cannot go as far as to say that Christ was *punished* in the strict sense of the word, we can say that he took upon himself our iniquities and that he suffered as he did for our sins (cf. Gal 3:13). The satisfaction made by Christ involves, then, true *expiation*. We are saved by his blood being spilt; his pain and death (the fact that they have been selected as the way to salvation) are linked to the pain and death due for our sins, and are why his death can be called expiation for the sins of men.

This is a constant theme in the Fathers whenever they discuss Christ's death and its redemptive character, in the course of commenting on the relevant passages of Scripture.[75] Thus, for example, St Eusebius of Caesarea (*c.*340) says that the Lamb of God "has borne on our behalf torment and torture which he did not deserve (whereas we do deserve them on account of our sins), for he accepted, for us, the death, beating and opprobrium that we deserved; transferring these to himself, he brought down on himself the curse that we merited, becoming our salvation. What was this but to substitute his life for ours?"[76] St Ambrose recalls that Jesus "made up to his Father for our sins".[77] St Augustine comments that "if Christ had not paid what was not his debt, he would not have freed us from our debt."[78]

The Creeds refer to the expiatory character of the life and death of Christ, who "for us men and for our salvation . . .,"[79] "who suffered for our salvation."[80] And the Eleventh Council of Toledo teaches that "according to the truth of the Gospel [. . .], he was conceived without sin, born without sin, and died without sin who alone for us 'hath been made sin' (2 Cor 5:21), that is, a sacrifice for our sins. Yet, his divinity unimpaired, he suffered his passion for our failings."[81]

Jesus Christ died "so that nature ruined by Adam should be repaired by Him;"[82] he "delivered himself for us, an oblation and a sacrifice."[83]

However, although the texts of the Magisterium frequently state that Christ died in order to repair a human nature wounded by Adam's sin, the term *satisfactio* is not used in connexion with Christ's passion until the Council of Trent and then only indirectly. When discussing the causes of justification, Trent says that Christ is the "meritorious" cause of our justification, because

God cannot be the author of sin, nor can he force an innocent person to become a sinner": M. González Gil, *Cristo, el misterio de Dios*, II, op. cit., 138.

75. Cf. J. Riviere, *Le dogme de la Rédemption. Essai d'étude historique* (Paris, 1906), 101-278; *Le dogme de la Rédemption chez S. Agustin* (Paris, 1928); "Rédemption", DTC, op. cit., 1935-42.
76. Eusebius of Caesarea, *Demonstr. evangel.*, X, 1 (PG 22, 724).
77. St Ambrose, *Enarrat. in Psalmos*, 37, 53 (PL 14, 1085).
78. St Augustine, *Sermo* 155, 7 (PL 38, 845).
79. Cf. *Symbolum Nicaenum* (DS 125).
80. Cf. *Symbolum Quicumque* (DS 76).
81. Eleventh Council of Toledo, *Symbolum* (DS 53).
82. Council of Orange, *De gratia*, canon 21 (DS 391).
83. Council of Ephesus, *Anathematismi S. Cyrilli*, 10 (DS 261).

"he merited for us justification by his most holy passion on the wood of the Cross and made satisfaction for us to God the Father;"[84] and when speaking of satisfaction as an act of the penitent it says: "add to this that while making satisfaction we suffer for our sins,. we are made conformable to Christ Jesus who satisfied for our sins (Rom 5:10; 1 Jn 2:1-2) [. . .]. Neither is this satisfaction which we discharge for our sins so much our own as not to be through Christ Jesus [. . .]."[85]

From this point onwards texts of the Magisterium frequently use "satisfaction" when referring to the manner in which Christ redeems us from sin. "The Only-begotten of God, made man", writes Leo XIII, "made satisfaction to God who had been offended by men, very abundantly and thoroughly with his blood."[86] The mystery of the Redemption is, says Pius XII, "in the first place and of its very nature a mystery of love; the dutiful love of Christ for his heavenly Father, to whom the loving and obedient sacrifice of the Cross rendered abundant, indeed infinite satisfaction for the sins of the human race."[87]

The notion of satisfaction is an integral part of doctrine on the mystery of the Redemption and should never be set aside.[88] "Jesus Christ, the Son of the living God, became our reconciliation with the Father (cf. Rom 5:11; Col 1:20). He it was, and he alone, who satisfied the Father's eternal love, that fatherhood that from the beginning found expression in creating the world [. . .]; He and he alone also satisfied that fatherhood of God and that love which man in a way rejected by breaking the first Covenant (cf. Gen 3:6-13) and the later covenants that God 'again and again offered to man' (Eucharistic Prayer IV)."[89]

(i) *The Anselmian notion of satisfaction*   Although Sacred Scripture and Tradition do make it clear that our Lord's sufferings had an expiatory value and therefore Christ's death was understood to be a reparation for our sins, not until St Anselm does the term "satisfaction" acquire the importance and legal

---

84. Council of Trent, Sess. VI, Decr. *De justificatione*, chap. 7 (DS 1529).
85. Council of Trent, Sess. XIV, chap. 8, *De sacramento poenitentiae* (DS 1690).
86. Leo XIII, Enc. *Tametsi futura*, 1 November 1900: AAS 33 (1900-1), 275.
87. Pius XII, Enc. *Haurietis aquas*, op. cit., AAS 48 (1956) 321.
88. The statement by the commission of cardinals which studied the text of the *Dutch Catechism* on this subject laid down the following: "The basic doctrine concerning Christ's satisfaction, which belongs to our faith, must be put forward unambiguously. God so loved sinners that he sent his own Son into the world to reconcile them to himself (cf. 2 Cor 5:19). . . . By this holy death, which in God's eyes compensated superabundantly for the sins of the world, it was brought about that divine grace was restored to mankind, as a reward merited by its divine Head": AAS 60 (1968) 688. And Paul VI, in a Letter to Cardinal Alfrink, also on the *Catechism*, says that there should be no room for ambiguity concerning "the nature of the satisfaction and the sacrifice offered by Christ to the Supreme Father, whereby our sins are blotted out and men are reconciled to him": cf. C. Pozo, *Las Correcciones al catecismo holandés* (Madrid, 1969), esp. 66.
89. John Paul II, Enc. *Redemptor hominis*, op. cit., no. 9.

connotation which marked its use in the Middle Ages. Unlike Peter Abelard (who, when stressing that Christ has saved us by his word and good example, seems to deny that his death truly made *satisfaction* for our sin),[90] St Anselm tries to provide "reasons of necessity" for the incarnation of the Word, basing his argument on man's need to be redeemed by Christ. Therefore, he stresses the infinite nature of sin (as an offence against an infinite God) and the requirements of divine justice—so much so that it would seem that God felt that justice required a satisfaction *ex toto rigore justitiae* (in accordance with strictest justice) and, therefore, a satisfaction which could only be made by someone whose actions had infinite value, that is, by the Son of God himself. The conditions laid down for Redemption, then, would demand the Incarnation of the Word (which was the principal objective of Anselm's treatise).[91]

This proposition, rigidly followed with an excessively legal idea of satisfaction and a rather feudal concept of divine honour, undermines the validity of the Anselmian theory of satisfaction.[92] St Thomas later corrected this theory by speaking of satisfaction not as something necessary but as something fitting. To bring about the salvation of the human race the death of Christ was the route most appropriate to justice and divine mercy—to justice, because through his passion Christ *made satisfaction* for the sins of all mankind and thereby man was liberated by Christ's justice; to divine mercy because, since man on his own cannot make satisfaction, God gave up his Son to do so, and by so doing he was being more merciful than if he had pardoned the sin without requiring any satisfaction to be made.[93]

As modified by St Thomas, St Anselm's doctrine has won universal acceptance. In fact, St Thomas' change is a substantial one, if one takes account of three key points: it safeguards the gratuitous and free nature of the Incarnation, as also that of the Redemption; it also sees the *satisfaction* offered

90. The Council of Sens condemned, among others, the following propositions of Peter Abelard: that Christ did not take flesh to free us from the yoke of the devil; that unaided free will is capable of doing good; that in Adam we contracted punishment but not guilt (cf. DS 723, 725, 728); ideas which in a sense makes it superfluous to speak of Christ's death in terms of satisfaction for our sins. Cf. J. Rivière, *Le dogme de la Rédemption au début du moyen âge* (Paris, 1934), 103-29.

91. Cf. St Anselm, *Cur Deus homo*, I, chaps. 19 and 20 (PL 158, 389-93); II, 6, 17-20 (PL 158, 403f; 419-28). Cf. J. Rivière, "Rédemption", DTC, op. cit., 1942f.

92. St Anselm's theory has often been exaggerated in order to ridicule it (particularly by Liberal Protestantism). However, as Greshake and Kasper have pointed out, in a feudal setting it was up to a point quite a reasonable theory. In the feudal period, recognition of the lord's honour was the basis for order and social peace; if that honour was injured, then the social order was injured. The re-establishing "of that honour therefore does not mean personal satisfaction for the Lord, but the restoration of the order of the whole. Anselm accordingly distinguishes between God's honour 'as it affects himself' and God's honour 'as far as it concerns the creature' ": W. Kasper, *Jesus the Christ*, op. cit., 219ff. However, it must be said that even the attempt to prove the Incarnation by necessary reasons is itself in need of profound correcting.

93. Cf. St Thomas Aquinas, *STh* III, q.46, aa.1-3, especially a.1, ad 3.

by Christ as the fruit of divine *justice* and *mercy*, using a theological concept of justice, and not just a legal one; finally, there is an underlying basis to all St Thomas' teaching on satisfaction—the affirmation of Christ's solidarity with the human race. For example, to the objection as to how is it possible for anyone to make satisfaction on behalf of someone else, he replies: "The head and members form as it were a single mystical person. Christ's satisfaction therefore extends to all the faithful as to his members."[94]

(ii) *Justice and mercy in God*   Discussing Redemption from the point of view of satisfaction implies discussing the justice of God. We have already examined the *justice of God* as the cause of the Redemption—looking on divine justice as sanctifying holiness (an aspect much stressed by St Paul). The initiative of redemption derives from this divine justice. This is the meaning St Thomas gave justice in the previous paragraph: the choice of satisfaction as the manner in which the redemption should take place was the option most appropriate to divine *justice* and mercy. But the notion of satisfaction also needs to be considered in the light of divine justice, understanding justice as requiring the restoration of a destroyed order, reparation for an offence. So, in one form or another, satisfaction involves the idea of reparation connected with something required by avenging justice.

When speaking of this aspect of divine justice, we must avoid conceiving divine justice in human terms or, worse still, confusing the virtue of justice with mere legalism. It should not be forgotten that justice exists in God in an eminent degree,[95] and that it is infinitely perfect and holy, because, in God, "justice is based on love, flows from it and tends towards it [. . .]. The divine justice revealed in the Cross of Christ is 'to God's measure', because it springs from love and is accomplished in love, producing fruits of salvation."[96]

This theological notion of divine justice (even the aspect of it that involves reward and punishment) requires that the correct kind of satisfaction be applied to the Redemption. The theological concept of satisfaction does contain something like the ordinary meaning of making reparation for an offence ("placating the anger of the offended party"), but there is an important difference.

Thus, in the case of man's sin, the "anger of the offended party", that is, the wrath of God, is manifested in the fact that he offers his own Son so that the world may not perish (cf. Jn 3:16-17). As we know, the wrath of God is something we can speak of only in a metaphorical way'[97] nor can we speak of

94. St Thomas Aquinas, *STh* III, q.48, a.3, ad 1.
95. Cf. St Thomas Aquinas, *STh* III, qq. 4 and 6.
96. John Paul II, Enc. *Dives in misercordia*, op. cit., no. 7.
97. "Anger and such like are attributed to God by similarity of effect: on account of its being proper to a person who is angry to punish, his punishment is metaphorically called anger": St Thomas Aquinas, *STh* I, q.3, a.2, ad 2.

his justice other than as part of divine holiness.[98] God's "anger" at man's sin is compatible not only with his justice but also with his faithfulness to the love which led him to create the universe. In Christ's suffering and death "has been revealed in a new and more wonderful way the fundamental truth concerning creation to which the Book of Genesis gives witness when it repeats several times: 'God saw that it was good' [. . .]. The God of creation is revealed as the God of redemption, as the God who is 'faithful to himself' (cf. 1 Thess 5:24), and faithful to his love for man and the world which he revealed on the day of creation. His is a love that does not draw back before anything that justice requires in him."[99]

(iii) *Penal substitution*   As indicated earlier, the idea that Christ was punished in our place lay at the heart of the soteriology of the early reformers.[100] This theory is called "penal substitution". It involves both the idea that Christ was punished (his suffering is truly a *punishment* inflicted by God) and the idea that he was punished *in our place*. This notion is closely connected with the typical Lutheran idea that both justice and sin can be imputed to man from outside; that is, that they are purely legal denominations. And, therefore, sin can be imputed to Christ (who is totally innocent) even to the point that he really deserves punishment for that sin;[101] in which case, the satisfaction offered by Christ would be merely a penal substitution: the vengeful justice of an angry God would have fallen on an innocent Christ, who would thereby have stood in for a sinful mankind to atone for the punishment sinners deserved.[102]

The theory of *penal substitution* is unacceptable as an explanation of the Redemption: it cannot be thought that the essence of the act of redemption lies in the Father inflicting suffering and death on the innocent Jesus as a *punishment* for the sins of men. A "penal substitution" of this kind (punishing

98. Cf. St Thomas Aquinas, *STh* I, q.6, aa. 2 and 3.
99. John Paul II, Enc. *Redemptor hominis*, op. cit., nos. 8–9.
100. This is a logical consequence of saying that Christ did not just take on himself the consequences of men's sin, but took the sin itself, to the point of becoming sin: "For which reason Christ is not only crucified and put to death, but through divine charity sin is imposed on him too. Sin being thus imposed on him, the law comes and says: every sinner shall die [. . .]. Rightly therefore does Paul apply the general law from Moses to Christ: 'Cursed is he who hangs from a tree' ": M. Luther, *In Epistolam S. Pauli ad Galatas Commentarius*, op. cit., ed. WA 40/1, 436, 24–29. Cf. B.A. Willens and R. Weier, "Soteriología. Desde la Reforma hasta el presente", in various authors, *Historia de los dogmas*, op. cit., 11.
101. Cf. J. Rivière, "Rédemption", op. cit., 1952f.
102. As already seen in the exegesis of Christ's words on the cross, "My God, my God, why hast thou forsaken me?" (cf. Mt 27:46), following Luther, and Calvin, who said that Christ bore "terrible torment such as befitted the damned and the lost" (Calvin, *Inst. Christ.* II, c.16, 10), some theologians went as far as to say that our Lord had felt eternal death, such was the nature and intensity of his sufferings; and even, if we look at the sublimity of the victim, that this suffering not only equalled but infinitely surpassed that of the damned (cf. J. Rivière, "Redemption", art. cit., 1952f).

an innocent man instead of punishing the guilty) would contradict the infinite justice of God and would also be incompatible with the loving regard the Father showed Jesus at his Baptism and Transfiguration: "This is my beloved Son, with whom I am well pleased" (Mt 3:17; cf. Mt 17:5). A God who *punishes* the innocent instead of the guilty would be neither just nor merciful; he would be arbitrary;[103] he would not be God. In fact, the theory of penal substitution, as such, along with what it is inseparably based on, goes against the basic principles of common sense. For, sin is a personal act, so it does not make sense to impute it to someone who has not committed it, because what is essentially a free and non-transferable attitude cannot be imposed from outside. Nor does it make sense to *punish* an innocent person instead of the guilty one; anyone who tried to obtain satisfaction for an offence in that way should be described as irrational.[104]

The theory of *penal substitution* was persistently held by the religious groupings which emerged from the Reformation. Faustus Socinus (+1604) does react against it; but in addition to criticizing the theory he denies the objective character of the Redemption, that is, he denies that Christ, the new Adam, out of the infinite love with which he obeys the Father even to the point of undergoing death, makes *objective* reparation for our disobedience. By denying Christ's death its satisfactory character, Socinus reduces its redemptive value to that of a mere "model", a simple "example" of charity which inspires us to imitate Christ's life.[105] The same rejection of *objective* redemption is to be found in the liberal interpretation of Schleiermacher (1786-1834) and Ritschl (1822-89), and of Sabatier (1839-1901), for whom our Lord's passion is merely "the greatest call to repentance ever made to mankind".[106] This reduction of the Redemption to mere moral influence (mere good example), denying its *objective* expiatory character, influences the Modernists, who attributed to St Paul the doctrine of the expiatory death of Christ and, as a consequence, denied that Christ was aware of the sacrificial character of his death, or that he ever referred to it.[107]

103. It is this arbitrary God that is to be found at the basis of the theory of penal substitution. "The majesty of the unknown God is for Luther, from the days of his youth, that of the irate judge. Through the word of the Ockhamist teachings this judge will later come to be converted into a God of caprice. Because this is the definitive point about the notion of God in Ockhamism: that God has to be free even to the point of caprice, free of all specification or rule that we could think or say": J. Lortz, *Historia de la Reforma* (Madrid, 1964), 191. Cf. L.F. Mateo Seco, *Lutero: Sobre la libertad esclava*, op. cit., 81-112.

104. "To represent 'God's anger' as a violent feeling, caused undoubtedly by sin but which has lost its reference to the sinner to the point of requiring (for appeasement) a certain amount of punishment to be borne by someone, it doesn't matter whom—that idea is not only impious; it is absurd": J.H. Nicolas, *Synthèse dogmatique*, op. cit., 502.

105. This teaching, along with others by Socinus concerning the Trinity, was rejected by Pius IV in the Const. *Cum quorundam hominum*, of 7 August 1555 (DS 1880).

106. A. Sabatier, *La doctrine de l'expiation et son évolution historique* (Paris, 1903), 107.

107. In the Decr. *Lamentabili*, the following proposition is condemned: "The doctrine of the expiatory death of Christ comes not from the Gospel but rather from St Paul" (DS 3438).

(iv) *Vicarious satisfaction*   The inaccuracies which arise when one forgets the analogy with which one has to use the words (satisfaction, punishment, etc.) when transferring them from a legal to a theological context, and the justified rejection of the theory of *penal substitution*, are not however sufficient reason for dropping the notion of satisfaction from the doctrine of the Redemption. The texts from Sacred Scripture, some of which we have cited, do not allow us to minimize what Christ's death means in terms of price, expiation, propitiation, ransom, and sacrifice for the sins of men. On the Father's part, there was no trace of vengeful justice with respect to Christ for the sins of men; yet, by his death Christ did atone for their sins, and the Father did accept that voluntary atonement as satisfaction. It is the Father himself who placed in Christ's heart the love necessary for him to give his life for the salvation of men.[108] But Christ's self-surrender was real and painful; one must not minimize what the Cross meant in terms of suffering and opprobrium (cf. Heb 12:2), in terms of atoning satisfaction.

The satisfaction Christ's death implies is to be seen all the more clearly when one considers that (as we have already pointed out) *the essential aspect of the satisfaction is not the expiation for sins through suffering, but love and obedience.* Christ made satisfaction for our sins principally (essentially) by offering the Father a love and obedience that more than made up for the disobedience and lack of love which sin implies. That is why not only Jesus' passion and death, but his whole life, every one of his human actions, made satisfaction for sin, because they were all expressions of his love for and obedience to the Father (cf. Jn 4:34; 8:29), a love and obedience whose highest manifestation was on the Cross (Phil 2:8).

It is often said that satisfaction necessarily includes a penal (painful) aspect of expiation. If this language were used, it would imply that not all Christ's actions were atoning ones, because not all involved suffering. It would be better to say that all Jesus' human actions had an expiatory value, both because they formed a continuum with the Cross, constituting one single salvific life, and because Christ's state of *kenosis* (involving the capacity to suffer) was present in all of them. Be that as it may, it is clear at any rate that their value as satisfaction is not dependent on the scale of the suffering but on the greatness of the love and obedience with which those sufferings are undergone.

As St Thomas explains, "someone effectively atones for an offence when he offers to the one who has been offended something which he accepts as matching or outweighing the former offence. By suffering in a loving and obedient spirit, Christ offered more to God than was demanded in recompense

---

108. St Thomas insists that Christ's self-surrender is an initiative of the Father's, who not only ordained our Lord's Passion as the route to bring about the salvation of mankind, but also inspired Christ to desire to die for us by imbuing him with a charity which led him freely to offer himself for our salvation: cf. *STh* III, q.47, a.3.

for all the sins of mankind, because first, the love which led him to suffer was a great love; secondly, the life he laid down in atonement was of great dignity, since it was the life of the God-man; and thirdly, his suffering was all-embracing and his pain so great."[109]

This kind of reparation is usually called "vicarious reparation", that is, satisfaction made on our behalf, reparation for the sins of others.[110] In a sense what this expression means is quite simple: Christ was absolutely innocent and therefore he did not offer his life in reparation for his own sins; he gave up his life as an expiation for the sins of others. This is what he means when he says that his blood is poured out for the forgiveness of sins (cf. Mt 26:28). This *vicarious* satisfaction should not be confused with *penal substitution*: our sin is not imputed to Christ, nor is he *punished* as if he were the guilty one; our Lord wipes out our disobedience by his obedience, our lack of love by his love. He does not take our place; but he takes us on himself (he unites himself in a certain way to every human being); he does not make satisfaction *instead of us*, but *as our Head*.

So, the Redemption is carried out by someone who not only is not alien to men but by one who has a special link with every man and woman. Christ is not only perfect man; he is also the new Adam. As St Paul teaches, by one man sin entered the world and with sin death. But where sin abounded, grace abounded all the more, in such a way that by the righteousness of Jesus Christ all might be given righteousness, for as by one man's disobedience all were made sinners, so too by the obedience of one man all will be justified (cf. Rom 5).[111]

When studying the Redemption, we must remember that Christ is Head

---

109. St Thomas Aquinas, *STh* III, q.48, a.2. Cf. R. Cessario, *Christian satisfaction in Aquinas. Towards a personalist understanding* (Washington 1980).

110. Although the expression "vicarious satisfaction" is relatively recent (it may come from M. Dobmayer, +1805), the *idea* goes right back to the Old Testament messianic prophecies, esp. that of Isaiah 53: cf. J. Galot, *La Rédemption mystère de'Alliance*, op. cit., 249. The New Testament contains many texts which show that Christ suffered for the sins of others, being himself completely innocent (cf. e.g., Mt 26:28; Mk 14:24; Lk 22:20; Gal 3:13; 2 Cor 5:21).

111. All the many different aspects of the Redemption need to be viewed in the light of the solidarity of the human race, especially its solidarity with Christ as the new Adam. All aspects of the Redemption "should be presented, yet they can be presented only one after another; moreover, all of them are incomplete, and it is because they have been isolated, one being exaggerated to the detriment of the other, that contradictory systems have been imagined, all insufficient in their narrowness and, above all, false by their exclusiveness [. . .]. Thus, whichever road is taken, unless indeed we halt on the way, we always end by coming to the principle of solidarity. This illuminating principle was not only perceived but clearly formulated by the Fathers of the Church. All of them say in about the same words that Jesus Christ had to become what we are, in order to make us become what he is; that he became incarnate in order that the deliverance should be accomplished by a man, as the fall had been accomplished by a man; that Christ, as redeemer, comprises and summarizes all humanity": F. Prat, *Theology of St Paul*, II, op. cit., 200-1.

of the human race, united with every human being.[112] His solidarity with all men (a mystery clearly stated in the New Testament: cf., e.g., Rom 5:12ff; Col 1:13-20;[113] and one whose depth is sensed in the mystery of the Incarnation itself) is seen most clearly in the light of the fact that Christ is the Head: "The subsistence in Christ of the divine Person of the Son which both surpasses and, at the same time, embraces all human beings, makes his redeeming sacrifice 'for all' possible."[114] Christ's solidarity with men and his position as their Head is, then, a consequence of the Incarnation of the Word—of the eternal Word in whom the Father "speaks" all created things (creation *through* and *in* the Word, according to John 1:3 and Colossians 1:16-17),[115] and who by becoming man *embraces* all men in full sight of the Father.

The Incarnation implies not only that Christ is true man but that he takes upon himself the weight of history. This happens to every human being when he or she is born: from birth onwards a person is joined by mysterious links to all those who have gone before, to one's people, to the entire human race. The solidarity that exists among men acquires deeper levels when viewed through theology: original sin and the communion of the saints are truths which show this very clearly. Christ's solidarity with mankind is located on an even higher level, a unique one: he is the new Adam, linked as Head to the human race even more closely that the first Adam was: "Adam, the first man, was a type of him who was to come, Christ the Lord [. . .]. Human nature, by the very fact that it was assumed, not absorbed, in him, has been raised in us to a dignity beyond compare. For by his incarnation, he, the Son of God, has in a certain way united himself with every man and woman."[116]

By linking himself mysteriously to every human being, He who did not know sin has been made sin (cf. 2 Cor 5:21); he lovingly took our history on himself to the point that, without having sinned, sin affected him; our sins were, in some way, sins of the holy and spotless Lamb through our union with him, and the satisfaction he made was our satisfaction. It is in the Heart of Christ that God reconciles the world to himself (cf. Col 1:20). Truly man, loving the Father with infinite charity, head of the human race, feeling all the sins of his members as his own, Jesus burns with a desire to make reparation,

---

112. Christ's being head of mankind should not be confused with his being head of the mystical Body; the former is the *presupposition* of Redemption by way of satisfaction; the latter is the *result* of the former in those men and women who personally accept the fruit of the (already brought down) Redemption.

113. Cf. St Thomas Aquinas, *STh* III, q.8, a.3. On the different way this solidarity is later explained (as substitution, representation, etc.). Cf. G. Oggioni, "Il misterio della Redenzione", in various authors, *Problemi e orientamenti di Teologia Dommatica* II, op. cit., 308-28.

114. John Paul II, *Address*, 26 October 1988, no. 5: *Insegnamenti*, XI, 3 (1988), 1332.

115. The Father, St Thomas says, *dicendo se (per Verbum), dicit omnem creaturam*: speaking himself (through the Word), speaks all creatures (*De Veritate*, q.4, a.5, in c.).

116. Second Vatican Council, Const. *Gaudium et spes*, no. 22.

to atone, to wipe out our disobedience with his obedience. And so Christ's love and adoration to the Father find their expression in satisfaction, reparation, sacrifice.

Our Lord lovingly takes upon himself the consequences which follow from his preaching the kingdom of God to a wicked and adulterous generation (cf. Mt 12:39). He will suffer extreme persecution *propter justitiam* (on account of justice or righteousness); and, faithful witness to the Father, he will consummate his life in sacrifice. "Christ was given grace", St Thomas Aquinas says, "not only as an individual but insofar as he is head of the Church, so that grace might pour out from him upon his members. Thus the deeds of Christ are to himself and his members as the deeds of another man, in the state of grace, are to himself. Now it is clear that if anyone in the state of grace suffers for justice's sake, he by that very fact merits salvation for himself, for it is written, 'Blessed are those who suffer persecution for justice's sake' (Mt 5:10). Therefore Christ by his passion merited salvation not only for himself, but for all who are his members."[117]

(v) *Adequate and superabundant satisfaction*   The satisfaction offered by Christ to the Father is a vicarious satisfaction by virtue of his being head of the human race. It is then a vicariousness which only Christ can deliver, because only he is head of mankind. This satisfaction is both *adequate* and *superabundant*.

An *adequate* satisfaction is one which proportionally compensates for the offence committed; whereas satisfaction is *inadequate* when it is not itself proportionate compensation but suffices simply because of the kindness of the offended person, who accepts it as compensation. To put it in classical language, adequate satisfaction is satisfaction which objectively makes reparation for the full weight of the offence committed.

In considering the satisfaction offered by Christ, we also need to look at what it is being offered for—the sin of mankind. However much one wants to avoid "legalism", it is not possible to discuss the Redemption without taking into account that sin is an offence against God and disrupts the order of creation desired by God. The texts of Sacred Scripture which speak of sin as an offence against God are numerous and clear. Besides, to say that God is not gravely offended by our sins amounts to denying not only God's justice but also his love.[118]

It is worth emphasizing that in speaking like this we are using analogous

---

117. St Thomas Aquinas, *STh* III, q.48, a.1, in c.
118. The general judgment as described by our Lord is a good proof of this: "Depart from me you cursed, into the eternal fire prepared for the devil and his angels; for I was hungry and you gave me no food" (Mt 25:41). Were God not offended by the injury done to man, it would be because he does not love man. And, also, we can offend God, among other reasons, because he loves us with infinite love. If his love brings him to desire our friendship, not to accept his friendship is an objective offence against him.

language, given that in God (who is love: 1 John 4:8) justice and holiness are identical and both grow out of one and the same love. But to use analogy is not being equivocal. Mysteriously and really, sin is an offence against God. This offence, in a sense, is infinite, given the infinite nature of the Love which is rejected, of the Holiness which is opposed. So, when speaking of satisfaction for sin, one may say that only a satisfaction of infinite value can *adequately* make up for what sin, objectively, means in terms of offence against God.

Whatever about the exaggerations and distortions it may have given rise to, St Anselm of Canterbury's approach had the merit of linking the satisfaction offered by Christ to the gravity of the offence done to God by men. The infinite gravity of the sin demanded infinite satisfaction.[119] Only the Man-God could offer that satisfaction, because only the acts of a Man-God have infinite value. St Thomas smoothed the edges of St Anselm's theory by retaining its basic intuition but softening its "legal" aspects, highlighting the moral aspect of sin insofar as it affects the interpersonal relationships between man and God, and stressing what St Anselm failed to stress—the sovereign freedom of God when it came to choosing the route to take to save man. The satisfaction made by Christ is thereby shown to be very fitting for man's salvation, but not necessary.[120] It is necessary only on the *hypothesis* that an *adequate* reparation for sin was called for, that is, *ex toto rigore justitiae* (in accordance with strictest justice). On this hypothesis (and only on it) one can say that, to save mankind it was *necessary* that Christ should make satisfaction. Only that kind of satisfaction is *adequate* to the gravity of the sin. But the Incarnation was not necessary for salvation (God could have saved men in all kinds of other ways), nor was Christ's death necessary for a perfect satisfaction, as St Anselm seems to argue.[121]

The satisfaction made by Christ was not only *adequate* but *superabundant*. What this means is that Christ offered the Father much more than was necessary to make adequate satisfaction for our sins. In fact, any act of love

---

119. Cf. St Anselm, *Cur Deus homo?*, 2, 6 (PL 158, 404). Some authors think that, given that sin is something done by man, one cannot exclude the possibility that man himself could make *adequate* satisfaction, for although sin is in some way infinite in view of the infinite holiness of the offended God, still from man's point of view it is something finite, not something infinite (cf. J. Rivière, "Redemption", art. cit., 1979). But this argument does not seem valid, because sin is not only an offence against God (and in this sense does have a certain infinity), but it is also the state of enmity towards God into which man falls due to sin. This is a state which no one can get out off except through supernatural grace. In other words, to be able to make satisfaction, man would need to be in the grace of God first, that is, liberated from sin (cf. J.H. Nicolas, *Synthèse dogmatique*, op. cit., 508-12). Besides, it is difficult to see how a mere man (even if he had the grace of salvation) could *adequately* make satisfaction for all men. As St Basil writes, "for the Redemption do not seek a brother but someone who is above you by nature; seek not an ordinary man but the Man God Jesus Christ; only he can render God satisfaction for us": St Basil the Great, *In Psalm. hom.*, 48, 4: PG 29, 440.

120. Cf. St Thomas Aquinas, *STh* III, q.46, aa. 1-3.

121. Cf. St Anselm, *Cur Deus homo?*, 2, 10-11 (PL 158, 408-12).

and obedience on Christ's part was sufficient to make such satisfaction, because the love of his human will was the maximum possible, and in some way had infinite value insofar as it was a human action of a divine Person. So, "the innocent Victim, shed not just one drop of his blood—which on account of the union with the Word would have sufficed for the redemption of the entire human race—but poured it out in abundance."[122]

This truth has been a frequent theme of Christian preaching in all ages. For example, St Cyril of Jerusalem said in AD 348: "The injustice of sinners was not as great as the Justice of Him who died for us. No matter how many sins we had, the Justice of Him who gave his life for us would exceed them."[123] The satisfaction Christ made was not only *superabundant* in this regard; it was also superabundant as far as its effects went: "where sin increased, grace abounded all the more" (Rom 5:20), which is the same as saying that Christ restored to man a state of grace higher than that which Adam had enjoyed before the fall.

(vi) *An infinite satisfaction*   To say that the satisfaction made by Christ is *adequate* and even *superabundant* to the gravity of the sin, implies that the work Jesus did had an infinite value. This raises a further question: what do we mean by "infinite value?"

Durandus, Scotus, Biel and other theologians close to Nominalism think that the satisfaction made by Christ is adequate, superabundant and of infinite value; but, as they understand it, this infinity derives not from its intrinsic value, but from outside, that is, from the value the Father gives it, from God's gracious acceptance of it.[124] According to this line of thinking, Christ's works would only have a limited value, and if his death had infinite value as satisfaction it was because God chose to take it as such. This position is consistent with what they have to say about the finite character of sin as offence against God.

On the other hand, St Thomas, St Bonaventure and many theologians think that Christ's works have an infinite value in themselves. Sin, St Thomas writes, "has a certain infinity because of the infinite majesty of God" and consequently, "for perfect satisfaction it is necessary that the work (of satisfaction) performed should have an infinite effectiveness, such as, for example, that of the Man-God."[125]

---

122. Clement VI, Bull, *Unigenitus Dei Filius*, 27 January 1343 (DS 1025).
123. St Cyril of Jerusalem, *Catecheses*, 13, 33 (PG 33, 812).
124. Cf. Durandus, *In III Sent.*, dist. 20, q.2; Duns Scotus, *In III Sent.*, dist. 19, q. un., n. 7; G. Biel, *In III Sent.*, dist. 19, q. un. Cf. R. Garrigou-Lagrange, *Christ the Saviour*, op. cit., 577-82.
125. St Thomas Aquinas, *STh* III, q.1, a.2, ad 2. On man's being saved through his Only-begotten's satisfaction, "we are shown, on the one hand, the severity of God, who did not wish to pardon sin without due satisfaction [. . .] and, on the other hand, his goodness, in giving man someone to make satisfaction for him, since man himself could

The infinite value of Christ's works as satisfaction derives from the hypostatic union, because actions are attributed to the person, in Christ's case the Word himself, who suffers in his Humanity.[126] It is true that his human actions, considered in themselves, like the good actions of all men have a finite dimension, and in this sense some are of more value that others; objectively, Christ's suffering on the cross has more value than his tears as a child. However, considered in the context of the Person who does them, they are actions of the Word, who is of infinite dignity. Therefore, it seems better to say that the satisfaction made by Christ has *an intrinsically* infinite value.

b) Christ's merit The concept of merit is completely bound up with the notions of sacrifice, expiation and satisfaction. It is a concept used to describe something which affects the deepest dimension of the personal sphere of the Redeemer in his work of salvation—the moral value of his actions. By his obedience unto death Jesus not only makes satisfaction for the human race but merits for himself and for mankind the blessings of God, that is, becomes deserving, in God's eyes, of his own glorification and of forgiveness for the sins of mankind.

Just as when speaking of satisfaction (when dealing with Christ's merit and its connexion with our redemption), we must try to avoid "legalism"; this means being careful about correct use of analogy. The concept of merit comes within the sphere of justice in that justice is "giving to each his own", giving each person what he or she deserves. And therefore one must not forget that if man can "merit" something in God's eyes, it is because prior to that he received as a gift the wherewithal to merit. From this perspective, meriting itself is a gift. The same happens in the case of Jesus Christ; if he can merit, it is because he first received the greatest of all possible gifts—the grace of union, that is, the gift of the hypostatic union.[127]

The merit aspect of human actions can be described as the moral value

not render sufficient satisfaction no matter how great sufferings he underwent" (ibid., q.47, a.3, ad 1). Cf. St Bonaventure, *III Sent.*, dist. 20, a.1, q.3-5.

126. This is the reason Clement VI gives when dealing with the value *qua* satisfaction of the blood shed by Christ (Clement VI, Bull, *Unigenitus Dei Filius*, op. cit.: DS 1025).

127. Even within this setting (that of the link between our actions and divine justice), theologians speak about *condign merit* and *congruous merit*. Condign merit, that is, perfect merit, obtains when there is equality between the quality of the action done and the reward it will receive, in such a way that the reward is due in strict justice; *congruous merit* applies when the reward is not due to the quality of the action done, but to the generosity of the one rewarding, that is to say, the reward is in keeping with the work done but the latter is not entitled to it in strict justice, only in accord with that generosity: cf. J. Rivière, "Sur l'origine des formules ecclésiastiques *de condigno* et *de congruo*", BLE 28 (1927) 75-83. When using this language, however, one should always remember that everything man has he has been given by God and therefore even the very fact of "meriting" is itself a grace from God, who generously chooses to "oblige himself" to reward human actions. However, given that God has set things up in this generous way, one can speak of genuine merit on man's part.

inherent in an action done in honour of someone; the action is worthy of being recognized, accepted and rewarded by the one in whose honour it is done.[128] This implies that a coherent moral order exists by virtue of which actions are worthy of reward or punishment and, in this sense, there exists an indissoluble connexion between merit and the justice of God. Performing good actions "demands" a reward, given the wisdom and justice of God.

To say, then, that Christ merits our salvation through his passion and death is equivalent to saying that these actions of his have been the true cause of our redemption because of their moral value in God's eyes. No other meaning can be attached to such expressions as Christ has "bought" us at the "cost" of his blood (cf. 1 Pet 1:18-21; 2 Cor 6:20; 7:23; Gal 4:5). Hence it can be said that his *meritum* lies in his true work of mediation in all its breadth and height and depth.[129] Christ's merit has to do with the personal relationship between Jesus and the Father—with that aspect of it whereby Jesus becomes deserving of reward in his Father's eyes due to the "honour" he does him by his love and obedience. This merit is to be found in Christ as something real and as something that makes a claim on divine wisdom and justice. To say that Christ merits implies, then, confirmation of his moral activity, that is to say, his behaving with genuine human freedom in the state of *viator*; it implies also saying that these moral actions of Christ really cause our salvation, because the quality of his obedience more than makes up for our disobedience, "requiring" from the Father our reconciliation with him; it also implies (given the hypostatic union) that Christ's merits are infinite because of the Person who is performing these moral actions.[130]

It is a matter of faith that Jesus Christ, by his passion and death, merited our salvation in God's eyes: he is the *meritorious cause* of our justification.[131] Although the word "merit" does not appear in Sacred Scripture applied to the manner in which Christ redeems us, its content is often implied. This is the case, for example, with these passages in which it is said that Christ obtained our salvation through his sacrifice, through his blood (cf., e.g., Eph 5:2; Heb 10:5-10; Rev 5:9, etc.). The very notion of redemption through the payment of a ransom implies the idea of merit, since the person who pays a fair price deserves to get what he pays for.

The New Testament does say that Jesus Christ merited his own glorification. In Philippians 2:8-9, Christ's exaltation is depicted as a reward for his earlier humiliation: "he humbled himself and became obedient unto death,

128. Cf. M. González Gil, *Cristo, el misterio de Dios*, II, op. cit., 251.
129. J. Auer, *Curso de Teología Dogmática*, IV/2, *Jesucristo, Salvador del mundo*, op. cit., 233.
130. Cf. J. Gallot, *Gesù liberatore*, op. cit., 235. On Christ's merit, cf. also R. Garrigou-Lagrange, *Our Saviour and his Love for Us* (St Louis, 1951), op. cit., 248-59.
131. Cf. Council of Trent, Session VI, Decr. *De justificatione* (DS 1529). Cf. also J. Rivière, "La doctrine de la Rédemption au Concile de Trente", BLE 26 (1925) 260-78.

even death on a cross. *Therefore* God has highly exalted him and bestowed on him the name which is above every name." This was already foretold by Isaiah: "Therefore I will divide him a portion with the great, and he shall divide the spoil with the strong; because he poured out his soul to death, and was numbered with the transgressors" (Is 53:12). And in Hebrews it is said that "we see Jesus [. . .] crowned with glory and honour because of the suffering of death" (Heb 2:9; cf. also Jn 17:4-5; Lk 24:26; Rev 5:12). The Fathers of the Church, when referring to Christ's merits, initially spoke mainly of the merit which Jesus earned for himself; only from St Gregory the Great onwards was the idea of merit also widely applied to our salvation.[132]

It is worth remembering that, in the work of redemption, merit cannot be separated from satisfaction. Christ merits the forgiveness of our sins because he renders satisfaction for them to the Father by his love and obedience; that is, because his love as manifested by his self-giving unto death (a self-giving made not only in an individual, personal, capacity but also as head of mankind) is deserving of acceptance by God.

Therefore, just as it was not only the Cross which had value as satisfaction but all Christ's human actions, so too all his actions, which are closely connected to the mystery of the Cross, had a parallel meritorious value for our salvation.[133] This meriting of our salvation is a true merit in the strict sense, *de condigno*. It must be borne in mind that only Christ could do this. *Condign merit* refers to personal merit, that is, merit for oneself; for others, we can only merit *de congruo*, that is, by having recourse to the absolute liberality of God, by entreating him or offering him actions backed by prayer. Christ, on the other hand, merited our salvation in strict justice, through his being the Head of mankind and his consequent solidarity with all men; he merited our salvation *de condigno*, as if he were meriting for himself.

The Scotists say (compare their ideas about satisfaction) that Christ's merits have finite value; and only through divine acceptance could they be said to have infinite extrinsic value. In fact, for Scotus, even the meritorious nature of any good act is extrinsic: a good action is meritorious only if God accepts it as such. Most theologians, on the contrary, defend the infinite intrinsic value of Christ's merits on the same grounds as they defended the infinite value of the satisfaction he offered the Father—by appealing to the *principium quod* of

132. Cf. C. Chopin, *El Verbo Encarnado y Redentor*, op. cit., 233f. This statement, however, can be found (though not as frequently as after Gregory the Great) in some earlier Fathers (cf. e.g., St Athanasius, *Orat. III adv. arianos* 33 (PG 26, 396).

133. The fact that Jesus had merited salvation from the very first moment of his life does not make the subsequent merits useless because "there is nothing to prevent something belonging to a person on several counts. According to this, the immortal glory which Christ merited at the first instant of his conception he could also merit by further actions and sufferings; not so that it would be more due to him but that it should be due for various reasons": St Thomas Aquinas, *STh* III, q.34, a.3, ad 3.

those actions, that is, the Word himself. "The merit of Christ," St Thomas suggests, "was not infinite in regard to the intensity of the act, because he loved and knew in a finite way; but it did possess a certain infinity because of the Person whose dignity was infinite."[134]

Christ's merit has the same characteristics as the satisfaction he made (abundant, infinite, etc.), and for the same reasons. However, we are dealing with different aspects of the same thing: the merit looks more to things to do with Christ himself (it is the reward his good work deserves), whereas the satisfaction has to do with reparation for the offence offered.

Meriting is something proper to the state of wayfarer. Therefore, it is said of Christ that he merited through all the actions he did in the course of his life on earth, but that his glorification was not meritorious, even though he merited it. While on earth, Christ merited for himself everything which his exaltation gave him and which he did not yet have; for us he merited superabundantly all the good things of grace and glory (cf. Rom 5:20-21; Eph 1:3; 2:5-10).[135] These include not just the grace of justification, which is infused into us "by Christ's meriting",[136] but even all the actual graces which prepare man for justification.[137] Jesus Christ also merits for us liberation "from the power of the devil".[138]

In a word, no one "can be just except him to whom the merits of the passion of our Lord Jesus Christ are communicated."[139] Christ has merited for us sanctifying grace, the actual graces which predispose us to justification, and eternal life itself. He is the only Mediator, and the mediator of all God's gifts to men.

c) **Christ, the efficient cause of our salvation**   Jesus Christ merited for us supernatural grace and definitive salvation in heaven, making satisfaction to God for our sins. His salvific work does not end there: Jesus not only merited for us the grace whereby he reconcilies us with God and frees us from sin, but he truly causes it in us; this causality belongs to a sphere distinct from that of merit.

Thus, whereas meritorious causality has to do with the moral sphere,

---

134. St Thomas Aquinas, *De Veritate*, q.29, a.3, ad 4; cf. also *In III Sent.*, d.13, q.1, a.2, sol. 2, ad 4; *STh* III, q.19, aa. 3-4.
135. Cf. St Thomas Aquinas, *STh* III, q.56, a.1, ad 3; cf. also P. Glorieux, "Le mérite du Christ selon S. Thomas", RSR 10 (1930), 622-49; H. Boüessé, "Causalité efficiente et causalité méritoire de l'humanité du Christ", RT 44 (1938), 256-98; J. Rivière, "Le mérite de Christ d'aprés le magistère de l'Eglise", RSR 21 (1947), 53-68; 22 (1948), 213-39; W.D. Lynn, *Christ's redemptive merit. The merit of its causality according to St Thomas* (Rome, 1962); B. Catao, *Salut et Rédemption chez S. Thomas d'Aquin* (Paris, 1965).
136. Council of Trent, Decr. *De justificatione*, chap. 16 (DS 1547).
137. Sixteenth Council of Carthage, can. 3 (DS 225)
138. Council of Florence, Bull *Cantate Domino* 4 February 1442 (DS 1347).
139. Council of Trent, Decr. *De justificatione*, chap. 7 (DS 1530).

efficient causality concerns the sphere of "physical" causality. Christ's infinite charity and obedience make him worthy to obtain from the Father our reconciliation, that is, Christ merits the Father's granting us forgiveness of sins and adoptive filiation. This means that we are justified in view of the merits of Christ. This justification, in turn, is something real: it is described as a re-birth, which makes us a new creature in Christ. This re-birth is caused in us in a real way by Christ, who has the power to produce supernatural effects. If Christ's meritorious causality is linked to his being a wayfarer, as we said in the previous page, his efficient cuasality stems from his power as Man-God. Strictly speaking, Christ now that he has risen no longer merits our salvation (though he continues in heaven to intercede for us: cf. Heb 7:25) but he does continue to cause our salvation by way of efficient causality.

The principal efficient cause of the grace of salvation can only be God (only he can change man into a child of his), but God causes this grace in us through the Humanity of Jesus. The Humanity of the Son of God is the *instrument* that his Godhead chose to use to bring about (not just to merit) all graces that men receive.[140] So, this Humanity of Jesus is truly the efficient cause of our salvation, just as it was "the instrument of our salvation".[141] This teaching is clearly expressed by many Fathers of the Church, including St Athanasius, St Gregory of Nyssa, St Cyril of Alexandria, St Epiphanius, St John Damascene; it is developed, especially, by St Thomas, who stresses very clearly that not only has salvation been won for us by Christ but that it is in union with him and with the mysteries of his life, death and glorification that this salvation is brought about, in fact, in every one of us.[142]

The effectiveness of Christ's humanity as regards our salvation is, certainly, the actual effective influence of Christ-in-glory on us, but it is also the actual effectiveness of the mysteries of his earthly life. The life, death and glorification of Christ are not just events of the past; they possess a transcendental (meta-historical) reality, because they pertain to the eternal Person of the Son of God. That does not mean, of course, that Jesus Christ is, even today, in some way, a child, or that he is dying on the cross, etc.; rather, the events of the past are so effective (not only in terms of satisfaction or merit) that they reach out and impact on every moment of history. As St Thomas explains,

140. Cf. St Thomas Aquinas, *STh* III, q.48, a.6.
141. Cf. Second Vatican Council, Const. *Sacrosanctum Concilium*, 5.
142. When it is said that by causing our salvation Jesus' humanity is an "instrument" of his divinity, it should not be thought of as a separate instrument (the way the brush is separate from the painter) but as a joined instrument, because it is the Person of the Word who is acting through his human nature. In that sense it is called an "instrumental cause", in the same kind of way as we say that we love with our heart or work with our hands. When using this expression one needs also to exclude from its meaning the idea that Jesus' human nature was only an instrument, a *means* to an end, as it were. As we have more than once stressed, Jesus is not a "means" of bringing about our salvation; he *is* salvation; our salvation lies in him—in becoming one with him, becoming like him.

"the things which Christ in his humanity accomplished or suffered were saving acts for us through the power of his divinity. [. . .] This power is extended by being present in all times and places, and this virtual contact is sufficient to explain this effectiveness."[143]

Thus, for example, when a person is baptized, Christ not only gives that person the grace He already merited twenty centuries ago, but also in a mysterious though real way Christ unites him or her to his life, death and resurrection: "Do you not know that all of us who have been baptized into Christ Jesus were baptized into his death? We were buried therefore with him by baptism into death, so that as Christ was raised from the dead by the glory of the Father, we too might walk in newness of life" (Rom 6:3-4). And when the Sacrifice of the Eucharist is celebrated, a true, sacramental, renewal of the Sacrifice of the Cross takes place.[144]

All the mysteries of the life, death and glorification of Christ, even though they happened successively in time past, constitute a single, unique cause of our salvation: all of them, together and at the one time, work our salvation, when in the Church (particularly in the sacraments) the fruit of the Redemption is applied to each person. This does not prevent particular mysteries of Christ's life from having a special connexion (by way of exemplary cause) to particular aspects of salvation. For example, the Resurrection of our Lord is, above all, the model (the exemplary cause) of our future resurrection at the end of time: "Christ has been raised from the dead, the first fruits of those who have fallen asleep. For as by a man came death, by a man has come also the resurrection of the dead. For as in Adam all die, so also in Christ shall all be made alive" (1 Cor 15:20-22).

Regarding the Ascension (the glorification of Christ), St Paul says: "When he ascended on high he led a host of captives, and he gave gifts to men. . . . He who descended is he who also ascended far above all the heavens, that he might fill all things" (Eph 4:8, 10). It is not only as an individual man that he is glorified; he is also gloroified as our head, and he in turn will glorify us by virtue of being our head.[144a]

3. THE REDEMPTION, A MYSTERY OF GOD'S LOVE AND SUFFERING

In his conversation with Nicodemus, Jesus pointed to the underlying reason why God, in his plan of salvation (in the "economy of salvation"), chose the death of the Son to be the cause of our salvation: "God so loved the world that he gave his only Son, that whoever believes in him should not perish but

---

143. St Thomas Aquinas, *STh* III, q.56, a.1, ad 3; cf. q.52, a.8; q.48, a.6, ad 2.
144. Cf. e.g., Second Vatican Council, Const. *Lumen gentium*, 28 which, in turn, refers to the Council of Trent (cf. DS 1739f).
144a. Cf. Roman Missal, *Solemnity of the Ascension*, collect.

have eternal life" (Jn 3:16). The Redemption is a product of love, and it is a divine initiative; it is also the product of suffering and death: God experiences pain and death in the Humanity of the Word. Just as Mary is said to be the Mother of God, because it is God himself who is conceived by her in his Humanity, so it can be said categorically that God dies on the Cross, because he experiences death in his Humanity.

a) **Redemptive love**   The entire mystery of the Incarnation and Redemption (the mystery of Christ) constitutes the supreme revelation of God's love—the love of the Father for the Son; the love of God for the world, his fidelity to his love for man; the love of Jesus for the Father, whom he lovingly obeys unto death; the love of Jesus for men, which he compares to the love of the Father for the Son: "As the Father has loved me, so have I loved you" (Jn 15:9); love which leads him to give his life, because "greater love has no man than this, that a man lay down his life for his friends" (Jn 15:13); the Holy Spirit, Love in Person, brings the work of our salvation to full completion.

As Pius XII writes, "the mystery of divine Redemption is in the first place and of its very nature a mystery of love: the dutiful love of Christ for his heavenly Father, to whom the loving and obedient sacrifice of the Cross rendered abundant, indeed infinite satisfaction for the sins of the human race [. . .]. It is the mystery too, of the merciful love of the august Trinity and of the divine Redeemer, for all men."[145]

It is true that divine justice also shines out in the Redemption, because God chose that adequate satisfaction should be made to him for sin. But what shines out above all is his merciful love, because it was God himself who, in the Humanity of the Son established as Head of mankind, has made that satisfaction. Here is revealed in a special way the mystery of God's infinite love, in which justice and mercy conjoin: "the Cross of Christ, on which the Son, consubstantial with the Father, renders full justice to God, is also a radical revelation of mercy, or rather of the love that goes against what constitutes the very root of evil in the history of man—against sin and death."[146]

b) **God's suffering in Christ**   In the work of Redemption, Christ's love (the human love of Jesus, which reveals God's infinite love) was manifested in a particularly eloquent way in suffering. This was true human suffering. The

---

145. Pius XII, Enc. *Haurietis aquas*, op. cit.: AAS 48 (1956), 321f. On the central role of love in the Redemption, cf. M. Richard, "La Rédemption, mystère d'amour", RSR 13 (1923), 193-217, 397-418.
146. John Paul II, Enc. *Dives in misercordia*, op. cit., no. 8. Cf. S. di Giorgi, "Il Mistero Pasquale, rivelazione del Mistero del Padre", in various authors, *Dives in misercordia. Commento all'Enciclica di Giovanni Paolo II*, op. cit., 94-5. On divine justice as love which justifies and saves, cf. J. Galot, *La Rédemption, mystère d'Alliance*, op. cit., 81-107.

Humanity of Christ was truly capable of suffering and truly subject to pain. We can see this clearly from the Gospels, which show Jesus experiencing hunger, thirst, fatigue (cf., e.g., Mt 4:2; Lk 4:7; Jn 4:6-8), having psychological emotions of joy and sorrow (cf., e.g., Mk 3:5; 9:19; Lk 19:41; Jn 11:33-38) etc., ending up with the greatest suffering of all, his death on the Cross.

Despite this evidence, the Docetists and some Monophysites refused to accept that Christ experienced pain or had any capacity to feel anything (any passibility). The underlying reason for the Docetists' stance (their rejection of the idea that Christ had a real body—they thought he only seemed to have one—and therefore could not feel pain) was because they thought both things (pain, a real body) unworthy of God.[147] Some Monophysites held the same sort of view; as they saw it the human was absorbed by the divine in the hypostatic union: and logically the capacity to suffer which is a feature of human nature was absorbed, overpowered, by the impassibility proper to the divine nature.[148]

Although for reasons contrary to those of the Monophysites, Nestorius' approach arrives at a similar conclusion: by conceiving the hypostatic union as a *moral* union, although he admits that the Humanity of Jesus does suffer, he does not realize that it is the Word himself who is suffering in this humanity. That is why the anathemata of St Cyril put such emphasis on the fact that the Word did suffer in the flesh.[149]

Some Fathers and some medieval theologians were of the opinion that the hypostatic union necessarily made the Humanity of the Lord impassible. They thought that so close a union as a union in unity of person must give the human nature (as far as possible) the attributes of the Person of the Word. This they see as taking place at the glorification of Christ—which led them to think that impassibility was natural to Christ, so a miracle was needed to make him capable of suffering;[150] therefore, given that they accepted that Jesus' sufferings *were* real, they were forced to conclude that his whole life on earth was one continuous miracle.

It seems much more logical to accept that the capacity to suffer was connatural to Christ, that is, that the Word assumed a human nature, intrinsically passible, which in the natural way suffered the actions of those things which make a normal human being suffer. In other words, in order to

147. As we have seen earlier, the Fathers of the Church reacted vigorously against any such denial of the reality of the Incarnation. Cf. e.g., S. Ignatius of Antioch, *Ad Polycarpum*, 3, 2 (PG 5, 721); St Justin, *First Apology*, 52 (PG 6, 404); *Second Apology*, 13 (PG 6, 465); Tertullian, *Adv. Praxeam*, 27 (PL 2, 190; *Adv. Marcionem*, 3, 8, PL 2, 331).

148. Cf. M. Jugie, "Monophysisme", DTC X, esp. 2225-6.

149. "If anyone should fail to confess that the Word of God suffered in the flesh and was crucified in the flesh and tasted death in the flesh [. . .], let him be anathema": *Anathem.* 12: DS 263.

150. Cf. Clement of Alexandria, *Stromata*, VI, 9, 71: 2 PG 9, 292.

suffer the fatigue of a journey, Jesus did not have to work a miracle; he simply had to walk for a long stretch; similarly, to be killed by the torments of the Passion, no miracle was called for; he had simply to undergo those torments.[151] As the Council of Florence says, Christ "was capable of suffering because of the condition of the nature that he had assumed".[152]

As we have said, the majority of theologians think that Christ enjoyed the "science of vision" while on earth. This form of knowledge is also called the "beatific vision", because it causes supreme happiness. That is what happens in heaven: intuitive, fact-to-face sight of God in inevitably followed by love, and supreme happiness is indissolubly linked to love. Science of vision in Christ must, then, be understood to co-exist with his capacity to suffer, since Sacred Scripture clearly shows that Christ was passible and that pain was connatural to him due to the flesh he assumed.

The existence of science of vision in Christ is supported by solid theological arguments.[153] And it is also clear that he experienced suffering. To explain this co-existence of pain and supreme happiness in Christ, theology usually offers a number of answers. The most general one is to say that his happiness lies, so to speak, "in the centre of his soul", whereas he feels pain in his faculties and potencies. This is the solution proposed by St Thomas and followed by the majority of theologians, and it means that the supreme happiness which comes with the beatific vision does not imbue all of Christ's human nature.[154]

This "non-impacting" of the glory of Christ's soul on all of his humanity is due, says St Thomas, to a special dispensation of divine providence.[155]

---

151. This does not mean that our Lord—the lord of life and death—did not have the power to reject those sufferings, but simply that they were co-natural to the nature he had taken on (cf. Jn 10:18; cf. also St Thomas Aquinas, *STh* III, q.47, a.1).

152. Council of Florence, Bull, *Cantate Domino*, op. cit. (DS 1337).

153. Cf. Chapter 4, section 3b(iii).

154. To the question whether in the Passion the whole soul of Christ enjoyed the beatific vision, St Thomas replies: "If 'whole soul' is taken in its essence, then Christ's whole soul rejoiced, inasmuch as the whole soul is the subject of the superior part of the soul which finds joy in the divinity [. . .]; if however 'whole soul' be understood as comprising the soul with all its faculties, then Christ's whole soul did not know bliss [. . .] because while on earth (*viator*), his glory did not spill over from the higher to the lower part, nor from his soul to his body. On the other hand, as the higher part of Christ's soul was not hindered in its proper function by the lower part, that higher part enjoyed perfect bliss all the while he was suffering": *STh* III, q.46, 1.8. The problem raised by St Thomas' solution lies in the fact that such a distinction between the higher and the lower part of the soul could seem more rhetorical than real, because sadness—which is a spiritual passion—forms part of the sufferings of the Passion. Saying that joy occurs in a different 'part' of the soul from that which suffers sadness is not something that is easily understood, especially when one takes into account the simplicity of the soul. However, St Thomas' solution should not be discarded too lightly because a soul can rejoice for one motive and suffer, at the same time, for another.

155. "From the natural relation which is between the soul and the body, glory flows into the body from the soul's glory. But this natural relation [*habitudo*] in Christ was subject to the will of his Godhead, and thereby it came to pass that the beatitude remained in his

It is worth pointing out that, in St Thomas' teaching, this "dispensation" is not miraculous, but is something connatural, resulting from the way divine Providence wanted the Incarnation to work.[156] Be that as it may, it is easy to see that in his approach to this mystery (of the co-existence of supreme suffering and supreme joy in the one subject) St Thomas tries to avoid the contradiction that would be involved if one were to say that the same subject experienced joy and pain at the same time and on the same point. His solution also makes it clear that Christ's body was not glorified until the Resurrection, which means that prior to then the glory of his soul did not fully impact on his entire body.

St Thomas' solution, however, does not satisfy everyone. Some, like Aureolus, say that Christ suffered only in the sensitive part of his soul; Melchor Cano and others said that Christ chose not to experience the joy which comes from the beatific vision.[157] Others prefer to sidestep the problem by speaking of Christ's science of vision and saying that "it is not like objectifying science but like subjective knowledge, like the intimate perception Jesus had of his divine filiation and his union with God."[158] The problem still remains: either this "subjective" perception is clear sight of God (and then it is necessarily something which gives joy) or else it is an experience in some way or other akin to mystical experience, in which case it has nothing to do with the beatific vision and therefore the problem they are trying to solve does not exist in the first place.

Besides, if human pain is already a mystery in some way, Christ's pain is a still greater one. This is so, as we have just seen, because of the unique and incomparable richness of his interior life. Thus, to say that Christ has the absolute fullness of grace involves saying that he enjoys the beatific vision, which is the height of grace; but it is categorically clear from Scripture that Christ did undergo suffering. The acceptance of both extremes implies, for theology, an attempt to plumb the deep mystery of Christ's soul, to try to discover how he could have had both joy and sorrow in the highest degree during his Passion.

There is another aspect of the mystery even harder for us to grasp, if we can say that. It is something which results from the hypostatic union: Christ's

---

soul, and was not shared by the body; hence the flesh suffered what belongs to a passible nature, as Damascene says: 'it was by consent of the divine will that the flesh was allowed to suffer and do what belonged to it' ": St Thomas Aquinas, *STh* III, q.14, a.1, ad 2.

156. Cf. J.H. Nicolas, *Synthèse dogmatique*, op. cit., 408f.

157. Cf. Capreolo, III d. 16, q. 1, a. 2. The refutation which the Salamancans make of this position is an easy one: the suffering of Christ was also a spiritual suffering, like the suffering for sins and sadness itself. Cano's position seems unacceptable too—though it does show the difficulty of the solution proposed by St Thomas—because it seems contradictory to see God face to face and yet not rejoice in this vision: cf. R. Garrigou-Lagrange, *Christ the Saviour*, op. cit., 552.

158. This is the view of M. González Gil, among others: cf. *Cristo, el misterio de Dios*, II, op. cit., 70.

suffering is God's suffering. Thus, "when the Humanity of Christ suffers, in body or in soul, it is the I of Christ that suffers, that is, the Person of the Word, not because pain affects the Godhead but because it is the Word which keeps that humanity in being; that Humanity subsists in the Word as in its own Person, and it is dependent on Him in its entire being and action. To think of Christ-Man as suffering like us, and the Word as knowing nothing of that suffering, is equivalent to eliminating all mystery from the passion of Christ and evacuating it of all its redemptive value."[159] This identifies the very core of the mystery of suffering in Christ: his pain is the Word's pain. True, the Word suffers *in* his humanity, or *with* his humanity, but the mystery cannot be solved by the easy expedient of understanding this in a Nestorian way (as if it were a matter of the suffering of two separate subjects more or less intimately connected); both terms of the mystery must be kept—that the Word suffers in Christ, that is, that the *subject* who suffers is God, and yet the Godhead is impassible. This incapacity of God to suffer which is mentioned in Revelation is a sign of God's infinite perfection, and should not be confused either with indifference or with *ataraxia* (stoical indifference or freedom from disturbance of mind).

When we speak about *the suffering of God in Christ*, we mean suffering in its plain, basic, human meaning. God chose to make *our sufferings* his sufferings, because "the man who suffers is the Only-begotten in person: 'God from God'."[160] Therefore, the mystery of God's suffering is, above all, the mystery of the Incarnation; it was the Incarnation that made it possible to us to see on Golgotha "God crucified",[161] for "the One who cannot suffer has suffered in the flesh, the One who cannot change has died."[162] In the light of this terrible fact that a God has suffered, meaning and value are given to human pain (even the suffering of the innocent), which God permits as a way for us to identify with Christ the Redeemer, a way of spiritual purification, and an opportunity for us too to show that we really do love.[163]

The expression "God's pain" or "God's suffering" has taken on a different meaning in the writings of some recent theologians. When they speak of God's suffering they are no longer referring to God's human suffering in Christ (that is, suffering within the framework of the mystery of the Incarnation of the Word); they are saying that there is a kind of suffering in God himself, in his inner being—viewing, therefore, the mystery of the cross as an intratrinitarian thing, of which Christ's suffering is only a reflection or an aspect.[164]

159. P. Parente, *Il mistero di Cristo* (Rome, 1958), 57f.
160. John Paul II, Apos. Letter, *Salvifici doloris*, op. cit., no. 17.
161. Tertullian, *Adv. Marcionem*, 2, 27 (PL 2, 345).
162. Hippolytus, *De sancto Paschate*, frag., 2 in GCS, *Hyppolitus Werke*, I, part II, 259.
163. Cf. John Paul II, Apos. Letter, *Salvifici doloris*, op. cit, 14-27; cf. also J.H. Nicolas, *L'amour de Dieu et la peine des hommes* (Paris, 1969).
164. A typical exponent of this approach (which has its roots in what Luther calls *theologia*

In one form or another, using the cross as a pretext, they depict the Godhead as a gigantic dialectic process of which human history is both the realization and the reflection. A good example of this is the philosophy of Hegel.[165] The various kenotic theologies of the nineteenth century are based on this. These see the *kenosis* of the Word in the act of becoming man as self-limitation on God's part; after the Resurrection, they say, the divine attribute of omnipresence gives ubiquity to Jesus' humanity.[166] In the last analysis, what this is an invalid application of the *communicatio idiomatum* (exchange of properties), deriving from a veiled Monophysitism. As Michel points out, these kenotic theories stem from difficulty in conceiving how two natures which are complete (yet each retaining its own properties without division or intermixing) can be joined in the unity of a single person. Hence the arguments they use and even the problems they raise are basically the same as those of Arius, Apollinaris and in general those of the Monophysites.[167]

The problem posed by this theory of God's suffering is, in a sense, not Christological but Trinitarian or, to put it more exactly, it is a Trinitarian problem caused by a mistaken Christological stance. Through wrongly applying the *communicatio idiomatum* (exchange of properties) in Christ, the holders of these views fail to accept the famous "*immutabiliter*" (unchangingly) of the Council of Chalcedon and all that follows from it, and they fall into a Monophysitism which collides head-on with divine omniperfection and immutability.[168] When these writers are speaking about God's suffering they are really saying that God is subject to change.[169] This kind of approach, whatever

---

crucis) is J. Moltmann, according to whom "one reaches a richer and deeper appreciation of the *trinitarian passion* of God" in the evangelical theology of the cross: J. Moltmann, "Ecumenismo bajo la cruz" in various authors, *Teología de la cruz* (Salamanca, 1979), 165. This "richer" understanding consists in thinking that "the Father sacrifices the Son of his eternal love in order to become the God and Father who sacrifices himself. The Son is given up to death and to hell in order to become the Lord of the living and the dead" (ibid., 177). And a little further on he says: "On the night of Golgotha, God experiences in himself pain, death, hell" (ibid., 177). It is, according to Moltmann, a matter of the cross being set in the very centre of the Trinity, in such a way that one can see it as the moment when the Trinity is constituted, because the Father is distinguished from the Son by the very fact of sacrificing him. Gherardini comments: "The fact is that Moltmann sets the cross in the very centre of God as that which, inside this trinitarian being, distinguishes and unites the divine Persons in their mutual relationships": *Theologia crucis. L'eredità di Lutero nell'evoluzione teologica della Riforma*, op. cit., 320.

165. On the Hegelian influence of these approaches and the aspects of them which are not acceptable, cf. ITC, *Theology, Christology, Anthropology*, op. cit., II B (Sharkey, op. cit., 219-23).

166. Cf. A. Gaudel, "Kénose", DTC, VIII, 2339-42.

167. A. Michel, "Hypostatique (union)", DTC, VII, 543. Cf. L.F. Mateo Seco, "Teología de la cruz", ScrTh 14 (1982), 165-79.

168. Cf. P. Henry, "Kénose", in DBS, V, 157.

169. For an eloquent outline of Moltmann's thought, cf. A. Ortiz Garcia, "La teología de la cruz en la teología de hoy", in various authors, *La teología de la cruz*, op. cit., 10.

form it takes, is akin to the ancient error of the Theopaschites, Monophysite in origin.[170]

It has to be said that passibility of this type cannot exist in God. Although it is true that the formulas used to speak about the suffering God underwent in Christ are only grasped by us in a very limited way, because we cannot fully understand the closeness of the union between the Word and his suffering flesh (it is the Word who suffers in his flesh), "the Christology of the Church does not allow us to affirm formally that Jesus Christ could suffer according to his divine nature";[171] nor can one speak formally of mutability and passibility in God.[172]

Finally, when speaking of God's suffering, other authors, respecting the statement of divine immutability, try to conceive this suffering as purified from everything that involves matter, passibility, imperfection,[173] thereby purifying the notion of pain of everything that is incompatible with the infinite perfection of God. This again brings us up against the great mystery of God's relationship with the world and with man. This is a question open to theologians to explore; but the key to the answer must lie in divine immutability (correctly understood), an immutability befitting the infinite perfection of the divine life, and therefore not opposed either to God's freedom or to his love; an immutability which has nothing to do with indifference on God's part or absence of life.

"Christian piety always rejected the idea of a Divinity indifferent to the vicissitudes of creatures. It was even inclined to admit that, just as 'compassion' is among the most noble human perfections, it can be said of God that he has a similar compassion without any imperfection and in an eminent degree, namely, the 'inclination of commiseration . . . and not the absence of power' (Leo I, *DS*, 293). It is maintained that this compassion can coexist with the eternal happiness itself. The Fathers called this total mercy toward human pain and suffering 'the passion of love', a love that in the Passion of Jesus Christ has vanquished these sufferings and made them perfect (cf. *Greg. Thaum. Ad Theopompum*; John Paul II, *Dives in Misericordia*, 7; AAS, 72, 1980, 1199ff.)."[174]

When, within the limits indicated, one speaks of God suffering in himself, what we have obviously is a use of analogy. What it means is that in God there is "something" similar and yet most dissimilar to what we understand by suffering. Because our notion of suffering largely has to do with mutability and passibility, if we apply it to God in himself we need to purify it of many

170. Cf. A. Amann, "Théopaschisme (controverse)"), DTC, XV, 502-12.
171. ITC, *Theology, Christology, Anthropology*, op. cit., II B.3 (Sharkey, op. cit., 221).
172. Cf. ibid., II B 4.
173. Cf. J. Maritain, "Quelques réflexions su le savoir théologique", RT 69 (1969), 3-27; J. Galot, *Il mistero della sofferenza di Dio* (Assisi, 1975). Cf. also P. Sequeri, "Cristologie nel quadro della problematica della mutabilità di Dio: Balthasar, Küng, Mühlen, Moltmann, Galot", SC, 1977, 114-51.
174. ITC, *Theology, Christology, Anthropology*, op. cit., II B, 5.1 (Sharkey, op. cit., 222).

of the intellectual overtones and, particularly, emotional overtones that the term carries for us. As John Paul II writes, "the concept of God as the necessarily most perfect being certainly excludes from God any pain deriving from deficiencies or wounds; but in the 'depths of God' there is a Father's love that, faced with man's sin, in the language of the Bible reacts so deeply as to say: 'I am sorry that I have made him' (cf. Gen 6:7) [. . .]. But more often the Sacred Book speaks to us of a Father who feels compassion for man, as though sharing his pain. In a word, this inscrutable and indescribable *fatherly 'pain' will bring about* above all the wonderful *economy of redemptive love* in Jesus Christ, so that through the *mysterium pietatis* love can reveal itself in the history of man as stronger than sin. So that the 'gift' may prevail! [. . .]. And on the lips of Jesus the Redeemer, in whose humanity the 'suffering' of God is concretized, there will be heard a word which manifests the eternal love of mercy: *Misereor* (I have compassion—cf. Mt 15:32; Mk 8:2)."[175]

4. THE UNIVERSALITY OF THE REDEMPTION

Our Lord died for all men and therefore "man—every man without any exception whatever—has been redeemed by Christ, and because with man—with each man without any exception whatever—Christ is in a way united, even when man is unaware of it."[176]

Jesus Christ has redeemed all men in all ages: Christ "died for all" (2 Cor 5:15; cf. Rom 5:18). Jesus, as St John says, "is the expiation for our sins, and not for ours only, but also for the sins of the whole world" (1 Jn 2:2). These words were later taken up by the Council of Trent to teach this truth of faith.[177] Earlier the Council of Quiercy (833) stated that "there is not, never was nor ever will be any person for whom Christ our Lord had not suffered,"[178] when referring to Gottschalk (*Gotteschalcus*) doctrine which said that men were predestined to glory and to condemnation. And when the Jansenists said that Jesus died only for those who are in fact saved, Pope Innocent X condemned that thesis as heretical.[179] Some years later, also against Jansenism, Alexander VIII reasserted the truth of the universality of the Redemption.[180] Christ died for all men.

---

175. John Paul II, Enc. *Dominum et vivificantem*, op. cit., no. 39. On the "suffering of God" in Christ in the teaching of John Paul II, cf. L.F. Mateo Seco, "Cristo redentor del hombre", in various authors, *Trinidad y salvación. Estudios sobre la teología trinitaria de Juan Pablo II* (Pamplona, 1990), 143-9.
176. John Paul II, Enc. *Redemptor hominis*, op. cit., no. 14.
177. Cf. Council of Trent, Decr. *De justificatione*, op. cit., (DS 1522).
178. Council of Quiercy (DS 624); cf. also Council of Arles, 475 (DS 340); Second Vatican Council, Decr. *Ad gentes*, 3; John Paul II, Enc. *Redemptor hominis*, no. 13.
179. Cf. Innocent X, Const. *Cum occasione*, 31 May 1653 (DS 2005).
180. Cf. Holy Office, Decr. of 7 December 1690 (DS 2304).

The universality of the Redemption does not mean that all men *necessarily* must be saved. It is true that every human being, without exception, has been redeemed by Christ; but each individual can reject the salvation offered; in order to be saved a person must make his own the effect of Redemption. The Church believes that Christ, who died and rose for all (cf. 2 Cor 5:15), gives man, through his Spirit, light and strength to be able to respond to his supreme vocation; no other name has been given on earth to men by which they may be saved (cf. Acts 4:12). Therefore, when a person is not saved, it is not because Christ has not redeemed him or her, but because he or she has rejected the grace of redemption. As St John Chrysostom taught, "Perhaps someone says, Why are we all not saved? Because you do not desire it. For grace, although it is a free gift, saves those who desire it, not those who do not desire it, those who reject it."[181] But even though some may reject the grace of Redemption, Christ "died truly for all, so as far as concerns him, to save all".[182]

This distinction between *objective redemption* (the redemption worked by Christ, which is absolutely universal) and *subjective redemption* (salvation made effective in each individual person, because people are able not to be saved) is a clear manifestation of God's respect for human freedom. "The Almighty, he who by his Providence rules the Universe, does not want forced slaves; he prefers free sons and daughters."[183] Therefore, as St Augustine writes, "he who has made you without you, will not save you with you."[184]

The Redemption is objectively universal not only because Jesus Christ made salvation *possible* for all, but because he in fact *offers* each and every human being the means necessary to attain salvation. God "desires all men to be saved and to come to the knowledge of the truth" (1 Tim 2:4); and to all he offers sufficient grace to enable them, if they freely accept it, to attain heaven.

Therefore, the Church teaches that no human being is condemned through not having had an opportunity to be saved. The possibility of salvation is offered to men principally through the preaching and sacraments of the Church; but it is also offered to all those who, through no fault of their own, have not received that preaching and those sacraments: God offers then, in a way hidden to us, the possibility of receiving Christ's grace and later attaining eternal life: "the universality of salvation means that it is granted not only to those who explicitly believe in Christ and have entered the Church. Since salvation is offered to all, it must be made completely available to all. But it is clear that today, as in the past, many people do not have an opportunity to come to know

---

181. St John Chrysostom, *In Epist. ad Rom*, 18, 5 (PG 60, 579).
182. Id., *In Epist. ad Hebr.*, 17, 2 (PG 63, 129); cf. St Thomas Aquinas, *STh* III, q.79, a.7, ad 2; *In Epist. ad Tim.*, cp. 2, lect. 1.
183. Blessed J. Escrivá de Balaguer, *Friends of God*, op. cit., no. 33.
184. St Augustine, *Sermo* 169, 11, 13 (PL 38, 923). On the distinction between objective and subjective redemption, cf. M.J. Scheeben, *Katholische Dogmatik*, V, 2, no. 1330 (Fribourg, 1954), 198ff.

or accept the Gospel revelation or to enter the Church. The social and cultural conditions in which they live do not permit this, and frequently they have been brought up in other religious traditions. For such people salvation in Christ is accessible by virtue of a grace which, while having a mysterious relationship to the Church, does not make them formally part of the Church but enlightens them in a way which is accommodated to their spiritual and material situation. This grace comes from Christ; it is the result of his sacrifice and is communicated by the Holy Spirit. It enables each person to attain salvation through his or her free cooperation."[185] However, this in no way reduces the importance of the evangelizing mission entrusted by Christ to his Church,[186] because Christ's teaching and sacraments enable a person more easily to live an upright moral life (indispensable for salvation) and because union with Christ through faith and the sacraments is a sovereign gift which prepares one, while still on earth, for incomparable glory in heaven.

5. CHRIST IS MAN'S SAVIOUR NOW

After the Ascension, Jesus did not "disappear" over the horizon of our lives, for he is the Head of the Church and "by the greatness of his power he rules heaven and earth, and with his all-surpassing perfection and activity he fills his whole body with the riches of his glory."[187]

The Church is the Body of Christ (cf. Eph 1:20-23), because from him as its Head it constantly receives divine life, the grace of salvation.[188] This is a truth of faith repeatedly taught by the Magisterium. It is particularly well developed in the encyclical *Mystici corporis*.[189] The analogy of Christ and the Church with a head and a body (found in Scripture: cf. Eph 1:20-23; Col 1:18) has a clear meaning: in the same sort of way as the head is the leading part and directs the rest of the body, so, because of his nearness to God, Christ has the most elevated grace and infuses all the members of the Church with grace.[190]

The relationship each member of the Church has with Christ (a multifaceted

---

185. John Paul II, Enc. *Redemptoris missio*, 7 December 1990, no. 10. Cf. Second Vatican Council, Const. *Lumen gentium*, 16; Const. *Gaudium et spes*, 22.

186. Cf. Second Vatican Council, Decr. *Ad gentes*, 7; Const. *Lumen gentium*, 13. In effect, "It is necessary to keep these two truths together, namely the real possibility of salvation in Christ for all mankind and the necessity of the Church for salvation. Both these truths help us to understand the *one mystery of salvation*, so that we can come to know God's mercy and our own responsibilty. Salvation, which always remains a gift of the Spirit, requires man's co-operation, both to save himself and to save others": John Paul II, Enc. *Redemptoris missio*, no. 9.

187. Second Vatican Council, Const. *Lumen gentium*, 7; cf. also 50.

188. On this subject, cf. e.g., B. Gherardini, *La Chiese oggi e sempre* (Milan, 1974).

189. Cf. Pius XII, Enc. *Mystici corporis*, 29 June 1943: AAS 35 (1943) 200ff.

190. Cf. St Thomas Aquinas, *STh* III, q.8, a.1.

one, expressing itself in various ways) is radically a type of spiritual union: "this union of Christ with man is in itself a mystery. From the mystery is born 'the new man', called to become a partaker of God's life (cf. 2 Pet 1:4), and newly created in Christ for the fullness of grace and truth (cf. Eph 2:10; Jn 1:14-16)."[191] The "new man, called to a share in the life of God, is born of his being united to Christ, because the principle of this new life is grace, and grace in man is a sharing in that grace which fills the human soul of Christ—capital grace, his grace as Head.

After presenting Christ to us as the One who is "full of grace and truth" (Jn 1:14), St John adds: "From his fullness have we all received, grace upon grace" (Jn 1:16). Grace, which makes man a son of God, like a "new man", not only comes to us through Christ but also comes to us from Christ; Jesus has not only merited grace for us and produced it in us: that grace is also a sharing in the fullness of grace which fills his holy human nature. The soul of Christ possesses grace in all its fullness; this enables him to communicate it to others; therefore, the habitual grace which sanctifies the soul of Christ and that grace which belongs to him as Head of the Church and source of holiness for all mankind are one and the same. There is only a distinction of reason between them—"habitual" referring to the sanctification of the soul, "capital" to the fact that that same grace causes grace in all men.[192]

Thus, he who was already like us in all things but sin, makes us like himself in the supernatural order of deification—in grace and glory. For this very reason we can say that *Christ is the source of all holiness in the Church.* Just as God is the universal principle of being, Christ as man is the principle of all grace, because just as God gives existence to all created things, analogically all the grace which men have is infused by Christ through his Humanity, as an instrument joined to the Godhead.[193] The Humanity of the Word is not just holy; it also sanctifies, because by its holiness are men sanctified.[194]

Sharing in Christ's grace brings with it *union* with him, through his *presence* in us. As St Augustine writes, the Lord, by making us his members, also brings it about that "in him we are Christ."[195]

This *being in Christ* (cf. also Rom 6:11; Gal 3:28; Eph 2:5-6), this union of Christ with each human being in grace, does not mean that Christ's humanity

---

191. John Paul II, Enc. *Redemptor hominis*, 18.

192. Cf. St Thomas Aquinas, *STh* III, q.8, a.5.

193. Cf. St Thomas Aquinas, *De Veritate*, q.29, a.5. See also F. Ocáriz, "La elevación sobrenatural como re-creación en Cristo", op. cit., 281-92.

194. St Thomas Aquinas, *STh* III, q.34, a.1, ad 3; cf. ibid., q.8, a.1.

195. St Augustine, *Enarrationes in Psalmos*, 26, 2, 2 (PI 36, 200). The expressions *in Christ, in Christ Jesus, in the Lord* are found 164 times in St Paul's letters; in many instances they refer to man's union and intimate identification with Christ. Cf. e.g., F. Buchsel, "In Christus bei Paulus", ZNW 42 (1942), 121-58; S. Zedda, "'Vivere' in Christo secondo S. Paolo", RBI 61 (1958), 83-92; M. Meinertz, "Teología del Nuevo Testamento", op. cit., 414-20; A. Wikenhauser, *Die Christusmystik des Apostel Paulus*, 2nd ed. (Fribourg, 1956).

is omnipresent (a notion condemned by the Second Council of Nicea in 787)[196] or that our Lord's body physically indwells in the faithful. What it means is a *virtual* presence, that is, an *operative* presence of Jesus' humanity in the person who is in the state of grace.[197]

This virtual, operative, presence brings about, on its own, the identification of man with Christ. Therefore, "the Christian is obliged to be *alter Christus, ipse Christus*: another Christ, Christ himself."[198] The sanctifying efficacy of the virtual presence in man of Christ's humanity is uninterrupted as long as man stays in the state of grace, and it acquires special salvific value in the sacraments, especially the Eucharist, in which there is not just a virtual but also a substantial presence of Christ's humanity. Therefore, in the Eucharist we not only find the sanctifying strength of Christ but Christ himself, truly, really and substantially present with his body, blood, soul and divinity. And so "in the most blessed Eucharist is contained the whole spiritual good of the Church."[199]

We might point out, in conclusion, that identification with Jesus (which can and should be something which steadily increases in every person's life on earth) will reach its fullness only at the end of time when we will actually see our Lord return to earth as universal Judge (cf. Mt 24:29-31), and "he will change our lowly body to be like his glorious body" (Phil 3:21). In other words, Sacred History does not end with the New Testament, there is still a mystery of Christ which we await—the Parousia; therefore, our time (the time of the Church on earth) is a time of salvation *already* attained, but also a time of salvation which has *not yet* reached its definitive fullness. The final words of the Book of Revelation express this eschatological tension: "Come, Lord Jesus" (Rev 22:20).

196. Cf. DS 606.
197. Cf. E. Hugon, *La causalité insturmentale dans l'ordre surnaturel*, 3rd ed. (Paris, 1924), 111.
198. Blessed J. Escrivá de Balaguer, *Christ is passing by*, op. cit., 96.
199. Second Vatican Council, Decr. *Presbyterorum ordinis*, 5. Cf. J.L. Illanes, "La Santa Misa, centro de la actividad de la Iglesia", ScrTh 5 (1975), 733-59.

Conclusion

The proclamation that "Jesus is the Lord" is a confession of faith, but a confession which implies something historical, something which really happened, for one is saying that the Word became flesh and that Jesus of Nazareth (born of the Virgin Mary at a particular point in human history, and who died under Pontius Pilate in the evening of a Friday in Spring) is the Son of God—the natural son of God, of the same substance as the Father, God from God, light from light. The Christian faith confesses historical facts and the mystery (a transcendental one) contained in those facts.

"Although *Christocentric* thought dominates the entire New Testament, that is in no way opposed to a *theocentric* view of things. Naturally, God is the beginning and end of all events; from God every salvific institution derives; and only with a view to him does life have any meaning. But God has made himself present and visible (in Christ) among men; Christ has been sent to the world by the Father; in Christ and through Christ divine salvation comes about. The person who reaches Christ reaches God; Christ leads to the Father. Christocentric orientation is grounded on and finds its fulness in theocentric orientation. The two are inseparable. Just as there is only one God, so too there is only one Son of God and only one bearer of God's revelation."[1]

When drawing near to Christ (and the study of theology is one way to do that), one should not forget that Jesus Christ is not only an *object* of knowledge or of teaching; he is above all a *Subject*, a divine Person, who is living and active, a Person to be loved. Loving Christ, however, implies keeping his commandments, so as to become true disciples of his (cf. Jn 14:23),[2] and attaining the *new life* in Christ by going to the sources of that life, the sacraments of the Church, particularly Penance and the Eucharist.[3]

We should also remember that "it is only in the mystery of the Word made flesh that the mystery of man truly becomes clear",[4] because only Christ is perfect man, and because his humanity is deified by the fullness of supernatural grace, a fulness in which we share (cf. Jn 1:14-16), after he himself merited

---

1. M. Meinertz, *Teología del Nuevo Testamento*, op. cit., 633.
2. Cf. P. Rodriguez, "Sobre la condición de discípulo y su significado para la cristología", ScrTh 1 (1969) 165-73.
3. Cf. John Paul II, Enc. *Redemptor hominis*, no. 20.
4. Second Vatican Council, Const. *Gaudium et spes*, 22.

for us that sharing, which makes us a new creature, children of God, removed from that sinful condition inherited from Adam.

Therefore, it is necessary to proclaim that only Christianity is the true, complete humanism; that is not the same as a mistaken "humanization of Christianity", which conceives the salvation Christ gave us as simply restoration to man of his natural dignity.[5] On the contrary, we should always remember that "the great boldness of the Christian faith—to proclaim the value and dignity of human nature and to affirm that we have been created to achieve the dignity of children of God, through the grace that raises us up to a supernatural level. An incredible boldness it would be, were it not founded on the promise of salvation given us by God the Father, confirmed by the blood of Christ, and reaffirmed and made possible by the constant action of the Holy Spirit."[6]

Finally, it should be remembered that the mystery of Christ "took shape beneath the heart of the Virgin of Nazareth when she pronounced her *'fiat'* (be it done). From then on, under the special influence of the Holy Spirit, this heart, the heart of both a virgin and a mother, has always followed the work of her Son and has gone out to all those whom Christ has embraced and continues to embrace with inexhaustible love [. . .]. Consequently, Mary must be on all the ways for the Church's daily life. Through her maternal presence the Church acquires certainty that she is truly living the life of her Master and Lord and that she is living the mystery of the Redemption in all its life-giving profundity and fulness."[7]

5. Cf. C. Fabro, *L'anima. Introduzione al problema dell'uomo* (Rome, 1955), 313.
6. Blessed J. Escrivá de Balaguer, *Christ is passing by*, op. cit., 133.
7. John Paul II, Enc. *Redemptor hominis*, no. 22.

Bibliography[1]

Adam, K., *The Christ of Faith*, London 1957.

Agnes, M., *La professione di fede nei concili ecumenici di Efeso e di Calcedonia*, Casino 1983.

Amann, A., "Nestorius et sa doctrine", DTC 11, 76-157.

—— "Théopaschisme (controverse)", DTC 15, 502-12.

Amato, A., *Gesù il Signore: saggio di cristologia*, Bologna 1988.

Aranda, G., "La historia de Cristo en la tierra, según Fil 2, 6-11", ScrTh 14 (1982) 219-36.

—— "Los Evangelios de la infancia de Jesús", ScrTh 10 (1978) 845.

Arduso, F., *Gesù de Nazaret è Figlio di Dio?*, Turin 1980.

Auer, J., *Kleine Katholische Dogmatik*, IV/1: *Jesus Christus Gottes und Maria "Sohn"*, Ratisbon 1986.

—— *Kleine Katholische Dogmatik*, IV/2: *Jesus Christus, Heiland der Welt. Maria, Cristi Mutter im Heilsplan Gottes*, Ratisbon 1988.

Bailleux, E., "L'impecable liberté du Christ", RT 67 (1967) 5-28.

Balthasar, H.U. v., *La foi du Christ*, Paris 1968.

Banks, R., *Jesus and the Law in the Synoptic Tradition*, Cambridge 1975.

Bardy, G., *Le Sauveur*, Paris 1939.

Basevi, C., "La humanidad y la divinidad de Cristo: las controversias cristológicas del s. IV y las cartas sinodales del Papa S. Dámaso (366-377)", ScrTh 11 (1979) 953-99.

Bellini, E., *Alessandro e Ario. Un esempio di conflitto tra fede e ideologia. Documenti della controversia ariana*, Milan 1974.

—— *Su Cristo: il grande dibattito nel quarto secolo*, Milan 1978.

Benoit, P., *The Passion and Resurrection of Jesus Christ*, New York 1969.

Biffi, I., *Il misteri della vita di Cristo in S. Tommaso d'Aquino*, Varese 1972.

Billot, L., *De Verbo Incarnato*, Rome 1949.

Bonnefoy, J.F., *La Primauté du Christ selon l'Ecriture et la Tradition*, Rome 1959.

Bonsirven, J., "Le Sacerdoce et le sacrifice de Jésus-Christ d'après l'épître aux Hébreux", NRT (1939) 641-60; 769-86.

—— *Theology of the New Testament*, London 1963.

Bordoni, M., *Gesù di Nazaret Signore e Cristo. Saggio de cristologia sistematica. I. Problemi di metodo; II. Il Gesù al fondamento della cristologia; III. Il Cristo annunciato dalla Chiesa*, Rome 1982-6.

---

1. This bibliography lists some of the works referred to in the text (but not Patristic or medieval texts or documents of the Magisterium), and only a small proportion of the immense bibliography on Christology and allied subjects. The use made of the diverse sources can be seen via the Index of Authors. [The translators of the English edition acknowledge with thanks the help provided by library staff at Maynooth College, Clonliffe College, Dublin and University College, Galway, in tracing English language editions of works cited.]

Boüessé, H., "Causalité efficiente et causalité méritoire de l'humanité du Christ", RT 44 (1938) 256-98.

—— *Le sauveur du monde*, 4 vols., Chambery-Leysse 1951-53.

Bouillard, H., *Sur la Resurrection de Jésus. Le point théologique*, Paris 1972.

Boularand, E., *L'heresie d'Arius et la "foi" de Nicée*, Paris 1972.

Bouyer, L., *La Bible et l'Evangile*, Paris.

—— *La Mystère Pascal*, Paris 1957.

—— *The Eternal Son: A Theology of the Word of God and Christology*, Huntington 1978.

Bover, J.M., *Vida de Nuestro Señor Jesucristo*, Barcelona 1956.

Boyer, C., *Luther: Sa doctrine*, Rome 1970.

Braun, F.M., *Oú en est le problème de Jésus?*, Brussels-Paris 1932.

Brito, E., *La Christologie du Hegel, Verbum crucis*, Paris 1983.

Bruckberger, R.L., *The History of Jesus Christ*, New York 1965.

Caba, J., *De los Evangelios al Jesús histórico (Introducción a la Cristología)*, Madrid 1971.

—— *El Jesús de los Evangelios*, Madrid 1977.

Camelot, T., *Efeso y Calcedonia*, Vitoria 1971.

Casciaro, J.M., *Estudios sobre la cristología del Nuevo Testamento*, Pamplona 1982.

—— "Las 'antítesis' de Mt 5, 21-48, ¿Halakôt de la Torâh o algo más?", RCatT 14 (1989) 123-32.

Castrillo, T., *Jesucristo Salvador. La persona, la doctrina y la obra del Redentor*, Madrid 1957.

Catao, B., *Salut et Rédemption chez S. Thomas d'Aquin*, Paris 1965.

Cazelles, H., "Les Poémes du Serviteur", RSR 43 (1955) 5-55.

—— *El Mesías de la Biblia: Cristología del A.T.*, Barcelona 1981.

Cerfaux, L., *Le Christ dans la Théologie de Saint Paul*, Tournai 1960.

—— *Jesus en los orígines de la Tradición*, Barcelona 1981.

—— *La theologie de l'Eglise suivant saint Paul*, Paris 1942

Cessario, R., *Christian satisfaction in Aquinas. Towards a personalist understanding*, Washington 1980.

Ceupens, P.F., *Theologia Biblica*, Rome 1939.

Chopin, C., *La Verbe incarné et redempteur*, Tournai 1966.

Comblin, J., *Jesus of Nazareth*, New York 1976.

Congar, Y., *Jesus Christ*, London 1966.

Coppens, J., *Le messianisme et sa relève prophetique*, Gembloux 1974.

—— "Le messianisme royal. Relectures christologiques", NRT 100 (1968) 834-63.

—— "Le Protoévangile. Un nouvel essai d'exégèse", ETL 26 (1950) 5-36.

—— "Le Serviteur de Yahvé. Vers la solution d'en énigme", in *Sacra Pagina*, I, Gembloux 1959, 434-54.

Cuervo, M., "Introducción al tratado de Verbo encarnado", in *Santo Tomás de Aquino. Suma Teológica*, vol. XI, Madrid 1960.

Cullmann, O., *The Christology of the New Testament*, London 1967.

—— *Jesus and the Revolutionaries*, New York 1970.

D'Ales, A., *Le Dogme d'Ephèse*, Paris 1931.

——, "Rédemption", DAFC 4, 542-82.

Daniélou, J., *Cristo e noi*, Alba 1968.

—— *Les évangiles de l'Enfance*, Paris 1967.

—— *En torno al misterio de Cristo*, Barcelona 1961.

De Fraine, J., *L'aspect religieuse de la Royauté israélitique*, Rome 1954.

De Galleux, A., "La définition christologique à Chalcédoine", RTL 7 (1976) 3-23; 115-70.

De la Potterie, I., "L'exaltation du Fils de l'homme (Jn 12, 31-36)", Greg 49 (1968) 460-78.

—— "L'Onction de Christi", NRT 80 (1958) 225-52.

—— *La passion de Jésus selon l'évangile de Jean*, Paris 1986.

—— *La verdad de Jesús*, Madrid 1979.

De la Taille, M., "Actuation créée par l'Acte incrée", RSR 18 (1928) 253-68.

Degl'Innocenti, U., *Il problema della persona nel pensiero di S. Tommaso*, Rome 1967.

Devreesse, R., *Essai sur Théodore de Mopsueste*, Vatican City 1948.

Dhanis, E., *Resurrexit (Actas del symposium sobre la resurrección de Jesú)*, Rome 1974.

Diepen, H., "L'assumptus homo patristique", RT 63 (1963) 225-45; 363-88; 64 (1964) 32-52, 364-86.

—— "La critique du baslisme selon Saint Thomas", RT 50 (1950) 82-118; 290-329.

—— "La psychologie humaine de Christ selon Saint Thomas d'Aquin", RT 50 (1950) 515-62.

Diez Macho, A., *La resurrección de Jesucristo y la del hombre en la Biblia*, Madrid 1977.

—— *El Mesías anunciado y esperado*, Madrid 1976.

Dreyfus, F., *Did Jesus know he was God?*, Chicago 1989.

Dupont, J., *La christologie de Saint Jean*, Bruges 1951.

—— *Les tentations de Jésus au désert*, Bruges 1968.

Durand, A., "La science du Christ", NRT 71 (1949) 497-503.

Durwell, F.X., *The Resurrection*, London 1960.

Esteve, H.M., *De caelesti mediatione sacerdotali Christi juxta Hebr 8:3-4*, Madrid 1949.

Fabris, R., *Jesús de Nazaret: Historia e interpretación*, Salamanca 1985.

Faynell, P. *Jesucristo es el Señor*, Salamanca 1968.

Feuillet, A., *Christologie paulinienne et tradition biblique*, Paris 1973.

—— *Il prologo del Quarto Vangelo*, Assisi 1971.

—— *L'Agonie de Gethsèmani*, Paris 1977.

—— "La personalité de Jésus à partir de sa soumission au rite de repentance du précurseur", RB 77 (1970) 30-49.

—— *Le Christ Sagesse de Dieu d'aprés les épîtres pauliniennes*, Paris 1966.

—— "Le coupe et le baptême de la Passion", RB 74 (1967) 356-91.

—— *Le prologue du IVᵉ évangile*, Paris 1973.

—— "Le Symbolisme de la Colombe dans les récits évangeliques du Baptême", RSR 46 (1958) 524-44.

—— "Le trois grandes prophéties de la Passion et de la Réssurection des évangiles synoptiques", RT 67 (1967) 533-60; 68 (1968) 41-74.

Fillion, L.C., *The Life of Christ*, St Louis and London 1928.

Forment, E., *Ser y persona*, Barcelona 1983.

Galot, J., *Cristo contestato. Le cristologie non calcedoniane e la fede cristologica*, Florence 1979.

—— *Cristo, ¿Tú quién eres?*, Madrid 1982.

—— *Il mistero della sofferenza di Dio*, Assisi 1975.

——, *Jesus our Liberator*, Rome and Chicago 1982.

—— *La conscienza di Gesù*, Assisi 1971.

—— *The person of Christ*, Chicago 1983.

—— *La Rédemption, mystère d'Alliance*, Rome-Bruges 1965.

Galtier, P., *L'unité du Christ, Etre Personne Conscience*, Paris 1939.

—— "La Conscience humaine du Christ", Greg 32 (1951) 525-56; 35 (1954) 225-46.

Garrigou-Lagrange, R., *Christ the Saviour*, St Louis 1950.

—— *Our Saviour and His Love for Us*, St Louis 1951.

Gaudel, A., "Kénose", DTC 8, 2339-42.

—— *Le mystère de l'Homme Dieu*, Paris 1939.

Gelin, A., "Messianisme", DBS 5, 1165-213.

Gherardini, B., *Theologia crucis, L'eredità di Lutero nell'evoluzione teologica della Riforma*, Rome 1978.

Gironés, G., *Uno de nosotros es Hijo de Dios*, Valencia 1971.

Glorieux, P., "La mérite du Christ selon S. Thomas", RSR 10 (1930) 622-49.

González Gil, M.M., *Cristo, el misterio de Dios*, 2 vols., Madrid 1976.

González Núñez, A., *Profetas, sacerdotes y reyes en el antiguo Israel*, Madrid 1962.

González, C.I., *El es nuestra salvación. Cristología y soteriología*, Bogota 1986.

Grandmaison, L., *Jesus Christ: His Person, His Message, His Credentials*, New York 1930.

Grelot, P., *Les poèmes du Serviteur. De la lecture critique a l'herméneutique*, Paris 1981.

—— *Sens chrétien de l'Ancient Testament*, Paris 1962.

Grillmeier, A., "De Jésus de Nazaret dans l'ombre due Fils de Dieu au Christ image de Dieu" in Comment être chrétien? La réponse de Küng, ed. J.R. Armogathe, Paris 1979.

—— *Gesü il Cristo nella fede della Chiesa*, Brescia 1982.

—— "La imagen de Cristo en la teología católica actual", in various authors, *Panorámica de la teología católica actual*, Madrid 1961.

—— "Los misterios de la vida de Jesus" in MS 111/11, Madrid 1969.

Grillmeier, A. and Bacht, H., *Das Konzil von Chalkedon. Geschichte und Gegenwart*, 3 vols., Wützburg 1954.

Guardini, R., *The Lord*, Cleveland 1969.

—— *La imagen de Jesús, el Cristo, en el Nuevo Testamento*, Madrid 1967.

Guillet, J., *Jésus devant sa vie et sa mort*, Paris 1971.

—— *La foi de Jésus-Christ*, Paris 1979.

Guitton, J., *Jesus*, New York 1967.

Hengel, M., *Victory over Violence: Jesus and the Revolutionists*, Philadelphia 1973.

—— *Jésus, Fils de Dieu*, Paris 1975.

Henry, P., "Kénose", DBC 5, 7-161.

Hirschberger, H., *Geschichte der Philosophie*, Freiburg im Breisgau 1963.

Hubaut, M., "Jésus et la Loi de Moïse", RTL 7 (1976) 410-25.

Hugon, E., *The Mystery of the Incarnation*, London 1920.

—— *Le mystère de la Rédemption*, Paris 1915.

Iammarrone, L., "La teoria chenotica e il testo di Fil 2, 6-7", DT 82 (1979) 341-73.

—— "La visione beatifica di Cristo viatore nel pensiero di San Tommaso", DC 36 (1983) 287-330.

Ibáñez, F. and Mendoza, J., "El valor terminológico del término hypóstasis en el libro I del Contra Eunomio de Gregorio de Nisa", in Mateo-Seco, L.F. (ed.), *El 'Contra*

Eunomium I' en la producción literaria de Gregorio de Nisa, Pamplona 1988, 329-39.

Illanes, J.L., "Jesucristo, Dios y hombre", GER 13, 439-53.

ITC (International Theological Commission), *Select Questions on Chrstology* (1979). *Theology, Christology, Anthropology* (1981). *Select Themes of Ecclesiology* (1984). *The Consciousness of Christ concerning Himself and His Mission* (1985). These documents are contained in Sharkey, M., *International Theological Commission, Facts and Documents 1969-1985*, San Francisco 1989.

Jedin, H., *Handbuch der Kirchgeschichte*, Frieburg im Breisgau 1973 and 1975.

Jeremias, J., *The Central Message of the New Testament*, London 1981.

——— *The Parables of Jesus*, New York 1972.

——— *New Testament and Theology*, New York 1971.

Jouassard, G., "L'abandon de Christ en Croix dans la tradition", RSR 25 (1924) 310ff; 26 (1925) 609ff.

Journet, C., *Les sept paroles du Christ en Croix*, Paris 1952.

——— *Théologie de l'Eglise*, Tournai 1958.

Jugie, M., "Monophisisme", DTC 10, 2216-51.

——— "Monothélisme", DTC 10, 2307-23.

Kasper, W., *Jesus the Christ*, London 1976.

Kürzinger, J., "Descente de Jésus aux enfers", DTB 259-64.

Lafont, G., *Peut-on connaître Dieu en Jésus-Christ?*, Paris 1969.

Lagrange, M.J., *The Gospel of Jesus Christ*, Westminster, Maryland 1938.

——— *Le Messianisme chez les Juifs*, Paris 1909.

Lamarche, P., *Christ vivant. Essai sur la cristologie du Nouveau Testament*, Paris 1966.

Lang, A. *Die Sendung Christi*, Munich 1966.

Larrañaga, V., *La Ascensión del Señor en el Nuevo Testamento*, 2 vols., Madrid 1943.

Latourelle, R., *The Miracles of Jesus and the Theology of Miracles*, New York 1988.

Lebreton, J., *History in the Dogma of the Trinity*, New York 1939.

——— "Jésus-Christ", DBS 4, 966-1073.

——— *The Life and Teaching of Jesus Christ our Lord*, New York 1968.

Leon-Dufour, X., *The Gospels and the Jesus of History*, London 1968.

Lepin, M., *Le Christ Jésus*, Paris 1929.

Leroy, M.V., "L'union selon l'hypostase d'après S. Thomas d'Aquin", RT 74 (1974) 205-43.

Lethel, F.M., *Théologie de l'agonie du Christ (La liberté humaine du Fils de Dieu et on importance sotériologique mises en lumière par Saint Maxime Confesseur)*, Paris 1979.

Liébaert, J., *L'Incarnation. I. Des origines au Concile de Chalcédoine*, Paris 1966.

Lobato, A., *La persona, I. Historia. Perspectiva metafisic*, Rome 1973.

Lohse, E., *History of the Suffering and Death of Jesus Christ*, Philadelphia 1967.

Loi, V., *San Paolo e l'interpretazione teologica del messaggio di Gesù*, L'Aquila 1980.

Lonergan, B., *On the Ontological and Pyschological Constitution of Christ*, California 1979.

Lopez Amat. A., *Cristo resucitado*, Valencia 1982.

Lortz, H., *Die Reformation in Deutschland*, 4th ed., Frieburg in Breisgau 1962.

Lyonnet, J.S., "De notione expiationis", VD 38 (1960) 241-61.

——— *Sin, Redemption and Sacrifice*, Rome 1970.

Mahieu, L., "L'abandon du Christ sur la Croix", MSR 2 (1945) 209-42.

Malevez, L., "La gloire de la Croix", NRT (1973), 1058-89.

—— "Le Christ et la foi", NRT 88 (1966) 1009-43.

Marinelli, F., "Dimensione trinitaria dell'Incarnazione, Div 13 (1969) 271-343.

—— L'Incarnazione del Logos e lo Spirito Santo", Div 13 (1969) 497-556.

Mateo Seco (ed.), L.F., *Cristo, Hijo de Dios y Redentor del hombre*, Pamplona 1982.

—— "La muerte de Cristo. La thanatología de Santo Tomás a la luz de sus precisiones en torno a la muerte de Cristo", EscV 12 (1982) 523-45.

—— "Sacerdocio de Criso y sacerdocio ministerial en los tres Grandes Capadocios", in various authors, *Teología del Sacerdocio*, vol. IV, Bruges 1972, 177-201.

—— "Boletín de crisología", ScrTh 17 (1985) 920-36.

—— *Estudios sobre la cristología de Gregorio de Nisa*, Pamplona 1978.

—— *W. Kasper: "Jesús el Cristo"*, ScrTh 11 (1979) 269-93.

Médebielle, A., "Expiation", DB Supl. 3, 1-262.

Meinertz, M., *Theologie des Neuen Testamentes*, Bonn 1956.

Michel, A., "Hyspostase. Hypostatique (union)", DTC, 7, 369-568.

—— "Incarnation", DTC 7, 1463-507.

—— "Jésus-Christ", DTC 8, 1108-411.

—— "Science de Jésus Christ", DTC 15, 626-1665.

Mondin, B., "La persona umana e il suo destino in San Tommaso e nel pensiero moderno", Aquin 17 (1974) 366-402.

—— *Le cristologie moderne*, Rome 1976.

Muñoz Iglesias, S., "Midrás y Evangelios de la Infancia", EE 47 (1972) 331-59.

Mussner, F., *Il messaggio dell parabole di Gesù*, Brescia 1986.

—— *La Resurrección de Jesús*, Santander 1971.

Navarro, A., *El sacerdocio redentor de Cristo*, Salamanca 1960.

Nicholas, J.H., "Aimante et bienhereuse Trinité", RT 78 (1978) 271-92.

—— "L'unité d'être dan le Christ d'après St. Thomas", RT 65 (1965) 229-60.

—— *Synthèse dogmatique*, Paris 1986.

Nicolas, M.J., "La doctrine christologique de saint Léon le Grand", RT 51 (1951) 609-60.

—— *Théologie de la résurection*, Paris 1982.

O'Collins, G., *Interpreting Jesus*, London 1983.

—— *Jesus Risen*, London 1987.

Ocáriz, F., *Hijos de Dios en Cristo. Introducción a una teología de la participación sobrenatural*, Pamplona 1972.

—— "La elevación sobrenatural como re-creación en Cristo", in *Atti del'VIII Congresso Tomístico Internazionale*, Vatican City 1981, vol. IV, 281-92.

—— "Lo Spirito Santo e libertà dei figli di Duo", in *Atti del Congresso Internazionale di Peneumatologia*, Vatican City 1982, 1239-51.

Oggioni, J., *El misterio de la Redención*, Barcelona 1961.

Orbe, A. *Cristología gnóstica*, Madrid 1986.

—— *Estudios Valentinianos*, Rome 1955-61, esp. vols. I & III.

—— *Parábolas evangélicas de San Ireneo*, Madrid 1972.

Ortiz de Urbina, I., *Nicea y Constantinopla*, Vitoria 1969.

Parente, P. *De Verbo Incarnato*, Rome 1953.

—— *Il mistero di Cristo*, Rome 1958.

—— *L'Io di Cristo*, Rovigo 1981.

Patfoort, A., *L'unité d'être dans le Christ d'après St. Thomas*, Paris-Tournai 1964.

Perez de Urbel, J., *Vida de Cristo*, Madrid 1966.
Piè i Ninot, S., *Tratado de teología fundamental*, Salamanca 1989.
Prat, F., *Jesus Christ: his life, his teaching and his work*, Milwaukee 1950.
—— *The Theology of St Paul*, London and Dublin 1945.
Quasten, J., *Patrology*, Westminster, Maryland 1960.
Quilliet, H., "Descente de Jésus aux enfers", DTC 4, 567-73.
Rahner, K., *Theological Investigations*, London.
—— and Thuesing, W., *Christologie systemarisch und exegetisch*, Basle 1972.
Ratzinger, J., *Dogma and Preaching*, Chicago 1985.
—— *Introduction to Christianity*, New York 1986.
—— "Orientaciones cristológicas", *Medellín*, 10 9184) 3-13.
—— *Principles of Catholic theology. Stories for a Fundamental Theology*, San Francisco 1987.
Riccioti, G., *Vada de Jesucristo*, Barcelona 1963.
Richard, L., *The Mystery of Redemption*, Baltimore 1965.
Riestra, J.A., "Cristo e la fede nella cristologia recente", in various authors, *Antropologia e Cristologia iere e oggi*, Rome 1987, 101-17.
—— *Cristo y la plenitud del Cuerpo Místico*, Pamplona 1985.
—— "La scienza di Cristo nel Concilio Vatticano II: Ebrei 4, 15 nella constituzione dogmatica 'Die Verbum'", AnTh 2 (188), 99-119.
Rigaux, B., "La historicité de Jésus devant l'exégèse récente", RB 65 (1958), 481-522.
Rivière, J., *Le dogme de la Rédemption. Essai d'étude historique*, Paris 1905.
—— *Le dogme de la Rédemption. Étude théologique*, Paris 1914.
—— *Le dogme de la Rédemption. Études critiques et Documents*, Louvain 1931.
—— "Rédemption", RTC 13, 1912-2004.
Robert, A. and Spico, C., "Médiation", DBS 5, 997-1083.
Rodriguez, P., "La Resurrección de Cristo en el pensamiento teológico de Santo Tomás de Aquino", in various authors, *Veritas et Sapientia*, Pamplona 1975, 318-51.
Sabourin, L., *The Names and Titles of Jesus*, New York 1967.
—— *Sin, Redemption and Sacrifice*, Rome 1970.
—— *La Cristologie à partir des texts clés*, Paris 1986.
Sabugal, S., *Christós. Investigación exegética sobre la cristología joannea*, Barcelona 1971.
Santiago-Otero, H., *El conocimiento de Cristo en cuanto hombre en la teología de la primera mitad del siglo XII*, Pamplona 1970.
Sauras, E., *El cuerpo mustico de Cristo*, Madrid 1956.
Sayés, J.A., *Jesucristo, ser y persona*, Bruges 1984.
Scheeben, M.J., *The Mysteries of Christianity*, London, 1946.
—— *Katholische Dogmatik*, V, 2, no. 1330, Tubourg 1954.
Scheffczyck, L. (ed.), *Grundfragen der Christologie heute*, Basle 1975.
Schillebeeckx, E., *Tussentijds Verdaal ouver Twe Jesus bocken* Holland 1978.
—— *Jesus Het Verhaal van een Levende*, Bloemendaad 1974.
Schlier, H., *Ueber die Auferstehung Jesu Christi*, Einsiedeln, 2nd ed., 1968.
—— *La Resurrection de Jesus Christ*, Mulhouse 1969.
Schmaus, M. and Grillmeier, A. (eds.), *Manual de historia de los Dogmas*, vol. III, *Cristología, Soteriología, Mariología*, Madrid 1973 and 1975.
Schmaus, M., *Katholische Dogmatik*, Munich 1951-60.
Schnackenburg, R., *God's Rule and Kingdom*, New York 1963.

Schürmann, H., *Jesu urelgener Tod*, 2nd ed., Freiburg im Breisgau 1976.

Segalla, G., *La Cristologia del Nuovo Testamento*, Brescia 1985.

Sequeri, P., "Cristologie nel quadro della problematica della mutabilità di Dio: Balthasar, Küng, Mühlen, Moltmann, Galot", SC (1977) 114-51.

Serentha, M., *Gesù Cristo ieri, oggi e sempre (saggio di Cristologia)*, Turin 1982.

Sesboüé, B., *Christ dans la tradition de l'Eglise*, Paris 1982.

—— *Jésus-Christ, l'Unique Médiateur*, Paris 1988.

—— "Le procés contemporain de Chalcédoine. Bilan et perspectives", RSR 65 (1977) 45-80.

Sharkey, M. (ed.), *International Theological Commission, Texts and Documents 1969-1985*. With foreword by Cardinal Ratzinger, San Francisco 1989. Cf. ITC above.

Spicq, C., *L'épître aux Hébreux*, 2 vols., Paris 1952.

Studer, B., *Dio salvatore nei Padri della Chiesa*, Rome 1986.

Taylor, V., *The Person of Christ in the New Testament Teaching*, London 1959.

Tournay, R., "Les chants du Serviteur dans la seconde partie d'Isaie", RB 59 (1952) 355-84; 481-512.

Vanderbroucke, F., *Les Psaumes et Le Christ*, Louvain 1964.

Vanhoye, A., *Structure and Message of the Epistle to the Hebrews*, Rome 1989.

—— *Le Christ, grande-prêtre selon Héb 2, 17-18"*, NRT 91 (1969) 449-74.

—— *Sacerdotes antiguos, Sacerdote nuevo según el N.T.*, Salamanca 1984.

—— *Situation du Christ. Hébreux 1-2*, Paris 1969.

—— *Textus de Sacerdotio Christi in epistula ad Hebraeos*, Rome 1969.

Virgulin, S., "Recent Discussion of the Title 'Lamb of God'", Scr 13 (1980), 74-80.

Various authors, *Jesucristo*, in *Iniciación teológica*, vol. III, Barcelona 1961, 18-185.

—— *Mysterium Salutis*, vol. III/1-2, Madrid 1971.

—— *La storia della cristologia primitiva. Gli inizi biblici e la formula di Nicea*, Brescia 1986.

Willam, F.M., *The Life of Jesus Christ in the Land of Israel and among its people*, London 1940.

Xiberta, B., *El Yo de Jesucristo. Un conflicto entre dos cristologías*, Barcelona 1954.

—— *Enchiridion de Verbo Incarnato*, Madrid 1957.

—— *Tractatus de Verbo Incarnato*, Madrid 1954.

Index